*The London Stock Exchange*

# The London Stock Exchange

## A History

RANALD C. MICHIE

# OXFORD
UNIVERSITY PRESS

Great Clarendon Street, Oxford OX2 6DP
Oxford University Press is a department of the University of Oxford.
If furthers the University's objective of excellence in research, scholarship,
and education by publishing worldwide in

Oxford New York

Athens Auckland Bangkok Bogotá Buenos Aires Calcutta
Cape Town Chennai Dar es Salaam Delhi Florence Hong Kong Istanbul
Karachi Kuala Lumpur Madrid Melbourne Mexico City Mumbai
Nairobi Paris São Paulo Singapore Taipei Tokyo Toronto Warsaw
and associated companies in Berlin Ibadan

Oxford is a registered trade mark of Oxford University Press
in the UK and certain other countries

Published in the United States
by Oxford University Press Inc., New York

British Library Cataloguing in Publication Data
Data available

Library of Congress Cataloging in Publication Data
Michie. R. C., 1949–
The London Stock Exchange : a history / Ranald C. Michie.
p. cm
Includes bibliographical references and index.
1. Stock Exchange (London. England) History. I. Title.
HG4577.MS23 1999 332.64'2421—dc21 99–25367
ISBN 0-19-829508-1

1 3 5 7 9 10 8 6 4 2

Typeset by Best-set Typesetter Ltd., Hong Kong
Printed in Great Britain
on acid-free paper by
Biddles Ltd., Guildford and King's Lynn

*This book
is dedicated to my wife, Dinah,
and our two children,
Alexander and Jonathan*

# Acknowledgements

This book was initiated by Sir Nicholas Goodison who suggested the idea of an independent and authoritative history of the London Stock Exchange. It was he who arranged access to the records still held—and used—by the Stock Exchange. Without his support this book would never have been written but he is not responsible for the views expressed here. They are mine and mine alone, though Sir Nicholas did share his knowledge of the 1980s with me. Similarly, though the Stock Exchange made available whatever I wanted to see, and I found the Council Minutes all I could manage, they have neither vetted nor commented on anything I have written. This is not an official history and I thank Sir Andrew Hugh Smith and Sir John Kemp-Welch—successive Chairmen of the London Stock Exchange for both their willingness to grant access and, even more, their ability not to try and influence. Louise Anstead was responsible for providing me with a room to work in and the volumes to work on, and I am very grateful to her. The Guildhall Library staff provided me with all the other original and secondary material with their usual efficiency. I conducted the research myself and so have no assistant(s) to thank! I also financed the research trips to London myself but am very grateful to the University of Durham for giving me a Sir Derman Christopherson fellowship for a year. That allowed me to write up my findings. I would like to record my thanks to David Kynaston for the use of his published and unpublished work, as it provides that human element that my own lacks. In addition, I would also like to thank Melissa Handley for all her hard work in producing the index. Finally, my wife and family have had to put up with a great deal while I worked on this book but, probably, less than the office staff in the Department of History at Durham University. This is probably the last book I will write for, after this one, Wendy and Tracy refuse to type another! I am very grateful that they have typed this one!

Ranald C. Michie

Durham
1998

# Foreword

The 'Big Bang' reforms at the Stock Exchange in 1986 were radical and essential. They came about chiefly because, following the abolition of exchange controls in the United Kingdom in 1979, the buying and selling of securities became more and more international. London, with its centuries-old tradition of international trade and investment, was a magnet for this business. But the London Stock Exchange's rules, which governed dealings in securities by its members were out of kilter with the method of operation of large market practitioners outside the Exchange, principally the big United States broking houses and continental European banks. Members of the London Exchange could not hope to compete in internationalized markets in stocks and shares if they continued to be bound by rules which did not reflect less restrictive international practices.

Ways had to be found, therefore, to maintain the London Exchange's traditional place in international securities markets, and to attract more of the growing market in overseas equities into London. If ways could be found, London would attract not only more of the secondary market in international securities but also, consequently, more of the primary money-raising business and more of the world's fund management business. If there had been no reforms, the London Exchange would have declined and London would have stood less of a chance of becoming the leading financial market in our time zone. So the Stock Exchange's rules were altered to attract the big international houses into membership and to allow everyone to compete on equal terms.

At the same time, the reforms needed to reflect the huge and rapid advances in technology, and particularly in the speed of communication. When I began work in the City of London in the 1950s, the telephone was slow and expensive, trunk-dialling did not exist and calls abroad had to be booked ahead. Many urgent messages were conveyed by telegram. By the 1980s, the world had shrunk, anyone could be instantly dialled, and information could be transmitted at the press of a button anywhere in the world. The effects of accurate up-to-date information and instant access to counterparties all over the world were profound. Money could move across frontiers in seconds, and did.

So in 1986 the London Exchange introduced a computerized price display system and a telephone market which did away with the traditional face-to-face trading-floor. The loss of the trading-floor to television news-screens was perhaps the most graphic public evidence of the 'Big Bang' reforms.

London was the first major exchange to abandon its traditional floor trading and thus to recognize the advantages of technology.

The reforms were a resounding success. The leading international firms found in the reforms an additional and compelling reason for establishing their European business in London. London's share of business in international equities leapt. The benefit to London's economy, and therefore to the United Kingdom economy, was enormous. London is now firmly established as the most international of all the financial centres of the world and looks set to maintain its position—providing, that is, that government does not do anything foolish such as raising personal taxes or introducing discriminatory taxes on securities or imposing a bureaucratic and heavy-handed degree of regulation.

The future of the Stock Exchange, like that of stock exchanges everywhere, is less certain. It has lost much of its regulatory role, including the regulation of the relationships of its members with their clients and, more remarkably, the regulation of the qualifications and the capital adequacy of its own members. It is no longer the provider of settlement services, and it is competing with other systems suppliers in the provision of the basic electronic tools of the market. I have always had doubts about the prospects for an exchange that simply becomes a supplier of an electronic market system and reporting mechanism. It needs a regulatory role in order to demonstrate to its members and their customers that it adds value to the market place. It is important, therefore, that the Stock Exchange has so far retained its role as the listing authority in the United Kingdom (and is recognized as such under European legislation), and maintains its role in the enforcement of its market rules. Both roles, however, are at some risk as the new Financial Services Authority assumes its comprehensive role. Indeed, the overall powers of the Financial Services Authority, which now include even the recognition of stock exchanges themselves, are without precedent in the United Kingdom. It is no exaggeration to say that its establishment changes the financial landscape. Nor is there any guarantee that the London Stock Exchange will, over the years, remain the only or the leading securities market in this country, although it will obviously try to do so as long as its members and owners want it to.

Perhaps its most promising future lies in cross-border development. There are no cross-border regulatory authorities, and as exchanges in different countries come to collaborate (as I am sure they will) they will need to develop their regulatory role to fill the vacuum and to assure investors of the integrity of their markets.

I have chosen to talk in this foreword about the 'Big Bang' reforms because they were the most far-reaching package of reforms in the long history of the Stock Exchange. The underlying theme—the need to alter rules and practices in order to meet or absorb potential competition while maintaining the standards of integrity needed to attract investors—was not a new theme. It is echoed by other events in earlier years, as the author of this history reminds us. It was not the first time that the Stock Exchange had accommodated new markets or welcomed practitioners from abroad who enhanced the range and level of business. But the extent of the reforms in 1986, and their effect, and the suddenness of their impact, were all unprecedented. They brought to a sudden resolution all the tensions that had built up in the Stock Exchange's markets over many years—tensions caused by the increasing power in the market of institutional investors, by the rapid growth of equity markets, by the development of large markets such as Eurobonds outside the Exchange, by the pace of technological change, by the relative lack of capital in Stock Exchange member firms, and as I have said above, by the internationalization of the securities business and the increasing flow of capital across national frontiers.

All these trends accelerated in the 1960s and 1970s. Ranald Michie reminds us not only of this but also of how some of them have their origins in much earlier times. He has established himself as the leading contemporary historian of the London Stock Exchange and its predecessors. He sets out in this book, which is based on painstaking research of the Exchange's archives, to show how the Exchange developed from its origins in the eighteenth century and how it found itself in the predicament which it faced in the 1980s. The story reflects the rise and decline of Britain as an industrial power, the constant value of the stock market as a source of stable long-term funding to government, and the remarkable survival against all the odds of London as an international market in the twentieth century. The story helps us also to understand the Stock Exchange's new predicaments today.

Sir Nicholas Goodison
*Chairman, London Stock Exchange, 1976–88*

# Contents

# List of Figure and Tables

# Introduction

There are two major strands to the history of the London Stock Exchange. The first concerns the growth and development of the modern securities market, both within Britain and internationally, for this was the reason that the London Stock Exchange existed. At the same time the London Stock Exchange played a very important role in the operation of this market for most of its existence. The second concerns the evolution of institutional control over that market as the number of participants and users grew, and the business became ever more complex. Again, the London Stock Exchange exerted a dominant influence in determining the structure of the modern securities market, both domestically and globally. It is only by bringing these two strands together, and tracing their interaction, that the history of the London Stock Exchange can be fully understood. The history of the London Stock Exchange is not simply the history of the British securities market and nor is the history of that market solely that of the London Stock Exchange. There were many distinctive features behind the origin and functioning of the London Stock Exchange that had serious consequences for the securities market at particular times, as well as influences on its day-to-day operations. Conversely, the scale and nature of the securities market that developed in Britain from the eighteenth century onwards, created particular challenges and opportunities for the London Stock Exchange. By combining the two strands of market and institution in the history of the London Stock Exchange over a long time-span it becomes possible to assess the contribution of each to

This introduction is culled from my research for the History of the London Stock Exchange and my previously published work on stock exchange history, especially the following: *Money, Mania and Markets: Investment Company Formation and the Stock Exchange in Nineteenth Century Scotland* (Edinburgh 1981); *The London and New York Stock Exchanges, 1850–1914* (London 1987); 'Different in Name Only? The London Stock Exchange and Foreign Bourses c.1850–1914', *Business History*, 30 (1988), repr. in R. P. T. Davenport-Hines and G. Jones (eds.), *The End of Insularity: Essays in Comparative Business History* (London 1988); 'The Canadian Securities Market, 1850–1914', *Business History Review*, 62 (1988); 'The London Stock Exchange and the British Economy, 1870–1939', in J. J. Van Helten and Y. Cassis (eds.), *Capitalism in a Mature Economy* (Aldershot 1990); 'The Development of the Stock Market', in P. Newman, M. Milgate, and J. Eatwell (eds.), *The New Palgrave Dictionary of Money and Finance* (London/New York 1992); 'The London and Provincial Stock Exchange, 1799–1973: Separation, Integration, Rivalry, Unity', in D. H. Aldcroft and A. Slaven (eds.), *Enterprise and Management* (Aldershot 1995); 'Friend or foe? Information Technology and the London Stock Exchange since 1700', *J. of Historical Geography*, 23 (1997); 'Stock Exchanges and Economic Growth, 1830–1939', in P. Cottrell and J. Reis (eds.), *Finance and the Making of Modern Capitalism* (forthcoming); 'The Invisible Stabiliser: Asset Arbitrage and the International Monetary System Since 1700', *Financial History Review*, 15 (1998).

what was happening, and then judge the outcome against the requirements of the time.

In many ways the London Stock Exchange appears a later comer in the history of securities markets for rival institutions, like the Amsterdam Bourse, trace a much longer ancestry for themselves. Certainly the transferable securities, for which stock exchanges were formed to ease purchases and sales, long existed in continental Europe. Such securities, such as those sold by Italian city-states, were bought and sold in medieval times. However they were issued in relatively small amounts which were held by a few people and generated sporadic and limited trading. This did not provide the conditions necessary for the appearance of specialized intermediaries, let alone specific markets. Instead, what transfers were required could be perfectly well handled by private negotiation or as one of the many items bought and sold in the mercantile exchanges. It was only from the seventeenth century onwards, with the appearance of both negotiable instruments representing national indebtedness and transferable stocks issued by corporate enterprise, that the volume of business generated by securities was such as to justify the beginnings of professional intermediation and organized markets.

Repeated wars waged by relatively stable nation-states provided ample need for governments to seek new means of financing their requirements, and one of the methods used was the creation of a permanent funded debt. This debt was attractive to investors as its yield was guaranteed by the state, but its indefinite duration meant that only a few could have afforded to purchase it with no date of redemption. The solution adopted was to make the debt transferable so that the government could borrow in perpetuity, committed only to pay a fixed rate of interest, while the holder was at liberty to sell to another, at the prevailing market price. A similar situation existed with large-scale joint-stock enterprise, especially the companies set up to pioneer the long-distance trade between Western Europe and India, namely the Dutch and English East India companies formed in 1612 and 1623 respectively. With these companies the holder of the stock was guaranteed a share of the year's earnings, in the form of the annual dividend. What was being established were markets in claims to future income whether this represented governments shifting the costs of current warfare onto generations of unborn citizens or commercial ventures spreading the costs of financing an expensive and risky undertaking among a wide body of investors. Both these types of securities generated extensive market activity. The very size of national debts created problems of matching buyers and sellers that could only be solved through organized markets. While the size of the capital required by the joint-stock companies was tiny in comparison to the needs of government, turnover in their securities was often high as each rumour about ship arrivals and current prospects produced speculative trading.

During the seventeenth/eighteenth centuries Amsterdam was the principal centre for securities trading in the world, with considerable activity in both domestic and foreign stocks. This volume of activity generated a group of specialist intermediaries who developed many of the modern techniques of stock exchange dealing, such as time bargains, price lists, and dealing for the account. These were then copied in other stock markets, especially London in the eighteenth century, aided by the migration there of a number of Amsterdam brokers. However, what Amsterdam lacked was any formal organization of this stock market. The brokers and their clients congregated around one of the 46 pillars of Amsterdam's general exchange building, and this inhibited the development of the rules and regulations necessary for the orderly conduct of business. It was only in 1787 that the brokers established some kind of organization as a protection against the menace of defaults, which undermined the trust element crucial to the conduct of business. Instead it was in Paris in 1724 that a formal stock exchange was first established, in the wake of the speculative boom inspired by John Law's financial schemes. This stock exchange both restricted entry to specialist intermediaries—*agents de change*—and had a code of conduct. However, the government limited its membership to only 60 and so a large and active alternative market continued to flourish in the streets outside the stock exchange building, and it was there that the advances in trading technique were being made.

Clearly the seventeenth and eighteenth centuries saw the development of securities markets, with Amsterdam in the lead, but Paris also prominent. However, in neither of these centres did there appear an organization called a stock exchange that controlled this securities market. It was either left largely uncontrolled, as in Amsterdam, or provided on such a restricted basis, as in Paris, that it had little influence of what was taking place. To this end it is essential to have a definition of a stock exchange which distinguishes it from a securities market. One such definition would be:

*Stock exchange*: A market where specialized intermediaries buy and sell securities under a common set of rules and regulations through a closed system dedicated to that purpose.

It is only when all those criteria are met can it be said that a stock exchange has come into existence and nowhere was that true in the eighteenth century, including London.

It was the French Revolution and Napoleonic Wars that led to the formation of the first stock exchange. The Revolution, and its aftermath, had the effect of destroying, temporarily, the securities markets of both Amsterdam and Paris and boosting that of London. London not only gained skilled personnel from the Continent but the prolonged European warfare that followed the Revolution led to a rapid growth in the National Debt and a period of extreme political uncertainty, which greatly stimulated turnover in that debt. The result was that a number of individuals saw the opportunity for creating an exchange in London where entry would be restricted to specialist intermediaries, but with no limit on membership. That membership would form their own rules and regulations reflecting the needs of the market. With the agreement of a large number of existing brokers and dealers in stocks this stock exchange was formed in March 1801.

The nineteenth century saw a great expansion in issues of transferable securities both by governments and corporate enterprise. In the United States the public debt of the Federal government increased from $64.8m. in 1860 to $1,193m. in 1913, largely due to the costs of the Civil War. At the same time the paid-up capital of the US railway system, which was the world's largest, rose rapidly from $318m. in 1850 to $19.8bn. in 1913. Altogether, it has been estimated that there were £32.6bn. (nominal value) of securities outstanding in the world by 1910, and these were owned by around 20 million investors. There was thus an increasing demand for the facilities provided by stock exchanges, with both new ones appearing around the world and old ones becoming larger, more organized, and increasingly sophisticated.

However, this distribution of both securities and investors was little related to either geography or population. Without organized markets there was little incentive to either issue or hold securities, rather than the assets which they represented but, without the existence of such securities, there could be no markets. It took time to acquaint both investors and borrowers with the benefits of securities, especially their ease of transfer without the need to disturb underlying operations. Consequently, it tended to be the most developed countries which possessed organized exchanges, educated investors, and experienced borrowers, and so it was there that securities were most frequently both issued and bought. In turn, the securities owned by investors in the richest nations not only represented assets of their own countries but also those of other places to a growing extent.

The estimate for 1910 suggested that of the total amount outstanding in the world British investors alone controlled 24 per cent, followed by the French with 18 per cent and the Germans with 16 per cent. This compared to only 5 per cent for the Russians, 4 per cent by the Austro-Hungarians, and 2 per cent each for the Italians and Japanese. Only the United States could challenge the overall dominance of Western Europe, for its investors owned 21 per cent of all securities, despite the fact that many of the stocks and bonds issued there were held abroad, especially in Western Europe. Even for an advanced economy like Canada, Western European investors owned a large proportion of all the securities issued, such as those of the Dominion government, all the major railroads, and, increasingly, minor industrial companies.

It was this distribution of the ownership of securities that created the general demand for stock exchanges as investors required facilities to buy and sell their holdings on a regular basis. With the concentration of ownership in Western Europe and the United States it was there that the largest, most active and best organized markets were established. Of the 89 principal stock exchanges in the world in 1907, 56 per cent were in Europe, especially Western Europe, with the rest being spread throughout the world, particularly in areas of European settlement or control.

At the simplest level were those exchanges that met a largely local need, providing a market for investors from a limited area in a restricted range of securities. In Britain numerous provincial stock exchanges were formed in the mid-nineteenth century and each of these provided a convenient forum for the securities of the growing numbers of local joint-stock companies, whether they were in insurance, textiles, shipping, or coal. Elsewhere in Europe the same phenomenon was observable at a later date such as in Germany, with stock exchanges being set up in Stuttgart, Düsseldorf, Cologne, Essen, and Bochum, or in France with Lille, Lyons, and Marseilles, or Spain with Barcelona and Bilbao. Abroad, it was the United States that was to see the formation of numerous local stock exchanges, such as Chicago and San Francisco, including some of only brief existence lasting no longer than the mining boom that had created them.

However, investors were interested in a far wider range of securities than those issued by local enterprise. The result was that these local stock exchanges both lost and gained business as orders were sent to markets offering a different choice while others were received for their specialities. Increasingly, these local exchanges were integrated into national markets so that they less and less catered for the general needs of their local investors but more and more offered an active forum in the securities of a limited number of companies operating in one or a few particular areas. They could even become of international importance as with the South African and Australian stock exchanges with their speciality gold-mining stocks.

Incorporating the functions of a local exchange for the vicinity within which they operated, but offering far more than that, were the national exchanges. These national stock exchanges attracted orders from throughout the country, and concentrated upon securities that could command a wide following and were actively traded. Initially this meant government stocks as these were held generally and required a central market, where they could be bought and sold. Without rapid communications this meant one place, frequently the capital city like London, Paris, or Madrid, though it could also be the major commercial, financial centre where that was not the capital, as with St Petersburg, Amsterdam, or New York. In the course of the nineteenth century the development of large-scale joint-stock enterprise with a national appeal and widespread ownership, such as the railways, considerably increased the volume and variety of securities traded on a national basis. At the same time improvements in communications, especially the telegraph and the telephone, allowed them to attract orders more easily from all over the country, which could result in business for their markets or be distributed to the most appropriate local exchange. The membership of the principal stock exchange in each country came to act as central co-ordinators of the securities market, as with Berlin in Germany and Milan in Italy after unification. As well as providing a central exchange and clearing-house, the principal exchange also acted as the main link with the banks and the money market, for it possessed the most actively traded securities with the greatest appeal, and it was securities of that kind that were ideal for either temporary holding or for collateral purposes. Thus, the difference between the local and national exchanges was not just one of the volume and variety of business, for there was a fundamental difference in the uses to which the securities traded were put. It was the national exchange that provided the most liquid market in which money could be readily employed or securities quickly sold, and so it attracted that kind of business from all over the country. In North America, for example, even Canadian banks did business in New York, rather than Montreal or Toronto, for that very reason.

This specialization was also carried a stage further with the development of exchanges that had an importance far beyond their national boundaries. With the developments of international telegraphic communications from the mid-nineteenth century onwards, the barriers that had preserved the independence and isolation of national exchanges were progressively removed, leading slowly to the creation of a world market for securities. Although many securities were of interest to only a small and localized group others came to attract a following from investors throughout the world, especially the major issues made by governments and railways. The result was that the securities quoted on each stock exchange became of interest to foreign investors, and so attracted external buying and selling. Increasingly, for example, arbitrage between different stock exchanges ensured that the same security commanded the same price on whatever market it was traded.

Although most of the major stock exchanges of Western Europe developed a trade in foreign securities, often with particular specialities by activity or country, it was London and Paris that became the major international markets, attracting business worldwide in an enormous variety of issues. Paris tended to fulfil the role of the central securities market for Europe and the Mediterranean area, while London emerged as the major market covering not only the securities of its extensive Empire but also issues made by countries as important as the United State, Argentina, and Japan. For North America it was New York that became the dominant stock exchange.

Consequently, though stock exchanges quoted different securities and met the needs of different investors, their trading was increasingly conditioned by forces beyond the confines of their own locality, or even country or continent. Some became specialist markets commanding a region or activity, while others gained a position as international centres, but all responded to developments throughout the world and, in turn, influenced trends. A reordering had taken place by the First World War in which the old stock exchanges continued to exist and flourish but the functions they performed had been altered, while new stock exchanges had been established which both competed with the established institutions and supplemented the market they provided, reflecting the rapid growth in importance of securities in finance and investment.

With international portfolio investment on a rising tide, governments finding new uses for funded debt, and business increasingly converting to the joint-stock form and the issue of securities, there was every sign that the fundamental forces underlying the growth of stock exchanges would continue into the twentieth century. However, beginning with the First World War the period after 1914 saw a progressive undermining of the role of stock exchanges within the economic system, both in individual economies and internationally. With the outbreak of the war all major stock exchanges closed temporarily as financial markets tried to cope with the consequences of the disruption caused by such a major military conflict. When the stock exchanges did reopen it was often under government supervision, as each country attempted to control the financial system in order to maximize finance for the war effort. The Berlin Stock Exchange did not reopen until October 1917. Consequently, when the war did end in 1918 not only had the Russian stock exchanges all but disappeared with the October revolution, but, more generally the climate of economic liberalism had begun to fade. Nevertheless most stock exchanges soon recovered their pre-war position aided by the needs of European governments to fund massive debts or to recapitalize industry, along with the resumption of established international lending and corporate borrowing. This was all reflected in stock market activity with the volume of sales on the New York Stock Exchange, for example, growing from 144m. in 1918 to 1,125m. in 1929, with a similar though more modest expansion taking place in London. One of the exceptions was in Germany, where, as hyperinflation had wiped out domestic savings, companies turned to foreign issues of stocks and bonds as a means of finance.

The crash of 1929 and the end of the gold standard in 1931 did more than bring this general recovery to an end. Stock exchanges were blamed for the ensuing economic depression of the 1930s, rather than being seen as the victims of underlying economic instability, with the result that there was a flurry of legislation aimed at controlling their operations. In 1933/4 the US government both established a Securities and Exchange Commission, to police new issues and secondary trading and, with the

Glass–Steagall Act, prohibited the direct involvement of commercial banks in the securities market, which had grown as a result of the government's own wartime need for finance through bond sales. Economic collapse in Germany in 1931 was followed by a prolonged period of stock exchange closure, and then a complete reorganization of the system by the government in 1934, when the stock exchange was reduced to minor importance. Similarly, civil war in Spain led to the closure of the Madrid Stock Exchange between 1936 and 1939. Internationally, the imposition and enforcement of exchange controls, with the collapse of the world monetary system, created major barriers to inter-stock exchange trading and led to the divergence of prices between markets. One of the few contrary trends was the establishment of an embryonic stock exchange in Tel Aviv in 1935, and that reflected the arrival there of Jewish migrants fleeing Nazi Germany. Generally, though most stock exchanges continued to provide an important service in the shape of a market for government and corporate securities, the interwar years represented a major set-back to the progress they had made in the nineteenth century.

Consequently, over the 1700–1939 period the history of the world's securities market can be depicted as a story of rise and fall. From humble beginnings in the seventeenth and eighteenth centuries they emerge as central to the dynamic expansion of a global economy. Without their existence governments and railroads would have been deprived of finance, and the integration of the world economy through trade, migration, and investment would have been considerably slowed down, if not stopped. By the beginning of the twentieth century the influence of stock exchanges was becoming ever more pervasive as all types of business reorganized themselves into the joint-stock form and appealed to investors for support. However, this triumph was to be cut short by the First World War which saw domestic and international finance severely disrupted and stock exchanges once again turned into instruments of government borrowing. After a brief revival for some in the 1920s the whole future of stock exchanges was plunged into doubt by the Wall Street crash and its financial and monetary repercussions. Political and economic nationalism severed the free flow of funds internationally upon which many stock exchanges had thrived, while domestically there was a growing preference for state provision or bank financing. The day of the stock exchange looked to have passed, to be replaced by a more corporate and interventionist future.

That pessimism appeared to be borne out with the Second World War and its aftermath. Following on from the 1930s depression, when capitalism itself was blamed for the world's economic problems, the era after 1945 saw a greatly enhanced role for the state. In socialist countries stock exchanges simply ceased to exist with central planning replacing financial markets. Even in market economies, government became much more involved in overall planning, and that included the direction of financial resources. Many industries, like entire railway systems, were nationalized and so their securities ceased to be traded on stock exchanges. At the same time the financial intermediation that was required was dominated by banks rather than markets. Only banks possessed the manpower and structure to cope with the huge increase in government regulation, both domestically with complex taxation, and internationally with exchange controls. Thus it was banks that dominated global financial flows and the domestic financing of business. For some twenty-five years after the Second World War stock exchanges appear to have settled for a minor role in the world's financial systems.

However, that was not to be the case. Beginning in the 1960s, and gathering pace from the 1970s onwards, government control over both national financial systems and global money and capital flows began to collapse. Market forces, for long held at bay, began to revive and this brought opportunities for the world's stock exchanges. At the very least a search by investors for securities that could cope with the effects of prolonged inflation directed their attention to corporate stocks rather than government bonds, and trading in these was very much the preserve of the likes of the New York Stock Exchange. The gradual abandonment of exchange controls also led to revival of an international market in securities, as financial institutions began to search for attractive investments beyond national boundaries. Finally, the recognition that nationalized industries had failed to deliver their promised benefits led to a programme of disposals from the 1980s, creating many new securities in the process. With the collapse of Communist economies around the world this was given a further boost as the new regimes sold off underperforming state assets for whatever they would bring. The outcome was both greatly increased activity on the long-established stock exchanges and the creation of numerous new ones around the world. By the end of the twentieth century stock exchanges had once again reclaimed much of the position in the financial system that they had held at the beginning.

Nevertheless, the conditions within which they operated were now radically different. The continuing development of communications and computing technology had made possible the creation of electronic market-places linking participants around the world. No longer was a physical trading-floor a necessity, endangering the position occupied by many of the world's major stock exchanges, such as New York and London. This electronic revolution was also combined by the active intervention of governments around the world to remove any restraints to trade, as was found in the rules and regulations of many of these long-established exchanges. Over the years since the First World War, and especially since 1945, stock exchanges had become much more bureaucratic organizations occupying quasi-official systems in the regulation of the financial system. This was not compatible with the more open economies of the late twentieth century and so stock exchanges had to change to survive, and many were slow to do so. Thus formally organized stock exchanges lost out to informal markets and electronic trading, and had to fight not only to recover their position but even to retain what they still had. Consequently, though the last two decades of the twentieth century witnessed a dramatic revival in the fortunes of securities markets around the world, it also created serious challenges for existing stock exchanges.

Though this history of the evolution of securities markets provides essential background to understanding the history of the London Stock Exchange, it is but part of the picture. There is a difference between a securities market and a stock exchange. A stock exchange is the institution that provides the forum for the sale and purchase of stocks and bonds, and the way it does that can affect the operation, appeal, and efficiency of the securities market. In turn the place of the securities market within the financial system can be affected with consequences for both other components, like banks, and the entire system itself. Essentially, the way the market is provided is not neutral in relation to its affect on the economy.

With an increase in the volume, variety, and velocity of transactions in securities, and as ever more buyers and sellers became involved, the difficulty of matching bargains, in respect of amount, time, place, type, and price grows enormously over time. The result is to create a need for improved facilities—such as a building which could accommodate all participants irrespective of weather conditions, and/or a communications system which would allow all to participate irrespective of location. In turn regulations are required so that all participants are aware of the conditions under which trading takes place, so as to ensure the smooth and orderly conduct of the market. To this end, in response to practical problems, a growing array of rules needs to be introduced governing such areas as admission of members, hours of trading, settlement of disputes, delivery of securities, charges to customers. Finally, the management of the facilities and the implementation of the rules require a permanent secretariat to handle the administration of the market while the members buy and sell securities. All this imposes costs and conditions upon those trading in securities, which alters the very market within which they are conducting business. The end result, however, is a modern securities market.

A modern securities market involves an inherent conflict of interest. Barriers to contact between buyers and sellers must be at a minimum so that all interested can participate when and where they want. Conversely, confidence in delivery or payment—as agreed—must be at a maximum, in order to both facilitate and encourage sales and purchases, and this requires strict controls on the admission and conduct of those permitted to participate. The number of participants has to be sufficiently small to permit the greatest contact between those with the most business to transact and there has to be a high degree of trust between those participants so that every bid to buy or offer for sale is equally acceptable, and so only price determines the counterpart to a deal. To this end a compromise between the legitimate requirements of an open market and a closed exchange has to be achieved, and the nature of this compromise changes as economic and financial circumstances alters. The success, or otherwise, of a stock exchange can be partly judged by how well it achieved this compromise at any one time.

There is also the question of cost. The provision of a sophisticated securities market is expensive, and that cost is normally borne by those who become members of the stock exchange. Naturally, they expect privileges compared to non-members in return for their payments. If non-members had the same access to the market as members, but were not subject to the same costs and rules, why would anyone become a member? Through membership of a stock exchange, participants in the market gain immediate access to numerous other participants, which greatly facilitates buying and selling. However, that position could be greatly enhanced, if existing members limited entry to the stock exchange. This would curtail the competition they faced and thus allow them to maintain or increase the charges they made to their customers. This was so as long as their membership of the stock exchange continued to give them a privileged position within the market and that could be achieved by using the rules to restrict access of non-members to such areas as current prices or major dealers. Conversely, those denied membership, or who were unwilling to pay the fees, would seek to circumvent the restrictions and so foster their own business, free of the rules that might hinder the ability of stock exchange members to compete. Here was another conflict of interest. Where all participants in the market were not members of the stock exchange, were members deliberately aiming to exclude potential competitors or were non-members seeking to avoid charges and controls? Again, the success or otherwise of a stock exchange can be judged by its ability to persuade most participants in the market to pay the fees required for the facilities and management necessary for the operation of that market. Again, the result would be an evolving compromise between the costs and privileges of membership and the freedom of non-members to conduct business as they saw fit.

Essentially, modern securities markets embody a series of compromises which may or may not provide the best service available at any one time. By studying the history of stock exchanges it is possible to see how these compromises evolved and how successful they were and thus make judgements about the relative importance of organized securities markets in different economies over time. Though it is the supply and demand for securities that created the market, the form that market took was by no means pre-ordained but reflected a complex interaction of economic and non-economic forces conditioned by the altering circumstances of the time. Out of that arose a variety of stock exchanges differing from each other in many substantial ways, such as the number and nature of the membership, the organization of the market-place, the securities that were traded, the charges made to customers, and the relationship with other powerful institutions, such as governments and banks, or markets, like those dealing in money and commodities. This diversity also meant that the place of the stock exchange within any national economy also differed enormously from one country to another. Generally, the more advanced the economy the more important was the stock exchange, but were stock exchanges a product of economic progress or a contribution to it? Similarly, where the role of stock exchanges differed between similar advanced economies was this a result of forces within the securities market itself or was it imposed from outside, with implications for comparative economic growth whatever the cause? It is only by studying stock exchanges both historically and internationally, and recognizing that they were institutions of considerable complexity and sophistication, that the answers to these type of questions can be found.

For example, in the nineteenth century the establishment of stock exchanges was very much a European phenomenon. Most were either formed in Europe or by Europeans abroad, as in the USA, Canada, Australia, or South Africa. However, despite their common European origins there was no single model which every country copied, while extensive variations of practice also appeared over time, reflecting modifications to suit local conditions. Rules were drawn up and frequently changed by the membership of these stock exchanges in order to protect their own interests and facilitate the business to be done by creating an orderly and regulated market-place. The nature of the demand, which varied from place to place and from time to time, was also a major force in determining the type of stock exchange that was formed and the way it developed.

These stock exchanges also differed from each other in significant respects, reflecting the way they had evolved, the relative power of groups within the membership, and the degree of government intervention. One illustration of the differences was their attitude to membership. Some stock exchanges, notably those in Germany, permitted commercial banks to become full members, and so helped to foster the development of the Universal Bank, whose business covered all aspects of financial activity from deposit-taking to new issues. However, most stock exchanges saw commercial banks, with their large capital and client bases, as major competitors, and tried to exclude them, as did both London and New York. Here, again, there were differences. London made admission easy and cheap for recognized brokers and dealers but restricted their additional activities. The result was a large, flexible, and dynamic market populated by numerous and competitive individuals and small firms, whose size ebbed and flowed with demand. In contrast, New York set a limit to membership which made entry expensive, but gave great freedom to its members in their other operations. This led to the growth of large brokerage firms able to provide a comprehensive service from new issues to trading and concentrating upon a high turnover in order to justify the cost of membership. Thus, the world market for securities was served by three different systems, and variations thereof—the German, the British, and the American—and each had advantages and disadvantages. Combined with attitudes to a fixed scale of charges to customers, willingness to quote new or different securities, and hostile or permissive government legislation, the consequence was that the role of the stock exchange was not the same in all countries, which had implications for the way financial and business systems were organized. In turn that had implications for the growth and operation of the economy. For too long the institutions that provided the markets through which supply and demand operated have been taken for granted and given no role in the success or otherwise of the markets they controlled. Stock exchanges as institutions grew out of the securities markets, and that itself indicates the need that existed for them. At the same time their very existence conditioned the way these markets then developed.

A modern stock exchange, of which London was the first, is not simply a securities market. A modern securities market needs to be provided with facilities, organized, regulated, and policed. At every stage of its development the London Stock Exchange and its membership had to take decisions that affected, either positively or negatively, the service that it provided to the securities market. The result was that the Stock Exchange was not a neutral bystander in the evolution of a complex securities market but an active participant conditioning the very form the market took and its ability to withstand competition at home and abroad. The study of the London Stock Exchange reveals a large and established institution evolving over time in the face of internal and external forces both pushing for and resisting change. The outcome of such a conflict is very important, for the London Stock Exchange was central to the operation of the financial system, and its performance can reveal much about the dynamism, or lack of it, in the British economy over time.

# I

# *From Market to Exchange,*
# *1693–1801*

## MARKET PLACE

There existed in London a securities market long before a formal stock exchange was ever established. As far back as the sixteenth century there is evidence of the buying and selling of shares, belonging to the few joint-stock companies then in existence. Though private negotiation between owner and purchaser was the normal means by which sales were accomplished, the growth in both the capital and the investors involved did lead to the use of public auctions. However, the ownership of shares remained concentrated within a very small group of wealthy individuals, and so there was little need for intermediaries to bring buyers and sellers together, and no justification for expensive and elaborate markets where business could be conducted on a frequent and regular basis. Typifying the time was the existence of the scrivener who combined in himself all the functions that would be performed later by the banker, lawyer, accountant, estate agent, and stockbroker. Land not securities formed the basis of investment before 1700, and credit not capital the principal object of finance.[1]

It was really not until the late seventeenth century that changes began to occur in the London securities market. There had already come into existence such substantial joint-stock companies as the East India Company before a flurry of activity in the 1690s transformed both the number and the capital. Before 1689 there were only around 15 major joint-stock companies in Britain, with a capital of £0.9m., and their activities were focused on overseas trade, as with the Hudson's Bay Company or the Royal African Company. In contrast, by 1695 the number had risen to around 150 with a capital of £4.3m. Though foreign trade remained significant, there had been a significant broadening of areas of interest, with domestic projects rising to the fore, as with banking and water supply. It was in 1694 that the Bank of England was formed.[2]

---

[1] W. R. Scott, *The Constitution and Finance of English, Scottish and Irish Joint-Stock Companies to 1720* (Cambridge 1910–12), i. 44, 155, 161; A. C. Coleman, 'London Scriveners and the Estate Market in the Later Seventeenth Century', *Ec. H. R.* 4 (1951/2), 230.

[2] K. G. Davies, 'Joint-Stock Investment in the Later Seventeenth Century', *Ec. H. R.* 4 (1951/2), 288, 291–2; Scott, *Constitution and Finance*, i. 460.

As a result of these developments there was a substantial increase in both the number of investors and the value of their holdings. Whereas before 1690 most joint-stock companies possessed a small capital provided by a closely connected group of shareholders, in that decade there did appear a number of well-capitalized concerns whose securities were widely held. The Bank of England, for example, obtained its capital of £1.2m. from 1,509 investors in 1694, or an average of £795 from each, whereas the Royal African Company, formed in 1671, raised £0.1m. from 200 subscribers, or £500 from each. Though individuals had already begun to appear who took a particular interest in the buying and selling of securities, either for others or on their own behalf, it was the 1690s that saw the emergence of specialized brokers and jobbers. Previously, with the number of securities in existence limited, and those held by a small number of people, turnover was both too low and too intermittent to justify the attentions of specialized intermediaries such as stockbrokers, or more than the occasional attentions of a dealer, or stockjobber, trading on his own account.[3]

Clearly the development in joint-stock company formation at the end of the seventeenth century had placed the securities market on a permanent and more substantial basis than before, and the focus of that market was London. It was in London that the richest members of society were concentrated, whether their wealth came from land or trade. Even the Scottish Company—the Company of Scotland trading to Africa and the Indies (Darien Company)—which was formed in 1695 expected to raise half its capital there.[4]

Similarly, of the first 500 subscribers for the shares being issued by the Bank of England, some 450 lived in London, and this was typical of the position for other major joint-stock companies at the time. There now existed a small number of companies that were fundamentally different in scale and nature from the joint-stock undertakings of the past. They had been, essentially, large partnerships with only a limited turnover in their nominally transferable securities. Instead there now existed stocks and shares that were regularly bought and sold publicly in sufficient amount, to justify the publication of current price lists and to attract the attentions of those willing to carry out such transactions on commission or be willing to buy or sell in the expectation of reversing the deal at a profit. For example, it was estimated that in 1704 turnover in the shares of the Bank of England and the East India Company totalled £1.8m., or 85 per cent of the combined paid-up capital of the two concerns.[5]

[3] Davies, 'Joint-Stock Investment', 292, 294–6.
[4] Scott, Constitution and Finance, ii. 210, iii. 478–9.
[5] E. V. Morgan and W. A. Thomas, The Stock Exchange: Its History and Functions, (London 1961), 14, 17; P. Mirowski, The Birth of the Business Cycle (New York 1985), 272; L. Neal, The Rise of Financial Capitalism: International Capital Markets in the Age of Reason (Cambridge 1994), i. 275, 279, 281; P. G. M. Dickson, The Financial Revolution in England: A Study in the Development of Public Credit (London 1967), 466, 490, 529–30; L. D.

In the early eighteenth century company shares continued to be an important driving force behind the expansion of the securities market in London. New companies were formed, expanding the amount of securities to be traded and the number of interested investors. During the speculative mania of 1719/20—the South Sea Bubble—some 190 new joint-stock companies were proposed. They expected to raise £220m. from an investing public convinced that the application of the joint-stock form to all areas of the economy would bring untold riches to their shareholders. Though most came to nothing, before the belief was shattered there was great activity in the securities market as shares changed hands at greatly inflated prices. Share prices more than doubled between 1719 and 1720 before collapsing by two-thirds by 1722. More lasting were the longer established concerns such as the Bank of England, which had attracted 4,837 investors by 1726.[6] However, corporate securities were not to be the foundation upon which the London Stock Exchange was built, despite their early significance. The problem was that business required to be both financed and managed and the joint-stock form, where ownership and operation were divorced, was inappropriate for most areas of the economy at that time. In such major sectors as agriculture and manufacturing the level of individual capital required was low but the need for personal involvement was high. The use and supervision of labour rather than the mobilizing of capital was what was crucial, and this was best achieved on an individual, family, or partnership basis. It was only in novel areas, like the development of trade to distant and unknown lands, like India, Africa, or Canada, that the joint-stock company could make a special contribution by raising a substantial capital and spreading the risk. Consequently, though the late seventeenth and early eighteenth century did see the widespread experimentation with the use of the joint-stock form in business, few of the companies survived outside trade and banking. Subsequently, the use made of joint-stock companies remained very low until the late eighteenth century. Though the Bubble Act, passed in 1720 and not repealed until 1825, did outlaw joint-stock companies, unless specifically permitted by Parliament, it is most unlikely that this was the explanation for the unpopularity of joint-stock companies after 1720. In Scotland, for example, where the Bubble Act was considered not to apply, the joint-stock company was also little in evidence outside banking and trade. Also when an area of business did appear in the late eighteenth century, for which the joint-stock company was ideal, namely the canal, many were promoted, obtained a charter, and attracted the interest of investors. Similarly, many businesses were operated as large-

Schwartz, *London in the Age of Industrialisation: Entrepreneurs, Labour Force and Living Conditions, 1700–1850* (Cambridge 1992), 226, 233.

[6] J. H. Clapham, *The Bank of England, 1694–1914* (Cambridge 1944), 281; B. R. Mitchell, *British Historical Statistics* (Cambridge 1988), 687.

scale partnerships no different in form from joint-stock companies but lacking any form of legal recognition.[7]

The real foundation of the securities market, that eventually led to the formation of the London Stock Exchange, took place in the year 1693 when the government, for the first time, borrowed by creating a permanent debt that was transferable. Previous to that the government's borrowings had been on a short-term basis, with the debt being either redeemed or refinanced, depending on the state of national finances, when it became due. Those who held this permanent debt now required a market where they could sell it, if they wanted to realize the funds that they had invested, in the same way as holders of joint-stock company shares did. The success of this issue was quickly followed by a series of private-sector initiatives in which joint-stock companies swapped the capital they raised from their shareholders for largely unmarketable government debt. As a result the government got its debt permanently funded, in return for regular interest payments, and so avoided the possibility of crisis when it tried to renew its borrowings. Conversely, the investor got a safe and remunerative investment that was readily saleable, in the form of shares in a joint-stock company whose principal asset was its holdings in government debt. The Bank of England, when formed in 1694, paid over its entire capital of £1.2m. to the government in return for a regular payment of £50,000 every six months, as well as exclusive banking privileges. Similarly, the East India Company lent its entire paid-up capital of £3.2m. to the government in 1708, as did the South Sea Company in 1711.

Altogether, by the middle of the eighteenth century the Bank of England, East India Company, and the South Sea Company had lent some £42.8m. to the government. As a result their shares were being valued by investors not so much for their banking or trading success and prospects but simply as a variety of government debt. From 1717 onwards the government itself was increasingly conscious of the advantages to be gained from having all its borrowings in a fully funded form, as the need to finance a succession of wars placed a continuing burden on normal government finances. A major cause of the South Sea Bubble was the climate of speculation fostered by the conversion in 1717 of government debt from a floating to a permanent basis, as this was then imitated by joint-stock companies. Eventually, in 1749 the government consolidated most of its remaining borrowings into one single loan, paying a fixed rate of interest of 3 per cent per annum, known as 3 per cent consols. The result was that, whereas in

---

[7] P. Mirowski, 'The Rise (and Retreat) of a Market: English Joint-Stock Shares in the Eighteenth Century', *J. Ec. H.* 41 (1981), 577; M. Patterson and D. Reiffen, 'The Effect of the Bubble Act on the Market for Joint-Stock Shares', *J. Ec. H.* 40 (1990), 163, 171; R. C. Michie, *Money, Mania and Markets: Investment, Company Formation and the Stock Exchange in Nineteenth Century Scotland* (Edinburgh 1981), 7; A. B. Dubois, *The English Business Company after the Bubble Act, 1720–1800* (New York 1938), 11–12, 34, 36, 38–40, 217, 219, 222, 225.

1691 the government owed £3.1m., none of which was funded, by 1750 it owed £78.0m., 93 per cent of which was permanently funded.[8]

As short-term government debt was little traded, being kept for redemption, but long-term debt was regularly bought and sold as the only means of disposing or acquiring it, the effect on the securities market was enormous. There now existed a large and permanent mass of securities in which there was a substantial and regular turnover. It is calculated that registered transfers in Bank of England, East India Company, and Government Stock, which fluctuated at between 1,000 and 6,000 per annum between 1694 and 1717, rose to 17,172 in 1718—the year after the conversion—and then reached 21,811 in 1720, before collapsing as the speculative boom died away. Even then transfers averaged between 4,000 and 7,000 per annum for the rest of the 1720s, through the 1730s, and into the 1740s, before peaking at the 25,000 level in 1749/50. It then fell back again but by then 20,000 transfers a year had become standard, suggesting a solid underlying volume of trading in the London securities market. Clearly this was the bedrock upon which an organized and established securities market could be built.[9]

With government consistently honouring its debts, and the payments it had to make upon them, and a market in existence whereby this debt could be bought or sold with little difficulty, transferable securities were an increasingly desirable investment in the eighteenth century. They attracted the interest of wealthy individuals like the Marlborough family or institutions such as the emerging insurance companies. Insurance companies or societies, for example, increased their investments from c.£0.3m. in 1720 to c.£4m. in 1800, by which time around 80 per cent was in securities, largely those issued by the government.[10] As Fairman, the accountant for Royal Exchange Assurance, explained in the 1790s:

The regular payment of the interest on the government funds, and the number of persons in this country preferring the interest they afford to the hazardous profits of trade, occasion continual purchasers for those shares in them which are brought to market for sale. The facility, also, and trifling expense, with which transfers are

---

[8] Dickson, *Financial Revolution*, 466–7, 529–30; Mirowski, 'Rise and Retreat' 560–2; Clapham, *Bank of England*, i. 19–20; A. C. Carter, *Getting, Spending and Investing in Early Modern Times* (Assen 1975), 127; H. V. Bowen, 'Investment and Empire in the Later Eighteenth Century: East India Stockholding, 1756–1791', *Ec. H. R.* 42 (1989), 188; H. V. Bowen, 'The Bank of England During the Long Eighteenth Century, 1694–1800', in R. Roberts and D. Kynaston (eds.), *The Bank of England: Money, Power and Influence 1694–1994* (Oxford 1995), 9.

[9] Dickson, *Financial Revolution*, 529–30; A. C. Carter, *The English Public Debt in the Eighteenth Century* (London 1968), 4–5, 18, 23; R. D. Richards, 'The Bank of England and the South Sea Company', *Economic History*, 2 (1930–3), 357–8; A. H. John, 'Insurance Investment and the London Money Market of the Eighteenth Century', *Economica*, NS 20 (1953), 138–40.

[10] Dickson, *Financial Revolution*, 482, 489, L. S. Pressnell, *Country Banking in the Industrial Revolution* (Oxford 1956), 417; Carter, *Getting, Spending*, 17.

made in these funds, are inducements to prefer vesting money in them to laying it out on mortgages or other private security, which, though probably yielding a greater interest, is frequently attended with trouble and uncertainty.[11]

Generally, by 1760, when the National Debt stood at £101.7m. there were an estimated 60,400 holders, of whom the great majority were to be found in and around London. Around 69 per cent of all transfers of government and Bank of England stock in 1755 were on behalf of Londoners, with a further 10 per cent being done for those resident in the immediate vicinity.[12]

## ORGANIZATION

Within London this securities market had a definite location as early as the 1690s. Having begun in the Royal Exchange, where all manner of commodities were traded and deals struck, it had gravitated to the street and coffee houses of the neighbouring Exchange Alley. Here in coffee houses such as Jonathan's or Garraways potential buyers and sellers could meet and agree terms. However, with the growing number and type of securities, the likelihood of matching exactly the requirements of both buyer and seller at one particular time receded. One solution to this was the use of an auction, where all interested could bid for the securities on offer. These appear to have been a regular occurrence at Garraways. The problem with an auction was that it suited the needs of the vendor—to dispose of what they owned—but it did not allow a potential purchaser to make known his requirements.[13]

Another solution was intermediation, with individuals being entrusted with the task of finding buyers or sellers on behalf of clients who wished to dispose of or purchase securities. In return the intermediary received payment for the time and effort involved. Clearly by 1700 such intermediaries—or stockbrokers—had come into existence though it is doubtful if any wholly specialized in the business. They were easily recruited, frequently combining stockbroking with the other tasks that they conducted for wealthy customers. Bankers, goldsmiths, or the clerks who registered changes of ownership in the Bank of England or the East India Company, were all obvious candidates to add the new profession of stockbroking to their list of activities. Certainly, whatever the occupation they came from the number of stockbrokers appeared to have grown rapidly in the 1690s as the government tried to restrict the total to 100 by a law passed in 1697.

[11] W. Fairman, *The Stocks Examined and Compared* (London 1798, 3rd edn.), 2.
[12] Carter, *Getting, Spending*, 19, 67, 76; Dickson, *Financial Revolution*, 489, 514, 529-30; Bowen, 'Investment and Empire', 201; Neal, *Financial Capitalism*, 93, 96.
[13] Dickson, *Financial Revolution*, 490-4, 499, 507-11; Neal, *Financial Capitalism*, 33; Carter, *Getting, Spending*, 73, 91, 125, 127, 134, 136; S. R. Cope, 'The Stock Exchange Revisited: A New Look at the Market in Securities in London in the Eighteenth Century', *Economica*, 45 (1978), 2-3.

This proved completely ineffective and the number of brokers continued to grow along with the market itself, with individuals being attracted either from other occupations in London or from other parts of Britain and abroad. Benjamin Cope, a stockbroker in London from 1733 had been a hosier while George Middleton arrived from Aberdeen and acted as a stockbroker in London in 1720, along with being a banker and goldsmith. Edmund and Philip Antrobus came from Congleton in Cheshire, and set up as stockbrokers in London in the 1770s. There was also a significant Dutch contingent who brought great expertise to London as Amsterdam was the leading securities market in the world at the time. One such was Abraham Ricardo who arrived in London around the year 1759, having been sent there by his father—Joseph—who was a successful stockbroker in Amsterdam. At the same time the profession of stockjobber or dealer became increasingly professional as wealthy individuals used their money or holdings of securities to buy and sell in the expectation of quickly reversing the deal at a profit. Samson Gideon, for example, the son of a London West India Merchant became a jobber in 1719 with a capital of £1,500 which had grown to £350,000 by 1759.[14]

Thus, fairly early in the eighteenth century there existed a group of individuals in London who made at least part of their living by handling the buying and selling of stocks and shares, on behalf of those who had neither the time, knowledge, opportunity, or inclination to do it for themselves. Nevertheless, stockbrokers could only arrange sales or purchases on behalf of clients when willing buyers or sellers could be found. For many securities this was no easy matter as the number of existing shareholders or interested investors were small, so restricting the potential to arrange a deal. In turn, this would reduce the incentive of individuals to specialize in stockbroking, rather than the other opportunities available to them in finance or trade. However, in the securities issued by the Bank of England, East India Company, or South Sea Company, plus the funded debt of the government, the possibility of easily and continually matching buyers and sellers was much greater because of the amount in existence and the number of investors involved. Furthermore, as it was the government that provided the final guarantee of payment, whether interest or dividend, all these securities were, to an extent, interchangeable. Hence investors looking for a safe and remunerative investment, secured on a trust in the government to service its borrowings, could be satisfied by any one of a number of securities that might be offered for sale. Consequently, as more and more

[14] E. Healey, Coutts and Company, 1692–1992: The Portrait of a Private Bank (London 1992), 45, 51; M. C. Reed, A History of James Capel and Company (London 1975), 1–3, 11–12; D. Wainwright, Government Broker: The Story of an Office and of Mullens and Company (East Molesey 1990), 1, 9; C. Wilson, Anglo-Dutch Commerce and Finance in the Eighteenth Century (Cambridge 1941), 97, 111, 116, 195; D. Weatherall, David Ricardo: A Biography (The Hague 1976), 3; Scott, Constitution and Finance, i. 345; L. Sutherland, Politics and Finance in the Eighteenth Century (London 1984), 387–9.

of the business of the securities market was composed of the buying and selling of government or related securities, it encouraged individuals not only to enter stockbroking but to specialize in it because of the steady income available, as well as the occasional bonus during a speculative boom. Despite that situation, when Edmund Antrobus was offered a partnership in the West End banking firm of Coutts & Co. in 1777 he gave up the stockbroking business he had established, leaving it to his brother Philip.[15]

This securities market became increasingly sophisticated in the eighteenth century, stimulated not only by the underlying growth of turnover but also by the arrival of Dutch Jews and French Huguenots who introduced continental practices. Even before 1700 buy/sell options were in use as was dealing for time. This became more refined in the eighteenth century with the custom of making deals for a month or more ahead, encouraged by a government attempt to reduce speculation by banning options in 1734. The ban on options had little effect but the use of a fixed date in the fixture, by which all stock had to be delivered and paid for, became standard practice in the London securities market. By the 1780s six-weekly settlements appear to have been in use, though by no means all bargains were done for time. Many transactions were also for cash or for varying periods depending on the preferences of buyer and seller. Nevertheless, the popularity of dealing for time also led to the use of other techniques such as continuation and backwardation. With continuation—or rescounters—a purchase could be continued from one settlement to the next by the payment of the difference in price between that prevailing when the deal was struck and that at the settlement date. Thus the buyers could delay payment of the purchase price at small cost until either the requisite funds became available or the price rose so as to make a profitable sale possible. Conversely, with backwardation the delivery of the stock whose sale had been agreed could be delayed until the next settlement date, for the similar payment of the price difference. The vendor could thus postpone handing over the securities in question until they became available, either from the client or through a price fall so that they could be bought in the market at a favourable price. Essentially, as these techniques and practices evolved in the eighteenth century, the securities market became better at meeting the varied needs of investors, ranging from those who simply wanted to buy or sell for immediate effect to those who sought to profit from a cycle of either rising or falling prices.[16]

Greatly assisting the flexibility of the market was the appearance, from

[15] Reed, *Capel and Company*, 1–3; Healey, *Coutts and Company*, 110.

[16] Cope, 'The Stock Exchange Revisited', 8–10, 12, 15, 17; C. F. Smith, 'The Early History of the London Stock Exchange', *American Economic Review*, 19 (1929), 207–8, 213; Dickson, *Financial Revolution*, 507, 510; S. R. Cope, 'The Goldsmids and the Development of the London Money Market during the Napoleonic Wars', *Economica*, NS (1942), 181, 201.

about 1700 onwards, of specialized dealers or jobbers, who bought and sold securities on their own account, and not for clients. Jobbers either employed their own money to buy securities in the expectation that the price would rise—and they could be sold at a profit—or had extensive holdings of stocks and shares available, which could be sold in the expectation that the price would fall, and they could be repurchased at a lower price—hence a profit would be generated. Between 1708 and 1755 a total of some 43 dealers in securities operated in the London market at various times. One, for example, was William Sheppard, a banker and goldsmith, who operated in Bank of England stock. In 1700 his 278 purchases and 371 sales of bank stock amounted to c.£0.5m. and represented a fifth of all such registered transfers. Similarly in 1754 William Cotsford made 870 purchases and 868 sales of 3 per cent consols, worth £0.6m. in total, and accounting for over one-third of all such transfers.[17]

These actions of the jobber, which were governed simply by self-interest and the desire for profit, made a major contribution to the London securities market. By being willing to either purchase or sell securities, without the prospect of immediate repurchase or resale, these jobbers were instrumental in creating a ready market for both securities and money in London. Those investors who wished to sell stocks could find a willing buyer—if the price was right—while those who wished to invest their money met with an available supply of securities—if the price was right. Naturally enough, jobbers were only willing to operate in the largest and most actively traded securities, like those issued by the government, as only in these could they have the expectation of reversing the deal reasonably quickly and safely, and so turn over their money and securities enough to generate a worthwhile return without accepting undue risks. Consequently, unlike many other types of investments, like property or mortgages, securities were more akin to short-term investments like bank deposits or 30- to 90-day bills of exchange, when they possessed an active secondary market serviced by jobbers.

It was this continuous buying and selling that astonished, and even appalled, contemporaries as they could not understand what lay behind it. As early as 1716 one anonymous contemporary had written a vitriolic attack on the securities market in general and stockjobbers in particular.

From this corruption of companies in Trade, breeds the vermin called stockjobbers, who prey upon, destroy, and discourage all Industry and honest gain, for no sooner is any Trading Company erected, or any villainous project to cheat the public set up, but immediately it is divided into shares, and then traded for in Exchange Alley, before it is known whether the project has any intrinsic value in it, or no, . . . If a design was never so solid to promote Industry and Trade, stockjobbing will eventually damn it in its infancy.

---

[17] Dickson, *Financial Revolution*, 494, 497, 511; Davies, 'Joint-Stock Investment', 294–5.

This writer even went so far as to demand the banning of transferable securities as the 'Buying and selling of shares, transferring or stockjobbing, ruins, and is a bane to all Honesty and Industry'.[18] Familiarity with the securities market did not necessarily lead to greater understanding.

Thomas Mortimer, writing in 1761 could see no role for either stockbrokers, apart 'for the conveniency of the ladies . . .', or the even worse stockjobbers, on whom he blamed the fluctuations in the value of government stock.[19]

Even at the end of the eighteenth century it is doubtful if most contemporaries had any greater knowledge of the function of the securities market, and its intermediaries, than was possessed at the beginning.

In *The Picture of London*, published in 1802, the curious stranger was encouraged to visit the rotunda of the Bank of England '. . . for the throng, the hurry, the seeming confusion, and the busy eager countenances, he will perceive there . . . although he comprehends nothing of the detail . . .'.[20] To most interested observers securities were no different from other forms of property, which were sold through extended negotiation and with little variation of price from year to year. Land or property for example, were sold for the rent they would bring, and that was fixed by the terms of the leases that the farmers or occupants had signed. In these cases a lawyer was of more value than a broker or dealer. However, those who bought, held, or sold securities in the eighteenth century did so for a variety of reasons, and only one of these was long-term investment for a permanent income.

Clearly, for many eighteenth-century investors the transferable nature of stocks and shares was of little significance as they bought and held their securities for either the regular and safe return it brought, as with government debt, or the prospects of windfall gains it offered, such as in the case of the small number of joint-stock companies. Among investors in East India Company Stock, for example, there were many who were content to receive their annual dividend payment without altering their holding by sales or purchases. An estimate for January 1767 suggested that as many as 44 per cent of those holding East India Company Stock were of this kind. To the passive investor government or related securities were very attractive as they could be easily acquired in variable amounts and when needed, and required no subsequent management. During the eighteenth century there developed an inverse relationship between investments in landed property and the purchase of government debt. When government borrowing was high as a result of foreign wars and military expenditure, as in the 1740s and 1770s, investors switched away from purchases of land and, instead, bought national debt. In contrast, in periods of peace, when

[18] *Thoughts on Trade and a Public Spirit* (London 1716), 4, 16–17.

[19] Thomas Mortimer, *Everyman His Own Broker or A Guide to Exchange Alley* (London 1761, 2nd edn.), pp. xi, 17, cf. Carter, *English Public Debt*, 23.

[20] *The Picture of London* (London 1802), 107.

government borrowing was low, there was strong interest amongst investors in the yield offered by land holdings, and so purchases and prices increased. Gains made, for example, as government securities rose in prices after a war, encouraged holders to sell out and switch their funds into land.

Increasingly, investors came to regard government debt and landed property as alternatives to each other. Increasingly, the safety, convenience, and liquidity of National Debt attracted investors who, in the past, might have placed their funds into land. London insurance companies gradually turned away from mortgages and land, towards government debt because of the greater ease of realizing securities when a shipping loss or major fire required a large and immediate payment to a policy-holder.[21]

While the yield on government debt was low it was both almost risk-free and easily realizable. Land and property could offer a higher rate of return but sales could take time to arrange, which was completely unsuitable if money was required quickly, as could be the case with a bank or insurance company. Similarly, sums lent by way of mortgages on property were not immediately recoverable if the owner was not able to repay and the assets had to be sold. Bank deposits also offered great flexibility but they were not without risks. During the 1720–1790 period a total of 82 private banks went bankrupt, or more than one every year, and this included 58 in London itself.[22]

To long-term investors all that was required was a means by which acquisitions or disposals could be made with little trouble or expense and as expeditiously as possible. Options, continuations, backwardations, and fluctuating prices, were of little concern to them. If investors had all been of this kind then there would have been little pressure for the development of a large and sophisticated securities market in London. Brokers would have been needed to match buyers and sellers at an acceptable price, considering the growing number of investors, but there would have been little scope for jobbers as the volume of turnover would be too low to provide them with an income. In turn, without jobbers the ability to buy or sell stocks and shares, at the time and in the amount required, would have been seriously affected, so undermining the attractions of securities to investors compared to other investments. Thus, though long-term investors made only infrequent and partial use of the ready market for securities the very existence of that market was an important influence in persuading them to place their savings in stocks and shares in the first place. The fluctuating

---

[21] Bowen, 'Investment and Empire', 199; Carter, *English Public Debt*, 18; C. Clay, 'The Price of Freehold Land in the Later 17th and 18th Centuries', *Ec. H. R.* 27 (1974), 184, 186; B. A. Holderness, 'The English Land Market in the 18th Century: The Case of Lincolnshire', *Ec. H. R.* 27 (1974), 559, 562–3; C. G. A. Clay, 'Henry Hoare, Banker, His Family and the Stourhead Estate', in F. M. L. Thompson (ed.), *Landowners, Capitalists and Entrepreneurs* (Oxford 1994), 117, 132; P. K. O'Brien, 'The Political Economy of British Taxation, 1660–1815', *Ec. H. R.* 41 (1988), 2, 4; John, 'Insurance Investment', 147.

[22] Pressnell, *Country Banking*, 536.

prices emanating from the market were a public manifestation to all that securities could be readily bought and sold, and thus an inducement to either subscribe to new issues or to purchase additional or different stocks being sold by others.

Luckily for the development of the market the transferable nature of securities was attractive to other investors. Obviously there were those who were always willing to speculate by buying for a rise or selling for a fall. However large-scale activities of this kind were of a spasmodic nature, as with the South Sea Bubble of 1720, and were hardly the basis upon which professionals like brokers and jobbers could expect to make a permanent and prosperous living. Instead, there were other investors who saw in transferable securities not some form of permanent investment but a temporary home for available funds. Merchants in London, for example, could employ funds released through sales, and not yet tied up in new stock, in buying securities which would be later sold when the funds were required. As securities reached the date at which interest and dividends were paid they rose in value to take account of the money their holders would receive. By buying for cash and selling for time it would be possible to take advantage of this fact on a relatively risk-free basis, and receive a modest profit as a result. That was only one of the ways that the ability to buy and sell quickly in the securities market, and at little cost, made it attractive to investors who were not in a position to lock savings away for a long period, as with property and mortgages.

Before the eighteenth century, temporarily idle funds would not have been attracted to long-term debt. Instead merchants, bankers, and others with cash not yet tied up in business or loans would purchase short-term bills or bonds with the expectation of holding them until the date when payment became due. Bonds issued by the East India Company to finance its trade, as well as the variety of short-term securities created by government to meet its differing financial needs, were ideal homes for temporarily idle funds. However, as the government increasingly converted its debt from a short- to a long-term basis, and provincial banks appeared providing credit for their local business communities, many of the obvious openings for temporary funds disappeared. This was where the transferable nature of the National Debt, and the market that existed to facilitate its buying and selling, became all important. To the issuer of the securities the debt created was permanent, but to the holder the ability to sell quickly rendered it temporary, and thus a suitable and remunerative home for short-term funds.[23]

What made this a widespread occurrence in the eighteenth century

[23] John, 'Insurance Investment', 140; D. M. Joslin, 'London Private Bankers, 1720–1785', *Ec. H. R.* 7 (1954/5), 171, 184–6; D. Hancock, ' "Domestic Bubbling": Eighteenth-Century London Merchants and Individual Investment in the Funds', in *Ec. H. R.* 47 (1994), 682–3, 690, 695–6.

was the development of the banking system as it greatly increased the volume of funds that were available for only short-term investment. Depositors expected to be able to withdraw their savings from a bank at their own convenience. However, banks could not force repayment of loans from those to whom they had lent the money. Loans could be tied up in unsold stocks of goods, for example, or in payments for raw materials. Consequently, banks had to maintain a margin between the funds they attracted in as deposits and those they lent out by way of loans. Unfortunately for the bank this margin—or idle balance—generated no income, making it necessary to charge a higher rate of interest on the amount that was lent and accept a higher level of risk as borrowers sought to service that debt. If the idle balance could be remuneratively employed, while at the same time remaining readily available to repay depositors, not only would banks charge lower rates of interest but the level of risk would be lower. In turn, fewer banks would collapse due to bad debts and panic withdrawals by depositors, and so more savings would be placed in the hands of bankers, greatly expanding the supply of credit available in the economy.

During the eighteenth century the practice grew up of banks, directly or indirectly, employing part of their idle balance in transferable securities. Either by investing directly in government or allied debt or lending to those that did, banks increasingly provided the funds that underpinned the growth of the London securities market. The stockbroker Edmund Antrobus, for instance, was largely employed by the West End bank of Coutts & Co. to buy and sell government stock on behalf of the bank and its customers from 1777. In 1786 around half of his firm's business, totalling £413,624, was from Coutts. Also it was not just London bankers who employed London brokers, for even provincial banks did so. The Worcester bankers, Berwick & Co., employed James Pilliner, a London stockbroker, from 1782. Between 1782 and 1787 Pilliner's buying and selling operations in, mainly, government stock averaged c.£150,000 per annum for that bank. More commonly, provincial banks deposited part of their idle balances at short notice with a London private banker, who paid interest upon it. In turn London bankers employed part of those funds in the securities market, through their broking connections there. As deposits that could be withdrawn at short notice paid a lower rate of interest than the irredeemable National Debt, the London banker could profit by purchasing government securities with depositors' funds. Without the existence of a market where these securities could be readily bought and sold, plus the growing sophistication of the operations conducted there, the risk involved in holding permanent debt with near-liquid funds would not have been sustainable. Consequently, what developed in the eighteenth century was the practice of banks but also of insurance companies and others, investing short-term funds in securities or lending to brokers and jobbers so that they could.[24]

Consequently, much of what the public saw as unnecessary speculation— and dismissed as such—was but the means necessary to ensure that bankers and others could employ short-term funds in long-term loans. As with a bank itself, where there was a continuous ebb and flow of funds as different customers deposited and borrowed, so the securities market witnessed continuous buying and selling of the most popular securities, reflecting supply and demand conditions in the money market.[25] Thus, though the London securities market was not directly involved in the provision of finance for economic growth in the eighteenth century, its ability to provide a large and remunerative outlet for short-term funds, for which it would be difficult to find an alternative use, did contribute to the maintenance of relatively low interest rates at the time and did give some partial stability to the emerging banking system. It also meant that the government could obtain the finance it required to wage war without putting such a strain on the capital market that productive areas of the economy would be disadvantaged. In the course of the eighteenth century, the London securities market thus became an integral part of both the nation's capital market, through the finance of the National Debt, and the money market, with the home it provided for bankers' balances. By expanding the supply of credit and capital, and facilitating the financial integration of the economy, the securities market made a significant contribution to eighteenth-century economic growth, though never central to the process.[26]

Internationally, the London securities market also played a role. During the eighteenth century it was the Dutch who were the major international investors, as well as large traders, and so it was through Amsterdam that flowed the currents of the world's payments system. The European economy was continuously moving away from a system where international payments were only in gold and silver currency and goods had all to be taken to and from specific locations where they could be traded. Instead, multilateral systems of payments and the use of credit were becoming standard practice. Inevitably this involved the continuous adjustment of balances between countries. At a time when internal currencies were denominated in terms of gold and/or silver this could be done in terms of the movement of metal. This was an expensive and time-consuming procedure much of

---

[24] Reed, *Capel and Company*, 11–12; Healey, *Coutts and Company*, 113; Pressnell, *Country Banking*, 36, 18, 76, 83, 85–6, 259–60, 264, 401, 412, 415, 417, 428, 431–2.
[25] Fairman, *Stocks Examined*, 20; R. W. Wade, *The Stock-holder's Assistant*, (London 1806), pp. iii, vi.
[26] J. Hoppit, *Risk and Failure in English Business* (Cambridge 1987), 63–4, 69–70, 133–4; M. Buchinsky and B. Polak, 'The Emergence of a National Capital Market in England, 1710–1880', *J. Ec. H.* 53 (1993), 18; B. L. Anderson, 'Provincial Aspects of the Financial Revolution of the Eighteenth Century', *B. H.* 2 (1969), 11, 18, 21; B. L. Anderson, 'Money and the Structure of Credit in the Eighteenth Century', *B. H.* 12 (1970), 85, 91.

which could be unnecessary as the balance of payments ebbed and flowed with shipments made and received. Instead, if a mechanism was in place which would match international credits and debits, even on a bilateral basis, then the transport of precious metals would only be required to settle the final balance, not every transaction. It was this service that merchant bankers, with connections and operations in two or more countries sought to provide. Essentially, a merchant banker not only provided the credit that international trade required, as payment was awaited on goods shipped, but also made available the means of payment at the place where it was required.

Thus, a market developed in the credits and debits arising from international commerce, and the securities market became a part of it by at least the middle of the eighteenth century. Foreign holdings of the National Debt, for instance, rose from 9 per cent in 1723/4 to 15 per cent in 1750, and most of this was Dutch. By then there was an active market in British government and related securities in Amsterdam as well as in London. As a result of this debt, and the market it produced, debits and credits could be produced in either London or Amsterdam which could be used to meet the needs of those merchants wanting to make payment in either country. If British government stock was sold in London to a British investor, but on behalf of a Dutch holder, the right to a payment in sterling in London would be created. This right could be sold to a Dutch merchant wanting to make a payment in London. Conversely, if the same stock was sold in Amsterdam, but on behalf of a British holder and to a Dutch investor, the right to payment in Holland would result. By the later eighteenth century the same procedure was in existence between London and New York. United States securities were being sent to Britain in order to pay debts incurred by American importers.

Thus, what contemporaries like Thomas Mortimer saw as unwelcome and undesirable speculation by the Dutch in the National Debt was, in reality, an integral part of the world's monetary system whereby the ability to make payments between countries was both facilitated and rendered less expensive by sales and purchases of securities in different markets. Inevitably this generated much activity in the securities market as prices of stocks rose and fell not only due to domestic monetary conditions but also those abroad, especially in Holland. Increasingly in the eighteenth century, until the French Revolution, London and Amsterdam interest rates were closely aligned, and the existence of active securities markets in both centres was of major importance in achieving this high degree of monetary integration. It was also becoming a transatlantic phenomenon with the inclusion of New York.[27]

[27] R. V. Eagly and V. K. Smith, 'Domestic and International Integration of the London Money Market, 1731–1789', *J. Ec. H.* 36 (1976), 207, 210–11; L. Neal, 'Integration of International Capital Markets: Quantitative Evidence from the 18th to 20th Centuries', *J. Ec. H.*

Consequently, in terms of turnover what was driving the growth of the London securities market was much less the general rise in the number of investors and the volume of stock—important as that was—but the constant need to buy and sell as money-market conditions altered at home and abroad. Mortimer, for example, castigated those who transacted

more business in the several government securities in one hour, without having a shilling of property in any one of them, than the real proprietors of thousands transact in several years.[28]

The requirements of those closely involved with the money market were also different from those acting on behalf of private investors. In particular, the brokers acting for private investors usually had ample time to arrange payment or delivery. In contrast, those acting on behalf of domestic banks, insurance companies, bill brokers, or foreign clients were required to act quickly before the opportunity was lost. This necessitated a much greater degree of understanding and trust among the participants in the market as they had to be certain that payment would be made and stock delivered, and they could not wait for evidence that that would be the case. It was for this reason that the Amsterdam stockbroker, Joseph Ricardo, sent his son David to London, as he was familiar with the way business was conducted and could be trusted. The clearest difference between the two types of market participant was that those using the market for long-term investment tended to buy and sell for cash, having the money or securities to hand, while the professionals, buying and selling for themselves or for money-market clients, dealt for time and did so frequently. The risk for them was that one default in the chain of operations could endanger their ability to pay or deliver in turn, and thus undermine the market itself. [29]

45 (1985), 225; L. Neal, 'The Integration and Efficiency of the London and Amsterdam Stock Markets in the Eighteenth Century', *J. Ec. H.* 47 (1987), 115; S. E. Oppers, 'The Interest Rate Effect of Dutch Money in Eighteenth Century Britain', *J. Ec. H.* 53 (1993), 40; E. S. Schubert, 'Arbitrage in the Foreign Exchange Markets of London and Amsterdam During the Eighteenth Century', *Explorations in Economic History*, 26 (1989), 17; Neal, *Financial Capitalism*, 21, 43, 90, 146, 151; Carter, *Getting, Spending*, 57, 77; Morgan and Thomas, *The Stock Exchange*, 20, 23, 49, 52; Bowen, 'Investment and Empire', 201; J. C. Riley, *International Government Finance and the Amsterdam Capital Market, 1740–1815* (Cambridge 1980), 122, 280; S. R. Cope, 'Bird, Savage and Bird of London, Merchants and Bankers, 1782–1803', *Guildhall Studies in London History*, 4 (1981), 209–12. Sutherland, *Politics and Finance*, 381–2; S. Quinn, 'Gold, Silver and the Glorious Revolution: Arbitrage Between Bills of Exchange and Bullion', *Ec. H. R.* 49 (1996), 473–4, 487–8; E. J. Perkins, *American Public Finance and Financial Services, 1700–1816* (Columbus, Ohio 1994), 200; G. Yoveb, *Diamonds and Coral: Anglo-Dutch Jews and the Eighteenth-Century Trade* (Leicester 1978), 55, 58, 194–5, 201, 204, 213; J. De Vries and A. Van der Woude, *The First Modern Economy: Success, Failure, and Perseverance of the Dutch Economy, 1500–1815* (Cambridge 1997), 142–4; M. Hart, J. Jonker, and J. L. Van Zanden, *A Financial History of the Netherlands* (Cambridge 1997), 55–8.

[28] Mortimer, *Everyman his own Broker*, 34.
[29] Cope, 'Stock Exchange Revisited', 17; Weatherall, *David Ricardo*, 3.

Therefore, it was not enough for the securities market to develop in terms of intermediation and technique in the eighteenth century. Also required was a system of control which guaranteed that sales and purchases would be honoured when they became due. This could not be done in law as Barnards Act, passed in 1734, had made time bargains illegal, regarding them as a form of gambling. It was thus left to the market participants themselves to create a code of conduct that enforced the conditions necessary for trade. Even without the legal impediments it was most likely that those who participated actively in the market would seek to find a solution to their own problems among themselves, without the use of either the law of the land or the government. London bankers, for example, set up the London Clearing House in 1773, with 31 members, in order to deal with inter-bank business while marine underwriters set up an organization—New Lloyds—in 1774 to meet the particular requirements of their business.[30] Essentially, what the professionals wanted so as to ensure speed and trust was a market in which all present were active participants, ready to buy or sell when the opportunity arose, and each possessing a reputation for honouring their part of a bargain. In turn, those who did not fit these criteria or meet the standards set would be excluded from the market. It was this that 150 brokers and jobbers attempted to establish in 1761 when they offered to pay Jonathan's Coffee House £8 each per annum for the exclusive use of the premises for about three hours every day in order to transact business. Though Jonathan's accepted the offer those who were excluded as a result objected, and in 1762 they obtained a court ruling declaring the action illegal. As Jonathan's had, by custom, been used as a market for buying and selling government securities, they could not refuse permission to anyone who wanted to participate.

The next attempt to develop an exclusive organization was in 1772 when a group of stockbrokers decided to construct a new building in Sweetings Alley which was to be called a Stock Exchange. This was opened on the 12 July 1773. Mindful of the legal rebuff that had been delivered some 10 years earlier, admission to this building was on payment of 6d. per day, so that all could participate if they wished. This payment would also remunerate the owners of the building for the cost of construction and maintenance. Interestingly, if a broker attended six days a week all year the cost would be £7.80 per annum, which was remarkably similar to the £8 which was to be paid to Jonathan's. Clearly that offer had made a group of the wealthier stockbrokers realize that they could personally profit by setting up an establishment for the use of their fellow intermediaries and then charging them a fee for its use. However, this new building was not an outright success as trading in securities continued to take place in a number of locations throughout the city of London. In particular, the

---

[30] John, 'Insurance Investment', 184; A. H. John, 'The London Assurance Company and the Marine Insurance Market in the 18th Century', *Economica*, NS 25 (1958), 129.

Rotunda of the Bank of England, which had been opened in 1765, was a very popular venue as it was there that transfers of both Bank of England and government stock had to be registered in any case. All these alternative locations were also free, and so attractive to those with only a limited business to transact. Consequently, the new Stock Exchange building failed to control the London securities market as it was neither exclusive not dominant. This Stock Exchange building appeared to have replaced Jonathan's to become an important centre for securities trading but without altering to any great degree the way the market was organized and controlled. It is thus difficult to date the origins of the London Stock Exchange to the opening of this building in 1773 as it appeared to offer little that was different from the securities market that had been developing throughout the century.

Until near the end of the eighteenth century the London securities market continued to be served in this way. The professionals could pay their daily entrance fee and conduct business with fellow professionals at the Stock Exchange building. They could also frequent other buildings, especially the Rotunda of the Bank of England, where they could deal directly with investors or with more casual intermediaries, like bankers or solicitors. Throughout, the size of the National Debt, and hence turnover in the London market continued to grow. The government's indebtedness rose from £130.6m. in 1770, when 98 per cent was funded, to £244m. in 1790 (96 per cent funded), again driven by the costs of foreign wars, such as the American War of Independence. This growth appears to have been easily accommodated within the London market, occasioning no substantial change, though the doubling, in nominal terms, of government debt during the American conflict did strain the market for public securities in London. Clearly investors were worried about accepting a never-ending increase in the National Debt especially when the military engagements that created them resulted in the loss of a major part of the Empire. In fact, in this period it was outside London that the new developments were taking place. In the provinces there was a growing interest in joint-stock companies and their securities. This focused especially on canal projects from the 1780s, reaching a mania in the early 1790s.[31] Though London investors were interested in the shares issued by these new canal companies, the focus for trading activity was in the towns and cities of Britain where they were being built and operated. In London the buying and selling of canal shares was very much a fringe activity within a securities market that remained completely dominated by the National Debt. Between 1780 and 1793 some 87 per cent of the

[31] Mortimer, *Everyman his own Broker*, p. xiv; S. R. Cope, 'The Stock-brokers Find a Home: How the Stock Exchange Came to be Established in Sweetings Alley in 1773', *Guildhall Studies in London History*, 2 (1977), 213, 217–18; Morgan and Thomas, *The Stock Exchange*, 52; Smith, 'London Stock Exchange', 206; O'Brien, 'British Taxation', 21.

holders of the National Debt were to be found in London and the Home Counties.[32]

The event that was to push the London securities market towards that final step of creating a stock exchange did not take place within Britain at all. That was the Revolution in France in 1789 and the subsequent period of instability and war that was to effect continental Europe until Napoleon's defeat at Waterloo in 1815. With the overthrow of the established order in France, and the terror that followed, the financial system in Paris was thrown into chaos. Bankers and others with wealth to lose fled to other centres, such as Amsterdam and London. Finally in 1793 the Paris Stock Exchange was closed down, leading to people such as Walter Boyd, a prominent Paris banker, transferring his operations to London. Worse was to follow for continental Europe for revolution in France was followed by war and revolution in other countries. Of crucial importance was the occupation of Amsterdam by French troops in 1795 and the disruption that caused to what had been the financial centre of Europe. Prominent bankers and brokers, such as Henry Hope, Raphael Raphael, and Samuel de Zoete, all left Amsterdam at that time and set up business in London as best they could. The German states were also engulfed by the turmoil, producing their own flow to London, including Johan Schroder from Hamburg and Nathan Rothschild from Frankfurt.[33]

The implications for London were twofold—simultaneous removal of rival financial centres, principally Paris and Amsterdam, and an influx of wealth and talent. As a consequence London was thrust into a position of financial leadership. Those bankers, brokers, and merchants who had fled to London brought with them their expertise and connections and now directed their affairs from London rather than the Continent. London was well placed to take advantage of this opportunity as it was already a centre of major importance, and this was further enhanced by Britain's ability to capture much of Europe's trade with the rest of the world. All this was bound to have repercussions for the London securities market considering its well-established links to the money and foreign exchange markets. The instability alone, coming from political and military events, created a very volatile environment within which securities trading had to take place, as prices responded to changing circumstances and prospects at home and abroad.

---

[32] J. R. Ward, *The Finance of Canal Building in Eighteenth-Century England* (Oxford 1974), 82, 100–6, 142; D. Wainwright, *Government Broker: The Story of an Office and of Mullens and Company* (East Molesey 1990), 1; Anderson, 'Provincial Aspects', 18; Mirowski, *Business Cycle*, 248–9.

[33] S. R. Cope, *Walter Boyd: A Merchant Banker in the Age of Napoleon* (Gloucester 1983), 3, 26, 29; S. D. Chapman, *Raphael Bicentenary 1787–1987* (London 1987), 5–7; H. Janes, *de Zoete and Gorton: A History* (London 1963), 6; R. Roberts, *Schroders: Merchants & Bankers* (London 1992), 3; Riley, *International Government Finance*, 8, 294; Neal, *Financial Capitalism*, 171, 180, 200, 217; A. Elon, *Founder: Meyer Amschel Rothschild and His Time* (London 1996), 84, 89, 130; Hart, Jonker, and Van Zanden *Financial History*, 51.

At the same time the amount of securities to be traded expanded enormously as the government sought to fund its greatly enlarged army and navy expenditure. By 1815 the National Debt stood at £744.9m. (92 per cent funded), having grown by some £500m. since 1790. This massive expansion of government debt sucked in investors from all over the country, ending the provincial flirtation with canal shares. In 1815 there were an estimated 250,000 holders of the National Debt, compared to the 60,000 of 1760. Also the only market for this debt was London, as Amsterdam no longer possessed a functioning securities market, though foreigners still held around 10 per cent of the total in 1806. One illustration of the increasing activity in the market was the business done by Benjamin Cole, the stockbroker who acted for the government. In 1786 he was handling £250,000 per annum but this had doubled to £550,000 by 1798 and reached £8m. in 1806. The consequence of all this was that the London securities market was being placed under greater and greater pressure as the volume and volatility of business increased, attracting in ever more participants—from home and abroad—who saw the daily fluctuations in prices as an ideal opportunity to make a quick fortune for themselves. Inevitably, this left the market professionals very exposed as it was difficult to know what trust to place in the new people with whom they were doing business.[34]

By the late 1790s a crisis had been reached in the London securities market. In December 1798 the Committee (Committee for General Purposes) responsible for the day-to-day running of the market in the Stock Exchange building were pressing for greatly increased powers so as to enforce discipline. In particular they wanted the authority to exclude from the building those who had defaulted on deals, unless there were clear and acceptable reasons why this had taken place. Generally, this committee was being forced to take more and more decisions on disputes between members concerning such matters as the penalty for non-delivery of stock or the acceptable commission on a deal. As all these committee members were practising brokers and jobbers this was becoming a serious diversion from their own business, through which they earned an income. Eventually, on 15 December 1798 they appointed a secretary to the committee. To this secretary could be devolved the administrative tasks related to the work that the committee carried out. However, this raised the matter of costs, for the secretary was to have a salary of 10 guineas per annum. The solution was the decision in January 1799 to charge those who frequented the Stock Exchange building 5s. each, which would meet the salary of the secretary and the other costs of the committee. Modest as this sum was, many who used the building on a casual basis would have

[34] Carter, Getting, Spending, 136; Neal, Financial Capitalism, 211; Wainwright, Mullens, 6, 8, 14, 17. For the experience of the Dublin securities market at this time see W. A. Thomas, The Stock Exchanges of Ireland (Liverpool 1986), 44, 48–9.

resented being expected to pay it. The result was a real dilemma for the committee—how were decisions to be enforced when the expansion of business was drawing into the market ever more new brokers who were unwilling to abide by accepted customs; and how was the necessary administration of the market to be financed if not all those using it would pay, voluntarily, the annual fee.[35]

On 7 January 1801 the Committee of Proprietors, representing those who owned the Stock Exchange building, suggested that it should be converted into a Subscription Room. These proprietors were also major users of the market like John Capel and David Ricardo. The proprietors calculated that they would get an acceptable return on their investment in the building if a minimum of 200 subscribers were recruited, with each paying 10 guineas per annum. The income of £2,100 per annum that would result was deemed sufficient to pay an acceptable return on their capital investment as well as to meet all running and administrative expenses. Clearly, the expansion of business and the appearance of an increasing number of full-time brokers and jobbers created sufficient optimism that those numbers would sign up as members. On 12 January 1801 the Committee for General Purposes, representing the users, met and endorsed the plan. On the following day, the following notice was posted in the Stock Exchange building under the signature of E. Wetenhall, secretary to the proprietors.

The Proprietors of the Stock Exchange, at the solicitation of a very considerable number of the Gentlemen frequenting it, and with the unanimous concurrence of the Committee appointed for General Purposes, who were requested to assist them in forming such regulations as may be deemed necessary, have resolved unanimously, that after 27 February next this House shall be finally shut as a Stock Exchange, and opened as a Subscription Room on Tuesday 3 March at ten guineas per Annum ending 1 March in each succeeding year. All persons desirous of becoming subscribers are requested to signify the same in writing to E. Whitford, Secretary to the joint committees on or before 31 inst. in order to their being balloted for by the said committees.[36]

Thus, on 3 March 1801 a London Stock Exchange formally came into existence that not only provided a market for securities but also incorporated regulations on how business was to be conducted. Furthermore adherence to these rules and regulations was monitored and adjudicated by a committee, including full-time administrative staff, and enforced by the threat of expulsion from the market. By this act the trading of securities in London had moved, decisively, from an open to a closed market as the only way of ensuring that all those who participated both obeyed the rules and

[35] Minutes of the Committee of the Old Stock Exchange, 19 Dec. 1798, 3 Jan. 1799, 9 Jan. 1799, 3 Apr. 1799, 8 Aug. 1799.
[36] Old Stock Exchange minutes, 12 Jan. 1801; Wainwright, *Mullens*, 8.

paid for the necessary administration. With 363 members by February 1802 the move did appear to have been a successful one.[37]

Though those who were members of this new Stock Subscription Room in 1802 traced their origins back to the opening of the Stock Exchange building in 1773, that was but a stage in the transition of a securities market into a stock exchange.[38] Close as they were to what was taking place they were unaware that by controlling admission, introducing full-time admin-istration, and enforcing rules and regulations, they had actually formed an institution that was far more than the collective actions of those who traded in securities. Certainly, the development of a securities market in London can be traced back to the seventeenth century, with the creation of a permanent government debt in 1693 being of fundamental importance. Certainly the opening of a building in 1773 which was dedicated to the provision of a market for securities was of importance in furthering that market. However, so were a series of other developments and improvements such as the appearance of brokers and jobbers and the use made of options, time bargains, and settlement dates. Taken together it can be suggested that the creation of the Stock Subscription Room in March 1801 was not simply another milestone in the progress of the London securities market but the beginning of a formally organized institution which was to have an impor-tant influence on the way the securities market itself developed at home and abroad, in the years to come.

[37] Old Stock Exchange minutes, 13 Jan. 1801, 23 Feb. 1801; LSE: Committee for General Purposes, minutes, 2 Mar. 1801, 4 Mar. 1801, 27 Mar. 1801, 17 Feb. 1802.
[38] LSE: General Purposes, 24 Feb. 1802.

# 2

# *From Money to Capital, 1801–1851*

## ORGANIZATION

The formation of the Stock Subscription Room in 1801 represented a major advance in the London securities market, though contemporaries appeared totally unaware of the significance of the change that had taken place. With the power to exclude there now existed an ability to enforce the rules and regulations that increasingly governed the conduct of business in the securities market. Rules and regulations were essential if those buying and selling securities were to cope with the volume, variety, and speed of transactions demanded of the market by that time. Nevertheless, it was to be a number of years before the authority of this new institution to control the market was accepted by all concerned. There were always to be those, not permitted to participate, who objected to the closed nature of the Stock Exchange compared to the absence of barriers in the past. Internally the institution had to resolve conflicts over the balance of power among the members as it was necessary to restrain the freedom of individuals, or even significant groups, in order to further the interests of the whole body. There was also the question of how far the rules and regulations could be extended into the private business affairs of members, including the relationships they maintained with clients.

The continuing development of the securities market was not stopped by the formation of the Stock Exchange, but it did change in nature. There was now a major institutional player in the process that could take collective action, co-ordinating the interests of different sections of the market and influencing the future course of events. Essentially, the emergence of a closed market in securities, and all that involved, represented both an end to one evolutionary process, related to the mechanisms and techniques whereby stocks and shares were bought and sold, and the beginning of another, that now included the control, distribution, and exercise of power and authority. Henceforth, the securities market was no longer an open one which participants could enter at will and act in without redress. Instead, it incorporated not only an enforceable code of conduct for business behaviour but also an institutional organization that demarcated member from non-member.

From the outset the Stock Exchange sought to control the admission of members, not so much in terms of absolute numbers but more with respect to type and character. The way the Stock Exchange was organized, with the building controlled by proprietors who gained their income from membership fees, precluded any exclusive policy that would seek to limit the numbers participating in the market. Instead, the aim was to exclude those who were untrustworthy, because of past actions or present reputation, or created risks for other members, due to their additional activities. On the eve of the establishment of the Stock Subscription room—23 February 1801—of those who had applied for membership at least eight were rejected by the committee, even after appeals had been heard. As members had to reapply annually for admission, and were then balloted for, there was a regular opportunity to refuse re-entry to those considered unsatisfactory by the rest of the membership. This was in addition to the ability to expel for specific misdeeds or to reject unsuitable new applicants. Altogether, over the period 17 February to 10 April 1802, covering the first renewal date, a total of 498 were admitted as members and 17 rejected, or some 3 per cent of the total. As the actual membership turned out to be double that envisaged when the idea of a subscription-only room was first raised, the response was not to try and restrict the number but to accommodate it with a new building. This was opened in 1802.[1] Clearly, almost all who wanted to become members of the subscription-only Stock Exchange were able to do so, suggesting that the barriers to entry were low. Abraham Goldsmid, for example, was a founder member of the London Stock Exchange despite operating as a bill broker and government loan contractor as well. Clearly a trustworthy reputation was the principal criterion for admission in the early years of the Stock Exchange and there was no attempt to exclude those categories of financial intermediaries who might be considered competitors to stockbrokers and jobbers, such as merchant bankers and bill brokers.[2]

Though the policy on admission to the Stock Exchange remained a liberal one in these early years, definite restrictions on the type of member slowly began to appear. In particular, applicants whose principal business was not that of stockbroking or jobbing now began to be refused. By 1807 applicants were being rejected because they were 'in trade' or 'in business', while the year before F. de Medina's request to join was turned down as he was a discount or bill broker.[3] In cases such as these the Stock Exchange was not making a judgement on the character of the applicant or even trying to limit the membership to a privileged few. Instead, they were forcing people

[1] Minutes of the Committee of the Old Stock Exchange, 23 Feb. 1801, 19 May 1801, 2 Feb. 1802, 17 Feb. 1802, 20 Feb. 1802, 23 Feb. 1802, 6 Mar. 1802, 10 Mar. 1802, 18 Mar. 1802, 1 Apr. 1802, 10 Apr. 1802.

[2] S. D. Cope, 'The Goldsmids and the Development of the London Money Market During the Napoleonic Wars', *Economica*, NS 9 (1942), 198.

[3] LSE: Committee for General Purposes, minutes, 15 Feb. 1809, 7 Mar. 1807, 9 Sept. 1807.

to choose between a commitment to the securities market or some other occupation. Eventually, this became enshrined in the rules and regulations of the Stock Exchange when they were collected together in 1811. From 1812 onwards all new members had to confine their business to the buying and selling of securities, while existing members were not permitted to engage in any additional activities, unless they were already so engaged before the rule became operative. In 1819 it was ruled, for example, that if a member had

... gone into any line of business independent of the stock exchange since the 1st of February 1812 he is ineligible to be re-admitted without undertaking to give up such business.[4]

Thus a Mr Bush had to decide between tea-dealing and the Stock Exchange whereas for Mr Shewell the alternative was banking.

Behind this limitation on the activities of members was a fear that a large loss made by a member outside the Stock Exchange, because of an involvement in trade or banking, could rebound on other members through availability to pay or deliver, causing them large losses in turn, and jeopardizing the stability of the whole market. Abraham Goldsmid, for instance, shot himself in 1810 faced with the bankruptcy of his business due to the bill broking side owing £466,700. As most of this was to the government (£419,000—for Exchequer bills taken and not paid for) disaster was averted by the government accepting delayed payment. At any one time outstanding sales and purchases between members could be very substantial, with the ability to deliver or pay taken on trust. When Thomas Manson, a member of six months standing, failed on 2 April 1814, due to a sudden decline in prices, he had outstanding commitments to his fellow members totalling some £134,000. Similarly, when a collapse in the market for foreign securities caused J. and L. Burnand to go under in 1835 their open sales and purchases of securities, on behalf of clients, amounted to £437,000. To settle these debts to fellow members the Stock Exchange expected the entire assets of the member concerned to be readily available, and not in dispute with external creditors. Most members of the Stock Exchange could not wait for long until a failed member's estate, especially the money and securities in his possession, were realized for their collective benefit. Obligations to either deliver or pay for stocks were of an immediate nature, and if one member could not complete an agreed deal, another had to be found who could, with the failed member's assets being seized in compensation. This position could be seriously jeopardized if the cause of bankruptcy lay outside the Stock Exchange, making a failed member's assets not readily available for redistribution as well as having to be shared among numerous creditors.[5]

[4] Ibid., 6 Mar. 1819, 29 Oct. 1811, 16 Nov. 1818, 15 Mar. 1819, 22 Mar. 1819.
[5] Ibid., 4 Feb. 1807, 17 Oct. 1814, 29 Apr. 1817, 16 June 1817, 29 May 1835, 3 July 1835; Cope, 'The Goldsmids', 203, 205.

Generally, the Stock Exchange had to exercise caution in whom it admitted. Once they became members they could run up large open positions with other members, which any sudden change in prices could make it impossible for them to fulfil. With falling prices clients were reluctant to pay for stocks worth less than the agreed purchase price. As early as 1821 those members who recommended new applicants were being asked to guarantee their losses up to £250, because of a sequence of recent failures. This was further increased in 1832 when each new applicant had to be endorsed by three members, each agreeing to provide £300 in the event of failure. It was in order to publicize the failure, so that all members were immediately aware and so would assess their own position, that the Stock Exchange decided in March 1833 that 'in future all defaulters shall be declared by the Hammer', instead of simply posting a notice as in the past.[6] Consequently, the restriction on bankers, merchants, bill brokers, and others as members originated with a legitimate concern to minimize the risk and extent of failure, and reduce the complications involved when it did incur. Naturally enough, it also excluded from membership certain groups that were involved in the securities market though it was not their principal business, let alone a speciality of theirs. There is no evidence that when the Stock Subscription Room was formed in 1801 bankers and others were to be excluded, though that is what eventually happened.

By insisting that not only had all members to be full-time stockbrokers or jobbers but also that any partner of a member must also join the Stock Exchange, and so be subject to those rules, a great encouragement was given towards the specialization already evident within the financial and commercial community in London.[7] London private bankers had, traditionally, employed stockbrokers to handle sales and purchases of securities, concentrating as they did on the relationship with their customers, whether individuals or country bankers, and the remunerative employment of the money deposited with them. Merchants who became bankers were extensively engaged in the finance of trade, and later the issue of securities, to which the buying and selling of stocks was but one aspect, and often the least important one. Discount or bill brokers were intermediaries who existed by borrowing the idle balances—or call money—of banks and employing it in the short-term bills of exchange used by manufacturers and merchants to fund their day-to-day operations. Again, to them, the purchase of government stocks or bills, as a temporary home for the funds at their disposal, was an important but not central part of their business.

Though the securities market might have evolved differently if these groups had been permitted membership of the Stock Exchange, most did not appear to want it at the beginning of the nineteenth century. One exception was the bill broker F. de Medina, who applied in 1806 and 1813, and

---

[6] LSE: General Purposes, 1 Sept. 1819, 9 July 1821, 13 Sept. 1832, 4 Mar. 1833.
[7] Ibid., 31 Aug. 1801, 5 June 1823, 13 Sept. 1832; Legal Opinion, 9 Apr. 1821.

was refused both times. Altogether, when the membership of the London Stock Exchange reached 488 in 1812, this represented some two-thirds of the 726 individuals estimated to be involved in the buying and selling of government stock. Among these would be included merchant bankers like Nathan Rothschild, who was clearly too busy in other directions to spend his time trading securities on the floor of the London Stock Exchange and would have employed someone to do it for him anyway.[8]

This exclusion could have had serious repercussions for bankers and others if the Stock Exchange had introduced and enforced minimum commission rates, regulating the charges that brokers made to their clients for transacting business. When the Dublin Stock Exchange had been formed in 1799 its rules had included a maximum commission rate of $\frac{1}{8}$th per cent, and this had become the minimum charge by 1824. Conventional commission rates did exist in London but there was no attempt to force members to charge these when the Stock Exchange was formed or until many years afterwards. Instead, brokers accepted payment from their clients in many different ways, ranging from an annual fee from major customers, like banks, to a straight commission on each transaction from small investors. When the stockbroker Benjamin Cole was appointed broker to the National Debt Commissioners in 1786, he accepted a payment of £400 per annum for his trouble, rather than charging commission for every sale or purchase made on their behalf. This arrangement was maintained after the formation of the Stock Exchange in 1801, of which Cole was a member, with the payment being increased to £750 per annum in 1806 because of the increased business he was having to do.[9]

Pressure to introduce a minimum scale of charges did arise in 1813, due to increasing competition between members. The Stock Exchange was already involved in trying to ensure that competition was orderly, with the poaching of clients from fellow members being strongly disapproved of. Members, for example, were prohibited from sending circulars to other than their own clients. It was inevitable that the question of commission would arise at some stage as the limitation on price competition was an obvious step for the members of a closed market. In September 1813 Luke Leake was accused by John Lloyd of taking business away from him through both not charging the full commission and being willing to make no charge. By agreeing a price with the client and obtaining a higher one in the market Leake could expect to make a profit that would compensate

[8] LSE: General Purposes, 15 Feb. 1806, 2 Apr. 1812, 13 Sept. 1813; S. D. Chapman, 'The Establishment of the Rothschilds as Bankers', *Transactions of the Jewish Historical Society*, 29 (1982/6), 187; S. D. Chapman, *The Rise of Merchant Banking* (London 1984), 4; D. M. Joslin, 'London Private Bankers, 1720–1785', *Ec. H. R.* ns 7 (1954/5), 173.

[9] Old Stock Exchange, minutes, 8 Aug. 1799; D. Wainwright, *Government Broker: The Story of an Office and of Mullens and Company* (East Molesey 1990), 1, 4, 8, 14; W. A. Thomas, *The Stock Exchanges of Ireland* (Liverpool, 1986), 63; R. Roberts, *Schroders: Merchants & Bankers* (London 1992), 358.

him for his time and trouble. Initially, the Committee for General Purposes, representing the collective interests of the membership, censured Leake for his actions, but, only for poaching clients not undercutting. In practice a standard rate of commission was in use. This was understood to be $\frac{1}{8}$th per cent with half-commission ($\frac{1}{16}$th per cent) being available to bankers. However, there was no attempt to force members to apply these rates, and the charges made to clients were left to their discretion. The matter did not arise again until 1838, when a move was made to introduce a fixed scale of charges to be followed by all members. Despite considerable pressure from some members this was, ultimately, not successful, though an unofficial scale did gain wide popularity. In fact, so common did the reference to this scale become that Mr Foster, of Foster & Braithwaite, complained in 1846 when he discovered a fellow broker undercutting him. He met with an immediate rebuff when the chairman of the Committee for General Purposes stated that

. . . they refused to interfere or decide in any way, what the scale should be.[10]

Therefore, though the rules and regulations of the Stock Exchange covered the relationships between members they did not encroach on that existing between member and client, even to the extent of setting a scale of charges. Members were equally conscious of the need both to introduce and enforce particular rules and the desirability of leaving unregulated particular aspects of their business. It was only through a process of challenge and consideration that the actual limits to regulation were set. The result was that members were left free to make whatever arrangements they liked with their clients. As a result, those investors generating a high volume of business, like the bankers, could have transactions carried out as cheaply and assiduously as if a partner or employee was involved. The brokers, Marjoribanks, Capel & Co. had a very close working relationship with two particular West End banks—Coutts and Drummonds—even extending to family connections at times. Similarly, the brokers Harrison & Cottle operated almost exclusively for Hoares Bank, with Hoares directing all its stock exchange business through them. Representative of the volume of business these institutional clients could generate was the fact that Capels handled 7,398 deals worth £22.1m. for Coutts, Drummonds, and their customers during 1829/30 and this generated £23,815 in commission. Rothschilds distributed its business among a small number of favoured brokers, including Montefiore Brothers, Menet & Cazenove, Laurence Whitmore and Co., and Helbert Wagg, with Cazenoves alone handling £1m. annually between 1830 and 1833.[11]

[10] LSE: General Purposes, 22 Apr. 1813, 15 May 1813, 15 Sept. 1813, 16 Oct. 1813, 14 Feb. 1818, 29 Jan. 1838, 19 Feb. 1838, 27 Mar. 1838, 18 Mar. 1839, 17 Jan. 1846.

[11] Roberts, *Schroders*, 358; M. C. Reed, *A History of James Capel and Company* (London 1975), 29–34, 44, 60; D. Kynaston, *Cazenove & Co.: A History* (London, 1991), 22, 25, 40; LSE: General Purposes, 3 Apr. 1846, 6 Apr. 1846, 20 Apr. 1846; D. Sebag-Montefiore, *The Story of Joseph Sebag & Co. and its Founding Families* (n.p. 1996), 6.

These close working relationships between the members of the Stock Exchange and their clients, especially major investors, was fostered by the location of the Stock Exchange in the heart of the City of London, next to the Bank of England, and convenient for the offices of most bankers, merchants, and money brokers. Interested clients were even able to congregate in the lobby of the Stock Exchange or wait in nearby coffee houses, with the broker running back and fore relaying current prices and receiving instructions. Of the clients served by the London stockbroker, George Davidge, between 1818 and 1853, some 80 per cent lived in London or its immediate vicinity. Brokers also regularly visited clients, certainly the important ones. The stockbroker William Mullens, spent half-an-hour each morning walking round different banking houses in the City, soliciting orders which he then completed at the Stock Exchange. Furthering these close personal contacts between stockbroker and client was the small scale of operation, encouraged by the fact that each partner in a stockbroking firm had to be a member of the Stock Exchange. There were no savings to be gained, in terms of membership fees, by one partner being a member, while the others handled the clients and other activities. All partners had to be members. Similarly, if stockbroking firms wanted to use their clerks to enter the Stock Exchange so as to deal for them, a subscription fee of 5 guineas per annum had to be paid. Even then the clerk was not permitted to deal on his own account but only for his employer, so preventing that means being used to reduce the individual cost of admission.[12]

The result was that many members operated alone, with the help of a clerk, while a firm with five partners was considered large for the time. Both Capels and Cazenoves had five partners in the mid-1840s reflecting their extensive business on behalf of banking clients. Foster & Janson, a stockbroking firm formed in 1825 by two brothers-in-law, managed with only two partners despite handling the securities business of the private bank, Brown, Janson, to which they were related. It was not until Richard Janson died in 1830 that a new partner, Isaac Braithwaite, was introduced, and he was a relative of James Foster, indicating the close family nature of these early firms. Even the firm of Templeman, Cole & Co., that acted as the government's broker, had usually only three partners before the second half of the nineteenth century, with death or retirement creating an opportunity for a relative or friend to join. In line with the size of the stockbroking firms, the number of clients was low. Templeman, Cole & Co. (which became Mullens & Co.) had only 85 clients, other than the government, in 1813. Though this rose steadily it only reached 127 in 1833 and 149 in 1841. Generally, among the clients of a stockbroker were numbered numerous

[12] Old Stock Exchange, minutes, 12 Jan. 1801, 31 Aug. 1801; LSE: General Purposes, 10 Dec. 1806, 6 Apr. 1808, 9 May 1814, 12 Jan. 1848; D. Kynaston, 'The London Stock Exchange, 1870–1914: An Institutional History', Ph.D. thesis, University of London 1983, 269.

friends, relatives, and acquaintances as well as connections with particular banks. There was a high degree of intimacy between the members of the Stock Exchange and the London financial and commercial community at this time, greatly minimizing the restriction on entry imposed upon those who were not full-time stockbrokers and jobbers.[13]

With this combination of easy entry, no fixed scale of charges, and close working relationships, the Stock Exchange increasingly dominated the London securities market, though never monopolizing it. The Rotunda of the Bank of England, the Royal Exchange, and coffee houses like Garraways, continued to be frequented by those buying and selling securities, while auctions were popular for the less well-known stocks and shares. Though the Stock Exchange did attempt to discourage its members from using these other markets it took no steps to prevent them so doing, recognizing that it was sometimes necessary if a broker was to fulfil the wishes of a client. The only prohibition on members was that they were not permitted to join another institution established as a market for securities.[14] The success of the Stock Exchange can be judged against the popularity of the Rotunda of the Bank of England, that had been its main rival before the formation of the Stock Subscription Room in 1801. By 1824 it was reported, regarding the Rotunda, that

... since the building of the Stock Exchange, the business of this nature (transactions in the public funds) here carried on had not only been much less, but of a less respectable description.[15]

In 1834 the Rotunda was closed as a market for securities. Though other locations waxed and waned as alternative markets for securities in London, and there were always threats of rival institutions being formed, the Stock Exchange was now supreme in London. Even the speculative booms of the mid-1820s and mid-1840s failed to produce a serious rival to it, though proposals did surface from time to time.[16] One of the most serious emerged in 1810 when a new stock exchange was planned for London involving no less than John Hemmings, who was then secretary to the Stock Exchange itself. This new stock exchange intended to capitalize on public dissatisfaction with the closed nature of the Stock Exchange set up in 1801. It was not to be the monopoly of its members but be open to the public on the payment of a daily subscription, in much the same way as the previous

[13] Reed, *Capel and Company*, 57; Kynaston, *Cazenove*, 30, 32; Wainwright, *Mullens*, 16, 26, 29; W. J. Reader, *A House in the City: A Study of the City and of the Stock Exchange Based on the Records of Foster & Braithwaite, 1825–1975* (London 1979), 10, 27, 37; Sebag-Montefiore, *Joseph Sebag & Co.*, 3–4.

[14] Old Stock Exchange, minutes, 13 Aug. 1801; LSE: General Purposes, 15 May 1805, 6 July 1815, 2 May 1817, 5 May 1817, 21 Oct. 1845.

[15] *The Picture of London* (London 1824), 104; *Knight's Cyclopaedia of London* (London 1851), 643.

[16] *The Picture of London* (London 1815), 180, 205 (1820), 150, 173 (1824), 121 (1826), 126, 129; J. Francis, *Chronicles and Characters of the Stock Exchange* (London 1849), 294–5.

institution. To this end the promoters of the new stock exchange presented a bill before Parliament, intending to gain the backing of that body for their project. It was this, rather than the rival market, that the proprietors of the existing Stock Exchange objected to. They argued that the existing Stock Exchange was not a monopoly, and thus in no need of legislative intervention to protect the interests of the public. In this they were successful, and the bill failed to be passed. Hemmings was dismissed for his disloyalty.[17]

As time passed contemporaries came to identify the London Stock Exchange with the entire securities market, recommending it as the place where trading took place and whose members were to be trusted to handle any sales and purchases on behalf of investors. As early as 1810 the public were informed that

The Stock Exchange is the market-place for buying and selling the national pledges or pawns, bearing interest by way of annuity, and called by the general term 'stocks'.[18]

This is not, of course, to say that the Stock Exchange was respected for what it provided. To the public mind the constant buying and selling of securities, behind doors closed to all but members, continued to be regarded as some form of gambling that was morally indefensible and made no contribution to the economic health of the nation. A satire in 1819 included the ditty,

These are the rooks
that prey on the pigeons
that flock around the House
that Jack built,

where rooks were jobbers, pigeons were speculators, and the House was the Stock Exchange.[19] Other criticisms were a lot less circumspect, such as this one in 1821 when the Stock Exchange was referred to as

. . . a body growing out of small beginnings in speculation, to a height that has given it the command of this nation—its destinies—its ministers of government—its resources—its morals—its private property; conducts all these vast relations with closed doors in a building of its own, and to the entire exclusion of all most materially concerned.[20]

[17] LSE: General Purposes, 19 Apr. 1810; House of Commons: Extracts from the Evidence and Further Observations Respecting Mr Hemings, 13 Apr. 1810; Proofs to Negative the Preamble of the Bill for a New Stock Market, 1810; London Stock Exchange: Trustees and Managers, minutes, 28 May 1810.

[18] *London: A Complete Guide to the British Capital* (London 1810), 452. See R. Hamilton, *An Enquiry concerning the Rise and Progress, the Redemption and Present State and Management of the National Debt* (Edinburgh 1818), 313–14; *A New Guide to the Public Funds* (London c.1825), 67.

[19] *The Financial House that Jack Built* (London 1819).

[20] *The Bank—the Stock Exchange—the Bankers—the Bankers' Clearing House—the Minister, and the Public: An Exposé* (London 1821), Preface; see pages 1–20.

The Stock Exchange had gained command over the securities market by 1820 but that had done little to alter the public's rather antagonistic views of what it represented or deepen their understanding of the functions it performed. Instead it had transferred a hostility to the market, or intermediaries like the stock jobbers, to the institution itself.

However, as the members' own spokesman—chairman of the Committee for General Purposes—indicated in 1846, the role played by the Stock Exchange was not only to bring order to the dealings between intermediaries but also to introduce safeguards and transparency to the securities market itself.

As a close market, from which the Public were excluded, it was particularly desirable that the interests of those persons, who confided their stock transactions to Brokers, should be rigidly guarded, and their business equitably done: to effect this two modes are adopted; the first and most important is, that all bargains should be made in the open market, and generally, as far as it was practicable by Brokers with Jobbers. Of course it sometimes happens that two Brokers may have orders to deal in the same particular stock or share, by which it is more advantageous for their respective principals to deal with each other at an intermediate price, without the intervention of a jobber; but generally speaking there is so much competition between respectable jobbers who have large capitals embarked for that purpose, and stand in the market all day, ready at all times to make fair prices, at which they will either buy or sell, that every Broker who resorts to that mode of dealing is sure to have his business done fairly. Another guard the public has, is the practice of having the prices marked by the official agent of the Stock Exchange, and an authorised list published of the prices at which business had actually been done, but there might be collusion in marking such prices, and fictitious quotations given. When there has been any suspicion of such, the Committee have instituted rigid enquiries.[21]

It was in the interests of the Stock Exchange to ensure that the investing public trusted the market which they used, for otherwise they would be discouraged from holding, buying, and selling securities, to the disadvantage of the membership. Thus mechanisms were put in place, and policed, that tried to ensure that the prices reported and obtained were an accurate reflection of the competing forces of supply and demand. Naturally enough when this fell short of expectations, there were always those who would continue to blame the institution and its members, whether they were guilty or not.

During those early years the Stock Exchange was also troubled by internal conflict, which it took time to finally resolve. Two parties were instrumental in the formation of the Stock Exchange in 1801. One was the group of proprietors who owned the building and derived an income from the fees paid by the members. These proprietors were running a business in which the fees had to be set at a level that was neither too low, and thus

---

[21] LSE: General Purposes, 3 Apr. 1846.

generate insufficient income, or too high, and so encourage the appearance of a cheaper rival. With a moderate entry fee a rise in membership was an obvious way of raising income, and thus their profits. The other group was the membership who used the building. Members desired as low a fee as possible, as it was yet another fixed cost, including staff and office rent, while their income was very variable. Foster & Braithwaite's income, before expenses, fell from c.£10,000 in 1834/5 to £3,170 in 1837, recovered to £4,183 in 1839, and then soared to £50,649 in 1845. Existing members therefore, were interested in restricting entry to the Stock Exchange as that could limit the number of potential competitors for the available business, which could be very slack at times. Clearly, the interests of both groups were not identical, though both wanted the Stock Exchange to succeed, and so a compromise had to be reached.[22]

In the period leading up to the opening of the Stock Subscription Room on 3 March 1801, the two committees, representing proprietors and members, met jointly, deciding upon who was acceptable as a member and the rules and regulations under which they would operate. However, when the Stock Subscription Room opened, this United Committee was dissolved, to be replaced, as before, with one representing the proprietors—Trustees and Managers, and one the members—General Purposes. The division of responsibility was spelled out from the outset, when the Committee for General Purposes resolved, on 4 March 1801, that,

... no proprietor of the Stock Exchange shall have the right to vote for the election of new members or any regulations respecting the Stock-Subscription Room . . .[23]

This left the proprietors with the ability to set the membership fee and the management of the building housing the market. The question of the number of members or the criteria for eligibility was left unresolved. Bereft of power over admissions and rules, all the proprietors serving on the Committee for General Purposes resigned on 27 March 1801, leaving the scrutiny and policing of applicants and members to the members alone.[24]

The resolution and the resignations did not end the conflict because issues arose from time to time which revealed these inner contradictions within the Stock Exchange. One such issue was over the hours during which the Stock Exchange was open. The members wanted a limit to the hours so that they would be free to attend their offices or, simply, enjoy more leisure. As long as the Stock Exchange was open there was the possibility of doing business, or missing out on a rapid change in circumstances if absent. Conversely, the proprietors wanted the Stock Exchange kept open for most of the day, so as to discourage the appearance of a before or after hours market

---

[22] Old Stock Exchange, minutes, 12 Jan. 1801, 4 Mar. 1801; Reader, *Foster & Braithwaite*, 38, 43.

[23] Old Stock Exchange, minutes, 4 Mar. 1801.

[24] Ibid., 27 Mar. 1801, 17 Feb. 1802.

that could develop into a serious rival. As it was, from about 1812 members began to put pressure on the managers to close the Stock Exchange at 4 o'clock. In 1814 they resolved that bargains done after that time would not be covered by the regulations, and from then on the Stock Exchange did appear to close at 4 o'clock. Nevertheless, all that happened was that, in periods of active trading, buying and selling switched to the alley beside the Stock Exchange. Clearly, in terms of hours the members were in control though even they were aware that any undue restriction could both prompt the growth of an outside market and stimulate criticism of the closed nature of the Stock Exchange. This tempered their demands some-what, though hours were changed from 10–4 o'clock to 10.30–3.30 in March 1845.[25]

The existence of a group of proprietors, with authority in the manage-ment of the Stock Exchange, did lead to some members trying to involve them on their behalf, when an unfavourable ruling was made. Generally, these were resisted by the Committee of Trustees and Managers, repre-senting the Proprietors, as they were well aware of the limits of their power. In 1809, for example, they replied to one request with the statement that,

. . . they have no authority to disturb the Resolution of the Committee of General Purposes.[26]

The one real dispute between the proprietors and the members took place in 1821/2. This concerned the question of whether option trading should be prohibited or not, and the outcome well illustrates the power exercised by the Stock Exchange over its membership at this time.

Many members had long been worried that extensive and extended dealing for time represented a real danger to the Stock Exchange. If one or more members failed, owing a large amount of either securities or money to other members, this could produce a chain reaction of collapses, to the detriment of all. The rules and regulations that had evolved over time were designed to limit the damage while allowing time bargains to take place, which were necessary because of the Stock Exchange's involvement with the money market. The ability of members to demand payment or delivery at regular and specific intervals moved from being a custom to a right in 1803, and was enforceable under the rules.[27] By 1850 it was reported that

. . . all bargains are usually made for certain days fixed by a Committee of the Stock Exchange, called settling days, of which there are about eight in the year . . .[28]

[25] LSE: General Purposes, 23 June 1812, 14 Feb. 1814, 24 Mar. 1814, 2 Feb. 1818, 13 Sept. 1832, 13 Mar. 1845, 19 Mar. 1845, 8 Sept. 1845, 29 Dec. 1847, 12 Jan. 1848, 7 Feb. 1848.

[26] LSE: Trustees and Managers, 27 Feb. 1809; Legal Opinion, 22 Mar. 1837.

[27] LSE: General Purposes, 29 July 1802, 30 Sept. 1802, 15 Nov. 1803, 6 Apr. 1808, 13 Dec. 1814.

[28] H. Keyser, *The Law Relating to Transactions on the Stock Exchange* (London 1850), 32.

With these settlement dates, when accounts of sales and purchases had to be completed by delivery and payment, or other arrangements made, there was a regular check on the ability of each member to honour their engagements. In effect, a compromise was arrived at that permitted constant buying and selling on credit, interrupted by intervals when either or both money and securities had to be produced, so restraining the speculative urges of members and their clients.

This still left the options, where the right to buy (a call) or sell (a put) could be sold covering much longer periods, and with no necessity that either delivery or payment would take place, and so provide a check on the ability of the member to complete his bargains. For example, a call option could be taken out with one member allowing another member to purchase a security at some specified price within a specified period into the future. If the price never rose above the one specified the option would be allowed to lapse. If the price did rise then the option would be executed and that might cause the failure of the member granting the option, if he possessed neither the securities nor the money to buy them in the market for immediate delivery. Conversely, a rise in price could prompt the member giving the option to make substantial purchases in the expectation that the call would be activated. All this increased the scale of risk if a failure took place as the open position would be greater and more extended.

The matter of options came to a head in 1819 when a number of brokers incurred large losses as their clients had reneged on time bargains. This prompted a call to abolish options in 1820. Eventually, in July 1821 a ruling was made that only time bargains done for 14 days or less would be recognized as being covered by the regulations of the Stock Exchange, and thus enforceable. Behind this was the aim of limiting the open position that could build up. Clearly this proved ineffective for in November of that year 283 members lobbied for a ban on options, claiming that they,

... are now so frequent as to constitute the greater part of the business done in the House and which operate materially against the interest of those who do not comply with this practice.[29]

In turn the banning of options was resisted by 92 members who considered it essential for their business. This was especially so by jobbers who used options to reduce the risks involved in their constant sales of stock that they did not possess at that moment but expected to buy in before they had to deliver it to the purchaser.

As it was the Committee for General Purposes resolved that from 25 March 1822, any member of the Stock Exchange caught dealing in options would be expelled. This then provoked 193 members to protest, indicating a major split within the Stock Exchange between those who conducted a regular commission business for permanent investors and those who either

[29] LSE: General Purposes, 13 Nov. 1821.

traded on their own account or operated for money market clients. Such was the seriousness of the dispute that the Trustees and Managers became involved, worried by the possibility that disaffected members would leave and form their own institution. However, when legal opinion was taken it was obvious that the power to introduce rules and regulations rested solely with the Committee for General Purposes.

In the end, though the prohibition was not repealed, it was considerably toned down. Those trading in options could be expelled but that was no longer automatic, and there was no sign that any action was taken subsequently, for options continued to be available in the Stock Exchange. The practice of dealing in puts and calls had become widespread again by 1832. Nevertheless an attempt then to have the prohibition removed failed. Essentially, what happened in the Stock Exchange was that options were and remained an accepted but unrecognized aspect of dealing in securities. As long as they did not intrude excessively into the normal conduct of business, they were tolerated by the majority of the membership who made no use of them. What the question of options revealed was that the proprietors had no control over the affairs of members and that members themselves were reluctant to impose or enforce regulations where a consensus did not prevail.[30] From the outset, dual control, and divisions within the membership itself, acted as a constraining influence on the power of the Stock Exchange as an institution to either confer undue privileges on its members or dictate the terms under which the securities market operated.

These developments within the Stock Exchange were taking place within an expanding membership, which reached 541 by April 1815. Government borrowing continued to expand on the back of the military expenditure necessary to wage war against Napoleon. The National Debt rose from £456.1m. in 1801 (95 per cent funded) to £744.99m. (92 per cent funded) in 1815, and then peaked at £844.3m. (94 per cent funded) in 1819, as the government struggled to get its income and expenditure into balance. This huge amount of stock held by numerous investors from all over the country needed a market and that was provided by the brokers and jobbers of the London Stock Exchange, as even a Scottish observer like Hamilton noted in 1815. Though the buying and selling generated by many of these investors could be, individually, quite small, collectively the result would be a steady turnover to be handled on a daily basis by the members. Thus, it was not surprising that the membership continued to grow.[31]

[30] LSE: General Purposes, 1 Sept. 1819, 1 Apr. 1820, 11 July 1821, 13 Nov. 1821, 10 Dec. 1821, 17 Dec. 1821, 24 Dec. 1821, 20 Feb. 1822, 4 Mar. 1822, 11 Mar. 1822, 14 Aug. 1832, 12 Sept. 1832; LSE: Trustees and Managers, 27 Feb. 1822; Letter from J. Ricardo *et al.* to the managers of the Stock Exchange, 22 Jan. 1822; Legal Opinion, 20 July 1822.
[31] LSE: General Purposes, 1 Apr. 1815, 1 Apr. 1820; Hamilton, *National Debt*, 313–15; R. C. Michie, *Money, Mania and Markets; Investment, Company Formation and the Stock Exchange in Nineteenth-Century Scotland* (Edinburgh 1981), 254–5; J. Lowe, *The Present State of England in Regard to Agriculture, Trade and Finance* (London 1823), 364–5.

What was surprising was the continued growth in membership after the end of the Napoleonic wars, reaching 737 by 1820, or an increase of a third. Much activity on the Stock Exchange before 1815 was speculative activity fuelled by both rumour and fact concerning the progress of war and the prospects of peace. Military success would suggest an end to war and thus a fall in government borrowing, lower inflation, and a decline in interest rates. These factors would drive the price of stock up. Conversely, defeat would suggest a prolonging of the conflict, and the costs attached to it, which would push prices down. Thus, when a group spread a false rumour on the Stock Exchange in 1814, purporting to come from France, and announcing that Napoleon was dead and Paris captured, the price of government stock rose, allowing the perpetrators to make a profit of £10,450 by selling the securities they had bought shortly before. Though this was a fraudulent scheme, the period generally was rife with speculative activity as the future value of government stock was dependent upon the course of political and military activity on the Continent of Europe, rather than long-term economic factors. Suggestive of the volume of business so generated was the fact that the stockbroker, Peter Templeman, bought and sold, on his own account, government securities worth £54,000 in May 1815 alone, emerging from the war a rich man as a result of his activities.[32]

With the end of the war the expectation would be that these speculative opportunities would fade away, so reducing both the activity and the membership of the Stock Exchange. Certainly, major players like the stockbroker David Ricardo, stopped speculating in government stock at this time. By 1815 Ricardo had amassed a fortune of around £0.5m. from buying and selling government stock, and over the next four years he switched that fortune to land. What speculation he did was in French *rentes* through the Paris market. Conversely, it was after 1815 that the Raphael brothers—Raphael and Joseph—moved from trade into stockbroking, which suggests, along with the membership figures, that there was an underlying vitality to the post-war securities market. The explanation seems to lie in a re-emergence of pre-war trends, where the securities market was a vital ingredient in the money and foreign exchange markets. Clearly, the Raphaels, as Amsterdam Jews, were exploiting their international connections to engage in the inter-country movement of securities, currency, and gold. This is also what Nathan Rothschild was engaged in at this time and what a Mr da Veiga, readmitted to the Stock Exchange in 1815, intended to do using his Dutch connections. Trading in government securities between London and Paris was now the pivotal element in European exchange operations. With French *rentes* held in London, Amsterdam, Antwerp, Frankfurt, Berlin, and Vienna until the 1820s, they constituted

[32] LSE: General Purposes, 15 Mar. 1814; Wainwright, *Mullens*, 16.

an internationally mobile asset whose ownership could be easily transferred via the securities market.[33]

## MARKET PLACE

Within Britain, the greatly increased size of government income and expenditure, due to the war, plus the expanded nature of Britain's trade, had led to the London money market becoming of far greater importance within the entire financial system of the country. The flow of funds to and from London, looking for temporary but remunerative employment, was far greater than in the past, with the proliferation of banks increasingly directing a portion of their deposits in that direction. Scottish banks, for example, now made far greater use of the London money market than in the eighteenth century, both to draw upon when money was required and to place money there when not otherwise taken up at home. In turn this fed through to the securities market as the National Debt offered excellent opportunities for short-term investment, which could be easily and quickly realized when required.[34] A mid-1820s guide to the Public Funds reported that they

. . . have become a kind of circulating capital, and in many respects answer the same purposes as the circulating medium of the country.[35]

Hence, as before the war, what the public took as meaningless speculation was but the ebb and flow of the money market adjusting to the constant fluctuations to the supply and demand for money at home and abroad. Of course some of this buying and selling was straightforward speculation or gambling. The members of the Stock Exchange, for instance, were also heavily involved in the sale and purchase of state lottery tickets, with an active secondary market in fractions of ticket before the draw was made. Much as it tried the Stock Exchange failed to stop the trading in lottery tickets within its premises, and it was only the end of public lotteries in 1826 that brought the practice to an end.[36]

The National Debt ceased to grow after 1819, though the economy— and the savings it produced—did continue to expand. Eventually, those

[33] LSE: General Purposes, 25 Aug. 1815, 30 Jan. 1818; D. Weatherall, *David Ricardo: A Biography* (The Hague 1976), 129, 131; S. D. Chapman, *Raphael Bicentenary, 1787–1987* (London 1987), 13; Chapman, 'Rothschilds as Bankers', 187; D. C. M. Platt, *Foreign Finance in Continental Europe and the United States, 1815–1870* (London 1984), 10–11; E. V. Morgan and W. A. Thomas, *The Stock Exchange: Its History and Functions* (London 1962), 80; J. C. Riley, *International Government Finance and the Amsterdam Capital Market, 1740–1815* (Cambridge 1980), 8.

[34] M. Collins, *Money and Banking in the UK: A History* (London 1988), 27, 29; R. G. Hawtrey, *A Century of Bank Rate* (London 1938), 88; M. Buchinsky and B. Polak, 'The Emergence of a National Capital Market in England, 1710–1880', *J. Ec. H.* 53 (1993), 18; LSE: General Purposes, 6 Sept. 1811, 2 May 1814, 7 Aug. 1820.

[35] *New Guide to the Public Funds*, 3.

[36] R. D. Richards, 'The Lottery in the History of English Government Finance', *Economic History*, 3 (1934–7), 57, 72–4; LSE: General Purposes, 6 Feb. 1809, 22 Feb. 1809.

savings were bound to seek an additional home to that of government securities. Over the period of the Napoleonic wars the National Debt stood at
approximately twice the level of National Income, as both borrowing and
the economy grew in line. With the post-war slump in the economy, combined with a continued expansion of government borrowing until 1819, the
National Debt reached a level almost three times larger than National
Income in 1821. From then on there was a steady decline, caused by a combination of debt repayment—down by almost £50m. between 1821 and
1851—and a strongly growing economy, with National Income up by
£230m. over the same period. The result was that ratio of National Debt
to National Income fell to 2:3 in 1831, 1:8 in 1841, and 1:5 in 1851, or
half the level it had been 1821. Inevitably this had implications for the
London Stock Exchange for it had originated as, and specialized in, the
market for the National Debt and related securities.

By the mid-1820s there were definite signs that investors were beginning
to look at investments that offered the same flexibility as a holding in
the National Debt but a better rate of return. The yield on 3 per cent
consols, which had stood at 5 per cent in 1816 had fallen to 3.8 per cent
in 1822 and declined further to 3.3 per cent in 1824. Naturally enough,
attention turned to the securities issued by other governments, especially
those of neighbouring Western European countries, as was observed in
the mid-1820s.

... in consequence of the high price of the British Funds, there is a considerable dis-
position in the public to speculate in Foreign securities ...[37]

The switch to foreign securities began in 1822 when the government itself
began converting that part of its debt paying 5 per cent per annum onto
a 4 per cent basis. A total of £2.8m. was repaid to holders unwilling to
accept the reduction in interest. In that same year at least five foreign
government loans, with a nominal value of £8.9m. were issued in London.
This was followed by another two in 1823 (£5m.), seven in 1824 (£14.7m.),
and six in 1825 (£11.5m.), making twenty loans with a nominal value
of £40.1m. in that four-year period. In particular, the newly independent
Latin American countries, such as Colombia, Chile, Peru, Mexico, and
Brazil borrowed heavily in London at this time, being responsible for twelve
of the loans and half the amount. They offered more attractive rates of
return than neighbouring European countries whose debt was taken by
their own nationals.[38]

Naturally enough once issued there developed an active secondary market
in these foreign government securities, especially as the speculative

[37] *New Guide to the Public Funds*, 117.
[38] F. G. Dawson, *The First Latin American Debt Crisis: The City of London and the
1822–25 Loan Bubble* (New Haven 1990), 21, 249; Corporation of Foreign Bondholders, *The
Principal Foreign Loans* (London 1877), listed by year; Platt, *Foreign Finance*, 11; Morgan
and Thomas, *The Stock Exchange*, 81; *Commerce in Consternation* (London 1826), 122–4.

potential was great. Little was known about many of the countries that issued the loans, with some such as Poyais being entirely fictitious. Prices thus fluctuated wildly as rumours and expectations abounded. When news was received from abroad, the financial prospects of the various governments—and thus their ability to service the loans—were reassessed, with obvious implications for the current price at which they were being traded. By August 1822 the London Stock Exchange itself recognized

... the great quantity of business transacted in Foreign stocks ...[39]

with many of its own members being extensively involved, executing orders on a daily basis. At that stage these dealings were taking place outside the Stock Exchange, such as in the street or at the Royal Exchange. This led to a request by six members of the Stock Exchange to be permitted to transact such business within the Stock Exchange. It was turned down on the pretext that the Stock Exchange was not permitted to trade in anything other than the Public Funds. Clearly, there was a reluctance among the membership to become involved with securities that involved far greater risk and uncertainty than British government debt.[40]

This request was repeated in October 1822, and this time it was supported by 30 members who referred to

The immense transactions that have taken place in the securities of foreign governments, within the last six months ...

and complained about

... the serious difficulties and risk which at present attend the negotiation of them.[41]

In particular, the lack of officially monitored prices for foreign securities made it extremely hazardous to know what current values actually were. This request met a better response as the Committee for General Purposes now decided that there was no reason why a market in foreign securities could not be established within the Stock Exchange with prices being officially quoted.[42]

The problem now existed of how to accommodate this new and active market within the existing building. This matter was referred to the Trustees and Managers as their responsibility. Unlike the members, the proprietors responded rapidly to this request. They were well aware that dealing in foreign securities, outside the Stock Exchange represented a real threat to their property's continued dominance of the securities market, for it created the possibility that a rival Stock Exchange would be set up. By 21 November 1822 the lease on an adjoining building—No. 6 Capel Court—had been purchased with the intention of converting it into a market for foreign securities. This was none too soon for the brokers and jobbers who were

[39] LSE: General Purposes, 5 Aug. 1822.     [40] Ibid.
[41] Ibid., 1 Oct. 1822.     [42] Ibid., 4 Oct. 1822.

involved in foreign securities, including members of the Stock Exchange, had been making plans to open their own separate market. They had gone as far as negotiating with William Melton, a property developer and he was ready to provide them with a room on a subscription basis. As it was, the prompt action by the managers forestalled Melton's plans, much to his annoyance, and the ground floor of No. 6 Capel Court was opened as a Foreign Funds market on 1 January 1823.[43]

The difficulties for the Stock Exchange, created by this switch to foreign securities, did not end with the admittance of their trading. The buying and selling of foreign government stock had attracted numerous new people to the occupation of stockbroking and jobbing and many of these were ineligible for entry into the Stock Exchange, because they had other occupations, such as bankers and money brokers. It was not a sufficient response to expand the Stock Exchange to accommodate this new market if many of those transacting the business were to be excluded. If this was done the possibility of a rival exchange being established remained a real one but the established members of the Stock Exchange were unwilling to change their rules so as to permit all concerned entry into their market. The solution devised was to set up a separate Foreign Funds market that would admit existing members of the Stock Exchange free but charge non-members 8 guineas per annum. Rothschild was a member of the Foreign Funds market though ineligible for admission to the Stock Exchange. This Foreign Funds market was to be jointly administered by the members of the Stock Exchange and those non-members who paid the subscription to use it. What was achieved was a physical and membership separation of the markets in British and foreign government securities, but a linking of the two in terms of the general rules and regulations under which they operated. In July 1823 the Trustees and Managers claimed for the Foreign Funds market,

... the security it would afford to the Public by those stocks being negotiated by persons acting under, and subject to, the Regulations by which the Stock Exchange is governed.[44]

Certainly, the result was a great success with some 200 people frequenting the Foreign Funds market when it opened, which was more than the room could cope with. Again the response of the managers was swift with the lease of No. 3 Capel Court, being purchased. As this lease had only a short time to run the intention was to expand the Foreign Funds market by incorporating this building as well. Altogether, the managers had spent £10,551 in acquiring and converting property in order to accommodate the move into foreign securities, and so pre-empted any challenge to their supremacy

[43] Ibid., 25 Nov. 1822, 6 Jan. 1823; LSE: Trustees and Managers, 21 Nov. 1822, 18 Dec. 1822, 7 Feb. 1823.

[44] Ibid., 19 Mar. 1823, 19 July 1824; LSE: General Purposes, 6 Jan. 1823, 26 Mar. 1823, 31 Mar. 1823, 4 Apr. 1823, 9 Apr. 1823, 14 Apr. 1823.

within the securities market. The membership of the Foreign Funds market, excluding those who also belonged to the Stock Exchange, reached 143 by March 1823 and 173 in March 1824, though falling back slightly to 169 in March 1825. If the running of the Stock Exchange had been completely dominated by its membership, most of whom were engaged in the sale and purchase of the National Debt, it has to be questioned whether the response would have been so swift and so positive. The members self interest was best served—in the short run—by protecting the market in the Public Funds, and they were antagonistic to the newcomers dealing in Foreign Funds. The proprietors self interest was in maintaining their position within the securities market as a whole, whatever was being traded, and that was best served by forestalling and accommodating competition.[45]

Investors and speculators did not remain satisfied for long with foreign government securities and soon turned their attention to the issues of newly formed joint-stock companies. Altogether, an estimated 624 joint-stock companies were promoted in 1824/5 with a nominal capital of £372.2m., or four times the numbers and eight times the capital of those already in existence at the end of 1823. These joint-stock companies covered a wide range of activities, ranging from domestic canal and railway projects to financial concerns aiming to channel British savings abroad. Among those that attracted the greatest interest from speculators were foreign and domestic metal-mining companies.[46] One observer in London, W. S. Davidson, wrote in January 1825:

All the town are mad just now, about mining shares—I never had or wished for any—and I dare say the Bubble will burst one of these days and ruin thousands.[47]

As the worth and prospects of these companies were even more unclear than that of foreign government bonds, many established members of the Stock Exchange were also reluctant to admit the shares they issued to their market. This was despite the fact that a number of their own members did deal in them outside the Stock Exchange, with the Royal Exchange again being a favoured location. Nevertheless, the proprietors of the Stock Exchange were well aware that they could not ignore this developing share market either, even though it only involved a minority of the membership. Consequently, having already met the problem of foreign securities by forming a separate market, the solution adopted by the managers of the Stock Exchange in March 1825 was to permit the buying and selling of shares within the Foreign Funds market.

[45] LSE: Trustees and Managers, 19 July 1824; LSE: General Purposes, 31 Mar. 1823, 4 Apr. 1823, 9 Apr. 1823, 14 Apr. 1823, 5 June 1823.

[46] Dawson, *Latin American Debt Crisis*, 67, 99, 120, 139–40; R. W. Randall, *Real de Monte: A British Mining Venture in Mexico* (Austin, Tex. 1972), 31, 33, 35, 80; J. Exter, *Causes of the Present Depression in our Money Market* (London 1825), 9–10; Morgan and Thomas, *The Stock Exchange*, 82–3.

[47] W. S. Davidson to W. Leslie 25 Jan. 1825.

Within these few months a great many companies have been formed for working mines, making Railroads and other purposes, and as the purchase and sale of shares in those companies are in general transacted by the Brokers of the Stock Exchange, the managers have directed that part of the business of the Stock Exchange to be transacted in the Foreign Funds Market.[48]

It was not possible to mount a direct challenge to the Stock Exchange, holding such a commanding position in the buying and selling of the National Debt, but the appearance of these alternative securities traded by different people, and treated with hostility by the members of the Stock Exchange, presented a new opportunity to compete. Certainly, by the end of March 1825 such moves were afoot, despite the efforts by the managers to accommodate the new markets and the new brokers and dealers.[49] However, as it was the volume of trading collapsed when the speculative boom burst towards the end of 1825. A tightening of the money market due to a poor harvest caused a flurry of selling that saw prices collapse leaving investors with large losses. Subsequently a number of banks that had lent money extensively on the security of speculative stocks and shares were bankrupted. This was compounded by the fact that many of the joint-stock schemes proved to be illusory, impractical or simply fraudulent while foreign states defaulted, unable to raise sufficient money out of taxes to pay interest on the loans. Of the joint-stock companies only 127, or a fifth, survived even to the end of 1826. Among the loans raised by Latin American republics only Brazil was still paying interest by December 1828, while in Europe, Greece, Portugal, and Spain had all defaulted. As a consequence, not only was there little incentive to open a rival stock exchange but membership of the Foreign Funds market slumped, reaching 30 in 1831, compared to 169 in 1825.[50]

This collapse of the market for both foreign government bonds and joint-stock company shares left the Stock Exchange with a problem of what to do with the Foreign Funds market, as its business disappeared after 1825. Those who were already members of the Stock Exchange drifted back to their original activities as brokers and jobbers in the Public Funds. Membership did drift down from the 804 of April 1826 reaching a low of 637 in April 1833, after a few ups and downs. Those who were subscribers to the Foreign Funds market could either abandon the securities business or attempt to join the Stock Exchange proper. The integration of the two markets was suggested in October 1827, becoming a formal proposal in December, only to be rejected. Negotiations then dragged on until March 1828 when it was proposed by the Foreign Funds market that its management should be placed in the hands of the Committee for General Purposes, on condition that

<hr />

[48] Foreign Funds Market: Committee Minute Book, 5 Mar. 1825.

[49] Ibid., 11 Dec. 1824, 29 Mar. 1825.

[50] Dawson, *Latin American Debt Crisis*, 114, 116, 123, 126–7, 132, 167, 173–4, 184–6, 191; Morgan and Thomas, *The Stock Exchange*, 83; Foreign Funds Market, 30 June 1831.

subscribers of five-years standing—30 in all—were then admitted as members of the Stock Exchange. This was accepted by the Stock Exchange but it still left some 50 subscribers to the Foreign Funds market who were not allowed to join the Stock Exchange. Among these were a number who also frequented the Royal Exchange, where an alternative securities market existed. They were deemed inadmissible along with those who had occupations other than stockbroking. There were six of these in 1829, including the Haes brothers who combined stockbroking with merchant banking.[51]

During the 1830s there was a gradual convergence of interest between the Foreign Funds market and the Stock Exchange proper. In July 1831 the rules and regulations covering both markets were amalgamated, with the Stock Exchange adopting a number of procedures from the Foreign Funds market relating to the method of dealing, the quotation of stocks, and the reporting of prices. Henceforth, though separate, the two markets were governed by exactly the same rules and regulations. The next step came in August 1832 when it was agreed to admit trading in foreign government securities onto the floor of the Stock Exchange itself, though the Foreign Funds room remained the location for any business outside the National Debt. Despite the fact that one of the Haes brothers—John—was already conducting business in the Stock Exchange unofficially, the Stock Exchange could not bring itself to admit the remaining subscribers, including five who made a formal application to join in March 1833. It was not until February 1835 that the Foreign Funds market and the Stock Exchange were finally unified with the remaining 22 subscribers being granted immediate admission, including the persistent John and David Haes.[52]

Behind this eventual change of policy was the renewed interest in foreign securities that developed in the mid-1830s. Between 1833 and 1837, inclusive, a total of 11 new foreign government loans were issued in London, with a nominal value of £23.2m. These, along with the existing loans, began to generate a growing activity in the London securities market, part of which was taking place outside the Foreign Funds room. By 1837, British investors were familiar with foreign government securities worth almost £400m., and though much of this was traded abroad, such as the massive French and Dutch debts, there was also an active market in some of the issues in London.[53] Consequently, on 18 February 1835 the Stock Exchange agreed that

[51] LSE: General Purposes, 3 Apr. 1826, 31 Mar. 1827, 31 Oct. 1827, 29 Nov. 1827, 10 Dec. 1827, 13 Feb. 1828, 21 Mar. 1828, 22 Mar. 1828, 29 Mar. 1828, 21 Apr. 1828, 16 Mar. 1829, 31 Mar. 1829, 6 Apr. 1829, 1 Apr. 1830, 29 Mar. 1831, 2 Apr. 1832, 1 Apr. 1833; Foreign Funds Market, 18 Dec. 1827, 24 Dec. 1827, 19 Mar. 1828, 20 Mar. 1828, 24 Mar. 1828, 7 Apr. 1828, 23 Nov. 1830, 30 June 1831.

[52] LSE: General Purposes, 30 July 1831, 14 Aug. 1832, 23 Feb. 1833, 23 Mar. 1833, 23 Feb. 1835; Corporation of Foreign Bondholders, *Principal Foreign Loans*.

[53] LSE: General Purposes, 22 Mar. 1832, 23 Mar. 1832, 24 Mar. 1832, 8 May 1832; C. Fenn, *A Compendium of the English and Foreign Funds* (London 1837), 50–1, 57–85; LSE: Trustees and Managers, 21 Feb. 1835.

Whereas from the great increase of investment of English capital, in Foreign securities, it is very desirable to terminate the distinction which exists between the English, and Foreign markets, and to unite the two rooms, thereby increasing the general accommodation, especially that now all rules and regulations which govern the Stock Exchange, govern the Foreign Stock Market . . .[54]

This decision was taken in the full knowledge that some of those who were admitted were also engaged in businesses other than stockbroking/jobbing but this was accepted as necessary if the merger was to take place, and was regarded in no way as an alteration to the rules. The trading in foreign securities continued to be regarded by many members as a much riskier business than the buying and selling of UK government debt. This was not simply because of the poor record of foreign states in securing their debts. More immediate was the question of price-sensitive information and its dissemination. It could take a long time for information from abroad to arrive in London—months in the case of Latin America—and then it filtered out into the market through a diverse number of sources. Consequently, trading in foreign securities was much more prone to manipulation and rumour than the market for British government debt, creating risks for the whole market. This problem of false or deficient information from abroad was not to disappear until international communications were transformed after 1851, when the international telegraph system began to transform the flow of messages around the world.[55]

The rehabilitation of foreign government securities in the 1830s was followed by a revival of interest in joint-stock company shares as well. Whereas in the mid-1820s the likes of canal shares were little traded on the London Stock Exchange, by the mid-1830s the Foreign Funds room was being used regularly as a forum where shares were being bought and sold. The London Stock Exchange increasingly comprised two markets, sharing both rules and members. The original building was devoted to UK government and related stocks while the Foreign Funds room was used for all other securities. By the late 1830s there was a considerable body among the membership who dealt in shares rather than government stock whether home or foreign. Most of these traded the securities issued by British joint-stock companies. In 1838 at least 278 brokers, out of a total membership of 675—or 40 per cent—were involved in the buying and selling of shares, with many dealers also participating. As early as 1835 15 members were engaged in dealings in the Blackwall Railway Company shares alone, while by 1838 37 members—21 dealers and 16 brokers—were handling large transactions in London and Brighton Railway stock. Certainly by the late 1830s there appeared to be little, if any resistance among the membership

---

[54] LSE: General Purposes, 18 Feb. 1835.
[55] Ibid., 10 July 1833, 9 June 1834, 4 Aug. 1834, 3 Aug. 1835, 29 July 1840, 17 Nov. 1847, 29 Dec. 1847, 29 July 1848.

as a whole to the buying and selling of corporate securities on the floor of the Stock Exchange.[56]

In fact, the very reverse was true for complaints gradually surfaced that brokers were transacting some of the business outside the Stock Exchange, such as in their own offices, to the disadvantage of the market as a whole. In 1843 all brokers were encouraged to bring all their orders to the Stock Exchange because,

. . . a large portion of the members of the Stock Exchange consisted of jobbers, who employed large capitals, and stood all day long in the market to make prices at considerable risk, often at serious loss to themselves, and whose only protection was their knowledge of the business, which was openly transacted in the House; but if undercurrents were to be going on, of which they could have no knowledge, their business would become too hazardous to be carried on, and Brokers would be unable to execute their commissions.[57]

As it was in the mid-1840s speculative boom, when the railway securities were all the rage, the value of share business being transacted threatened to swamp the Foreign Funds room. By April 1845 it was reported that the '. . . vast majority of members . . .' were dealing in railway shares in the Foreign Funds room, to the great disadvantage of those who normally transacted foreign business there. Rather than try to restrict this growth of business in shares the Stock Exchange responded by allocating more space to share-dealing. As a temporary measure this was done via a rearrangement of markets within the Stock Exchange, to the annoyance of dealers in consols. More permanently, the Stock Exchange was itself extended again. No. 9 Throgmorton Street had been purchased for this purpose in 1844, as business and membership picked up after the lull at the beginning of the 1840s.[58]

By April 1846, the London Stock Exchange could claim for their share market, that

in addition to the numerous and wealthy members who had from the first commencement of the share business, acted as jobbers in that market, there had been such an influx from the English market of old and responsible consol jobbers with large capital at command, that business of any extent might at all times be done, in every description of share or stock with the most perfect fairness and safety.[59]

Clearly, the episode of the Foreign Funds market in the mid-1820s had been a watershed for the London Stock Exchange, and marked the beginning of

---

[56] LSE: General Purposes, 15 Mar. 1824, 27 Dec. 1824; 31 Oct. 1835, 27 Jan. 1838, 29 Jan. 1838, 27 Mar. 1838, 29 Mar. 1838, 13 May 1840, 10 May 1843, 19 May 1843; LSE: Trustees and Managers, 21 Feb. 1835.

[57] LSE: General Purposes, 8 Feb. 1843.

[58] Ibid., 8 Apr. 1845, 18 Apr. 1845, 28 Apr. 1845, 17 Sept. 1845, 23 Oct. 1845; LSE: Trustees and Managers, 25 Mar. 1844, 20 Mar. 1845, 11 Sept. 1845, 26 Sept. 1845, 25 Mar. 1846.

[59] LSE: General Purposes, 3 Apr. 1846.

the move away from a complete reliance on business in the National Debt to a variety of other transferable securities.

Though business remained dominated by transactions in UK government debt, as would be expected because of its connections to the money market, other securities were of growing importance. Though increasingly inappropriately named, the Foreign Funds room was increasingly used as a market for corporate securities, meeting no opposition from members, apart from those dealing in foreign securities who were being crowded out. The failure of a rival Stock Exchange to appear in London in the mid-1840s, despite the great enthusiasm for railway securities, testifies to the ability of the London Stock Exchange to accommodate the new business. All that did appear, despite the volume of turnover was a twice-weekly auction of railway shares at the Hall of Commerce erected in Threadneedle Street in 1842 at a cost of £70,000. An attempt by Edward Moxhay, the owner of the Hall of Commerce, to establish it as an alternative to the Stock Exchange in 1845 failed as did the idea of creating a public stock exchange in the Royal Exchange.[60]

Nevertheless, despite this positive response to corporate securities the dominance of the London Stock Exchange within the British securities market was under threat from the mid-1830s onwards. That threat was coming from a direction about which it could do little. With the establishment of the Dublin Stock Exchange in 1799 London possessed a formal rival within the British securities market. However, Dublin posed no real threat, as even significant Irish sales and purchases of government debt continued to be channelled to the members of the London Stock Exchange. Instead, it was the growth of an alternative market in securities in the industrializing areas of Britain that ended London's virtual monopoly. As the British economy grew in the nineteenth century, and especially as savings and confidence returned after the post-war depression, there was a rising tide of investment outside London and the National Debt. In particular, local investors became interested in local projects as had been the case with the canal mania of the early 1790s. However, instead of canals, joint-stock company formation focused on utilities like gas and water supply plus, increasingly, railways, followed by financial concerns like insurance companies and banks. By 1840 there were some 106 Scottish joint-stock companies, with a paid-up capital of £18.6m. that had issued securities that could command a public market. Generally, the 1820s and 1830s saw a growing and vigorous promotion of all forms of joint-stock enterprise outside London. Much of the bank and railway

[60] *The Economist*, 5 Apr. 1845; *Railway Record*, 31 May 1845, 17 Oct. 1846; A. D. Gayer, W. W. Rostow, and A. J. Schwartz, *The Growth and Fluctuation of the British Economy 1790–1850* (Oxford 1953), 358, 362, 376, 409; C. Duguid, *The Story of the Stock Exchange* (London 1901); H. Pollins, 'The Marketing of Railway Shares in the First Half of the 19th Century', *Ec. H. R.* 7 (1954/5), 237.

company promotion of the 1830s took place in Lancashire not in London for example.

Unlike UK government debt, or even foreign securities, the shares issued by these provincial joint-stock companies tended to be held on a very localized basis. These companies providing services like gas or banking, attracted investors who were familiar with their operations on a day-to-day basis, through residing in the area in which they did business. This was not a simple division between London and the rest of the country, because all over the country joint-stock enterprise had a particular bias in the location of its shareholders. Each locality had its group of investors who preferred the immediate and familiar in terms of joint-stock company securities. Consequently, what was required was not an improvement or extension of the London Stock Exchange's market in corporate securities, because this did come about, but a mechanism for facilitating transactions between local investors in local securities. With transport and communications slow, before the national railway and telegraph system, there was no way the London Stock Exchange could provide the service required. It took, for instance, at least five days to communicate between London and Dublin in the 1820s.[61]

Gradually, from the 1820s onwards the informal securities markets, that had long existed in the major British cities outside London, became more sophisticated, with the appearance of stockbrokers specializing in buying and selling securities for investors. Within Scotland, John Robertson in Edinburgh and James Watson in Glasgow were among the earliest stockbrokers to appear. Their regular correspondence regarding securities on offer or required was tantamount to a Scottish Share market. Typical of their correspondence was the following for March 1834:

If the seller of the Shotts Iron Coy would take £16 a share I would take them but £20 is out of the question. I have not fallen in with any Glasgow Union but will inform you if I do.[62]

Turnover was limited in the securities of provincial joint-stock companies, with days if not weeks and months taken to negotiate a sale or purchase. Nevertheless there was a growing and regular turnover in an increasing number of securities that was sufficient to justify the appearance of stockbrokers in most of the major British cities from the 1820s onwards. The Dublin Stock Exchange, which had been formed with 13 members in

[61] W. A. Thomas, *The Stock Exchanges of Ireland* (Liverpool 1986), 123, 128, 141; Michie, *Money, Mania and Markets*, 27–41, 50–62, 78–99, 284–5; W. A. Thomas, *The Provincial Stock Exchanges* (London 1973), 17, 22; R. C. O. Matthews, *A Study in Trade-Cycle History: Economic Fluctuations in Great Britain 1833–1842* (Cambridge 1954), 196, G. H. Evans, *British Corporation Finance, 1775–1850: A Study of Preference Shares* (Baltimore 1936), 31, 37.

[62] James Watson to John Robertson, 10 Mar. 1834; see esp. 18 Jan. 1834, 17 Feb. 1834, 3 Mar. 1834, 14 Mar. 1834, 22 Mar. 1834, 3 Apr. 1834, 12 June 1834, 16 June 1834, 17 June 1834, 19 June 1834, 4 July 1834, 3 Feb. 1837.

1799, boasted between 25 and 30 in the 1820s and 1830s. In fact, such was the volume of business that stock exchanges were formed in both Liverpool and Manchester in 1836, the former with a membership of 37 and the latter with only seven, though that quickly rose to 23 by 1839. Though speculative activity in shares did contribute to the formation of the two stock exchanges in Lancashire, it was but a reflection of an underlying growth in the provincial popularity of corporate securities.[63]

The next major change came with the railway mania in the 1840s. Popular as railway shares were on the London Stock Exchange, threatening to overwhelm all other business, their impact on the provinces was even more dramatic. Whereas in 1825 the paid-up capital of Britain's railways was a mere £0.2m., rising to £7.5m. in 1835, by 1840 this had increased more than sixfold to £48.1m. and then almost doubled again to £88.5m. in 1845. Nevertheless, compared to the National Debt, static as its growth was, the paid-up capital of the railways equated to only 11 per cent of the National Debt in 1845. In contrast, the appearance of numerous well-capitalized railway companies, whose shares were actively traded among new and enthusiastic groups of provincial investors, represented a major challenge to the provincial securities market. Membership of existing provincial stock exchanges shot up, with Liverpool reaching 220 in 1846 and Manchester 89, while a rash of new stock exchanges appeared all over the country. By the end of 1845 there were some 18 stock exchanges in existence compared with three at the beginning of the decade, and most major provincial towns possessed one. In Dublin, at one time there were 4 separate stock exchanges, as the established Dublin Stock Exchange, controlled by its membership, limited entry and enforced high commission changes. It was only after an official enquiry ordered by the Lord Lieutenant, that the Dublin Stock Exchange was forced to liberalize entry.[64]

Generally, the appearance of these numerous provincial stock exchanges, beginning in 1836 and culminating with the wholesale expansion of 1844/5, represented a fundamental extension of the British securities market, taking in a greatly expanded body of both securities and investors. The London Stock Exchange responded to this shift as well as it was able, and the absence of any rival exchanges within London, compared to Dublin, does testify to its success in that respect. However, it was impossible for a market based in London to cater for the local interests and needs of investors from a distance. They had to accept that, try as they might, provincial markets were better informed about local securities than they were. The very vitality of local investment by local investors in local securities, combined with

[63] Thomas, *Stock Exchanges of Ireland*, 55; Thomas, *Provincial Stock Exchanges*, 17, 22–3; J. R. Killick and W. A. Thomas, 'The Provincial Stock Exchanges, 1830–1870', *Ec. H. R.* 23 (1970), 99, 102; J. R. Killick and W. A. Thomas, 'The Stock Exchanges of the North of England, 1836–1850', *Northern History*, 8 (1970), 114–16, 118–20.

[64] Thomas, *Provincial Stock Exchanges*, 21, 23, 51–2, 55, 58, 59, 287; Michie, *Money, Mania and Markets*, 101–11; Thomas, *Stock Exchanges of Ireland*, 55, 79, 81–3.

the excitement of speculation in the mid-1830s and, especially, the mid-1840s, underlay the formation of stock exchanges outside London. It is difficult to see what actions the London Stock Exchange could have taken to prevent their appearance, committed as it was to no ceiling on membership and, by then, a willingness to trade in whatever securities were popular. Membership did reach 906 in 1851 compared to 617 in 1844, or an increase of almost 50 per cent, over the period.[65]

Once the speculative boom passed, a number of these provincial stock exchanges faded away, as with Huddersfield and Nottingham, while the number of provincial stockbrokers slumped by around 20 per cent, from c.500 in 1846 to c.400 in 1850. During those years the London Stock Exchange did recover its position within the securities market, reclaiming more and more of the business in railway shares from the provinces. By then, though, the British securities market was, clearly, a multi-centred one with cities like Glasgow, Edinburgh, Manchester, Liverpool, Leeds, Birmingham, and Bristol all possessing established and active stock exchanges providing a local forum for the trading of locally held securities, whether they were the issues of local joint-stock companies or the holdings of local investors in national securities.[66]

By 1853 the paid-up capital of the securities quoted on the London Stock Exchange amounted to £1.2bn. Of this three-quarters had still been issued by governments, especially the British government. In contrast that representing corporate undertakings was very much in the minority, at one-quarter of the total, with British railways being by far the biggest component, at £194m., or 16 per cent. Most of the securities were also domestic in origin with those foreign stocks issued in London comprising only 8 per cent of the total. Overall, the British National Debt, which had completely dominated the activities of the London Stock Exchange at the beginning of the nineteenth century had shrunk to 70 per cent of quoted securities by the mid-nineteenth century. A decisive shift had taken place in the role of the securities market for it was now firmly placed within the national capital market, helping to meet the financial requirements of the British economy, particularly the transport infrastructure, rather than the needs of government, determined by military spending during wars.[67]

[65] D. M. Evans, The Commercial Crisis, 1847–8 (London 1848), 7; M. C. Reed, Investment in Railways in Britain, 1820–44: A Study in the Development of the Capital Market (Oxford 1975), 93, 212, 262; B. C. Hunt, The Development of the Business Corporation in England, 1800–1867 (Cambridge, Mass., 1936), 105, 107; M. C. Reed, 'Railways and the Growth of the Capital Market', in M. C. Reed (ed.), Railways in the Victorian Economy (Newton Abbot 1969), 162–3, 166, 172–4, 179, 182; LSE: General Purposes, 25 Nov. 1846, 1 Dec. 1846, 30 Jan. 1847.

[66] Thomas, Provincial Stock Exchanges, 72, 287; Reed, 'Railways and the Capital Market', 181–2; see R. C. Michie, 'The London and Provincial Stock Exchanges 1799–1973', in D. H. Aldcroft and T. Slaven (eds.), Enterprise and Management (Aldershot 1995).

[67] R. C. Michie, London and New York Stock Exchanges, 1850–1914 (London 1992), 52, 54.

With the railways the Stock Exchange made a material contribution to the financing of economic growth. Railways required large injections of capital at the outset, if they were to provide the continuous transport connections attractive to passengers, and of use for the movement of freight. The return to that investment came over the years as those using the service paid for that privilege. Thus the financial needs of railways were much more akin to that of a government, funding sudden military expenditure, than the gradual accumulation of capital in agriculture, manufacturing, or even housing. However, as with the National Debt there were few in society who could afford to lend indefinitely, without any immediate prospect of repayment, and, when they did, a high rate of interest would be requested. By making the stocks and shares issued by railways transferable, the companies obtained the large initial amounts required on a permanent basis, while the investors were presented with the ability to sell their holdings when, or if, required.

Whereas in 1760 corporate debt was only 7 per cent of all financial assets in Britain, by 1850 it had doubled to 16 per cent. Government debt had also grown as a proportion over the same period, from 28 to 36 per cent, reflecting the vast increase during the French Revolutionary/Napoleonic wars. What had been squeezed was mortgage finance, down from 25 to 16 per cent, and trade credit, falling from 28 to 9 per cent, indicating that the requirements of the economy were increasingly for long-term finance, which the issue of transferable securities were ideally placed to provide.[68] Initially, the Stock Exchange was little involved in providing a forum for the sale and purchase of this new corporate debt, leaving it to the outside markets in London and their provincial equivalents. The *Bankers' Circular* observed in 1835, that

It is a remarkable fact, that the Railway system advanced and became established in the public confidence, almost wholly without the assistance of the Stock Exchange.[69]

True as that was at the time, it was already becoming inaccurate. The members of the London Stock Exchange were even then involved in the trading of railway securities, with a market for them developing in the Foreign Funds Room. Thus, by 1845, when the paid-up capital of British railways was some twelve times greater than in 1835, the London Stock Exchange was a major market for the securities that they issued. On the back of the railway mania, for instance, the firm of stockbrokers, Foster and Braithwaite, saw their income rise from a mere £4,183 in 1839 to £50,649 in 1845, suggesting a twelvefold growth in business. Though contemporaries could, and did, complain about the speculation that

[68] Michie, 'Introduction', in R. C. Michie (ed.), *Commercial and Financial Services* (Oxford 1994), pp. xli–xlii, l–li.
[69] The *Bankers' Circular*, 6 Nov. 1835.

accompanied this involvement, and pointed to the widespread appearance of stock exchanges outside London, there could be no doubt that the London Stock Exchange was playing a major role in the whole process of railway finance at the time—a role that grew in importance once the speculation died away. By 1850 the railway track open for use in Britain reached 6,621 miles, and three-quarters of that had been built since 1840, or two-thirds since 1845. Similarly, the paid-up capital totalled £246m., and of that 80 per cent had been raised since 1840 or 64 per cent since 1845. When in 1853 the capital invested in the British railway system amounted to £278.4m., the London Stock Exchange quoted 70 per cent of it, with the prices set by its trading dominating provincial markets.[70]

Despite the repositioning of the Stock Exchange from the 1820s onwards, so that it came to play a small but strategic role in the capital market through railway finance, the prime role it played continued to be as a market in the National Debt and the connection to the money market. By permitting the formation of joint-stock banks in England, outside London, in 1826, and extending that privilege to London itself in 1833, more and more of the nation's banking became London based. At the same time a growing sophistication of banking technique made bankers increasingly aware of the opportunities for the profitable employment of idle balances in the London money market. The result was to direct not only an increasing amount, but a rising proportion, of the country's short-term funds to London for remunerative employment. This was especially so within the branch–head office relationships of the expanding joint-stock banks. In turn, this had implications for the Stock Exchange for one way of utilizing these short-term funds was to either buy, hold, and then sell government stock or to lend, at low rates of interest, to those who made a profession of so doing, such as certain members of the Stock Exchange.[71]

Any fluctuations in the supply of, or demand for, money had immediate implications for the price of government stock, and so sustaining an active market. The *Bankers' Circular* reported in July 1829

The difficulty of finding safe employment for money, . . . has caused almost all public securities to advance in price.[72]

These were also the times when promoters could form joint-stock companies, like railways, as the stocks they issued increased the supply of securities to which these funds could be applied. Conversely, there were brief periods when the speculative interest on the Stock Exchange was sufficient

[70] Michie, *London and New York*, 52; Reader, *Foster & Braithwaite*, 39, 43, 45; Reed, 'Railways and the Capital Market', 181–2; *The Times*, 30 Aug. 1845, 14 Oct. 1845; *The Economist*, 4 Oct. 1845, 25 Oct. 1845; *Railway Record*, 27 Oct. 1846.

[71] *The Economist*, 8 May 1847; J. Sykes, *The Amalgamation Movement in English Banking, 1825–1924* (London 1926), 1, 4; Collins, *Money and Banking*, 27, 29, 55.

[72] *The Bankers' Circular*, 24 July 1829; see also 20 Aug. 1830, 19 Oct. 1832, 11 Apr. 1834.

to absorb funds from the money market, to the detriment of other users. The East India merchant, James Bruce, complained in May 1835 that

... the pressure for money is so great (arising out of the transactions in the Stock Exchange) that I have had difficulty in raising money myself.[73]

There was thus a very close and intimate relationship between the London money and securities markets at this time, with one constantly interacting with the other as conditions changed from minute to minute during the day. It was thus not surprising that so many of the brokers, who were members of the Stock Exchange, numbered banks among their most active clients. Foster and Braithwaite, for example, were extensively used by the London bankers Glyn Mills, Mastemans, and Hanbury Taylor and Lloyd, to buy and sell securities from 1825 onwards, as well as the emerging provincial joint-stock banks, like Manchester and Liverpool District Bank, the Bank of Liverpool, and the Lancaster Bank.[74]

Generally, money was forever being lent and borrowed on the Stock Exchange, as London, provincial, Scottish, and merchant bankers all sought the best openings for what they had temporarily available. R. Hichens, who acted as the 'broker to the London Joint-Stock Bank and to several Lombard Street Bankers...' was reported in 1848 as being '...a large dealer in money'. He himself claimed then that

The Stock Exchange is the channel through which all money business of London flows...[75]

Generating much of the turnover on the Stock Exchange at this time, as before, was, therefore, the need of bankers and others to constantly invest or realize the funds entrusted to them. During the year 1850 the merchant bank, Barings, lent a total of £13.6m. to the stockbroker Cazenove, who then re-lent to jobbers for their operations in government stock and other securities.[76]

Despite the rise of railway securities the focus of money market transactions on the Stock Exchange continued to be the National Debt. The debt of the British government possessed a large and active market where stock could be bought and sold in any amount at any time for either cash or credit and for either immediate or future delivery. An assessment made of the market for 3 per cent consols between 1821–60 concluded that it was very efficient, judged by the standards of the late twentieth century.[77] It was the

[73] James Bruce to William Shand, 29 May 1835; see H. B. Kerr, 'Report on the Law of Partnership: House of Commons Sessional Paper', XLIV (1837), 5.

[74] P. Ziegler, Central Bank, Peripheral Industry: The Bank of England in the Provinces, 1826–1913 (Leicester 1990), 40–6; Reader, Foster and Braithwaite, 10, 27, 37; Roberts, Schroders, 355–8.

[75] LSE: General Purposes, 16 Feb. 1848; see also 24 May 1842, 17 Sept. 1845.

[76] Kynaston, Cazenove, 30, 32–3, 39–40.

[77] R. L. Brown and S. D. Easton, 'Weak-form Efficiency in the Nineteenth Century: A Study of Daily Prices in the London Market for 3 percent Consols, 1821–1860' Economica, 56 (1989), 68.

existence of this market that allowed those with short-term funds to hold, directly or indirectly, long-term securities, and those holding such securities to easily and quickly obtain short-term funds when required.

In a place of so extensive commerce as London, opulent merchants who possess property in the funds and are unwilling to part with it have frequently occasion to raise money for a short time. Their resource in this case is to sell for money and to buy for account . . .[78]

So reported Henry Keyser in 1850. The differential in price between selling for money and buying for account, plus the commission paid to the broker, would represent the cost of the money obtained, while preserving owner-ship of the government stock and the yield it produced.

By 1850 it was not only British banks and merchants who were making use of the ready market for securities provided by the London Stock Exchange for their money market operations. In that year Cunningham referred to the London Stock Exchange as the ready-money market of the world, while the following year *Knights Cyclopaedia* claimed that

No Stock Exchange in Europe affords such facilities for speculation as that of London, for the dealings are not confined to English government securities, but embrace every description of transferable security, shares in railways, mines, canals, insurance companies, joint-stock banks, and indeed all property, the sign of which can be passed from hand to hand, besides including every description of foreign funds. The foreign capitalist is attracted from every capital in Europe to the English Stock Exchange, and the Jews flock to it from every quarter under heaven.[79]

Though this is a rather exaggerated account, the ability to invest and realize at will on the London Stock Exchange was becoming attractive to investors outside Britain at this time, if only to facilitate payments in dif-ferent centres. The American merchant George Peabody, based in London from 1838, traded extensively in US bonds. By buying in the United States and selling in London, or vice-versa, payments in dollars made to him by American importers could be converted into the sterling required to pay British exporters. The same requirements, and practices, existed between Britain and the Continent, and all would generate continuous trading in foreign securities on the London Stock Exchange which contemporaries would simply ascribe to speculation in rising and falling values.[80]

Between 1801 and 1851 the London Stock Exchange had come a long way. Whereas in 1802 it had a membership of 363, by 1851 it was 906. In 1801 it traded, exclusively, British government debt, or proxies for it, which

[78] Keyser, *The Law Relating to Transactions on the Stock Exchange*, 32–3.

[79] Cunningham, *Hand-Book of London* (London 1850), 472, *Knight's Cyclopaedia of London* (London 1851), 647.

[80] K. Burk, *Morgan Grenfell, 1838–1988: The Biography of a Merchant Bank* (Oxford 1989), 11, 13; H. Janes, *de Zoete and Gorton: A History* (London 1963), 6, 16, 21; Platt, *Foreign Finance*, 13–14, 19.

amounted to £456m. By 1853 it quoted securities capitalized at £1.2bn., and these now included 8 per cent issued by foreign governments and railways and 20 per cent by British companies. Over the same period it had consolidated, and even extended, its position within the domestic money market, which was an increasingly integrated one. Internationally, its influence was growing as London was the centre of the world money market, for Amsterdam never recovered from occupation and revolution, Paris remained troubled by political instability, and Germany was disunited. Though the raising of capital at home and abroad, continued largely to bypass the Stock Exchange, apart from the needs of governments, the appearance of railways did see the securities market begin to make a contribution to financing economic growth. As the financial requirements of the railway system began to reach large-scale proportions from the mid-1830s onwards, Stock Exchange involvement grew. Even European railways, as with those in France, issued stocks and shares in London, in the 1840s, and these were then traded on the Stock Exchange. Despite the appearance of rival stock exchanges within Britain at this time London played a central role in developing this new market for corporate debt.[81] As an institution the London Stock Exchange established itself as a permanent element in the City of London during these years. It successfully blended the need for access and participation with that for control over the conduct of members.

In the eyes of the public the London Stock Exchange became identified with the entire securities market, though it never succeeded in monopolizing that. The very lack of serious competitors in London, however, was evidence of the Stock Exchange's ability to meet the interests of all users, and their clients, despite the considerable changes that took place in the securities market over that half-century. Accepting that institutional arrangements needed to be made so as to permit the securities market to both function effectively and to meet the demands made upon it, the assessment must be that the London Stock Exchange, on the whole, had achieved that by mid-century. Nevertheless, problems did remain even in the very fundamentals of its organization, with many members remaining unhappy with the residual influence of the proprietors in the conduct of their business.[82] At the same time the growing integration of securities trading was bringing the London Stock Exchange into closer and closer contact with potential rivals both at home, such as Liverpool, and abroad, such as Paris. These were to be the challenges of the future.

[81] Michie, *London and New York*, 52, 54; Michie, *Commercial and Financial Services*, pp. xli–lv.

[82] LSE: General Purposes, 17 Nov. 1847, 29 Dec. 1847, 12 Jan. 1848; Legal Opinion, 11 Jan. 1851, 14 June 1851.

# 3

# *From Domestic to International,*
# *1850–1914*

MARKET PLACE

In 1850 the London Stock Exchange was the biggest and most important of its kind in the world. This was mainly a reflection of the strength and vitality of the British economy at that time. Though international influences and connections did exist they were completely overshadowed by the needs of domestic investors and borrowers. On the eve of the First World War the London Stock Exchange remained the most important in the world despite the challenge to Britain's economic position from the United States and Germany. An American economist who was very familiar with the securities business, C. A. Conant, noted in 1904 that, 'Great Britain easily leads the world in the volume of her Stock Exchange business'. Another well-informed American, S. F. Streit of the New York Stock Exchange, was of the opinion after a tour of Europe, that turnover on the London Stock Exchange was ten times greater than on his own in 1914.[1] Whatever measure is applied there was no sign that London's dominant position among the hierarchy of stock exchanges was under threat by the beginning of the twentieth century. Behind this success lay a fundamental shift in orientation for the London Stock Exchange. Increasingly it was not domestic but international opportunities that underlay its growth. Though activity in domestic securities continued to provide a large, expanding, and even dynamic business for its members, that was increasingly overshadowed by the rapid expansion of both foreign securities and foreign clients. The interests of European investors and trading in American securities, in particular, became significant areas of activity for the London Stock Exchange over the 1850–1914 period, attracting the attention of numerous members. Yet another American observer, R. M. Bauer of New York, was of the opinion in 1911 that 'The London Stock Exchange is the only really international market of the world. Its interests branch over all parts of our globe.'[2] By the First World War the London Stock Exchange was not simply

[1] C. A. Conant, *Wall Street and the Country: A Study of Recent Financial Tendencies* (New York 1904), 147; S. F. Streit, *Report on European Stock Exchanges* (New York 1914), 16–17.
[2] LSE: General Purposes, minutes, 15 May 1911.

still the largest in the world, it was also in a different class from all its counterparts, judging from the views of informed contemporaries.

Certainly the years between 1850 and 1914 were ones of unparalleled opportunity and challenge for the London Stock Exchange. It was at that time that transferable securities became commonplace as a means of finance for both governments and businesses around the world, creating in the process an ever expanding demand for the facilities of securities markets. Simultaneously, the transformation of communications, begun with the telegraph and culminating with the telephone, destroyed the sovereignty of localized markets leading to direct competition between distant stock exchanges for the first time. Radically altered circumstances like these inevitably tested the organizational structure of the London Stock Exchange. If the London Stock Exchange was to both profit from the opportunities and surmount the challenges, its structure had to be, at one and the same time, sufficiently durable to ensure its survival and sufficiently flexible to accommodate the momentous changes taking place. Considering the growth of domestic business one response could have been to concentrate upon that, controlling the British market for securities. However, that would have left the rapidly expanding international securities market for others to exploit, most notably the Paris Bourse for European investors and the New York Stock Exchange for North American borrowers. How well the London Stock Exchange served the domestic market and how successful it was in taking command of the emerging global market before 1914 both need to be considered. It is, therefore, against this background that the performance of the institution and its members needs to be judged.

In 1850 financial assets represented an estimated 39 per cent of all assets owned by the British people, and comprised such items as mortgages, bank deposits, trade credit, and government and corporate debt. By 1912/13 the proportion had risen to 64 per cent, or by two-thirds, at the expense of real property such as land and buildings. At the same time the stock of total assets was itself growing strongly. The value of domestic fixed assets in the UK tripled from £4.2bn. to £12.9bn., at constant (1930) prices, between 1856 and 1913. Within this rapid growth of financial assets the most rapidly expanding proportion was that of transferable securities. In 1850 an estimated 56 per cent of financial assets could be classified as domestic or foreign debt, much of which would be transferable, whereas in 1913 this had reached 64 per cent of the total. This was despite the rapid growth of the banking system and stagnation in the size of the British government's own debt. In particular, the share taken by foreign assets had grown from 8 per cent to 28 per cent between 1850 and 1913. Though Britain was very much at the forefront of the use of transferable securities the move was apparent in all the leading economies, to a greater or lesser degree. Generally, the more sophisticated the financial system the greater the proportion of wealth in the form of securities, because of their mutual convenience for holders and issuers. Altogether, it is estimated that the total stock of transferable securities in the world increased from £6.7bn. in 1878 to £23bn. in 1910, or an almost fourfold expansion at current prices in a deflationary era. Of these securities approximately a quarter were in the hands of British investors.

Reflecting this growth in the popularity of securities in Britain was an increase in the number of investors holding part of their wealth in this form. Estimates suggest that the number of serious holders of securities also quadrupled over the 1870–1914 period, rising from 250,000 to 1m. Large as this growth was it still represented a very small minority of the British population, though the proportion was growing. In 1870 only 0.8 per cent of the population could be classified as investors and this had grown to only 2.2 per cent by 1913. These investors were holding a growing variety of securities, though. An examination of the shareholders of 6,120 joint-stock companies, excluding railways, which was conducted in 1901, revealed a cumulative total of 3,369,000 names. Allowing for duplication because of multiple holdings, this was reduced to 445,000 or almost half the investing public. Whereas at mid-century most investors concentrated upon the securities issued by either governments or the railways, by 1900 the shares and debentures belonging to both home and overseas industrial, commercial, mining and other such companies had become popular. Also, by then the average investor was holding between seven and eight different securities.[3]

One illustration of the simultaneous widening and deepening of the investing public can be seen from the situation of British joint-stock banks. In 1902 the paid-up capital of the 10 largest banks totalled £22.7m. and this was held, collectively, by 80,093 shareholders, or an average holding of £283 per person. Ten years later, in 1912, the number of shareholders had reached 135,982 though the capital had only grown to £29.2m., bringing the average holding down to £215. Among those with significant savings in British society the direct holding of securities became increasingly popular and this led more and more to experiment with types of securities which had once been the preserve of small groups of well-informed insiders. When Barclays Bank was formed in 1896, as an amalgamation of private banks, it had only 110 shareholders. By 1902 the total was still only 650 but in that year the stock was quoted on the Stock Exchange. As a result, by 1907, the number of shareholders had expanded to 4,150 and then reached 6,800 by 1912, or a more than tenfold increase over a

[3] Association for the Reform and Codification of the Law of Nations: Summary and Report on Negotiable Instruments to Bearer, February 1879; M. A. Neymarck, *La Statistique Internationale des Valeurs Mobilières* (La Haye 1911), 3, 23; R. C. Michie, 'Introduction', in R. C. Michie (ed.), *Commercial and Financial Services* (Oxford 1994), pp. l–lii; R. W. Goldsmith, *Comparative National Balance Sheets: A Study of Twenty Countries, 1688–1978* (Chicago 1985), 216–32; G. W. Edwards, *The Evolution of Finance Capitalism* (New York 1938), 89.

10-year period. In the process capital per shareholder shrunk from £3,717 in 1902 to £471 indicating that it was investor demand that lay behind the increase, not the financial needs of the company. Generally, British investors appear to have been among the most sophisticated in the world, judging by their willingness to purchase the securities issued by companies operating in emergent fields or countries earlier than investors elsewhere.

Though the number of individuals directly investing in securities remained but a small proportion of the population, their indirect involvement was greatly widened by the investment of institutions. Joint-stock banks, insurance companies, and investment trusts were among the most important of the financial institutions who directed a growing proportion of collective savings into stocks and shares over the 1850–1914 period, and did so in an increasingly professional manner. Insurance companies, for example, moved away from channelling most of their premium income into the National Debt and mortgages on land, as they were still doing at mid-century. Instead they invested in a much more diversified portfolio involving domestic and foreign securities. The assets of British life insurance companies, for instance, rose from £108.8m. in 1870 to £530.1m. in 1913, with the proportion in the form of securities growing from 24.4 per cent to 50.6 per cent over the same period. This represented a tenfold increase in their absolute holding of stocks and shares. With the growing importance of these financial institutions, and their increasingly diverse nature, moving beyond banking, there was created a powerful group of institutional players interested in the professional management of portfolios of securities. Naturally, these developments further complicated the operation of the securities market, in which the London Stock Exchange was the central element, as the requirements and activities of these new and large institutional investors could be very different from those of the individual investors and the private bankers of the past.[4]

Complicating even more the environment within which the London Stock Exchange had to perform was the revolution in communications that occurred at this time. With the invention of the telegraph in 1837 it was possible to separate the flow of information from its physical transportation by converting information into a series of electrical impulses, transmitting it along a wire, and then decoding it at the other end. As these electrical impulses could travel much faster that any known form of transport the result was revolutionary. From 1840 onwards London became linked by telegraph to all the major cities of Britain with Glasgow, for instance, being reached in 1847. Consequently, by 1850 there was in place a national communications system which placed the members of the London Stock Exchange in rapid contact with any centre where securities

[4] Y. Cassis, *City Bankers, 1890–1914* (Cambridge 1994), 68, 72; L. E. Davis and R. J. Cull, *International Capital Markets and American Economic Growth 1820–1914* (Cambridge 1994), 71.

were also bought and sold. Subsequent refinements in technology reduced the delay to negligible proportions. By the 1890s it was estimated that the time to transmit a telegraphic message from London to Glasgow was only 2.5 minutes but, by then, the existence of the telephone ensured that constant voice-to-voice contact could be maintained. Domestically, first the telegraph and then the telephone, ensured that between 1850 and 1900 the isolation of individual securities markets, due to the time taken to relay and receive information, had been overcome. Other factors would now dictate to which stock exchange buying and selling orders would be sent, creating both risks and possibilities for London in the process.

From 1851, with the completion of the submarine cable across the Channel, London was linked to Paris, and then other continental markets, by telegraph. Though the initial cost of a message was almost prohibitive the result was to remove rumour and uncertainty from the London Stock Exchange's pricing of major European securities, such as French *rentes*, by constant reference to trading on, for example, the Paris Bourse. This was made even easier in the 1890s with the London–Paris telephone line. Even more dramatic than the European-wide links was the London to New York submarine cable, with the first permanent connection coming in 1866. Instead of the 16-day-old American prices that the London stockbroker, Satterthwaite, was using in 1854, a member of the London Stock Exchange now had access to those arrived at on the floor of the New York Stock Exchange only 20 minutes previously. Again, as the technology improved this delay fell to a mere 30 seconds by the First World War. Telegraphic contact with other non-European financial centres was also established with far distant Melbourne in Australia being reached as early as 1872. By the mid-1870s rapid and reliable communication was in existence between London and all major foreign Stock Exchanges, with only a slight delay in the transmission and receipt of information. For the first time it became possible to identify a global securities market where individual stock exchanges both complemented and competed against each other for business.[5] The London Stock Exchange itself observed in November 1906 that

The increased rapidity of communication has made everyone want to deal at the closest possible price . . .[6]

Such was the speed and sophistication of the international communications system in existence by then that there was an almost continuous interaction between securities markets despite being separated by thousands

[5] R. C. Michie, *The London and New York Stock Exchanges 1850–1914* (London 1988), 7–10, 38–48, 101, 118–22; W. A. Thomas, *The Stock Exchanges of Ireland* (Liverpool 1986), 90, 92, 104, 124, 127; LSE: General Purposes, 3 Dec. 1851, 26 Mar. 1857, 30 Mar. 1857, 3 Apr. 1857, 24 Oct. 1872, 10 Mar. 1881, 6 Apr. 1909.
[6] Ibid., 20 Nov. 1906.

of miles. Both nationally and internationally the market within which each stock exchange and its members operated was ceasing to be secure monopolies by virtue of geography and so had to develop alternative roles if they were to survive and prosper.

The challenges faced by the London Stock Exchange, and its membership, were thus both profound and varied over the 1850–1914 period. At the simplest level was the need to increase capacity to cope with the growing volume of securities to be traded. This necessitated both further expansion to the trading-floor and a willingness to accept a substantial number of new members. At the same time more people had to be attracted to the stockbroking and jobbing professions. However, the changes experienced over this period, with new securities from different countries and companies, allied to the transformation of communications, meant that the response could not be more of the same. Both the institution, and those who belonged to it, would have to alter the way they operated, and their relationship to others, if they were to retain a central and influential position within the evolving securities market.

## ORGANIZATION

Facing these momentous changes, the organizational structure of the London Stock Exchange continued to be influenced by the division of authority between the owners and the members, with both positive and negative consequences. 'The administration of the Stock Exchange is vested in two bodies whose functions are distinct . . .' reported Frances Levien, secretary to the Committee for General Purposes, when questioned in 1878 by the Royal Commission on the London Stock Exchange.[7] This dual control continued to be a source of conflict within the Stock Exchange, and came under attack from the membership on more than one occasion between 1850 and 1914. In the mid-1870s, for example, when the management of the Stock Exchange was raising the level of both the initial entrance fee and the annual subscription, in order to pay for improvements, the membership resented their ability to do so without consulting them. Eventually, in 1876 it was agreed that all future purchasers of shares in the company owning the Stock Exchange must also be members of that institution and that all new members had to purchase a share. The aim of this move was to create a greater identity of interest between the members and the proprietors, by gradually eliminating those who had only a financial interest in the success of the Stock Exchange. Of course, this did not preclude ex-members holding shares in the Stock Exchange, and many retired members did have substantial stakes, creating potential conflict.

[7] Royal Commission on the London Stock Exchange (London, 1878), Minutes of Evidence, p. 4. See *Report*, 5.

Conflict arose again in both the 1880s and the 1890s with, this time, the issue being the size of the membership. An obvious solution to any downturn in the amount of stockbroking business to be handled, which occurred after every speculative boom, was to limit the number of new members admitted to the Stock Exchange. This would allow the existing members to monopolize what buying and selling there was. However, any reduction in membership would reduce the revenue of the Stock Exchange, with serious consequences for the profits of the institution, for running costs would remain at the same level. Thus the proprietors of the Stock Exchange, especially those who regarded it as an investment, were, inevitably, opposed to any policy of restriction on membership. Schemes were suggested to end Dual Control but they all foundered on the question of cost. The proprietors could only be bought out by the membership at a price that reflected the value of the Stock Exchange building and its capacity to generate income from fees. This would be very expensive and would have to be borne by the membership as a whole, and this many were in no position to finance. There was also the continuing fear that if the Stock Exchange became too exclusive a cheaper alternative might emerge or the government might decide they were a monopoly acting against the public interest. Thus, divisions of interest and opinion within the membership and a worry about buy-out costs prevented any change to the dual structure of control before 1914.

The long-term consequence of the 1876 change was that the number of shareholders in the Stock Exchange grew from only 268 in 1876 to 2,366 in 1914, creating an increasing but not complete overlap between member and proprietor. Whereas in 1876 there were seven members to every proprietor, by 1914 the ratio was only 2:1. However, though the power of members to control the institution to which they belonged did grow over time, there continued to remain a distinct group of proprietors which continued to have an influence on the running of the Stock Exchange. It would always be the older and wealthier of the membership who dominated the ownership of the Stock Exchange, as they could afford more than one share, and they tended to represent the interests of the larger and more established firms. As such they were always an actual, or potential, moderating influence on the collective stance of the majority of the members.[8]

The attitude of the proprietors was well summed up in 1891 when it was reported that,

The managers desired to make the Stock Exchange not only the best but the only place for dealings in stocks and shares.[9]

---

[8] D. Kynaston, 'The London Stock Exchange, 1870–1914: An Institutional History', Ph.D. thesis, University of London 1983, 54–7, 59, 60, 72; E. V. Morgan and W. D. Thomas, *The Stock Exchange: Its History and Functions* (London 1962), 142, 144.

[9] LSE: Trustees and Managers, 14 Oct. 1891.

This striving for 'best' was the positive aspect of their aim, and was reflected in a progressive expansion in the space and facilities available to the members of the Stock Exchange. On the negative side the desire to be the 'only' market for securities indicated a hostility to any other exchange or trading mechanism that threatened their monopoly position.

By 1850 the London Stock Exchange was under severe pressure to accommodate the increase in members, and their clerks, that had arisen as a result of 'the Railway Mania'. The trading-floor, in particular was felt to be severely crowded and this continued to be the case despite a rearrangement of markets in 1851 in order to make better use of available space. In 1853 a radical decision was taken to demolish the existing Stock Exchange building and construct a new one. This was completed in 1854, with the space available to members being doubled. Further improvement took place in 1872 when a settling room was provided in the basement. There stockbrokers' clerks could meet together to arrange the delivery of, or payment for, the securities being bought and sold on the floor. Previously, this had been done on the floor itself and so its removal reduced congestion arising from expanding numbers. By 1876 membership had reached 1,900 or more than double the 1851 figure. Expecting even greater numbers the proprietors were always interested in purchasing adjacent property into which the Stock Exchange could expand. In May 1879 they offered £5,778 for the house next door and, when that was refused, came back with a substantially higher offer of £7,133 in June. Eventually these purchases led in 1884 to a new building on the eastern side of the Stock Exchange, adding substantially to the space available when it was opened in 1885. By 1884 the Stock Exchange covered a floor space of 8,406 square feet which was shared by 2,573 members and 1,463 clerks, providing 2.08 square feet per person. With the extension, which virtually doubled the size of the Stock Exchange, as in 1854, the floor space rose to 4.07 square feet per user. Further extensions in 1896 and 1905 pushed the floor space up to 25,650 square feet and maintained it at around 3 square feet per user up to the First World War, or a more generous allocation than in 1884. However, in the period before 1914 the proprietors were increasingly unable to purchase adjacent property into which they could expand further. The site occupied by the Stock Exchange, being so close to the Bank of England, was a popular one with financial institutions generally as well as being very restricted because of the adjacent streets. With the City of London expanding as a whole at this time and residential property having been eliminated around the Bank of England, the physical expansion of the Stock Exchange was constrained by the site it occupied. Considering the physical difficulties of the site the proprietors of Stock Exchange clearly responded to the needs of members for space in which to trade and to complete the bargains made. An official clearing house was also set up in 1880. This replaced an earlier private initiative and matched bargains in designated active stocks, leaving members to deliver or pay for the balance, rather than complete every transaction.[10]

The cost of these facilities to every member remained relatively modest. The annual subscription fee at 10 guineas was not raised to 12 guineas until 1872. By 1900 a differential scale had come into operation with those being members of 20 years or more paying 20 guineas compared to 30 for those dating from 1880. Those joining after 1900 had to pay 40 guineas per annum. In addition, in 1854 there was introduced an entrance fee payment for new members, initially set at 50 guineas, with a reduction to 30 guineas for those who had been clerks. In contrast to the membership fee this one-off charge had risen substantially, reaching 500 guineas (250 for clerks) by 1914. As the facilities of the Stock Exchange were progressively improved, financed out of the annual fees of existing members, it was felt to be fully justified to charge those newly joining a substantial sum for the privilege of sharing in what had been created. Overall, even at its most expensive, which would exclude reductions for clerks, or long-standing members, by the First World War it cost only £525 to join the London Stock Exchange plus an annual payment of £42. Though this represented a substantial increase in the cost of membership, compared to the subscription of 10 guineas in 1850, it was by no means prohibitive. With most new members having served their time as clerks, the real expense of joining was substantially less. There was no sign that either the entrance fee or annual subscription discouraged interest.[11]

The proprietors of the Stock Exchange also showed themselves very responsive to changes in the requirements of the market in other ways. With transatlantic telegraph communications in place from 1866 onwards, trading in American securities became not only increasingly active but also heavily influenced by conditions on the New York Stock Exchange. Consequently, it was at its busiest during the hours when the New York Stock Exchange was open. The 10 a.m. opening of New York took place at 3.00 p.m. UK time. However, the London Stock Exchange closed at 4 p.m. forcing the brokers and jobbers in American securities to conduct business outside the building in Shorter's Court, next to the transatlantic cable companies' offices. Business there could continue until 8 p.m. at night, regardless of weather conditions. As in the past the existence of this outside market worried the owners of the Stock Exchange for it represented an embryonic rival that could be transformed into a fully fledged competitor if it received sufficient support. On more than one occasion they tried to

---

[10] Kynaston, 'London Stock Exchange', 51, 54; Morgan and Thomas, *The Stock Exchange*, 142–4; LSE: General Purposes, Appendix, 4 Feb. 1874, 26 July 1874; LSE: General Purposes, Settlement Department Subcommittee, 17 Apr. 1882, 18 June 1891; LSE: Trustees and Managers, Subcommittee on the Enlargement of the House, 26 May 1879, 10 June 1879; LSE: General Purposes, Committee of Members, 20 Apr. 1904.

[11] Kynaston, 'London Stock Exchange', 55, 72; Morgan and Thomas, *The Stock Exchange*, 144, 151.

offer a home for the American market within the Stock Exchange, as in
October 1891.

The managers are desirous of making some attempt to provide them with suitable
accommodation in a place where they may be sheltered from the inclemencies of an
English winter, where sufficient light shall be provided for the due transaction of
business in an orderly and proper manner, and where the jurisdiction of the Committee shall be free from any doubt or question.[12]

The easiest way to achieve this was to extend the opening hours of the
Stock Exchange but this the membership as a whole would not agree to. If
the Stock Exchange was open, even if restricted to American transactions,
there would be a pressure to continue transacting other business, forcing
the rest of the membership to remain as well. The result was that the
American market remained out-of-doors and less regulated. Similar problems emerged over the rearrangement of markets on the floor of the Stock
Exchange in order to accommodate the need for access to the telegraphic
offices. In 1884, for example, the managers suggested moving the foreign
market as near the office of the Post Office telegraph as possible. Those
who frequented the foreign market were in constant telegraphic contact
with continental Europe and any delay in communications created a risk
as prices rose and fell. Inevitably these proposed changes were objected to
by those members happy with the existing arrangements, and they were
sufficiently powerful to block them at that time. However, the subsequent
extension of the Stock Exchange allowed individual markets to be located
close to the communications systems they required. Thus, trading in American securities was clustered around the office of Anglo-American Telegraph
and Commercial Cable as these provided the transatlantic links. Similarly,
close to the telephone boxes for calls to Paris and Brussels were to be found
not only the Foreign Market, where European government securities were
bought and sold, but also dealers in such mining stocks as Rio Tinto, which
was popular among European investors. Again, it was the managers who
were readiest to respond to changes rather than the membership, as the
majority saw little need to accommodate the needs of a minority.[13]

  The one facility which the proprietors were reluctant to provide for the
membership was short-distance communications, through which changing prices and conditions within could be made known outside the
Stock Exchange. Long-distance communications to the Continent, North
America, and the rest of world extended the reach of the institution allowing its membership to trade foreign securities on an equal footing with the
members of overseas exchanges. Initially, at least, there was little fear that

[12] LSE: Trustees and Managers, 7 Oct. 1891; see Michie, London and New York, 83–4.
  [13] LSE: Trustees and Managers and General Purposes, Subcommittee to Confer on the
Arrangements of the Markets, 22 Aug. 1884; J. E. Day, Stock-Broker's office Organisation,
Management and Accounts (London 1911), 78; D. Kynaston, The City of London (London
1994), i. 355–6, 362.

London would lose business to rival centres as orders flowed out. Rather the aim was to retain, enhance, or gain such orders for the members of the London Stock Exchange. In contrast, local communications posed a direct threat to the London Stock Exchange as a club which brokers and dealers had to join if they wanted to buy and sell securities successfully. If non-members had constant access to the prices being determined on the floor of the Stock Exchange, and could communicate with members without needing to gain admittance to the building, there would be an incentive to not apply for membership, especially as costs of admission rose. Conversely, the membership saw benefits in both developments. The constant relaying of price information to interested non-members, such as major institutional investors, could encourage buying or selling orders which would increase the overall volume of business. Similarly, the ability to communicate rapidly from the floor of the Stock Exchange could keep a member in touch with events back in his office, and so respond quickly to the needs of customers.

With the introduction of the ticker-tape machine in 1867 it became possible to transmit prices as they changed on the floor to anyone who rented a receiver. This gave them instant access to the state of the market, and allowed them to buy and sell at current prices. Thus, when the Exchange Telegraph Company requested access to the floor, in order to collect and transmit prices, this was refused by the managers. As they said in 1868.

The managers decided that it would not be desirable to admit any person on the House for such a purpose as they had no guarantee but that prices might be wired to other places than the offices of brokers, and might tend to the formation of markets elsewhere.[14]

It was not until 1872 that the opposition of the proprietors was overcome and the ticker-tape was introduced. The members always had the ultimate weapon, if they were sufficiently united, that they would form an alternative Stock Exchange. Even then the service provided by the ticker-tape in London was poor as the Stock Exchange restricted both the number of operators allowed to collect prices on the floor and those permitted to receive them. In 1886, for example, it was discovered that some 80 non-member brokers subscribed to the ticker-tape, and used the prices it relayed to buy and sell securities on behalf of their clients, and so diverted business away from the members of the Stock Exchange. This led to further controls on the clients that the Exchange Telegraph Company was allowed to accept.

Though the delay in introducing the ticker-tape and the restrictions on the service were obstacles placed in the way of technological progress, they amounted to little more than minor inconveniences for the development of

[14] LSE: Trustees and Managers, 7 Oct. 1868.

the market. The ticker-tape provided information but did not allow a response. If a price change produced a flurry of interest investors needed to contact their brokers in order to buy or sell. For major clients, brokers kept them informed anyway in the hope that some business would result, allowing the giving of information to be followed, immediately, by a response if warranted. Thus, in addition to the ticker-tape there was a constant stream of prices being relayed from the Stock Exchange by the membership itself, and this went directly to those most interested in minute-to-minute changes. Similarly, the periodic bouts of speculative manias in Britain, such as in the 1880s, the 1890s, and the 1910s does not suggest any failure on behalf of the British public to become involved in stocks and shares because of the less than perfect stream of prices via the ticker-tape.

With the appearance of the telephone in 1878, the Stock Exchange faced a threat far greater than that posed by the ticker-tape. A direct two-way communication could be opened up between the floor of the Stock Exchange and an interested party outside. Through the use of the telephone, buying and selling prices quoted on the floor of the exchange could be instantly matched against those obtainable elsewhere, creating the possibility that business would be diverted away from the Stock Exchange. Furthermore, through the wider telephone system an inter-office market could be established that traded on Stock Exchange prices but was conducted between non-members. Due to this possibility the management of the Stock Exchange resisted the introduction of the telephone into the confines of the building. They rejected an application made in November 1879 to establish a telephone service linking the Stock Exchange with outside subscribers. However, pressure from members forced the management to reconsider. In February 1880 they agreed to have a telephone installed and by 1883 a telephone room was in use within the Stock Exchange.

Nevertheless, the service provided was considered inadequate by the membership who lobbied for improved facilities. When little was done the Committee for General Purposes, representing the members, issued this ultimatum to the managers in July 1888.

If they threw obstacles in the way of business or rather if they did not increase the facilities and show the public that business could be done cheaper and better on the Stock Exchange than elsewhere it would flow into other channels.[15]

The proprietors backed down and from thenceforth placed few obstacles to the introduction and use of the telephone into the Stock Exchange. The result was that the telephone became an indispensable tool for the transaction of business.

During October 1908, for instance, 81,883 outward and 23,916 inward calls were made or received at the Stock Exchange telephones linked to brokers' offices. This meant, approximately, one telephone call every five

[15] LSE: General Purposes, 11 July 1888.

seconds during the working day, and suggested a constant interaction between the members on the floor of the Stock Exchange and their partners or staff liaising with clients. In 1904 it was revealed, for instance, that those members dealing extensively in mining securities had direct telephone lines connecting their offices with the London offices of the major South African finance houses. Similarly in 1909 it was evident that those brokers buying and selling tea and rubber company shares were in constant communication with the members of the Mincing Lane Tea and Rubber Brokers Association, creating an active inter-exchange market in those securities. In 1911, the stockbroking firm of de Zoete and Gorton's office switchboard maintained two dozen private telephone lines to important clients so that the information and orders could be simultaneously relayed. In turn their office was directly connected to the floor of the Stock Exchange.

Generally, from the late 1880s onwards the management of the London Stock Exchange found themselves powerless to resist the leakage of prices from their trading-floor and the direct trading between member and non-member. Inevitably brokers would use the telephone to relay information to clients like the banks, insurance companies, investment trusts, and finance houses, in the hope that they would be given orders in return. For the same reason dealers belonging to the Stock Exchange would keep in close contact with non-member dealers if a substantial business was being done outside, as happened from time to time in such securities as South African gold mines, Eastern plantations, or American railways. This was all to be welcomed in extending the securities market beyond the confines of those present at any one time on the floor of the Stock Exchange for it fostered closer pricing, stability, and liquidity. By 1900 the management of the Stock Exchange had also come to accept that the future of their institution was not threatened by developments in local communications. In November 1908 a complaint about the capacity of the telephone service linking the Stock Exchange with the rest of the City of London was met by an agreement, in June 1909, to expand the provision, once the matter had been discussed and investigated.[16] This was hardly resistance to change.

Dual control had exerted a crucial influence in maintaining the balance between an open market in respect of access and a closed market in terms of regulation. One overriding principle maintaining this balance was that any qualified applicant was acceptable for membership, regardless of the number already there. As H. Rokeby-Price, Chairman of the Committee for General Purposes, put it in 1890,

[16] Generally see Michie, *London and New York*, 13–14, 19–20, 251–2; also LSE: Trustees and Managers, Subcommittee on the Enlargement of the House, 3 Feb. 1880; LSE: General Purposes, Subcommittee on Exchange Telegraph Company, 21 Feb. 1887; LSE: General Purposes and Trustees and Managers, Conjoint Committee, 5 Nov. 1908, 8 June 1909; LSE: General Purposes, 18 Feb. 1903, 11 July 1904, 26 July 1909: H. Janes, *de Zoete and Gorton: A History* (London 1963), 54.

... from the earliest days it had been a leading principle with the governing bodies of the Stock Exchange, that any person of respectability, who might be duly recommended, can become a subscriber.

The implications of this policy on admissions, continued Rokeby-Price, was that,

... by showing that character, and not money, was a chief qualification for membership, the governing bodies had been able more than once to prove that the Stock Exchange was to all intents and purposes an open market, and not, as alleged, a monopoly.[17]

There was always the fear that any restriction on entry, which could enhance the position of members within the securities market, would be seen as an abuse of power and provoke calls from the public for government to intervene and exert outside control.

Many were critical of the Stock Exchange seeing it as a private monopoly whose members were immune to public scrutiny. Henry Roy declared in 1860 that

The Stock Exchange is a closed market, pregnant with facilities for collusion having no pretence to comparison with an Auction mart.[18]

He demanded instead an open Stock Exchange regulated by the government. Certainly in the 1860s and 1870s the London Stock Exchange received a bad press. The commission set up in 1875 to enquire into the disastrous losses made by investors in certain foreign loans led to serious questions being asked regarding the role and functions of the Stock Exchange. That investigation concluded that

... the Stock Exchange practically require nothing more than the production of documents showing the authority of the agent to issue the loan, of the prospectus, and of a certificate stating the amount subscribed for and allotted to the public ... they make no further inquiry into the circumstances or conditions of the proposed loan, nor into the truthfulness of the prospectus, nor into the solvency of the borrowing state.

Nevertheless, the Stock Exchange was not asked to change its procedures because

The business of the Stock Exchange is to buy and sell, not good securities only, but all securities that are dealt in, and it is hardly fair and hardly wise to entrust to it the power of suppressing those questionable proposals by which it alone, of all the public, is certain to benefit.[19]

[17] LSE: General Purposes, 27 Jan. 1890, quoted in Kynaston, 'London Stock Exchange', 72.
[18] Henry Roy, *The Stock Exchange* (London 1860), 13, cf. 12, 22, 34; see also *Exposure of the Stock Exchange and Bubble Companies* (London 1854), 3.
[19] Select Committee on Loans to Foreign States, *Report* (1875), pp. xlvi, xlviii.

However, the matter did not end there. The revelations regarding foreign loans were followed by others concerning fraudulent company promotions whereby the public were encouraged to invest through the creation of an artificial market in the shares. Once the shares had all been sold by the promoters, support for this market was abandoned, and the price collapsed, leaving the investors with, at best, greatly overvalued securities or, at worst, a worthless enterprise. This resulted in a Royal Commission being set up in 1878 to investigate the Stock Exchange itself. Despite a sense of unease that the Stock Exchange was too lax on whom it admitted as members and the securities it quoted, again no action was taken. By the time the Commission reported those particular abuses had died away while there was also an unwillingness to suggest greater regulation or outside intervention as that could undermine the functions the Stock Exchange performed. Despite the criticisms and suspicions of the public, Parliament was loath to legislate for, on investigation, self-regulation did appear to be operating successfully. As Rokeby-Price said in his evidence to the Commission,

Our rules have gone on like the laws of the land, wherever there has been a nefarious thing we have endeavoured to stop the gap.[20]

Consequently, though the Stock Exchange continued to receive a hostile press, as with the writer in 1885 who compared it to betting on horses, no action was ever taken by the government to police its operations before 1914. It also appears that after the investigations of the 1870s the public's antipathy towards the Stock Exchange abated somewhat, possibly as investment in securities became more professional and better understood.[21]

Generally, up to the twentieth century the fear of being seen as a monopoly and provoking intervention, helped to maintain an open policy on admissions by the London Stock Exchange, along with the interest of the proprietors in increasing income and discouraging competition. Between 1886 and 1903 a total of 3,854 people applied for membership of the London Stock Exchange and only 39, or 1 per cent, were rejected. Whereas in 1850 there were 864 members of the Stock Exchange, by 1905 that number had reached 5,567, or a more than sixfold growth. In absolute numbers each decade saw a growth in the number of new members admitted, up to 1905. After that date membership began to fall gradually, reaching 4,855 in 1914. This decline in membership coincided with the introduction of a policy deliberately designed to contain the expansion of membership. Though attempts had been made in this direction before, none had been successful. However, by 1900 the membership had obtained greater control over the management of the institution through

---

[20] Royal Commission on the London Stock Exchange, *Report* (1875), 22; Minutes of Proceedings (1875), 71.

[21] H.M., *On the Analogy between the Stock Exchange and the Turf* (London 1885); see Kynaston, 'London Stock Exchange', 81.

the progressive effects of the deed change of 1876, while outright public hostility to the Stock Exchange had diminished. By the early twentieth century there was certainly a feeling that the securities market could not support a membership greatly in excess of 5,000, plus an additional 3,000 clerks who were also authorized to trade on behalf of their firms. At the most basic level the floor could not accommodate a potential 8,000 people entitled to congregate there, let alone unlimited expansion.

After much pressure from the majority of the membership, and resistance by a minority who wanted to maintain the principle of admitting every qualified entrant, a scheme was accepted in 1904, and introduced in 1905, to cap the numbers. Henceforth an applicant for membership had to buy the nomination of an existing member, as well as pay an entrance fee and the annual subscription. Though the Committee for General Purposes reserved the right to create nominations, mainly for the use of clerks, this effectively set a ceiling on membership. One immediate response was a rapid rise in membership as clerks converted into members under the previous rules. During the two-week period in November 1904 when the new rule was passed but not yet in operation a total of 664 clerks became members. With this pre-emptive increase, and the fact that the price of nominations remained relatively modest, it is difficult to suggest that the change in policy proved a particularly restrictive one before 1914. The price of a nomination, for example, ranged from a high of £170 in March 1910, to a low of £15 in June 1907, reflecting activity in the securities market.[22] Overall, it can be seen that those with access to the floor of the Stock Exchange— members and their clerks—peaked not in 1904/5 but in 1910, when it stood at 7,665 (see Table 3.1).

Nevertheless, this restriction on entry was followed by the formation in 1909 of the Mincing Lane Tea and Rubber Broker's Association, to provide a market for the vast speculative business in plantation company shares being generated at that time, stimulated by the inflated prospects for rubber tyres from the bicycle and motor car industries. This was not the first specialist securities market formed in London after 1850, to compete with or complement the Stock Exchange. Between 1855 and 1895 at least four different mining exchanges were established and operated in London, with the last one appearing in 1888. These provided a market for the shares of British metal-mining companies that tended to be ignored by the members of the London Stock Exchange, because of the extreme unpredictability of their prospects and their small size, with most of the shares being held in the mining districts themselves.

As the British metal-mining industry disappeared in the late nineteenth century, in the face of foreign competition, these mining exchanges closed. In contrast, foreign metal-mining did result in a number of major

---

[22] LSE: General Purposes, Committee of Members, 20 Apr. 1904; Kynaston, 'London Stock Exchange', 56, 59, 60, 63, 66, 70, 73, 78.

Table 3.1. London Stock Exchange: Membership, May 1904–November 1914

| | Members | | Clerks | | | | Total |
|---|---|---|---|---|---|---|---|
| | No. | % | Authorized | Non-authorized | Total | | |
| | | | | | No. | % | |
| May 1904 | 4,779 | 64 | 609 | 2,058 | 2,667 | 36 | 7,446 |
| Nov. 1904 | 5,481 | 73 | 322 | 1,725 | 2,047 | 27 | 7,528 |
| Nov. 1905 | 5,463 | 71 | 438 | 1,762 | 2,200 | 29 | 7,663 |
| Nov. 1906 | 5,397 | 71 | 493 | 1,714 | 2,207 | 29 | 7,604 |
| Nov. 1907 | 5,266 | 71 | 534 | 1,637 | 2,171 | 29 | 7,437 |
| Nov. 1908 | 5,047 | 71 | 526 | 1,531 | 2,057 | 29 | 7,104 |
| Nov. 1909 | 5,034 | 69 | 652 | 1,606 | 2,258 | 31 | 7,292 |
| Nov. 1910 | 5,102 | 67 | 795 | 1,768 | 2,563 | 33 | 7,665 |
| Nov. 1911 | 5,070 | 66 | 806 | 1,758 | 2,564 | 34 | 7,634 |
| Nov. 1912 | 5,052 | 66 | 828 | 1,732 | 2,560 | 34 | 7,612 |
| Nov. 1913 | 4,971 | 67 | 816 | 1,669 | 2,485 | 33 | 7,456 |
| Nov. 1914 | 4,822 | 67 | 765 | 1,562 | 2,327 | 33 | 7,149 |

*Source*: LSE: Committee for General Purposes, Selected Appendices, Membership 1922/3.

companies being formed whose size and prospects attracted a widespread investing public, and trading in their shares was conducted on the floor of the London Stock Exchange. Even the speculative boom in the shares of South African gold-mining companies in the 1890s, which spilled over into an after-hours street market, did not lead to the creation of a rival exchange specializing in mines, because both the securities and the brokers/jobbers involved, were admitted to the Stock Exchange. One might have expected the same to occur with the plantation companies because many were well capitalized concerns with a fairly certain future. However, though the London Stock Exchange did provide a market for plantation company securities, and a number of members undertook the business, this response did appear inadequate.[23]

Throughout the years before the First World War the Stock Exchange permitted its members to buy or sell whatever securities attracted them, and this permission extended to trading on the floor itself. Over the same period the physical expansion of the floor allowed a home to be found for virtually any group of securities whose popularity warranted one. As particular securities attracted interest members would begin to make a market in them with brokers flocking around jobbers. In turn this crowd would squeeze

[23] R. Burt, 'The London Mining Exchange, 1850–1900', *B. H.* 14 (1972), 124, 131, 142; J. R. Pike, *Britain's Metal Mines* (London 1864), 53; Michie, *London and New York*, 253–4.

adjoining markets on the floor, to everyone's discomfort. Where trading became so animated it spilled out-of-doors, into the streets and courtyards adjacent to the Stock Exchange, as with the Kaffir market in gold-mining securities from time to time from the 1890s onwards. In turn, that was a signal for physical expansion if the business became a large and permanent feature of the floor. Consequently, the Stock Exchange exhibited a clear propensity to meet the needs of new securities requiring a market place, once these were brought to its attention by the members.[24]

The one real control the Stock Exchange did exercise in this area was its willingness, or otherwise, to grant a quotation for a particular issue or whole categories of securities. By refusing to grant a quotation the Stock Exchange was not denying that security a market, even on the floor itself. What was being denied was access to a publicly recognized market, and all that went with that. By obtaining a quotation on the Stock Exchange there was an implicit statement that these securities could be, relatively easily, bought or sold, and that the prices in the Official List were an accurate reflection of current value. As a result quoted securities were more attractive to the investing public as they could be acquired or disposed of with little difficulty. Financial institutions were happy to lend on their collateral as they had an independently arrived at value and the expectation that they could be sold if the loan was not repaid. In turn this made both governments and companies anxious to have their securities quoted because it would lower the return they had to offer to investors in order to attract interes: '. . . an official quotation does certainly confer an increased marketability and value upon the quoted security' observed *The Economist* in 1885.[25] Thus, by restricting those securities placed on the Official List the Stock Exchange could influence the behaviour of investors and the access to finance of borrowers.

Reluctance to quote new and different securities after 1850 could have had important ramifications for the Stock Exchange for its traditional business was of diminishing importance. Whereas in 1850 the funded National Debt stood at £775.7m. by 1913 it had dropped to £593.5m. or by a quarter. Over the same period the wealth of the United Kingdom grew from £3.6bn. to £15.4bn. Thus, as an outlet for savings the National Debt's importance had shrunk dramatically from being equivalent to 21 per cent of total wealth down to 4 per cent. Much of the debt still in existence was tied up in the hands of savings banks and other institutions, and so was not actively traded in the market. This National Debt had represented some 70 per cent (Tables 3.2 and 3.3) of the securities quoted in

[24] Kynaston, 'London Stock Exchange', 160–1, 201, 225; Royal Commission on the London Stock Exchange, Minutes, 66, 149; *Financial Times' Investor's Guide* (London 1913), 67.

[25] *The Economist*, 30 May 1885; cf. M. S. Rix, *Stock Market Economics* (London 1954), 36–7; A. J. Merrett, M. Howe, and G. D. Newbould, *Equity Issues and the London Capital Market* (London 1967), 2.

**Table 3.2. Nominal values of securities quoted in the Stock Exchange Official List, 1853–1913 (£m.)**

| Class of security | 1853 | 1863 | 1873 | 1883 | 1893 | 1903 | 1913 |
|---|---|---|---|---|---|---|---|
| British government | 853.6 | 901.9 | 853.6 | 871.6 | 810.2 | 936.2 | 1,013.0 |
| UK public bodies | — | — | 5.3 | 43.0 | 91.4 | 166.0 | 277.1 |
| TOTAL | 853.6 | 901.9 | 858.9 | 914.6 | 901.6 | 1,102.2 | 1,290.1 |
| Colonial governments | — | 24.7 | 47.3 | 130.6 | 264.9 | 334.6 | 401.4 |
| Foreign governments | 69.7 | 146.7 | 403.9 | 831.5 | 722.8 | 1,028.6 | 1,421.9 |
| Colonial/Foreign public bodies | — | — | 35.3 | 13.0 | 43.9 | 48.1 | 156.5 |
| TOTAL | 69.7 | 171.4 | 486.5 | 975.1 | 1,031.5 | 1,411.4 | 2,034.4 |
| UK railways | 193.7 | 245.2 | 374.0 | 658.1 | 854.8 | 1,104.6 | 1,217.3 |
| Indian railways | 31.3 | 65.7 | 102.0 | 80.0 | 105.5 | 134.0 | 150.6 |
| Imperial railways | | | | 51.6 | 119.0 | 154.5 | 313.4 |
| American railways | | 132.0 | 82.7 | 307.6 | 743.7 | 1,107.5 | 1,729.6 |
| Foreign railways | | | 168.8 | 378.0 | 596.1 | 581.9 | 736.1 |
| TOTAL | 225.0 | 442.9 | 727.6 | 1,475.3 | 2,419.0 | 3,082.4 | 4,147.1 |
| Banks and discount houses | 6.5 | 17.7 | 103.7 | 55.8 | 62.6 | 200.2 | 294.4 |
| Financial, land, and investment | — | — | 7.3 | 33.5 | 75.5 | 105.4 | 133.4 |
| Financial trusts | | | | | 49.1 | 71.1 | 115.3 |
| Insurance | 6.6 | 8.5 | 2.2 | 12.8 | 12.4 | 63.8 | 66.4 |
| TOTAL | 13.1 | 26.3 | 113.2 | 102.2 | 199.5 | 440.5 | 609.1 |
| Canals and docks | 16.6 | 15.3 | 9.8 | 33.2 | 41.7 | 41.4 | 19.9 |
| Gas | 5.7 | 7.3 | 12.8 | 21.8 | 34.9 | 70.2 | 75.4 |
| Electric light/power | — | — | — | | | | 74.2 |
| Telegraph and telephone | — | — | 12.2 | 29.6 | 34.9 | 41.8 | 141.1 |
| Tramways and omnibus | — | — | 1.7 | 6.4 | 11.9 | 24.4 | 117.5 |
| Waterworks | 2.1 | 4.5 | 6.2 | 10.8 | 16.9 | 22.2 | 7.2 |
| TOTAL | 24.5 | 27.1 | 32.9 | 101.8 | 140.3 | 200.1 | 435.8 |
| Commercial/Industrial | 21.9 | 26.7 | 19.7 | 18.9 | 93.3 | 256.5 | 438.6 |
| Breweries/Distilleries | | | | | 52.1 | 118.4 | 103.8 |
| Iron, coal, and steel | | | 5.8 | 13.4 | 15.4 | 287.2 | 329.8 |
| Shipping | | | 7.1 | 10.7 | 11.8 | 28.7 | 45.8 |
| TOTAL | 21.9 | 26.7 | 32.6 | 43.0 | 172.6 | 690.9 | 917.6 |
| Mines | 7.4 | 5.2 | 7.6 | 20.8 | 32.9 | 41.1 | 60.3 |
| Nitrate | | | | | | | 7.5 |
| Oil | | | | | | | 23.6 |
| Tea, coffee, rubber | — | — | 1.1 | 1.6 | 1.7 | 9.7 | 25.0 |
| TOTAL | 7.4 | 5.1 | 8.8 | 22.4 | 34.6 | 50.8 | 116.4 |
| TOTAL | 1,215.3 | 1,682.9 | 2,270.4 | 3,634.4 | 4,899.2 | 6,978.2 | 9,550.5 |
| TOTAL* | — | — | — | 5,677.3 | 6,561.1 | 8,833.8 | 11,262.5 |
| Foreign government bonds | ? | ? | ? | 2,042.8 | 1,661.8 | 1,855.6 | 1,712.0 |

\* Includes those foreign government bonds payable abroad but quoted on the London Stock Exchange. As the market for these was mainly abroad, turnover in London was low.

*Sources: Stock Exchange Official Intelligence, 1884, 1894, 1904, 1914.*

**Table 3.3. Nominal values of securities quoted in the Stock Exchange Official List, 1853–1913 (%)**

| Class of security | 1853 | 1863 | 1873 | 1883 | 1893 | 1903 | 1913 |
|---|---|---|---|---|---|---|---|
| British government | 70.2 | 523.6 | 37.6 | 24.0 | 16.5 | 13.4 | 10.6 |
| UK public bodies | — | — | 0.2 | 1.2 | 1.8 | 2.4 | 2.9 |
| AS PERCENTAGE OF TOTAL | 70.2 | 53.6 | 37.8 | 25.2 | 18.4 | 15.8 | 13.5 |
| Colonial governments | — | 1.5 | 2.0 | 3.6 | 5.4 | 4.8 | 4.2 |
| Foreign governments | 5.7 | 8.7 | 17.8 | 22.9 | 14.8 | 14.7 | 14.9 |
| Colonial/Foreign public bodies | — | — | 1.6 | 0.4 | 0.9 | 0.7 | 1.6 |
| AS PERCENTAGE OF TOTAL | 5.7 | 10.2 | 21.4 | 26.8 | 21.1 | 20.2 | 21.3 |
| UK railways | 15.9 | 14.6 | 16.5 | 18.1 | 17.4 | 15.8 | 12.7 |
| Indian railways | 2.6 | 3.9 | 4.5 | 2.2 | 2.2 | 1.9 | 1.6 |
| Imperial railways | | | | 1.4 | 2.4 | 2.2 | 3.3 |
| American railways | | 7.8 | 3.6 | 8.5 | 15.2 | 15.9 | 18.1 |
| Foreign railways | | | 7.4 | 10.4 | 12.2 | 8.3 | 7.7 |
| AS PERCENTAGE OF TOTAL | 18.5 | 26.3 | 32.0 | 40.6 | 49.4 | 4.2 | 43.4 |
| Banks and discount houses | 0.5 | 1.1 | 4.6 | 1.5 | 1.3 | 2.9 | 3.1 |
| Financial, land, and investment | — | — | 0.3 | 0.9 | 1.5 | 1.5 | 1.4 |
| Financial trusts | | | | | 1.0 | 1.0 | 1.2 |
| Insurance | 0.5 | 0.5 | 0.1 | 0.4 | 0.3 | 0.9 | 0.7 |
| AS PERCENTAGE OF TOTAL | 1.1 | 1.6 | 5.0 | 2.8 | 4.0 | 6.3 | 6.4 |
| Canals and docks | 1.4 | 0.9 | 0.4 | 0.9 | 0.9 | 0.6 | 0.2 |
| Gas | 0.5 | 0.4 | 0.6 | 0.6 | 0.7 | 1.0 | 0.8 |
| Electric light/power | — | — | — | | | | 0.8 |
| Telegraph and telephone | — | — | 0.5 | 0.8 | 0.7 | 0.6 | 1.5 |
| Tramways and omnibus | — | — | 0.1 | 0.2 | 0.2 | 0.3 | 1.2 |
| Waterworks | 0.2 | 0.3 | 0.3 | 0.3 | 0.3 | 0.3 | 0.1 |
| AS PERCENTAGE OF TOTAL | 2.0 | 1.6 | 1.4 | 2.8 | 2.9 | 2.9 | 4.6 |
| Commercial/Industrial | 1.8 | 1.6 | 0.9 | 0.5 | 1.9 | 3.7 | 4.6 |
| Breweries/Distilleries | | | | | 1.1 | 1.7 | 1.1 |
| Iron, coal, and steel | | | 0.3 | 0.4 | 0.3 | 4.1 | 3.5 |
| Shipping | | | 0.3 | 0.3 | 0.2 | 0.4 | 0.5 |
| AS PERCENTAGE OF TOTAL | 1.8 | 1.6 | 1.4 | 1.2 | 3.5 | 9.9 | 9.6 |
| Mines | 0.6 | 0.3 | 0.3 | 0.6 | 0.7 | 0.6 | 0.6 |
| Nitrate | | | | | | | 0.1 |
| Oil | | | | | | | 0.2 |
| Tea, coffee, rubber | — | — | 0.1 | — | — | 0.1 | 0.3 |
| AS PERCENTAGE OF TOTAL | 0.6 | 0.3 | 0.4 | 0.6 | 0.7 | 0.7 | 1.2 |

*Sources:* As Table 3.2.

London in 1853. One area that had been growing rapidly before 1850 as an alternative to the National Debt were the securities of British railway companies. In 1850 their issued capital totalled £234.9m. and this increased by over £1bn. to reach £1,282m. in 1913. Despite this enormous increase it did little more than keep pace with the growing wealth of the country, for it represented 7 per cent of the total in 1850 and 8 per cent in 1913. In addition, London had to compete with the provincial Stock Exchanges for this market though the process of amalgamation did encourage trading to concentrate in London. Consequently, the London Stock Exchange needed to further diversify its list of quoted stocks and shares if it was to continue to command a central position within the British, let alone the world securities market.[26]

Three major possibilities existed. The first, and most obvious, were overseas government bonds as these had been able to command a place on the Stock Exchange since the mid-1820s. By 1853 foreign government securities with a paid-up value of £69.7m. were quoted, and this only covered those payable in London. A large mass of other foreign government securities were also bought and sold but their main market was to be found abroad, especially in the countries that had issued them. This was always to be a problem for though government borrowing via transferable debt did increase enormously over the 1850–1914 period, so did the interest of investors in the securities issued by their own authorities. During the American Civil War, for example, the US Federal government's interest-bearing debt escalated by some $2.3bn. By 1875, when the debt still stood at $1.7bn., some 37 per cent, or $0.6bn., was held abroad, especially in Britain. Within five years, that element held abroad fell to 12 per cent, or $0.2bn. In addition, the British were not the only investors interested in foreign government securities with the French, Dutch, and later the Germans all being active holders of the securities issued by indebted nations like Russia, Spain, or Turkey. This meant that British investors were forced to take an interest in the debts of emergent nations, like the Latin American republics, or Far Eastern borrowers, such as China and Japan. Again, such securities were readily quoted by the London Stock Exchange as well as the more secure issues of the countries of the British Empire. A few exceptions were the refusal to quote the Confederate Loan during the American Civil War and an unwillingness to quote Japanese domestic loans while the country was still on the silver standard. Both these involved exceptional risks due to political or currency instability and represented understandable caution at the time. There was also a reluctance to quote new issues by states who were in default on previous loans, as this was one of the few means, available to holders, to try and force repayment. Generally, this willingness by London to grant a quotation to foreign government securities was in marked contrast to stock exchanges abroad. Paris, for example, greatly restricted the quotation of foreign government bonds, and so diverted much of the buying and selling of its own nationals to London.

[26] C. H. Feinstein and S. Pollard (eds.), *Studies in Capital Formation in the UK, 1750–1920* (Oxford 1988), 464; B. R. Mitchell, *British Historical Statistics* (Cambridge 1988), 601–3; Morgan and Thomas, *Stock Exchange*, 119, 123.

Japanese loans, for instance, were welcomed in London in the 1870s but not until after 1900 in Paris. By then Japan was an established borrower with a good record of maintaining interest payments. The result of this liberal policy towards foreign and colonial government issues was that the amount quoted, and payable, in London rose to £2bn. by 1913, by which time they represented 21 per cent of all quoted securities. In relative terms the peak had been reached in the 1880s, when, in 1883, 27 per cent of quoted securities were those of foreign and colonial governments. Consequently, one major response by the Stock Exchange to the potential decline in business was to offer a home to those securities issued by overseas governments that were not absorbed by their own national investors. Inevitably this necessitated a willingness to take risks as the nature of borrowers was constantly changing. New countries appeared while the issues of older ones were repatriated. There was also the growth of lesser government bodies, with British and foreign municipalities becoming important borrowers by the early twentieth century, and these also found a welcome in London.[27]

The second possibility was also overseas for the introduction of railways in Britain was copied by other countries world-wide before 1914. The capital employed in the US railroad system grew from a mere $0.3bn. in 1850 to $21.1bn. in 1916. By 1853 securities amounting to £31.3m., belonging to foreign railways, were already quoted on the London Stock Exchange, with an active market in American railways in existence. However, this represented a mere 3 per cent of all quoted securities (Tables 3.2 and 3.3). Thenceforth, as successive countries developed railway systems the companies concerned tapped London for funds. As with foreign government securities, though, once the merits of railways, and the securities they issued, became known to their own investing public, there was a continuous process of repatriation. French railway issues, for example, which had been popular in London at mid-century, were largely held at home by 1860. Again, it was often the newer countries, with large land masses and sparse populations, like Argentina and Australia, that continued to rely heavily on foreign investors for their finance. Thus, the London market had to continually respond to offerings from new companies developing new routes in often relatively new countries. The one exception to this was the continued growth in popularity of American railway securities in London, for they came to comprise a large, distinct, and active

[27] J. J. Madden, *British Investment in the United States, 1860–1880* (New York 1985), 2, 116; D. C. M. Platt, *Foreign Finance in Continental Europe and the United States, 1815–1870: Quantities, Origins, Functions and Distribution* (London 1984), 33, 84, 86–7, 92, 129, 154; T. Suzuki, *Japanese Government Loan Issues on the London Capital Market, 1870–1913* (London 1994), 9, 10–11, 21, 55, 58–63, 65, 129, 132, 134, 152, 183; D. C. M. Platt, *Britain's Investment Overseas on the Eve of the First World War* (London 1986), 52; Kynaston, *City of London*, i. 217; J. F. Wilson, 'The Finance of Municipal Capital Expenditure in England and Wales, 1870–1914', *Financial History Review* 4 (1987), 38, 48.

market on the London Stock Exchange. This was not simply because the Americans were unable to finance the rapid extension of their own railway system but because the London Stock Exchange was almost more welcoming to the securities they issued than New York. Thus, though the popularity of foreign railing securities peaked in the 1890s, with 32 per cent of all quoted securities in 1893, the importance of US railroad securities continued to expand throughout, reaching 18 per cent of the total in 1913. Again, there is little sign that the London Stock Exchange proved at all resistant to the growth of this new market, for the evidence suggests quite the reverse. Certainly from the 1880s onwards London was not only the major market for the railroad issues of such countries as India, Canada, and Argentina, but it was also an important alternative market to New York for US railroads. London's willingness to quote such securities again drew in business from continental investors, such as the French, denied an official market in Paris.[28]

Whereas in 1853 foreign government and railway securities composed only 8 per cent of quoted securities in London, by 1893 the position had been transformed, for they were now in the majority, at 53 per cent of the total. Though the next 20 years saw a decline this was marginal as they still provided 51 per cent of the total in 1913. Over the 1850–1914 period the London Stock Exchange had created a large new business for itself by its willingness to provide official quotation for numerous governments and railroads from around the world, and to do so more readily than most other Stock Exchanges, including some of those in their homelands.

By the late nineteenth and early twentieth centuries this welcome had been extended to a variety of other corporate securities, most notably those belonging to foreign mines, industrials, and utilities. In 1853 companies operating in these areas were hardly in existence, even in Britain, apart from a few canals. The foreign mining boom of the 1820s had left few survivors. Consequently, they attracted little attention from investors and thus no need for a quotation on the Stock Exchange. This began to change in the 1890s with the appearance of numerous large and well-capitalized mining companies, operating in such places as South Africa and Australia, as well as companies producing such commodities as tea, coffee, and rubber in countries like India and Malaya. In addition, the amalgamation movement in the United States produced a few giant industrial enterprises, like United States Steel, that attracted investors world-wide. The need to build docks and harbours or provide telecommunications and tramways in less

---

[28] S. Chapman, *The Rise of Merchant Banking* (London 1984), 91; A. H. Woolf, *The Stock Exchange: Past and Present* (London 1913), 112; Platt, *Foreign Finance*, 33, 157, 172; W. E. Rosenbaum, *The London Stock Market: Its Features and Usages* (New York 1910), 4; E. S. Woolf, 'The American Market before 1914', *Stock Exchange Journal*, 8 (June 1963), 14; Davis and Cull, *Capital Markets*, 21, 63, 67, 78; Madden, *British Investment*, 88, 319; M. Wilkins, *The History of Foreign Investment in the United States to 1914* (Cambridge, Mass. 1989), 97–8, 190, 194.

developed economies also led to the formation of companies that sought finance from the more affluent investors of Britain. Again, these companies met a ready response from the Stock Exchange in obtaining a quotation for the securities that they issued. Nevertheless though the speculative booms that took place in their stocks and shares, as with South African gold-mines in the mid-1890s or Malayan rubber plantation companies in 1909–11, did attract much public attention, their overall importance was very limited. The entire mining and plantation sector provided only 1.2 per cent of quoted securities in 1913 though that was double its share in 1853. Though the London Stock Exchange had become the world market for mining shares such securities did not dominate activity on the floor even though the public might have gained that impression.[29]

Instead, the great growth in non-government and non-railway securities, especially from 1890 onwards, was in domestic corporate securities. For the first three-quarters of the nineteenth century these were of little interest to investors, partly because they were simply not available. Industry, commerce, shipping, and related activities were financed from personal savings and reinvested profits and so made little or no appeal to the investing public. This began to change from the mid-1870s onwards with the conversion of established enterprises into the joint-stock form, giving outsiders access to their capital structure for the first time. Over the entire 1863–1913 period a total of 147,932 enterprises were registered as joint-stock companies under the limited liability acts. Collectively these companies were stated to have a nominal capital (*not* paid-up or *market*) of £7.8bn. The formation of these companies was growing rapidly over time with the 4,998 formed in the 1863–9 period, or 714 per annum, contrasting with the 30,420 in the four-year-period, 1910–13, before the First World War, or 7,605 per annum. Though most of these joint-stock companies remained private, closely held concerns, a growing number did issue securities for which a public market was sought. Initially this was the stock exchange proximate to the company's head office and main focus of operation, which tended to be in Northern England or Scotland, rather than London and the South-East. As the Stock Exchange Year Book reported in 1874, regarding the Sheffield steel-makers, Charles Cammell Co., 'The Company is not quoted in the London list, the shares being chiefly held and dealt in locally'. Even where a London quotation had been obtained little business often resulted. Regarding Muntz's Metal Co., a Birmingham concern, the same Year Book noted '. . . the chief dealings are in Birmingham' and a similar statement was made regarding Young Paraffin Light and Mineral Oil

[29] LSE: General Purposes, 23 Sept. 1909; Kynaston, 'London Stock Exchange', 225; J. J. Van Helten, 'Mining, Share Manias and Speculation: British Investment in Overseas Mining, 1880–1913', in J. J. Van Helten and Y. Cassis (eds.), *Capitalism in a Mature Economy: Financial Institutions, Capital Exports and British Industry, 1870–1939* (Aldershot 1990), 159–61, 163; Wilkins, *Foreign Investment*, 262, 292; A. Lougheed, 'The London Stock Exchange Boom in Kalgoorlie Shares, 1895–1901', *Australian Economic History Review*, 35 (1995), 87.

Company, 'The Company is quoted in the London Share List, but the dealings are chiefly in the local markets'.[30] Thus, even where London did grant a quotation to a non-local industrial company the market remained, firmly, in the local exchanges. This was only to be expected as these institutions were trying to maintain their existence by finding new securities to replace the trading in railway issues, which was being lost to London.

However, beginning in the 1880s an increasing number of large and established companies converted to the joint-stock form and combined that with an issue of stocks and shares to the investing public as a whole, as with Guinness in 1886. The result was a far greater awareness of, and interest in, domestic industrial and commercial securities on the London Stock Exchange. The paid-up value of such securities quoted rose from a mere £43m. in 1883 to £690.9m. in 1903 and then to £917.6m. in 1913, or from only 1 per cent of the total to almost 10 per cent. Though there was some relative relapse in the 10 years before the war, the absolute total continued to expand rapidly especially in the miscellaneous categories of commercial and industrial companies, thus indicating the continued interest of the London Stock Exchange in quoting securities of companies in ever more diverse fields. Altogether, it is again quite clear that, once London began to attract the buying and selling of domestic and industrial securities away from the dominance of the provinces, this was accompanied by a ready willingness to grant these companies recognition on the official list of the London Stock Exchange.[31] In fact, the London Stock Exchange appeared much more interested in industrial and commercial companies than those providing insurance. Despite the importance of London in insurance, with both large companies and the Lloyd's market, the Stock Exchange was never a good market for insurance shares, compared to centres like Liverpool and Edinburgh. Possibly this reflected the continuing liability attached to insurance company shares due to the uncalled proportion on the shares. This had certainly undermined the growing interest in the shares of the joint-stock banks, after the City of Glasgow bank collapse in 1878 had exposed the fact that the banks did not possess limited liability, resulting in their shareholders being liable for all losses, not just their shares becoming valueless. It took time for this sector to revive but the growing process of bank amalgamation, and the quotation of the securities in London, did lead to an increasing concentration of business there. The London, County & Westminster, for instance, had a capital of £3.5m. and 23,000 share holders in 1912. The ability to get a quotation on the Stock Exchange also

[30] The Stock Exchange Official Yearbook (London 1927), 1990; The Stock Exchange Year Book (London 1874), 187, 200, 201, 212; The Stockbrokers' Directory of Great Britain and Ireland (London 1873/4), 3.

[31] W. A. Thomas, The Provincial Stock Exchanges (London 1973), 63–4, 68–9, 71; W. A. Thomas, The Stock Exchanges of Ireland (Liverpool 1986), 145, 154; J. R. Killick and W. A. Thomas, 'The Provincial Stock Exchanges, 1830–1870', Ec. H. R. 23 (1970), 99, 105.

attracted to London a number of the banks being formed in the Empire and Latin America, to provide banking services in these developing economies. Thus, again, whereas in 1853 the London Stock Exchange had virtually no interest in the securities of any kind of financial institution, apart from the Bank of England, by 1913 some £609m. (paid-up value) was quoted and these reflected a diverse variety of concerns operating in Britain and abroad. In the process a whole new kind of financial institution had been created— the investment trust. This operated by issuing shares and debentures, which were then quoted on the Stock Exchange. The funds so obtained were used to purchase a portfolio of assets, both foreign and domestic, and so generate an income to investors obtained through an acceptable combination of risk and return. These assets could also be used as collateral so as to obtain bank loans, which could also be invested in stocks and shares.[32]

Clearly, between 1850 and 1914 the Stock Exchange proved itself very receptive to the demands made upon it to quote not only ever more securities but also ones of an increasingly diverse nature, whether judged by the countries they came from or the activities they indulged in. Only foreign plantations and domestic insurance appear to have experienced any difficulty in becoming accepted in London. Generally, some 90 per cent of all applications for a quotation were accepted with the commonest reason for refusal being the size of the capital involved. As the number of securities expanded exponentially from mid-century onwards it became impossible for the Stock Exchange to offer a home to them all. Between 1853 and 1913 the number of different securities quoted in London rose from under 500 to over 5,000. As a result, the Stock Exchange increasingly discriminated on the grounds of size alone, for its trading mechanisms were becoming clogged with large numbers of securities. Many issues of securities were of small size and narrowly held, resulting in an inactive market. Despite the rise in membership it was unrealistic to expect dealers to be ready to buy and sell, on demand, every security quoted let alone those that had not even been granted that privilege. At any one time only around 10 per cent of all quoted securities could command a ready market as jobbers had to have a realistic expectation of undoing the deals they made. Even in 1877 it was estimated that, at least, 1,082 out of the 1,367 separate issues, quoted on the Stock Exchange, were unmarketable at any one time. As The Economist noted in 1885:

Admission to a quotation in the 'Official List' is based, to some extent, upon the importance of the security to the public, and, generally speaking, this depends upon its amount. Hence, multitudes of small undertakings are excluded, not because there

---

[32] M. Collins, *Money and Banking in the UK: A History* (London 1988), 52; J. Sykes, *The Amalgamation Movement in English Banking, 1825–1914* (London 1926), 197; Thomas, *Provincial Stock Exchanges*, 119, 122; G. Jones, *British Multinational Banking, 1830–1990* (Oxford 1993), 30; Cassis, *City Bankers*, 47, 68; Kynaston, 'London Stock Exchange', 162–3, 172, 175, 185–6, 223, 245; Royal Commission on the London Stock Exchange, *Report*, 369.

is any doubt as to their bona fides, but simply because their admission to the List would render the latter so bulky as to impair its utility . . .[33]

This situation continued right up to the First World War. In fact the 'challenge' system was introduced in 1885 as a way of providing a mechanism whereby the mass of inactively traded quoted securities could be more easily bought and sold. By listing a security on the Exchange Telegraph tape a member could broadcast his interest to others and so stimulate a sale or purchase. Use was made of this system as well as telephoning around but there continued to be many securities that had been given a quote but generated little buying or selling.

Essentially, if there was the expectation that a security would generate a significant amount of business for the membership the Stock Exchange would quote it, so as to advertise that a market existed for it there. This might only result in the occasional bouts of activity or the steady trickle of business, as opposed to the active trading that took place in the major stocks. Conversely, if there was no evidence, either because of the small size of the capital or the absence of interest, no quotation would be granted. It was only in rare cases, where something adverse was known about the security and the circumstances surrounding its issue, that reasons other than a lack of potential trading, would prevent it being granted a quotation. The Stock Exchange itself did not possess the administrative resources to conduct investigations of its own and left that to the membership itself, who could and did bring adverse comment to the knowledge of the relevant committee. More importantly, however, the Stock Exchange never saw itself as fulfilling any role in vetting the securities for which a quotation was applied, and this was a generally held belief at this time. Gibson, in a comparison of the London, Paris, and New York Stock Exchanges in 1889 indicated that,

. . . the Stock Exchanges guard the public, in so far as they are able, in declining to admit to quotations the questionable enterprises of 'shady' promoters, but they do not in any manner thereby indicate any opinion, personal or official, as to the value of such issues, or their real genuineness or soundness. That is entirely beyond their province, and persons buying issues that have been 'listed' should scrutinise the property and investigate the value for themselves.[34]

Trapped between possible accusations of the abuse of monopoly power, as a private club or association, and the complaints of aggrieved investors who had lost money on ill-conceived or fraudulent schemes, the Stock Exchange was open to criticism from either direction before 1914. As it was it stuck

[33] *The Economist*, 30 May 1985; see J. E. Day, *Stock-brokers Office Organisation, Management and Accounts* (London 1911), 44; Kynaston, 'London Stock Exchange', 223; LSE: General Purposes, Exchange Telegraph Company, June 1890.

[34] G. R. Gibson, *The Stock Exchanges of London, Paris, and New York: A Comparison* (New York 1889), 37.

to what it could do best which was to expand the business of its members, and the securities market as a whole, by its willingness to quote those securities most likely to benefit from official access.

Important as was the institutional framework that the Stock Exchange provided for the London securities market, ultimately its competitive position at home and abroad depended upon the skills, enthusiasm, and connections of those who became members. This meant that the Stock Exchange had to remain attractive not only to the great majority of those involved in the buying and selling of securities but also to the particular individuals or groups whose abilities and knowledge were essential within a business that was fast becoming more specialized, more technical, and more international than ever before. There was always the risk that if a specific component of the securities business was ignored, either because of capacity constraints or restrictions on the type of person admitted to membership, then it would develop outside the Stock Exchange itself. The Stock Exchange had no absolute monopoly over the British securities market, despite its size and longevity, and with much business being of an international nature, there was no necessity that it would always take place within Britain itself. Like the institution to which they belonged the members of the London Stock Exchange lived in a very competitive world and, if they were to multiply and prosper, they had to show themselves able to take advantage of the opportunities that were available.

## MEMBERS

The regulations of the Stock Exchange did continue to restrict those eligible for admission. No incorporated bodies could become members, despite the increasing use of the joint-stock/limited liability form by British business generally, even in the financial field. Banks, discount houses, and investment trusts were among the numerous financial concerns that were converted into, or formed under, the joint-stock company laws, and none were eligible for membership. Instead, each member of the Stock Exchange possessed unlimited liability with all their business and personal property forfeit in the event of failure. Though failure was not commonplace, and fellow members could be forgiving in the event of losses due to defaulting clients or unforeseen price fluctuations, considerable risk continued to be attached to Stock Exchange business. This commitment to the Stock Exchange for a livelihood was further reinforced by the continued restriction on outside occupations, for all members had to confine themselves to the buying and selling of securities or activities closely related to that, such as company promotion or handling new issues. Finally, all partners of members' firms had also to be members themselves, precluding the possibility of combining stockbroking and jobbing with other activities or raising additional capital through offering a share in the profits generated. All these conditions of membership were motivated by a desire to restrict the commitments of members so that all their assets would be immediately available to settle debts to fellow members and the risk of bankruptcy due to losses made outside the Stock Exchange would be small. Of course, a by-product of these restrictions was the continuing exclusion of other financial intermediaries from membership. On the Continent the large commercial banks played an important role in the securities market while in the United States the investment banks were heavily involved, but neither they nor other emerging groups like the investment trusts, were able to play a direct role in London. Over the 1850–1914 period this need not have been of much consequence for the securities market, if strong and close relationships were formed between the members and those non-members much involved with the sale and purchase of securities. In particular the commercial banks were most in touch with the investor through their customer base of depositors whereas the merchant banks were most involved with those wishing to create and sell new securities, namely governments and companies. There was no reason why either or both of these activities needed to be combined with the buying and selling of securities as long as that facility was easily and cheaply available whenever required. In fact there was much to be said for specialization considering the size and complexity of the British financial system, as long as no barriers existed to limit co-operation between its various elements. It is against that need that the nature and activities of the membership of the Stock Exchange need to be judged.

Throughout the 1850–1914 period membership of the Stock Exchange for all candidates who met the entry requirements appeared a relatively easy matter. As long as three existing members would sponsor a candidate, and stand surety for £750 each, admission was assured.[35] Even after the restrictions of 1905, membership did not appear particularly difficult to achieve as long as the prospective candidate could convince the existing membership that his inclusion would generate business. In 1909, for example, Max Karo became a member once he had built up a client base operating as an outside, or non-member, broker. In fact, the criticism throughout was that the Stock Exchange's policy on admission was too lax with virtually no scrutiny of prospective members. Always conscious that any major restriction on membership, not only by number but also by type, could provoke the accusation of acting as a monopoly, the Stock Exchange was loath to vet applicants. As with the quoting of securities the overriding policy appears to have been to admit if no one could put forward specific reasons for refusal.[36]

---

[35] LSE: General Purposes, Committee of Members, 20 Apr. 1904; Rokeby-Price quoted in Kynaston, 'London Stock Exchange', 72.

[36] Max Karo, *City Milestones and Memories: Sixty-five Years in and Around the City of London* (London 1962), 24; Royal Commission on the London Stock Exchange, *Report*, 22; Kynaston, 'London Stock Exchange', 80–1.

With no formal qualifications required, or compulsory period of apprenticeship to serve, the London Stock Exchange appeared to be the last bastion of the British amateur, to which the children of the aristocracy drifted from the 1870s onwards. Certainly, a number of aristocrats did become members, such as Lord Walter Campbell who joined Helbert Wagg in 1877, or George Eden, son of Lord Aukland, who joined Mullens. However, the underlying reality was somewhat different. As the securities market grew in scale, reach, and sophistication a far greater knowledge and expertise was being required from both brokers and jobbers. The result was that it was becoming routine for applicants to have served a period of training as a clerk before joining the Stock Exchange. The number of clerks elected to membership rose throughout. Whereas in the 1886–1902 period 70 per cent of new members were clerks by 1909 the proportion had risen to 80 per cent. As the membership grew and then stabilized it became an increasingly professional body for even those who had not served time as clerks had often undergone other forms of training, such as in banking and accountancy. Both Thomas Greenwood and Alexander Henderson trained as accountants with the London firm of Deloittes, before entering the Stock Exchange in 1867 and 1872 respectively. Business on the Stock Exchange required a diversity of skills and this drew on a wide range of talents, not all of which were acquired through a period of apprenticeship with an existing member. Max Karo, for example, had originally trained as a banker in Germany before moving to London in 1896. The converse of the Stock Exchange's lax control on admission was that there was no exclusive route to membership, and thus no stereotypical member.[37]

Certainly, many of the new members had been brought up to the business, being the sons, brothers, or nephews of existing members. John Akroyd, who had been a member since 1848, was joined by his three sons. Two of them—John and Swanson—became brokers, like their father, while the other—Bayly—became a jobber, forming Akroyd & Smithers. In Mullens, Marshall & Co. there was a steady progression of sons joining fathers. William E. Marshall joined his father, William B. Marshall, in 1862, and was joined by his son, William D. Marshall in 1905. Alexander Henderson was joined at Greenwoods in 1881 by his brother Henry, who became a partner in 1884. Similarly, the jobber Fred Durlacher was joined by his brother Neville in 1884. Thus, with or without a period of formal training with a member, the Stock Exchange was able to rely increasingly on a pool of young men to whom the world of broking and jobbing was very familiar because of family connections. In addition, as partners

[37] R. Roberts, *Schroders: Merchants & Bankers* (London 1992), 358; *The Stock Exchange Clerks' Provident Fund Centenary, 1874–1974* (London 1974), n.p.; Kynaston, 'London Stock Exchange', 75, 77, 80, 86; D. Wainwright, *Henderson, A History of the life of Alexander Henderson, First Lord Faringdon, and of Henderson Administration* (London 1985), 14–15; Karo, *City Milestones*, 1.

and their clerks had all to work very closely together and rely upon the actions and words of each other, trust was of major importance. Though family ties were no guarantee that this trust would not be broken, it was less likely to happen because of long familiarity and the risk to other relationships. With unlimited liability and the constant risk that clients would default or the market would turn, a broking or jobbing partnership was very vulnerable to any mistake or dishonest action by a partner authorized to trade. All deals had to be honoured or the firm failed. Spencer John Herepath, for example, joined the prosperous stockbroking firm, established by his father, which specialized in South American railway securities, but it failed in 1888 owing £135,000, after one of the partners, Delmar, disappeared.[38]

Nevertheless, a family connection was by no means essential for a career on the Stock Exchange or even a partnership. An old established firm like Foster & Braithwaite regularly recruited from outside the family orbit. It expanded from two to six partners between 1860 and 1873 and none were relatives. The same was true of Pember & Boyle in the 1890s when they acquired five new partners. Even a religious divide was no obstacle to partnership. Arthur and Edward Wagg were both Jews but from 1877 onwards they recruited non-Jews as partners in their stockbroking firm of Helbert Wagg. Though family and religion helped steer individuals towards a career in the Stock Exchange, possessing the right connections did not mean automatic entry while their absence did not create major barriers. There were many sons, for example, who did not join the family firm. The stockbroker Spencer Herepath had four sons but only one, Spencer John, joined him on the Stock Exchange. Family connections were also not sufficient to ensure success, as Spencer Herepath's grandson, Roy Samborne, discovered. Despite admission to the Stock Exchange and a capital of £5,000 provided by his mother in 1910, Roy never developed a successful stockbroking business.

Generally, whether among relatives or others the search was on for people who were interested in a career on the Stock Exchange, possessed abilities of use there, and could be trusted. In addition, established firms in particular were looking for individuals that could further the interests of the firm through the connections they possessed, whether at home or abroad. Self-interest in the survival and expansion of the business was, probably, far more important than family loyalty or dynastic succession in determining entry into the Stock Exchange. Wealth could always be inherited but if talent and aptitude were absent there was little point in leaving the fortune

---

[38] D. Kynaston, *Cazenove & Co.: A History* (London 1991), 77; D. Wainwright, *Government Broker: The Story of an Office and of Mullens and Company* (East Molesey 1990), 37, 39, 44, 57, 58; *Wedd, Durlacher, Mordaunt and Company, Members of the Stock Exchange, London* (n.p. 1984); Wainwright, *Henderson*, 18; S. Nicholson, *A Victorian Household* (London 1988), 18, 96

of the firm to sons if others were available. The Wagg's deliberately recruited Lord Walter Campbell in 1877, and then Arthur Haydon and Cyril Russell in 1888, in order to develop a private client business, and so reduce their dependency upon Rothschilds for orders. Similarly, Pember & Boyle in the 1890s greatly widened the range of activities they covered by recruiting as partners F. C. Stapylton who brought in private clients, O. C. Bevan and C. A. Campbell who had strong banking connections, and F. H. Anderson who had links with the discount houses. For the same purpose de Zoete & Gorton recruited William Mackenzie in 1896 because of his Far Eastern connections and then extended that to Greece, Egypt, and the Middle East with Pericles Nassif in 1900 and Hugh Pritchard in 1910. New partners could also consolidate an existing business as in the case of the stockbroking firm Panmure Gordon recruiting the son of the Hong Kong and Shanghai Bank's London manager in 1905, for that firm had a very strong Far Eastern connection. Though favouritism based on class, religion, and family existed on the Stock Exchange it was by no means an exclusive body. Entry was available to any that had something extra to offer by way of expertise or connections. Typical of this type was someone like Robert Nivison who, after working for the Westminster Bank, became a member of the Stock Exchange. In 1887 he formed Robert Nivison & Co., and specialized in colonial government securities having become familiar with them whilst with the Westminster Bank as they were involved in their issue. This was a business that Mullens had turned down because of conflict with their existing activity in UK government debt. Clearly, where a need arose for a new speciality, as with colonial government securities, either an existing firm would move into the business, recruiting suitable personnel or new members would join having acquired their expertise outside the Stock Exchange. Though established partnerships could afford to be conservative and ignore new types of business, as with Mullens, there were plenty of new members who were eager for anything that was on offer. Of the membership of 4,834 in 1903/4 half had been there in 1894/5 but half had not. If there was business to be done in the securities market, gaining entry into the Stock Exchange in order to do it seemed to present no barriers, no matter the background or training of the individuals concerned.[39]

This openness also extended to foreigners with a constant influx of members from abroad throughout the period, especially from Germany. Many of these brought valuable connections and particular specialities, that allowed the market as a whole to develop a wide range of new activities,

[39] Ibid., 33–6, 185, 210; W. J. Reader, *A House in the City: A Study of the City and of the Stock Exchange Based on the Records of Foster & Braithwaite, 1825–1975* (London 1979), 60; Roberts, *Schroders*, 355, 358; Kynaston, 'London Stock Exchange', 99, 186; B. H. D. MacDermot, *Panmure Gordon & Co., 1876–1976: A Century of Stockbroking* (London 1976); Janes, *de Zoete and Gorton*, 43–5; Kynaston, 'London Stock Exchange', 93, 97–8, 100, 102; Wainwright, *Mullens*, 55; Madden, *British Investment*, 97.

at home and abroad. Members from continental Europe, for example, were of major importance in allowing the Stock Exchange to serve, increasingly, investors from that area. Ludwig Messel, a Darmstadt banker, moved to London after the Franco-Prussian War of 1871. There he set up the stock-broking firm of L. Messel & Co., which became very successful serving the interests of German banking clients. His son, Leonard Messel, succeeded him in the firm, after a period of training with a bank in Germany. Similarly, the broking firm of Nathan & Rosselli also prospered on the back of a largely European client list, employing one German, five Swiss, and two Dutch clerks in 1914 in order to undertake the business. It was not just from Europe that such individuals flowed but from around the world. As a market in Australian corporate securities developed in Britain from the late nineteenth century a number of experienced Australian brokers moved to London and joined the Stock Exchange, such as L. Aarons & E. L. Samuel, from Sydney, E. L. Bailleu from Melbourne, and Lionel Robinson from Adelaide. They were representative of that group of members, including Canadians, South Africans, and others, who were British but had been born outside the British Isles. There were even those, such as Harry Panmure Gordon, who had spent all or part of their business careers abroad, especially in India and the Far East, and on return to Britain made use of their expertise as brokers or jobbers in securities of Australian mines, Indian tea plantations, or Malayan rubber plantations. Clearly, the Stock Exchange sucked in talent from throughout the world and these members repaid by providing London with the connections necessary to make it a global centre.

However, it was not just connections that foreigners brought for they were also recruited for their skills, not least in language. In particular, the growing business in foreign securities and the techniques required for trading between markets required individuals skilled in such operations. Continental Europe, especially Germany, was a major source of such talent. There the skills learnt by bankers in coping with not only exchange rate fluctuations but also a multitude of currencies, as in Germany before unification, could be equally well applied to the buying and selling of securities between different stock exchanges. Thus, even by the 1870s much of the dealing in foreign securities on the Stock Exchange was the preserve of Europeans. Even British firms recruited Europeans for these specialities. Panmure Gordon, for example, hired William Koch, a Belgian of German origin, in 1877, and he became their specialist in Chinese and Japanese government loans. By 1888 he was a partner and in 1902 he became head of the firm. Similarly both Helbert Wagg and Raphaels relied heavily on the abilities of German-born partners, namely Adolph Schwelm and H. H. Struckmeyer respectively. Foreigners were valuable to London not simply because of their ability to extend its geographic reach and range of securities, but also because their experience in less stable monetary systems had given them skills that could be applied to the emerging global securities market.[40] Nevertheless, in 1891 the Stock Exchange tried to restrict the membership of such people. In that year a rule was passed that any foreigner applying for membership had to have been resident in Britain for 7 years and naturalized for 2. At that time new foreign members were being accused of initiating a round of reductions in commission rates as they competed for business, which was experiencing one of its periodic downturns. Though this rule probably delayed foreigners becoming accepted as members, it appears to have done little to restrict their access to the market. In 1876 it was estimated that 60–70 members were of foreign birth, which was around 3.1–3.7 per cent of the total. By 1914, when some 218 were registered as being of foreign birth, this was 4.5 per cent of the total. Over the 1900–9 period 99 new members of foreign birth were admitted, which was just over 4 per cent of the total who joined at that time.[41]

Consequently, with some 5,000 members recruited from a wide variety of backgrounds at home and abroad, and largely trained in broking, jobbing, or related activities, the Stock Exchange became an increasingly professional and cosmopolitan body. Though many of its new recruits comprised one generation of the same family succeeding the last, this was by no means exclusive and even rules aimed at denying foreigners membership, proved ineffective. Certainly up to 1914 the evidence points to the Stock Exchange's continued willingness to admit every qualified candidate. Once admitted these members both co-operated and competed, with partnerships both breaking up and reforming. Cazenoves, for example, recruited partners from other brokers with Claud Serocold coming from Rowe & Pitman in 1901/2 and Charles Micklem from Bulett, Campbell & Grenfell in 1912. The Stock Exchange comprised a vast pool of talented individuals all needing to generate business if they were to survive. Nevertheless, once admitted these members had to operate under the rules and regulations imposed by the Stock Exchange.

One of these restrictions was on the number of clerks that a member could employ on the floor of the house, either authorized to trade on his

[40] Nicholson, *Victorian Household*, 137, 145; M. C. Reed, *A History of James Capel and Company* (London 1975), 95–6; MacDermot, *Panmure Gordon & Co.*, 50; S. D. Chapman, *Raphael Bicentenary* (London 1987); LSE: General Purposes, Subcommittee on Rules and Regulations, 13 Apr. 1910; S. Salisbury and K. Sweeney, *The Bull, The Bear and the Kangaroo: The History of the Sydney Stock Exchange* (Sydney 1988), 223, 276; G. P. Marchildon, 'British Investment Banking and Industrial Decline before the Great War; A Case-study of Capital Outflow to Canadian Industry', *B. H.* 33 (1991), 73, 75, 79.

[41] Kynaston, 'London Stock Exchange', 88–9, 200; Michie, *London and New York*, 88–123; Kynaston, *Cazenove*, 87; R. C. Michie, 'Dunn Fischer & Co. in the City of London, 1906–1914', *B. H.* 30 (1988), 200; Lougheed, 'Kalgoorlie Shares', 87; LSE: General Purposes, 4 Jan. 1915.

behalf or to carry out other duties. In 1874 the limit was set at two authorized clerks and an attempt in the early 1900s to increase it to three was
defeated. Altogether in 1902 a member was allowed up to two authorized
and three non-authorized clerks on the floor. This reduced the potential
advantages possessed by large firms of brokers or jobbers, channelling business through numerous employees. Along with the refusal to admit corporate members, those not solely engaged in broking or jobbing, or accepting
partnerships between members and non-members, there was imposed a
definite restraint on the size of partnerships formed among members. In
1862 the average number of partners per firm, whether broking or jobbing,
was only 2.25, and though this did rise it remained low, at 2.38 in 1887
and 3.14 in 1914. Within this there were many single-member firms as well
as some large operations. The number of firms with five or more partners
grew from three in 1862 to 10 in 1887, reaching 163 in 1914. Among these
were some relatively large firms like Lazarus Brothers with 16 partners,
Lemon Brothers with 13, and L. Hancock & Co. with 12. Nevertheless,
the large firm remained untypical. In fact, the ratio of clerks permitted
access to the floor and members remained remarkably constant over the
entire period, indicating little real growth in scale. In 1877, of the 3,245
people admitted to the floor of the Stock Exchange a total of 2,009 (62 per
cent) were members and 1,236 (38 per cent) were clerks. By May 1904,
before the restriction on membership came into force, of the 7,446 permitted on the floor 64 per cent were members and 36 per cent were clerks,
whereas in 1913, of the 7,456 admitted to the floor two-thirds were
members and one-third were clerks. There were, however, no controls over
the number of clerks that a member or his firm employed in his own office
and these played a major role in maintaining contact with clients and processing sales, purchases, and payments aided by the new office technology
available. Day, writing in 1911, estimated that the typewriter had doubled
the amount of correspondence a clerk could handle, compared to pen and
ink, while the telephone made possible direct contact with clients without
leaving the office.

Whether firms would have been larger in the absence of Stock Exchange
regulations is difficult to answer. What appeared to be happening was
expansion along the entire front of single-man operations to large firms.
There continued to be numerous one-man, or two-partner broking or
jobbing operations employing a capital of around £1,000, and generating
a decent living for those involved. At the same time there were also emerging some large firms employing a capital very much greater. Between 1853
and 1887 the capital employed by Cazenoves doubled to £90,000 reflecting
their large domestic broking business while, by 1890, Raphaels employed
some £3m., to transact a large international business. Illustrative of the
range of capital employed was the survey of the 74 members who died
between 1894 and 1896. This revealed that their average wealth was

£40,042 but this included one, James Renton, a dealer, who left £852,515, and 39 who left under £10,000.[42]

What appeared to be happening at this time was an increase in the specialization of the membership. This was not simply in the obvious distinction between broker and jobber but also within each of these categories. Of the membership of c.2,000 in 1877 it was estimated that some one-third were jobbers while two-thirds were brokers. By 1908 the position was reversed with two-thirds being jobbers. Among these jobbers specialization reflected the increasing diversity of securities quoted. Durlachers, formed in 1881, initially concentrated upon railways but then moved, successively, into brewing and distilling, and then rubber. In contrast, Wedd Jefferson, formed in 1885, stuck with fixed-interest securities, especially government stock, while Bone, Oldham, created in 1889, concentrated upon the brewing, food, dairies, and hotels sector. In all cases there was little sign of jobbing firms attempting to cover most of the market through numerous partners and a large number of clerks. Instead, the development of expertise in a particular area was the normal situation, and as the number and variety of securities expanded so did the jobbing fraternity, without any apparent pressure to amalgamate in order to achieve economies of scale. Within jobbing there was also a division in terms of the risks taken. James Renton, for example, reported the distinction in the 1870s between a dealer and a jobber. A jobber squared his book every day, which meant that he had sold whatever he had agreed to buy and bought whatever he had agreed to deliver. Thus, it was only the profit or loss resulting from the transaction that was carried forward to the next day's trading. In contrast, a dealer was willing to go uneven, which meant that they were willing to pay for and hold the securities they bought until a favourable opportunity to sell arose, and hold off buying the securities they had contracted to deliver until the last possible moment in expectation of finding a lower price. As Renton died a very wealthy man, skill as a dealer could yield large rewards for large risks, though one does wonder how many died penniless.[43]

Clearly, a jobber could operate on a small scale, little capital, and limited expense. An office was not even required as all the business would be done on the floor of the house. Conversely, a dealer could seek to spread his risks by operating on a larger scale and this required substantial capital, and the need to maintain an office and staff in order to handle transactions and contacts. In between were a whole range of operations and all appear to have had a presence on the floor of the Stock Exchange. However, there was some suggestion that the restrictions on non-member partnerships, was

---

[42] Kynaston, 'London Stock Exchange', 66–7, 76, 107, 122; J. E. Day, *Stock-broker's Office Organisation, Management and Accounts* (London 1911), 100; Kynaston, *Cazenove*, 45, 78; Chapman, *Raphael Bicentenary*, 30, 3.

[43] Royal Commission on the London Stock Exchange, 44, 102; *The Times*, 17 Mar. 1908, quoted in Kynaston, 'London Stock Exchange', 255.

denying dealers the level of capital required to carry stocks until the market changed. *The Times* quoted a jobber in 1908 saying that

We have only lost part of the American Bond market because it got too big for Stock Exchange capital . . .[44]

Dealers on the Stock Exchange were not able to attract capital by promising a share in the profits that resulted and so were dependent upon the capital of the partners and that which could be borrowed. As partners died and retired, capital was continually withdrawn though the family nature of many firms ensured it stayed in the business. Borrowed capital was readily available but required that the securities bought were used as collateral, and they could be of questionable value, as with some mining securities. Borrowed funds also could be easily withdrawn forcing securities to be sold on disadvantageous terms. However, there was no general sign that the Stock Exchange was losing business due to a lack of capital among its dealers.

Nevertheless, there were certain niche markets, like American railroad and industrial stocks or bonds, or South African gold-mining shares, in which well-capitalized non-member firms were posing a competitive threat to the Stock Exchange dealers. In American securities, for example, a banker/broker like Saemy Japhet flourished in the after-hours market where there were also to be found branches of New York and Chicago brokerage firms. Similarly, in the South African market a number of mining finance houses, with large holdings in numerous individual companies, were willing buyers or sellers, and so provided an alternative to the dealers on the floor of the Stock Exchange. However, as both these markets continued to be active ones for members of the Stock Exchange itself, there is little sign that the restriction on access to outside capital was, before 1914, a significant problem for the membership. Certainly, an American, W. E. Rosenbaum, writing in 1910, was of the opinion that it was easier and cheaper to finance positions in American securities in London than in New York. Bank finance was readily available while the fortnightly settlement system meant that purchases only needed to be financed at the end of the account period, before which time a dealer might very well have bought and sold the stock many times over. Similarly, it was only at that time that securities needed to be delivered, reducing the need to hold large amounts of stock, as there was ample opportunity to buy in before then.[45]

Among stockbroking members there was also increasing specialization, with some concentrating upon servicing the needs of numerous private clients while others looked after the interests of a small number of corporate or institutional investors. A firm like G. S. Herbert & Sons did a

[44] *The Times*, 17 Mar. 1908; quoted in Kynaston, 'London Stock Exchange', 255.
[45] LSE: General Purposes, 15 Oct. 1906; Rosenbaum, *The London Stock Market*, 5–6; Michie, *London and New York*, 267.

largely private client business, with the number of investors it catered for growing almost sixfold between 1881/4 and 1909/13, as it rose from 548 to 3,209. Possibly the majority of the Stock Exchange's brokers were of this kind, each serving a client list built up over many years of business, and doing so through a great deal of personal contact and trust. Even a firm like Foster and Braithwaite, that had long-established banking connections, was heavily committed to serving the needs of long-established individual customers. Over 83 per cent of their 1,930 clients in 1885/9 were individuals, for example, with the wealthiest and most well-informed among them possessing extensive portfolios of securities that were slowly altered over the years, both in size and composition, as circumstances changed. Foster & Braithwaite's commission income, rose from c.£15,000 per annum in 1882/3 to £25,000 per annum in 1911/13, and this provided a dependable element to an otherwise variable income.

Conversely, there were other brokers who catered for mainly institutional clients. Capels extended its institutional connections, built upon private banks like Coutts and Drummonds, by acting for the London and County Bank and the fledgling investment trusts being formed by Robert Fleming. Cazenoves, with only 50 clients in the 1890s did most of its business for merchant banks like Barings, Rothschilds, and Gibbs. In particular, the merchant banks were major sources of Stock Exchange activity as they managed the portfolios of individual and institutional clients, as well as maintaining extensive holdings of their own, reflecting the issues they were currently handling. In 1905 half of Hambro's own holdings of securities were almost equally split between American (24 per cent) and British and colonial (22 per cent) securities. Five years later, in 1910, the American securities had almost doubled their share to 46 per cent, whereas the British and colonial element had virtually disappeared to 4 per cent. All this necessitated large and regular sales and purchases on the Stock Exchange through their brokers. Foreign banks also appeared as major customers at this time as they made growing use of the London market. Nathan & Rosselli, for instance, had only 14 clients in 1892 and 55 in 1897, but these were mainly German banks channelling their own and their clients business, though London.

However, the division between brokers was not as simple as that between private and institutional clients, and any combination in between. As the size of the market expanded, both in terms of the range of securities and spread of investors, so stockbroking firms changed accordingly. Brokers like Robert Nivison & Co. and Heseltine, Powell & Co., that became prominent in this period, did so by specializing in the new securities that appeared, namely colonial government issues and American railroad stocks and bonds respectively. The driving force behind Panmure Gordon was the growth in Chinese and Japanese bonds being traded in London, and the expertise, contacts, and familiarity they developed in this market. As new securities appeared so existing or new brokers moved in to serve the needs of the investors who became interested. A firm like de Zoete & Gorton, formed in 1863, began with a specialization in European government loans and then dabbled in Latin American securities, gold-mining shares, Far Eastern rubber plantations, and Middle Eastern issues, all before 1914. This was not only with the growth of international securities at this time but was also to be found among domestic issues. These were to be found, initially, in the miscellaneous market from which they would gravitate to a distinct space of their own on the floor if the volume of business justified it, as happened with sectors like breweries and iron, coal and steel. In 1899 there were 103 members operating in this miscellaneous market and only 19 of them had been there in 1886. Thus, three-quarters of those in that market had moved in during the 1890s, when there was a boom in domestic joint-stock company flotations and conversions. In fact, if the opportunities for profitable employment were there brokers from any speciality, whether home or overseas, would quickly move in. Greenwoods, with a long-standing interest in Latin America railways also became involved in the markets for UK and African railways as well as British industrials like Imperial Tobacco. In addition, some brokers also undertook specialist functions. Some like Laurie, Milbank and Sheppards & Co. became money brokers lending out bank money to fellow brokers and jobbers. Others, like Raphaels, became arbitrageurs, buying and selling securities between London and foreign countries.

Looking at what was happening among the stockbroking members of the Stock Exchange at this time, one detects both a high level of flexibility and response as different types of business waxed and waned. As long as there were clients to be served and securities to be bought and sold brokers appeared to do the business. At the same time the level of competition between members was high, with long-established contacts, or even religious affinity, proving of little value if it stood in the way of increased business. Helbert Wagg, for instance, had conducted much of the Rothschild's stock exchange business in the nineteenth century, with the partners in both firms being Jewish. However, in the late nineteenth century Rothschilds became involved in Far Eastern government loans, where the stockbroking firm of Panmure Gordon was well established. In return for Panmure Gordon favouring Rothschilds in handling the issues, Rothschilds passed much of their broking through Panmure Gordon. This forced Helbert Wagg to move into other areas of stockbroking, such as private clients.

In fact, it was from the competitive and heavily populated world of stockbroking that the City of London drew numerous recruits for other financial activities. Established merchant banks like Barings and Rothschilds could afford to ignore governments and companies, about which little was known but who were anxious to raise funds in London. This was not so with stockbrokers who appeared ever ready, if not over-anxious, to handle any new issue that came their way if the price and conditions were sufficiently attractive. When Japan, for example, first tried to raise a loan in the 1870s she was spurned by the major merchant banks in London and the Continent. However, with the assistance of Panmure Gordon the loan was brought out successfully. Panmure Gordon retained a role even after the likes of Rothschilds had become involved when Japan became a recognized and creditworthy borrower. Similarly, Helbert Wagg moved into handling the issues of British and Canadian industrial and commercial companies. Thus, the members of the Stock Exchange, with their knowledge and contacts, provided a constant source of competition for the established merchant banks, with some, like Helbert Wagg in 1912, deciding to concentrate entirely in that activity, and leave the Stock Exchange. In fact, numerous leading broking partnerships became involved in new issues and company flotations. Cazenoves handled about fifty company flotations between 1884 and 1914, with many being in the armament industry. Foster & Braithwaite were closely involved with both US railroad and British electrical company issues. Similarly, the issuing house of Cull & Co., was created by four jobbers just before the First World War, after experience in the oil shares market, while Stanley Christopherson, a stockbroker, moved into South African mining finance.[46]

One restriction the Stock Exchange did impose on its membership, which did affect the brokers but not the jobbers, was a ban on any form of advertising. A member was only allowed to circulate his own clients, giving advice about new issues or suggesting possible sales and purchases. The purpose of this rule was to prevent one member competing with another for clients and to distinguish a member of the Stock Exchange from a non-member by making clear to the public that their members did not advertise. The problem for brokers was how to capture the orders of the growing class of new investors without the use of advertisements, which non-members inserted in national newspapers. The device used was the sharing of commission, especially with banks, accountants, and lawyers. These were the very people who were in regular contact with potential investors as they handled the money and assets of their customers and clients. In return for channelling sales and purchases through a member of the Stock Exchange, the broker rebated to them a share of the commission charged. There were even half-commission men who made a living by developing a client base, with whom they kept in regular contact, and

[46] Kynaston, 'London Stock Exchange', 66–7, 117, 186, 205, 263–4, 312–13, 319–20; Reader, Foster & Braithwaite, 53–4, 93, 98, 109, 111, 113, 117; Janes, de Zoete and Gorton, 28, 40, 42–3, 45, 49; Reed, Capel and Company, 65, 95–6; Kynaston, Cazenove, 82–4, 104; Wainwright, Mullens, 55, 138; P. G. Warren, Heseltine, Powell and Company: One Hundred Years of Stockbroking, 1851–1951 (London 1951), 1–6, 15; MacDermot, Panmure Gordon & Co., 11, 42, 45; LSE: General Purposes, Committee of Members, 20 Apr. 1904; Cassis, City Bankers, 1890–1914 (Cambridge 1994), 110–11, 173, 219; Roberts, Schroders, 84–5, 104, 362–4; Wainwright, Alexander Henderson, 14, 41, 42, 54–5; T. Balogh, Studies in Financial Organization (London 1946), 290.

whose business they brought to a particular broker in exchange for half the commission generated. West End clubs seemed a particular haunt of these men, where they 'preyed' on relatives, old school friends, and the like for business. Some of these even had the use of a desk in the stockbroker's office, and access to the telephone, stationery, and clerical help, though remaining self-employed.

Nevertheless, extensive as this network of links were, and persuasive as was the inducement given to channel business to members of the Stock Exchange, the whole process was rather passive. The broker did not stimulate business, apart from among their existing client base, but waited for it to come to them. Certainly by the late nineteenth/early twentieth century there was a feeling that some business was bypassing the Stock Exchange as a result, having being siphoned off by non-members who tried to match bargains themselves without using the Stock Exchange. The non-member brokers, Cornforth & Teacher, certainly claimed in 1894 that their advertising brought in business from investors that otherwise would have been directed to bank and building society deposits or house purchase. However, though non-members did compete with members for business, they also complemented each other. It was estimated in 1893 that outside brokers paid £53m. in commission to 294 members of the Stock Exchange for business transacted on behalf of their clients.

On the whole, the restrictions imposed by the Stock Exchange did not appear to be particularly onerous, being a balance between the desire to maintain an open and competitive environment and a need to control and police the standards and behaviour of the membership. The one effect they had was, probably, to limit the size of stockbroking firms, as there were few economies of scale. Larger firms, for example, could not generate business by advertising while the restrictions on non-member or corporate partners stopped the creation of large integrated firms. However, a stockbroking firm like Mullens, for example, grew from three partners in 1850 to only five in 1910, and that was sufficient to handle sales and purchases of the National Debt on behalf of the government and a private client business. In fact, the size of stockbroking firms does not appear out of line with equivalent firms in the City. When the three original partners of the merchant bank, Samuel Montagu & Co., were faced in 1868 with the prospect of expanding to a 12 partnership operation, in order to provide openings for their collective sons, they decided instead, to form a new but allied merchant bank, Keysers & Co. Eventually in 1909 these two banks became completely separate. This suggests that a partnership of about six, with the requisite support staff, was ideal for that type of financial business.[47]

[47] Kynaston, 'London Stock Exchange', 66, 93; Roberts, *Schroders*, 362; Wainwright *Mullens*, 55, 58, 138; LSE: General Purposes Subcommittee on Exchange Telegraph Company, 24 Oct. 1893, 13 Aug. 1894.

The problem was that considerable fluctuations in the scale and nature of the business done by both jobbers and brokers took place, and so firms had to maintain relatively lean and flexible operations. Capels, for example, generated an income of £93,000 in 1888/9 of which 80 per cent was distributed to the partners, once all salaries and office expenses had been met. The next year, 1889/90, this income had fallen to £71,380, or by 23 per cent, and by 1896/7 it was down to £43,040, or less than half the 1888/9 level, but they were still managing to distribute 71 per cent of it to the partners. Generally, fixed costs were kept low whether it was rent for office space or the number of clerks, and it was the income taken out of the business by the partners that varied enormously from year to year. Compared to banking, for instance, stockbroking remained a less attractive career. Isaac Braithwaite's son Basil turned down an invitation to join the family firm in 1888, preferring to remain with Brown Janson, the bankers, whom he had joined in 1880. As it was, Foster & Braithwaite almost collapsed in the early twentieth century, when moving into oil company shares, after a great deal of success in the 1880s and 1890s as specialist brokers in British electricity companies and American railroads. The firm had tied up much of its capital in Piccadilly Hotel Ltd., which went bankrupt, and in the Kansas City, Mexico & Orient Railway, which went into receivership. Thus, it was ill placed to survive downturns in income and only survived by mortgaging its office and borrowing from relatives.

Consequently, both broking and jobbing continued to involve considerable risk in this period, though the number of firms failing did appear to be declining. Whereas the number of defaults per year was 28.6 per annum over the 1870–6 period, it fell to 24.6 in 1878–96, to 23.6 in 1897–1910, and reached only 16 per annum in 1910–14. The growing professionalism among the membership encouraged a greater awareness of the risks involved and a greater ability to avoid large losses. For most broking or jobbing operations it was credit not capital that was important and that was readily available from the City of London's unrivalled money market. Similarly it was trust and contacts, not size, that mattered whatever the clients.[48]

What emerges from an investigation of the members of the London Stock Exchange over the 1850–1914 period is their diversity and their responsiveness, both to opportunities on and off the floor. Any boom provoked interest, with brokers and jobbers moving in from other markets, while any downturn produced resilience and a search for alternative sources of income. On the whole the balance between regulation and freedom seemed to be maintained. It was at this time that stockbroking emerged as a

[48] Reed, *Capel and Company*, 68–71; Reader, *Foster & Braithwaite*, 56, 97, 109, 111–12, 113, 115, 117, 125–8, quoted in Kynaston, 'London Stock Exchange', 124–5; LSE: General Purposes, Subcommittee of Non-Permanent Character, 19 Nov. 1930.

respectable profession in the eyes of the public with very few cases of members defrauding clients. Broker/client relationships were normally left to the member apart from the cases when a client complained. It was then investigated by the Stock Exchange. If dishonourable conduct was shown the member could be expelled but, generally, it was left to the criminal courts to extract retribution. Within the Stock Exchange the mechanism of settling disputes between members was now well established and the authority of the Committee for General Purposes was largely unquestioned. In terms of competition, the result was a general narrowing of the spread between bid and sell prices especially in the actively traded securities where numerous brokers and jobbers were involved. This was also reflected in rates of commission. In the American market, where outside and foreign competition was extreme, the rate of commission fell from 2s. 6d. per share in the 1880s to 6d. a share by 1899, or by 80 per cent. By 1904 Canadian Pacific shares, a popular international stock, were being bought and sold at 3d. a share commission or half the 1899 level. In many cases the transaction costs were far less than that as major users of the Stock Exchange, like British and foreign banks, made specific arrangements with brokers to buy and sell for an annual fee, or even for nothing, in the expectation of making a profit on the transaction. The merchant bank Anthony Gibbs & Sons, reported in 1896 that

. . . we made special terms with Williams (broker) as to the commission. Essex, the small red-headed clerk of Williams, is told off, specially to attend on us, which he does very efficiently, being sharp and industrious . . .[49]

J. Silverston & Co., for instance, acted as brokers, for an Austrian bank from 1907 onwards in return for an annual fee. This had been set at £3,000 for 1907/8 but when the amount of business did not justify that level of remuneration it was reduced to £1,000 per annum for 1909/10. Thus, up to 1912, when the minimum commission rules came in, members were left to make whatever arrangements they wished with their clients in terms of the charges made. The result was that small investors paid the conventional commission charges, which were falling anyway, while major institutions, like the banks, could commute the entire cost into an annual salary or settle on any other mutually agreeable terms. With over 5,000 members of the Stock Exchange, and no firm of any large size, there were plenty to choose from and negotiate with if any major investor was unhappy with the arrangement.

[49] Kynaston, 'London Stock Exchange', 218, 231–2, 261, 275, 277, 279, 286, 343; quotation from ibid. 329.

## RELATIONSHIPS AND RIVALRY

However, following on from the victory achieved in 1904, which capped future expansion of the membership, the London Stock Exchange was beginning to introduce and enforce other rules and regulations that cut across the intimate relationships that had come to exist between the members of the London Stock Exchange and the rest of the financial community. As long as it was both easy and cheap for banks and other financial institutions to employ a member of the Stock Exchange to buy and sell securities, their exclusion from the trading floor was of little real consequence. With the banning of dual capacity in 1909, and the introduction of minimum commissions in 1912, this free and easy relationship was undermined. In particular, the combination of the two rule changes posed a serious threat to the particular role the Stock Exchange had played in the City of London since its foundation.

Conventionally the members of the Stock Exchange acted either as brokers or jobbers, with brokers buying and selling for investors and jobbers acting as intermediaries between brokers. This division was even formally enshrined in the rules, as in 1847, 1877, and 1903, despite some attempts among the membership to abolish it. In 1887 each member was obliged to declare their status though not all did. However, though the rule did exist and blatant transgressions were punished, there was no blanket enforcement. Thus brokers with an interest in particular securities made markets in them in order to stimulate interest, as with Heseltine, Powell and Foster & Braithwaite in American stocks and bonds in the 1870s. Conversely jobbers had direct contacts with major outside investors, like merchant and foreign banks, to whom they would quote prices and do deals. This became much easier with the coming of the telephone as jobbers could communicate directly with clients from the Stock Exchange itself. During one week in 1909 a total of 6,127 calls were made from the Stock Exchange via the National Telephone, and of these 63 per cent were made by 124 firms or by only 24 per cent of the firms using National Telephone. As this was an outside line it would allow direct contact with a client. Resentment gradually built up from brokers, and smaller jobbers, who felt they were being bypassed in the transaction of business as major institutional investors went direct to the jobber. The result was that in 1909 they managed to pass a rule that dual capacity—acting as both broker and jobber—was prohibited, and that this was to be enforced. Technically this cut direct contact between the jobbers and non-members like the merchant and foreign banks. In reality it did not, as the Stock Exchange had little way of knowing what jobbers were doing unless they were informed upon, and few clients were eager to spoil a relationship that had been established over many years. In addition jobbers had many contacts among the broker members who were willing to pass the business through their books, for a nominal fee, allowing the jobber to retain his outside connections.

Walter Bennett, for example, was a jobber while his brother Charles, was a broker. Similarly, while Charles Micklem was a broker with Cazenoves his brother Hugh was a jobber.[50]

Thus, though the banning of dual capacity, and its attempted enforcement, did affect the service that jobbers could provide to major users it, by no means, ended it, and the practice carried on much as before. Instead, the real restriction came with the introduction of minimum commission rates in June 1912. Again this was an attempt by individuals or small partnership members who did not cater for the large users, to reduce the level of competition in the Stock Exchange, which was driving charges down. After the 1907 crisis there was a downturn in business while membership remained at the c.5,000 level. The introduction of minimum commission rates had been a recurring demand among a part of the membership throughout the nineteenth century, and such was the pressure and insistence that, this time, they managed to have the rule introduced, despite the opposition of many of the largest firms. The majority of the membership were small brokers and jobbers who expected to benefit from minimum commission through the passing of the charges onto their customers and the greater distribution of transactions on the floor. With the introduction of minimum commission charges the flexibility that brokers had once enjoyed to meet the individual requirements of their customers was now undermined. In July 1914 Akroyd & Smithers, representing 416 members, complained that

... owing to the existing official score of commissions, much of the business that used to be done on this Exchange has been lost, or diverted to other channels.[51]

Clearly that was not the case as the Stock Exchange and its membership continued to dominate the British, and indeed global, securities market right up to 1914. Jobbers such as Akroyd & Smithers, Medwin & Lowy, and Chinnery Brothers even claimed that, before the First World War, they were regaining the business in American bonds that had been lost to outside houses in the past. Though an official scale of charges was now in place established broker/client relationships, combined with a series of concessions and an unwillingness to enforce the rules too vigorously, did ensure that past practices did continue. Nevertheless, it was difficult to make arrangements that represented major transgressions of the rules. Mullens, for example, were permitted to continue receiving a fee rather than a commission from the National Debt Commissioners for sales and purchase, but could not do the same for other bodies, like the Ecclesiastical

[50] Kynaston, 'London Stock Exchange', 31, 90, 252, 256; LSE: General Purposes, 29 Oct. 1877, 21 May 1903, 13 July 1914; LSE: General Purposes, Subcommittee on Commissions, 21 May 1912; LSE: Conjoint Committee, 3 May 1909; LSE: General Purposes, Readmission of Defaulters, 23 Nov. 1911, 25 Sept. 1912; Morgan and Thomas, *Stock Exchange*, 145, 154; Reader, *Foster & Braithwaite*, 51, 53; Michie, *London and New York*, 21–2.
[51] LSE: General Purposes, 13 July 1914.

Commissioners, the Charity Commissioners, and London County Council. Similarly, J. Silverston & Co.'s arrangement with the Anglo-Austrian bank was deemed to be against the rules. There were even alternatives to the Stock Exchange begun. The *Daily Mail* advertised a service whereby readers could use its columns to advertise sales and purchases. In response to this competition, as well as ongoing complaints from a substantial minority of its own membership, the Stock Exchange was driven to revise the charges and even to consider the value of the whole scheme, though consideration of that was interrupted by the First World War.

Thus, it was not until almost the First World War that the Stock Exchange began to use the power it possessed, in order to regulate and police the securities market, to assist its own members through the introduction of minimum charges. Combined with the prohibition of dual capacity this represented a major change with far-reaching implications. However, even before the war broke out there was a strong rearguard action being fought against the changes, especially the imposition of minimum charges, and, like a number of rules in the past, there was the distinct impression that those running the Stock Exchange were most reluctant to take strong measures to enforce a policy against which so many members were opposed. The same had happened before with a prohibition of pre-allotment dealing. This had been banned in 1864 in the face of public pressure, as it had been used as a way of stimulating investor interest in a new issue of securities, which in some cases turned out to be worthless or grossly over-valued. However, in 1865 the ban was withdrawn as unenforceable, and never reintroduced before 1914. Consequently, though major changes had been made shortly before the First World War there was no guarantee that they would remain in place for long. Even if they had, the prevailing attitude was one of permissiveness where member/client relationships were concerned, and so enforcement of any ban on jobber/non-member contact or broker/client charging arrangements was going to be difficult.[52]

The changes introduced in 1909, with the ending of dual capacity, and in 1912, with minimum commission rates, had implications not only for the relationship between the members of the Stock Exchange and existing or potential investors. They also had implications for the securities market as a whole for the London Stock Exchange was not the only such institution in existence either in Britain or abroad. Nor were its members the only intermediaries at work. There existed, and continued to exist, other stock exchanges as well as individual stockbrokers and finance houses, who did not belong to any formal institution. The revolution in communications that came with the telegraph and the telephone had the potential to mould these spatially disparate elements into one market if established

---

[52] Ibid., 13 July 1914, 16 Mar. 1915; LSE: General Purposes, Subcommittee on Commissions, 21 May 1912; LSE: General Purposes, Subcommittee on Exchange Telegraph Company, 13 June 1912; Kynaston, 'London Stock Exchange', 142, 281.

institutional barriers could be broken down and individuals could devise ways of co-operating over long distances. On the one hand the London Stock Exchange's monopoly over its immediate vicinity was threatened as communications allowed investors to direct their orders to other markets, especially where provincial or foreign securities were concerned. Conversely, the members of the London Stock Exchange could, themselves, seek to serve more distant clients and so bring business to their market from ever further afield. The choice was there but it had to be grasped.

With the telegraph it was now possible to communicate between different centres not only at the beginning or the end of the trading day but on a constant basis. Thus activity in each exchange did not simply adjust to conditions elsewhere but merged into a national market. In addition to the disappearance of separation by distance, changes in the nature of securities being bought and sold also began to erode separation by function. As railways linked major centres, they attracted investors from a far wider area than did the more local joint-stock companies of the past. Railway securities were also more attractive to the investing public in that they were issued in far greater numbers, being expensive infrastructure projects, and attracted both speculative interest during the construction phase and investment interest once established and running. At a stroke railway securities provided an important link between the London and provincial markets, as the buying and selling of railway securities became the most important element in all the provincial exchanges and one of the most active on the London Stock Exchange. The railway mania of 1844/5 was but a short-lived speculative bubble, collapsing in 1846 but it left as a legacy a vast mass of railway securities many of which were held by investors far distant from the area of operation. Thus, as investor confidence returned in the early 1850s railway securities again came to play the major role in linking trading in the London and provincial markets. This was further enhanced by a series of alliances and amalgamations which created a small number of highly capitalized railway companies whose securities offered a secure and predictable rate of return. As such they appealed to investors from all parts of the country.

With common securities and a rapid means of communications there existed by the 1850s the conditions of rivalry between the London and provincial stock exchanges for the securities market of the British Isles. Though the London Stock Exchange retained its dominance of government issues and each provincial stock exchange had its pool of purely local stocks and shares, there was a large and growing volume of railway securities the trading in which could gravitate to any exchange offering the best market and lowest costs. In 1853 the London Stock Exchange quoted UK railway securities with a paid-up value of £194m., and this had become the second most important category after UK government debt. Despite the ability and experience of the London Stock Exchange in catering for a high volume business for investors from all over the country, the London Stock Exchange never completely captured the market for railway securities. On the Aberdeen Stock Exchange, for example, which was one of the smallest of the provincial markets, over one-third of turnover by value was in railway securities in both the 1860s and 1870s, declining to 17 per cent in the 1880s and 15 per cent in the 1890s. Evidence from the other provincial exchanges suggests a continuing vitality of trading in railway securities, most of which were also quoted in London. Generally, the period between 1850 and 1914 saw not only the continued existence of the provincial stock exchanges but their expansion, judged from membership figures. In fact, the late nineteenth and early twentieth century saw a rash of provincial stock exchanges being formed, such as Dundee in 1879, Cardiff in 1892, and Nottingham in 1909. Over the same period the London Stock Exchange itself continued to expand. Consequently, though one might have predicted the appearance of a national securities market centred on the London Stock Exchange, what actually happened was a multi-centred market expanding on all fronts before 1914.[53]

The reasons for the growth and co-existence of separate institutions serving the one market was twofold. First, the volume and variety of securities to be traded grew enormously between 1850 and 1914. These years saw the London Stock Exchange come to occupy a central role in the emerging international securities market, with its members transacting business both for foreign clients and between different foreign stock exchanges.[54] With a world to serve the London Stock Exchange could expand without the need to compete with the provincial stock exchanges for domestic business. To an extent the provincial stock exchanges survived and grew because the London Stock Exchange left gaps in the national securities market that needed to be filled.

At the same time the provincial stock exchanges also benefited from the continued vitality of joint-stock company formation outside London. Their very existence may even have encouraged this vitality as the market they provided stimulated the continued supply of local securities from often small and diverse enterprises. These securities derived from both new and established activities. Though nothing rivalled railways as a major new use of the joint-stock form, numerous local companies were established to provide tramways, telephone services, and electricity. More dramatic was the growing number of conversions of existing industrial and commercial concerns into public joint-stock companies from the late nineteenth century onwards. Most of these continued to be managed and owned on a local basis, and so their securities were ideal material for trading on provincial

[53] Thomas, *The Provincial Stock Exchanges*, 28–46, 63–4; Thomas, *The Stock Exchanges of Ireland*, 102; R. C. Michie, *Money, Mania and Markets: Investment, Company Formation and the Stock Exchange in Nineteenth-century Scotland* (Edinburgh 1981), 117–21, 212, 214, 216, 226–7; Michie, *London and New York*, 10–12, 52.
[54] Ibid., chs. 2 and 3.

stock exchanges. The paid-up capital of the Irish joint-stock companies quoted on the Dublin Stock Exchange grew from £4m. in 1862 to £19.3m. in 1914, and only the largest of these—the brewers Guinness—were also quoted in London. Similarly, trading in industrial and commercial securities grew from 2 per cent of turnover on the Aberdeen Stock Exchange in the 1850s to 16 per cent in the 1890s. Neither Dublin nor Aberdeen were in the industrial heartland of Britain and the importance of such securities appeared to be much greater for exchanges like Manchester, Glasgow, or Birmingham. Behind the creation of the new provincial stock exchanges from 1890 was the need to provide a market for the securities of local industrial and commercial enterprises.[55]

However, it was not simply the fact that the London and provincial stock exchanges continued to serve separate parts of the securities market that explained their lack of rivalry for much of the period. There was growing competition between the two as London provided, increasingly, a market for the securities of the largest provincial corporate enterprises in addition to railways. Provincial stock exchanges also developed markets in securities which had been largely the preserve of London, such as those of American railroads and foreign mining companies. Throughout the period the interests of investors were broadening so that they did not simply concern themselves with government debt or local securities but took in stocks, bonds and shares issued by a growing variety of enterprises at home and abroad.[56] This posed problems for the provincial stock exchanges if they were to retain the market in securities issued by the largest industrial and commercial companies, including those based and operating in the same city as the provincial stock exchange. Investors in those companies required, increasingly, the facility of being able to buy and sell easily and quickly in order to realize their capital or employ their liquid funds. In contrast, the securities of provincial stock companies did not, normally, possess a ready market and so took time to sell as brokers consulted clients looking for suitable vendors or purchasers and negotiating a price. None of the provincial stock exchanges possessed the jobbers or dealers who were always willing to buy and sell actively traded securities in the expectation of reversing the deal when the circumstances changed. When acting independently no single provincial stock exchange could generate the daily volume of business to generate both sufficient income for a dealer and provide the opportunities for undoing sales and purchases quickly and with only limited risk. Only on the London Stock Exchange did such conditions exist, and so this was where its competitive advantage lay over its provincial counterparts.[57]

[55] Thomas, *Stock Exchanges of Ireland*, 145, 151, 154, 157, 159, 221; Thomas, *Provincial Stock Exchanges*, 63–71, 119, 123, 133, 147; Michie, *Money, Mania*, ch. 12; Michie, *London and New York*, ch. 1.

[56] Michie, *Money, Mania*, 198–9, 201, 259.

[57] Thomas, *Provincial Stock Exchanges*, 73, 77, 171, 187; Thomas, *Stock Exchanges of Ireland*, 123, 126, 128; Michie, *Money, Mania*, 256–7.

However, the provincial stock exchanges retained a continued importance in the market, even in the securities of major companies, by altering their relationship with the members of the London Stock Exchange. This change was greatly facilitated by the transformation of communications wrought by the telegraph and then the telephone. By using the pre-existing correspondence networks, linking individual brokers in the provinces with individual brokers in London, provincial brokers could, with the telegraph, quickly test the London market for any large corporate issue, as well as try their own. There thus developed a joint market where a provincial broker could either buy or sell locally, if the opportunity existed, or pass the business to a London broker for transaction there, sharing the commission payable. In turn, this encouraged London brokers and jobbers to provide a market in these corporate securities as they were receiving similar orders from all over the country. The telegraph link to London allowed the provincial brokers to provide, locally, the ready market that investors sought and so encouraged investors to continue to channel business through the members of the provincial stock exchanges. Though no exchange on its own, with the possible exception of London, possessed the critical volume of business to support the dealers who would provide a ready market in all these corporate securities, the directing of so much of the buying and selling to London from all over the country, even on a residual basis, created the necessary conditions there and met with a ready response. In 1909 20 times more business was directed to London from the provinces than came in return. The result was an active market for the securities of numerous large industrial and commercial enterprises, encouraging the supply of more of the same. One explanation for the greatly increased use of the joint-stock form for British industrial and commercial firms in this period, and the popularity of their securities among the investing public, must lie in the ready market provided by the London and provincial stock exchanges acting in combination. The joint-stock form, for example, was much more prevalent in Britain than in other European countries. Within the domestic securities market integration and specialization was taking place rather than rivalry as the members of each exchange co-operated on an individual basis in order to serve the needs of their clients and generate an ever-growing volume of business for themselves.

Initially, this growing relationship between the members of the London and provincial stock exchanges provoked no institutional response, even though it blurred the distinctions between each. As it merely expanded and intensified the existing contacts between brokers in London and the country it did not pose any new threat to any existing stock exchange. The London broker continued to receive commission on the business that flowed to and from the country, and the London jobber got his 'turn' on the difference between the buying and selling price, wherever the order originated. However, gradually a conflict of interest on the London Stock Exchange did develop, especially from the 1870s onwards. As the speed and reliability of the telegraph grew, and the cost fell, it became easier and easier to communicate between London and the provinces. However, a differential opened up between those firms that invested in direct lines and those that continued to rely upon the public system. With direct lines contact became almost instantaneous and when direct telephone lines became available after the 1880s, it was also continuous. The result was to concentrate the business between the London and provincial stock exchanges into the hands of the few London firms with the dedicated communications links and the specialized staff, as they could offer the fastest and most expert service. This development was matched on the provincial stock exchanges with the emergence of the broker who specialized in maintaining contact with London and 'shunting' business to and from that market. These shunters came to act as the channel through which most buying or selling orders flowed from the provinces to London. Essentially, on each provincial stock exchange there arose one or a few members whose function it was to maintain the flow of information and orders to and from the London Stock Exchange, where there also existed a larger but similar group who possessed such contacts all over the country. By acting in partnership with the London firm, and often sharing costs and dividing profits and losses, the provincial brokers constituted joint operations that acted as nation-wide dealers in those securities of mutual interest to the London and provincial markets. Whether in London or the provinces they were always ready to buy or sell according to supply and demand, expecting to undo the deal either within the same exchange or in another. If any price differential arose in a security traded in both London and a provincial exchange, or between provincial exchanges, they could also make a profit by buying where the price was lower and selling immediately where it was higher—an arbitrage operation. With provincial business increasingly concentrated, and communications so swift, a final step was now possible. This was the direct contact between provincial brokers and London jobbers. The London jobber quoted two prices—a lower one for purchases and a higher one for sales—and generated his income from the differences or spread, between the two. With the telegraph, and especially with the telephone, the jobber could quote these prices to anyone likely to provide sufficient sales or purchases to make the maintenance of contact worthwhile. In the past this had all been done on the floor of the London Stock Exchange in direct contact with brokers, who were also members. Now, with specialized shunters there were provincial brokers with whom it was worthwhile to maintain direct control. From the jobbers perspective this contact allowed them to extend their business beyond the floor of the London Stock Exchange with the expectation that both a greater volume of turnover—and thus increased profits—would ensue and that more opportunities would exist to undo deals—and thus reduced risks. For the provincial shunter the great attraction was the ability to bypass the London broker, and thus avoid paying any commission charged on a transaction. Therefore in the provincial stock exchanges most inter-market activity fell into the hands of shunters while in London it became the preserve either of those jobbers who maintained direct contacts with the shunters, or those brokers, possessed of the contacts, who were willing to quote buy and sell prices to shunters. The original commission business was confined to those securities that could only be sold by negotiation and could not command a ready market.

As a result of this relationship the provincial stock exchanges obtained a dealing service they had not previously enjoyed, and so the activities of the shunters were accepted and business practices adjusted accordingly. In London the consequences were more wide-reaching and provoked friction between particular groups. Inevitably those brokers—the vast majority—who had lost provincial business as a result resented what had happened as they regarded exclusive and direct access to jobbers, and the ready market they provided, as one of the privileges of membership of the London Stock Exchange, which they had to pay for. Similarly, those jobbers who were not involved in provincial business were unhappy with brokers who were now quoting prices to country brokers. In essence, brokers saw their commissions now threatened by jobbers' direct contacts outside the Stock Exchange while jobbers felt their livelihoods threatened by brokers making markets. The consequence was a steady build-up of hostility to the whole way that the London and provincial business was being conducted because of its potential ability to undermine the value of the London Stock Exchange to its members. If jobbers could deal directly with non-member brokers and brokers could bypass jobbers by making their own markets in conjunction with outsiders, how could the market be regulated, as rules only covered the conduct of members, and why should anyone pay for membership when the privileges were available to all?

The solution was either to extend membership, reflecting the integrated nature of the domestic securities market, to those outside London, or to limit direct access to the market by non-members. The former never appears to have been considered, by either London or the provincial stock exchanges, and the latter provoked fierce resistance by those who would be most affected. Nevertheless, in 1909 jobbers were prohibited from trading with non-members, within the United Kingdom, and brokers were banned from making markets, again in the United Kingdom. The expectation was that provincial business would still come to London but now it would have to pass through the hands of brokers. This did not prove the case until 1912, when minimum commission rates were introduced. Before then jobbers could, nominally, pass business through a friendly broker for a small annual fee. These minimum commission rules did more than simply add a cost to inter-market activity for it also changed the way business was done, by outlawing joint-account trading. Not only were jobbers prevented from dealing directly with the provinces but brokers had to make a fixed charge for any sales or purchases done for a provincial broker. If the flow of business had been equal this could have resulted merely in the two offsetting charges, but as many more orders were sent to London as received from it, this placed a heavy cost burden on provincial brokers. Part of London's aim in this was to force more business to come directly to London, rather than via the provincial brokers. By dealing directly with a London broker an investor paid only the one commission charge while an indirect contact through a provincial broker could result in commission being paid to both brokers, unless the provisional broker gave up his fee. The London brokers, for example, continued to be willing to share their commission with banks and their branches, as well as lawyers and accountants, and so attracted business from all over Britain via that route.[58]

Therefore, on the eve of the First World War the growing integration of the domestic securities market was being threatened by the London Stock Exchange, many of whose members saw the provincial stock exchanges as rivals for this business. The feeling of many brokers was that the market for the domestic securities quoted in London should be the London Stock Exchange, and that the provincial stock exchanges should deal solely in local securities, directing all other transactions to London, as had always happened in government stock. Nevertheless, there existed many members of the London Stock Exchange who regarded the 1909/12 rule changes as a retrograde step and they continued to make representations accordingly. Instead of the new rules driving business to London they tried to show that it was diverting existing business away because of the high commission charges and inflexible means of operation. There existed in London finance houses that were ineligible for membership of the London Stock Exchange, because they incorporated a banking operation as well, and there was the ever-present threat that they would occupy the dealing role for the provinces once taken by the jobbers. Consequently, in July 1914 some 415 members, around 10 per cent of the total, petitioned the London Stock Exchange to consider revising the commission structure regarding provincial business. This was taken seriously and it was agreed to look at the matter in October. By then, however, the First World War had broken out and the discussion never took place, replaced by considerations of more pressing urgency. Whether a revision and relaxation would have taken place it is impossible

[58] Michie, *London and New York*, 8–10, 14–20, 23–6; Thomas, *Provincial Stock Exchanges*, 88–90, 102–4, 123, 131, 133; Thomas, *Stock Exchanges of Ireland*, 90–2, 127; Michie, *Money, Mania*, 258–61; R. C. Michie, 'The Stock Exchange and the British Economy, 1870–1939', in Van Helten and Cassis (eds.), *Capitalism in a Mature Economy*, 103–4, 107–9; R. C. Michie, 'Different in Name Only? The London Stock Exchange and Foreign Business, c.1850–1914', in R. P. T. Davenport-Hines and G. Jones (eds.), *The End of Insularity: Essays in Comparative Business History* (London 1988), 51–61.

to say but there appeared at that time every reluctance by the London Stock Exchange to police the rule changes it had introduced, and which had taken so long to be passed in the first place.[59]

Consequently, though within the British Isles the London Stock Exchange dominated the securities market it by no means monopolized it. There continued to exist and flourish numerous other stock exchanges and unattached brokers who filled regional and sectoral roles within the securities market, and even acted as overspill venues when business reached very high levels. Rather than reflecting a lack of interest in the domestic market by London, or an inability to compete, this was part of the growing specialization that was taking place at this time, brought about by the transformation of communications and the vast expansion in the scale and spread of transferable securities. The same process that was integrating British securities market was taking place internationally, creating vast new opportunities for the London Stock Exchange. Beginning with the London–Paris telegraphic link of 1851, and then extended by the Paris and Brussels telephone connections from the 1890s, the members of the London Stock Exchange were now in a position to serve an international clientele. This took place both directly and indirectly. To a large extent the business came to London in the form of the branches and agencies of foreign financial houses, especially banks. With London established as the world's premier financial centre, and the growth of international trade and investment, a presence in the City was of growing importance to non-British banks and other financial concerns. This could be done through correspondent relationships with established British banks but, increasingly, a growing number of foreign banks, brokers, and investment companies opened their own branches and agencies in London. By 1910 there were 26 branches of foreign banks in London, with the majority being from continental Europe.

These banks had, traditionally, played an active role in their domestic securities market and so were well positioned to direct some of that business to London, when it offered the best opportunities. The French ambassador to London observed in 1903 that 'so close to France, the London market attracts more and more of our capital and gives the Paris Stock Exchange ever-increasing competition. Many of our stockbrokers and credit companies have either correspondents or branches in London and they say that it is through their English broking that they make the greatest profit.' In particular, London's active market in American securities, which were popular all over Europe, brought much foreign buying and selling to the members of the Stock Exchange. Brokerage firms from both the United States and Canada were also increasingly represented in London at this time. Harris, Winthrop & Co., who were members of the New York Stock

[59] Michie, London and New York, 20–2; Thomas, Provincial Stock Exchanges, 89–90; Thomas, Stock Exchanges of Ireland, 67; LSE: General Purposes, 13 July 1914.

Exchange, had an office in London by 1912, for instance, and this serviced clients from all over Europe.[60] The importance of these foreign bankers and brokers in bringing business to London was stressed in 1912 by Eugène Karminski, the manager of the Crédit Lyonnais branch in London:

... the Banks have always been the natural channel through which orders have been brought to the London Stock Exchange from abroad, and it has been largely through their intermediary that the London Stock Exchange has developed into an international market for stocks and shares. By their organisation the Banks are in direct touch and personal intercourse with their clients, who look to them for advice and guidance.[61]

In turn these foreign banks and brokers employed members of the Stock Exchange to carry out the mechanics of buying and selling securities. Mosenthal and Samuelson, for example, were but one firm of brokers employed in 1900 by the London agency of the Banque Française de L'Afrique du Sud, while Harris, Winthrop & Co. used the brokers Rowe & Pitman to transact business.[62] Thus, almost without any action on their behalf foreign securities business was brought to London for execution.

However, by the early twentieth century there was a growing reaction among the membership of the Stock Exchange to the presence of these foreign bankers and brokers in London. Though there was a recognition that they had brought the orders of foreign clients to London there was also the feeling that they were now drawing business away from the Stock Exchange. Cheap and rapid telecommunications was a two-edged weapon for it could as easily transmit orders to or from London. Again, it was the single operators or the small partnerships among the membership who feared they were being bypassed. Jobbers believed that brokers were using these foreign finance houses as alternative dealers to themselves while brokers felt they were losing out through the direct contacts that jobbers maintained with foreign banks and brokers. The suspicion was that the general level of business passing through the Stock Exchange was being reduced though a few jobbers and brokers were gaining through their connections with the foreign finance houses.[63] As the *Financial Times* reported in 1908:

[60] Quoted in H. Bonin, *Société Générale in the United Kingdom, 1871–1996* (Paris 1996), 16, cf. R. C. Michie, *The City of London: Continuity and Change, 1850–1990* (London 1992), 73, 112; Michie, *London and New York*, 146; LSE: General Purposes, Commissions, 16 July 1912; LSE: General Purposes, 27 Nov. 1914.

[61] LSE: General Purposes, Subcommittee on Commissions, 16 May 1912.

[62] LSE: General Purposes, 19 Apr. 1900, 27 June 1900; LSE: General Purposes, Subcommittee on Commissions 16 May 1912, 16 July 1912.

[63] LSE: General Purposes, 15 Oct. 1906.

The average London broker has, as a rule, very few foreign connections. Our international market is almost entirely in the hands of Germans and Frenchmen, who keep in close touch with the great international banks and finance houses.[64]

Hence, here was yet another reason why the membership as a whole were keen to protect their position by enforcing the ban on jobbers dealing with non-members and introducing minimum commissions which might spread business more widely. Though both restrictions reduced the appeal of the London Stock Exchange to European bankers and American brokers they appear to have made little impact before 1914.

Foreign business coming to London was but one way that the members of the Stock Exchange exploited the growth of an international market in securities. Increasingly from 1850 onwards members of the Stock Exchange began to acquire foreign clients directly. In 1854 the brokers Simon & Co. had a banking house in Paris as a client, while J. B. Samuel & Co. had clients in Berlin in 1878. In 1912, Roberts & Buckingham had a client in Moscow. As these contacts grew and the business expanded more formal and extensive arrangements were put in case. In particular, London brokers began to organize networks of agents or remisiers who circulated investment material on their behalf and solicited orders, all in return for a share of any commission generated.[65] In 1912 the brokers Salomon and Company described the development of the system that was then in place:

A large proportion of the business coming to London from the Continent consists of orders from Banks and their branches in most of the provincial towns, and also from Brokers who are willing to induce their clients to invest or speculate on the London Stock Exchange provided that they, as Agents, are remunerated by a return of part of the commission, and that the necessary information is supplied to them in a sufficiently attractive and intelligible form. As information by cable to a number of different towns is not only too costly but too brief to be of value, a wire is sent daily to the Remisier, who, with the aid of his staff, draws up an interesting circular on the information supplied, and delivers or posts the same to the above-mentioned Institutions in his own name. For introducing these clients, and for his valuable services, the Remisier has always shared in the commission which is left to us after remunerating Agents.[66]

Clearly, by the early twentieth century a complex web of contacts, clients, agents, and organizers linked the London broker to investors abroad and

[64] *Financial Times*, 25 Jan. 1908, cf. Bonin, *Société Générale*, 17–18, 23; Y. Cassis, 'Financial Elites in Three European Centres: London, Paris, Berlin, 1880s–1930s', *B. H.* 33 (1991), 53–5; T. Balogh, *Studies in Financial Organisation* (London 1946), 229.

[65] LSE: General Purposes, 6 Dec. 1854, 25 Oct. 1870; LSE: General Purposes, Subcommittee on Commissions, 11 June 1912.

[66] LSE: General Purposes, 23 May 1912; see also 15 May 1911 for the comments of their remisier in New York, R. M. Bauer.

produced an expanding flow of orders to buy and sell. The brokers, William Asch & Co. had remisiers in both New York—Henry S. Straus—and in Gothenburg—Ludwig, Levisson & Co., suggesting the role being played by the London Stock Exchange as the very centre of the web that comprised the international securities market. The vital role played by these remisiers was recognized and the sharing of commission with them accepted, again mitigating the effects of the rule changes.[67]

Telecommunications did not simply allow the members of the London Stock Exchange to extend their reach world-wide, it also opened up the whole business of international arbitrage. Arbitrage was defined by the Stock Exchange itself as:

The business of buying and selling a security as a Principal in one centre, with the intent of reversing such transaction in a centre in a country different from that in which the original transaction has taken place, in order to profit from the price difference between such centres and which business is not casual but contains the element of continuity. It is therefore essential that there is a market in the security in both centres independently.[68]

For arbitrage to be carried out continuously, consistently, and on a large scale required organized security markets which offered the certainty of being able to buy and sell quickly. Thus, the combination of the ability to communicate between one separate financial centre and another and the existence of sophisticated stock exchanges in these locations created an entirely new situation for the securities markets from mid-century onwards.[69]

The problem of arbitrage was that its very operation eventually ran counter to the desire of most members of the London Stock Exchange to ensure that non-members were denied access to the market on the same terms as members. By its very nature arbitrage involved the completion of a transaction in another market. What was bought or sold in London had to be reversed—or undone—elsewhere in order to profit from the spatial price difference. To this end the arbitrageur had to be in constant contact with non-members, exchanging both current prices and instructions in the expectation that an opportunity would arise for a profitable matching buy/sell order. When that did occur a member of another stock exchange was used to either buy or sell. Hence the arbitrageur was concerned to broadcast current market conditions to non-members as quickly as possible and to use the members of other exchanges to conduct business. This clashed with the interests of most fellow members who wanted to see all business take place on their exchange so that they could derive benefit from the transactions through commission payments or profits. As at all times

---

[67] LSE: General Purposes, Subcommittee on Commissions, 16 May 1912, 23 May 1912, 31 May 1912.
[68] Council of the London Stock Exchange, Minutes, 28 Jan. 1957 (repeated 31 July 1973).
[69] J. E. Meeker, *The Work of the Stock Exchange* (New York 1930), 44–5.

those engaged in arbitrage were but a small minority of the membership the possibility of restrictions on their activities was an ever-present one.

The beginning of international arbitrage came with the London–Paris submarine cable of 1851. Though it took time to overcome the delays and interruptions to the service, and bring the costs down to a level that encouraged constant use, the opening up of the telegraphic contact between the London and Paris Stock Exchanges meant both an end to their isolation during the trading day and the opportunity for arbitrageurs to monitor continuously the fluctuating prices of jointly traded securities, ready to buy/sell in both markets whenever the opportunity of profit existed. Risk was still present but was now greatly reduced. Gone, for example, were the frequent accusations of spreading false rumours regarding prices, which had characterized the market for French *rentes* in London, and which had allowed a number to profit unfairly. Instead, an increasing air of certainty regarding Paris prices increasingly pervaded the floor of the London Stock Exchange.[70]

The problem for the arbitrageurs was the lack of securities which could command an active market in both London and Paris. In both countries securities issued domestically tended to be held domestically, including those of foreign governments and corporations. This did change briefly with British investment in French railways in the 1840s, but these were taken over, increasingly, by French investors in the 1850s once the merits of these securities were recognized in that country. Thus arbitrage had to take the more risky course of buying/selling British consols against French *rentes* under the assumption that they would perform in the same way. Consequently, though the telegraph transformed communications between London and Paris, and there were already those skilled in inter-market trading, the possibilities of arbitrage were actually quite limited as there was little overlap in securities. Thus the challenge to London in terms of competition with an established rival stock exchange was quite limited, and so the activity of arbitrageurs could be allowed to grow in an unrestricted fashion. A far greater opportunity for the arbitrageurs came with the opening of a permanent London–New York cable connection, which finally took place in 1866. The United States was already a major area of interest for British investors, and this was not confined to those American securities tailored for the British market and even denominated in sterling. Dollar securities issued by, among other, US railroads were also well known in Britain. Brokers like E. Satterthwaite regularly dealt in stocks and bonds issued domestically in the United States, taking their prices from those in New York. Thus, with the transatlantic cable there now existed the final

[70] LSE: General Purposes, 9 June 1834, 3 Aug. 1835, 17 Nov. 1847, 17 Jan. 1848, 28 July 1848, 17 Nov. 1851; LSE: Committee of Trustees and Managers, Minutes, 7 Sept. 1824; Foreign Funds Market, minutes 9 Sept. 1823, 6 Sept. 1824, 7 Sept. 1824; Michie, *London and New York*, 36–8, 41.

element required for arbitrage, namely active markets in the same security in more than one centre.

Nevertheless, it took time after 1866 for the reliability and regularity of telegraphic contact to be proved, and for costs to be brought down. However, by 1870 transatlantic arbitrage did appear to be in full operation while the rapid expansion of the telegraph system during the 1870s extended the reach of the arbitrageurs to organized stock exchanges world-wide. By 1900 there were some 350,000 km. of submarine cables in existence, connecting all major financial centres, with the result that communication delays were reduced to minutes rather than days, weeks, or months of the past. At the same time arbitrageurs grew in skill, experience, and connections enabling them to spot, and profit from, any spatial price difference that appeared in actively traded securities. Particular securities also appeared to fulfil this role, one being the common stock of the Canadian Pacific Railroad. By 1910 there was $180m. of this in existence, held by 24,000 investors world-wide, with 65 per cent of the stock being held in Britain, 15 per cent in continental Europe, 10 per cent in the United States, and 10 per cent in Canada.[71]

Illustrating the volume of arbitrage activity was the fact that by 1909 the members of the London Stock Exchange were sending to, or receiving from continental Europe a telegram every second of the working day with the members of the Amsterdam, Berlin, Brussels, Frankfurt, and Paris Stock Exchanges being the main recipients or sources. The cost of each telegram was, by then, less than 3 per cent of that when the service had begun in 1851. However, the telegraph was also giving way to a superior form of communications, namely the telephone, with connections to Paris in 1891 and Brussels in 1903. With an open telephone line it was now possible to have continuous two-way communication between London and the Continent so even the small delays of the telegraph were eliminated. Though the transatlantic telephone was a long way off, such was the efficiency of the transatlantic cable that communications between London and New York was down to 30 seconds each way by 1911, and the cost was a mere 0.5 per cent of the 1866 level. Between London and New York the exchange of telegrams was running at around one every six seconds during the working day, with most being concentrated into the time when trading was taking place in both centres simultaneously (3–8 p.m. UK/10 a.m.–3 p.m. USA). No wonder a close correlation existed between the yields on first-class US railway bonds in London and New York over the 1871–1913 period, as these were the very securities that the arbitrageurs were most active in.

The more efficient arbitrage became the more the general membership of the stock exchange recognized the threat it posed to the exclusiveness of their market. As arbitrage became increasingly a matter of calculation and

[71] Michie, London and New York, 45–57; E. F. Satterthwaite: Circular, 10 May 1854; R. F. Pocock, The Early British Radio Industry (Manchester 1988), 19.

speed, so it became the preserve of a small number of specialists who devoted themselves to its conduct. Many of these were German Jews who moved to London faced with a decline in opportunities at home. The unification of the German currency and its link to gold in the early 1870s greatly reduced currency speculation while the outlawing of stock exchange speculation in the 1890s removed that activity. Conversely, security arbitrage offered a growing and attractive field for their talents, and they became the élite of their profession in London before 1914. The result was that the brokers who had conducted sporadic arbitrage with their correspondents abroad, as the need of opportunity arose, now found themselves supplanted by the specialists who did nothing else. These arbitrageurs thus became the principal conduits of contact between London and foreign markets attracting to themselves business that might otherwise have been shared with brokers and jobbers in general. Essentially, they were not simply conducting arbitrage but they were becoming the London market for the securities in which they specialized as they were the ones who were constantly in touch with the situation in the other markets where those securities were traded. This process of specialization cut across the interests of other members, both brokers and jobbers, who were now losing business to the arbitrageurs because of either the speed of transaction or closeness of buy/sell prices that they could offer.

However, it was only when the activities of the arbitrageurs began to cut across the accepted practices of the London Stock Exchange that they became vulnerable to attack, rather than a general air of hostility and an unwillingness to accommodate their particular requirements, as with the hours of business. In the later nineteenth century, as the competition in arbitrage increased and London tried to hold its position as the central intermediary in the process, it became necessary to both speed up the transaction time and to lower the costs involved. For the brokers the response was to cut out the jobbers and become the market for the securities they arbitraged. In that way they attracted all buying/selling interest in London and so could quote with certainty current prices and conditions, and quickly either initiate or undo a transaction in conjunction with their arbitrage partner in the other exchange. The brokers Heseltine, Powell & Co., with long-standing interests in a range of US securities, increasingly became the market in those, attracting orders from other brokers in competition with the jobbers in the American market. Similarly Morton Brothers, with connections in Australia, became the market in London for a variety of Australian stocks and shares. Though jobbers complained about this competition from brokers, it only involved a restricted range of securities and so was tolerated as an exception required by the nature of the arbitrage business.

The growing connections between jobbers and non-members was regarded more seriously. Brokers valued highly the ready market created by the jobbers and were keen to restrict access to it to themselves, and so enhance their position against non-members. However, by cutting out the brokers, and establishing direct contact with members of other stock exchanges, the costs of arbitrage could be cut, as the broker's commission on each purchase/sale could be avoided. Essentially, non-members were being placed in the same position as member brokers, for all could go to the jobber, obtain a buy/sell price, and then conclude a bargain. Members did so on the floor of the Stock Exchange while non-members did so by telegraph or telephone to the jobbers office. All the jobber had to do was maintain constant communication between those dealing on the floor and in the office, which pneumatic tubes and the local telephone service greatly facilitated. Furthermore, arbitrage could involve much less risk to a jobber than a normal deal on the floor, as that usually resulted in the need to undo a bargain at some time in the future—hence the spread in the buy/sell prices quoted. In contrast arbitrage frequently involved an almost simultaneous buy/sell operation, though half the bargain was done on their behalf elsewhere. As the ability to conduct these simultaneous transactions grew, so jobbers were willing to narrow their buy/sell prices to very small margins indeed, as long as a profit resulted. Thus the outsider could actually get a better price from an insider than the member because the resulting risk was now less, as no position resulted. Nevertheless, there was a perception that arbitrage was a specialized activity and for it to be done at all required jobbers to be permitted to transact business for non-members on very fine margins.

This tolerance towards jobbers and brokers conducting arbitrage, and breaking conventions as a result, began to break down from the 1890s as a result of two developments. Undermining certain jobbers were the appearance of a number of mining finance houses that, possessed of both ample securities and funds, began to act as a market in South African and other mining securities. Instead of taking their business to the jobbers in the mining market inside the Stock Exchange, brokers telephoned the mining finance houses for rival quotations and did deals with them if favourable. These mining finance houses were in constant touch with the producing countries and so could arbitrage between London and Johannesburg as efficiently as any member of the London Stock Exchange. Their threat, though, was limited to activity in one very volatile market. More general was the growing role being played in London by the continental banks. Unlike Britain, banks on the Continent played an active role in the securities market, including membership of stock exchanges in such countries as Germany, and had well-established client networks in place. Denied membership of the London Stock Exchange they could achieve the same position by establishing direct access to the jobbers. By telephoning jobbers' offices these banks could be quoted current buy/sell prices and so do business on the same terms as brokers who were members of the Stock Exchange. Naturally, this annoyed the brokers who saw valuable clients bypass them and go direct to the jobbers. As these banks were large customers, especially for North American stocks and bonds, the jobbers were happy to deal direct with them, and without any formal prohibition on jobbers having outside contacts it was impossible to prevent the relationship.

As the volume of business between the banks and brokers grew, so did the hostility to the relationship. If foreign banks based in London could deal directly with London jobbers why could not domestic institutions like the UK banks, investment trusts, and insurance companies, or even large individual investors. Brokers had a position in the market to defend that was greater than the simple issue of the relationship between foreign banks with London offices and London jobbers. There was also the position of a number of the jobbers in the foreign market. They felt they were losing business because brokers were going to the London branches of these foreign banks to transact business, and being quoted better prices than inside the Stock Exchange because of the contacts maintained with continental centres. Deutsche Bank, for instance, maintained a direct telephone line between its London and Paris branches, and then telegraphic contact between there and Germany.

With so many members—both brokers and jobbers—feeling threatened by the ability of non-members to deal directly with jobbers, a movement grew up to make the rules prevent jobbers having such contacts—jobbers were to only deal with members. Along with that came the equivalent ruling preventing brokers making a market, and so force them to bring all business into the Stock Exchange. Nevertheless, it took until 1909 for such a ruling to be passed because many members also recognized that it could limit the flexibility which had brought so much international business to the London Stock Exchange, and so benefited the market as a whole. Even then it was not until 1912, when minimum commission rates were introduced, that the ruling was made effective. Those commission rates also fixed the minimum charges that brokers could make their clients, resulting in the resignation of at least one firm of brokers, Helbert Wagg & Co., who arbitraged with William A. Read & Co. in New York.

As sophisticated arbitrage had relied on jobbers having direct contact with non-members and brokers making markets, rather than charging commission, these rule changes should have seriously undermined London's position, at least after the introduction of minimum commission in 1912. However, this was not the case. The rule changes were never aimed at foreign competitors of the London Stock Exchange but at domestic ones, such as the foreign banks and mining finance houses multiplying in London. Thus accompanying both the banning of dual capacity—jobbers dealing with non-members (role of brokers), and brokers making markets (role of jobbers)—and the introduction of a schedule of charges, were exceptions and rebates for arbitrage business. Outside contacts were permitted for jobbers as long as those concerned were domiciled abroad while brokers could both make prices and reduce considerably the fees charged if the clients were foreign. In addition to these dispensations there was no willingness among the members of the Committee for General Purposes, who ran the Stock Exchange, to interfere in arbitrage operations, even when complaints were made that the new rules were being ignored. Arbitrage was a little understood and rather separate business which did not readily come within the general rules and regulations of the Stock Exchange and, where possible, it was left to formulate its own practices and conventions. This position was further reinforced by the fact that much arbitrage activity took place after 4 o'clock in the afternoon when the London Stock Exchange was closed but New York was still open. At that time the members of the London Stock Exchange, whether brokers or jobbers, with an interest in American securities, were joined by a variety of non-members. In fact the most prominent firm of arbitrageurs before 1914 were S. Japhet & Co., who, as merchant bankers, were not eligible for membership of the London Stock Exchange. This after hours market did not simply involve London and New York but continental Europe as well, for dollar securities were the main mobile currency whose ownership flowed from country to country. Illustrative of the level of co-operation in this after-hours market was that the direct telephone link to Brussels was shared by Japhet & Co., H. Salmony (both non-members), and Stamm & Co. (members) who used it to arbitrage in traction shares, where the main market was on the Brussels Stock Exchange.[72] Generally, before the First World War there was little sign that London's position in international arbitrage had suffered to any appreciable extent as a result of the changes in regulations and charges, especially as the London Stock Exchange was not alone in trying to restrict the growth of trading outside the exchange.

## MONEY AND CAPITAL

The period 1850–1914 also witnessed a transformation of the role performed by the London Stock Exchange in terms of the extent and the intensity of its relationship to the money and capital markets. With the formation of London-based national banking groups a growing proportion of the nation's short-term funds were directed from London. Whereas in 1871, when British commercial bank deposits totalled £446m., 36 per cent were controlled from London, by 1913 the proportion had risen to 64 per cent, and the total to £1,032m. In addition, it was at this time that even those British banks without a London head office, such as the Scottish banks, began to direct an increasing stream of funds to the money market there. It was not only a build-up of domestic short-term money that was taking place. London was also the home to a growing number of British banks that operated overseas, especially in Asia, Africa, and Latin America. In

---

[72] Michie, *London and New York*, 42–8, 66–7, 69, 70–2, 76–88, 90–2; Roberts, *Schroders*, 370; LSE: General Purposes, 14 Apr. 1914.

1860 there were 15 such banks with a mere 132 branches and assets of £45m. By 1913 the number had doubled to 31, the branches had grown tenfold to 1,387 and the assets eightfold to £366m. Like their domestic counterparts in Britain these overseas banks built up large deposit bases and looked to the London money market for the employment of a growing volume of short-term funds. Even without the mechanism of these British banks the London money market was acting as a magnet for foreign funds from the 1850s onwards. Altogether, the deposits of foreign and colonial joint-stock banks directly represented in London rose from £112m. in 1880 to £1,855m. in 1914. In addition numerous other overseas banks and financial institutions channelled funds to the London money market via established British banks who acted on their behalf.[73]

The result of this build-up of short-term money in London was to intensify the use traditionally made of the securities market by those looking for a temporary home for their funds. In 1909 it was noted by the Stock Exchange itself that

... the large English banks, Discount, Insurance and Trust companies ... continually enter into large transactions in stock exchange securities for short periods at rates calculated to give only a slight profit over the Bill rates for money.[74]

The same year they also observed that

A very considerable amount of foreign capital is employed on the London Stock Exchange for carrying-over purposes.[75]

Essentially those with short-term funds to employ had a choice. They could invest directly in securities expecting a return from the interest or dividend paid or the rise in price as the date approached when the dividend/interest became due. Many banks and financial institutions did just that, continuously buying and selling securities as the availability of funds waxed and waned.

However, that involved a degree of risk that was not always acceptable, because both governments and companies could default on payments, and prices could also fall due to unforeseen political or economic circumstances. Instead, an increasingly common practice was to lend funds to brokers and jobbers who would invest it on their own behalf, and accept the risks involved. This also disposed of the need to maintain a staff with a thorough knowledge of the nature and timing of security investment. In 1914, around half of the money being lent by banks in London at call and at short notice consisted of loans to brokers and jobbers, with securities as collat-

[73] Michie, London and New York, 136–8, 146–8; D. Ziegler, Central Bank Peripheral Industry: The Bank of England in the Provinces, 1826–1913 (Leicester 1990), 50, 66–7, 106, 118; M. Collins, Money and Banking in the UK: A History (London 1988), 40, 106, 149; G. Jones, British Multinational Banking, 1830–1990 (Oxford 1993), 30, 93, 414–15.

[74] LSE: General Purposes, 4 Oct. 1909.

[75] Ibid., Memorandum to the Chancellor of the Exchequer, 13 May 1909.

eral. The popularity of this method of employing funds meant that certain members of the Stock Exchange specialized in acting as intermediaries between those with money to lend and brokers and jobbers seeking to borrow for themselves or their clients.[76] In 1877 Percival Spurling, a money broker, reported that

we can lend at times almost any amount which is given into our hands, on short loans. Both fortnightly and day-to-day.[77]

By using their capital as margin for loans both brokers and jobbers could and did employ very large sums lent to them, either directly or indirectly, by banks and other financial institutions present in the London money market. The Deutsche Bank's London branch, for example, was increasingly involved in providing credit for Stock Exchange transactions rather than trade, while it was from 1881 onwards that the Midland Bank began lending to London stockbrokers. Overall, it was estimated that around 80 per cent of the purchases made on the Stock Exchange were financed by credit in 1894, and this proportion had risen to 90 per cent in 1909. Capels, for instance, lent £1,045,482 to clients and fellow members in 1906/7 and financed this by borrowing £937,000, with their margin being £108,482 or 11.6 per cent. Assuming an average capital of £10,000 per Stock Exchange broker or jobber the c.5,000 members would collectively possess a capital of £50m. and a borrowing capacity of a further £500m., assuming an average 10 per cent margin. As it was the members of the Stock Exchange owed £80.8m. to banks and other financial institutions on the eve of the First World War, but, in all likelihood that sum had been much reduced as the threat of war loomed. Clearly, by this time holding, or lending upon, transferable securities had become a major element within the operation of the London money market as it sought to employ safely and remuneratively the vast and growing volume of short-term funds that was directed to it from all around the world.[78]

With the growing use being made of the Stock Exchange for money market purposes the availability of a large volume of suitable securities was of crucial importance. It was vital that they could be easily and quickly bought and sold in large amounts with little alteration in their price, if the risk involved was to be kept at an acceptable level. At mid-century only the

---

[76] Ziegler, *Central Bank*, 66–7, 106, 118; F. Playford, *Practical Hints for Investing Money* (London 1856), 30; P. L. Cottrell, 'Great Britain', in R. Cameron and V. I. Bovykin (eds.), *International Banking, 1870–1914* (New York 1991), 36.

[77] Royal Commission on the London Stock Exchange, *Report*, 40, 150.

[78] Kynaston, 'London Stock Exchange', 109–10, 122, 281; Reed, *Capel and Company*, 69–70, Chapman, *Raphael Bicentenary*, 30, 35–6, 38; Michie, *London and New York*, 142; Kynaston, *Cazenove*, 98; M. Pohl, 'Deutsche Bank London Agency Founded 100 Years Ago', in M. Pohl (eds.), *Studies on Economic and Monetary Problems and on Banking History* (Mainz 1988), 236–8; Madden, *British Investment*, 116, 147; P. L. Cottrell, 'The Domestic Commercial Banks and the City of London 1870–1939', in Y. Cassis (ed.), *Finance and Financiers in European History, 1880–1960* (Cambridge 1992), 50.

National Debt really filled that role but, increasingly, a variety of other securities could be used for that purpose, as with US Federal bonds in the 1870s or Japanese Imperial Government stock in the 1900s. In addition the securities created by the largest companies were also suitable, whether they were British railways, American railroads, or South African gold-mining companies. All were heavily capitalized, widely held, and commanded active markets. Generally, it is estimated that the number of separate issues of securities which could be used for money-market purposes expanded some tenfold between 1870 and 1914, increasing from c.40 to c.400.[79] As J. B. McKenzie, a broker, observed in 1908, 'stick to the active issues, and you can either buy or sell and stock at practically any moment'.[80] Consequently, both the type of securities quoted and the volume of trades that took place on the London Stock Exchange reflected the importance of that market as a home for funds only temporarily available. In turn the range and nature of the securities traded attracted to London the banks and other financial institutions with funds to employ. This interaction between supply and demand underpinned the growth of the London Stock Exchange and conditioned the way it operated and the market it provided.

As a result of the service provided by the Stock Exchange and its members the London money market could operate very flexibly. Whether throughout the year, with the seasons, or from year to year, due to fluctuating economic conditions, the ability to employ money remuneratively in securities and realize it when required, greatly reduced the need for banks and others to maintain large reserves or be subject to extreme variations in inflows and outflows. Instead, an excess of deposits could be recycled through the securities market while any upsurge in withdrawals could be met by calling in loans to brokers/jobbers and selling securities. This could bankrupt a few brokers, as in the monetary stringency of 1907, but the major financial institutions were secure. The jobbers, Medwin & Lowy, clearly recognized the role being played by the Stock Exchange when they wrote in 1909,

To curtail in any degree the facilities of the London market means that in time of financial stress those who are compelled to realise securities would have no means of disposing of their holdings, and what might have been a temporary stringency could easily develop into an alarming crisis.

They went on to indicate that the London Stock Exchange played this role not only for Britain but for the world's financial system, for they added that

. . . the International character of the London market forms the safety-valve of financial disturbance . . .[81]

[79] Michie, *London and New York*, 141–2; Kynaston, 'London Stock Exchange', 159, 219, 225, 231, 245; Royal Commission on the London Stock Exchange, *Report*, 369.
[80] J. B. McKenzie, *The Story of a Stock Exchange Speculator* (London 1908), 9.
[81] LSE: General Purposes, 3 June 1909.

Over the 1867–1913 period Britain was free of major monetary crises despite events such as the collapse of the City of Glasgow Bank in 1878 or the insolvency of Barings in 1890. Instrumental in achieving this stability was the liquidity given to the monetary system by the ability to employ and release funds, virtually at will, through the mechanism of the Stock Exchange. It was this rather than any development of central bank policy by the Bank of England or the developments in a national banking system, that was the crucial force at work.[82]

The London Stock Exchange also played a major role in allowing the world's monetary system to operate under the fixed exchange rate regime of the gold standard. With a large mass of securities common to many markets, such as US railroad bonds, there existed a class of mobile assets. By buying these securities on one exchange and, simultaneously, selling them on another—arbitrage—a transfer of funds could be achieved. In turn these funds could be used to make payments where and when required, without any need to transfer gold or arrange credit. Consequently, the continuous pressure put on exchange rates as open economies interacted could be absorbed in the constant buying and selling operations on the London Stock Exchange and its counterparts abroad. In a memorandum to the Chancellor of the Exchequer in 1909 the London Stock Exchange tried to explain the role it was now playing,

. . . operations in International Stocks and Shares largely influence the money markets of the world, . . . arbitrage operations, especially as regards American securities, are of great value to the money market and provide at times a very useful set-off to the remittances, which might otherwise have to be made in the shape of gold to pay for the imports of produce.[83]

With international securities commanding virtually the same price over the world, any slight divergence between exchanges would produce a rapid flurry of activity from the arbitrageurs, resulting in a transfer of money from one country to another. In particular, a tightening of credit in one country would, immediately, depress security prices there, signalling an inrush of external buy orders, especially from those countries where an easing of credit was pushing up prices.[84]

By forging an ever closer link to the money market the London Stock Exchange made itself a central and indispensable force behind the stability and flexibility that characterized domestic and international monetary arrangements at this time. Not only were short-term funds, that might have remained idle, released for profitable employment but the existence of active

[82] Ziegler, *Central Bank*, 88, 132; *Financial Times' Investors' Guide*, 13, 21; Michie, *London and New York*, 150–1; A. Cairncross, 'The Bank of England and the British Economy', in R. Roberts and D. Kynaston (eds.), *The Bank of England: Money, Power and Influence 1694–1994* (Oxford 1995), 60–1.
[83] LSE: General Purposes, 13 May 1909.
[84] Ibid., 1 July 1909; Michie, *London and New York*, 155–7.

markets for a large mass of securities, both domestically and world-wide, provided a means of absorbing the full force of either monetary stringency or excess that had proved disruptive at earlier times. Though crises continued to occur, the relationship between the securities and money markets were now such that their worst consequences could be absorbed and diffused. Essentially, the London Stock Exchange and its members were that vital mechanism that allowed open and unmanaged economies to interact and develop without producing such strains and imbalances that would lead governments to intervene, restrict and control for national self-interest. Few members of the Stock Exchange realized that their continuous buying and selling was of such significance, taking for granted the combination of stability and expansion that appeared to come from the Bank of England, the gold standard, and economic liberalism.

Instead of recognizing the role being played by the Stock Exchange in the operation of the domestic and international money markets, attention has tended to focus on the relationship, or lack of it, with the domestic capital market. In particular, a contrast is drawn, in this period, between the more interventionist role played by banks in continental Europe compared to the practice in Britain where banks were more reluctant to become involved in the financing of industry. Instead, domestic business obtained finance through the issue of securities traded on the Stock Exchange, where they were valued by investors for their immediate return and not their long-term potential.

Whereas European banks took the long view and financed the development phase of businesses, British investors simply compared the risk versus return of the wide range of securities open to them, and opted for American railroad bonds or Japanese government stock instead. Such, at least, is the conventional wisdom leading to the conclusion that the Stock Exchange has made a significant contribution to Britain's long-term decline through denying promising enterprises the finance they required to grow, and, instead directed the flow of savings abroad into safe but low-yielding bonds.[85]

However, there is very little evidence that continental European banks were that much more interventionist than their British counterparts, especially when they are compared not with commercial banks alone but the spread of British financial institutions including the merchant banks, investment trusts, and company promoters. After an initial enthusiasm at mid-century, European banks began to retrench on direct investment in manufacturing industry from the 1870s onwards. In countries like Germany, France, and Belgium the earlier experience had all revealed to banks how difficult it was to combine short-term deposits

[85] F. Capie and M. Collins, *Have the Banks failed British Industry?* (London 1992), 17; W. P. Kennedy, 'Capital Markets and Industrial Structure in the Victorian Economy', in Van Helten and Cassis (eds.), *Capitalism in a Mature Economy*, 25–6.

with a commitment to long-term lending, and remain solvent. The result was to encourage a much more cautious policy, leading to a growing emulation of British banking practice in continental Europe. Hence their heavy reliance upon the London money market for the remunerative employment of short-term funds, and thus the increasing dependence upon the facilities provided by the London Stock Exchange. This was even true for the less-developed economies of Europe, like Russia, where banks concentrated much more upon short-term lending rather than development finance from the mid-1870s onwards. By 1913 there were three branches of Russian banks in London. Consequently, though it is possible to point to examples of industries aided by bank finance in individual continental European countries, such as the electrical industry in Germany, there also exist others that prospered without such assistance, as with chemicals in Germany.[86]

Conversely, the London Stock Exchange gave an enthusiastic welcome to securities that could only be categorized as involving a high degree of risk. The companies involved in the nascent oil industry, for example, found in London an excellent market for their shares despite the absence of any domestic experience with the activity. Generally, probably the riskiest of all investments was the exploitation of the earth's resources, considering the state of scientific knowledge and the remote regions involved, but the companies involved found in London the most receptive market for the securities they issued. Thus, even though those who invested in such securities were drawn from throughout Europe, with the French heavily involved in South African gold-mining, the market was to be found on the London Stock Exchange.[87] This was true even for risky domestic investments where the opportunities existed, as in the early development of the radio industry. The

[86] Cameron and Bovykin (eds.), *International Banking*, ch. by H. Bonin, 'The Case of the French Banks', 72–3, 77, ch. by R. Tilly, 'International Aspects of the Development of German Banking', 108–9, ch. by H. Van der Wee and M. Goossens, 'Belgium', 123, 129, ch. by V. I. Bovykin and B. V. Ananich, 'The Role of International Factors in the Formation of the Banking System in Russia', 143, 156, ch. by A. Broder, 'Banking and the Electrotechnical Industry in Western Europe', 475; T. Balderson, 'German Banking 1913–1939', *University of Manchester: Working Papers in Economic and Social History, No. 2*, 1990, 2–3; Y. Cassis, 'British Finance: Success and Controversy', in Van Helten and Cassis (eds.), *Capitalism in a Mature Economy*, ch. by Y. Cassis, 'British Finance: Success and Controversy', 8–9, ch. by J. Armstrong, 'The Rise and Fall of the Company Promoter and the Financing of British Industry', 115, ch. by Y. Cassis, 'The Emergence of a New Financial Institution: Investment Trusts in Britain, 1870–1939', 141.

[87] A. A. Fursenko, 'The Oil Industry', in Cameron and Bovykin (eds.), *International Banking*, 458; J. J. Van Helten, 'Mining, Share Manias and Speculation: British Investment in Overseas Mining, 1880–1913', 159, 163, 176, and M. Cowen, 'Capital, Nation and Commodities: The Case of Forestal Land, Timber and Railway Companies in Argentina and Africa, 1900–1945', in Van Helten and Cassis (eds.), *Capitalism in a Mature Economy*, 192; Suzuki, *Japanese Government Loan Issues*, 10–11; Madden, *British Investment*, 301; M. Wilkins, *The History of Foreign Investment in the United States to 1914* (Cambridge, Mass. 1989), 156, 197.

principle upon which this industry was based was the discovery of invisible electromagnetic radiation by the German scientist, Hertz, in 1887. Subsequently, the practicality of wireless communication was then established by an Italian, Marconi, in 1897. However, the financing of the whole operation took place in Britain with the formation of the Wireless Telegraph and Signal Company in 1897, and the subsequent enthusiastic following their shares received on the London Stock Exchange. Unlike the telephone, whose development was blocked by the Post Office's monopoly over communication using wires, the progress of the radio was not restricted in that way, and both investors and the market provided a positive response.[88]

Unfortunately, another important development at the time, the electrical industry, was blighted not by investor indifference or resistance in the securities market, but by central government legislation and local authority hostility limiting the activities of interested companies. As the stockbroker, J. Bevan Braithwaite, complained in 1907,

...the market in electric securities has been almost destroyed. People decline to invest their money in these concerns while municipalities maintain their present attitude.[89]

His firm, Foster & Braithwaite, was greatly involved in the market for electricity company shares, and he himself was Chairman of the City of London Electric Supply Company and a personal friend of Emile Garcke, one of the early pioneers of the British electricity supply industry. Clearly, there was no lack of interest from the Stock Exchange, either collectively or individually, in new technological developments and their potential, but there was a problem in persuading investors to purchase the securities required for their finance, and maintaining an active secondary market, against the hostility of local authorities as owners of the gas supply or the Post Office, as controllers of the telegraphy network, when they had the support of the law to prevent or restrict competition.[90]

Similarly, the criticism made of the Stock Exchange for its late and limited involvement in the market for industrial securities fails to recognize that London was but a part of the domestic securities market. The provincial stock exchanges played a very active role in providing a market for the securities of industrial and commercial companies among the very investors who were likely to be most interested and most knowledgeable. This was the business community of the locality in which they operated with each provincial stock exchange developing its owns speciality. The number of individual and commercial companies quoted on the Manchester Stock Exchange rose from c.70 in 1885 to c.220 in 1906, with many having

[88] Pocock, *The Early British Radio Industry*, 2, 66, 105, 124, 142, 144, 149.
[89] *Daily News*, 18 Nov. 1907.   [90] Michie, *London and New York*, 112.

a capital of as low as £50,000. Through links between stock exchanges securities issued by these companies were available to all investors, with the London Stock Exchange playing a central co-ordinating role.

There was no lack of a market for industrial securities in Britain before 1914 for it existed both in and between the numerous stock exchanges in existence. In fact, compared to other stock exchanges in Europe and abroad there appeared a greater interest and a more active market in industrial securities in London than elsewhere. In the entire period before the First World War there was little interest in industrial securities on the Paris Bourse.[91] For New York a recent verdict was that:

As the demand for finance for new industry—industries often located in the south and west—grew, the British exchange reacted quickly, the New York Stock Exchange much more slowly . . . the London market supplied capital to firms still incapable of attracting finance on the New York Exchange.[92]

Similarly the London Stock Exchange was more welcoming to major Dutch companies than the Amsterdam Stock Exchange, while Canada could only offer a narrow market for such securities.[93] Most stock exchanges increasingly quoted and traded foreign stocks and bonds where and when permitted. Between 1892/3 and 1908/14 the proportion of foreign securities quoted in Paris rose from one-quarter to one-third while in Berlin one-fifth of all new issues listed were foreign. Both these stock exchanges restricted the access of non-domestic securities to their market with the result that investors in these countries used London for trading in the likes of US railroad stocks and bonds.[94]

Generally, where a market for securities was required on the London Stock Exchange it was readily forthcoming. Of course, most financing operations took place without the need to issue stocks and shares and provide for their subsequent purchase and sale. Most activities in the economy were quite capable of being financed from the private savings of individuals or small groups while businesses traditionally reinvested profits to provide for further expansion. Consequently, though the Stock Exchange had moved closer to occupying a central position in the financial mechanism of the economy, it still remained somewhat tangential. In industrial

---

[91] Thomas, *Provincial Stock Exchanges*, 133; Thomas, *Stock Exchanges of Ireland*, 145; Capie and Collins, *Have the Banks Failed?*, 33; Y. Cassis (ed.), *Finance and Financiers in European History, 1880–1960* (Cambridge 1992), ch. by A. Aveslin, 'Banks and State in France from the 1880s to the 1930s', 72, ch. by A. Broder, 'Banking and the Electrotechnical Industry in Western Europe', 475.

[92] Davis and Cull, *Capital markets*, 65, see also 68–9.

[93] M. Hart, J. Jonker, and J. L. Van Zanden, *A Financial History of the Netherlands* (Cambridge 1997), 114; C. Armstrong, *Blue Skies and Boiler Rooms: Buying and Selling Securities in Canada, 1870–1940* (Toronto 1997), 56.

[94] W. J. Greenwood, *Foreign Stock Exchange Practice and Company Laws* (London 1911), 115, 187, 192, 210, 211; Cameron and Bovykin (eds.), *International Banking*; Bonin, 'French Banks', 80, Tilly, 'German Banking', 95.

finance, for example, the conversion of established enterprises into the joint-stock form, and then the issue of securities to the investing public, seemed much more conditioned by the willingness of the public to purchase the securities than the need of business for the funds so raised. Even by 1914 the role played by the Stock Exchange in the capital market was still heavily oriented towards meeting the needs of governments and large infrastructure projects like railways. The real change was that the role it played in this had become world-wide rather than, largely, domestic.[95]

Furthermore, the particular role played by the Stock Exchange was not to raise the finance required by governments, railways, and other enterprises but to provide the market place where the resulting securities could be bought and sold, so satisfying the needs of investors. As the *Financial News* observed in 1905,

The public will not purchase mining shares unless it is assured that when it wants to sell, a price will always be made by dealers.[96]

The existence of an active and permanent secondary market for securities gave investors the confidence to invest in the first place, in the full knowledge that they could realize their holdings if required. By continually providing markets in new types and categories of securities the Stock Exchange encouraged investors to become more adventurous in their choices and interests, as there was always the possibility of either exit and entry. Whereas in the 1865–74 period two-thirds of the issues of foreign securities were on behalf of governments, or guaranteed by governments, by 1905–14 the proportion had been reversed, with now two-thirds coming from business of all descriptions. Increasingly, investors using the London Stock Exchange were sufficiently confident to purchase, hold, and trade securities belonging to individual enterprises and not backed by the authority of a state. On the one hand the result was to expand enormously the savings available for long-term investment and, on the other, to encourage their diversification into ever more varied and productive aspects of the economy. Though an increasing proportion of the securities so created were non-British there is no sign that this was at the expense of the British economy itself. The ability to expand the supply of savings in step with demand, as short-term funds were increasingly attracted to London, ensured that the financial requirements of the British economy, either in total or in composition, were met with little trouble at this time. Those seeking to blame Britain's economic problems on the capital market, and especially the role played within it by the Stock Exchange, have, so far, singularly failed to produce a causal connection rather than mere coincidence.[97]

[95] Michie, *London and New York*, 101, 112.

[96] *Financial News*, 23 Mar. 1905, quoted in Kynaston, 'London Stock Exchange', 247.

[97] Michie, *London and New York*, 114, 117–24; M. Dintenfass, *The Decline of Industrial Britain, 1870–1980* (London 1992), 44–5; Michie, *Financial and Commercial Services*, 'Introduction'.

Certainly there were signs immediately before the First World War that the London Stock Exchange was becoming a more restrictive and less flexible institution than in the past. However, the position of stock exchanges in other countries was by no means perfect. In Germany government legislation, as with the Bourse Law of 1896, greatly circumscribed the operation of all stock exchanges, driving much business abroad or into an inter-bank market that bypassed the established institutions. In France, the continuing power of the officially sanctioned *agents-de-change*, plus government controls on what could be quoted, drove much activity away from the Paris Bourse and onto outside markets. In the United States the control of the New York Stock Exchange, by its members, and its rules which both capped numbers and maintained high minimum commission rates, made it an unattractive market for all but high volume business with, again, much trading taking place outside. Accepting that any stock exchange involves a less-than-ideal situation, compared to the free and open market place, then the situation of the London Stock Exchange did not compare unfavourably with any rival or alternatives on the eve of the First World War. On the whole it maintained a balance between access and control that allowed it to expand rapidly in terms of membership and respond to the new opportunities that were becoming available within the securities market. Considering that the London Stock Exchange was already the largest and most well-established of its kind at mid-century, it is remarkable how willing to change it was in the years that followed. The result was that the London Stock Exchange not only continued to dominate its domestic securities market but also occupied a commanding position within the evolving global market, playing a central role in the world's financial system.[98]

---

[98] Michie, *London and New York*, 88–9; Davis and Cull, *Capital markets*, 78.

# 4

# *Shattered Dominance: The First World War, 1914–1918*

## Outbreak of War

On the eve of the First World War the London Stock Exchange was the dominant institution of its kind in the world, whether measured by activity, variety, connections, or sophistication. Its members were at the heart of a world-wide network linking the most important individual and institutional investors with the largest corporate and state borrowers. Simultaneously, the relationship with the numerous and thriving provincial stock exchanges ensured that the contribution of London to the development of a global securities market was not at the expense of its domestic counterpart. The functions performed by the London Stock Exchange also made it central to the operation of the world's money and capital markets. Dealings in securities gave to the money market the liquidity and mobility that ensured that crises were diffused before they could threaten the stability of the entire financial system, whether within Britain or internationally. Similarly, the range and depth of trading in securities made that form of finance the preferred option throughout the world as both governments and business sought long-term funding for capital intensive projects. By the end of the First World War all these accomplishments of the previous century had been damaged in some way, to the detriment not only of the Stock Exchange itself but also the stability and flexibility of the entire world economy. Inevitably a major and prolonged conflict, involving the principal economies in the world, would have serious repercussions for an institution that was both open and international in its orientation and operations. However, the Stock Exchange was not simply an innocent bystander but an important player in the events as they unfolded and the reactions they produced.

Certainly the outbreak of war, on 1 August 1914, came as a shock to the members and management of the London Stock Exchange. Rumours of war had always been an influence on market sentiment but no thinking, let alone planning, had been carried out on what to do if a major conflict did break out. Kirkaldy noted in 1915 that '. . . the outbreak of war took the financial world by surprise . . .', while Hartley Withers view, in the same year was

Table 4.1. London Stock Exchange: Members and clerks of foreign birth, 1914

| Country of Birth | Members | | Clerks | | Total | |
|---|---|---|---|---|---|---|
| | No. | % of total | No. | % of total | No. | % |
| Germany | 153 | 70 | 21 | 68 | 174 | 70 |
| Austria | 20 | 9 | 3 | 10 | 23 | 9 |
| Netherlands | 18 | 8 | 3 | 10 | 21 | 8 |
| Switzerland | 7 | 3 | — | — | 7 | 3 |
| France | 3 | 1 | 2 | 6 | 5 | 2 |
| Belgium | 3 | 1 | 2 | 6 | 5 | 2 |
| Italy | 2 | 1 | 1 | 3 | 3 | 1 |
| Greece | 2 | 1 | — | — | 2 | 1 |
| Russia | 1 | — | 1 | 3 | 2 | 1 |
| EUROPE | 210 | 96 | 31 | 100 | 241 | 97 |
| United States | 7 | 3 | — | — | 7 | 3 |
| Venezuela | 1 | — | — | — | 1 | — |
| TOTAL | 218 | 100 | 31 | 100 | 249 | 100 |

*Source*: LSE: Committee for General Purposes, Minutes, 4 Jan. 1915.

that 'It came upon us like a thunderbolt from a clear sky.'[1] This was especially so in the case of a war with Germany, for so much business was done with, and on behalf of, that country on the Stock Exchange. Among the membership no country exhibited such strong ties of birth or relationship. Germans were the single most important group of non-British among both members and clerks (Table 4.1). Among the wider financial community the ties to Germany were equally strong. While any major war would have serious implications for the London Stock Exchange, one involving a conflict between Britain and Germany posed the severest challenge.

Possibly because the implications of such a conflict were so horrendous for the Stock Exchange, no strategic planning took place. When the outbreak of war did become inevitable towards the very end of July 1914 the Stock Exchange was forced to devise and implement emergency measures, with little thought given to their long-term implications. There was no awareness of how severe and extended the conflict was going to be, and thus no pressure to devise measures that were more than temporary. The Chairman of the Committee for General Purposes, Sir R. W. Inglis, recorded in his diary the daily sequence of events leading up to the outbreak of war.

[1] A. W. Kirkaldy (ed.), *Credit, Industry and the War* (London 1915), 245; H. Withers, *War and Lombard Street* (London 1915), 1.

Thursday 30 July 1914
Dealings in the House practically nil and markets all flat. About 7 p.m. Mr Satterthwaite [Edward Satterthwaite, Secretary, Committee for General Purposes] called and said war was certain and that to prevent a panic and widespread failures we ought to close the House at 10 a.m. tomorrow for which hour the Committee was summoned. He also outlined the proposal for postponing the impending settlements. We got a motor, drove to Town and saw Mr Koch [William M. Koch, member of the Committee] (arranged by telephone before we left) and heard such news that I agreed with Mr Satterthwaite's suggestion and drove back home.

Friday 31st July 1914.
Went up by 8.15 [train] and was with Mr Satterthwaite by 9.15 and agreed his Resolutions. Committee met at 10 and passed and confirmed them. It is believed this action will save the House from great disaster but whatever happens I wish to place on record that Mr Satterthwaite is entitled to the credit. He thought out the idea from first to last and drew up the Resolutions before he came to see me on Thursday night and I agreed that at once as I saw what would be the result of taking no action at all.[2]

Edward Satterthwaite, as a reserve Colonel, had connections in the War Office while William Koch possessed friends in the Treasury. It was through these contacts, not via official channels or the Bank of England, that the London Stock Exchange learnt that war was imminent. They then took what action they could to save their fellow members from the consequences of a likely collapse in the prices of securities and a severe contraction of credit. Growing panic on continental Europe was already producing a crisis on the London Stock Exchange as foreign clients were unable to complete agreed transactions, either by payment for or delivery of securities, while the sources of credit were drying up. With every possibility that the outbreak of war would be followed by both a substantial and general fall in the prices of securities and a major interest rate rise, a large number of members, operating on credit and with open positions, would face immediate ruin. Loans would be called in, securities would be liquidated at low prices, and members' capital, being used as margin, would be lost. This would lead to widespread failure as members would be unable to repay their borrowings. In turn, this would bring down other members owed money or securities by those who had failed and so become a wholesale collapse among the membership with only a few surviving. By closing the Stock Exchange and postponing the settlement, this crisis was averted, temporarily, until either the threat of war disappeared or measures could be put in place to cope with its consequences. The same course of action was followed around the world with not only the London Stock Exchange, but also Paris, Berlin, and New York, closed by 31 July 1914.[3]

---

[2] Diary Entry Reprinted in LSE: Committee for General Purposes, 24 Mar. 1915.
[3] J. E. Meeker, *The Work of the Stock Exchange* (New York 1930), 606; A. W. Kirkaldy (ed.), *British Finance During and After the War, 1914–21* (London 1921), 1–2.

As the members of the Stock Exchange financed so much of their operations upon credit it was essential that the banks were involved at an early stage in finding a solution to the problems that brokers and jobbers now faced. If the banks called in their loans, members could not repay as the closure of the Stock Exchange removed the market for the securities used as collateral. Conversely, if the Stock Exchange was reopened the predicted depreciation in prices would mean that the collateral no longer covered the loans with the result that members would be bankrupted and the stability of banks called into question. Furthermore, as much of the Stock Exchange's business was with German investors and banks, it was going to be impossible to enforce either payment for or delivery of securities in many cases, creating havoc in settling deals when the current fortnightly account was completed. Consequently, before the Stock Exchange could be reopened decisions had to be taken regarding the fate of the loans made to members of the Stock Exchange and the status of outstanding sales and purchases made between brokers and jobbers. Without some action any reopening would be accompanied by panic selling that could destroy the whole basis of trust and credit upon which the market existed. This was the situation all round the world.

In response to the crisis the government had introduced a temporary moratorium on loans, so that they could not be called in. This, combined with the closure of the Stock Exchange and the suspension of the account, was sufficient to provide a breathing space during which discussions could take place between the Treasury, the Bank of England, and the Stock Exchange. By the end of October a scheme was in place under which the settlement of the pre-war account was suspended until twelve months after the war was over, leaving until then the complex question of what to do about deals entered into on behalf of German and Austrian clients. Similarly, the banks agreed to an equivalent delay on the calling in of their loans as long as minimum prices were introduced that ensured that the market value of the securities used as collateral was greater than the loan made. Anything that was not covered by the suspension of the account and the moratorium on loans was then dealt with, on a case-by-case basis, by the Committee for General Purposes. As it was some 17 member firms failed in the opening months of the war, being unable to obtain payment from clients in Germany or cover the interest on the loans they had expected to repay with the sale of securities used as collateral. However, the action taken did prevent a far greater collapse, giving members time to make arrangements with each other and their banks.[4]

[4] E. V. Morgan and W. A. Thomas, *The Stock Exchange: Its History and Functions* (London 1962), 217–18; LSE: General Purposes, 14 Aug. 1914, 10 Feb. 1916; LSE: Subcommittee on Rules and Regulations, 30 Aug. 1917; LSE: Subcommittee on Readmission of Defaulters, 11 Apr. 1918, 15 Apr. 1919, 11 Mar. 1920; Withers, *War and Lombard Street*, 123–4.

As the immediate emergency passed, trading in securities gradually resumed. Investors holding shares in companies likely to profit from the war sought to realize capital gains while others sought to shift their savings in that direction. With the Stock Exchange remaining closed this buying and selling took place outside, such as on the street, in brokers' offices, or at convenient meeting places. Durlachers, the jobbers, dealt in the shares of rubber plantation companies at the Savoy and housed a night shift of clerks in the Great Eastern Hotel in order to maintain contact between London and the Far East. There was also an increased use of the Exchange Telegraph's challenge system, whereby subscribers could broadcast prices for particular securities and await a response. Before the war this had only been used for the most inactive of securities but, with the Stock Exchange closed, one firm of jobbers, Wedd Jefferson, complained that it was being employed to buy and sell consols. Between 1 January and 31 July 1914 only 29 subscribers used the challenge system, quoting 70 prices, whereas from 1 August until 31 December 1914, the number of subscribers rose to 96 and the prices quoted to 428. Auctions of securities even reappeared with the likes of Goddard & Smith and Knight, Frank & Rutley both finding it worthwhile, especially in the interests of solicitors who had difficulty in valuing or settling estates. The *Daily Mail* also restarted its service to readers whereby they could use its columns to indicate prices for the securities they wanted to buy or sell.[5]

Though all this annoyed the Stock Exchange and led to demands from members for action to be taken, it was but an inadequate substitute for the reopening of the Stock Exchange itself. At the very least the underlying business of the realization, acquisition, and valuation of securities went on, whether there was a war or not, and the Stock Exchange was being by-passed as a market because of its closure. Pressure, therefore, began to build up to find a way of reopening the Stock Exchange as soon as possible without precipitating the financial crisis that its closure was designed to avert. During September and October certain obstacles were removed, the most important being the agreement to continue the suspension of the pre-war account and the moratorium on loans. In order to cope with the complex and ongoing nature of the transactions on the Stock Exchange, the scope of this suspension and moratorium had to be widened in November. T. R. Stokes of A. Hirch & Co. had pointed out that,

if it be insisted that those who have lent money are bound to continue so doing for the specified period, while on the other hand, they are required to make payment for securities previously or subsequently purchased, the result must be disaster

[5] LSE: General Purposes, 25 Aug. 1914, 29 Aug. 1914, 4 Sept. 1914, 7 Sept. 1914, 9 Sept. 1914, 14 Oct. 1914, 7 Apr. 1915, 22 Sept. 1915; LSE: General Purposes, Subcommittee on Exchange Telegraph Company Limited, 20 Aug. 1914; Wedd, Durlacher, *Wedd, Durlacher, Mordaunt, and Company, Members of the Stock Exchange* (n.p. 1984). W. Hamilton Whyte, *The Stock Exchange: Its Constitution and the Effects of the Great War* (London 1924), 55.

to a very large number of our members and an entirely untenable position thereby created.

In response it was agreed that all unsettled transactions would be included, including sales, purchases, options, or loans.[6]

With a number of the provincial stock exchanges conducting informal sessions by November, the London Stock Exchange and its members were losing out in the securities market that was being re-established. One firm, Morton Brothers, suggested on 24 November that,

A lot of business is going past the market at present owing to the Stock Exchange not being open and we see no reason why it should not now be opened for cash bargains, even although the Official List is not issued. It would tend to again consolidate all business passing into our market and give brokers and jobbers something to do.[7]

By the end of that month the Edinburgh, Manchester, and Liverpool Stock Exchanges were already providing a market for domestic securities while New York reopened, officially, in December, providing a threat on the international front. As the war was showing no sign of drawing to a close, a way had to be found of reopening the London Stock Exchange if it was not to lose out to its rivals.

The problem that made it difficult for London to reopen, despite the steps taken in October and November, were the worries of the banks. If prices fell dramatically on the reopening of the Stock Exchange, as was expected from unofficial trading, the bankers' loans with securities as collateral would not only be uncallable, because of the moratorium, but they would also be uncovered. Once this was revealed the safety of deposits in banks could be called into question, leading to panic withdrawals and endangering the entire financial system. Consequently, the Treasury would only agree to the reopening of the Stock Exchange on condition that severe restrictions on trading were observed. Minimum prices had to be maintained, with no transactions taking place at lower values, despite the strong probability that these were no longer realistic. These minimum prices would preserve the fiction that loans were fully covered while, at the same time, making it easier and cheaper for the government to raise finance for the war effort, as new debt could be priced below the minimum set but above that prevailing in the unofficial market.

Furthermore, all transactions were to be for cash, with immediate payment on delivery. In essence this meant a delay of up to five days, simply to cope with the administration of deals, but even that was a considerable change from the minimum 14-day delay under fortnightly accounts. The objective here was to reduce the sensitivity of transactions on the Stock

---

[6] LSE: General Purposes, 7 Nov. 1914, cf. 27 Aug. 1914, 28 Oct. 1914, 6 Nov. 1914.
[7] Ibid., 24 Nov. 1914, cf. 6 Nov. 1914, 23 Nov. 1914, 25 Nov. 1914.

Exchange to news from the war front, as this could have destabilizing effects on the entire financial system. A military reverse could result in plunging prices, resulting in large losses for certain brokers and jobbers at the end of the account, with consequences for those who had financed their positions. For the same reason the use of options was banned as that could also lead to the build-up of a large speculative position, and its collapse in a reversal of fortune militarily. Arbitrage was also prohibited as it could have a similar destabilizing influence on the international value of the pound through sales and purchases on behalf of foreigners converting into or out of sterling. Finally, in order to deny the enemy access to the London market, all securities bought and sold on behalf of foreigners were to be vetted. It was well known that German banks and investors were large holders of many American securities for which the London Stock Exchange was the principal market. However, by the end of December, even before the Stock Exchange had reopened, that restriction on enemy access to London had been widened to encompass all foreigners. All non-UK investors were virtually prohibited from selling all or part of their holdings in London, even though that was the principal or sole market for the securities that they owned. By denying them access to the London Stock Exchange, the Treasury prevented any pressure on sterling, as foreigners sold to British investors, or competition for government loans among British savings.[8]

Having agreed to these rather onerous conditions that reversed so many pre-war practices, the Stock Exchange was allowed to reopen on 4 January 1915. The following notice, drawn up by Edward Satterthwaite, was posted informing all members that,

The restrictions upon business are great, but as they have been imposed by the Treasury and are recognised by the Committee as being 'absolutely necessary in the national interests' at the present time, the Committee are sure that they can rely upon the loyal acceptance of them by the members of the Stock Exchange.[9]

In order to ensure that these restrictions were observed, the Stock Exchange banned its members from doing deals before 11 o'clock in the morning and after 3 o'clock in the afternoon (1 o'clock on Saturdays).

## EFFECTS OF WAR

The Stock Exchange was now no longer master of its own market, being forced to accept a severe curtailment of its normal methods of conducting business and the freedom allowed to its members. It had little option but to agree to the Treasury's demands as there was always the threat to end the moratorium on loans. If that moratorium was ended and the banks

---

[8] Ibid., 10 Nov. 1914, 18 Dec. 1914, 22 Dec. 1914, 31 Dec. 1914; ibid., Temporary Regulations for the Reopening of the Stock Exchange, 1914.

[9] Ibid., 23 Dec. 1914.

called in their loans, a large number of brokers and jobbers would be ruined. As the broker S. N. Braithwaite, had explained in a letter to Edward Satterthwaite as early as 23 September 1914:

The working capital of a Stock Exchange business is generally represented mainly by Bank balances, margins in values over loans, and money lent without margin on loans. If all these are not freely available few would be justified in carrying on business at all . . .[10]

The broking firm of de Zoete & Gorton had loans from banks of over £1m. outstanding in July 1914, for example. If the pre-war loans could not be continued and new ones obtained from banks, most members would be unable to operate, and so it was better to accept the restrictions and carry on as best they could.[11]

When the Stock Exchange did reopen it began immediately to reclaim business from the alternatives that had been developing. The use of the challenge system on the Exchange Telegraph, for example, fell by half during 1915 while the *Daily Mail* ceased to offer its 'Stock Exchange' service in the September of that year. However, the five-month closure of the London Stock Exchange had allowed the larger provincial stock exchanges, like Liverpool and Edinburgh, to establish a market in consols for the first time, and this remained in place after London's reopening. Part of the problem was that the restrictions imposed greatly interfered with the ability of members to maintain the active and liquid markets, with close pricing, that had existed in the past and which clients expected. The Committee for General Purposes was besieged with a flood of complaints from members as it was forced to adjudicate on whether particular deals were in contravention of the restrictions or not. The simple necessity of forever filling in forms slowed down the buying and selling of securities while the restrictions on foreign investors hampered the ability of brokers and jobbers to make deals. With regard to foreign investors, the Treasury rules were relaxed during 1915 so as to allow them to buy securities in London. Even the Treasury could be persuaded that Americans and Australians buying securities in London, especially from British investors, would both release funds that could be lent to the government for war finance and relieve pressure on the exchange rate. Other than in cases like this, the Treasury was most unwilling to accept any variation of the restrictions imposed on the London Stock Exchange even though they did not apply to other institutions and non-members.[12]

One area where the Stock Exchange tried to achieve a relaxation of the conditions imposed on it was that of minimum prices. In certain cases they

[10] LSE: General Purposes, 10 Feb. 1916.
[11] Ibid., 18 Dec. 1914, 29 Dec. 1914; H. Janes, *de Zoete and Gorton* (London 1963), 55–6.
[12] LSE: General Purposes, 7 Jan. 1915, 18 Jan. 1915, 7 Apr. 1915, 20 Sept. 1915, 10 Feb. 1916; W. A. Thomas, *The Provincial Stock Exchanges* (London 1973), 171, 180.

were completely unrealistic and so prevented any business in those securities being done on the London Stock Exchange. Included among these were consols. With War Loan yielding 4 per cent, the minimum price set for consols, equally guaranteed by the state, meant that it was seriously overvalued and could not be sold. Hence consols were traded on the less-regulated provincial stock exchanges. Despite a meeting with representatives of the banks and insurance companies on 25 February 1915, the Stock Exchange failed to get any agreement on lowering minimum prices. These institutional investors were not willing to accept a depreciation in the value of securities used as collateral because of the implications it had for the cover on their loans. The Treasury was also unsympathetic because it wished to see all investor attention focus on new War Loan issues, which had no minimum price, rather than existing government debt and alternatives like railway stocks. Nevertheless, the Stock Exchange tried a direct approach to the Treasury arguing that the maintenance of minimum prices was inflicting long-term damage on the capital market, which had implications for the government's war finance. The artificial price regime was stifling investor activity which often involved a continuous process of realization and reinvestment. Brokers had numerous clients who wished to sell existing holdings, even at a loss and use the proceeds to buy new government debt, but were unable to do so because of minimum prices.[13]

At this stage the Stock Exchange had no wish to abandon minimum prices for it recognized that

. . . so long as its conceivable that bad news may come from the seat of war, the maintenance of minimum prices is a necessary dam against a panic which such news might cause; thus endangering much of the good which the action of the Treasury, of the Banks, and of the Stock Exchange Committee has accomplished since the beginning of the war.[14]

What the Stock Exchange wanted was more flexibility in adjusting minimum prices so as to bring them into line with prevailing market conditions, but it was precisely this that the Treasury and the banks were unwilling to permit.

Eventually, on 5 March 1915, Lord St Aldwyn, on behalf of the bankers, accepted that minimum prices were preventing the revival of trading on the Stock Exchange as well as creating serious anomalies in the pricing of securities. By then at least 50 per cent of the money borrowed from banks by Stock Exchange members had been repaid, so reducing the need to maintain fictitious prices. However, Lord St Aldwyn also drew the attention of the Chancellor of the Exchequer to the serious consequences of any major collapse in the price of securities if minimum prices were suddenly

[13] LSE: General Purposes, 22 Jan. 1915, 2 Feb. 1915, 4 Feb. 1915, 1 Mar. 1915.
[14] Ibid., 1 Mar. 1915.

abandoned. Smaller banks, insurance companies and other financial institutions did not have sufficient reserves to cover a heavy depreciation in the value of their assets, and thus their very existence would be jeopardized. With the bankers now accepting that the minimum price regime, for all its merits, had serious flaws, the Treasury signified that it was willing to accept an immediate reduction in minimum prices, agreed by all parties. This set in train a regular process through which minimum prices were gradually adjusted to take into account prevailing market conditions, while preserving them to cope with sudden fluctuations. All agreed that this was unsatisfactory but it did meet the needs of the banks, in preserving asset values, and the Treasury, in maintaining the relative attractions of war loan.

There could be no end to the minimum price regime until a solution was found to the continued over-pricing of consols, as this was the direct competitor for current government debt and the main security used for collateral purposes. This solution was found in June 1915 when it was agreed that consols could be converted into War Loan at the minimum price set by the Stock Exchange. By this device holders could now swap it for a security which was actively traded and thus commanded a market price. By November 1915 it was possible to end minimum prices for consols. Once that had happened without adverse consequences for either war finance or financial stability, it was followed by constant pressure from the Stock Exchange to end the entire minimum price regime. Eventually colonial and provincial government securities were freed from minimum prices in January 1916, UK railways in May 1916, and then all other securities on 3 July 1916. Throughout this entire period, of almost two years, a market in those securities had been developing outside the Stock Exchange, where transactions were being done at below minimum prices. In particular, the provincial stock exchanges and non-members in London, such as banks and foreign brokers, were able to gain both the expertise and the connections that were going to make it difficult for the Stock Exchange to regain its pre-war position.[15]

Though pressure from the Stock Exchange did lead to the end of the minimum price regime the other restrictions remained in place, most notably the suspension of the account and the ban on arbitrage. This did lead to occasional protests from members, especially when they realized that they were losing out to non-members, who were not covered by the restrictions. Despite these complaints the Stock Exchange generally accepted the conditions imposed upon it and tried to ensure that they were not transgressed by their members. In this they were successful.[16] The

---

[15] LSE: General Purposes, 8 Mar. 1915, 18 Mar. 1915, 23 June 1915, 12 July 1915, 19 July 1915, 22 July 1915, 19 Nov. 1915, 22 Nov. 1915, 10 Jan. 1916, 11 Mar. 1916, 29 Mar. 1916, 11 May 1916, 26 June 1916; Whyte, *The Stock Exchange*, 56–9; Kirkaldy, *British Finance*, 124–6.

[16] LSE: General Purposes, 29 Mar. 1915, 6 Dec. 1915.

Chancellor of the Exchequer, Reginald McKenna, congratulated Sir Robert Inglis, Chairman of the Committee for General Purposes, in August 1916, for

> ... the admirable way in which the Stock Exchange Committee has carried out its very difficult task of administering the restrictions which have been necessitated by the war.[17]

Apart from the campaign on minimum prices there was no suggestion that trading for the account, the use of options or the conduct of arbitrage would be revived. All that was requested was a greater degree of flexibility in dealing with foreign clients and overseas securities.

This experience of monitoring and policing the activities of its members, to a much greater degree than ever before, began to change attitudes within the Stock Exchange. Those on the Committee for General Purposes began to learn that much more was possible in terms of regulation than before the war while members themselves became accustomed to accept a far greater degree of intervention and control. In April 1916 the attitude towards the restrictions was still one that saw them as a necessary evil that should be dispensed with as soon as possible. Alfred Waley, Chairman of the Trustees and Managers, publicly expressed this in a speech in April 1916.

> I trust the restrictions under which we now conduct our business may be modified and shortly entirely removed, for regulations which impose restrictions on the Stock Exchange and are not enforced on transactions outside, not only defeat their own end but are actually an injustice to the Stock Exchange, which after all has provided both the Government and the Public with a market for their securities.

He then went on to praise the pre-war arrangements under which the Stock Exchange was left to regulate itself

> I have always believed that the ease with which transactions have been carried out in the past and the facility which we have shown for adapting our methods to the ever changing conditions of business have been the secret of the pre-eminence of the London Stock Exchange amongst the Bourses of the world.[18]

Though this remained a common view, there also grew up an opinion that much could be learnt concerning the better conduct of the market from the wartime restrictions under which it operated. At the end of August 1916 it was decided to ask the Subcommittee on Rules and Regulations

> ... to consider and report on the principles on which Stock Exchange procedure should be altered on the resumption of normal business.[19]

The aim was to extend and tighten up the regulations, making them more effective in the process. It was recognized that the pre-war regulatory

---

[17] Ibid., 14 Aug. 1916.   [18] LSE: Trustees and Managers, 18 Apr. 1916.
[19] LSE: Subcommittee on Rules and Regulations, 31 Aug. 1916.

regime, while achieving the objective of an orderly market, was a fairly lax one with major loopholes in the interpretation and enforcement of certain rites, such as in the recently introduced commission charges or dual capacity. Thus, behind the scenes, from September 1916 onwards, the Stock Exchange began to review the whole way it operated. There was a re-examination of rules and regulations covering such areas as the admission of new members, dealing before allotment, use of options, size of firms, outside activities of members, and the precise nature of arbitrage. The outcome was a much more prescriptive regime than before the war, with the intention being to remove those abuses that had resulted in the Stock Exchange being seen as a place of speculation rather than investment.[20]

Certainly by April 1917 another influential member, John Mullens, was expressing satisfaction about how well the Stock Exchange was coping with the restrictions imposed on it.

After over two-and-a-half years of this ghastly war, we can take credit from the fact that the Stock Exchange is carrying on its business without unnecessary restrictions, with free markets, and unfettered by minimum prices, and we can only hope that this will continue.[21]

A subtle change in the attitude towards regulation was taking place with an increasing emphasis on intervention rather than freedom as the war dragged on and on. By the end of the war there was an acceptance that the Stock Exchange had to take into account the interests of the Treasury and the opinions of the public more than ever before, and this meant controlling some of the practices and excesses that had previously been tolerated. As one member, Sir Walter Nevill, warned in December 1918,

. . . Press and Government were not favourably disposed towards the Stock Exchange and to such dealings as might be termed 'Gambling'.[22]

There were some, such as H. T. Campbell, who advocated no return to account trading. The immediate payment for and delivery of securities reduced the possibility of serious default. Certainly, during the years of war, members became accustomed to a mode of dealing that involved much less risk than when securities were being carried by brokers, jobbers, and their clients from account to account through large loans from banks and other financial institutions. The First World War left a legacy of control and caution in the Stock Exchange that would not be easily dispelled in the years to come. Within the Stock Exchange as an institution there was always an uneasy balance between those whose priority was to maintain stability and preserve existing business and those willing to accept risks in order to expand into new areas. What the war did, was to tilt the balance towards

[20] LSE: Rules and Regulations, 31 Aug. 1916, 6 Sept. 1916, 11 Oct. 1916, 21 Nov. 1916.
[21] LSE: Trustees and Managers, 17 Apr. 1917.
[22] LSE: Rules and Regulations, 11 Dec. 1918.

Table 4.2. London Stock Exchange: Membership, 1914–1918

| Year | Members | | | Clerks | | |
|------|---------|------------|--------------|--------|------------|--------------|
|      | Total   | Authorized | Unauthorized | Total  | Authorized | Unauthorized |
| 1914 | 4,822   | —          | —            | 2,327  | 765        | 1,562        |
| 1915 | 4,230   | 614        | 170          | 1,860  | 571        | 1,289        |
| 1916 | 4,057   | —          | —            | 1,757  | 540        | 1,217        |
| 1917 | 3,895   | —          | —            | 1,688  | 517        | 1,171        |
| 1918 | 3,884   | 546        | 150          | 1,685  | 515        | 1,170        |

*Source*: LSE: Trustees and Managers 1914–1918.

the conservative element who favoured capping the activities of members for the good of an orderly and regulated market.[23]

The effect of the war, however, was not confined to the Stock Exchange as an institution for it also had direct consequences for the membership as a whole and especially particular groups. Military demands made an immediate impact. By June 1915 it was estimated that over 1,000 members of the Stock Exchange—brokers, jobbers, clerks—were engaged in military service while in September it was felt that '. . . practically the whole Stock Exchange population of military age is engaged on some form of National Service'. Whereas in 1914 those with access to the Stock Exchange numbered 4,822 members and 2,327 clerks, or 7,149 in all, by 1918 there had been considerable shrinkage with only 3,823 members and 1,677 clerks, or 5,500, being eligible. This fall of almost a quarter was compounded by the fact that many of those eligible were only nominally so, being engaged in military service or other war work. In November 1917 it was estimated that, of the members numbering c.4,000, only 2,500 were still active in the Stock Exchange (Table 4.2).

However, this reduction of manpower appeared to be more than matched by the decrease in Stock Exchange business. Firms such as James Capel, Cazenoves, and Foster & Braithwaite all reported greatly reduced turnover and profits over the war years, for example. Some members switched to diferent activities, such as the jobbers Oppenheim & Greenwood who took to trading in aluminium. Others resigned completely from the Stock Exchange, as in the case of Nelke Phillips & Co., when they became private bankers. There was also a great decline in recruitment on the Stock Exchange with few clerks becoming members at this time. In fact, so limited was business in some areas that a number of established members started acting as clerks for fellow members. Consequently, during the course of the

[23] Ibid., 5 Feb. 1919; Whyte, *The Stock Exchange*, 60–3, 78, 81.

war there was a cessation of the normal exit and recruitment that had kept the Stock Exchange such a lively and dynamic body in the pre-war years. In addition to which there was the loss of life itself in the conflict, with 124 members and 235 clerks being killed.[24]

However, the war did not make an equal impact on the membership as a whole. Two groups in particular were most affected, those born in enemy countries and those engaged in international operations. As Germans had played a prominent role before 1914 in furthering London's position in the global securities market, because of both expertise and contracts, they were to be doubly affected by the war. Shortly after war was declared the Stock Exchange ruled that only those born in the UK or naturalized were permitted to enter the building, whether as clerks or members. That is where matters stood until May 1915 despite the fact that this left a core of members who had either been born in Germany, but were now naturalized, or were of German parentage but born in the British Isles. As the conflict wore on they did not have an easy time on the Stock Exchange, being identifiable by their names, with one member voicing the opinion in April 1915 that,

... for many years past I think it has been very derogatory to us as a British Institution the amount of German we have heard in the Stock Exchange and I should like to make the suggestion that no language but English be heard upon the floor of the House.... Before the war, in the Tinto (copper mining) and American markets we heard more German than English.[25]

Despite this evident hostility no action was taken and those of German origin could continue in business as best they could. The problem was that the outbreak of war left them very exposed because so many had German or Austrian clients. Julius Stamm, for instance, had his main business with continental Europe but could neither demand or make payment nor accept or deliver securities for those resident in enemy countries. The banning of arbitrage with the reopening of the Stock Exchange dealt an even greater blow. Leon Brothers complained in January 1915 that the result was '... absolute hardship to a firm like ourselves whose only business practically is arbitrage'.[26]

[24] M. C. Reed, *A History of James Capel and Company* (London 1975), 74; D Kynaston, *Cazenove & Co.: A History* (London 1991), 91–2; D. Reader, *A House in the City: Foster & Braithwaite, 1825–1975* (London 1979), 131–2; LSE: General Purposes, 22 Feb. 1915, 31 May 1915, 7 June 1915, 6 Sept. 1915, 10 Apr. 1917, 21 Nov. 1917; LSE: Trustees and Managers, 18 Apr. 1916, 14 Apr. 1919; LSE: General Purposes, Appendix on Membership, 1922/3; LSE: Subcommittee on Settlement Department, 17 Dec. 1915; *The Stock Exchange Clerks' Provident Fund Centenary, 1874–1974* (London 1974), 22. For estimates of turnover see LSE: Committee for General Purposes, Minutes, 14 July 1924 and F. Paukert, 'The Value of Stock Exchange Transactions in Non-Government Securities, 1911–1959', *Economica*, 28 (1962/3), 304. These suggest a considerable decline.
[25] LSE: Trustees and Managers, 20 Apr. 1915.
[26] LSE: General Purposes, 22 Jan. 1915, cf. 10 Nov. 1914.

Treasury rules on dealing for foreign clients and in foreign securities made it almost impossible for firms like Julius Stamm and Company and Leon Brothers to operate. Even when they attempted to develop a new market, such as in the internal loans being issued by Britain's allies, the French and Russian governments, the Treasury blocked their involvement as it could reduce demand for the UK's own war loan. One of the few areas left to them was the purchase in London and resale in New York of American securities. However, even that began to be lost from July 1915 onwards when the government itself started to requisition American securities held by British investors in a desperate search for dollars. Though the government's action initially generated activity in London it increasingly replaced established transatlantic links with its own mechanisms. It bought in London at prices cabled from Wall Street and then sold in New York through its own agents.[27]

As the war progressed the Treasury's restrictions and activities, along with the ban on arbitrage, gradually destroyed much of the Stock Exchange's international business. What remained faced increasing competition from non-members as the Chancellor of the Exchequer himself accepted, though he did claim in March 1916 that they also abided by a voluntary code

Although these rules only apply to members of the Stock Exchange, most financial houses have throughout voluntarily observed the restrictions . . .[28]

The outcome of all this was that those members of the London Stock Exchange who had established over the years an expertise in foreign securities and the connections necessary to facilitate it, saw it both fade and disintegrate during the course of the war. Many gave up the business or moved to New York.[29]

However, the destruction of the Stock Exchange's international business was not solely due to the actions of the Treasury, for much damage was caused by the growing hostility to Germans among the membership from May 1915 onwards. The sinking of the *Lusitania* at the beginning of that month resulted in a wave of anti-German hysteria on the floor of the Stock Exchange. On 8 May 1915 the Stock Exchange sent the following circular to all members of German and Austrian birth.

[27] K. Burk, *Morgan Grenfell, 1838–1988: The Biography of a Merchant Bank* (Oxford 1989), 128; C. Lewis, *America's Stake in International Investment* (Washington 1938), 117; LSE: General Purposes, 10 Nov. 1914, 11 Nov. 1914, 31 Dec. 1914, 4 Jan. 1915, 29 Jan. 1915, 8 Feb. 1915, 17 Feb. 1915, 22 Feb. 1915, 16 Mar. 1915, 29 Mar. 1915, 19 Apr. 1915, 3 May 1915, 16 June 1915, 20 Oct. 1915, 23 Nov. 1915, 6 Dec. 1915, 15 Dec. 1915, 20 Dec. 1915, 21 Dec. 1915, 10 Jan. 1916, 12 Jan. 1916, 6 Mar. 1916.
[28] Ibid., 3 Apr. 1916.
[29] Ibid., 23 Sept. 1914, 28 Feb. 1916, 5 Mar. 1916, 21 Mar. 1916, 14 Aug. 1916, 18 Dec. 1916, 26 Jan. 1917, 29 Jan. 1917, 27 Aug. 1917; Janes, *de Zoete and Gorton*, 55–6; D. Sebag-Montefiore, *The Story of Joseph Sebag & Co. and Its Founding Families* (privately printed 1996), 43.

Feeling in the Stock Exchange today has run so high that members of German or Austrian birth are advised to keep away from the House at present. Members employing clerks of German and Austrian birth are requested to convey this intimation to them.[30]

This worry about the physical safety of German and Austrian members and clerks was still evident in November, when they were warned, yet again, not to enter the Stock Exchange.[31]

Rather than dying away, this hostility to Germans, in particular, took root within the Stock Exchange, with calls to exclude permanently all those of enemy birth. One member, H. Frisby, wrote in December 1915 that

There was a very strong feeling that no one of German birth should return to the Stock Exchange unless he had given evidence of his loyalty by some special act of patriotism.[32]

The problem was that many of German and Austrian birth had outstanding liabilities to fellow members which did not have to be liquidated until one year after the end of the war. Realizing this wider problem the Stock Exchange resisted calls for their expulsion. However, any that turned up on the floor of the Stock Exchange were subjected to verbal and sometimes physical abuse by fellow members and this led them to transfer what business they still had away from the Stock Exchange. H. H. Struckmeyer, a skilled arbitrageur, resigned as a partner in Raphaels in 1915. Similarly, Michael Manasse of Singer Manasse, an important arbitrage firm before the war, was operating from New York by 1916. Eventually in March 1916 a meeting of members voted 408 for and 41 against, with 36 abstentions, to oppose the re-election of all those of enemy birth who had become members after 1895, and were not serving with the Imperial forces, or had sons serving there. As members had to be re-elected annually this provided a convenient way of excluding Germans and Austrians without formally expelling them. An estimated 113 members were affected by this resolution, comprising 103 of German birth, nine Austrian, and one Turkish. Though the Committee for General Purposes rejected the resolution, in the annual re-election, held that month, many with German names were deemed unacceptable. These included such prominent members as Nathan Cassel, Victor Koch, Alfred Marx, Maurice Oppenheim, Max Salomon, and Julius Stamm. On appeal some were readmitted, like Alfred Marx and Max Salomon, but most were not. The partners in Grumbar & See had successfully argued that, having been born in Lorraine and Alsace respectively, they were not really German. With these expulsions the Stock Exchange deprived itself of the very people who possessed the expertise and the contacts that had made the London Stock Exchange such a centre for the global

---

[30] LSE: General Purposes, 10 May 1915.     [31] Ibid., 2 Nov. 1915.
[32] Ibid., 8 Dec. 1915, cf. 15 Nov. 1915.

securities market. They would now operate in London, but outside the Stock Exchange, or from New York.[33]

The predicament of those individuals was put to the Stock Exchange by Nathan Cassel's solicitor when he appealed in July 1916 against his client's continued exclusion.

Largely owing to the war he has lost nearly all his capital and in fact his resources have been reduced to such an extent that he has been compelled to dispose of his car and works of Arts in order to provide for his living expenses during the war.[34]

Despite the plea, Nathan Cassel was not readmitted and the anti-German campaign grew in intensity. Those members of German origin, who had anglicized their names to escape persecution, were forced to include their former designation in all correspondence from July 1916 onwards. In the re-election of March 1917 more with German names continued to be rejected, including some who were in the forces, while appeals from those previously excluded were ignored.

Eventually, in February 1918 a rule was introduced that those born in Germany, Austria, Hungary, Bulgaria, and Turkey were not eligible for membership of the Stock Exchange, though some discretion was allowed the Committee. Other foreigners had to have lived in Britain for 10 years and be naturalized for five. As a result the likes of Julius Stamm, Ernest Friedlander, Carl Goldschmidt, and Jules Singer were all deemed unacceptable, despite requests to be readmitted. Even Alfred Marx was now ejected from the Stock Exchange despite his earlier success on appeal. This hostility to Germans, in particular, did not subside with the end of the war. In January 1919 a new rule was introduced that members were not even allowed to employ any person of enemy birth, as some ex-members had become clerks in order to survive. Similarly in the March 1919 re-elections the likes of Julius Stamm, Victor Koch, and Leo Hatry continued to be refused.[35]

Before the war the London Stock Exchange had prospered by attracting from abroad talented and well-connected people who could provide both the expertise and contacts necessary to further its international business. Many members of British birth resented the intrusion and success of these individuals, and this partly fuelled the unwillingness to grant concessions for arbitrage on the American market, but this resulted in little direct action. The largest single group among these foreigners was German and the war, and its course, converted this resentment into hatred and gave it official recognition. Most of those of German origin, including some of the major players in the Stock Exchange, were now excluded, and continued to be

---

[33] Ibid., 17 Jan. 1916, 26 Jan. 1916, 10 Feb. 1916, 10 Mar. 1916, 11 Mar. 1916, 15 Mar. 1916, 14 Aug. 1916; S. D. Chapman, *Raphael Bicentenary, 1787–1987*, (London 1987), 36.

[34] LSE: General Purposes, 17 July 1916.

[35] Ibid., 6 Nov. 1916, 6 Mar. 1917, 19 Mar. 1917, 8 Feb. 1918, 15 Mar. 1918, 14 Jan. 1919, 19 Mar. 1919.

even after the end of the war. Combined with the prohibition of arbitrage, the difficulties in maintaining any international links, and the sell-off of American securities, this amounted to a serious blow to the global role played by the members of the London Stock Exchange. At the same time, rival stock exchanges had not been idle with much trading in foreign securities being repatriated to national markets, like Montreal and Johannesburg, or seeking refuge in neutral centres like Amsterdam or Zurich. The New York Stock Exchange, bolstered by the repurchase of dollar securities and the arrival of expertise from London, now became a serious challenger in international markets.[36]

The First World War also encouraged a realignment of London's relationship with the other stock exchanges in the British Isles, though the result was much less severe than what happened internationally. Initially the war brought London and the provincial stock exchanges closer together as they tried to co-ordinate policy on the conditions necessary for reopening. Once achieved, this led to co-operation on increasing charges towards the end of 1915, as costs rose but business remained depressed. Edgar Crammond, representing the provincial stock exchanges, put the case for joint action at the beginning of November.

... the restrictions which have been imposed on the stock exchanges by the Treasury have not only caused a great reduction in the volume of business, but they have involved a mass of detailed work which has rendered the cost of conducting the reduced amount of business now passing extremely onerous. ... the increase in the cost of public services, such as telephones and the telegraphs, and the advance of the Income Tax, afford further justification for a substantial increase in the charges made by stockbrokers for their services to the Public.[37]

The London Stock Exchange responded positively to these provincial overtures, being willing to agree to national minimum rates of commission. At this stage the aim was to create a national scale in which no stockbroker undercut another and so eliminate price competition between stock exchanges in their quest for the custom of investors. However, despite this intention, it proved difficult to agree the details. The provincial stock exchanges were reluctant to include as equal members in any national scale those 600 or so stockbrokers who were not members of any stock exchange. They saw them as potential competitors while London regarded them as vital sources of business, feeding in the orders of country clients. Nevertheless, by June 1916, agreement had been reached on a national scale, with

[36] C. P. Kindleberger, 'The Formation of Financial Centers', in C. P. Kindleberger, *Economic Response: Comparative Studies in Trade, Finance and Growth* (Cambridge, Mass. 1978), 103; M. Hart, J. Jonker, and J. L. Van Zanden, *A Financial History of the Netherlands* (Cambridge 1997), 141–2; C. Armstrong, *Blue Skies and Boiler Rooms: Buying and Selling Securities in Canada, 1870–1940* (Toronto 1997), 73–82; C. R. Geisst, *Wall Street: A History* (Oxford 1997), 147–52.

[37] LSE: General Purposes, 2 Nov. 1915, cf. 23 Nov. 1914.

preferential terms being denied to those brokers who resided within 5 miles of a stock exchange but were not members of it. This would exclude, for London, the members of the Mincing Lane Tea and Rubber Brokers Association. In addition, brokers who advertised were not to be given preferential rates.[38]

One major stumbling block still remained—and that was the London Stock Exchange's custom of sharing commission with recognized agents, especially bankers, solicitors, and accountants. The provincial stock exchanges wanted London to abandon this practice so that all investors would deal directly with a stockbroker. Any other intermediary would have to add their charge on top of commission, making their services expensive. The London Stock Exchange was reluctant to do this as the half-commission paid to agents was an important device in attracting business to its market. Without a branch network or the use of advertising it was impossible for London brokers to maintain contact with the investing public, especially outside London. Naturally the members of the provincial stock exchanges saw themselves as the sole channel through which investor business would flow to London, whereas the members of the London Stock Exchange wanted to maintain their existing widespread and diverse contacts. Here was a fundamental divide on how each stock exchange perceived the functions it performed. The London Stock Exchange saw the provincial exchanges simply as markets for a restricted range of local securities while London was the market for all stocks and shares that commanded national, and international, attention. Within this the geographical residence of the investor was irrelevant. In contrast, the provincial stock exchanges saw themselves meeting the needs of those investors who resided within their catchment area by either completing deals locally or passing orders to London. Within that role was the market they provided for local securities as these were of greatest interest to local investors.[39]

Despite discussions during 1916 and 1917, no agreement could be reached that would resolve this fundamental difference. London regarded all investors as its legitimate constituency while each provincial stock exchange wanted exclusive contact with those in its own locality. Before the introduction of minimum commission charges in 1912, London brokers were left to make what arrangement they liked with clients and agents, depending upon the nature and amount of business generated. Thus a provincial broker channelling a great many orders to London could obtain low rates of commission, leaving considerable scope for profit when clients were charged on the official scale imposed by his own local exchange. However, in London's own official scale members of the provincial stock

[38] Ibid., 3 Aug. 1915, 22 Nov. 1915, 22 Feb. 1916, 1 June 1916, 20 July 1916; LSE: Subcommittee on Commissions, 8 Feb. 1916, 14 Apr. 1916.

[39] LSE: General Purposes, 4 Sept. 1916, 2 Oct. 1916, 8 Dec. 1916, 23 July 1917, 31 Oct. 1917, 12 Nov. 1917, 27 Dec. 1917.

exchanges were placed in the same category as other agents, like bankers and solicitors, and offered the same discount of half-commission rates. This made it more difficult for provincial brokers to compete with other intermediaries in their area when orders had to be sent to London for completion. Even before the war there had been a sustained attack, inside and outside the Stock Exchange, on the effects these commission charges were having on the relationship between London and provincial brokers.

With the outbreak of war demands for revision and relaxation fell into abeyance, but the general discussion of a national minimum scale brought them to the fore again. The June 1916 agreement between London and the provincial stock exchanges had included a concession that, it was hoped, would resolve the problem. Whereas provincial brokers would be entitled to a rebate of half the commission charged, other agents would only receive one-third. It was hoped that this would satisfy the provincial brokers while leaving London with its widespread web of contacts. Though the provincial stock exchanges did reluctantly agree, the banks, as the other principal agents, did not. When consulted they refused to accept any reduction in the rebate and then proceeded to mobilize resistance to change within the Stock Exchange itself. With bank amalgamation a growing proportion of the orders they collected from clients was being channelled through fewer, but larger, brokers who, in turn, used fewer but larger jobbers. Thus while many of the smaller brokers, doing a largely private client business, were happy to support the reduction or elimination of rebates, aided by the small jobbers, the largest brokers and jobbers were not. Thus brokers like James Capel & Co. and jobbers such as Wedd Jefferson, being among the largest, put pressure on the Stock Exchange to leave commission rates and rebates alone. By October they had been successful and it was decided to leave the rebate unaltered. The unstated threat that the banks might try to bypass the Stock Exchange by establishing their own market mechanism was more powerful than any possible advantages that might come from greater co-operation with the provincial stock exchanges.[40]

Though any arrangement with the provincial stock exchanges was now ended, agitation for a general increase in commission charges and a reduction in rebates continued, in the face of increasing costs and depressed activity. This was led by the smaller brokers who wanted to pass on their increased costs to their clients but were worried that any action by any individual member would result in a loss of business, especially to the larger firms who could spread their costs better. By March 1917 the jobbers were sufficiently worried by the campaign to mount a counter-offensive, as they were worried that it would drive business away from the Stock Exchange. A total of 376 jobbers warned that,

[40] LSE: General Purposes, 13 July 1914, 1 June 1916, 14 Aug. 1916, 31 Aug. 1916, 2 Oct. 1916; LSE: Subcommittee on Commissions, 3 Feb. 1914, 5 May 1914, 15 Oct. 1915, 19 Oct. 1915, 27 Jan. 1916, 16 Aug. 1916; Whyte, The Stock Exchange, 75, 77.

It is unwise, at a time when business in the House is already seriously affected by the absence of members on public service, by the diminution of general business owing to the war, and by the restrictions placed upon free dealing by Government Regulations, to make proposals that must inevitably lead to the disturbance of existing relations between the Stock Exchange and other commercial interests in the country.[41]

At all costs the majority of jobbers and the larger brokers wanted to prevent any large increase in commission charges that would encourage banks and others to bypass the Stock Exchange entirely. The banks had already gained an enhanced position for themselves because they were better able to cope with the complicated paperwork that new regulations and increased taxation introduced. At the same time they were more in touch with the numerous small investors who were purchasing securities for the first time, encouraged by the government's need to tap savings at all levels for war finance. An increase in commission charges by brokers could result in more investors putting their sales and purchases through banks, and any reduction in the rebate to banks might encourage those institutions to co-operate in the creation of an alternative market. As it was a new schedule of commission rates was introduced in October 1917 but this involved very modest increases, mainly at the bottom end of the scale. The Stock Exchange was happy to leave the small investor to the banks, who could then aggregate it before passing it on to a broker.

However, this did not end the demands for further revision. Many brokers demanded that the rate of commission on UK government debt, which now dominated trading, be doubled from $\frac{1}{8}$ to $\frac{1}{4}$ per cent because of the costs of handling the large number of small deals. This was coupled by suggestions that the commission rate on foreign government stocks and bonds be raised because of the extra work involved in meeting government regulations. Private client brokers also continued to demand an end to the sharing of commission. This pressure finally paid off in October 1918, when a new scale of commission on UK debt was introduced, ranging from $\frac{1}{8}$ to $\frac{1}{4}$ per cent. The rate on foreign securities was also raised despite mounting worries about competition from abroad, especially Amsterdam. At the same time the threshold above which rebates would be paid was increased to £2,500. In future only large orders from agents would receive a discount so removing some of the competition from solicitors and accountants for the business of private investors.[42]

The consequence for the Stock Exchange was that it emerged from the war not only with its system of fixed commissions intact but also reinforced

[41] LSE: General Purposes, 15 Mar. 1917.

[42] Ibid., 13 Nov. 1916, 21 May 1917, 29 May 1917, 9 July 1917, 12 Sept. 1917, 10 Oct. 1917, 31 Oct. 1917, 12 Nov. 1917, 2 July 1918, 15 July 1918, 6 Aug. 1918, 7 Aug. 1918, 7 Oct. 1918; LSE: Subcommittee on Commissions, 1 June 1916, 26 July 1916, 28 July 1916, 20 June 1917, 24 July 1918.

through higher rates and fewer concessions. The rift with the members of the provincial stock exchanges had not been healed and may very well have been aggravated by the abortive discussions on a national minimum. At the same time the position of the banks in the securities market had been strengthened and they had been able to maintain their access to a discount on volume business. Internationally, the higher charges for transactions on foreign securities undermined London's competitive position, already weakened by government controls and the expulsion of German members. In the end the Stock Exchange had opted for a policy of trying to squeeze greater commission income out of what business there was, through raising the minimum commission rates, rather than increasing that business by permitting greater competition among the members. That might have led to larger firms with lower costs per transaction, more economical ways of operating, or greater co-operation with banks and others. It might even have led to advertising as one member, Charles Ensell, recommended in 1917 because

... it will bring us into touch with large and ever increasing sections of the public, who know nothing about the business of the Stock Exchange owing to its hedged-in and isolated position. Publicity is the only way of reaching them.[43]

This could have been accompanied by a guarantee scheme, as suggested by J. Galloway in the same year. That would give the small investors the confidence of trusting their business to a stockbroker, who was a member of the Stock Exchange. Both schemes aimed at addressing the increased competition that small brokers were experiencing from banks, but both were rejected as too risky and ambitious for the time.

Consequently, over the short period of the First World War, many of the strengths possessed by the London Stock Exchange were reduced, negated, or reversed. Freedom of entry for foreigners, especially Germans, was considerably circumscribed while military demands resulted in a serious loss of staff and expertise plus a hiatus in training. Flexibility in terms of regulations was greatly lessened for the experience of the war encouraged a much more interventionist and restrictive attitude. Charges were increased with much of the discretion and many of the loopholes being closed. Relationships with members of other stock exchanges, both at home and abroad, had been damaged or lost. Finally, the very operation of the Stock Exchange had been transformed with the ending of account trading, options, and arbitrage, leaving much to be relearnt when the war ended. The inevitable result of all this was to alter the role played by the Stock Exchange in domestic and world money and capital markets, notwithstanding any changes that came with Britain's altered economic position due to the war.

---

[43] LSE: General Purposes, Subcommittee of a Non-Permanent Character, 13 June 1917, cf. 16 May 1917, 30 May 1917; LSE: Rules and Regulations, 5 Mar. 1917.

## MONEY AND CAPITAL

When the war broke out, despite attempts to reduce commitments, the members of the Stock Exchange still owed £60m. to banks and another £20m. to other financial institutions in London. Of this £80m. 17 per cent was without margin and 83 per cent with. In addition, at least a further £25m. was outstanding in open transactions between members, dependent upon payment or delivery at the end of the account, while banks had lent a further £250m. to customers with securities as collateral. This was at a time when uncertainty had acted to greatly depress such business. What this illustrated was the central role played by the Stock Exchange in the London money market. With the closure of the Stock Exchange, the moratorium on the debts, and the suspension of the open contracts, this constant ebb and flow of finance between the Stock Exchange and money market was frozen. As one member, R. L. Chapman, observed in October 1914, '. . . the Stock Exchange being closed, very few people come up to the City', while another member firm, Erskine, Neville and Company, complained in November that, 'The network of credit is destroyed . . .'[44]

Even when the Stock Exchange reopened in January 1915 it was unable to resume its position in the money market. There was the overhang of the unfinished pre-war account while the ending of account trading, options, and arbitrage removed much of the flexibility and liquidity that had allowed so much money to be employed in securities with relatively little risk. Nevertheless, lending to brokers and jobbers with securities as collateral did resume, with war loan and American securities being the most preferred. However, the whole money broking business, whereby particular members lent money borrowed from banks to fellow members on the floor, almost came to an end. Heseltine, Powell & Co., for example, gave it up for the duration of the war, though some 20 money brokers did try to stay in business, with Greenwell & Co., Sheppards & Co., de Zoete & Gorton, and Pember & Boyle being numbered among them.[45] The problem they faced was the vast expansion of the Treasury's own short-term borrowing. The government's unfunded debt rose from a mere £31.5m. in 1913 to £7,096.7m. in 1919, mostly in the form of short-dated securities, and this greatly reduced interest in the long-term debt traded on the Stock Exchange. As Pember & Boyle explained in September 1918, with regard to the discount houses,

[44] LSE: General Purposes: 26 Oct. 1914, 16 Nov. 1914, cf. Withers, *War and Lombard Street*, 18, 24, 48, 77, 120–1.

[45] P. G. Warren, *Heseltine, Powell and Company: One Hundred Years of Stockbroking, 1851–1951* (London, 1951), 24; Janes, *de Zoete and Gorton*, 55–6; LSE: General Purposes, 6 Mar. 1916, 11 Mar. 1916, 23 Nov. 1916, 29 May 1917, 4 Apr. 1918; LSE: Rules and Regulations, 22 Nov. 1915, 9 May 1918; LSE: Treasury Subcommittee, 29 Feb. 1916.

At a time when there was a scarcity of short-dated securities, coupled with an easy money market, the Discount Houses were tempted to carry consols and other Government stocks as a temporary employment of money but, with the present enormous creations of Exchequer and National War Bonds irredeemable or long-dated stocks are not likely to constitute any material part of their holdings.[46]

The result was that the Stock Exchange became much less central to the operation of the City of London's money market. Bank lending to members of the Stock Exchange, for example, shrank from c.11 per cent of deposits in 1913 to a mere 1.2 per cent in 1919.[47] The finance bill, which was an instrument usually created as a result of international transactions in securities, virtually disappeared from London. The banning of arbitrage, the absorption of available funds by government borrowing, and disapproval by the Bank of England and the Treasury made it virtually impossible for members of the Stock Exchange to participate in the international movement of money. Instead, what business there was fell into the hands of the major British joint-stock banks with their foreign agencies and correspondents.

Within London itself, the closure of the branches of the German banks had removed a major source of short-term funding from members of the Stock Exchange. The three London branches of the German banks—Deutsche, Dresdener, and Disconto—were holding securities worth £30.3m. on the eve of the war. Of these c.77 per cent belonged to German clients leaving 23 per cent (c.£7m.) for British clients, many of whom were brokers and jobbers depositing securities as collateral for loans. In 1914, H. Carlebach and Company, members of the Stock Exchange had borrowed from the Deutsche Bank to carry 4,766 shares in 10 different mining companies.[48]

Thus, on all fronts the London Stock Exchange's central role in the money market was all but destroyed during the duration of the First World War. Instead, its place was taken by governments and banks. The same process was taking place in the capital market. Inevitably, the priority during the war was to fund the government's sudden and vast demand for funds, in order to finance purchases and payments at home and abroad. Taxation levels were raised with the standard rate of income tax reaching 25 per cent at the end of the conflict compared to 6 per cent at the outset. This could only meet part of the requirement and so borrowing on a massive scale took place. The government's total indebtedness stood at £0.7bn. in

---

[46] LSE: Subcommittee on Commissions, 3 Sept. 1918, cf. Kirkaldy, *British Finance*, 155, 160, 162.

[47] G. A. Fletcher, *The Discount Houses in London* (London 1976), 253; B. R. Mitchell, *British Historical Statistics* (Cambridge 1988), 602–3; T. Balogh, *Studies in Financial Organization* (London 1946), 57–60.

[48] Enemy Banks (London Agencies): *Report of Sir William Plender*, 16 Dec. 1916, 22–5; *Financial News, The City 1884–1934* (London, 1934), 31; R. S. Sayers, *The Bank of England, 1891–1944* (Cambridge 1976), 275–8; LSE: General Purposes, 1 Feb. 1918.

1913 compared to £7.5bn. in 1919, or a more than tenfold increase. Also, by then £1.4bn. had been raised abroad, primarily in the United States.[49] Though patriotism, an attractive rate of interest, and the security of the state were powerful inducements for private and institutional investors to subscribe to each new issue, the Treasury also ensured that there was little competition in the market:

It appears to the Treasury that in the present crisis all other considerations must be subordinated to the paramount necessity of husbanding the financial resources of the country with a view to the successful prosecution of the war. Accordingly they wish it to be understood that until further notice they feel it imperative, in the national interest, that fresh issues of capital be approved by the Treasury before they are made.

Such were the instructions issued in January 1915. New issues by British companies could only be made if they were '... advisable in the national interest ...', which meant, essentially, the finance of war work. Issues by companies operating outside Britain, but within the Empire, would only be permitted if '... urgent necessity and special circumstances exist', which made it highly unlikely that they would be allowed. Issues by foreign governments and companies would, simply '... not be allowed'.[50] Faced with these draconian measures, implemented without consultation, the Stock Exchange sought a meeting with the government minister, Lord Reading. This took place on 2 February 1915 when it was made clear that

... the question of the advisability of new issues from the National point of view must rest with the Treasury and not with the Stock Exchange.[51]

For the rest of the war this remained the steadfast view of the Treasury as it sought to close every loophole through which funds drained away from UK government loans, especially abroad. Quite quickly members of the Stock Exchange were prevented from any form of participation in new foreign issues, such as an offer by the New York Central Railway of $10m. in bonds in February 1915. As early as December 1915 a number of members were worried about the long-term consequences of this for the London Stock Exchange, but the Treasury proved completely intransigent in the face of pleas for some relaxation in the rules.[52] Even subscription to the French and Russian loans was prevented as John Bradbury, from the Treasury, made clear to the Stock Exchange in March 1916,

Provision has been duly made where necessary for financial assistance to the Allies of this country in the present war by special agreements between His Majesty's

[49] Mitchell, *British Historical Statistics*, 602–3.
[50] LSE: General Purposes, 19 Jan. 1915.     [51] Ibid., 4 Feb. 1915.
[52] Ibid., 17 Feb. 1915, 22 Feb. 1915, 19 Apr. 1915, 16 June 1915, 23 Nov. 1915, 20 Dec. 1915, 10 Jan. 1916, 12 Jan. 1916, 7 Feb. 1916, 22 Feb. 1916, 6 Mar. 1916; LSE: Treasury Subcommittee, 16 July 1915.

Government and the Allied governments, and it is not desirable that these arrangements should be interfered with by private investments in the internal securities of those governments to an undefined and uncontrolled total.[53]

Thus it was impossible to extend the Stock Exchange's involvement in foreign securities during the war, with no new issues being granted a quotation. At the same time the stock of existing foreign securities was being substantially reduced in order to finance the government's foreign exchange requirement, especially for dollars. One estimate suggested that investors sold securities worth £850m. during and immediately after the war, with over two-thirds of these being dollar denominated. The result of all this was to greatly diminish the international dimension of the London Stock Exchange, replacing it only with the short-term debt of the UK government much of which was handled by the discount houses.[54]

In terms of the world economy, the wartime reduction of American securities held abroad, from $5.4bn. to $1.6bn. represented a major disaster for the world economy. As it was the most negotiable of these securities that were sold by the likes of Britain and Germany it removed, at a stroke, the most mobile assets within the international money markets. It was the continuous sale and purchase of these securities, and the credit and debt balances created as a result, that had ensured that economies remained in equilibrium in an era of fixed exchange rates. At the same time capital markets became much more nationally orientated. Whereas UK holders had holdings of $3.7bn. in US securities when the war began, American investors held only $0.8bn. in UK securities at its end.[55]

The London Stock Exchange thus emerged from the war a fundamentally different institution from what it was at the beginning. Apart from the internal changes that it made itself, or were forced upon it, the world within which it operated was now very different. The experience of working closely with the Treasury, Bank of England, and the major banks during the war led to a continuance of regulation and control into the post-war world. Once government intervention had taken place, exercising effective control over the Stock Exchange, it was inevitable that it would be used again in the difficult economic conditions that followed any war. At the same time the role played by the Stock Exchange within the money and capital markets

[53] LSE: General Purposes, 21 Mar. 1916.

[54] Lewis, *America's Stake in International Investment*, 117, 544; P. L. Cottrell, 'Great Britain: The International Markets, 1918–1939', in G. D. Feldman, U. Olssen, M. Bordo, and Y. Cassis (eds.), *The Evolution of International Financial Institutions in the Twentieth Century* (Milan 1994), 38; Royal Institute of International Affairs, *The Problem of International Investment* (Oxford 1937), 6, 65, 130, 155–6, 166–7; R. M. Kindersley, 'A New study of British Foreign Investments' *E. J.* 153 (1929), 9; Kirkaldy, *British Finance*, 175, 184, 196.

[55] Meeker, *Work of the Stock Exchange*, 516; C. H. Feinstein, P. Tenin, and G. Toniolo, 'International Economic Organisation: Banking, Finance and Trade in Europe between the Wars', in C. H. Feinstein (ed.), *Banking, Currency and Finance in Europe between the Wars* (Oxford 1995), 14; Kirkaldy, *Credit, Industry and the War*, 246; Withers, *War and Lombard Street*, 50, 85.

at home and abroad had been severely diminished.[56] In terms of the money market, domestic conditions were once again supreme, while for the capital market UK government debt now dominated as it had before 1850. Between 1913 and 1920 the nominal value of the National Debt quoted on the London Stock Exchange rose by £5.4bn. or from 9 per cent of all quoted securities in 1913 to 33 per cent. With foreign securities still quoted that had been liquidated during the war, the importance of UK government debt was even greater than those figures suggest.[57]

Faced with the enhanced position of international rivals like New York and Amsterdam, and the continuing competition of the provincial stock exchanges, along with the greater role of banks and other non-members in the buying and selling of securities, there was no guarantee that the London Stock Exchange was in a position to recover its pre-war position in the domestic and global securities market. There was also no guarantee that the conditions which had allowed the London Stock Exchange to acquire such a central position in the world's money and capital markets would ever reappear as alternative monetary and financial systems were put in place. Whatever else had happened during the four years of war their effects had been to greatly change the conditions within which the London Stock Exchange operated.

[56] A. Cairncross, 'The Bank of England: Relationships with the Government, the Civil Service, and Parliament', in G. Toniolo (ed.), *Central Banks' Independence in Historical Perspective* (Berlin 1988), 43, 46; M. Collins, *Money and Banking in the UK: A History* (London 1988), 212; D. Kynaston, 'The Bank of England and the Government', in R. Roberts and D. Kynaston (eds.), *The Bank of England: Money, Power and Influence, 1694–1994* (Oxford 1995), 25.

[57] Stock Exchange Official Intelligence, 1913 and 1921.

# 5

# *Challenges and Opportunities,*
## *1919–1939*

### LEGACY OF WAR

Though the Stock Exchange had begun to review its rules and regulations from September 1916 onwards, there was very little planning to meet the problems and competition likely to be faced in the post-war world. Despite all the changes inside and outside the Stock Exchange, that had taken place since August 1914, there was only a limited recognition that these had more than temporary consequences. One retired broker, J. Coles, probably spoke for most, when he observed in April 1916,

I do not suppose anybody thinks the centre of finance will ever go away from London and I believe the prosperity of the Stock Exchange will increase with a rush when peace comes. I most certainly believe in the future and look forward to the future of the Stock Exchange with a great deal of confidence.[1]

Even this war was expected to come to an end, and with it the circumstances that had done so much to undermine the traditional strengths of the Stock Exchange. After a century during which the London Stock Exchange had grown from strength to strength, both domestically and internationally, it was difficult to believe that a few years of war could make much difference.

Nevertheless, the occasional member with time to reflect did experience some unease about the future. One such was J. Underhill. While on military service at the front he wrote to Colonel Satterthwaite in February 1916 expressing his concern.

Conflicting stories reach us as to the attitude of the people in England. As far as I can judge there appears to be depression about the war but optimism about the financial condition. Out here it is the reverse, we all feel optimistic about the war but pessimistic about the cost of it all.[2]

---

[1] LSE: Trustees and Managers, 18 Apr. 1916.
[2] J. Underhill to Colonel Satterthwaite, 8 Feb. 1916 in LSE: General Purposes, Selected Appendices.

Those closest to the events, whether it was the war or the Stock Exchange, appeared least able to perceive future difficulties. In Underhill's case the end of the war was over two years away, in November 1918!

By the middle of 1917 there was a growing awareness on the Stock Exchange that the war had affected its standing at home and abroad, and efforts would have to be made to remedy that once the conflict was over. In a memorandum to the Chancellor of the Exchequer, in February 1917, the Stock Exchange made it clear that action would have to be taken if it was '. . . to maintain its position as the leading market for securities in the world'. However, the nature of this action was a plea for an end to government intervention and control, not a desire for assistance in any way. '. . . the freedom of markets in securities should not be impaired and that London should remain as heretofore a clearing house for transactions in such securities', was the most the Stock Exchange requested, believing that if left to their own devices they would be able to recover their previous position.[3] A few rules and regulations were to be tightened up and certain abuses more rigorously policed but nothing fundamental was required.

Certainly it was by no means inevitable that the damage inflicted on the Stock Exchange by the war was permanent. Members and staff would flow back from military duty or war work, Treasury controls would be relaxed, and normal methods of trading would be restored. In addition, there would remain a vast increase in the British government's indebtedness that would have to be funded in some permanent form. That would require and sustain an active secondary market. Corporate issues, suspended during the war, would resume as British businesses sought capital to re-equip and expand and, again, this would generate much subsequent buying and selling. Internationally, traditional borrowers would return to the London market, as both governments and corporations made good the financial shortages of the war years, while new countries would seek to raise large loans in order to fund reconstruction projects or service reparation payments. Obviously, the financial world within which the London Stock Exchange operated would be different, with the most marked change being the greatly enhanced status of New York, while taxation and asset disposals reduced the financial power of the British investor. However, out of this combination of opportunities and challenges it was up to the London Stock Exchange as an institution, and its members as independent operators, to maximize the gains and minimize the losses. Success in the past had only been achieved through the Stock Exchange responding to ever-changing circumstances. What was now required was a similar degree of flexibility and innovation that would both preserve the integrity of the regulated market and position it to profit from the new situation. Whatever else had happened the fundamental need for a securities market remained.

[3] LSE: General Purposes, 28 Feb. 1917.

Despite the massive sell-off of foreign securities during the war British holdings of transferable debt had increased enormously. The principle cause of this was the great growth of UK government borrowing in order to finance the war effort. Whereas the British government entered the war with debts of c.£0.7bn., it finished it with c.£7.5bn., of which over £6bn. had come from British savers. Much of this was in the form of short-term borrowing, like Treasury Bills, which were redeemed and renewed rather than traded on the Stock Exchange. Nevertheless much was in longer-dated stocks, whose ownership was transferred in the market. Altogether, while in the five years before the war (1910–13) some £1.1bn. was raised in London through new issues, or £210m. per annum, the figure for the war years (1914–18) was £4.5bn. or £900m. per annum. The years immediately after the war witnessed the creation of even more transferable debt as, firstly, governments and then businesses sought to tap the capital market in order to fund past expenditure or future plans. The year 1919 alone saw new issues totalling £1.0bn. while the total for the 1920s (1920–9) as a whole was £3.2bn., or some 50 per cent greater than the pre-war annual average. Even the economically depressed 1930s (1930–9) experienced a further £1.6bn. in new issues. Overall, the war and inter-war years added around £10.3bn. in new securities to the steady accumulation of the past, which more than outweighed the losses, sales, redemptions, and defaults of those troubled times.

The result of this was that the proportion of UK national wealth held in the form of transferable debt, which had already reached 41 per cent in 1912/13, rose even higher to 47 per cent in 1927/9, before falling back slightly during the 1930s, dropping to 44 per cent by 1937/9. This had been, and remained, a much higher level than in other major economies, such as France, Germany, or the United States, reflecting Britain's more advanced stage of financial sophistication. However, as a proportion of all domestic financial assets the First World War marked something of a watershed in Britain's financial history. Before 1914 holdings of securities were rising not only absolutely but as a proportion of all financial assets, especially bank deposits. Subsequently, though the absolute value of securities continued to rise, it did so much more slowly than deposits with banks and building societies or investments with insurance companies and other financial institutions. In 1913 73 per cent of financial assets were in the form of securities but only 62 per cent in 1929 and 51 per cent in 1939. The main cause of this change was a switch from foreign to home investment as overseas holdings were mainly in the form of securities while domestic assets involved mortgages for house purchase and bank lending to fund car ownership. Nevertheless, the UK's proportion of domestic financial assets in the form of securities remained among the highest of any major developed economy. Prior to the Second World War there was to be no sustained move, absolute or relative, away from transferable securities, towards more tangible assets, and this implied a continued need for the Stock Exchange to fulfill its traditional function as a securities market.

Lying behind the continued importance of transferable debt as a home for savings was a substantial shift in its composition. Before the war the London capital market was heavily international in its orientation, with 71 per cent of the capital raised between 1910 and 1913 being for overseas borrowers. This ceased with the war itself when access to the market was denied to all but the British government. After the end of the war this position was only gradually relaxed. Consequently, even in the 1920s only around one-third of the new issues made in London where on behalf of foreign borrowers, and this fell to one-quarter in the 1930s, or a complete reversal of the pre-war position. Instead of London many issues of foreign securities were now being made in New York where American investors proved receptive subscribers. As a result the proportion of Britain's national wealth held in the form of foreign securities shrunk from c.18 per cent in 1912/13 to 11 per cent in 1937/9. In contrast, domestic stocks and shares rose from 23 per cent in 1912/13 to 36 per cent in 1927/9, at which it remained in the 1930s. The challenge for the London Stock Exchange was to both reorientate towards domestic issues and to face up to the competition coming from New York in foreign issues that London had once dominated.

A shift was also taking place in the type of securities that investors held. Before the war the trend had been away from government debt, especially that of the British government, and towards corporate securities, particularly those of railways. Inevitably the needs of war reversed this. In 1912/13 only 5 per cent of national wealth was in the form of domestic public debt contrasted to 18 per cent in domestic corporate debt. By 1927/9 the proportions were identical—18 per cent—despite the revival of corporate issues in the 1920s. The 1930s saw little change in this picture with domestic public debt only falling back to 17 per cent with corporate debt rising to 20 per cent in 1937/9. It would take a long time before the massive government borrowing of the First World War worked its way through the financial system. As the National Debt was the very security whose trading the London Stock Exchange had dominated before the First World War, its great increase had positive implications for that institution if it could remain unchallenged. Similarly, from the late nineteenth century onwards London had begun to provide a market for British industrial and commercial issues, even though the companies concerned were largely based in the North or Scotland. As these companies grew in size and scope between the wars, and sought finance through the issue of shares, the London Stock Exchange offered the obvious central market for their securities. Thus, the shift towards UK government debt and then domestic corporate issues, over the 1914–39 period, played to the London Stock Exchange's strengths for they all required a national rather than a provincial market. Though the loss of foreign government and railroad securities was a blow to the London Stock Exchange the vast increase in the National Debt and the stocks and shares belonging to large national companies should have more than compensated. Certainly the nominal value of securities quoted on the London Stock Exchange rose from £11.3bn. in 1913 to £16.6bn. in 1920 and then to £18.5bn. in 1933. It then fell back slightly in the 1930s, falling to £18.0bn. in 1939, as domestic new issues failed to compensate for the de-listing of inactive foreign securities. Even so, the value of securities in which trading could take place was 60 per cent greater in 1939 than in 1913. (Table 5.1.)[4]

Not only was the size of transferable debt expanding, with much in a form ideal for trading on the London Stock Exchange, but the size of the investing public had also been greatly increased. Spurred on by patriotism and the government's voracious need for funds, a large proportion of the British people became investors for the first time as they bought War Bonds. One contemporary, Comyns Carr, writing in 1918 estimated that the number of investors now stood at 13m., or a quarter of the British population, compared to a mere 1m. on the outbreak of war. 'We have seen during the war a remarkably widespread diffusion of money, and a wonderful growth in the habit of investment, among classes of the population to whom both are a novelty', was his observation, but his plea for greater scrutiny of new issues because of this vast increase in inexperienced investors went unheeded.

After the war it may be expected that a large number of people who never were investors before will be willing to entrust their savings to commercial companies, but will not be very well equipped to select those which are worthy of their confidence. Simultaneously there will be a large crop of new schemes appealing for public support, mostly bonâ fide, but offering unique opportunity to the fraudulent and over sanguine. In my opinion it would be a disaster if by such means the money of the new class of investors were to be lost, and they were ultimately to be frightened away.[5]

Though the holdings of most of these new investors were small, and confined to War Bonds, they did represent an enormous potential market for the members of the Stock Exchange. The question was whether they

[4] B. R. Mitchell, *British Historical Statistics* (Cambridge 1988), 602–3, 685; J. M. Atkin, *British Overseas Investment, 1918–31* (New York 1977), 61; R. W. Goldsmith, *Comparative National Balance Sheets: A Study of Twenty Countries, 1688–1978* (Chicago 1985), 216–32; R. Roberts, *Schroders: Merchants and Bankers,* (London 1992), 230; C. Lewis, *America's State in International Investments* (Washington 1938), 454; F. W. Hirst, *The Stock Exchange: A Short Study of Investment and Speculation* (London 1948, 4th edn.), 178; F. W. Paish, *Business Finance* (London 1961, 2nd edn.), 134.

[5] Company Law Amendment Committee: Report (1918) (Cd. 9138), Minority Report, 13–14, cf. A. W. Kirkaldy (ed.), *British Finance During And After The War, 1914–21* (London 1921), 137.

Table 5.1. Nominal values of securities quoted in the Stock Exchange Official List, 1913–1939 (£m.)

| Class of security | 1913 | 1920 | 1933 | 1939 |
|---|---|---|---|---|
| British government | 1,013.0 | 5,418.2 | 6,526.1 | 6,922.5 |
| UK public bodies | 277.1 | 335.0 | 466.0 | 934.4 |
| TOTAL | 1,290.1 | 5,753.2 | 6,992.1 | 7,856.9 |
| Colonial governments | 401.4 | 541.0 | 908.1 | 859.9 |
| Foreign governments* | 3,133.9 | 2,394.2 | 2,868.5 | 2,197.7 |
| Colonial/Foreign public bodies | 156.5 | 159.5 | 187.3 | 161.3 |
| TOTAL | 3,691.8 | 3,094.7 | 3,963.9 | 3,218.9 |
| UK railways | 1,217.3 | 1,259.5 | 1,125.4 | 1,140.3 |
| Indian railways | 150.6 | 159.5 | 138.3 | 136.5 |
| Imperial railways | 313.4 | 323.3 | 263.3 | 314.7 |
| American railways | 1,729.6 | 2,534.7 | 1,418.9 | 865.4 |
| Foreign railways | 736.1 | 870.9 | 845.3 | 637.3 |
| TOTAL | 4,147.0 | 5,147.9 | 3,791.2 | 3,094.2 |
| Banks and discount houses | 294.4 | 392.0 | 232.5 | 195.0 |
| Financial, land, and investment | 248.7 | 255.8 | 418.5 | 487.9 |
| Insurance | 66.4 | 67.2 | 32.6 | 36.3 |
| TOTAL | 609.4 | 715.0 | 683.6 | 719.2 |
| Canals and docks | 19.9 | 14.8 | 31.8 | 30.7 |
| Gas | 75.4 | 70.6 | 96.6 | 126.4 |
| Electric light/power | 74.2 | 105.8 | 189.1 | 218.5 |
| Telegraph and telephone | 141.1 | 146.0 | 447.2 | 441.4 |
| Tramways and omnibus | 117.5 | 119.7 | 79.0 | 59.6 |
| Waterworks | 7.2 | 8.8 | 25.6 | 28.5 |
| TOTAL | 435.3 | 465.7 | 869.3 | 905.1 |
| Commercial/Industrial | 438.6 | 669.2 | 1,215.7 | 1,279.5 |
| Breweries/Distilleries | 103.8 | 120.8 | 188.0 | 215.0 |
| Iron, coal, and steel | 329.8 | 413.1 | 370.0 | 306.2 |
| Shipping | 45.8 | 66.8 | 101.1 | 73.6 |
| TOTAL | 918.0 | 1,269.9 | 1,874.8 | 1,874.3 |
| Mines | 60.3 | 61.4 | 76.1 | 76.2 |
| Nitrate | 7.5 | 6.5 | 17.8 | 9.1 |
| Oil | 23.6 | 79.6 | 148.3 | 162.3 |
| Tea, coffee, rubber | 25.0 | 32.3 | 69.1 | 60.0 |
| TOTAL | 116.4 | 129.8 | 311.3 | 307.6 |
| TOTAL | 11,208.0 | 16,626.2 | 18,476.2 | 17,976.1 |

* Including foreign government bonds payable abroad. (In 1920 £1,241.9m. were payable in London and £1,152.3m. were payable abroad.)

Sources: Stock Exchange Official Intelligence, 1913–1939.

would continue to take a permanent interest in securities, as a home for their savings, in the post-war years. This did appear to be the case for Hamilton Whyte, writing in 1924, estimated that there were 17 million holders of British government securities by March 1923 and that many of these had become keen investors for he was of the opinion that,

The effects of the war have been to enlarge the interest of the public in the movements of the prices of stocks and shares, and many of the smaller sums which previously lay dormant in current accounts, or we were allowed to remain on deposit or in savings banks accounts are now finding their way into stocks and shares.[6]

Not only did there continue to be numerous individual holdings of War Loan but British industrial and financial companies also acquired a large following among the investing public. With many of these companies firmly entrenched in the domestic market, and dominating particular branches of the economy, they offered some immunity from the problems of the world economy that affected both foreign government bonds and British companies operating overseas, like Argentinian railways or Far Eastern rubber plantations. In 1926 seven of the largest British companies (Imperial Tobacco, Courtaulds—textiles, Anglo-Persian Oil (BP), Brunner-Mond-Chemicals, Vickers—engineering, Dunlop Rubber—tyres, and Cunard Steamship) were owned by a collective total of 385,500 shareholders with a paid-up capital of £120m. The average holding was only £311 and 85 per cent of the shareholders owned £500 or less of the stock. By the mid-1930s the number of shareholders in five of the largest companies totalled 381,510 suggesting a continuance of interest among the investing public. Imperial Chemical Industries boasted 124,690 shareholders, while Imperial Tobacco had 94,690, Courtaulds 59,940, Dunlop Rubber 52,620, and J. & P. Coats (cotton thread) 49,570. Similarly, the top five domestic banks that had been formed at the end of the war also attracted investor support with around 400,000 shareholders by the late 1930s. Clearly the war did leave as a legacy a greatly expanded investing public, many of whom moved from holding only government debt to other forms of securities. However, in order to tap these new investors the members of the London Stock Exchange would have to change. Before the war brokers were used to dealing with a relatively small number of wealthy and informed investors whereas the post-war situation involved a greatly expanded number of investors of more modest means and with little personal knowledge of the securities that they held.[7]

---

[6] W. Hamilton Whyte, *The Stock Exchange: Its Constitution And The Effects of the Great War* (London 1924), 71.

[7] H. Wincott, *The Stock Exchange* (London 1946), 42; B. Ellinger, *The City: The London Financial Markets,* (London 1940), 121; Atkin, *British Overseas Investment,* 110–23; J. Foreman-Peck, 'Industry And Industrial Organisation in the Inter-war Years', in R. Floud and D. McCloskey (eds.), *The Economic History of Britain Since 1700* (Cambridge 1984, 2nd end.), ii. 196.

To that end this new investing public required more advice from stock-brokers but generated less business as their individual holdings were smaller. Nevertheless, they did offer some compensation for the loss of foreign investors due to London's diminished international role. The restrictions on trading in overseas securities, combined with the loss of German nationals as members, had removed many foreign investors who had traditionally bought and sold through the London Stock Exchange. In particular, the wholesale repatriation of American railroad securities, for which London had been the principal European market, meant that even those brokers who still retained foreign clients had much less business to transact for them.[8] Nevertheless, even here there was some compensation because foreign, especially European, investors were attracted to British War Loan because of the stability it offered in comparison to that of their own countries. As the Stock Exchange itself observed in 1919:

...the investor abroad has ever regarded Great Britain as politically more secure and less liable to upheaval than many foreign countries and ...this has prompted him to deposit securities in this country ...the financial stability of Great Britain has also fostered a predisposition for foreigners to invest their money in British securities. The British Government War Loans have been largely subscribed for by foreigners.[9]

It was not only the safety guaranteed by British government debt that attracted foreign investors for the changed financial circumstances of Britain relative to other countries made other domestic securities attractive. In particular the war had meant great prosperity for the United States, as well as neutral nations such as the Netherlands, with the result that their populations had substantial savings to invest. In the United States the number of investors rose from a pre-war maximum of 2m. to around 20m. by 1929. Naturally enough a number of these investors began to look overseas for investments with some being attracted to Britain.[10] The members of the Stock Exchange became aware of this soon after the war's end, as in this comment in 1919:

...in comparison with the rates of interest current abroad, the yield obtainable on British industrial securities (before the war) was too low to attract foreign buyers. Now conditions have materially altered we are informed by persons closely in touch with America and Holland that there are constant enquiries for English industrial investments. A representative of a well-known English financial house recently visited Switzerland, and he informs us that at nearly all of about eighty institutions

---

[8] A. S. J. Osborn, *The Stock Exchange: Its Method and Practice* (London 1927), 30–1.

[9] LSE: General Purposes, 30 June 1919, cf. Hirst, *Stock Exchange*, 202–3; Atkin, *British Overseas Investment*, 24–5, 29.

[10] J. E. Meeker, *The Work of the Stock Exchange* (New York 1930), 587; C. R. Geisst, *Visionary Capitalism: Financial Markets and the American Dream in the Twentieth Century* (New York 1990), 4; W. Lazonick and M. O'Sullivan, 'Finance and Industrial Development', *Financial History Review*, 4 (1997), 12.

he visited, he was told that their clients were enquiring for English industrial invest-ments—recent political events having frightened them in regard to Foreign Gov-ernment loans. And that many investors were also looking for a higher rate than could be obtained from Government Stocks. We also have reliable information that even in France with the present adverse conditions in exchange, there is a constant demand for good English industrial investments.[11]

Though a reversal of the pre-war position, where London brokers and jobbers helped channel the savings of European investors into American, Australian, Asian, and African securities, the attractions of British invest-ments for foreign investors did provide some compensation for the business that had been lost, providing that the members of the Stock Exchange could position themselves so as to conduct it.

Within Britain itself it was not just the size of the investing public that had been expanded, for it was also changing in nature. Increasingly insti-tutions were playing a growing intermediary role between the saver and the ultimate holding of securities. During the war, banks, insurance companies, and other financial institutions channelled a large part of their funds into the purchase of government debt. British life insurance companies had invested 51 per cent of their assets in securities by 1913 but 66 per cent by 1921, with the total rising from £280m. to £530m. Much of this now con-sisted of UK government debt, which had grown from 1 per cent of total investments in 1913 to 35 per cent in 1921. This made institutions such as these a far more important force in the securities market than ever before, and this continued into the inter-war years as they remained important investors in securities, especially corporate stocks and shares. By 1937 the insurance companies had holdings of £1.2bn. in securities, or 68 per cent of their total assets, and they had moved heavily into corporate debt.[12]

By the early 1930s these institutions had emerged as a major force within the British securities market, particularly the insurance companies, invest-ment trusts, and the newly formed unit trusts. Unit trusts only came into existence in Britain in 1931 but by 1940 there were around 100 in opera-tion with holdings of c.£82m. in securities. Though dwarfed by older financial institutions they reflected the growing institutionalization of investment that was taking place. As early as 1932 the *Financial News* had identified the growing importance of the institutional investor, with hold-ings of around £1.7bn. and responsible for an estimated one-fifth of Stock Exchange business. Nevertheless, the overwhelming bulk of securities con-tinued to be owned by private investors and they were responsible for some 80 per cent of activity on the Stock Exchange.[13] As the *Financial News* itself

---

[11] LSE: General Purposes, 30 June 1919.

[12] J. Johnson and G. W. Murphy, 'The Growth of Life Assurance in the UK Since 1880', *Manchester School of Economic and Social Studies*, 25 (1957), 155.

[13] *Financial News, The Stock Exchange: An Investor's Guide* (London 1933), 22; A. Gleeson, *People and their Money: 50 Years of Private Investment* (M & G Group 1981), 2; Atkin, *British Overseas Investment*, 110–11.

observed in 1932, 'Investors, on the whole, seem to prefer to have the fun of managing their investments themselves through their own stockbrokers rather than to entrust their savings to an insurance company, an investment trust or a building society.'[14]

Throughout this entire period the continuing revolution in communications technology was also extending and deepening the reach of the London Stock Exchange and its membership. During the war the military had been given priority in the use of both national and international telephone and telegraph circuits. This led to both considerable delays and inadequate capacity on what was available for members of the Stock Exchange. Even after the end of the war this situation continued for a number of years. In March 1919 delays of between 1 and 2½ hours on the London–Dublin route were being reported, with London–Glasgow communication being a problem until the end of 1920. Internationally, delays on the service to both Paris and Brussels also continued into 1920, with the Stock Exchange being given a much lower priority than military or government use. Generally it was only towards the end of 1921 that the members of the Stock Exchange were receiving the fast and reliable telephone and telegraph service that they expected. Though complaints were still made thereafter there was general satisfaction with the service now provided.[15] This was only to be expected for the quality and capacity of both domestic and international communications steadily improved at this time. Domestically the inter-war years saw the continued growth of the telephone system and its increasing refinement. The introduction of omnibus circuits in the 1920s created country-wide networks of brokers all linked into the same communications system. Thus no matter the location it was possible to communicate instantly with any other member of the network.

During the 1930s the introduction of telex provided a high speed and automatic teleprinter service, through which large amounts of information could be despatched by London brokers to offices all over the country.[16] Even by 1920 it had been noted by the Stock Exchange itself that 'It is now possible for anybody to get through to the House from any part of the kingdom and speak to a member.'[17] What subsequent improvements did were to greatly increase the speed, coverage, and sophistication of the communications available to every member, whether on the floor of the Stock Exchange or in their own offices.

The telephone quickly moved from being an important element in the

[14] *Financial News, The Stock Exchange*, 22.
[15] LSE: General Purposes, 28 Oct. 1918, 2 Dec. 1918, 17 Mar. 1919, 22 Apr. 1919, 30 June 1919, 22 Dec. 1919, 26 Jan. 1920, 9 Apr. 1920, 20 Dec. 1920, 23 May 1921, 2 Aug. 1921, 2 Nov. 1921, 26 Nov. 1928, 25 Mar. 1930.
[16] C. Cherry, *World Communication: Threat or Promise: A Socio-Technical Approach* (London 1971), 81.
[17] LSE: Subcommittee, Exchange Telegraph Company, 11 Feb. 1920.

stockbroker's business to becoming an indispensable one.[18] In response to a proposal by the Post Office to increase domestic telephone charges, 102 broking firms, led by Morison & Morison, lodged a strong complaint, indicating how serious the consequences would be.

It is of supreme importance to London as the great financial centre that it should be in constant communication with the provinces and the Continent. Thus communications is provided for either by the use of private lines, or by 'trunk calls', and the cost of these falls on individual firms, but the benefit resulting is shared by the public as a whole in the greatest fluidity of markets, and the immediate reflection of price changes. If the charges become prohibitive these services will cease to be rendered and business as a whole must suffer . . .[19]

Of course improved communications between London and major provincial centres was a two-edged weapon. The same facilities that allowed members of the London Stock Exchange to establish contact with clients and fellow brokers nation-wide, also allowed those very same people to communicate with each other directly. As the *Financial News* noted in 1933, 'The telephone has linked up markets so closely that the investor, no matter what broker he employs, can never be certain in what market his deal has been concluded.'[20] If the members of the London Stock Exchange did not offer their clients the service they required the telephone made it increasingly possible to contact brokers in other cities and use them to buy or sell as required. The telephone threatened both the London Stock Exchange's role as the central element within the domestic securities market and its monopoly of the business coming from London's own financial institutions and investors. Improving telecommunications allowed provincial centres not only to bypass London, dealing with each other, but also gave London investors direct access to members of other stock exchanges.[21]

Internationally, the inter-war years saw the continuance of the telecommunications revolution begun with the telegraph. Now it was focused more on the telephone and the wireless. When the telephone connection between London and Johannesburg was made in the early 1930s it replaced a delay of 10 minutes through the telegraph with constant and immediate contact. Small as this improvement was, compared to the 20 days that the mail took, it did lead to a great growth in business for now no time barrier existed.[22] As those doing an international business explained in 1921, time was of the essence and any delay, even of minutes, made it impossible to undertake the simultaneous buy/sell orders at acceptable levels of risk. 'One of

---

[18] LSE: Subcommittee, Exchange Telegraph Company, 27 Feb. 1923. LSE: Trustees and Managers, 16 Apr. 1926, 23 Apr. 1928.

[19] LSE: General Purposes, 10 Jan. 1921.       [20] *Financial News, The Stock Exchange*, 18.

[21] LSE: General Purposes, 26 June 1933, 11 Mar. 1933, 17 Apr. 1939; LSE: Subcommittee on Country Jobbing/Country Business, 4 Oct. 1934.

[22] LSE: General Purposes, 11 Dec. 1933, 3 May 1937; LSE: Rules and Regulations, 12 Nov. 1919; *Financial News, The Stock Exchange*, 16.

the main factors governing all arbitrage business, is rapidity of communication between centres concerned: this is essential.'[23] Even a 10-minute
delay greatly reduced the volume of business taking place between the two
markets whereas its elimination expanded it substantially. For that reason,
therefore, it was surprising that more use was not made of short-wave radio
communication, as this allowed voice contact over long distances. As early
as 1927 the radio-telephone was introduced on the North Atlantic route,
offering immediate communication compared to the 3-minutes or less via
the submarine cable. Though cost was a problem, with a 3-minute call
costing £15 in 1927, this did fall, being only £4. 4s in 1936, while cable
charges rose. Instead, the main difficulty with short-wave radio was its
limited capacity and its unreliability being subject to fading, blackouts, and
extensive interference. As such it was simply not possible to base a business requiring rapid, clear, and guaranteed contact, on the service it provided. Thus, for international stock exchange business Europe and later
South Africa was increasingly served by the telephone while for farther
afield, such as North America, Australia, and the Far East, the telegraph
remained dominant.[24]

Consequently, though the First World War was a highly disruptive time
for the Stock Exchange it did not represent a complete disaster. If the institution and its membership could reorientate themselves to meet the new
needs developing in terms of those both issuing and purchasing transferable securities, then it might not only recover its pre-war importance but
build upon it. However, to do this required both an effort to recapture business lost during the war, as from New York, and to develop in new directions. The world securities market had not stood still during the war and
both domestic and international financial systems had been greatly affected
as a result. The post-war years would involve a simultaneous move back
to the peacetime conditions that existed before 1914 and developments
based upon the transformations that had taken place, and which could not
be easily reversed. The massive sell-off of dollar securities, accumulated over
a century of investment, could not be replaced within a decade. The vast
increase in the number of people who had become acquainted with investment for the first time would not wither away. At the same time the continuing elimination of time and distance through telecommunications was
both exposing the London Stock Exchange to new competition and allowing it to serve an ever-widening community. As before 1914 the London
Stock Exchange possessed substantial assets in terms of size, expertise, and
connections that would allow it to take advantage of these new opportunities. Conversely, it also possessed the handicap of an established position
and accepted customs that might prevent it from adapting sufficiently to
profit from the new situation.

[23] LSE: General Purposes, 18 Apr. 1921.
[24] Cherry, *World Communication*, 82, 159; LSE: General Purposes, 27 Dec. 1933.

However, unlike the pre-war years there was one area that was largely beyond the control of the Stock Exchange to influence and that was government policy, whether at home or abroad. The war had witnessed an unprecedented increase in government intervention into the affairs of the Stock Exchange, and these controls were maintained in place when peace came. The Stock Exchange was too important an element within the money and capital markets to be left unsupervised in the difficult monetary and financial conditions that followed the end of the war. As H. Eustace Davis, of the Ministry of Reconstruction explained to the Stock Exchange in November 1918, the controls were to remain in force 'In order to prevent undesirable speculation during the Reconstruction period . . .'[25] The Stock Exchange accepted the maintenance of wartime controls partly out of a sense of patriotism and also because they were reluctant to antagonize the government and provoke stricter measures or other actions. In March 1919 they were worried that the railways were to be nationalized, so removing an important part of their market. As it was, from April 1919 onwards there was a gradual relaxation of controls.

Nevertheless, matters did not return to the pre-war position where the Stock Exchange was left entirely free to run its affairs as it saw fit, and its members to conduct whatever business they liked with whomsoever they chose. Behind the scenes the Treasury and the Bank of England, either singly or jointly, continued to exert an influence in the manner they had become accustomed to during the war. This was especially so in the early years after the war, the return to the gold standard in 1925, and its abandonment in 1931, and the approach to war in 1939. On all these occasions the Stock Exchange was asked to behave in a particular way, and in each case it responded accordingly.[26]

For most of the inter-war years, for example, the government tried to restrain investment abroad and sought the co-operation of the Stock Exchange and its membership in order to achieve that end. In May 1925 Montagu Norman, Governor of the Bank of England, wrote to the Stock Exchange,

It seems essential that for the present all moneys available for investment shall, as far a may be possible, be retained in this country for the purpose of reducing the strain on the Exchanges.

This was echoed in June 1933 when the Chancellor of the Exchequer, Neville Chamberlain, wrote to the Stock Exchange,

The large inflow into London during this year of short-term money from abroad may have obscured, but it certainly has not removed, the intrinsic weaknesses of

[25] LSE: General Purposes, 25 Nov. 1918.
[26] Ibid., 16 Dec. 1913, 17 Mar. 1919, 7 Apr. 1919, 4 May 1925, 5 Oct. 1931, 14 June 1933, 14 June 1937, 18 July 1938, 26 Apr. 1939; Royal Institute of International Affairs, *The Problems of International Investment* (Oxford 1937), 76–7, 79–81.

our position, and this country is not in my judgement at present in a position to invest large sums at long-term in foreign countries.[27]

Without the need for legislation or an official embargo the Stock Exchange was being used by the government to restrain purchases of overseas securities by British investors and to make itself less attractive to foreign issues of stocks and bonds.

As a result of these extensive contacts with the government and the Bank of England the Stock Exchange had come to regard itself as a national institution by the 1930s.

... although the Stock Exchange is by its constitution a private undertaking it has come to be an institution of national importance with heavy obligations to the public...

was its own view of itself in February 1937. It possessed the power to influence the investment habits of the nation

... by the withholding or withdrawing of permission to deal in securities which for one reason or another appear to be unfit for sale to the public ...[28]

Like the Bank of England, another privately owned financial institution acting increasingly in the public interest, the Stock Exchange had come to occupy a semi-official position as supervisor of the securities market.

This even led to consideration in 1937 of the question of having a full-time chairman and deputy chairman, paid by the Stock Exchange for the duties they performed. The custom was that those occupying these positions continued in business as brokers or jobbers, merely chairing committees where the administrative duties were carried out by paid officials. However, in the inter-war years the work and responsibility attached to being chairman and deputy chairman had increased enormously, especially as the government used the Stock Exchange to control the securities market. Despite the acceptance that the positions did demand a great deal of time it was decided not to pay either the chairman or his deputy because this could lead to them losing touch with the work of the market. Clearly the membership still saw the function of the Stock Exchange as administering the securities market in the interests of its members, not implementing the policies of the government.[29]

The Stock Exchange appeared to receive few, if any, privileges in return for its co-operation with the government and the Bank of England. While the members of the Stock Exchange could be persuaded to follow

---

[27] LSE: General Purposes, 4 May 1925, 14 June 1933; see Atkin, *British Overseas Investment*, 29, 31, 41, 49, 56; A. Cairncross, 'The Bank of England and the British Economy', in R. Roberts and D. Kynaston (eds.), *The Bank of England: Money, Power, and Influence, 1694–1994* (Oxford 1995), 62–3; ibid., P. L. Cottrell, 'The Bank of England in its International Setting, 1918–1972', 94, 103; ibid., R. Roberts, 'The Bank of England and the City', 162.

[28] LSE: General Purposes, 1 Feb. 1937.      [29] Ibid., 6 Dec. 1937.

Table 5.2. Nominal values of securities quoted in the Stock Exchange Official List, 1913–1939 (%)

| Class of security | 1913 | 1920 | 1933 | 1939 |
|---|---|---|---|---|
| British government | 9.0 | 32.6 | 35.3 | 38.5 |
| UK public bodies | 2.5 | 2.0 | 2.5 | 5.2 |
| AS PERCENTAGE OF TOTAL | 11.5 | 34.6 | 37.8 | 43.7 |
| Colonial governments | 3.6 | 3.3 | 4.9 | 4.8 |
| Foreign governments* | 28.0 | 14.4 | 15.5 | 12.2 |
| Colonial/Foreign public bodies | 1.4 | 1.0 | 1.0 | 0.9 |
| AS PERCENTAGE OF TOTAL | 32.9 | 18.6 | 21.5 | 17.9 |
| UK railways | 10.9 | 7.6 | 6.1 | 6.3 |
| Indian railways | 1.3 | 1.0 | 0.7 | 0.8 |
| Imperial railways | 2.8 | 1.9 | 1.4 | 1.8 |
| American railways | 15.4 | 15.3 | 7.7 | 4.8 |
| Foreign railways | 6.6 | 5.2 | 4.6 | 3.5 |
| AS PERCENTAGE OF TOTAL | 37.0 | 31.0 | 20.5 | 17.2 |
| Banks and discount houses | 2.6 | 2.4 | 1.3 | 1.1 |
| Financial, land, and investment | 2.2 | 1.5 | 2.3 | 2.7 |
| Insurance | 0.6 | 0.4 | 0.2 | 0.2 |
| AS PERCENTAGE OF TOTAL | 5.4 | 4.3 | 3.7 | 4.0 |
| Canals and docks | 0.2 | 0.1 | 0.2 | 0.2 |
| Gas | 0.7 | 0.4 | 0.5 | 0.7 |
| Electric light/power | 0.7 | 0.6 | 1.0 | 1.2 |
| Telegraph and telephone | 1.3 | 0.9 | 2.4 | 2.5 |
| Tramways and omnibus | 1.0 | 0.7 | 0.4 | 0.3 |
| Waterworks | 0.1 | 0.1 | 0.1 | 0.2 |
| AS PERCENTAGE OF TOTAL | 3.9 | 2.8 | 4.7 | 5.0 |
| Commercial/Industrial | 3.9 | 4.0 | 6.6 | 7.1 |
| Breweries/Distilleries | 0.9 | 0.7 | 1.0 | 1.2 |
| Iron, coal, and steel | 2.9 | 2.5 | 2.0 | 1.7 |
| Shipping | 0.4 | 0.4 | 0.5 | 0.4 |
| AS PERCENTAGE OF TOTAL | 8.2 | 7.6 | 10.1 | 10.4 |
| Mines | 0.5 | 0.4 | 0.4 | 0.4 |
| Nitrate | 0.1 | — | 0.1 | 0.1 |
| Oil | 0.2 | 0.5 | 0.8 | 0.9 |
| Tea, coffee, rubber | 0.2 | 0.2 | 0.4 | 0.3 |
| AS PERCENTAGE OF TOTAL | 1.0 | 1.1 | 1.7 | 1.7 |

* Including foreign government bonds payable abroad. (In 1920 £1,241.9 m. were payable in London and £1,152.3 m. were payable abroad.)

*Sources*: As Table 5.1.

government guidelines, because of the control their own institution exercised, it was much more difficult to police non-members. Consequently, while the activities of members were restricted, especially in terms of international business, banks and non-member brokers were still able to take advantage of the opportunities that were available. Though the government and the Bank of England accepted that this was inequitable there was little they could do about it.[30] Where the government could have been more responsive was in the realm of taxation, which concerned the Stock Exchange throughout the inter-war years. In order to fund its massive wartime debts the government sought to tap all possible sources of funds. The maintenance of high rates of income tax, with the standard rate in 1919/22 at 30 per cent being five times the pre-war level, affected the Stock Exchange indirectly. It deprived large investors of the sums they had traditionally used to purchase securities, and so reduced their use of the Stock Exchange. Of more immediate consequence was stamp duty as it directly discouraged transfers. At a rate of 1 per cent in 1920 it encouraged foreigners to buy and sell in markets other than London especially when it was doubled in 1923.[31]

In the October of that year 109 member firms with strong international interests, such as Medwin & Lowy, L. Messel & Co., and J. Sebag & Co., spelled out the consequences for London of the tax imposed on transfers.

The London market provides facilities for free dealing in securities unequalled by those of any other centre in the world. It can afford the imposition of a certain tax on the securities in which it deals and still compete with others on favourable terms. But when such taxation is imposed beyond a certain point it defeats its own ends and business which formerly passed through London is diverted to other channels to the loss of the trading community and of the Exchequer alike. Our experience since the tax was raised from £1 per cent to £2 per cent has furnished many examples to support our contention.

They then went on to explain how the tax was hurting their business in two ways. First it was discouraging the issue of new foreign securities in London which would then be traded on the Stock Exchange on behalf of investors from home and abroad. As they said,

Competition among issuing countries is keen and in many cases the heavy stamp duty now in force has just turned the scale against London in favour of some other centre, particularly New York.

Secondly, sales and purchases of existing securities on behalf of foreign clients were bypassing London.

[30] LSE: General Purposes, 5 Oct. 1931.
[31] Ibid., 7 Apr. 1919, 23 June 1919, 10 Mar. 1920, 10 May 1920, 14 Apr. 1920, 21 Apr. 1920, 7 June 1920, 11 Aug. 1920, 30 Aug. 1920, 6 Sept. 1920, 19 Feb. 1923, 17 May 1923.

Many stocks of an international character, the business in which formerly passed from one centre via London to another, are now dealt in for direct delivery and therefore pass without the English Stamp.[32]

With pressure of this kind from its membership, and evidence that London was losing out in the international business, the Stock Exchange lobbied the Chancellor of the Exchequer, Winston Churchill, for at least a reduction in the level of stamp duty. However, their pleading was ignored. The only concession the Stock Exchange was given was in 1920. At that time jobbers, who bought and sold constantly, were allowed to replace stamp duty on every transaction with a nominal flat rate. Consequently, during the inter-war years the Stock Exchange suffered on two fronts. As it was perceived to represent the securities market the government implemented its policies through it, in the same way as the Bank of England was being transformed into an arm of the state. This had the result of subjecting the Stock Exchange's membership to a much greater degree of control than those who did not belong. In particular this had implications for the international role played by the membership of the Stock Exchange because this was an area that the government were keen to influence in the interests of monetary and exchange rate stability.[33] More generally the imposition of taxation, especially stamp duty, added an extra cost to transactions in London which domestic investors could not avoid but foreigners were in a position to do so. Thus, foreign investors tried to avoid routing transactions through London if they would incur stamp duty and, instead chose another centre, such as New York or Johannesburg. There was little the Stock Exchange could do about either of these impositions for there is little evidence that its opinions carried much weight in government circles, compared to the need to stabilize the pound or raise revenue. Exchange instability and exchange controls, for example, made international dealing both hazardous and difficult for most of the inter-war years but international monetary stability had become a function of government not the markets by then, and so there was little the Stock Exchange could do but accept the situation and operate the best it could within it.[34]

However, even before the Stock Exchange could reach the position of meeting the post-war challenges and grasping the new opportunities it had to make the transition from wartime controls to peacetime operation. Over the duration of the war so much of the normal operation of the Stock Exchange had been either suspended or curtailed, that it was not possible

---

[32] LSE: General Purposes, 29 Oct. 1923.

[33] Ibid., 14 July 1924, 5 Jan. 1925, 9 Mar. 1925, 27 Apr. 1937, 5 May 1937; LSE: Subcommittee, Non-Permanent, 29 Apr. 1924; Royal Institute of International Affairs, *Problem of International Investment*, 80.

[34] LSE: General Purposes 18 Apr. 1921; LSE: Subcommittee on Disputes and Buying In/Selling Out Cases, 22 Nov. 1939.

to revert to peacetime practice as soon as the Armistice was declared. For a start there was the suspended pre-war account to be settled, and that did not have to be completed until twelve months after the end of the war. Four years of wartime operation had also changed attitudes, ideas, and personnel, with much of the international/foreign dimension greatly reduced. Consequently, the transition from war to peace was itself fraught with difficulties and involved much more than a simple return to the conditions that had prevailed before August 1914. Even before the war there had been conflicting views in the Stock Exchange over such major issues as the size of the membership, the desirability of fixed commission rates, the distinction between broker and jobber, and the relationship between London and other stock exchanges. None of these issues had been resolved by the war, only suspended in many cases while a greater conflict was fought out. Undoubtedly they would emerge again once the war was over, with different groups using the opportunity to push the Stock Exchange in a direction of their choosing, rather than return to the uneasy balance that had previously existed.

The restricted conditions under which the Stock Exchange operated during the First World War were very different from the lightly regulated regime prevailing in the pre-war years. Some of the membership welcomed the change, relishing the reduced risks that cash trading created. Nevertheless, the expectation was that, in a somewhat modified form, pre-war practices would be restored as soon as practicable. However, this proved much more difficult to achieve than anyone envisaged. The first problem to be tackled, before trading for the account was to be resumed, was the completion of the pre-war settlement. There could be no restoration of buying and selling for future payment and delivery, until all members had made good their bargains. Under the system of fortnightly accounts trading between members on the floor of the Stock Exchange was based on a belief that purchases would be paid for and that securities sold would be delivered, when the due date arrived. This trust could not exist if members were permitted to default on their obligations, whatever the circumstances. As it was, the moratorium, under which the pre-war account had been suspended, gave members 12 months to complete deals once the war ended. However, even by November 1919, a full year since hostilities had finished, the pre-war account still remained unsettled, making it difficult for the Stock Exchange to reintroduce trading for the account.[35]

Nevertheless, by then unresolved bargains had been reduced to such a low level that the Stock Exchange was contemplating the reintroduction of dealing for the account. It now met the opposition of the government expressed through the Governor of the Bank of England. This continued

[35] LSE: General Purposes, 22 Apr. 1919, 27 Nov. 1919; LSE: Treasury Subcommittee, 18 May 1920; Whyte, *The Stock Exchange*, 47, 63.

into 1920. In February 1920 it was reported by the Chairman to the Committee for General Purposes that

... with Mr Robinson he had informally approached the Governor of the Bank of England with reference to the resumption of dealings for the account and has been met with a polite but flat refusal. In the Governor's opinion the only terms on which such a proposal would be entertained by the Government would be if they were assured that the whole pre-war Account in London and all the Provincial Exchanges had been liquidated.[36]

Consequently it was not opposition within the Stock Exchange that prevented a speedy resumption of account trading, and all that implied for the money market, but from the government and the Bank of England worried about the effects a build-up of speculative activity would have upon monetary stability.

The difficulty the Stock Exchange faced in bringing to a close the pre-war account was reaching an agreement on when the war actually ended. This was not interpreted as the date when the fighting ended but when the peace treaties were signed. As it was these ranged from the 10 January 1920 for Germany through Austria on 16 July and Hungary on 26 July 1920 to Bulgaria on the 9 August 1920. Some countries had disintegrated, such as the Austro-Hungarian Empire, while others had virtually disappeared, as in the case of the Ottoman Empire. This made it very difficult to negotiate an end to the war, even though the conflict was long over. Without an end to the war the Stock Exchange could not force members to complete their pre-war accounts, especially when it could have severe financial penalties for them considering the changed value of securities they might have to deliver or pay for. The Stock Exchange tried to get the government to declare an official end to the war, suggesting the date of the German peace treaty, but got no response until the middle of 1921.[37] In the May of that year they wrote to the Chancellor of the Exchequer, Sir Robert Horne, stating their dilemma and asking again for an official date for the end of the war, as it looked likely that Turkey would never sign a peace treaty.

When the Emergency Rules were passed in accordance with the Treasury Scheme of the 31st October 1914 for providing Government assistance in dealing with account to account loans on the Stock Exchange and the Temporary Regulations for the reopening of the Stock Exchange were made in the December of that year, it was not anticipated that the war would last as long as it did, or that so long a period would elapse between the termination of hostilities and the ratification of the Peace Treaties ... The Committee [for General Purposes] are very anxious that all outstanding Stock Exchange obligations should be completed at the earliest possible date and it seems to them that there is at the present time no reason political or financial which should prevent the realisation of this desire.[38]

[36] LSE: General Purposes, 18 Feb. 1920.     [37] Ibid., 14 Mar. 1921, 10 July 1922.
[38] Ibid., 23 May 1921, cf. 25 July 1921.

By then the government were inclined to agree and they set as the official date for the end of the war, 1 September 1921, or almost three years after the fighting finished. Effectively, the government had prevented the return to normal trading on the Stock Exchange not through any official or unofficial restriction but through not declaring an official end to the war and holding to the precise terms under which the Stock Exchange had been allowed to reopen in 1915.

Immediately an official date for the end to the war was announced members petitioned the Stock Exchange for a resumption of account trading, only to be met with the reply that

As long as the pre-war account remained unsettled the Treasury had refused to allow dealings other than for cash.[39]

With the war long over the patriotism of members was being tested to the limit by the government's reluctance to accept a return to traditional methods of trading on the Stock Exchange. There was also a growing feeling among many members that the Treasury had been able to dictate to the Stock Exchange because only those brokers and jobbers doing a safe investment business had their views considered, and they were relatively happy with cash trading. As one member, Gerald Williams, had observed in November 1918,

The one outstanding feature in dealings in the 'House' during the past four, inherently difficult, years has been the well-nigh perfect safety for all concerned. Not only did the cash basis of our transactions effectively reduce to—practically—zero the risk involved in the ultimate completion of each bargain, but it tended to stabilise markets in a most salutary and hitherto unknown manner.[40]

Certainly he was not alone among the membership in holding this view, while much outside opinion also identified dealing for the account as a form of gambling.[41]

Spurred by the growing criticism from those among the membership who were unhappy with the continuance of cash trading, the Stock Exchange began to lobby the government, asking it to allow a return of the fortnightly account before the 12 months were up. Though this was met with a refusal in September 1921 the Chancellor of the Exchequer agreed in November 1921 to an early resumption of account trading. With official approval granted the Stock Exchange then began to plan the return to its normal trading practices. This did not come about until 1922 suggesting a definite reluctance on behalf of many on the Stock Exchange to return to pre-war conditions. Further evidence of this reluctance was the fact that when the fortnightly account was reintroduced in May 1922 its use was denied to certain categories of business. Sales and purchases for foreign

---

[39] Ibid., 25 July 1921.    [40] LSE: Rules and Regulations, 27 Nov. 1918.
[41] Ibid., 5 Feb. 1919, 19 June 1919; Whyte, The Stock Exchange, 78.

clients still had to be for cash. The Stock Exchange was worried that sudden foreign exchange fluctuations could have disastrous consequences for the membership as a whole if a large speculative account was allowed to build up over a two-week trading period. Similarly, the buying and selling of government debt could not be done for the account because of the risk of a major default due to violent fluctuations in price. Clearly, the Stock Exchange had noted the greatly reduced number of failures during the war when only cash trading was allowed, and sought to apply that to those areas of business where the risks were greatest.[42] (Table 5.3)

Naturally many of those being denied access to account trading objected, mainly the members involved in foreign business. In response to the proposals to deny them the use of the account, Leon Brothers, on behalf of 40 firms, protested in March 1922 that it would lead to the loss of such business to non-members. By trading for the account members doing an international business could minimize the capital required as they only had to pay for the securities taken up at the end of each fortnightly period. This allowed them to compete with better capitalized outside houses, such as British and foreign banks. If they were denied access to the account that advantage would be lost, and with it some, at least, of the foreign business. In essence the conflict over access to the account encapsulated the conflict in the Stock Exchange over the degree of risk that was acceptable. Leon Brothers, for the arbitrageurs, downplayed the risks while pointing out

... what an enormous amount of business arbitrage firms bring to the Stock Exchange, which would otherwise never come to London at all. As an instance, Paris deals with London, and London distributes that business to New York, Japan or other centres. Paris and other countries would cut out London, if London could not give the best, quickest, and most efficient facilities ...

In contrast a broker like Kemp-Gee focused on the threat to the Stock Exchange arising out of the post-war monetary turmoil,

... forward dealings with the present fluctuations in Continental Exchanges might lead to disaster, as fluctuations in exchange such as had recently occurred in Germany might swamp the capital of either the London or Foreign House or the foreign speculator.

In the end the fear that excessive exposure to foreign business, under the conditions of the time, could so threaten the financial well-being of so many members that the whole market place would be forced to close, temporarily, as at the outbreak of the war, persuaded the Stock Exchange not to restore account dealing for foreign business.[43]

[42] LSE: General Purposes, 26 Sept. 1921, 17 Oct. 1921, 8 Nov. 1921, 3 Jan. 1922; LSE: Rules and Regulations, 11 July 1922; Kirkaldy, *British Finance*, 347; Whyte, *The Stock Exchange*, 64, 78, 82.
[43] LSE: General Purposes, 29 Mar. 1922.

Table 5.3. Failure of brokers, 1905–1930

| Year | No. defaulting | No. bankrupt | Liability to clients (£) | Amount paid (£) | Amount outstanding (£) |
|------|------|------|------|------|------|
| 1905 | 16 | 1 | — | — | — |
| 1906 | 8 | 1 | 2,020 | 1,958 | 62 |
| 1907 | 22 | 3 | — | — | — |
| 1908 | 3 | 1 | — | — | — |
| 1909 | 6 | 3 | 156 | 113 | 43 |
| 1910 | 4 | 1 | 734 | 734 | — |
| 1911 | 7 | 1 | 8,571 | — | 8,571 |
| 1912 | 6 | 1 | 1,283 | 1,283 | — |
| 1913 | 11 | 3 | — | — | — |
| 1914 | 11 | 2 | 12,302 | 12,302 | — |
| 1914 | 12 | 3 | 2,371 | 1,025 | 1,346 |
| 1915 | 2 | — | 234 | 234 | — |
| 1916 | 2 | 1 | 6,192 | 301 | 5,891 |
| 1917 | 5 | — | 3,512 | 1,090 | 2,422 |
| 1918 | 2 | — | 531 | 501 | 30 |
| 1919 | — | — | | | |
| 1920 | 2 | — | | | |
| 1921 | 2 | — | ? | ? | ? |
| 1922 | 4 | 1 | 199,227 | 52,415 | 146,812 |
| 1923 | 2 | — | 2,211 | 1,639 | 572 |
| 1924 | 1 | 1 | — | — | — |
| 1925 | 3 | 1 | 11,608 | 4,841 | 6,767 |
| 1926 | 2 | — | 3,517 | 823 | 2,694 |
| 1927 | 2 | 1 | — | — | — |
| 1928 | 3 | — | 11,922 | 2,547 | 9,375 |
| 1929 | 4 | — | 25,875 | 7,540 | 18,335 |
| 1930 | 1 | — | 1,448 | — | 1,448 |

*Source*: LSE: General Purposes, Subcommittee of a Non-Permanent Character, 19 Nov. 1930.

Clearly the experiences of the war, from its outbreak to its aftermath, had inclined the membership of the Stock Exchange towards a more cautious approach to the risks they were willing to accept, collectively. This was to be seen in the way other features of the pre-war trading system were introduced. Before the war not only had dealing for the account been such an important element in the way the London Stock Exchange operated, attracting custom from New York as a result, but so had the ability to continue sales and purchases from account to account—contango. Through the simple payment of the difference between current and agreed prices at the end of each account, a deal could be continued for much longer than a fortnight, if both parties were willing. Again, there was always the risk that this allowed an insolvent member to continue trading with the eventual collapse being much larger than it needed to be. Consequently, the government also opposed the resumption of contangos, but that ended in late 1921 when they accepted that account dealing could be restored. This then brought out the opposition among the membership, worried about the buildup of risk that contangos involved. A total of 1,289 members (789 brokers/500 jobbers) opposed the reintroduction of contangos in May 1922, arguing that,

Since dealings have taken place for cash only, the prestige of the Stock Exchange has risen, and we doubt if it has ever stood so high in the estimation of the public, as it does at the present time. In pre-war days the Stock Exchange was regarded by many as little more than a 'Gambling Institution', but since the war we have done genuine and clean business, and the Stock Exchange may be fairly said to have justified its claim to play a very important part in the public life.

They, reluctantly, accepted the necessity of account trading for domestic business but wanted all purchases paid for and all securities sold delivered at the completion of each account, not carried over from one to another, because of the risk involved,

we consider that the contangos system, in providing an uncontrollable measure of credit to the public, is inimical to the best interests of the Stock Exchange, a source of great danger in all times of political or financial stress, and weighs especially heavily on Brokers who have far the greater share of responsibility for the due fulfilment of obligations.[44]

Despite these protests the Stock Exchange realized that many of its members—possibly the majority—could not survive without the ability to carry over deals from one account to another. So much of the activity on the Stock Exchange was of an ongoing nature—investing in securities money only temporarily available—that restrictions placed on the length of a time a deal was open, would drive away much business. It would also discourage those investors backing their judgement on whether an individual stock, or the whole market, would rise or fall, and requiring more than two weeks to be proved right or wrong. As a consequence it was decided to reintroduce contangos from September 1921, indicating that, though caution was uppermost in the minds of members, there was a realization that traditional market practices had to be restored or business would be lost, perhaps permanently. Similarly, it was decided to allow the use of options even though their reintroduction was also opposed by many members. However, mindful of the build-up of risk, especially in foreign business, options were restricted to a maximum length of three months and were not available to foreign

---

[44] LSE: General Purposes, 8 May 1922.

clients. Consequently, though trading in government debt was denied the use of the account, they did have access officially to options as compensation. This meant that a sale or purchase of government stock could be matched by a reverse option, allowing banks and others to lend or borrow on the Stock Exchange without the risk of losing out due to price fluctuation.[45]

Throughout the slow process involved in the dismantling of wartime restrictions and practices the Stock Exchange met opposition from the government, through both the Treasury and the Bank of England, and from its own membership. As a result it was not until towards the end of 1922, or eight years after the war had begun, that some semblance of normal trading practices had been restored. Even then, there remained one major casualty of the whole process and that was the London Stock Exchange's international business. Though there was understandable caution in exposing the Stock Exchange to the currency turmoil of the post-war years, with sterling itself not returning to the gold standard until 1925, much trading in foreign securities did take place in London though now increasingly outside the Stock Exchange.

One problem was the continuing refusal of the Stock Exchange to readmit ex-members of German origin. Even when the Board of Trade made a request in November 1925 for the Stock Exchange to drop its hostility towards Germans, reciprocating the ending of anti-British discrimination in Germany, it was refused. As late as 1930 10 ex-members were still reapplying for admission and being refused.[46] By then some relaxation had taken place in individual cases but the strong feeling remained that,

. . . the re-election of members of ex-enemy birth 'en bloc' would be extremely unpopular . . .[47]

Many of those members of German origin, who had been born in Britain and served in the forces, anglicized their names in order to deflect hostility. A. Bredermann & Co., who had been members since 1858, became Cuthbertson & Co. in January 1920, for instance.[48] A consequence of this continued hostility to these ex-members of German birth, led them to establish themselves elsewhere in the City of London doing business in foreign securities. By 1924 M. V. Salomon was a manager with the British North-European Bank while Sydney Wedel, who had helped pioneer South African business on the Stock Exchange, was continuing to do so but as an outside house.[49]

[45] Ibid., 11 May 1922, 15 May 1922, 23 May 1922; LSE: Rules and Regulations, 27 Nov. 1918.

[46] LSE: General Purposes, 19 Mar. 1919, 28 July 1919, 10 Mar. 1920, 30 May 1921, 14 Mar. 1922, 3 July 1922, 19 Feb. 1923, 10 Sept. 1923, 17 Mar. 1924, 23 Mar. 1925, 3 Nov. 1925, 23 Nov. 1925, 11 Apr. 1927, 14 Apr. 1930. LSE: Trustees and Managers, 18 June 1930.

[47] LSE: General Purposes, 23 June 1930.    [48] Ibid., 5 Jan. 1920, 8 Mar. 1920.

[49] Ibid., 4 Sept. 1922, 28 Oct. 1924, 24 Nov. 1924.

Consequently, as members of the London Stock Exchange gradually re-established contact with overseas clients after the war, and tried to revive the London market in foreign securities, especially American stocks and bonds, they faced competition from a group of skilled and experienced ex-colleagues. As it was, the Treasury only slowly and reluctantly gave permission for members of the Stock Exchange to start transacting business for overseas clients. It was only in August 1919 that the restriction on dealing in securities held outside the country was withdrawn, and even then there remained a prohibition on those owned by enemy nationals. All Germans, for example, were expected to surrender holdings of foreign securities so that these could be used to finance their country's reparations payments. This applied to Germans wherever they were located, and so included some living in Britain with investments in British securities. This complicated the trading in foreign securities, as the nationality of the owners had to be established in all cases, and it was not until 1 August 1923 that a declaration of non-enemy ownership was dispensed with. It also made it difficult for some members to settle their pre-war account. Firms like Joseph Sebag & Co. and Messel & Co. still had money due from German clients in December 1919, but the only way they could be repaid was if those clients were able to sell the foreign securities they held. Without these payments these firms had difficulty re-establishing an international business.[50]

Generally, the war had given a boost to those non-members who had conducted an international trade in securities, as the Stock Exchange was better able to force adherence to the restrictions. Though members did begin to reclaim the business in the post-war years the restrictions imposed by the Stock Exchange itself, as on access to the account or the use of options, did not assist. Foreign investors, for example, were increasingly using a London bank or other financial institution to conduct their business in London rather than dealing themselves with a broker or jobber. By that means they could deal for the account and use options denied to foreign clients if they had direct contact with a member. Inevitably, this encouraged the outside houses to bypass the Stock Exchange entirely in arranging trans-actions. By 1924, for example, members of the Stock Exchange were losing their intermediary position in handling transactions between Johannesburg and Paris in South African gold-mining shares. Instead the business was either taking place directly or was being undertaken by non-members.[51]

Nevertheless, despite all the problems and the competition an international business did reappear on the London Stock Exchange as Treasury

[50] LSE: General Purposes, 16 Dec. 1918, 3 Feb. 1919, 25 Mar. 1919, 3 Apr. 1919, 14 Apr. 1919, 19 Aug. 1919, 15 Sept. 1919, 1 Oct. 1919, 1 Dec. 1919, 15 Dec. 1919, 25 Mar. 1920, 31 July 1923; LSE: Treasury Subcommittee, 25 Mar. 1920.
[51] LSE: General Purposes, 29 Mar. 1922, 29 May 1922, 16 Oct. 1922, 8 Mar. 1923, 28 Oct. 1924.

controls lessened. As early as September 1919 permission had been given to resume arbitrage though this was fraught with difficulty because of the volatility of the foreign exchanges and the absence of appropriate securities. The government, for example, continued to be a major purchaser of American securities for resale in New York, and it was not until June 1921 that it stopped and began to return unsold securities to investors. In the Rhodesian market such was the low level of activity that one jobber, Ernest Keene, retained his job with a firm of woollen merchants. However, transactions between London and Paris began to become important from the end of 1919, to be followed with a revival of dealings with New York.[52]

The problem with the New York connection, which had been the mainstay of London's international business before the war, was not simply the lack of marketable securities but also the restrictions imposed by the Treasury and, later, by the Stock Exchange itself. In the immediate post-war year the exchange rate most under pressure was that between the dollar and the pound. One way of alleviating that pressure was to prevent British purchases of American securities, and this the Treasury sought to do. S. F. Streit of the New York Stock Exchange explained in October 1920, '. . . your Treasury Regulations prevent a free and open market with you . . .' However, he also went on to explain that an alternative was appearing which was much more acceptable to the British government as it involved American purchases of British and European securities, '. . . although in a reverse movement from that in former years, there is developing an arbitrage business between your country, Holland and the United States . . .'

He also indicated that the New York Stock Exchange was keen to encourage this having become much more confident of their ability to compete with London during the war. In contrast, the London Stock Exchange was much less sure of its standing vis-à-vis New York but had no option but to respond. Consequently, with Treasury permission it agreed to permit joint-account arbitrage between London and New York from 1 December 1920. Even then, though, it tried to restrict the flexibility of the arbitrageurs to operate as they saw fit because of a suspicion that their foreign contacts gave them an unfair advantage over fellow members.[53]

Finally, links with Germany also began to recover in the early 1920s though much business was now routed via Amsterdam. The German markets were in disarray while the London branches of the main German banks had been closed during the war. Thus, in 1924 Cassel & Co. conducted arbitrage between London and Germany, in German government, bank, and industrial securities, through the firm of S. Schoenberger & Co. in Amsterdam.

---

[52] Ibid., 1 Sept. 1919, 29 Sept. 1919, 20 Nov. 1919, 22 Dec. 1919, 26 Jan. 1920, 24 Mar. 1920, 9 Apr. 1920, 12 Apr. 1920, 20 Dec. 1920, 10 Jan. 1921, 18 Apr. 1921, 23 May 1921, 27 June 1921.

[53] Ibid., 11 Oct. 1920, cf. 18 Oct. 1920, 8 Nov. 1920, 25 Apr. 1921.

In the early years this link had posed problems as Germans were not allowed to sell foreign securities but had to surrender them for reparations use. However, Dutch investors—as a neutral nation during the war—began purchasing them and so giving German investors the foreign exchange they required. In turn Dutch investors were selling their holdings of American railroad stocks and bonds in New York, with London brokers and jobbers acting as intermediaries, as they traditionally had. Inevitably, amongst these Dutch holdings appeared securities once held, or even currently owned, by German investors. The British government expected the Stock Exchange to prevent this happening and those members caught trading such securities, as with Crews and Company in 1920, were suspended. Again, however, the result was to add another complication to international business and force the Stock Exchange to police its own members to a much greater degree than was possible with non-members.[54]

Consequently, though Treasury controls had been removed by the 1920s and international business had recovered, the London Stock Exchange was now in a much weaker position than before the war. Both New York and Amsterdam offered serious competition in particular segments of the global securities market due to their greatly enhanced financial situation. Even within London the members of the London Stock Exchange faced greatly increased competition. Business that had once largely flowed through the Stock Exchange was now conducted by non-members, such as the Germans expelled during the war, American brokers dealing direct with New York, and British banks with branches and correspondents abroad. These non-members had always been a threat to the London Stock Exchange because of the capital and connections they could command but direct access to all the trading facilities of the Stock Exchange had allowed members to offer strong competition before the war. By denying members doing an overseas business access both to the account and to options, and trying to restrict their freedom to operate, the Stock Exchange greatly diminished the benefits to be derived from membership. All this came after a war and its aftermath where members of the Stock Exchange had their international business more closely policed and regulated than non-members. The inevitable result was that not only had much international business moved from London itself but it had also moved away from the membership of the Stock Exchange. The Stock Exchange and its membership was going to have to work hard to recover that business from the mid-1920s onwards.[55]

## ORGANIZATION

Instead, the Stock Exchange appeared much more concerned with its own internal affairs in the immediate post-war years than in any concerted effort

[54] LSE: General Purposes, 19 Apr. 1920, 20 Apr. 1920, 22 Apr. 1920, 19 May 1920, 15 Sept. 1924.
[55] Ibid., 28 Jan. 1924, 8 Dec. 1924.

to recover international business. In particular, the perennial debate over dual control with members versus proprietors, flared up again. During the war membership had fallen from 4,855 in 1914 to 3,994 by 1918, or by some 1,000. When the post-war revival in activity came, those members who had survived the war and stayed in business during the lean years (Table 5.4) did not want to see their expected profits quickly disappear in a rapid expansion of new members competing for clients. They knew that, once the post-war speculative boom was over, lean times would return again, as they had in the past, leaving a greatly expanded membership to share what was available. Instead, they wanted to cap the membership at around the 4,000 level, for many believed the pre-war numbers had been too large anyway. In contrast, the proprietors who owned the Stock Exchange were keen to expand the membership as a means of increasing its income. Increasingly the proprietors and the membership were the same people but the overlap was by no means complete. In 1918, of the 20,000 shares issued by the Stock Exchange a total of 16,272 or 81 per cent was owned by members, leaving almost a fifth in the hands of those who regarded it as an investment and not simply a necessary expense of business. In addition those members who controlled most of the shares tended to be the larger firms, who did not always have the same attitude to membership as the smaller firms.

Certainly the Stock Exchange as an institution had a great need to increase income in the post-war years. During the war subscriptions totalling £198,888 had been forgone for those on active service but still, nominally, members. This, along with the expulsion of Germans, retirements, death, and emigration resulted in a drop of subscription income from £231,462 in 1914 to £97,485 in 1918. Income from the rent of offices and other services also fell at this time. Though efforts were made to control expenditure by not replacing staff as they left, it was difficult to do so with inflation, and so costs remained at much the same level, being £127,383 in 1914 and £114,409 in 1918. To cover some of the deficit the Stock Exchange sold property in Throgmorton Street in 1918, but that provided only a temporary respite. Essentially, they had to increase income as staffing costs, in particular, remained high in the post-war years. An estimate made in February 1922 suggested that whereas salaries cost £31,241 annually before the war, this had risen to £57,574 post-war, making an increase of £26,333 or 84 per cent. Whatever course of action the proprietors chose was going to be unpopular with the membership as it would either be an increase in subscription fees or an expansion in numbers. However, the membership had their own solution which was to take direct control of the institution themselves by buying out the shareholders. This was suggested by the likes of Rowe & Pitman, W. Greenwell & Co., and de Zoete & Gorton in April 1919 and was under serious consideration by June. A vote that month among the membership produced 1,908 in favour and only 95

against. Motivating this move was a feeling among the membership, as expressed in April 1919, that

Under the present arrangement, the greater the exertions of the members to get more business, the higher become the entrance fees and subscriptions, and the bigger is the dividend paid to the proprietors.[56]

The difficulty in this plan was the cost involved for the valuation made in November 1919 suggested a figure of £3.6m. Either every member would have to find in excess of £900, which was difficult after the war years, or a large loan would have to be serviced, involving a substantial rise in the membership fee. In addition, a Parliamentary Bill would be required with all the public scrutiny that would bring regarding the potential monopoly that was to be created. This led to an amended plan whereby a new company would be set up to own the Stock Exchange but in this case it would be owned equally by the membership, with a maximum set at 4,000. This was put to the proprietors who rejected the proposal in May 1921. As no voluntary scheme could be agreed upon, and the members were reluctant to put forward a Parliamentary Bill, the matter was allowed to drop. However, the consequence was that the proprietors were well aware of the hostility of the membership to any general expansion of numbers and the figure of 4,000 became an unofficial ceiling. Instead, the proprietors had to make do with increasing entrance fees and subscription charges.[57]

As it was, when the speculative post-war boom died away in the early 1920s so did the debate over the size of membership. It was not until the late 1920s, with activity rising once again that the issue revived. As before the membership opposed any large increase beyond 4,000, with 2,493 signing a petition in May 1928 requesting that the limit be maintained. By then there was a serious risk that membership was set for a persistent decline not because of a lack of demand for admission but the inability to purchase a nomination. Since the 1904 ruling anyone wishing to be admitted had to purchase the nomination of a retiring member. These nominations lapsed if not used within a certain time period, which had happened during the war and in the depressed years of the mid-1920s. In addition, if a member failed his nomination was lost. Between 1904 and 1914 a total of 803 nominations had lapsed while over the war years (1914–18) a further 845 went. Added to these were the 226 that were unsold in the 1920s (1918–28) in the years when business was low, making 1,874 in total. As a result nominations were fetching up to £1,800 each in 1928, and were reported to be very scarce. The one exception to this dispensation was that clerks could become members by putting their names on a waiting list.

---

[56] LSE: General Purposes, 7 Apr. 1919.

[57] Ibid., 25 June 1919, 30 June 1919, 20 Oct. 1919, 3 Nov. 1919, 6 Nov. 1919, 25 Nov. 1919, 23 Feb. 1920, 3 May 1921, 12 May 1921; LSE: Conjoint Committee, 7 Dec. 1932; LSE: Trustees and Managers, 16 Apr. 1918, 14 Apr. 1919, 25 Nov. 1920, 14 Dec. 1920, 9 Feb. 1922.

However, by June 1928 there were 360 names on the waiting list and only a few were admitted each year. Over the entire 1904–28 period only 367 such nominations were granted, leaving a net shortfall of 1,507. Many among the membership also wanted that list abolished. As it was, the collapse of the speculative boom in 1929, followed by two years of depressed levels of business, again removed the possibility of any great expansion in membership. However, this time the members did not let the matter drop as they wanted an agreed limit. By then they were in control of the Stock Exchange. A total of 2,878 out of the 2,987 shareholders, or 96 per cent, were also members by October 1931. In the end the proprietors agreed in January 1931 that the membership would only be through the purchase of a nomination, that additional nominations would only be created if numbers were felt to be too low, and that these new nominations would be sold at a minimum price of £2,000 each.[58] The result was to cap the membership at the 4,000 level desired by the majority. (Table 5.4.)

Thus, though the membership failed to end the system of dual control they had emerged, by the early 1930s, as dominant within the Stock Exchange. This meant that each member, whatever volume of business he undertook or capital he commanded, had equal power. In the past, through ownership of shares in the Stock Exchange, the larger firms could compensate for their lack of numbers through their greater wealth. Thus the interests of the broad spectrum of members was represented. Now the sole criteria for influence was membership and this obviously favoured the individual rather than the firm. As it was, the policy was now to restrict membership at the 4,000 level with the result that, when recovery in business took place, the price of nominations also rose, reaching a high of £1,975 in 1937.[59]

This power of the individual member was reflected in the restrictions placed upon the number of clerks that a member was allowed to employ to transact business in the Stock Exchange. The larger firms wanted to employ more clerks, both authorized to deal for them and not, so that their partners had more time to meet clients and generate business. When they requested this in 1923 they were refused as too many of the membership saw this as a threat to their livelihood. If firms were allowed to employ as many clerks as they liked to buy or sell on the floor of the Stock Exchange it would render the limit on membership completely ineffective. It could also lead to the concentration of business in the hands of a few large broking firms, to the disadvantage of the independent broker. Thus, when a renewed attempt was made in both 1928 and 1930 to expand the number of per-

[58] LSE: General Purposes, 30 Apr. 1928, 29 May 1928, 29 Oct. 1928, 21 Oct. 1929, 1 Dec. 1930, 26 Jan. 1931; LSE: Subcommittee of a Non-Permanent Character, 28 June 1928, 13 Dec. 1928, 25 June 1929; LSE: Conjoint Committee, 24 Oct. 1928, 7 June 1932; LSE: Trustees and Managers, Appendix, Apr. 1928; ibid., Subcommittee on Nominations, 3 July 1929; Osborn, *The Stock Exchange*, 15.

[59] H. Wincott, *The Stock Exchange* (London 1946), 32.

mitted clerks it was again blocked. A firm of five or more partners could introduce a maximum of five clerks (three authorized/two unauthorized) into the Stock Exchange. Consequently, there were few benefits to be achieved if a firm became larger than that for it would not be permitted to employ any more clerks in the Stock Exchange, though it could do so in its own office. One way around this problem was for a firm to employ a member as an authorized or unauthorized clerk, and this was an increasingly common practice between the wars. Whereas in 1918, 696 members, or 18 per cent of the total, operated in this capacity the number had risen to 957 by 1939, or 24 per cent, with most of them authorized to deal for their firm. (Table 5.5.) Clearly this indicates that the rules of the Stock Exchange were restricting the expansion of capacity not only through a limit on membership but also through preventing existing members from undertaking more business through increasing their staff. Before the war this control on the use of clerks had posed little of a problem as the number of members was so large. Now, with maximum inter-war membership at 4,076 in 1939 some 25 per cent below the maximum pre-war figure of 5,481 in 1904 (Table 5.5), the restriction on clerks was a restraint, as it discouraged members from forming larger units that could handle proportionately more business. This was so even though the limit on the number of partners a firm could have had been dropped in January 1922.[60]

Whether it was part of a general desire to limit membership and reduce competition or simply sex discrimination, the inter-war years also saw the Stock Exchange take a stance on the admission of women. This had never arisen before the war as no women had applied for membership, nor did any during or immediately after the war. The Sex Disqualification (Removal) Act of 1919 had outlawed the exclusion of women from incorporated societies but that had not led to any applications at the time. It was not until a Miss Oonah Mary Keogh, the daughter of a Dublin stockbroker, was admitted to the Dublin Stock Exchange in May 1925, that the Stock Exchange even realized that a woman might apply for membership of their institution. As that case received publicity in the press, being reported in the *Financial Times*, the Stock Exchange took legal advice from its solicitors, Travers, Smith, Braithwaite & Co., who concluded:

The profession or vocation carried on by members of the Stock Exchange is that of Brokers or Dealers; there is nothing to prevent either a man or a woman carrying on that profession or vocation although not a member of the Stock Exchange; and the Stock Exchange is not an incorporated society. Membership of the Stock Exchange only enables persons to carry on such profession or vocation in a particular place, which is a private building, to which only such stock and

[60] LSE: General Purposes, 25 Jan. 1922, 8 Oct. 1923, 15 Oct. 1923, 22 Oct. 1923, 27 Feb. 1928, 30 Apr. 1928, 29 May 1928, 22 Oct. 1928, 19 May 1930, 23 June 1930; LSE: Non-Permanent, 6 May 1930, 13 May 1930; LSE: Conjoint Committee, 14 Jan. 1924.

Table 5.5. Stock Exchange membership, 1938

| Stock exchange | Members | Firms | Members per firm |
|---|---|---|---|
| London | | | |
| Brokers | 2,491 | 465 | 5.4 |
| Jobbers | 1,433 | 342 | 4.2 |
| TOTAL | 4,132* | 807 | 5.1 |
| Glasgow | 263 | 140 | 1.9 |
| Liverpool | 160 | 96 | 1.7 |
| Manchester | 142 | 76 | 1.9 |
| Birmingham | 105 | 50 | 2.1 |
| Dublin | 81 | 50 | 1.6 |
| Edinburgh | 67 | 32 | 2.1 |
| Bristol | 44 | 18 | 2.4 |
| Belfast | 42 | 25 | 1.7 |
| Newcastle | 37 | 20 | 1.9 |
| Sheffield | 31 | 14 | 2.2 |
| Leeds | 30 | 13 | 2.3 |
| Cardiff | 25 | 22 | 1.1 |
| Huddersfield | 19 | 9 | 2.1 |
| Bradford | 18 | 12 | 1.5 |
| Nottingham | 17 | 12 | 1.4 |
| Cork | 15 | 10 | 1.5 |
| Greenock | 14 | 7 | 2.0 |
| Dundee | 13 | 7 | 1.9 |
| Swansea | 12 | 11 | 1.1 |
| Aberdeen | 11 | 7 | 1.6 |
| Halifax | 8 | 5 | 1.6 |
| Newport | 4 | 3 | 1.3 |
| Provincial stock exchanges | 1,158 | 639 | 1.8 |
| Provincial brokers** | 321 | 230 | 1.4 |
| TOTAL | 5,611 | 1,676 | 3.3 |

\* 208 members inactive.
\*\* Operating in 124 provincial towns.
*Source*: LSE: Subcommittee on Country Jobbing/Country Business, 4 Apr. 1939.

Sharebrokers and Dealers as are elected members, have the right of access and to which the public in general have no such right.[61]

Put simply, women had no right of admission to the Stock Exchange and it was up to the membership to elect them or not as it saw fit. The issue was not put to the test until 1936. That year publicity was again given to the case of a female stockbroker, a Miss Edith Midgley, who was carrying

[61] LSE: General Purposes, 6 July 1925; see W. A. Thomas, *The Stock Exchanges of Ireland* (Liverpool 1986), 102.

on business in Bradford and even employed a male managing clerk. This led to a Mrs M. Gosnell applying for membership of the Stock Exchange, provoking some debate within the institution and publicity outside. She was refused, being told that she was not eligible. The matter was taken no further at the time as she accepted the decision most graciously, writing in July 1936, '. . . while I regret their decision I fully appreciate that such an innovation has difficulties which time may or may not remove'.[62] As the pre-war Stock Exchange had never been tested in this way it is difficult to know whether this symbolized the growing conservatism of the institution or not.

In addition to the restrictions placed on the number of clerks a member could employ on the floor of the Stock Exchange there were other controls that also limited the growth of large stockbroking firms. The millions of new investors created by the war offered the prospect of much additional business for a stockbroking firm that could devise ways of attracting their custom. One obvious way was advertising. Traditionally a broker had catered for a relatively small number of clients, such as wealthy individuals or financial institutions, each of whom generated a substantial volume of business. This could all be done through direct service from an office in the City with contact being of a personal nature, reinforced through family, educational, or other ties. Advertising was not required for this type of business. However, it left untapped the orders of the small investor who knew little about the service a stockbroker offered, let alone possessed a personal contact. This mattered little before the war when the collective activities of the small investor were of limited significance and catered for by lawyers, accountants, bank-managers, provincial brokers, and others who acted as intermediaries between them and the London stockbroker. At that time advertising was associated more with the outside broker, who was not a member of a Stock Exchange and, to a large extent, offered a service where the public could bet on the rise and fall of share prices without a sale or purchase taking place.

Consequently, before the war there had been little need for stockbrokers to advertise and little damage caused by their neglect of the small investor. However, the sudden and rapid expansion of the number and importance of small investors during the war did change the situation significantly. There continued to exist much business for brokers generated by wealthy individuals and financial institutions, where advertising was, simply, not necessary. Nevertheless, a new and expanding market for stockbrokers was available, as the advertising agents, Street and Company, pointed out to the Stock Exchange in 1925.

. . . a great deal of peoples' savings are put into pianos, houses, land, etc. instead of into stocks and shares because of an ignorance of how to start about making investments. So many regard the Stock Exchange as a place where Jobbers and Brokers

[62] LSE: General Purposes, 25 May 1936, 8 June 1936, 22 June 1936, 27 July 1936.

gamble between one another and thus make their profits, but do not realise that there is room for the outside person to come along and get sound advice on invest-ing earnings and be advised as to when to sell, and further they are nervous because they do not understand the terms on which business is conducted.[63]

The result of this advice was the Stock Exchange itself improved its offi-cial advertising but continued to deny its membership the opportunity to advertise on their own account and so attract custom directly. This was already happening among the membership of the Mincing Lane Tea and Rubber Brokers' Association in a concerted effect to cater for the interests of the small investor generally, and not only in plantation shares. By August 1925 the Stock Exchange had forced the Mincing Lane Exchange to drop both advertising and dealing in other than tea and rubber shares. An uneasy and informal relationship existed between the members of both exchanges which could be made much more difficult if the London Stock Exchange wished.[64]

Though a few members were interested in experimenting with adver-tising, and it had been discovered that members of the New York Stock Exchange were permitted to do so, the prevailing mood was against it. There was always the worry that it would lead to poaching of clients and unseemly rows between members about what was permissible or not.[65] As it was, the personal introduction of new investors through direct contact or an existing client still appeared to be normal practice in the 1920s. C. G. Singleton, for example, who was a clerk with John Prust & Co., met a Mr Merrick at a dance, and then again on the Reigate train. The result was that

During the conversation which followed he mentioned that he sometimes had a little business on the Stock Exchange and asked if I would care to do it for him. I agreed to do so. He also said that he could introduce me the business of some of his friends.[66]

Such was the way a private client business was built up and maintained, and many on the Stock Exchange saw little need to change, especially if there was a risk that a few firms, running large advertising campaigns, would emerge and monopolize the business to the detriment of all the others.

However, demands to be allowed to advertise resurfaced among a section of the membership in the mid-1930s, in the wake of another downturn in activity. Some members could see that there was an investing public which could not be reached by private introductions and was currently served by banks and solicitors if they bought and sold securities at all. It was even pointed out that non-member brokers, who could advertise, were attract-ing large numbers of clients.[67] One jobber, K. D. Drewitt, went so far as to suggest in 1934 the ending of the ban on advertising because,

[63] LSE: General Purposes, Non-Permanent, 10 Nov. 1925.     [64] Ibid., 21 Dec. 1925.
[65] LSE: General Purposes, 15 Oct. 1928, 15 July 1929.     [66] Ibid., 13 Apr. 1927.
[67] Ibid., Commissions, 27 Apr. 1933; LSE: Trustees and Managers, 22 Apr. 1932, 21 Apr. 1933.

... if we want to obtain more business from the public, I feel quite sure we have got to go out for it a great deal more than we are doing today.[68]

With business picking up, however, the demands from the membership for a relaxation on the prohibition of advertising faded away. Those among the membership, whether broker or jobber, who were content to share the business that did come the Stock Exchange's way had emerged victorious. Those who suspected that the Stock Exchange was losing out to non-members, or simply failing to capitalize on a greatly enlarged investing public who needed to be advised, educated, and assisted if they were to become permanent investors in securities, were in the minority. Instead the Stock Exchange campaigned for a government ban on advertising by all stockbrokers, believing in 1937 that '... advertising serves no useful purpose to the stockbrokers profession or is a source of danger to the public ...'[69]

The same conflict and the same result, was to be found on the issue of branch offices. A stockbroker was only allowed to have an office in the City, which, ideally should be as close to the Stock Exchange as possible. By the later 1920s a number of members were wanting to set up additional offices elsewhere in order to serve an expanded client base. Again, this was permitted by the New York Stock Exchange. However, this request was refused by the London Stock Exchange despite requests in 1929 and 1936. This meant that stockbrokers could not establish national networks of offices channelling business to and from London, as on the American pattern. With corporate bodies denied membership of the Stock Exchange it was also impossible to emulate the European pattern where bank branches were fully integrated into the securities market, and so could provide a means of accessing the small investor. In the inter-war years the commercial banks had some 8,000 branches while the Post Office had around 15,000 outlets. These presented a vast retail network that could have been utilized for the sale and purchase of securities by the greatly enlarged investing public. However, both the banks and the Post Office had to operate through brokers rather than have a direct presence on the Stock Exchange and this reduced their incentive to actively cultivate such a business. Conversely, even if the Stock Exchange had permitted its members to establish branches they could never have expanded sufficiently to tap more than a tiny proportion of the small investors now in existence. Nevertheless, the fact that the Stock Exchange threw so many obstacles in the way of its members doing a retail business indicates an unwillingness to respond to the needs of a mass investing public, preferring to act through the banks.[70]

Another means through which the Stock Exchange could have done more to attract the custom of the small investor was in setting up a

[68] Ibid., 17 Apr. 1934.    [69] LSE: General Purposes, 1 Feb. 1937.
[70] Ibid. 15 Oct. 1928, 14 Jan. 1929, 30 Nov. 1936; Whyte, *The Stock Exchange*, 75–6; Osborn, *The Stock Exchange*, 53.

Compensation Fund. Publicity given to the failure of brokers, many of whom were not members of the Stock Exchange, discouraged small investors from investing in securities. Where they did they also had a tendency to use the banks, which were large and well known, and so offered the confidence of size and familiarity. Certainly, members of the Stock Exchange did fail and clients did lose money as a result, some of it fraudulently. Between 1923 and 1939 there were 25 failed brokers whose estates were wound up by the Official Assignee. This resulted in only £36,522 being realized through the sale of their assets, such as house and contents, against debts of £140,559, leaving clients to shoulder a loss of £104,037. In addition, other brokers failed whose debts were settled privately or by the Stock Exchange itself. Over the 1923-35 period the Stock Exchange received 190 claims on the estates of members who had defaulted on their clients, through either non-delivery of securities or non-return of money held on their behalf. In all there was only £24,839 available from the estates to pay out claims of £84,499, leaving a loss of £59,660.[71] (Table 5.3.)

These losses were very small in proportion to the total business being carried out on the Stock Exchange. Between 1922 and 1930 a total of 22 brokers defaulted. This amounted to less than three per annum or 0.06 per cent of the membership. An estimate of their liability to clients suggested a total of, at least £255,808, of which £186,003 still remained after the sale of assets, or £20,667 per annum. This period did include the particularly bad failures of 1922.[72] One such failure in the early 1930s was that of Frank White, the senior partner in the broker, Thomas Coleman & Co. He had appropriated £1,529 in cash and £1,861 in securities from the accounts of clients which he had then used for speculative purposes. When the fraud was discovered, through the collapse of speculation, Frank White committed suicide and the firm failed. His partner, Ernest Haines, lost £1,010, plus £1,085 put up by his family. He eventually returned to the Stock Exchange in 1933 but only as an authorized clerk with Davey & Candy.[73]

Whereas for large investors and financial institutions the trust that was essential in any relationship with a stockbroker could be created through intimate knowledge, regular contact and personal acquaintanceship, that was not available to the small investor dabbling occasionally in the market. They were easily discouraged by stories of deception, rare as they might be, and thus looked for some form of reassurance when trusting a stockbroker with either securities or money. This the reputation of a lawyer or an accountant could give, backed by a professional body, while bankers were employees of a large and well-known companies. In reality it was brokers who were much more at risk than their clients. A broker was much more

[71] LSE: Compensation Fund Committee, Report and Recommendations, 27 Feb. 1950; LSE: Conjoint Committee, 15 Sept. 1936, 4 Nov. 1937, 19 July 1938.
[72] LSE: General Purposes, Non-Permanent, 19 Nov. 1930.
[73] Ibid., Readmission of Defaulters, 6 Apr. 1933.

likely to be bankrupted because of one or more clients defaulting on a deal that had turned out unfavourably, than any other cause. Brokers themselves bought and sold for their clients very much on trust, expecting the client to pay for securities when delivered and to deliver securities when sold. In the meantime the price could change resulting in a loss, tempting the client not to pay or deliver. In contrast, the broker had to honour all deals made on the Stock Exchange, regardless of the actions of the client. If brokers could not meet their obligations to fellow members they had to cease to trade, and so their business was lost.[74]

Essentially, the Stock Exchange ignored the client and expected all brokers to be responsible for the sales and purchases they made. If they could not complete a deal it was their responsibility. This then forced the broker to be cautious in the clients they accepted, though even then problems continued to occur leading to failure. Typical of what happened was the firm of brokers Sewill, Baillie, Hamilton & Co., who failed in 1930. According to Herbert Sewill in 1938:

In the depth of the depression the sum of £143,000 became due by a client of the firm in respect of 168,000 shares, this being the balance owing after the retention of a margin of 20 per cent of the average market value which was retained by us as Brokers. The client defaulted and the responsibility therefore fell on my firm.

Herbert Sewill was ruined, eventually becoming a clerk with another broking firm, Vanderfelt & Co.[75] However, failures of stockbrokers through clients defaulting was not newsworthy, compared to clients being defrauded, and so the impression among the less informed investor was of the potential risks involved in placing business with a stockbroker.

One solution to the problem, initially suggested during the war, was the establishment of a Guarantee or Compensation Fund.[76] By the mid-1930s, such a fund was under active discussion as a means of both distinguishing between brokers who were members of the London Stock Exchange, and those who were not, and competing with the banks who accepted responsibility for any fraud committed by their own employees. The problem was, of course, cost, which was put at c.£20,000 per annum. Members who were jobbers did not deal with the public and were, accordingly, reluctant to contribute to a scheme that brought them no direct benefit. Similarly, those members who did scrutinize clients very carefully and operated a cautious policy of limited sales and purchases without accompanying documentation and payment, were also unwilling to provide funds that would compensate the clients of fellow members who did not follow such a conservative line, and possibly gained more business as a result, and at their expense. In the end, by July 1938, a compromise had

[74] Ibid., 31 Jan. 1923, 15 Apr. 1930.    [75] Ibid., 5 Apr. 1938.
[76] LSE: General Purposes, Non-Permanent, 10 May 1917, 30 May 1917, 13 June 1917, 21 June 1917.

been reached. A Compensation Fund was to be established, with participation voluntary for existing members but compulsory for all new members. However, with the threat of war looming ever closer the establishment of such a fund appeared a less pressing priority and was not implemented, despite the acceptance of the principle behind it.[77]

Clearly, the majority of the members of the London Stock Exchange were unwilling to allow a minority to experiment with new ways of doing business, whether through advertising or branch offices. They also resisted the creation of a Compensation Fund, and blocked the expansion of individual firms through denying them the privilege of putting more clerks on the floor of the Stock Exchange. The emphasis was very much on creating a level playing field on the basis of the individual member or small partnership, with any tendency that would permit the growth of larger units being resisted and, on the whole, blocked. The result was to make it difficult for brokers, who were members of the Stock Exchange, to establish retail operations catering for that new segment of the investing public brought into being by the First World War. Instead, it was non-members that increasingly filled that vacuum. The outside stockbroker, Sir Arthur Wheeler, who did advertise extensively was reputed to have some 50,000 clients in the 1920s, served from an office in Leicester. He had built up his client base during the war when he sold War Loan to the public, and had a potential mailing list of half a million names.[78] In contrast the Stock Exchange appeared to oppose any move that would allow member firms to operate on a large scale. Foster & Braithwaite, for example, had set up in 1929 a nominee company as a simpler way of holding the stocks and shares of clients, rather than in the names of individual partners while a sale was arranged or payment by the client awaited. When this was brought to the Stock Exchange attention in 1934, it was only agreed to, once the suspicion that the firm was converting into an incorporated company was dispelled.[79]

The problem for jobbers was more complex. Beginning with Frisby Brothers in 1934, who were major traders in the rubber market, there was a growing demand for permission to convert into unlimited liability companies. By doing so they could average profits over good and bad years and so reduce the tax liability they were incurring as a partnership. At the same time it removed the necessity to pay tax on unrealized, and frequently unrealizable profits arising out of holding securities which had risen in value over the year. Such securities might very well represent the capital of a jobber being used as collateral with the bank to finance extensive borrowing. However, as what was being requested amounted to corporate

[77] LSE: General Purposes, 1 Feb. 1937, 28 June 1937, 23 May 1937, 11 July 1938.

[78] LSE: Trustees and Managers, Appendices, 22 Apr. 1932; L. Dennett, *The Charterhouse Group 1925–1979: A History* (London 1979), 16–17.

[79] LSE: General Purposes, 24 Sept. 1934, 15 Oct. 1934, 22 Oct. 1934.

membership that was unacceptable to the Stock Exchange. It would allow the creation of large and well-capitalized stockbroking firms which could threaten the livelihood of many individual members. As a result the simple device of conversion to an unlimited liability company was rejected and an alternative way of reducing the tax burden was sought through negotiations with the Treasury.

After a great deal of discussion no other solution could be reached and that was the position reached by January 1939. Even then it was not until the April of that year before the amendment to the rules was ready, allowing members to register as private unlimited liability companies for tax purposes.[80] Even then, it was stated quite clearly in March 1939 that this implied no change in the rule banning corporate membership, only a more tax efficient status for members.

From the point of view of the Stock Exchange, the carrying on of business as a private unlimited liability company is for all practical purposes indistinguishable from the present practice of carrying on business in partnership.[81]

Clearly, the fear of both banks demanding admission and the appearance of large stockbroking or jobbing firms enjoying company status prevented the Stock Exchange from reforming its members' rules and so made it difficult for its members to respond to many of the new opportunities of the inter-war years, as with more retail-focused stockbroking. The result was that the average firm continued to remain small, catering for a limited number of wealthy individuals or financial institutions.

As the rules of the London Stock Exchange prevented members from developing into large firms with an extensive retail operation or the direct participation of those who possessed such operations, such as commercial banks, it was vitally important that the charges made by members encouraged not only investors to make direct use of their services but also attracted the custom of intermediaries who were in contact with all sections of the investing public. There was no necessity for members to advertise, possess branch offices, or be especially large, if the service that they offered was competitive in terms of price and execution. However, the prices that brokers charged were now not open to their own discretion but controlled by commission rules laid down by the Stock Exchange itself. Opposition to the imposition of a fixed scale of charges had largely ended with the war for in the post-war years it was seen as an essential aid to limiting competition between members and a means of dividing out business during a slump. Whereas before the war there had been serious doubt about whether fixed commissions would survive, the debate between the wars was not on

---

[80] See ibid., 29 Oct. 1934, 12 Nov. 1934, 9 Jan. 1939, 6 Mar. 1939, 3 Apr. 1939; ibid., Non-Permanent, 23 Oct. 1934; ibid., Selected Appendices, 24 Mar. 1939; LSE: Trustees and Managers, 20 Feb. 1939. LSE: Rules and Regulations, 8 Feb. 1939.

[81] Ibid., 3 Mar. 1939.

their abolition but on their modification to suit changing conditions. Among the membership were many different types of broker.

A private client stockbroker did a regular investment business for a small number of wealthy investors, and he wanted to maintain reasonably high fixed commissions in order to repay himself for the personal service being offered.

The greater part of a stockbroker's work consists of advising clients for which technical professional knowledge is as important as in any recognised learned profession,

was the claim by the Stock Exchange itself in 1920 when they compared themselves to doctors and lawyers and felt justified in demanding the remuneration they enjoyed.[82]

In contrast the larger firms, who tended to carry out the business of financial institutions and provincial broker, operated in a much more competitive environment. They were always conscious that the clients they served would be tempted to look for alternative means of buying and selling shares if they found a London stockbroker too expensive. Consequently, what they wanted was a great deal more flexibility, which would allow them to tailor charges to suit individual clients. In particular they were keen on being able to offer substantial discounts for the volume business generated by banks, both merchant and commercial, or the non-member brokers, such as those in the provinces and abroad. The fixed scale of commissions had to be made to satisfy these varied interests of the membership and that would, inevitably, cause problems.

Though the volume of stock exchange business did revive in the post-war years, brokers found that their costs, especially wages, which had escalated during the war, continued to remain high. It was also impossible to economize on staff because the war's creation of large numbers of small holders of War Loans meant that deals were for a lower average value. In the transactions in government stock handled by the Post Office, the average deal fell from £140 before the war to £50 in 1923. Whatever the size of the deal the administrative cost was the same, which pushed up the clerical costs for brokers. Larger firms of brokers were able to absorb this across the range of business that they did and the office staffs that they maintained, but it was a burden on the smaller partnerships doing a largely private client business. The result was pressure to increase commission charge for small deals. This was achieved in 1920 when commission at the bottom of the scale was doubled from either 2/6 to 6/- or from 5/- to 10/- per transaction, depending upon the type of business being done. Though, in terms of the existing cost structure of such deals the increase was more than justified it did mean that the London Stock Exchange was denying itself the opportunity to cater for the large number of small investors now in existence. New types of

[82] LSE: General Purposes, 11 May 1920.

stockbroking operations would be required if such an operation was to be financially viable. A survey in 1930 found that the average cost of a transaction handled by a broker was £1. 2s. 3½d. but that 30.6 per cent generated a commission of £1 or under. Such business would only be viable for large stockbroking firms, where economies of scale and a diversity of activity, could make such business profitable. However, those were the very firms that Stock Exchange rules prevented from appearing. Nevertheless, despite the evidence of the lack of profitability in small deals and agitation for further increases in rate of commission, this course of action was resisted.[83] Instead there is evidence that brokers were trying to cut costs by making greater use of office technology, such as duplicators and electric calculators, and by employing more clerical and secretarial staff. This would allow the routine processing of sales, purchases, bills, and payments to be done in greater numbers and lower costs.[84]

However, it was not only the small investor who was not attracted to use the Stock Exchange because of the rate of commission. From 1922 onwards firms catering for institutional customers were suffering resistance to their charges, especially as the rules on commissions were progressively tightened. It had been accepted that the official scale of commissions, and the rebates allowed, was so complex that there was considerable scope for ambiguity, misunderstandings, and evasions without deliberately flouting the rules. This had greatly reduced resistance to minimum commissions before the war and continued to do so for some time afterwards.[85] Even by 1934 one member, Warwick Smith, was of the opinion, regarding the scale of commissions, that

We do not understand them ourselves and we have a sub-committee appointed which has endless work in trying to explain them to their own members.[86]

Nevertheless, the longer the fixed scale of commissions was in place the more experienced the Stock Exchange became at closing loopholes and punishing members who transgressed, either accidentally or deliberately. Unlike the pre-war era the great majority of members appeared solidly committed to minimum commissions as a means of preserving their business in difficult times, and so were less willing to ignore breaches of the rules by fellow members.

The permanence of commission rules was certainly accepted by 1922 by the likes of C. P. Serocold, a partner in Cazenoves, a broking firm with much institutional business.

[83] LSE: Commissions, 15 July 1919, 27 Mar. 1924, 22 June 1920; LSE: General Purposes, 7 Nov. 1919, 26 July 1920, 3 Aug. 1920, 23 Aug. 1920, 29 Dec. 1930; Whyte, *The Stock Exchange*, 73; F. Paukert, 'The Value of Stock Exchange Transactions in Non-Government Securities, 1911–1959', *Economica*, 28 (1962/3), 304.

[84] *Financial News, The Stock Exchange*, 20; M. C. Reed, *A History of James Capel and Company* (London 1975), 80; D. Kynaston, *Cazenove & Co.: A History* (London 1991), 129.

[85] LSE: General Purposes, 12 Jan. 1925, 23 Apr. 1928, 6 Oct. 1930.

[86] LSE: Trustees and Managers, 17 Apr. 1934.

It is generally recognised that there should be a minimum commission, but it should be at a considerably lower scale than that which at present obtains, and the rules which deal with commissions should be greatly modified where large lines of stock are concerned. The latter modification of course applies mainly to the market in Government and Colonial securities.

In framing these requests Serocold was responding to pressure from Casenoves' mainly institutional clients, as he candidly admitted.

In the ordinary course of every day business, I meet businessmen of high position in the City of London, both Bankers, merchants and others who are accustomed to dealing on the Stock Exchange, and I find them of the opinion that if the Stock Exchange is to remain the chief centre of dealings in securities, there will have to be a radical alteration in the existing rules and scales of commissions.

Reflecting Casenoves' links with brokers outside London he also indicated that:

The present scale of commissions between the provinces and us also needs revision in order to attract more business to London.

Generally, what Serocold was doing was voicing the opinion of the large and well-established broking firms among the membership who felt confident about this position in the securities market, if only they were freed from the restrictions imposed by commissions rules.

It is pretty obvious that with lower minimum commissions and *in certain cases* a greater freedom permitted to brokers to charge their clients what they think right and deal where they might, a much greater volume of business will come to the Stock Exchange, and after all that is the result which must benefit the House in general.[87]

Supported by other large brokers, such as Joseph Sebag & Co., the commission rules were modified somewhat to meet the needs of institutional customers but only with great reluctance. The hope was that the competition that had taken hold during the war, as with Glasgow and Liverpool brokers in War Loan, would gradually fade away as business resumed its pre-war channels. As early as June 1924 another large firm of brokers, Fielding, Son & Macleod did point out that this was not happening but the Stock Exchange remained reluctant to alter its rates. Though much of the business passing through the Stock Exchange originated with the larger firms of stockbrokers, with their institutional clients, the majority of brokers among the membership were small partnerships doing a private client business, and they resisted any reduction in minimum commissions rates. For them there would be little or no compensation through an increased volume of transactions. Consequently the commission rate structure remained essentially unaltered between the wars, despite constant

[87] LSE: Commissions, 14 Dec. 1922.

complaints from the larger firms that business was being lost to non-members, especially where it involved numerous and regular purchases, as with financial institutions. In those cases it was worthwhile to seek out alternative means of doing business which was not the case with the individual investor with a close and long-established relationship with a broker.[88]

However rigid fixed commissions regime appeared to be, many clients generating a substantial business were able to obtain discounts. In addition deliberate or accidental evasion of the rules continued to occur throughout the inter-war years. For example, in 1925 brokers on the Mincing Lane Exchange wanted to share commissions with members of the London Stock Exchange which would, effectively, halve the commission charges. This was denied to them as the London Stock Exchange saw them as a threat but in 1926 it was acknowledged that the sharing of commissions was happening unofficially. Similarly in 1930 it was discovered that rebates of commissions were being given, regularly, to large investors even though it was meant only to be given to agents, so as to encourage them to bring business to members of the Stock Exchange. When dealing with the likes of banks, insurance companies, investment trusts, and others it was never easy to be certain whether an order was on behalf of a client or for the institution itself.[89]

However, the whole system of rebates and sharing commissions, which had greatly reduced the inflexibility of the minimum commission rules when applied to large investors, itself came under attack between the wars. Agents were used extensively by the larger firms as introducers and collectors of business, for which they were remunerated by a share of the commissions resulting. The most important among the agents were the banks, with their extensive branch networks and numerous depositors, as they were well connected to those who had any interest in buying and selling securities. There had always been a somewhat uneasy relationship between the banking and broking communities, as brokers saw banks as potential competitors as well as important sources of business. In the days when there were numerous individual banks the broking business they generated was spread among numerous brokers. This ensured that the broking community as a whole saw co-operation not competition as the preferred arrangement. However, the growing amalgamation among banks and the centralization of their operations, virtually completed with the banking amalgamations at the end of the war, led banks to channel more and more business from their separate branches through a London head office and thence to a few larger brokers. By 1916 it was estimated that less than 20 per cent of brokers received orders from banks and the proportion fell

[88] Ibid., 18 Jan. 1923, 22 Feb. 1922, 26 June 1924, 10 May 1932; LSE: General Purposes, 12 Mar. 1923, 11 Feb. 1924, 25 Feb. 1924, 7 July 1924, 15 June 1925; ibid., Non-Permanent, 12 Apr. 1938, 31 May 1938, 9 June 1938, 14 June 1938, 16 June 1938.
[89] LSE: General Purposes, 15 June 1925, 12 Apr. 1926, 17 Nov. 1930.

thereafter. The result was that many of the small brokers saw banks in the 1920s as very much as a threat to their business, not as a source of it. In contrast solicitors were regarded as important sources as they spread their clients buying and selling among numerous brokers.

Consequently, small brokers questioned the value of sharing commissions with agents in general, but banks in particular. Though banks were the main target of the attack on the sharing of commissions they were also the most powerful. It was recognized by the brokers that the banks could always decide to try and by-pass the Stock Exchange and develop an inter-bank market instead. As a result it was other agents, like the solicitors and accountants, who were most likely to be excluded from a share of the commissions, as they were felt to have no alternative but to transact the business through a broker. This was despite the fact that they were the agents the small brokers were less worried about. However, despite the complaints in the early years after the war, no action was taken on the whole subject of rebates, discounts, and the sharing of commissions, and considerable flexibility remained. There was a recognition in the 1920s among the majority of the membership that once the sharing of commissions had been enshrined in the scale of charges, as it was from the outset, it was very difficult to abandon it without creating a tremendous disruption in the way business was done, which could have major consequences for both individual brokers and the Stock Exchange as a whole. At least, temporarily, business would be lost if banks and other agents did not receive a share of the commissions resulting from the orders they were directing to members of the Stock Exchange.[90]

Nevertheless, the collapse in business in the early 1930s prompted a renewed attack on the sharing of commissions, with demands that it be either banned or reduced from 50 per cent to 25 per cent. Again, banks were the main focus of attack, which was backed by around two-thirds of all brokers. In a survey of brokers it was shown that, over the 1927-9 period, of the commissions received from clients some 26 per cent was returned to those introducing the business while a further 31 per cent was taken up in office expenses and wages. This left 43 per cent as profit from the brokers themselves. With the subsequent collapse of business, over the 1930-2 period expenses/wages absorbed 51 per cent of the brokers, commissions income, while commission returned to agents/banks remained constant at 27 per cent. The result was that profits had collapsed to only 22 per cent of commission income. At the same time commission income was also severely reduced. As it was difficult to reduce office expenses and wages greatly, and remain in business, the level of discounts given to banks and others proved an obvious target for reduction for many brokers trying to

[90] LSE: Commissions, 16 Aug. 1916, 23 July 1919, 5 Jan. 1922, 10 Apr. 1922; LSE: General Purposes, 23 Oct. 1922, 5 Feb. 1923, 23 Jan. 1929, 20 Dec. 1930; ibid., Non-Permanent, 16 Oct. 1930.

survive under very difficult circumstances.[91] This time the campaign did have limited success despite the opposition of the brokers. By February 1933 the maximum share of commissions that could be rebated was reduced to one-third, for certain categories of agents. What the Stock Exchange was trying to do was to restrict access to the full discount of 50 per cent to those who were clearly acting in an intermediary capacity, on a full-time regular basis, like banks, provincial brokers, and remisiers abroad. Those who acted on a casual basis, referring orders to a broker when it arose, were to be rewarded with only one-third of the commission resulting. For them there was always the suspicion that they were acting on their own account or being used by certain brokers to offer reduced rates to important individual clients.[92] Though banks had been the main focus of the campaign against discounting there continued to be a strong reluctance to take action against them because of fear of reprisals.

As the Stock Exchange itself recognized in 1932

. . . by virtue of the fact that there are few towns of any importance in the British Isles which have not a bank, or a branch of a bank, the banks are in a position to institute business from the very small capitalists in every part of the country who has no means of getting into touch with stockbrokers . . .

Along with the commercial banks it was felt that financial institutions, like the merchant banks, possessed connections that were 'extremely valuable' for stockbrokers, in contrast to the weaker links of lawyers and other agents. If any change was made in the arrangement with banks and other financial institutions the Stock Exchange had to recognize that there was '. . . considerable danger of them forming some kind of arrangement among themselves by which they would, at least, transact their big gilt-edged orders between themselves and boycott the Stock Exchange in so far as the big orders, which carry the biggest commissions are concerned'. There was definite concern that the discount houses would emerge as alternative intermediaries to brokers/jobbers in the gilt-edged market to be followed by others in industrial securities. The banks, led by Sir Harry Goschen, also made it clear that they would resist any reduction in their half-share of commission even to the extent of bypassing the Stock Exchange—a threat that was taken seriously.[93]

The result was that in 1932 a list of those entitled to a share of commissions was to be drawn up, with the Stock Exchange vetting all applications to be put on the list. This list would then have two elements with banks and related financial institutions/intermediaries being entitled to a 50 per cent rebate while all others, such as solicitors and accountants were

[91] LSE: General Purposes, 23 May 1932.
[92] LSE: Commissions, 3 Dec. 1931, 30 Mar. 1933, 7 Mar. 1935, 11 July 1935. LSE: General Purposes, 11 Jan. 1932.
[93] Ibid., 18 Jan. 1932.

only to receive back a third. Those placed on the one-third list, did complain, like the solicitors and insurance companies, but eventually in October 1932 the new commission rules were approved, and they were in force by the following February 1933. In all this there was the recognition that business might be lost but, with members desperately seeking to enhance their income, that risk was accepted. Once this list was established the Stock Exchange now had the power to regulate those to whom rebates were given. In 1937, for example, 279 country brokers applied to be put on the register of agents entitled to a 50 per cent reduction, as financial intermediaries, but 121 or 43 per cent were rejected. Only those with a substantial and recognized stockbroking business were deemed acceptable. The Stock Exchange was clearly attempting to transform stockbrokers outside London into full-time professionals with a pecuniary interest in bringing business to the members of the London Stock Exchange. Those who operated only casually were to be discouraged.[94]

As it was, the attack on the sharing of commissions was renewed in December 1938 only to be swallowed up by the threat and arrival of war. Clearly many members, especially the small brokers, would not rest until all exceptions to the minimum commission rules were removed.[95] Generally, the inter-war years saw commission rules being enforced to a far great degree than before 1914. Loopholes were being closed while the ability to vary fees was reduced. Undoubtedly this effected the ability of members of the Stock Exchange to attract business on the basis of price, both at the bottom and the top of the scale. Certainly the likes of Serocold of Casenoves, whose business was with large investors, believed the Stock Exchange was being bypassed as a result. Similarly, the business of the small investor was lost. In the period after the war the Post Office handled much of the buying and selling of War Loan and consols for small investors as its charges were less. In 1922 a stockbroker belonging to the London Stock Exchange made a minimum charge of 10s. while the Post Office only charged 2s.3d., though this was later doubled. In 1921 the Post Office and Trustee Savings Banks carried out 260,000 such transactions, with 90 per cent being for less than £500. Essentially, the minimum commission charge meant that the Stock Exchange did not compete at this level. Instead, it left the business to the likes of the savings banks who could consolidate all the little orders into a few big deals and then pass them on to a broker and have the sales or purchases done at a discount.

At least in the case of the Post Office the business did end up with members of the Stock Exchange. This was not the case when banks and mining finance houses matched deals between themselves when the opportunity arose, rather

[94] LSE: General Purposes, 21 Jan. 1932, 26 Jan. 1932, 28 Jan. 1932, 26 Feb. 1932, 20 June 1932, 29 Aug. 1932, 15 Sept. 1932, 17 Oct. 1932, 19 Dec. 1932, 28 Dec. 1932, 15 Apr. 1937, 20 May 1937.
[95] Ibid., 19 Dec. 1938.

than use a broker. With the centralization of transactions in securities for their customers, banks were ideally placed to complete sales and purchases themselves. Similarly, mining finance houses had traditionally acted as both brokers and dealers, releasing securities from their own holdings in the face of demand and absorbing them when the price was favourable. The activities of Arthur Wheeler in the 1920s also indicated the success that could be made of a stockbroking business freed from minimum commission and other rules imposed by these on its membership.[96]

Certainly the minimum commissions rules did reduce the attractions of the London Stock Exchange for provincial brokers and see the emergence outside London of an alternative to the service it offered. What the provincial stock exchanges wanted was the abolition of any fixed scale of commission for buying and selling between members of all the British stock exchanges. This existed for all major stock exchanges outside London, and the Associated Stock Exchanges, which represented the likes of Liverpool and Glasgow, wanted it extended to include London.[97] As they explained, the current situation was that

. . . your Exchange requires members of other Exchanges to pay to your members on nearly all transactions the same commissions as your members charges to their clients . . .

Whereas they wanted the position to be that

. . . Brokers in the country who send a continual stream of orders to their correspondents in London should be exempt from the charge . . .[98]

This would be tantamount to regarding all the members of the individual stock exchanges in Britain as forming one integrated market, who operated a common scale of commissions for non-members but charged each other as circumstances dictated. London would not agree to this believing that it would give provincial brokers immediate access to London jobbers, via a friendly broker. It would also mean an end to any system of sharing commissions, especially with the banks. On the whole, the membership of the London Stock Exchange felt they stood to gain more by denying provincial brokers access to London jobbers and persuading banks to channel business to London through the inducement of a share of the commissions—a facility the provincial brokers did not offer. Throughout the 1920s the London Stock Exchange turned down all requests by the provincial stock exchanges, even the more modest ones, for a reduction in the existing rates, as the feeling was that much provincial business did not pay even at the current rates.[99]

[96] Ibid., 14 Mar. 1922, 24 Mar. 1922, 30 May 1922, 7 Mar. 1927, 23 July 1934, 7 Aug. 1934.
[97] Ibid., 2 Nov. 1921.     [98] Ibid., 7 May 1923.
[99] Ibid., 29 Oct. 1923, 17 Dec. 1923, 9 Jan. 1924, 21 Jan. 1924, 23 Apr. 1928, 3 Sept. 1928, 18 Feb. 1929. LSE: Commissions, 11 May 1928, 8 Oct. 1928, 14 Feb. 1929.

It was not until 1930 that there was an acceptance that the commission rules, as applied to provincial brokers, had cost the London Stock Exchange business. In a survey of brokers, covering the 1927–9 period, it was reported that '. . . country brokers say that they now do a lot of business between themselves . . .'[100]

Developing from the 1920s onwards, and well-established by the 1930s, there came into existence a much more active inter-stock exchange market in the provinces. Whereas before the war provincial brokers directed those sales and purchases that could not be done locally to London, that was less and less the case between the wars. As a result London did appear to be losing out not only on the trading in local securities between local investors, which it had never captured anyway, but also bargains in London quoted securities between investors in different parts of the British Isles. This did appear to be attributable to the minimum commissions rules which left little scope for profit for the provincial broker as he could not charge his client more than the local branch of a national bank would. Essentially, the London Stock Exchange was competing with the provincial stock exchanges through sharing commission with the banks, and so gaining country business that way. In the process it lost some provincial business it once had by its failure to be flexible on the commissions it charged provincial brokers, encouraging them to bypass London where and when it was convenient to do so.[101]

The rules on the fixed scale of commissions also affected the ability of its members to command the London market in foreign securities as they had done in the past. As the market in American securities reappeared in the 1920s, particularly after the return to the gold standard at the pre-war parity in 1925, a growing number of American firms set up business in London, offering a service to British investors. Firms such as de Saint Phalle Ltd., and Harvey Fisk & Sons, were all branches of US brokerage houses while large US banks, like National City Bank, or investment houses like Bankers Trust Co., Guaranty Trust Co., and Higginson & Co., were all established in London by 1921 and did an increasing business during the 1920s. Saint-Phalle Ltd. had partners operating on both the New York Stock Exchange and the Paris Bourse in 1927 as well as branches in London and Brussels. They saw themselves as international brokers. Even New York brokerage houses without offices in London, such as Joseph Walker and Sons, advertised that they would conduct business directly on the New York Stock Exchange for British clients.[102]

Added to the presence of North Americans brokers was the growing international business of the British commercial banks. The Westminster

---

[100] LSE: General Purposes, 29 Dec. 1930.

[101] Ibid., 4 May 1931, 11 July 1932, 11 Mar. 1935, 30 Dec. 1935, 13 June 1938, 11 July 1938, 26 June 1939.

[102] *Stock Exchange Year Book for 1929* (London 1929), pp. iv, cvii; LSE Commissions, 23 Feb. 1921, 7 Oct. 1924, 4 Mar. 1926, 8 Dec. 1927, 12 Jan. 1928; LSE: General Purposes, 28 Nov. 1927; ibid., Subcommittee, 28 Mar. 1927.

Foreign Bank, which was a wholly owned subsidiary of the Westminster Bank, was an active player in foreign securities, with its own representative on the Paris Bourse. Through these banks and non-member brokers British investors had the ability to tap into trading in foreign stock exchanges, most notably New York and Paris. These competitors were not bound by obligation to adhere to the London Stock Exchanges minimum commissions rates while they could offer a rapid dealing service at a competitive price for British investors interested in particular foreign securities, especially dollar-denominated ones.

By the late 1920s the competition from the American houses in London had reached such a level that the London Stock Exchange complained to the New York Stock Exchange, as most of the firms in London were offshoots of their members. By 1928 there were 10 members of the New York Stock Exchange with offices in London, and many more prepared to do business there from their New York offices.

The last thing we wish to do is to curtail facilities for dealings between your market and ours, but if the tendency of our members to set up Branch Offices in London with a view of attracting business direct from the British Public without the intervention of a London Broker is to increase, the question will become a serious one for our Exchange.[103]

This was the implied threat sent by Archibald Campbell, Chairman of the London Stock Exchange to E. H. H. Simmons, President, New York Stock Exchange in January 1928. The reply received from Simmons, though not until the October of 1928, made clear that New York had no intention of restraining the territorial expansion of its membership and explained what lay behind it.

For many years the New York Stock Exchange has permitted its members to establish branch offices and to advertise, and many of our members are firmly persuaded that this policy has been a fundamental factor in the development of New York as the financial centre of the United States. Our strict prohibition against splitting commissions with banks or other non-member concerns or persons—prohibition which we consider absolutely vital to the future success and independent of this Exchange—made the use of branch offices and advertising necessary in the United States and by a natural development our members have established branch offices in several foreign countries.[104]

In the face of this refusal by New York to take action, and prodded by those among its membership who were losing business to these outside firms, like Rowe and Pitman, the London Stock Exchange did reduce its commission rates on 'American' securities.[105]

However, it was the Wall Street crash of late 1929 that really reduced the competition being felt in London from these New York brokers in

---

[103] LSE: General Purposes, 16 Jan. 1928.     [104] Ibid., 15 Oct. 1928.
[105] LSE: Commissions, 26 Jan. 1928, 15 Mar. 1928; 3 May 1928; LSE: General Purposes, 14 Jan. 1929.

particular. Both Saint Phalle and Harvey Fisk disappeared at that time and the interest of British investors in American securities collapsed. However, competition soon reappeared both from the American brokers and bankers who had survived and from new arrivals. The New York brokerage firm of Fenner, Bean & Ungerleide set up an office in London in 1932 adding it to their Paris branch, while another New York broker, Batsell and Co., appeared in 1933. Altogether, by 1937 there were a total of 25 branches of American and Canadian brokers operating in London, providing intense competition for members of the London Stock Exchange in American securities. Clearly, in the 1930s the London Stock Exchange was losing the market in American securities to London branches of American firms who could trade direct with New York.[106]

As early as October 1932 R. Raphael & Sons plus 78 other firms heavily engaged in the market in American securities warned the Stock Exchange of what was happening.

If we were to discontinue the street market and cease dealing at 4 o'clock, a very considerable amount of the American business would be lost to the Stock Exchange members, and as a consequence, be driven into the hands of the outside houses, more particularly to the American firms who have established their own offices in London, or else the public would deal direct with New York. There is no doubt that this is already being done to a certain extent, but it would undoubtedly be greatly increased if there were no street market.[107]

Only the existence of the more lightly regulated after-hours market allowed the London Stock Exchange to retain a share of the trading in American securities taking place in London. By refusing to permit members to share commissions with American brokers in London, as they were regarded as competitors, the American brokers directed more and more of their buying and selling to and from New York, greatly diminishing the spread and depth of London's own market in American securities, and so further discouraging their use of it.

The problem was that much of the business in foreign securities involved contact with non-members both in London and abroad. These non-members, especially banks and brokers, could not be treated as ordinary clients in the way they were charged. Some, like the foreign remisiers, were introducing business to London brokers and would only continue to do so if rewarded by a share of the commissions. Though they could be given 50 per cent in some cases this was not deemed sufficient for the trouble and expenses they incurred. Nevertheless, the commission rules did leave substantial discretion in dealings with fellow financial intermediaries abroad,

---

[106] LSE: Commissions, 1 Sept. 1932, 1 Dec. 1932, 21 Dec. 1933; LSE: General Purposes, 7 Nov. 1932, 28 Dec. 1932, 1 Feb. 1937; *Stock Exchange Yearbook for 1937* (London 1936), p. lxxxvii.
[107] LSE: General Purposes, 17 Oct. 1932.

though not always enough for the arbitrageurs. Arbitrageurs worked on very small margins and so any net commissions payment at all could make the business unprofitable. As Grumbar & See, representing 63 firms who did an extensive arbitrage business, pointed out in 1930.

... in view of the small margin of profit obtainable at present on arbitrage operations, those houses will not be able to afford to pay the full scale of commissions and that an important shrinkage in the volume of the business which this class of operation brings to the Stock Exchange is bound to result.

In fact, they claimed it was already happening

This form of business originates entirely from genuine international supply and demand from all over the world. These transactions are not clients orders in the ordinary sense, but business created by outside Houses with large capital resources and facilities. Under no circumstances could it be created or undertaken to any such extent by firms in the London Stock Exchange ...

We know that many big transactions take place between one outside house and another, and also that business is taken to such Houses direct without going to the Stock Exchange. The margin on which this class of business is transacted is in most cases so small that the full commissions will force outside Houses still more to deal between themselves.[108]

Though some members wanted no discounts to be given, the Stock Exchange was able to accept a sharing of commissions in these cases which, with so much international business being of a two-way nature meant, effectively, that the commissions charges on each side were cancelled out.

The real problem was those brokers and bankers who had established themselves in London and conducted a large business with their parent firms, whether in Europe or North America. Banks could be classified along with UK banks and given a half-share of commissions, but that left out non-member brokers. The London Stock Exchange could not accept a role for brokers in London who were not members and so refused to allow them any share of commissions. However, they were not eligible for entry to the Stock Exchange as they did not confine themselves to broking operations and often included partners from abroad who were members of other stock exchanges. Thus, even though these American brokers were keen to use the London Stock Exchange as an alternative to New York, where a market already existed, the charges made by brokers for so doing were prohibitive. Consequently they directed as much of their business abroad as possible.[109] Clearly, the minimum commissions structure imposed, in certain cases, too expensive a charging structure on the trading in foreign securities, with the result that it increasingly bypassed members of the London Stock Exchange in the

[108] Ibid., 17 Nov. 1930.
[109] Ibid., 19 Nov. 1930, 22 Dec. 1930, 22 Feb. 1932, 29 Jan. 1934, 18 June 1934.

1930s. This did not necessarily mean that it bypassed London. As de Zoete & Gorton pointed out in 1934, in the case of French clients.

Our clients say quite frankly that they want to put the business through the Stock Exchange, but that they feel that if this rate is to be maintained, they will not be able to do so on further occasions.[110]

Instead, the option open to them was to deal through an English bank with a branch in Paris. It was also increasingly difficult to evade these rules. In that same year one firm of brokers, Shaw & Co., were suspended from the Stock Exchange for six months for charging clients in Calcutta and Bombay a lower rate of commissions than the one laid down for such business. The special needs of the arbitrageur were recognized, where simultaneous buying and selling took place, but any concessions to foreign investors could lead to either a re-routeing of domestic business through foreign intermediaries in order to gain the lower rates, or a demand for the lower rates from domestic investors. Clearly this could not be allowed, and so foreign investors, who were not acting as remisiers or involved in arbitrage, had to pay the higher rate.[111]

Overall, the attitude of the Stock Exchange to new developments in the inter-war years was probably typified by its position on the public broadcasting of Stock Exchange prices. The London Stock Exchange was reluctant to permit this to take place, and only agreed to it in 1926, though the request had been first made in 1923. Even then no prices were to be broadcast before 7 p.m., by which time trading would be finished. The worry here was that non-members could trade on London Stock Exchange prices and thus compete directly with it. The London Stock Exchange did not see itself in the role of providing current information on the state of the market, of which it was the central element.[112]

MEMBERSHIP

Between the wars the controls imposed upon its membership by the London Stock Exchange became more and more restrictive. As these controls were not accompanied by new advantages, other than access to the market, inevitably they reduced the ability of the membership to compete with non-members. One explanation for this development might lie in the nature of the membership itself. This was capped at around the 4,000 level making it more difficult and more expensive to gain admission. At the same time particular groups were excluded, especially the Germans who had been such a dynamic element in the pre-war years. As a result the Stock Exchange began to resemble a members-only club for the first time. It had given this

---

[110] LSE: General Purposes, 9 Apr. 1934.      [111] Ibid., 18 June 1934.
[112] Ibid., 11 Jan. 1926; LSE: Subcommittee, Exchange Telegraph Company, 27 Feb. 1923, 13 Mar. 1923, 23 Dec. 1926.

appearance in the past but that was false because it was both relatively easy and cheap to gain admission. Admission was easy and cheap at times between the wars, but only when business was at a low ebb, as in the wake of the post-war speculative boom or the early 1930s. Generally, entry was either difficult or expensive or both. In the mid-1930s it was estimated that membership could cost £3,000, and that was presuming a nomination was available for purchase. For a clerk the cost did fall to £650 but the number of clerks becoming members was running at half the pre-war level. Thus there was not the same influx of new members constantly challenging the regulations of the past and desirous of experimenting with new ways of doing business.[113]

Many brokers with an established domestic business were quite content with the existing regulations, receiving a regular income from fixed commissions and enjoying limited competition. Foster and Braithwaite, for example, after being nearly bankrupted before the war, and then experiencing the boom–bust conditions of the immediate post-war years, adopted a very cautious policy between the wars. They recruited only family members as partners and concentrated upon doing a commission business for private and institutional investors. As a result their income ranged from c.£70,000 to c.£160,000 between 1919 and 1939. Similarly, Capels continued to recruit many of its partners from among those connected with the West End banks, for these continued to provide it with the bulk of its business. P. K. Stephenson, whose brother was a partner in Coutts, was recruited in 1921, with A. D. Malcolm, whose father was chairman of Coutts, coming in 1932. C. R. V. Holt, whose father was the managing partner of another West End bank—Holts—joined in 1936. Similarly, Mullens, the government broker, continued the tradition of sons or nephews entering the firm with both Terence Eden and Derrick Mullens being recruited between the wars. With no expansion in the overall numbers belonging to the Stock Exchange, openings were more restricted with the result that relationships and friendships, would, inevitably, determine to a greater degree who was admitted to membership.[114]

Nevertheless, it would be a mistake to see the inter-war Stock Exchange as comprising only a self-perpetuating group. The need for expertise and business connections remained strong and this created openings for those from different backgrounds and little capital. Cazenoves, in particular,

---

[113] Sir Stephen Killik, *The Work of the Stock Exchange* (London 1933), 18; *The Stock Exchange Clerks' Provident Fund Centenary, 1874–1974* (London 1974), 22; Share-Pushing: Report of the Departmental Committee Appointed by the Board of Trade, 1936–37 (London 1937) (C. 5537), 39.

[114] W. O. Reader, *A House in the City: Foster & Braithwaite, 1825–1975* (London 1979), 132, 134, 179; Reed, *Capel and Company*, 75–7, 79–80; D. Wainwright, *Government Broker: The Story of an office and of Mullens and Company* (East Molesey 1990), 70; A. Gleeson, *People and Their Money: 50 Years of Private Investment* (M & G Group 1981), 82; D. Sebag-Montefiore, *The Story of Joseph Sebag & Co.* (n.p. 1996), 18, 28.

recruited a steady stream of talented individuals who possessed one or both of these attributes. Ludlow Vigers was recruited in 1922 because his experience in Java made him an expert on rubber plantation company shares, which were then exceedingly popular. He had also connections with two banks, Glyns and Hambros. Algy Belmont joined in 1925 creating a link to the merchant bank Lazards, as his father-in-law was Sir Robert Kindersley. In 1928 Cecil Breitmeyer and John Scaramanga appeared, each bringing a particular area of business to the firm. Breitmeyer was the son of a South African mining magnate and brought a knowledge of the gold-mining industry while Scaramanga was a skilled arbitrageur between London and Paris, and had connections with two merchant banks, Singer & Friedlander and Seligman Brothers. From 1933 Cazenoves' money-broking operations were bolstered by David Shaw-Kennedy, who was recruited because of his mathematical ability and connections with the discount houses. Similarly, in that same year Anthony Hornby appeared in order to enhance the firm's connections with British business, as his father had transformed W. H. Smith into a modern retailer. Finally, in 1936 Derek Schreiber was made a partner, cementing the relationship with Henderson Administration, a major client, as his grandfather had been Lord Faringdon. This was not an isolated example. The stockbrokers Bevan & Co. recruited Sidney Perry in 1922 to handle their gilt-edged business because of his technical expertise as an insurance company actuary. They also brought in Tom Ismay, son of the Chairman of the White Star Line, for his private client connections, and Neville Williams, an Australian, who had links with financial institutions there. In turn, all three eventually left to join Phillips & Drew, a small private client firm. William Piercy, a City timber broker, joined the stockbroking firm of Capel, Cure & Terry as a partner in 1934, where he played a key role in the development of unit trusts. Clearly, membership of the Stock Exchange continued to be open to those whose skills and background offered the promise of sustaining an existing business or developing a new area. As ever, talent was as much in demand as connections, but one or the other was required for success.[115]

Despite the restriction on aliens, and bar on Germans, membership of the Stock Exchange was also gained by a succession of individuals whose experience and connections had been acquired overseas. In particular, a growing British interest in Indian securities between the wars encouraged a few individuals from there to transfer to London. R. G. Cruickshank and Victor Butler, both from India, formed the stockbroking firm of Cruickshank & Co. in 1929. They were joined by Henry Turle, who had been the senior partner of the Calcutta broking firm of Place, Siddons & Gough. He was

[115] Kynaston, *Cazenove*, 100–1, 105, 131; Wainwright, *Mullens*, 71. H. Janes, *de Zoete and Gorton* (London 1963), 243–316; LSE: General Purposes, 3 Feb. 1919; W. J. Reader and D. Kynaston, *Professional Stockbrokers: A History of Phillips & Drew* (London 1998), 14–15, 18, 32; Whyte, *The Stock Exchange*, 83; Osborn, *The Stock Exchange*, 49; R. Coopey and D. Clarke, *3i: Fifty Years Investing in Industry* (Oxford 1995), 30.

then recruited by Capels in 1934. Similarly, Nathan & Rosselli, who did a large transatlantic arbitrage business, recruited J. B. Doge an American in 1926, The jobbers, Smith Brothers were set up in London in 1924 by two South Africans with an expertise in the gold-mining market. They joined the Stock Exchange in 1926. A similar route was followed by Joseph Sebag & Co. who had possessed a large continental business before the war. They were a closely connected Jewish family firm but grafted onto that new partners with good connections like Sir Edward Goschen, ex-British ambassador to Vienna, Sir John Gilmour, whose father had been Lord Provost of Edinburgh, and Edmund Telfer, an Edinburgh chartered accountant.[116] The problem was that, unlike the pre-war years, international business offered many fewer openings for either brokers or dealers and so attracted many fewer from overseas with expertise and connections to sell. Instead, brokers and jobbers whose orientation had been largely foreign sought to develop a domestic business in order to survive. A firm of stockbrokers like de Zoete & Gorton, who had done a substantial overseas business before 1914, attempted to replace it by recruiting new partners whose connections were with British banks and solicitors. Actions such as these ensured the survival of both de Zoete & Gorton and Joseph Sebag & Co.[117]

There was also an active internal recruitment market within the Stock Exchange itself, as members moved from one firm to another, and from being independent to becoming partners. In 1930, for example, the brokers Mullens, recruited Hugh Priestly from the jobbers, Wedd Jefferson, as they needed someone with dealing experience. Similarly in 1932, they were joined by Edward Cripps, from the brokers, Simpson & Cripps, as he could help extend their move into equities and away from government debt. Within the Stock Exchange there were constant shifts in alliances as members and clerks left or joined firms, set up on their own or abandoned independence for a salary. In 1936 Peter Kemp-Welch linked up with Foster & Braithwaite as a half-commission man, despite having established a successful business himself as an independent member.[118] Suggestive of the movement among the membership, was the brief résumé given by Clifford Stiles, himself the son of a member killed during the war, of his career on the Stock Exchange. In December 1935 he noted,

I was for several years a Clerk with P. N. Kemp-Gee and Company and then with my own money made myself a member and went jobbing with Smith Brothers. Unfortunately I made a mess of jobbing . . .[119]

[116] Reed, *Capel and Company*, 71, 88; *Financial Times*, 15/16 July 1995; Sebag-Montefiore, *Joseph Sebag & Co.*, 30.

[117] Reed, *Capel and Company*, 97, Janes, *de Zoete and Gorton*, 60; B. H. D. MacDermot, *Panmure Gordon & Co., 1876–1976: A Century of Stockbroking* (London 1976) 59; P. A. Warren, *Heseltine, Powell and Company: One Hundred Years of Stockbroking, 1851–1951* (London 1951), 24; Sebag-Montefiore, *Joseph Sebag & Co.*

[118] Wainwright, *Mullens*, 64–5, 70, 91; Reader, *Foster & Braithwaite*, 179.

[119] LSE: Trustees and Managers, 18 Dec. 1935.

As no firm, whether broker or jobber, was particularly large and most were small, individual members could either operate on their own, join with another as a small partnership, or combine with one of the larger firms either formally or informally. As circumstances changed, either in the market or among partners, these combinations could split apart and reform. Even those expected to join the family firm often spent time with another broker or jobber, gaining experience before finally deciding whether to make the Stock Exchange a career or not.

However, also noticeable in the inter-war years were the mergers that took place between member firms. One reason for this was the loss of experienced partners during the war, accompanied by a cessation of training and replacement. Thus, mergers were an obvious way of sharing the talent that was available. However, this was also accompanied by a desire among firms to spread themselves into new fields, and thus be less vulnerable to changes in the fortunes and fashions of particular markets. Mullens merged with Steer, Lawford & Co. in 1921 which not only brought in four new partners but also extended the firm into the equity market, and so reduced dependence upon government business. Cazenoves, which was already a relatively large broking firm, merged in 1919 with J. E. Tomkinson, Brunton & Co. This added two new partners with experience in money broking as well as connections with Barings. This was followed in 1932 with a merger with Greenwood & Co., a well-established stockbroking firm with a major interest in South American and British railways. Nevertheless, the average size of broking firms remained very small. In 1938 there were 2,491 brokers belonging to the Stock Exchange and these were grouped in 465 different firms, or an average of 5.4 members each (Table 5.5). Even among the larger firms the number of partners remained small. Mullens, for example, grew from four partners in 1920 to seven by 1930, at which level it remained in 1939. This was despite its extensive business on behalf of the government and its move into equities. Similarly Nathan & Rosselli handled an extensive arbitrage business, as well as growing sales and purchases on behalf of institutional clients, with only nine partners in 1936. Despite Cazenoves expansion between the wars, with its mergers and new partners, its staff only rose from around 40 at the beginning of the 1920s to about 70 at the end of the 1930s. Similarly Capels staff grew from c.26 to c.40 over the same period.[120]

Those who were members of the London Stock Exchange did appear to be making a reasonably good living between the wars, despite difficult conditions. Few failed, even in the wake of the 1929 crash, while firms like Foster & Braithwaite, Capels, and Cazenoves all returned healthy profits. Cazenoves, in particular, were generating profits of c.£400,000

---

[120] Wainwright, *Mullens*, 64–5, 138; Reed, *Capel and Company*, 89, 94, 97–8; Kynaston, *Cazenove*, 94, 111, 126–7, 129; LSE: General Purposes, Country Jobbing/Country Business, 4 Apr. 1939.

in the mid-1930s, or a return of 80 per cent per annum on their capital. At the other end of the scale Phillips & Drew, generated £7,651 in 1935/6, which was divisible between five partners, and this was probably typical of private client brokers. As a consequence the incentive to develop difficult segments of the securities market, such as serving the small investor or competing with European banks/American brokers, was limited, especially if Stock Exchange rules made it difficult anyway. Increasingly this could be left to others.[121] The Melbourne stockbrokers, J. B. Were & Co., for example, opened a London office in 1928 to deal directly with investors interested in Australian securities in the City of London.[122]

In the area of stockjobbing, firms also remained small, with the 1,433 jobbers of 1938 being grouped into 342 separate firms, or an average of 4.2 members per firm (Table 5.5). This was despite the fact that jobbers were also under pressure between the wars as better capitalized outside firms and banks competed for their business. Nevertheless, few mergers resulted and existing firms expanded little. A firm like Wedd Jefferson for example, merged with no other jobber between the wars.[123] Instead what took place were informal alliances between jobbers to handle the market in a specific security. These were referred to as 'market partnerships' and their purpose was explained in 1919.

There were cases where an issue was too big for one firm to handle and too small for a public issue. In these cases two strong firms in market partnership prevented the business going outside. It also often occurred that a member who had a special knowledge of some stock was not strong enough to finance his business and it was an advantage to the House that he should become allied with a strong firm.[124]

It might have been expected that the justification for market partnerships would also have encouraged the emergence of jobbing firms with a large number of partners. However, that was not the case. For both jobbers and brokers the inability to expand the number of clerks placed on the floor of the house set a ceiling to the expansion of the size of firms. Judging from the need to form market partnerships and the activities of large outside dealers, like S. Japhet & Co., there were benefits of scale to be obtained but these were not available to members.[125]

During the 1920s Stock Exchange jobbers were actually a privileged

[121] LSE: General Purposes, 21 Feb. 1931, 28 Dec. 1932, Reed, *Capel and Company*, 83–4, 94–5; Kynaston, *Cazenove*, 100–1, 117, 119, 123, 125, 134, cf. Reader, *Foster & Braithwaite*, 134; Reader and Kynaston, *Phillips & Drew*, 10; Share-Pushing: Report, 17, 29, 67; Dennett, *Charterhouse Group*, 14, 16, 32.

[122] S. Salsbury and K. Sweeney, *The Bull, The Bear and the Kangaroo: The History of the Sydney Stock Exchange* (Sydney 1988), 319.

[123] *Wedd, Durlacher, Mordaunt and Company, Members of the Stock Exchange, London* (n.p., 1984).

[124] LSE: Rules and Regulations, 3 July 1919, 9 July 1919.

[125] Dennett, *Charterhouse Group*, 77.

group. Whereas brokers and others paid a 1 per cent stamp duty on all the sales and purchases they carried out, from August 1920 onwards jobbers were only subject to a nominal stamp of 10s. per transaction on all stock held for less than two months. This was a recognition of the role played by jobbers in holding securities they had purchased until a favourable opportunity for resale arose. Nevertheless, competition from brokers in selected securities did continue, as it did from those provincial brokers who began to offer a dealing service to their members because of the cost of using London. W. J. Richardson & Co., began to job in gilt-edged securities in Belfast in 1923, for example, despite having to pay the 1 per cent duty. This protection of the tax privilege was less secure against foreign competitors, like European banks or New York brokers, because they could lodge the securities abroad and so carry out transactions away from British jurisdiction, and so contributed to the erosion of international business.[126]

The competition faced by the jobbers intensified in the 1930s. After much campaigning the provincial jobbers managed to have the concessionary tax extended to themselves in 1931. The Stock Exchange did not take this matter very seriously and so did not oppose the extension of the tax privilege to provincial jobbers. As it was, by the mid-1930s the London Stock Exchange recognized the increased competition they now faced from country jobbers who could now operate under the same tax privilege as London jobbers.[127]

It was reported in 1935 that:

An outstanding example of a country jobber who is prepared to make prices and deal in securities the market for which is in London is Messrs J. W. Nicholson and Sons of Sheffield. There is clear evidence that this firm transacts a very considerable business which would otherwise come to London.[128]

Certainly, by the end of the 1930s there was no doubt on the Stock Exchange that country jobbers had carved out for themselves a role in industrial and commercial securities that had once been the monopoly of dealers in London.[129]

Competition in overseas securities also intensified in the 1930s as banks exploited their expertise in foreign exchange and international connections to offer finer prices and a readier market than jobbers on the floor of the Stock Exchange. The market in American securities, for example, had moved almost entirely off the floor of the Stock Exchange. Thus, like the

---

[126] LSE: General Purposes, 6 Sept. 1920, 7 May 1923, 14 Sept. 1925, 17 Nov. 1930; Thomas, *Stock Exchanges of Ireland*, 235; W. A. Thomas, *The Provincial Stock Exchanges* (London 1973), 171, 180.

[127] LSE: General Purposes, 26 May 1931, 7 July 1931, 7 Aug. 1934; 27 Aug. 1934; Thomas, *Provincial Stock Exchanges*, 221.

[128] LSE: General Purposes, 11 Mar. 1935.

[129] Ibid., 17 Apr. 1939; LSE: Country Jobbing/Country Business, 4 Oct. 1934, 7 Oct. 1934, 7 Mar. 1935, 30 May 1935.

brokers, the jobbers lost to outside competition between the wars. The ability of country jobbers to deal directly with large investors, either individuals or institutions, which was denied to jobbers who were members of the London Stock Exchange, gave them a competitive edge in those securities in which they specialized. Similarly, the large capital possessed by the banks, mining finance houses, and American brokers, gave them an advantage in international operations involving large deals at fine prices being done for exchange purposes. It was recognized on the Stock Exchange that jobbers could not compete in this area and could only survive if they complemented the banks rather than competed with them. Requests to either allow jobbers to deal directly with non-members, or to prevent brokers from using outside dealers as easily as they did, were refused in the 1930s. As with the brokers the cap of expansion on membership, and the generally satisfactory level of business, especially in government stock, did reduce the incentive for jobbers to pursue other areas as aggressively as they might, especially in the face of strong competition from the country and abroad.[130]

However, though both the brokers and dealers belonging to the Stock Exchange appear to have become less aggressive in their search for business between the wars, a considerable degree of dynamism was exhibited, within the confines of the restrictions placed upon them by the Stock Exchange. Though much of the business of brokers remained the same— buying and selling on behalf of large investors, both private and institutional—one major area that developed was handling new issues on behalf of domestic industrial and commercial concerns. The merchant banks that proliferated in London before 1914 had largely handled overseas issues, especially for railroads and governments, leaving the smaller issues of British industrial and commercial companies to others, including brokers. With foreign borrowing much reduced after the First World War, and a growing interest in the securities of British industrial and commercial companies, brokers stepped in to handle the issues of securities that they made. Capels, Cazenoves, and Foster & Braithwaite, were for example, much involved in such issues as were a host of other brokers. Mullens even became involved though they withdrew after 1930 after having been warned by the Bank of England that it could jeopardize the business they did for it. One estimate, made for 1937, indicated that some 92 stock-broking firms were actively involved in the new issues business. If the opportunity was there brokers became involved. C. N. Whittington, a stockbroker specializing in shipping company shares, moved into the actual finance of shipping from 1934 onwards, as the industry faced growing problems due to the collapse of world trade. Though brokers had long been

---

[130] LSE: General Purposes, 9 Mar. 1931, 7 Aug. 1934, 5 May 1937, 7 Nov. 1939; ibid., Non-Permanent, 27 Nov. 1930, 2 Dec. 1930, 3 Dec. 1930, 4 Dec. 1930, 12 Apr. 1938, 4 June 1938, 9 June 1938, 13 Oct. 1938; LSE: Commissions, 10 Mar. 1938.

involved in the new issue business it does appear that they became more active in this regard between the wars. They were often more familiar with the domestic economy than the merchant banks and possessed better contacts among the business community. Thus it was the broker S. J. Lovell & Co. that handled such issues as George Wimpey, Richard Costain, and Marley Tile, benefiting from the housing boom, and Currys, Ilford Camera, and British Tyre and Rubber, whose involvement in new products attracted investor interest. Similarly, it was another broker, E. R. Lewis, who floated the record company Decca. At the same time many brokers were also involved with established finance houses in handling issues of securities by domestic industrial and commercial concerns. Greenwoods co-operated with Schroders in many new issues while John Prust & Co. acted with the Charterhouse Trust. It was a stockbroker, Richard Jessel, who advised Siegmund Warburg when setting up Mercury securities in London in 1933. The switch towards domestic finance clearly operated in favour of stockbrokers and many responded to the opportunities it opened up.[131]

Brokers also responded positively to some of the new opportunities created by the changes in the investing community. The unit trust movement, for example, was largely the creation of stockbrokers, especially Burton-Baldry, Ian Fairbairn, and W. Piercy. It was Burton-Baldry who brought the idea from the United States of an unmanaged portfolio of securities held for 20 years and then redeemed. That was then converted into a flexible trust by Ian Fairbairn, with the units representing the underlying assets being able to be bought or sold at valuation. Thus, though Stock Exchange brokers were unwilling or unable to reach out, directly, to the small investor, the development of the unit trust movement from 1931 onwards did exhibit their ability to respond to the growth of a mass investing public and devise ways of meeting their needs.[132]

Brokers also responded to those new openings that developed abroad, faced as they were by the loss of business in such major areas as American and Russian securities. For example, firms like L. Messel & Co. and Nathan & Rosselli had by 1921, developed an extensive business between London and Paris. As post-war restrictions eased this was extended into a London–Paris–New York–Amsterdam connection involving such stocks as Royal Dutch Shell.[133] Such was their success that by January 1925 P. N. Kemp-Gee were able to claim that '. . . practically every foreign Government and other Dollar Loans issues in America can be bought or

[131] Reed, *Capel and Company*, 77–8; Kynaston, *Cazenoves*, 103, 145, 158; Wainwright, *Mullens*, 65, 69, 73; Reader, *Foster & Braithwaite*, 148–9; Roberts, *Schroders*, 389; Ellinger, *The City*, 300–1; E. Green and M. Moss, *A Business of National Importance: The Royal Mail Shipping Group, 1902–1937* (London 1982), 166; Dennett, *Charterhouse Group*, 22, L. Hannah, *The Rise of the Corporate Economy* (London 1976), 76; J. Attali, *A Man of Influence: Sir Siegmund Warburg, 1902–1982* (London 1986), 126, 136; J. Kinross, *Fifty Years in the City: Financing Small Business* (London 1982), 78; LSE: General Purposes, 2 Aug. 1921.

[132] Kinross, *Fifty Years*, 119; Gleeson, *People and Their Money*, 1–2.

[133] LSE: General Purposes, 11 Oct. 1920, 10 Jan. 1921, 18 Apr. 1921, 8 Mar. 1923, 12 Mar. 1923; S. D. Chapman, *Raphael Bicentenary, 1787–1987* (London 1981), 43.

sold immediately inside the Stock Exchange today . . .'[134] The result of these brokers' actions was to retain a large international market on the floor of the London Stock Exchange, despite the increased importance of New York, Paris, and Amsterdam in the business. This was only done by aggressive risk taking as A. D. Overy, of the brokers H. Carlebach & Co., explained in 1930, '. . . as soon as he got a $^3/_8$ margin in a stock like Brazil Tractions he started buying and selling. If he waited for a margin he would never be able to deal in Brussels. Outsiders did not wait for cables but acted on tendencies . . .'[135] Clearly the business had to be captured by taking the same risks as outside firms, like the European banks. In addition, brokers were in the forefront in the development of new overseas markets as with trading to the Far East. By the mid-1920s, for example, they were establishing strong contacts with Singapore and Kuala Lumpur in order to serve clients interested in tin shares.[136]

Generally, what brokers did between the wars was to rebuild their domestic and international contacts to reflect the changed circumstances of the securities market at home and abroad. Domestically, this meant establishing closer relationship with banks, solicitors, provincial brokers, and others who were in close contact with the greatly expanded investing public. Deprived of the ability to advertise, create branches, or compete on price but still possessing the right to share commission, this was one of the few ways they could gain access to the new investors. For example, it was estimated that over the 1927–9 period 9 per cent of an average broker's business came via the clearing banks, 7.5 per cent via county brokers, and a further 17.1 per cent through other agents, or a third in total. Obviously, the proportion varied enormously as each firm tended to specialize. Morison & Morison and P. M. Vaughan & Co. did an extensive country business, Capels served the West End banks, and L. Jacobs dealt for merchant banks and mining finance houses, for instance. In fact, certain brokers were very closely tied to particular banks—clearing, foreign, and merchant. W. Greenwell & Co. acted for Credit Lyonnais, Grumbar & See for A. Keyser and Co., H. Carlebach & Co. for S. Japhet & Co., Rowe & Pitman for Higginson & Co., or Schwab & Snelling for Société Générale Foncière. Such was the closeness of the relationship that in 1938, for example, Schwab & Snelling acted on a telephone order from the Paris Office of Société Générale Foncière to buy £160,000 in French *rentes*. In particular it was the larger firms that relied heavily on the business being generated by other financial institutions. They had the established contacts and could command trust. The clearing banks were valued especially for the business they brought in as they collected orders from all over the country, centralized them at head office, and then had the sales and purchases carried out by favoured brokers. Pember & Boyle estimated in 1939 that 70 per cent of the total number of orders handled by the

---

[134] LSE: General Purposes, 5 Jan. 1925.    [135] Ibid., Non-Permanent, 25 Nov. 1930.
[136] LSE: General Purposes, 28 Dec. 1926.

clearing banks originated in their county branches. It was also possible to compete on quality of service rather than price. When at Phillips & Drew from 1935 onwards, Sydney Perry used his actuarial knowledge and insurance company connections to generate a growing business through the specialist investment advice they could give in return for orders to buy or sell.

Those brokers without contacts in the banks and other financial institutions had to rely on other ways of generating business. Vanderfelt & Co., for instance, did an extensive business with solicitors, both in London and the provinces. Those brokers without even these contacts used other means to generate business such as employing clerks or engaging half-commission men. These brought in orders from their circles of friends and relatives.[137] Such was the case of the broker, T. G. Hensler & Co.:

Captain P. Guthrie-Davidson has for a very short time past introduced some of his friends and relations as clients to us, and has been receiving half-commission on these introductions. For the purpose of being able to look after his clients, he has the privilege of using our telephone and of using notepaper giving the address and the telephone number of our firm but not the name of the firm.[138]

Consequently, brokers were at the very centre of a vast web of contacts which, daily, brought into the Stock Exchange a huge volume of business from throughout the country, ranging from the constant stream of sales and purchases of the large financial institutions to the intermittent stream from the half-commission men.

Inevitably such a system could lend itself to abuse as the brokers themselves recognized. C. E. Stevenson & Co., for example, along with 13 other brokers, complained in 1938 about the 'Individuals who are usually only in evidence when markets are active and who tout for business round West End Clubs and in golf Clubs and on race Courses etc., and may be in touch with more than one Broker.'[139] However, without altering the entire way stockbroking was organized and operated through the London Stock Exchange it was very difficult to exclude those who preyed upon their friends, acquaintances, and relatives, from the vastly greater legitimate business that the system generated.

This system also operated overseas with brokers retaining contacts in major centres. In 1927 R. Layton & Co. employed a Swiss clerk simply to maintain contact with Swiss, German, and Italian banks. Other firms had the overseas equivalent of half-commission men—remisiers—based abroad who collected business and directed it to London. The brokers, de Zoete

---

[137] LSE: General Purposes, 9 Jan. 1923, 27 June 1927, 29 Dec. 1930, 9 Mar. 1931, 11 Jan. 1932, 10 Jan. 1938, 19 Dec. 1938, 28 Dec. 1938, 2 May 1938; Reed, *Capel and Company*, 79, 98; Gleeson, *People and Their Money*, 35; LSE: Commissions, 8 Nov. 1934; LSE: General Purposes, Non-Permanent, 16, Oct. 1930; Whyte, *The Stock Exchange*, 83; Reader and Kynaston, *Phillips & Drew*, 19–21.
[138] LSE: General Purposes, 15 July 1929.      [139] Ibid., 19 Dec. 1938.

& Gorton, were in close contact with J. H. Perez who ran a brokerage firm with offices in Cairo and Alexandria, using as an intermediary his brother Sam Perez, who was based in London.[140] Gerald Williams, of the brokers Williams de Broe & Co., explained the procedure in 1934: 'we send prices everyday to our remisier, and he hands them round to his clients with my firms' initials at the bottom.'[141] This was a well-established procedure dating back to long before the First World War. Though it did continue between the wars, the decline of international business reduced its popularity. The number of remisiers appeared to have dropped from 84 to 65 between 1921 and 1931 and then recovered to 78 by 1938. In addition, the foreign firms were reversing the process. Batsell & Co., a London and New York brokerage firm, were employing Norman D'Arcy in London to bring business to them in the 1930s while another firm of London and New York brokers employed Alexander Abel Smith. Similarly, foreign banks with branches or representatives in London could direct business to the London Stock Exchange or away, depending on where the best markets at the lowest costs were to be found.[142]

Thus, though the number of investors directly served by London Stock Exchange brokers may have remained relatively small between the wars, through their network of contacts at home and abroad they continued to attract a vast volume of business. The main loss appears to have been internationally, for though the contacts did remain they appear to have been much less and much reduced in importance. Here, the exclusion from the Stock Exchange of foreign firms who brought ready-made networks with them, must have been a major loss.

Deprived of outside contacts it was more difficult for jobbers to develop new lines of business. They were dependent upon what brokers brought in. They could only buy and sell those securities that brokers approached them about. Nevertheless the preferential stamp duty and the vast volume of government debt to be traded did provide them with a secure place within the Stock Exchange. However, they were involved in attempting to revive markets that had once been important. The jobbers Bristowe Brothers, for example, who had been major players in dealing between London and Paris, resumed that activity as early as 1921. There was also much jobbing activity in both rubber plantation company shares and South African gold-mining shares in the 1920s, as well as a revival of the American market, but in the 1930s many of the jobbers involved in areas outside UK government stock did badly. Exchange controls and competition from European banks/New York brokers made many of their traditional markets difficult, notably orders from European investors or dealings in American

[140] Ibid., 27 June 1927; LSE: Commissions, 31 Mar. 1921, 26 Mar. 1931, 2 Feb. 1933, 1 Apr. 1937, 31 Mar. 1938.
[141] Ibid., 26 Apr. 1934.
[142] LSE: General Purposes, 28 Dec. 1932; LSE: Commissions, 21 Dec. 1933.

securities. Competition from country jobbers undermined the market in individual shares while Argentinian rail collapsed as a market.[143]

Faced with this, jobbers tried to develop other interests. A number, for example, attempted to move into the market for Indian securities which was largely an inter-broker market.[144] Jobbers like G. T. Pulley & Co. explained the background.

It is difficult to sell in bulk in London without depressing the market out of proportion, and by sending a cable to Calcutta you can avoid these violent fluctuations. It is not the money, but the fact that you can get the stock sold out there without making an effect on the London market. It enables you to keep a nice steady market price in London . . .[145]

Furthermore, this need to deal in the East in order to maintain their position in London led jobbers to provide the service to brokers out in the Far East and Pacific itself, because there were no jobbers in Australia, India, or the Far East generally.

This inevitably provoked the opposition of the brokers as it undermined the business they were doing in those areas. Unlike the domestic situation the rules did permit jobbers to offer a service directly to non-members overseas but the Stock Exchange was reluctant to permit this in areas outside those where jobbers were already operating. Such was the case with the Far East Pacific area which brokers regarded as their own. Thus, it was difficult for jobbers to establish new roles for themselves as competition was coming not just from better capitalized and better connected firms outside the Stock Exchange but also from brokers inside the Stock Exchange.[146]

With brokers in the majority on the Stock Exchange they could use their powers to limit the service jobbers could provide to non-members, when that threatened their business. During the inter-war years the rules of the Stock Exchange, designed to create an orderly market, were increasingly being used by the membership to limit the competitive environment within which they operated. This was true both in terms of outside competition, with restrictions on admissions, and internally, with minimum commissions and other controls. The end result was a lessening of those forces for change that had forced the membership in the past to respond to challenges and to seize opportunities. Though change continued to take place and many firms exhibited dynamic tendencies, the membership as a whole became much more conservative, seeking to maintain what they had rather than expand into new areas.

---

[143] Roberts, *Schroders*, 315; LSE: General Purposes, 7 May 1923, 14 Sept. 1925, 17 Nov. 1930, 7 Aug. 1934; LSE: Commission, 12 May 1921.

[144] LSE: General Purposes, 22 Nov. 1937.    [145] LSE: Commissions, 20 Jan. 1938.

[146] Ibid., 27 Jan. 1938, 10 Feb. 1938, 24 Feb. 1938, 10 Mar. 1938.

# 6

# *The Changing Market Place Between the Wars*

## COMPETITION

The competitive environment within which the London Stock Exchange existed between the wars was itself changing. Communications were allowing the London Stock Exchange to serve, directly, a much wider constituency in terms of the investing public. With the introduction of omnibus telephone circuits and the teleprinter within Britain, and the continuing development of wireless telegraphy and submarine telephone cables internationally it was becoming as easy and cheap to communicate between London and other centres as within London itself. As it was, the use of the telephone by London brokers, both for local and national purposes, grew enormously in this period. Cazenoves went so far as to have private lines installed between its office and those of its largest clients, such as Barings and Schroders. Though regular face-to-face contact was still important, with partners in Capels, Cazenoves, and Sebags continuing to do a daily round of regular clients, that was being supplemented, and then steadily replaced, by telephone calls. With a telephone call a client could be immediately updated as market circumstances changed and new orders received and carried out. It was an easy matter to extend that service to clients outside London.[1]

However, though technology was continuing to eliminate distance as a barrier to direct participation in the market, institutional impediments still remained or were introduced. The imposition of exchange controls made it difficult to obtain the foreign currency necessary to pay for the purchase of securities owned outside a country. Domestically each stock exchange jealously guarded its own independence while manœuvring for position within an evolving market-place. Communication was a two-edged weapon as the direction of any flow of business was dependent upon the competitive power of the markets at either end, and the numerous stock exchanges still

[1] LSE: Trustees and Managers, 16 Apr. 1926; C. H. Holden and W. G. Holford, *The City of London: A Record of Destruction and Survival* (London 1951), 182; D. Kynaston, *Cazenove & Co.: A History* (London 1991), 111, 136; M. C. Reed, *A History of James Capel and Company* (London 1975), 79; D. Sebag-Montefiore, *The Story of Joseph Sebag & Co.* (n.p. 1996), 39.

in existence between the wars fully understood this. Though the London Stock Exchange increasingly recognized the competition now posed by its provincial counterparts between the wars it was incapable of developing a strategy that could cope with it. For most London brokers provincial orders were a marginal part of their activity and thus easily sacrificed. A survey done in 1930 found that only 31 firms of brokers did more than 20 per cent of their business with provincial brokers. When this survey was repeated in July 1939 only 11 per cent of all firms indicated that more than 20 per cent of their business was done with the country while 80 per cent did under 10 per cent. Under these circumstances little could be done to persuade the membership as a whole to adopt a more flexible attitude towards the provincial stock exchanges, especially at a time when costs had risen and income was under pressure. All that was achieved was that when the general rebate on commission was reduced from one-half to one-third in 1933, that for provincial brokers remained at the same level—as did that for banks.[2]

Throughout the inter-war years the provincial stock exchanges did not remain passive onlookers to a battle being fought—and lost—on their behalf between members of the London Stock Exchange. The very restrictions and charges imposed by London created opportunities for a new group of dealers to emerge who did not belong to the London Stock Exchange but could offer the market-making facility that provincial brokers had been used to receiving from that institution. Though no provincial stock exchange could, of itself, support even one full-time dealer, collectively their volume of business could. In 1934, when the London Stock Exchange had some 4,000 members, the largest provincial stock exchange, Glasgow, had only 250. Collectively, though, there were some 1,319 stockbrokers in the provinces of whom 1,045 were attached to one or other of the 21 recognized stock exchanges. With the London Stock Exchange proving uncooperative there was now every incentive to develop trading links between these provincial stock exchanges so that London could be bypassed wherever possible.[3]

By the end of the 1920s such a means was not only in place but was being actively and regularly used by the members of the provincial stock exchanges. In 1928 the London Stock Exchange had been informed by one member that much Belfast business was now going to Glasgow and Liverpool rather than passing through the London Stock Exchange

---

[2] LSE: General Purposes, 9 Jan. 1924, 29 Oct. 1928, 29 Dec. 1930, 10 Apr. 1933, 11 Mar. 1935, 13 June 1938, 11 July 1938, 14 July 1941; Kynaston, *Cazenove*, 137; F. E. Armstrong, *The Book of the Stock Exchange* (London 1934), 139; LSE: Subcommittee on Exchange Telegraph Company, 11 Feb. 1920; LSE: Subcommittee of a Non-Permanent Character, 6 May 1930.

[3] LSE: General Purposes, 26 May 1931; Armstrong, *Book of the Stock Exchange*, 141–62; W. A. Thomas, *The Provincial Stock Exchanges* (London 1973), 171, 180, 196, 206, 219, 221; W. A. Thomas, *The Stock Exchanges of Ireland 1918–1976* (Liverpool 1986), 226.

as in the past. The threat to London was still perceived to be small however.

County brokers say that they now do a lot of business between themselves, but the general belief was that 'we believe that this forms but a small proportion of their total business in securities which have a London market'.[4]

In contrast, by the middle of 1933 there was a realization that the competition provided by the provincial stock exchanges was both a real and growing one because their members could: '. . . deal with some rapidity and ease with practically any part of the country as they can with London'.[5] Not only were London brokers and thus jobbers being bypassed as provincial brokers matched sales and purchases between each other using a web of direct telephone lines, but there was ever the impression that they were siphoning away some London business as well, because of the competitive markets, in terms of prices and transaction times, that they offered.[6]

The clearest example of this competition was the appearance and growth of provincial jobbers who offered their services not simply to members of the provincial stock exchanges but to the public at large. On the provincial stock exchanges there were no rules prohibiting jobbers from dealing directly with non-members for there was no distinction made between brokers—who transacted the orders of clients—and jobbers, who bought and sold on their own account. Consequently, jobbers who belonged to a provincial stock exchange could offer the very dealing service that the London jobbers were prohibited from doing by the 1909 and 1912 rule changes. Among the most prominent of these was J. W. Nicholson & Son of Sheffield, who had become, possibly, the largest firm of jobbers in the country by the 1930s. They had been established in 1909 as a firm of stock-brokers but from 1921, along with a number of other provincial brokers, they began to operate as dealers for members of the provincial stock exchanges, who could contact them by telephone for a price quotation and to make a buy/sell order.[7] By 1935 the London Stock Exchange was forced to recognize that '. . . this firm transacts a very considerable business which would otherwise come to London' and that the competition they provided was now well-established because

The gradual improvement in telephone and telegraph communications between local centres would appear to facilitate this class of business and under existing conditions there seems no reason to believe that it will not increase in volume.

[4] LSE: General Purposes, 29 Dec. 1930.   [5] Ibid., 26 June 1933.
[6] W. H. Whyte, *The Stock Exchange* (London 1924), 4; A. S. J. Osborn, *The Stock Exchange* (London 1927), 45.
[7] LSE: General Purposes, 7 Aug. 1934, 11 Mar. 1935; LSE: General Purposes, Subcommittee of a Non-Permanent Character, 13 Apr. 1928; Thomas, *Provincial Stock Exchanges*, 218, 221, 237; Thomas, *Stock Exchanges of Ireland*, 225–6.

Furthermore, there was the prospect that the provincial stock exchanges appeared to be mounting a real challenge to the London Stock Exchange as there was the prospect that

... the future will see the country brokers uniting to form an organisation of their own with their own dealers and machinery for settlement and making a market which in time might come to rival London.[8]

Despite the alarmist tone of these statements, and pressure for change from such important firms of brokers as Vickers da Costa & Co., and jobbers like Wedd, Jefferson & Co., the Stock Exchange resisted responding to this rivalry by altering its practice and charges, so as to permit its members to become more competitive in this area. By 1939 it was estimated that Nicholsons were handling 1,000 transactions a day—up from 400 in 1934—and were in regular contact with some 900 brokers, through a highly automated communications and dealing room in Sheffield. As early as 1934 Nicholsons had spent some £40,000 on equipment and employed around 100 staff in order to maintain an accessible and responsive dealing service for any registered client.[9] In that year the following description of that office was given to the London Stock Exchange,

As the amount of business coming over the telephone has been too large to be handled by his principal dealers, we hear he has recently installed in his office an expensive giant, electronically operated, price board. This board contains the names of the main stocks in which he deals. On one side of the board sit his chief dealers, who each have a form of electric typewriter which controls the prices appearing on the indicator board. As the position of their 'book' changes as a result of jobbing, so they alter the prices on the board. On the other side of the indicator board sit a large staff of sub-dealers who are empowered to deal in a limited number of shares on the basis of the prices which appear on the indicator board.[10]

Utilizing the latest technology and maintaining direct telephone lines to selected brokers' offices Nicholsons could provide a dealing service to rival any that was available in London, and they were not alone. In 1939 there were nine major firms of country jobbers and they were making a market in 385 different stocks, specializing in those of most interest to the provincial stock exchanges. Thus they traded in 193 industrial and commercial stocks, 60 insurance, and 50 mining. Though the London Stock Exchange continued to dominate the securities business in Britain a significant and growing part of the market was now in the hands of the provincial stock exchanges who were in active competition with London.[11]

---

[8] LSE: General Purposes 11 Mar. 1935.

[9] Ibid., 11 Jan. 1939, 14 Aug. 1939, 28 Jan. 1941, 13 June 1941, 14 July 1941; LSE: Subcommittee on Country Jobbing, Subcommittee on Country Business, 4 Oct. 1934.

[10] Ibid., 4 Oct. 1934.

[11] Ibid., 7 Mar. 1935, 30 May 1935, 20 June 1935, 21 Nov. 1935, 21 Mar. 1939, 4 Apr. 1939, 10 Aug. 1939, 6 Feb. 1940, 11 Apr. 1940 (with attached papers).

There was a recognition of this state of affairs among the members of the London Stock Exchange from the mid-1930s onwards but it was not until June 1939 that there was a willingness to open full discussions with the provincial stock exchanges in order to try and resolve the rivalry. What London wanted was an end to country jobbing, at least in those securities which were also quoted on the London Stock Exchange. This would leave the provincial stock exchanges with the market for local securities. What the provincial stock exchanges wanted was either direct access to the London jobbers or major concessions on the fixed rate of commission charged by London brokers for passing such business to the jobbers. For direct access the provincial stock exchanges would sacrifice their country jobbers, as they only provided an alternative to London in a restricted range of securities. Where the country jobbers did not make a market provincial brokers had to use London, which put them in the same position as the banks and other agents competing for the business of country clients. However, the London Stock Exchange remained unwilling to concede direct access. Instead a compromise was agreed whereby the London Stock Exchange agreed to give provincial brokers more privileged access to the London market in return for the provincial stock exchange restricting the activities of country jobbers. In particular, the provincial stock exchanges agreed to enforce single capacity, and so prevent country jobbers making a market for anyone other than a broker. With the outbreak of the Second World War these agreements quickly evaporated in the face of changed circumstances.[12]

Though London was losing out in competition with the provincial stock exchanges between the wars, it was also making gains at their expense. In particular, the one weapon London had was its willingness to share commission with a wide range of intermediaries, which the members of the provincial stock exchanges were unwilling to countenance. Scottish sales and purchases of bank and insurance shares, for example, were more and more directed to London by banks, solicitors and others in return for participation in the fees paid by investors in the form of commission. Generally, the merger or amalgamation of railways, banks, and industrial enterprises did create large companies whose securities were attractive to a wide cross-section of the investing public. Inevitably the greatest concentration of ownership was to be found in London among the individually wealthy and the large financial institutions. In addition, London remained the only market where large sales and purchases could be done quickly and without large adverse price changes, whether in government stock or popular corporate issues. This factor was of importance to the major

[12] Conference between representatives of the Committee for General Purposes, the Stock Exchange, London, and the Council of Associated Stock Exchanges, 14–16 June 1939; LSE: Country Jobbing, 28 Feb. 1940, 19 Mar. 1940, 20 Mar. 1940, 9 Apr. 1940, 11 Apr. 1940; LSE: General Purposes, 17 Apr. 1939, 26 June 1993, 14 Aug. 1939, 6 May 1940.

financial institutions, like insurance companies and investment trusts, that were important holders of such securities. Consequently, the fundamental forces at work were encouraging a centralization of domestic securities business in London, but the London Stock Exchange diminished its own attractions by a failure to accommodate the needs of the broking community operating in the provinces by the restrictions it placed on its own membership in terms of single capacity and minimum commissions. The London Stock Exchange did not possess a monopoly over the domestic securities market but tended to act as if it did.[13]

Thus, domestically the Stock Exchange's own actions had cost it part of the business that it could have done, and had given an opportunity to non-members to exploit gaps in its service to both investors and securities. Nevertheless, important as these were there can be no doubt that the London Stock Exchange, and its membership, continued to dominate the domestic securities market though not quite to the same extent as it had before 1914. Internationally, however, the problems were of a different order and nature. Here the problem lay with the decline and collapse of much of the global market for securities, and its growing complexity. This created opportunities for better capitalized and better connected players, placing members of the Stock Exchange at a disadvantage. The rules barring membership to anyone other than full-time brokers and jobbers, kept banks—merchant and commercial—out of the Stock Exchange. However, it was operators like Helbert Wagg, Japhets, Westminster Bank, or Crédit Lyonnais, which saw the international movement of securities as part of the ebb and flow of foreign exchange under uncertain monetary conditions, that were able to prosper at this time. The smaller and more isolated Stock Exchange members were much less able to operate in these areas, being used simply to buy and sell or to serve smaller markets like Calcutta, Melbourne, or Johannesburg. Without changing its rules, radically, on membership the Stock Exchange was not able to hold its position in the vastly more complicated areas of global securities trading.

The international business of such major players as de Zoete & Gorton or Panmure Gordon, was at a much reduced level between the wars, compared to the pre-1914 position. Nevertheless, others did continue to find a role for themselves in the global market, such as Raphaels, Heseltine, Powell & Co., Nathan & Rosselli, Cazenoves, and Robert Nivison & Co. Part of this was luck as they happened to be in an area which now attracted increased interest, as with Robert Nivison in colonial securities. Similarly, the revival of interest in American securities in the second half of the 1920s,

[13] Thomas, *Provincial Stock Exchanges*, 171, 180, 293, 316; Thomas, *Stock Exchanges of Ireland*, 171, 189; J. Attali, *A Man of Influence: Sir Siegmund Warburg, 1902–1982* (London 1986), 126, 136; J. Kinross, *Fifty Years in the City: Financing Small Business* (London 1982), 41–3, 60; *Share-Pushing, Report of the Departmental Committee appointed by the Board of Trade, 1936–7* (London 1937), cf. 44–5.

with the speculative boom on Wall Street, favoured firms like Heseltine, Powell with the requisite contacts and expertise. However, even in these areas members of the Stock Exchange faced greater competition than ever before. Some of this was from within London itself for there had always existed non-members who specialized in an international business. As before the war Japhets continued to be very active in providing a market in international securities for European investors, in competition with dealers belonging to the London Stock Exchange. By 1921 they had a capital of £750,000 which allowed them to be much more adventurous in taking up a position than most jobbers. Similarly an ex-member, like Helbert Wagg also did an extensive international business especially in American securities. Established merchant banks like Schroders were also always interested in any opportunities for trading securities that their international connections could bring them. It was between the wars that they recruited Albert Sam, from the brokers, Vivian Gray, and he became their expert on South American securities.[14] One of the most concerted challenges for this international business came from New York brokers who opened offices in London in the 1920s. In 1933, for instance, Fenner, Beane & Ungerleider, who were members of the New York Stock Exchange offered 'A complete brokerage service in the world's markets'.[15]

In international arbitrage, for example, the London Stock Exchange lost most of its position. Dollar securities issued by US corporations, especially railroad stocks and bonds, had been the main currency of the arbitrageurs before 1914 but these had been largely sold off by European governments to finance the war, with investors compensated with domestic government debt. Though new securities did come to take their place they had neither the volume nor the wider appeal of those either repatriated or repudiated during the war. Consequently the ability to find multiple active markets in the same security, which the arbitrageurs required, was considerably circumscribed. In April 1921, 20 member firms of the London Stock Exchange, who were engaged in arbitrage complained that, 'The difficulties surrounding Arbitrage business today are far greater than in the pre-war period, largely owing to the restricted state of markets, consequent upon the altered conditions ruling the violent exchange movements.'[16] Nevertheless, firms like L. Messel & Company, Leon Brothers, and Nathan & Rosselli, who were experienced in arbitrage from the pre-war era,

[14] D. H. D. MacDermot, *Panmure Gordon & Co., 1876–1976: A Century of Stockbroking* (London 1976), 59; P. G. Warren, *Heseltine, Powell and Company: One Hundred Years of Stockbroking, 1851–1951* (London 1951), 24; H. Janes, *de Zoete and Gorton* (London 1963), 55–6; S. D. Chapman, *Raphael Bicentenary 1787–1987* (London 1987), 43; Reed, *Capel and Company*, 96–7; Kynaston, *Cazenove*, 137; R. Roberts, *Schroders: Merchants & Bankers* (London 1992), 179, 243, 370, L. Dennett, *The Charterhouse Group* (London 1979), 77; W. L. Fraser, *All to the Good* (London 1963).
[15] *Stock Exchange Yearbook for 1929* (London 1929), p. iv; *Stock Exchange Yearbook for 1933* (London 1933), p. lxxxvii.       [16] LSE: General Purposes, 18 Apr. 1921.

all attempted to re-establish the business once they were permitted to do so in 1919. However, they were given little support in this. Under the influence of the Bank of England and the Treasury, who continued to regard arbitrage as potentially destabilizing for the currency, the Stock Exchange placed restrictions in the way of the arbitrageurs.[17] Joint-account arbitrage, which was the easiest and simplest form, was not permitted until December 1920, and only then because threatened competition from the New York Stock Exchange made it imperative from then to do so.[18]

The London Stock Exchange increasingly regarded international arbitage as a threat, and so limited the freedom of the arbitrageurs to operate. Attempts were made in 1921, for example, to confine arbitrageurs to a restricted range of securities, so as to prevent transactions being completed on exchanges abroad, and so avoid commission charges. As arbitrageurs were desperate to find any security that could command an active market in both London and overseas, even temporarily, such a restriction had serious implications for arbitrage, and was, in the end, repealed. Similarly, attempts in 1922 to restrict arbitrage to cash transactions, though rooted in the desire to prevent the buildup of large speculative positions, was also detrimental to arbitrage as it was now more difficult to close a transaction as quickly as in the past and so trading for the account was more required. Again this was resisted and account trading restored.[19]

Gradually, however, there was a growing recognition on the London Stock Exchange, among those who had the responsibility for implementing and policing the regulations, that arbitrage did have a role to play in the functioning of the market, and that those who conducted it were faced with an increasingly difficult and competitive environment. In 1934, for example, in the semi-official *Book of the Stock Exchange*, Armstrong highlighted the complexity of arbitrage when he stated that,

When it is remembered that there must be taken into account exchange rates, commission charges, interest, cables, insurance, fluctuations in money, settlement days, and the possibility that a commitment entered into in one centre may not be successfully undone or closed in another, it will be seen that arbitrage is a highly skilled and technical business.[20]

By then, the demands by 448 member firms in 1930 that those engaged in arbitrage not be given any further concessions in the increasingly restrictive minimum commission rates was rejected by the Committee for General Purposes, despite only 63 member firms supporting the request for concessions.

---

[17] Royal Institute of International Affairs, *The Problem of International Investment* (Oxford 1937), 108; R. M. Kindersley, 'British Foreign Investments in 1928', *E. J.* 158 (1930), 176.

[18] Reed, *Capel and Company*, 96; Chapman, *Raphael Bicentenary*, 43; LSE: General Purposes, 3 Feb. 1919, 11 Oct. 1920, 8 Nov. 1920, 18 Apr. 1921, 25 Apr. 1921, 15 Sept. 1924.

[19] Ibid., 25 Apr. 1921, 29 Mar. 1922, 15 May 1922, 29 May 1922.

[20] Armstrong, *Book of the Stock Exchange*, 167.

Left to the membership as a whole the arbitrageurs would have been forced to conform to a set of regulations and charges designed to extract the maximum advantage from a largely captive domestic market. In contrast those members in authority in the Stock Exchange were reluctant to make the arbitrageurs conform as they were well aware that the business would simply drift away to non-members or other centres.[21]

Nevertheless, the restrictions that were placed on the arbitrageurs, and the changes they were being forced to make, was resulting in more and more of the business taking place outside the Stock Exchange. In particular, the 1920s saw a growing number of New York banks and brokerage firms establish branch offices in London, such as Guaranty Trust, Equitable Trust, National City Bank, and Blair & Co. By 1927 there were 10 members of the New York Stock Exchange with offices in London and this had risen to around 25 in 1937, despite the bankruptcy of some firms in the wake of the 1929 crash. These firms maintained direct telegraph contact with their head offices, and so they were able to buy or sell US securities for British clients at current New York prices. As there were insufficient holdings of dollar securities in London in the 1920s to sustain much active trading on the Stock Exchange, these firms increasingly constituted the American market in London, and so they were well placed to arbitrage between New York and London using the different offices of the same firm. In fact by 1929 these firms had extended their activities to British stocks and shares, as these were being held across the Atlantic in the form of American Depository Receipts (ADRs). The nascent market, however, was killed off by the Wall Street crash and interest in the 1930s again focused exclusively on the transatlantic trading of dollar securities.[22]

In addition to North American competition members of the London Stock Exchange also faced the rivalry of continental banks. Especially after 1931, when sterling left the gold standard, the relative price of the same security being traded on different exchanges was determined more by currency fluctuations than any other factor. By buying a security in one financial centre and selling in another an exchange of currency was automatically created. Security arbitrage offered a way of participating in currency speculation or simply a convenient way of transferring funds from one country to another, especially if that was blocked by exchange controls. Banks, with large capitals at their disposal were much better placed to participate in these operations than the specialist arbitrageur and so they became a growing force in arbitrage in the 1930s. Consequently, in the inter-war years

[21] LSE: General Purposes, 17 Nov. 1930, 19 Nov. 1930, 22 Dec. 1930, 2 Feb. 1931, 14 Mar. 1932, 5 Sept. 1932; LSE: General Purposes, Non-Permanent, 25 Nov. 1930, 2 Dec. 1930, 4 Dec. 1930, 16 Dec. 1930, 27 Jan. 1931.

[22] J. E. Meeker, *The Work of the Stock Exchange* (New York 1930), 507; LSE: General Purposes, 29 Mar. 1922, 15 May 1922, 29 May 1922, 29 Oct. 1923, 15 Dec. 1924, 5 Jan. 1925, 8 June 1925, 28 Nov. 1927, 14 Jan. 1929, 24 June 1929, 12 Aug. 1929. (ADRs appeared in 1927).

members of the London Stock Exchange were losing out to New York brokerage houses for American securities while transactions with other European countries were increasingly done by those continental banks with
London branches. Even in the case of South African gold-mining shares,
the mining finance houses continued to provide an alternative means of
arbitraging with Johannesburg. Though London remained at the centre of
what international arbitrage there was in the inter-war years, having
reclaimed that position from New York by the mid-1920s, the brokers
and jobbers who belonged to the London Stock Exchange lost out to
non-members.[23]

This was not through any want of effort among the arbitrageurs. For
example, as early as 1922 they were promoting Indian securities as a substitute for the American stocks and bonds lost during the war. L. Powell,
Sons & Co., claimed in that year that the Indian market '. . . will some day
be almost as large as the American market was in 1913, now unfortunately
reduced to very small proportions'.[24] Unfortunately, there was nothing like
the same investor interest in Indian securities, either in Britain or India, to
generate the type of active markets that the arbitrageurs really required.
Thus, though the business was cultivated between the wars, and did develop
along with Far Eastern and Australian securities, it never came near to
replacing the securities lost during the war. At the same time there was a
problem of timing as the trading day in Calcutta, Singapore or Melbourne
did not coincide with that in London. G. T. Pulley & Co., a firm of jobbers
who arbitraged with Calcutta, received cables at 7.30 a.m. (UK time) from
the East, transacted business in London before 10 a.m. and sent return
cables at 11 a.m., which caught the close of business in India (5 p.m., Indian
time). For Australia there was not even that narrow overlap, which made
the London Stock Exchange sceptical about whether arbitrage was being
conducted at all, as no simultaneous buy/sell transaction was possible. If
no arbitrage was being conducted then normal regulations and charges
would prevail.[25]

By the end of the 1930s, though international arbitrage was still a force
within the London Stock Exchange it was but a pale shadow of what it had
been before 1914. Currency instability and exchange controls had made
the whole process of buying and selling between countries, and remitting
payment, either difficult or impossible while the closing down of stock
exchanges through government action, as in Russia and Germany, removed

---

[23] LSE: General Purposes, 28 Dec. 1932, 10 Apr. 1933, 29 Jan. 1934, 9 Apr. 1934, 7 Aug.
1934, 27 Aug. 1934, 1 Feb. 1937, 7 Nov. 1938, 25 Sept. 1939; LSE: Non-Permanent, 27 Nov.
1930, 2 Dec. 1930, 3 Dec. 1930; Royal Institute of International Affairs, *Problem of International Investment*, 107; Kindersley, 'British Foreign Investments', *E. J.* 46 (1936), 654; 47
(1937), 650-2; 48 (1938), 623; 49 (1939), 689.
[24] LSE: General Purposes, 16 May 1922.
[25] Ibid., 16 May 1922, 20 Dec. 1926, 28 Dec. 1926, 10 Apr. 1928, 22 Nov. 1937, 14 Mar.
1938; LSE: Subcommittee on Commissions, 20 Jan. 1938, 10 Feb. 1938, 24 Feb. 1938.

the organized and active markets needed for arbitrage. Substitutes for dollar securities had been found in the form of the issues of European multinationals like Shell and Unilever, along with South African gold-mining shares, which had a ubiquitous appeal at a time of uncertainty about the value of money. These were traded between those exchanges which were still open, especially London, Paris, Amsterdam, and Brussels in Europe, and New York, Montreal, and Johannesburg abroad.[26] However, with the outbreak of the Second World War even this modest level of arbitrage was threatened. In November 1939 Sternberg Brothers, who arbitraged between London and Paris, remarked that even with a 10 per cent differential in the price of French *rentes* '. . . it is only on very rare occasions that advantage can be taken of these discrepancies owing to the very rigid restrictions imposed both by the Bank of England, and the Bank of France, on transfers of currency'.[27] Clearly, between the wars a business that had been a major force on the London Stock Exchange before 1914 virtually came to an end, despite the efforts of individual members to preserve it by seeking out new markets and new securities. The defaults, exchange controls, and other restrictions of the 1930s had destroyed investor confidence in international investment, and so undermined the opportunities for doing business in those areas, while the restrictions imposed by the Stock Exchange had helped drive what remained into the hands of non-members.

## MONEY

Another activity that had generated much activity on the London Stock Exchange was buying and selling in response to money market conditions. Banks and other institutions in London, with money temporarily unemployed, readily employed it by lending to brokers and jobbers. In turn, these, either on their own account or through lending to other members, used the funds to purchase and hold securities, profiting from the yield differential between short- and long-term financial instruments. The result was a close and direct relationship between short- and long-term interest rates, with fluctuations in one being readily transmitted to the other.[28] It was this role that had made the members of the London Stock Exchange so vulnerable on the outbreak of war, as so much of their activity depended upon borrowed funds that could be withdrawn at little notice. Naturally, such a relationship between the money and securities market required a high degree of trust among the individual participants. Bankers and others had to believe that not only could they employ remuneratively whatever idle

---

[26] Armstrong, *Book of the Stock Exchange*, 163–9, Reed, *Capel and Company*, 97; LSE: General Purposes, 8 Apr. 1940.

[27] LSE: Subcommittee on Disputes and Buying and Selling-out Cases, 22 Nov. 1939.

[28] S. Howson, *Domestic Monetary Management in Britain, 1919–38* (Cambridge 1975), 48.

funds they possessed but also that such loans would be quickly repaid when asked. Otherwise, they would be more reluctant to lend, would lend less, would charge more and would be more ready to withdraw from the business. Conversely, brokers and jobbers had to believe that funds would be readily available in sufficient amount and at low cost so that the risk taken would be worthwhile. Furthermore, brokers and jobbers had to know that the securities they purchased and held could be quickly sold at little loss if loans were recalled. Otherwise, they would be reluctant to undertake the activity. Inevitably, the war, with its closure of the Stock Exchange and its moratorium on loans, undermined the trust that had underpinned the relationship between the money and securities market. The result was a greater hesitation among all participants to engage in the operations to the same extent as before, because of the risks involved, of which they were now only too aware.

It was now clear to all members that maintaining large open positions, funded by extensive short-term borrowings, was a very risky activity, unless accompanied by large capital reserves. Unfortunately, the membership rules of the London Stock Exchange restricted access to capital. Without such capital the exposure of a few members to large losses from such operations, if there was a simultaneous shortage of funds and a sudden collapse of prices, could endanger the membership as a whole for both payments and deliveries would be defaulted upon. Considering the unstable monetary conditions that characterized the immediate post-war years, with the currency turmoil in Central Europe, the priority was to minimize all risks rather than quickly permit the resumption of such activities. Consideration was given to the maintenance of cash trading, or the introduction of compulsory margins between the value for securities purchased and the amount financed on credit. As it was, the exclusion of government debt from the use of the account was one positive measure taken to limit the buildup of large positions. By its very nature the securities purchased on credit were those that could command a wide and active market, where large sales and purchases could be done with little effect on prices. Naturally, the vast debts created by the war were ideal for such purposes.[29] As Fielding, Son & Macleod explained in May 1922:

The world is still in great unrest, and any political upheaval, international crisis, or material improvement in trade, would induce the Banks to call in their loans, and precipitate a serious position on the Stock Exchange.[30]

The 1920s did witness a slow recovery in trust and a growing confidence that short-term money could be safely lent on, and borrowed for, stock

---

[29] E. V. Morgan and W. A. Thomas, *The Stock Exchange: Its History and Functions* (London 1962), 190–1; Armstrong, *Book of the Stock Exchange*, 105–6; R. G. Hawtrey, *The Art of Central Banking* (London 1932), 299; LSE: General Purposes, 8 May 1922; LSE: Rules and Regulations, 27 Nov. 1918, 5 Feb. 1919, 27 Feb. 1919.

[30] LSE: General Purposes, 9 May 1922.

market operations. Loans to members of the Stock Exchange, by British banks, for example, grew from only £18m. in 1921 to £48m. in 1928, while foreign and overseas banks were attracted to the better rates on offer in New York. Gradually, some of the pre-war relationships and practices were revived as stock-market conditions improved. Nevertheless, the level of activity appeared markedly less than before the war. Banks remained more cautious about lending to members of the Stock Exchange, and tried to restrict the amount lent. As it was, the ability of the Stock Exchange to offer a home for such funds had been reduced by the disappearance of international securities during the war and continued inability to buy and sell government debt for the account, keeping the position open from account to account. Instead, all such deals had to be financed by borrowings which placed members of the Stock Exchange in the same position as outside operators, like the discount houses.[31] Also, the nature of the debt created by the government to finance the war gave far greater scope for employing short-term funds remuneratively outside the Stock Exchange. In 1919, of the government's debt in the hands of investors—amounting to £6.6bn.—a total of 27 per cent was itself short-term, being redeemable within 5 years. Half that was floating debt, such as Treasury bills. Much of this short-term debt was neither quoted on nor traded in the Stock Exchange, being the preserve of the discount houses and other money-market operators. As a result, though there continued to be a link between the money and securities markets it was much weaker than before the war, with most of the short-term funds available in London being directed towards short-term instruments like Treasury bills. This meant that it was the British government's own financing requirements that drove the money market rather than the monetary needs of the British or world economy. This helps explain the divergence between short- and long-term interest rates between the wars compared to the close relationship before 1914. Nevertheless, as the government gradually extended the redemption dates on its debt, with the floating element down from 13 per cent of the total in 1919 to 7 per cent in 1929, the Stock Exchange did slowly gain a position as a valuable component of the money market.[32]

However, this recovery never approached the pre-war position. In 1929 British bank lending to members of the Stock Exchange was a mere 2.5 per

[31] R. J. Truptil, *British Banks and the Money Market* (London 1936), 96; Morgan and Thomas, *The Stock Exchange*, 190–1, 222–3; M. Collins, *Money and Banking in the UK: A History* (London 1988), 213; Sir Stephen Killik, *The Work of the Stock Exchange* (London 1933), 52; C. Maughan, *Markets of London* (London 1931), 8; Committee on Finance and Industry (MacMillan Committee), *Minutes of Evidence* (London 1931, cmnd. 3897), answers by J. W. Beaumont Pease, Chairman of Lloyds Bank (Q2088), F. Hyde, Managing Director of the Midland Bank (Q891, 894), T. Scott, Bank of Scotland (Q2769).

[32] *Stock Exchange Yearbook for 1919* (London 1919), 23; Howson, *Domestic Monetary Management*, 161; Collins, *Money and Banking*, 250; G. A. Fletcher, *The Discount Houses In London: Principles, Operations and Change* (London 1976), 253; D. E. Moggridge, *British Monetary Policy, 1924–1931* (Cambridge 1972), 35.

cent of deposits, or a quarter of that proportion prevailing in 1913. Thus when the Wall Street crash took place in October 1929 it had little immediate impact in London because the volume of credit-financed operations was at a low level compared to New York, which had sucked in short-term funds from around the world. Nevertheless the Wall Street crash and then the abandonment of the gold standard in 1931 further undermined confidence in both the value of securities as collateral and the stability of the financial system itself. The result was to encourage banks and others to take even fewer risks with their lending. Loans to members of the Stock Exchange by British banks fell from a peak of £48m. in 1928 to a low of £16m. in 1932 before starting to recover. More importantly, the banks themselves started to hold government debt directly rather than lending to those that did, as the gap between long- and short-term interest rates left little scope for the middleman.[33] As Ellinger reflected at the end of the 1930s

Formerly there was considerable business done on these by money brokers who lend money for the purpose of carrying over shares, but there is now very little done in this way. Funds for carrying over are usually borrowed from banks, either directly by the buyers or indirectly through the intermediary of their stockbrokers.[34]

Consequently, though a semblance of the pre-war relationship between the money and securities markets continued to exist between the wars its strength and importance had been fundamentally altered. Banks were now lending more to either specific brokers or directly to investors rather than via the money brokers, as there was now little scope for both banks and money brokers to profit from the process. At the same time banks were tending to hold government debt directly both for the higher return it gave than lending to intermediaries and in the belief that it involved little greater risk than if a broker or jobber defaulted on loans where securities were being used as collateral. Where banks did want to lend money at call the discount houses remained major competitors for what was available. The discount houses emerged as successful jobbers in government debt in the 1930s as they were better capitalized than Stock Exchange firms and were equally well connected to the banks. In addition they possessed the backing of the Bank of England, which wanted to see their preservation as an important buffer between itself and the clearing banks.

Therefore, the inter-war years saw the members of the London Stock Exchange fail to reclaim the role they had once played in the domestic money market. Partly this was due to their own restrictions, as on access

---

[33] LSE: General Purposes, Non-Permanent, 28 Sept. 1931; B. Ellinger, *The City: The London Financial Markets* (London 1940), 138, 161; Truptil, *British Banks*, 96, 105; J. R. Winton, *Lloyds Bank, 1918–1969* (Oxford 1982), 59–60; E. Nevin and E. W. Davies, *The London Clearing Banks* (London 1970), 147, 180, 298–9; T. Balogh, *Studies in Financial Organization* (London 1946), 57–62; F. W. Hirst, *Wall Street and Lombard Street: The Stock Exchange Slump of 1929 and the Trade Depression of 1930* (New York 1931), 29, 80.

[34] Ellinger, *The City*, 337, cf. LSE: General Purposes, Non-Permanent, 28 Sept. 1939.

to capital or use of the account for government debt. However, it was mainly due to the completely altered nature of the money market. This was now dominated by the British government's need to finance its massive wartime debt, much of which was of a short-term nature. Even when a large element of this had been converted into a more permanent form, as in 1932, the narrow gap between short- and long-term interest rates made it difficult to make a profit by borrowing from banks and employing the money in securities. Only discount houses were able to survive in this role, and that was because they were given a somewhat privileged position. The result was that the money market lost some of its flexibility and responsiveness to market conditions and, instead, became much more controlled by the government and Bank of England.[35]

Internationally the consequences for the world's monetary system were even more serious. The London money market was a truly global one, employing short-term funds from around the world in securities from around the world and so permitting banks to balance their accounts internationally, and so maintain currency equilibrium between nations. As the Royal Institute of International Affairs observed in 1937:

It is true that a large movement of capital from one stock exchange to another is likely to be followed in due course by a movement in the opposite direction and such movements help to preserve rather than destroy international equilibrium.[36]

With the disposal of the dollar securities that had permitted this to take place so easily before 1914 the London money market was less able to perform its role of employing, releasing, and redistributing money around the world in response to supply and demand. In turn this had implications for the London Stock Exchange for it deprived it of the vast volume of business which such activity had generated. Though British investors did retain large foreign holdings at the end of the First World War, as with Argentinian and Indian railways, few commanded the international appeal of the pre-war American securities. Without realizing the underlying needs the members of the Stock Exchange did try to respond to the lack of international securities by trying to create replacements. A few North American

[35] Armstrong, Book of the Stock Exchange, 86, 105–6, 112; Collins, Money and Banking, 204, 213–14, 216, 218, 232; Ellinger, The City, 138, 161; Truptil, British Banks, 96, 176–80, 313; R. Saw, The Bank of England, 1694–1944 (London 1944), 102; Fletcher, Discount Houses, 253; Kynaston, Cazenove, 125; Balogh, Financial Organization, 190, 204; Committee on Finance and Industry, Q891, 894, 2088; J. M. Atkin, British Overseas Investment, 1918–1931 (New York 1977), 27, 300; Roberts, Schroders, 189, 213–14; Y. Cassis and J. Tanner, 'Finance and Financiers in Switzerland, 1880–1960', in G. D. Feldman, U. Olssen, M. Bordo, and Y. Cassis (eds.), The Evolution of Modern Financial Institutions in the Twentieth Century (Milan 1994), 301; K. Burk, 'Money and Power: The Shift from Great Britain to the United States', in Feldman et al. (eds.), Modern Financial Institutions, 362, 364; Moggridge, British Monetary Policy, 35, 232–3; H. W. Greengrass, The Discount Market in London: Its Organisation and Recent Development (London 1930), 7–8, 35, 166.
[36] Royal Institute of International Affairs, Problem of International Investment, 108.

securities still continued to be widely held and actively traded, as with US Steel and Canadian Pacific Railway. In addition, a small number of large mining companies, especially those involved in South African gold but including International Nickel of Canada, had always attracted world-wide interest. Also, a few companies by their very nature were international such as the Anglo-Dutch concerns of, firstly, Shell and, later, Unilever. They were also joined by a few international holding companies, like the Brussels-based International Hydro-Electric, that controlled a portfolio of power and traction companies operating in a number of different countries. Securities such as these were actively traded internationally, as Kindersley noted in 1936:

Royal Dutch, Unilever, Mexican Eagle, Brazilian Traction, International Nickel, the South African gold-mines, are only a few examples of companies whose shares are subject to international trading on a substantial scale whenever currency fears, disturbed political situations and other international complications occur. From a national standpoint the mobility of these assets and the ease with which they are realisable give them an important advantage over the shares of British companies, since in times of national emergency they may be mobilised to provide a reservoir of foreign exchange.[37]

However, compared to the billions of dollars worth of securities floating between the world's stock exchanges in the pre-1914 era, these represented but small compensation. Collectively, they did not possess the weight to move markets and were only sufficient to allow minor adjustments.[38] (See Figure 6.1. and Table 6.1.)

British investors did begin to rebuild their foreign holdings of securities in the 1920s. There was no attempt to replace holdings in major US corporations, such as the railroads, for these were now well held by the American investing public, both institutional and individual. Instead British interest focused on colonial securities and a diverse range of US industrial securities, especially the lesser known stocks quoted on the New York Curb market. The yields offered by major US securities were no longer attractive in Britain, especially with the higher interest rates prevailing in London and New York. Consequently, it was more speculative stocks with the potential for rapid rise in prices that were attractive. It was estimated that by 1931 the holding of British investors in dollar securities stood at £100m. though much of this included pre-war investments.[39]

More importantly, was the growth of interest among American investors

[37] Kindersley, 'British Foreign Investments', E. J. 46 (1936), 654.

[38] Howson, Domestic Monetary Management, 56; Roberts, Schroders, 230; C. Lewis, America's Stake in International Investments (Washington 1938), 454; Kindersley, 'British Foreign Investments', E. J. 44 (1934), 379; Moggridge, British Monetary Policy, 35, 232–3, 260; Financial News, The Stock Exchange: An Investor's Guide (London 1933), 14.

[39] Atkin, British Overseas Investment, 311, 314; LSE: General Purposes, 22 Mar. 1920, 24 Oct. 1927, 7 Jan. 1929, 14 Jan. 1929, 4 Feb. 1929.

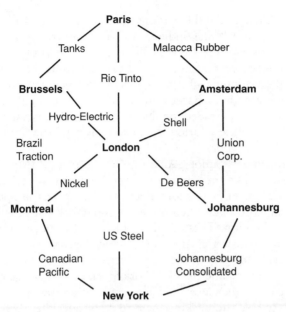

**Fig. 6.1.** Market connections of representative internationally traded securities in
1933

**Table 6.1.** Extent of links of internationally traded securities in 1933: Number of
international securities in common

|  | London | Paris | Brussels | Amsterdam | New York | Montreal | Johannesburg |
|---|---|---|---|---|---|---|---|
| London | — | 14 | 6 | 11 | 15 | 5 | 5 |
| Paris | 14 | — | 2 | 8 | 9 | 1 | 5 |
| Brussels | 6 | 2 | — | 4 | 5 | 4 | 0 |
| Amsterdam | 11 | 8 | 4 | — | 9 | 3 | 2 |
| New York | 15 | 9 | 5 | 9 | — | 5 | 3 |
| Montreal | 5 | 1 | 4 | 3 | 5 | — | 0 |
| Johannesburg | 5 | 5 | 0 | 2 | 3 | 0 | — |
| TOTAL | 56 | 39 | 21 | 37 | 46 | 18 | 15 |

*Source: Financial News, The Stock Exchange: An Investor's Guide (London 1933), 14.*

in British industrial securities. As speculation developed in New York
during the 1920s it was only natural that it would spill over into securities
quoted on other markets, and the longest established links already existed
with London. With the move towards a return to the pre-war parity
between the pound and the dollar, achieved in 1925, American investors
could then judge the value of British shares without the risk—or so it

seemed—of exchange-rate fluctuations. Compared to the United States the yield and potential of British industrial shares appeared attractive, such as technology stocks like the General Electric Company. One estimate suggested that 40 per cent of the shares of GEC were held by American investors at the beginning of 1929. Generally, it was reported in January 1929 that there were a '. . . large number of shares of English incorporated companies now being traded on New York Stock Exchange and Curb markets . . .'[40] Purchases during 1928 were felt to run into millions of dollars.

Such was the interest among American investors in British securities that New York banks, like the Guaranty Trust Company, repackaged them in the form of American Depository Receipts. The ADRs of specific British companies, like GEC, were then traded in New York with the actual holdings lodged in London. These ADRs represented a much more attractive way of holding British securities for American investors but the London Stock Exchange refused to quote them, fearing a loss of business to American brokers in London and the New York Stock Exchange itself. The Chairman of the New York Curb Exchange even wrote to the London Stock Exchange in August 1929 asking them to reconsider their ban.

. . . we are trading in over 50 English issues in this market all through the medium of American Depository Receipts issued by Guaranty Trust Company of New York and other New York banks. Under this method, . . . shares purchased by American brokers in your market are, instead of being shipped to this country, delivered to the London office of the American bank against which their New York office issues and delivers to the broker here American Depository Receipts which are traded in and are good delivery on the New York Curb Exchange.

If London could be persuaded to recognize these ADRs it would greatly facilitate trade between the two exchanges, and thus provide a growing volume of securities that commanded an international market. However, London was not willing to agree as they were worried about the potential loss of business. Much British buying and selling of American industrial securities was already taking place directly with brokers in New York and ADRs offered a means by which these US markets could compete with London in active British securities. There would be nothing to stop British investors buying and selling British securities in New York, through brokers there, if the market was better and the charges lower. As it was, the reply of Archibald Campbell, Chairman of the Committee for General Purposes was both arrogant and dismissive.

This country has had greater experience of dealing in every kind of international security and the Committee see no reason to substitute a new system for one which has worked well for considerably more than half a century.[41]

[40] LSE: General Purposes, 14 Jan. 1929, cf. 11 Mar. 1929, 24 June 1929, 14 Aug. 1929, 19 Aug. 1929.    [41] Ibid., 12 Aug. 1929.

London was not going to agree quickly to a change that would undermine the command it had over its own market even for the prospect of expanding a transatlantic business that had once been of major importance, if this involved any risk to its own position domestically.

Consequently, even after the revival of interest in foreign investment during the 1920s, by investors both in Britain and abroad, the number of securities that could command an international market by the end of that decade remained very limited. With the Wall Street collapse, the interest of foreign investors in speculative American securities largely disappeared as they became either unsaleable or only capable of disposal at way below their original price. Similarly, American interest in foreign securities also evaporated faced with the double blow of falling prices and exchange losses as currencies were devalued against the dollar.[42]

Nevertheless, the interest of British investors, especially institutions, in foreign securities did not disappear. However, it was an activity of growing complexity and risk because of the increasing involvement of government, as with exchange controls, and the greater uncertainty with exchange rates, as with the collapse of the revived fixed-rate regime in 1931. As a result it became more and more the preserve of banks as only they had the capital, short-term funds, and large numbers of trained staff capable of handling most situations. They also had the need to maintain some system in operation as the ability to receive and make payments internationally was an important part of their operations. Unfortunately, the rules of the London Stock Exchange made them unacceptable for membership while the minimum commission charges were considered prohibitive for certain regular and high volume transactions.[43] The banks, therefore, increasingly conducted the international buying and selling of securities between themselves without the use of the Stock Exchange. As 63 brokers, led by Grumbar and See, pointed out to the Stock Exchange in 1930:

This form of business originates entirely from genuine international supply and demand from all over the world. These transactions are not clients' orders in the ordinary sense, but business created by outside Houses with large capital resources and international capabilities and facilities. Under no circumstances could it be created or undertaken to any such extent by firms in the London Stock Exchange.

We know that many big transactions take place between one outside House and another, and also that business is taken to such Houses without going into the Stock Exchange.

[42] Atkin, *British Overseas Investment*, 317; A. Gleeson, *People and Their Money: 50 Years of Private Investment* (M & G Group 1981), 23; LSE: General Purposes, 7 Jan. 1929, 4 Jan. 1992, 4 Feb. 1929, 9 Aug. 1929.

[43] W. A. Morton, *British Finance 1930–1940* (Maddison, Wis. 1943), 270; *Financial News, The City of London 1884–1934* (London 1934), 31; R. S. Sayers, *The Bank of England, 1891–1944* (Cambridge 1976), 275–8, 298; Fletcher, *Discount Houses*, 137; Moggridge, *British Monetary Policy*, 9, 35, 232–3; D. Williams, 'London and the 1931 Financial Crisis', *Ec. H. R.* 15 (1962/3), 517, 519; D. Williams, 'The 1931 Financial Crisis', *Yorkshire Bulletin of Economic and Social Research*, 15 (1963), 93–4, 107.

What these members wanted was a relaxation of the commission rules because the low margin upon which it was conducted, and the considerable increase in the risks, was driving the business outside the Stock Exchange. Instead, they felt 'it should be fostered, encouraged, and allowed every facility and freedom, in order to retain for London, its position of the most free international market in the world.'[44]

Finally, limited as was the recovery in the 1920s in the Stock Exchange's international business, linked to the money market, the financial crises of the 1930s, culminating in the collapse of the new monetary order, provided a major setback. When Britain left the gold standard on 20 September 1931 the Stock Exchange had been consulted beforehand but only as to whether it intended to remain open on the day of the announcement, and then only by the Deputy Governor of the Bank of England.

The Chairman informed the Committee that he, with the Deputy Chairman, had been summoned to a meeting at the Bank of England on Saturday. The Deputy Governor had informed them that notwithstanding every effort that had been made it was impossible to remain on the Gold Standard, he had asked their opinion as to whether the Stock Exchange should be opened or closed on Monday when the announcement would be made. He (the Chairman) had told the Deputy Governor that they had come to the conclusion that in the interest of the country the Stock Exchange should not open. They were then informed that the Banks shared their opinion.[45]

The following notice was then posted in the Stock Exchange:

The Chancellor of the Exchequer wished it to be stated that any British Citizen who increased the strain on the Exchange by purchasing Foreign Securities himself or assisting others to do so was deliberately adding to the country's difficulties.[46]

Thus, even before the imposition of exchange controls the Stock Exchange was being pressurized into a position where it could not operate internationally. The Stock Exchange reopened on 24 September 1931 but only for cash dealings with option business banned. Dealing for the account was not restored until 16 November while options trading reopened on 18 December.[47]

With the ending of the link to gold, sterling became a managed currency with an office for that purpose being established at the Bank of England. Faced with fluctuations in the value of the currency and subject to pressure by the government and the Bank of England to limit purchases of foreign securities, international business became even more difficult on the Stock Exchange. Though international dealings in securities did recover somewhat in the 1930s the complications and controls it now involved removed it

[44] LSE: General Purposes, 17 Nov. 1930.    [45] Ibid., 21 Aug. 1931: 'Financial Crisis'.
[46] Ibid., 21 Aug. 1931: 'Notice'.
[47] Ibid., 20 Aug. 1931, 27 Aug. 1931, 31 Aug. 1931, 26 Sept. 1931, 28 Sept. 1931, 5 Oct. 1931, 12 Oct. 1931, 9 Nov. 1931, 30 Nov. 1931.

more and more from the members of the Stock Exchange and into the hands of the bankers, especially the large international banks. It was they who were well placed to profit from the newly emerging international monetary system in which organized markets were supervised and policed by governments and subject to exchange and other controls, as they could internalize operations or employ staff to understand and interpret the regulations to their advantage.[48]

In 1938, R. B. Pearson, the Chairman of the Stock Exchange, noted that,

There is not a bank of any consequence in any country of the world that has not a London Office or Agency; and so, each day, from every quarter of the globe, a great business in stock and shares gravitates to London, which possesses and maintains, beyond all comparison or competition, the greatest stock market in the world.[49]

True as this was, the reality was that much of this international money market business never reached the members of the Stock Exchange but was actually transacted between the offices and agencies of these banks even in London itself.[50]

The relationship between the London Stock Exchange and the London money market had underpinned much of the trading activity of its members. Over the course of the nineteenth century this relationship had grown in importance and intensity through the ability to employ short-term funds in long-term investments, using the medium of transferable securities. Additionally, that facility had greatly eased the need to move funds geographically and across currencies. Unfortunately, for the future of both the international monetary system and the health of the world economy, few recognized the contribution made by these developments. Instead, the post First World War years saw an attempt to recreate a system that had long since decayed in use, with inevitable failure. The result was serious weakening, though never breaking of, the links between the money and securities markets so that financial resources were no longer being fully employed and the mechanism of transfer was no longer operating successfully. Clearly this harmed the London Stock Exchange itself as a major source of business died away. Though the Stock Exchange did nothing to try and retain or sustain this business, and even alienated part of it by its actions, it has to be doubted that this was a principal cause of what happened between the wars. Instead, those causes are to be found in the actions of

[48] Ibid., 14 Dec. 1931, 14 July 1933, 12 Jan. 1939; LSE: General Purposes, Non-Permanent, 23 Sept. 1931, 29 Sept. 1931, 25 Sept. 1931, 1 Oct. 1931, 1 Mar. 1932, 18 Dec. 1931, 26 Jan. 1932,
[49] LSE: General Purposes, Appendix, 24 Mar. 1938.
[50] G. Jones, *British Multinational Banking, 1830–1990* (Oxford 1993), 139, 149, 182, 192–3; Collins, *Money and Banking*, 221; Armstrong, *Book of the Stock Exchange*, 163–5, 167; Ellinger, *The City*, 339, 373; Truptil, *British Banks*, 136; Morton, *British Finance*, 270; J. R. Winton, *Lloyds Bank 1918–1969* (Oxford 1987), 87; T. Balderston, 'German Banking 1913–1939', in *University of Manchester: Working Papers in Economic and Social History, No. 2* (1990), 29–32.

governments and central banks as they sacrificed the long-term health of the world economy for the short-term interests of national economies.

## CAPITAL

In contrast to the loss of so much of the business generated by the London money market, and the international dimension that this had stimulated, the members of the Stock Exchange turned more and more to domestic securities between the wars. This was not simply a reflection of the vast increase in the size of the National Debt but also a continuance of the pre-war trend where domestic corporate securities had been of growing importance. Nevertheless this increasing focus by the London Stock Exchange on not only British securities but those issued by companies operating within the UK, went largely unnoticed by contemporaries, such as the government's own committee on finance and industry.[51]

Though overseas investment had come to a standstill with the war, and its financial needs, there was every expectation that it would revive thereafter, and so the major London issuing houses saw no immediate need to steer their activities away from international issues and compete for domestic clients. Certainly in the 1920s British overseas lending did recover. Over the decade (1920–9) as a whole loans totalling £1.2bn. were made in London on behalf of overseas borrowers, or £118m. per annum. However, this was noticeably lower than before the war, even before any adjustment was made for inflation, and this was reflected in the smaller share occupied by overseas loans in total new issues made in London. Whereas in the immediate pre-war years (1910–13) they had comprised 71 per cent of all such issues, during the 1920s their share was only 37 per cent.

The problem was that London now faced far greater competition for such international business than before the war. As a result of the war a significant proportion of the savings of the British people had been expended in sustaining the conflict, fundamentally altering the balance between the wealth of Britain and other countries. Previous overseas borrowers, like the governments of Canada, Australia, South Africa, or India, were now as able to raise money at home rather than by tapping the London market. Those countries and their enterprises, that continued, or needed, to borrow abroad, such as the Latin American republics or newly emergent European states, found a welcome in New York together with lower interest rates and a stronger currency. Schroders, for example, were in the 1920s handling foreign loans through their New York rather than their London office.

---

[51] MacMillan Committee, *Report and Minutes of Evidence*; J. Armstrong, 'The Rise and Fall of the Company Promoter and the Financing of British Industry', in J. J. Van Helten and Y. Cassis (eds.), *Capitalism in a Mature Economy* (Aldershot 1990), 132; F. Lavington, *The English Capital Market* (London 1921), 212; LSE: General Purposes, 2 Jan. 1918, cf. 11 Jan. 1918, 21 Jan. 1918.

Generally, London was largely deserted both by overseas railway companies seeking new finance and by foreign governments. What remained were colonial governments, whose securities found favour in London because of the imperial links, and companies involved in such activities as oil production, metal-mining, and rubber plantations. In addition, Central European enterprises turned to London as a means of rebuilding their capital after the financial and monetary turmoil of the early 1920s. There were a rash of issues in London for German industrial companies and utilities, for example.[52]

As before these types of foreign issues continued to be handled by the merchant banks as they possessed the established expertise and connections. However, the recovery of London's position in the international new issue business was cramped by government restrictions, though Britain was not unusual in this as French controls also restricted Paris. Throughout the 1920s the British government was ever-conscious of the need to refinance its own short-term borrowings and saw itself in competition with foreign borrowers. Also, from the mid-1920s onwards, even before the return to the gold standard in 1925, there was the need to maintain the value of the pound. This could best be done by a high interest rate regime. Naturally, this discouraged foreign borrowers from placing loans in London rather than New York, where the rate was lower. Finally, the government itself discouraged the use of London as a centre for issuing international loans. A stamp duty of 2 per cent on foreign loans raised in Britain, was sufficient, in keenly priced issues, to switch them to New York. In addition, British-based companies with international operations were taxed on their world-wide income, and with the high levels of post-war taxation this was sufficient both to discourage such companies from operating from a London base and encourage those so doing to move abroad. This was especially so where a company was taxed on its income both where it operated and then, again, on what it remitted to Britain. Consequently, even with the revival of the overseas loans business many merchant banks found themselves with a reduced business, and so looked for other activities in which to occupy their capital and their talents.[53]

As it was, domestic issues in the 1920s totalled £2bn. or 63 per cent of

[52] Atkin, British Overseas Investment, 11, 14–16, 27, 41, 49, 56–61, 77, 85, 132, 149, 154, 160, 171–2; K. Burk, Morgan Grenfell, 1838–1988: The Biography of a Merchant Bank (Oxford 1989), 90; Roberts, Schroders, 230; LSE: General Purposes, Non-Permanent, 7 May 1924; A. S. J. Baster, 'A Note on the Colonial Stock Acts and Dominion Borrowing', Economic History 2 (1930/3), 604; H. Bonin, Société Générale in the United Kingdom (Paris 1996), 34; P. Marchilden 'Hands Across the Water: Canadian Industrial Financiers in the City of London, 1905–20', B. H. 34 (1992), 79–80; R. Geisst, Wall Street: A History (Oxford 1997), 161, 169.

[53] Atkin, British Overseas Investment, 107, 123, 132, 149, 154, 160; S. Diaper, 'The Sperling Combine and the Shipbuilding Industry: Merchant Banking and Industrial Finance in the 1920s', in Van Helten and Cassis (eds.), Capitalism in a Mature Economy, 72–3, 75; Roberts, Schroders, 373; LSE: General Purposes 23 June 1919, 30 June 1919; Balogh, Financial Organization, 249–55.

the total made in the London market for that decade. Though the average was £204m. per annum this came in two bursts. One followed the relaxation of government controls on new capital issues in the early 1920s (1920–2) and the other in the late 1920s (1927–8), when British investors shared in the speculative excitement spilling over from Wall Street. Underlying these domestic new issues was a growing interest by investors in corporate securities, especially equities, as a counter to the fixed interest—and increasingly long-term stock available from the government. In an era of currency turmoil abroad and financial uncertainty at home a direct stake in the fortunes of British industry seemed an ideal safeguard. There was also the added advantage that whereas dividend or interest income was taxed, capital gains were not, and a stake in a successful business would see the value of the holding rise. At the same time companies saw an issue of shares as a cheap and attractive way of both releasing capital from an established business, on behalf of the partners and their families, and raising new or additional capital so as to finance expansion. Having said that, self-finance through the savings of entrepreneurs and the profits generated in the business, continued to remain by far and away the most important source of finance for British business. Though the capital requirements of individual enterprises were continuously on the increase, putting increased pressure on the savings of the community, so were both collective and individual wealth. An entrepreneur with a successful record and with the right contacts among family friends and business associates, could obtain the necessary finance for a promising new venture, without the need to attempt a public issue of shares. Certainly in the late 1920s, £50,000 could be raised with little difficulty.[54]

However, these informal methods of finance were under pressure because of the depressed state of the British economy, and the greatly increased level of taxation. Hints of difficulties did emerge in the inter-war years. E. L. Payton, representative of the National Union of Manufacturers, with 3,000 small firms nation-wide, told the MacMillan Committee that, because of the depressed state of the economy, 'most of your friends have got their own commercial difficulties and have not their money free to put into that business, and so you retard it'.[55] Even Sir Robert Kindersley, director of the

---

[54] W. A. Thomas, *The Finance of British Industry, 1918–1976* (London 1978), 6–7, 102, 115, 117; F. W. Paish, *Business Finance* (London 1961), 62, 94, 134; L. Hannah, *The Rise of the Corporate Economy* (London 1976), 71–3; C. Brooks, *Something in the City: Men and the Markets in London* (London 1931), 99; Howson, *Domestic Monetary Management*, 9–10, 25, 27, 34, 38, 56, 161; Moggridge, *British Monetary Policy*, 155, 211–12; Atkin, *British Overseas Investment*, 60, 66; M. Cowen, 'Capital, National and Commodities: The Case of Foresstal Land, Timber and Railway Company in Argentina and Africa, 1900–1945', in Van Helten and Cassis (eds.), *Capitalism in a Mature Economy*, 203; J. B. Jeffreys, *Trends in Business Organisation in Great Britain since 1856*, Ph.D. thesis (London University 1938), 130; A. Essex-Crosby, *Joint-Stock Companies in Great Britain, 1890–1930*, M. Comdiss. (London University 1938), 228–30, D. H. MacGregor, 'Joint-stock companies and the Risk Factor', *E. J.* 39 (1929), 495–6.

[55] MacMillan Committee, *Minutes*, Q 22511.

City merchant bank, Lazard Brothers & Co., admitted before the same committee, 'I think for small concerns the probability is that there is something lacking in our financial organisation.'[56] Nevertheless, even in the interwar years firms in growth areas, like motor vehicles, do not appear to have experienced any real problems in raising funds through both informal and formal avenues. The likes of Austin and Daimler never found themselves deprived of finance either from reinvested profits or public issues of securities.[57] It was Sir Mark Webster Jenkinson, an accountant with extensive experience of company finance, who clearly identified in his evidence to the MacMillan Committee, the central problem that arose after the war: 'I think new industries generally can find the capital. I am thinking more particularly of some of the older industries.'[58]

Between the wars there was a prolonged fall in business income, with the gross profit rate between 1924 and 1937 averaging around one-third of the pre-war level, at constant prices. Inevitably this reduced the supply of funds available for self-financed growth, especially in those established industries most badly affected, like shipbuilding. Added to this contraction in profits was the increased level of taxation owing to the need to service the vastly increased National Debt. Thus, even out of the profits that were being made, less was left at the disposal of business to fund either new projects or existing operations. Overall, after depreciation, new savings were just over half the 1873–1913 level between 1925 and 1937.[59]

Even the act of taxation itself, though it may be regarded as merely redistributing income from one group in society to another, undermined the mechanism of self-finance, as Sir Josiah Stamp pointed out:

You cannot expect these private businesses to be financed as they were by people who knew them once the money has left them by high taxation and gets into the hands of rentiers who do not know them, and if it is bid for by home enterprise it goes into the very large concerns. No *rentier* getting his war loans return and looking round for further investment is going to put the money into the business of John Jones or Tom Smith whose securities are not marketable, he will put them into the securities of some large combine. You have altered the whole direction of savings by that very fact.[60]

Consequently, by the mid-1920s, companies in the major sectors of British manufacturing, most notably the export industries, were being forced to look for external finance for the first time if they were to avoid bankruptcy

[56] MacMillan Committee, *Minutes*, Q 1530.
[57] D. Thomas and T. Donnelly, *The Motor Car Industry in Coventry Since the 1890s* (London 1985), 17, 20, 23–4, 50–5, 58–9, 105, cf. MacMillan Committee, *Minutes*, QQ 3921, 6760, 7901, 7976, 8351, 8742; Thomas, *Finance of British Industry*, 91–2, 102.
[58] MacMillan Committee, *Minutes*, Q 3607.
[59] R. C. O. Matthews, C. H. Feinstein, and J. C. Odling-Smee, *British Economic Growth, 1856–1973* (Oxford, 1982), 140, 149, 178, 190–2, 383–6, 518, 527; Thomas, *Provincial Stock Exchanges*, 256, 317; Thomas, *Finance of British Industry*, 91–2, 96, 102, 107, 115, 117.                    [60] MacMillan Committee, *Minutes*, Q 3950.

and closure, as they had exhausted the traditional sources. The difficulty was that the very firms looking to solve their financial problems, by the issue of securities, were the ones least attractive to investors because of the commercial difficulties they were in. Sir Roland Nugent, of the Federation of British Industry, explained the problem:

> I think you are in a vicious circle, you cannot go to the public for capital, because your dividend or profit record is pretty bad, for the same reason you have not accumulated reserves, yet you cannot get on the profit-earning scale again until you recondition your plant, and there you are.[61]

From all the basic industries the complaint was the same—depression and taxation had undermined the means of finance that had served them well until the war, but now they could not obtain the funds they required to modernize their plant and keep this businesses going.[62]

Therefore, the 'MacMillan Gap' was only incidentally the problem of financing new manufacturing enterprises. More importantly, it was the question of what to do with long-established and once-successful firms that could no longer generate profits, had exhausted their reserves and were a poor risk for further lending. In 1930, one banker, Sir W. N. Goschen, Chairman of the National Provincial Bank, expressed the view that, 'I think when the industry has reached such a point that it has exhausted all its capital and credit that it is entitled to have there is only one thing—to disappear.' Harsh as this viewpoint was it was shared by both other bankers, like J. W. Beaumont Pease of Lloyds Bank, and industrialists like the shipbuilders Sir William Lithgrow and W. L. Hickens.[63] Any efforts by the Stock Exchange or its members could not have persuaded investors to buy securities issued by firms with a record of losses and little prospect of future success, no matter their prosperity in the past.

Issues of securities were of growing importance to the finance of British industry between the wars, with many medium-sized companies participating. This switch to issues by the smaller British companies favoured the stockbrokers who, inevitably, numbered among their clients wealthier industrialists from all over Britain. Consequently, it was natural that they would be approached, in the first instance, when the idea of making an issue of securities arose, for whatever reason. Stockbroking firms like Capels and Cazenoves, for example, all became involved in new issues through their clients. Charles Micklem, of Cazenoves, was a personal friend and later relative of William Shearer, the managing director of Balfour Beatty,

---

[61] MacMillan Committee, *Minutes*, Q 8380.

[62] Ibid., QQ 1530, 1537, 2511, 2536, 3607, 3651–3, 3695, 3706, 6760, 7976, 7980, 8351, 8365, 8372, 8382, 8400, 8494, 8548, 8576, 8694, 8696, 8742, 9267. Statements by Sir Mark Webster Jenkinson, 27 Mar. 1930, Central Landowners' Association, 27 Mar. 1930, H. Lakin-Smith, 11 July 1930.

[63] Ibid., QQ 1934 of 2257, 2271, 7980, 8382, 8494. For a discussion of the 'MacMillan Gap' see R. Coopey and D. Clarke, *3i: Fifty Years Investing in Industry* (Oxford 1995), 9–18.

the electrical contractors. When that firm formed Power Securities in 1922, as a means of handling new issues of electrical securities, Cazenoves were involved form the outset. Even without these personal connections the handling of small issues for medium-sized British companies was exactly the type of business that a stockbroker could undertake. In contrast, a merchant bank was used to much larger and more international issues of securities. The result was that London stockbrokers carved out for themselves an expanding niche in the capital market, between the issue that could command only local attention and those that required national/international marketing. They did this either independently or in association with a number of specialist issuing houses that were set up at this time. Cazenoves, as indicated, worked with Power Securities, while Foster & Braithwaite handled issues for Charles Hatry's Corporation and General Securities, which was set up in 1924. Similarly, the brokers, John Prust and Company were involved in the commercial and industrial issues originated by the Charterhouse Trust, set up in 1925 to undertake such business.

Also, it was not simply in domestic securities that stockbrokers grasped opportunities in the new issue market. One of the remaining active areas in overseas loans was for the smaller colonies, without large capital markets of their own or an ability to appeal to New York. These were the very countries that had used stockbrokers to handle issues before 1914 as they were too small to attract the merchant banks like Barings and Rothschilds. Hence, Scrimgeour, and Mullens were well placed to exploit their existing connections in the 1920s whereas the merchant banks had lost theirs. Unfortunately for Mullens, the Bank of England warned that this growing involvement in colonial issues could jeopardize their position as government brokers and so they withdrew at the end of the 1920s.[64] Consequently, though the nature of the capital market was substantially altered in the 1920s, compared to the pre-war years, the changes actually favoured London stockbrokers because of their experience in handling second-class issues, and their connections with British investors.

Inevitably some of those involved were less than scrupulous in evaluating the quality of the issues that they handled, and these included members of the Stock Exchange. An investigation by the Stock Exchange itself in 1930 uncovered the fact that a member, Cyril James, was involved in sharepushing, whereby investors were recommended to buy shares, through false reports of a company's prospects in newspapers like British Industry and Finance. This had begun with Gondar Tin Mines in 1926, followed by, among others, Australian Commonwealth Carbide in 1927, Sunbeam

[64] Reed, Capel and Company, 77–9; Kynaston, Cazenove, 100–3, W. J. Reader, A House in the City: Foster & Braithwaite, 1825–1975 (London 1979), 148–9; Armstrong, 'Rise and Fall of the Company Promoter', 132–3; Thomas, Finance of British Industry, 50; D. Wainwright, Government Broker: The Story of an Office and of Mullens and Company (East Molesey 1990), 65, 69, 763; Roberts, Schroders, 389; Atkin, British Overseas Investment, 104–6; Dennett, The Charterhouse Group, 22.

Gramophone and Record Company in 1928, and the Patent Coals Carbonisation Trust in 1929. All had been orchestrated by a shadowy figure called Jacob Factor. The role of the broker was to create a false market in the securities of these companies so as to give an impression that the issues were being well received by the public. As a consequence of activities of this kind much of the funds raised by the companies involved was expended in promotional costs, leaving the enterprise heavily over-capitalized but under-funded, and so endangering its long-term future. The brokers T. Gordon Hesler & Co., for example, were involved in the promotion of seven companies in the late 1920s. These were in such novel fields as film production, and the manufacture of gramophones, recording apparatus, and refrigerators, reflecting the current interest in the prospects of new industrial products. Altogether they had raised subscriptions totalling £1,048,916 for these seven companies though, in the end only £722,593 or 69 per cent, had actually materialized from investors. However, the expenses involved came to £172,761, which was 16.5 per cent of the subscribed capital or 24 per cent of the sum actually received. Generally, a survey by the Stock Exchange of 26 companies promoted by 12 brokers between December 1927 and March 1929 revealed that of the £3.8m. in capital promised by investors only £2.3m. was delivered and the expenses involved absorbed £0.6m. or 27 per cent of that.[65]

These practices all came to light in the wake of the Hatry scandal of September 1929. In order to provide himself with the finance required for his more speculative financial operations, Charles Hatry had taken to creating additional securities on behalf of well-respected companies whose issues he handled. This provided a simple and low-cost source of temporary finance. As long as he bought back the securities before dividends or interest had to be paid, so that the number authorized matched those in existence, the device remained undiscovered. At one stage in 1929 it was estimated that these sale and buy-back operations involved some 400,000 shares, especially those belonging to Photomaton, a manufacturer of automatic photography equipment. The problem came when Hatry and his associates could no longer buy back the extra shares because of the falling prices. This had begun in February 1929 when the bank rate was raised, forcing them into ever more expensive support operations to cover their losses. For the Stock Exchange the consequence was to leave members holding securities which were now worthless as their issue was unauthorized. The losses created were alleviated by a subscription collected from among the membership.[66]

[65] LSE: General Purposes, 12 Aug. 1929, 17 Mar. 1930, 14 Apr. 1930.
[66] M. Karo, City Milestones and Memories (London 1962), 87; LSE: General Purposes, 25 Sept. 1929, 17 Mar. 1930, 24 Mar. 1930, 15 May 1930; LSE: General Purposes, Non-Permanent, 25 Oct. 1929, 20 Feb. 1930, 24 Feb. 1930; LSE: Subcommittee on Country Jobbing, 4 Oct. 1934; Reader, House in the City, 148–9; E. Green and M. Moss, A Business of National Importance: The Royal Mail Shipping Group, 1902–1937 (London 1982), 96–7, 100, 147; The Economist, 28 Sept. 1929.

Interestingly, the London Stock Exchange was of the opinion that the Wall Street crash was due to the revelations that came from the Hatry scandal, as it had '. . . caused great uneasiness in the United States, and the confidence, which the public had in the stability of the stock markets was rudely shaken.'[67] Certainly, when the Wall Street crash did come in October it had little direct impact on London because prices there were already falling and it had its own crisis to cope with. As *The Economist* noted on 2 November 1929, regarding the Wall Street crash, the '. . . role of the London Stock Exchange during the past week has been largely that of an interested but impassive spectator.'[68] However, a financial crisis in both London and New York, of such magnitude, could hardly be blamed on the actions of one man handling small and fairly marginal issues. As the merchant banker James Kinross reminisced regarding 1928/9, 'During this period practically any rubbish could be sold.'[69]

As early as 1921 Lavington had noted that the issues of small industrial companies were difficult to sell, with the result that those that succeeded in so doing expected to be amply rewarded. One way of doing that was to persuade the public that the issue was going to be a success by creating a fund that bought up any shares that were sold by investors during the issue period. This gave other investors the confidence to subscribe and thus made the issue a success, with the company getting sufficient capital to establish itself in business, generate profits, and reinvest in the future.[70] Sir Robert Kindersley, a director of the merchant bank Lazards, pinpointed the problem in his evidence to the MacMillan Committee in 1930, when discussing the problems of handling small issues

. . . the average investor today does not like to have anything without a market, and you cannot possibly have a market with £50,000 of stock or £100,000 of stock for that matter, there is bound to be no market in stock and it is very difficult of negotiation in consequence.[71]

The problem was that the methods used to give an illusion of marketability, and thus persuade the reluctant investor to purchase the securities of small and untried ventures, were also open to abuse, as was the case with Hatry.

It was interesting that *The Economist* reported, on 10 November 1928:

A feature of the year has been the repeated over-subscription of speculative issues, the attraction of whose deferred shares as gambling counters were more regarded by the public than their merits as an investment.[72]

---

[67] LSE: General Purposes, 15 May 1930. Credence to this view is given by Geisst, *Wall Street*, 186.

[68] *The Economist*, 21 Nov. 1929.     [69] Kinross, *Fifty Years in the City*, 73.

[70] Lavington, *English Capital Market*, 221.

[71] MacMillan Committee, *Minutes*, Q 1526.     [72] *The Economist*, 10 Nov. 1928.

This was probably true in many cases but in others—and certainly those associated with Hatry—it was but an illusion created by operations in the stock market designed to allow the offloading of unsold securities in an active after-market.

Unfortunately, in the aftermath of the Hatry scandal, and the general collapse in prices, the shares of those small companies in novel fields fell most heavily, or disappeared entirely. In a comparison of new issues made in 1928 it was discovered that those that represented conversions of established companies had fallen 18 per cent in value by 31 May 1931 while those for entirely new enterprises had fallen by 83 per cent.[73] With evidence of this kind it was only natural to blame abuses in the market place rather than the judgement of investors, the inevitable risk associated with untried enterprises, and the prevailing financial conditions. 'The great new issue boom of 1928 foisted a great deal of worthless trash on the public and very few securities of permanent worth',[74] wrote Valance in 1935, and he placed the blame on the Stock Exchange itself for allowing it to happen. The prevailing orthodoxy of 'caveat emptor' which had come under attack even in the less interventionist days before 1914, was now under pressure, with expectations that either the Stock Exchange took steps to prevent a repeat performance, or the government would. There was certainly a widespread belief that investors now required greater protection from worthless company promotion and market manipulation than had been the case before 1914, and they had the right to expect it from the likes of the Stock Exchange.[75] Thus, from both the government and the Stock Exchange there were attempts to limit access to the market by those seeking to finance new developments, and to curb the ways used to persuade investors to become interested in such activities.

The company legislation of 1928/9, for example, attempted to enforce greater disclosure on new companies so that at least investors were more aware of what they were investing in. It also prohibited the selling of unmarketable securities to the public. However, both these measures had little long-term effect, once the scare of the Hatry scandal had died away. Disclosure could force companies to reveal their real worth but it did not force potential investors to read the documents produced or allow them to understand complex financial structures and arrangements. As the Departmental Inquiry into Share-pushing noted in 1937, the main victims of fraud were inexperienced investors who exhibited a '. . . curious reluctance to seek any advice before parting with money or securities'.[76] Similarly, those inter-

---

[73] A. T. K. Grant, *A Study of the Capital Market in Post-War Britain* (London 1937), 144–6, 178.

[74] A. Vallance, *The Centre of the World* (London 1935), 234, cf. 244.

[75] *The Times, The City of London* (London 1929), 182–3; Royal Institute of International Affairs, *International Investment*, 363.

[76] *Share-Pushing, Report*, 17.

ested in selling securities directly to the public found a simple means of evading the restrictions on advertising their wares. As the Stock Exchange itself noted in 1934:

... by buying out a country broker, an outside finance group obtains a list of clients which they can circularise freely. We know the names of a number of country broker firms which have been bought up in this manner and we know of other firms who have been approached from London with an offer, on the death of a partner or the equivalent.[77]

As it was, when the abuse reappeared in the mid-1930s the government was at a loss to know what to do for any action they proposed would interfere '... with the smooth running of the delicate machinery of legitimate "finance" in the City of London'.[78] Their only recommendation was to restrict participation in new issues to those belonging to a stock exchange or another recognized body. In essence, self-regulation was deemed to be the only solution with greater power to be given to organizations like the Stock Exchange that policed the conduct of their members.

The London Stock Exchange had already begun to take measures to reduce the use made of its trading facilities by those trying to sell new securities to the public. There had always been a sizeable group among the membership who believed existing regulations had been too lax in this respect. When Gerald Williams wrote to the Stock Exchange in November 1918, regarding possible new post-war rules and regulations, he raised the matter of the ability to unload new shares on the floor.

In the interests of the public, which is also that of the 'House' a change ought to be made in all requirements concerning the introduction on the London market of shares in newly floated companies.

The problem, as he saw it, was the fact that London allowed securities to be traded on the floor not only before obtaining the right to be listed but also before they had been fully issued. This allowed '... the unscrupulous company promoter ... to take advantage at any time and in any market of a "boom" during which he can get rid of great numbers of intrinsically unsound shares issued at temptingly low nominal values'.[79] The Stock Exchange did tighten up somewhat by forcing brokers to ask permission to deal in a security before starting to create a market for it on the floor. Furthermore, in November 1919, they insisted that an advertisement regarding the security had to be placed in the press before permission to deal was given, if any issue had been made without a prospectus or circular.[80]

However, neither of these restrictions proved particularly onerous as

---

[77] LSE: Subcommittee on Country Jobbing/Country Business, 4 Oct. 1934.
[78] *Share Pushing, Report*, 37, cf. 67.
[79] LSE: Rules and Regulations, 27 Nov. 1918.
[80] LSE: General Purposes, 27 Nov. 1919, 12 Mar. 1928; W. T. C. King, *The Stock Exchange* (London 1954, 2nd edn.), 83–4.

members were, naturally, keen to trade in any securities with a potential for an active market. Also, if they did not provide a market there were plenty who would, such as the outside brokers in London or the members of the provincial stock exchanges. Nevertheless, in the wake of the abuses exposed by the Hatry scandal the London Stock Exchange was forced to tighten up further its regulations on dealings in new issues. However, these amounted to little more than a demand for greater documentation and increased scrutiny of what was provided. At this stage there was a great reluctance to abandon the freedom given to members to develop markets in new securities as that benefited the whole membership through increased turnover. The Stock Exchange itself noted in 1930 that

... the existing system has worked well for a great number of years, has provided facilities for settling transactions in an efficient and speedy manner, and ... the Hatry frauds have themselves made their recurrence less likely by drawing attention to the risks attaching to temporary documents.[81]

Though the procedures thus survived the Hatry frauds the Stock Exchange was now much more aware of the need to police the new securities to which it was giving a market. As a result it became more difficult to get permission to deal in a particular security on the floor, and thus dubious—or simply novel—securities found it more difficult to attract the interests of investors, and those who were in regular contact with them.[82]

This general tightening up was sufficient in the immediate aftermath of the frauds, and the Wall Street crash, but they were tested again in the mid-1930s when there was a revival in company promotion. Again, this involved securities whose worth was far from certain, especially those of overseas mining companies and domestic industrial companies developing a new technology. The Stock Exchange itself was worried that mining companies were being brought to the market at too early a stage of their development, before the worth of the reserves was established, while even the government was concerned about the flotation of companies designed to exploit processes based on unproven scientific principles. Again the response was to further tighten up the inspection of the documents submitted in any request for permission to deal, and demand even higher standards, such as three years of accounts.[83]

By the mid-1930s, however, a new problem had arisen that was the reverse of share-pushing. This was the growing practice of making issues to only a restricted group of investors, and not making it available to the public at large. This grew up as a way of dealing with the large number of small issues that would not justify the costs of a public offering. Those

---

[81] LSE: General Purposes, 21 July 1930.
[82] F. W. Hirst, *The Stock Exchange: A Short History of Investment and Speculation*, (London 1948, 4th edn.), 212–13; King, *Stock Exchange*, 121; Balogh, *Financial Organization*, 284–6.
[83] LSE: General Purposes, 1 Oct. 1934, 8 Apr., 1935, 21 Oct. 1935, 11 Nov. 1935.

issuing securities had the choice between a placing, an introduction, and a public offer for sale. In a placing the securities in question were placed with a small group of interested investors, such as among the clients of a particular broker. This was a very inexpensive way of raising capital for the company concerned. In an introduction the securities were placed in the hands of a broker, or even a jobber, who then released them to other brokers and jobbers depending upon demand. There was thus no formal issue, or even pricing, but a gradual dissemination of the securities among the investing public. In both these cases the market for existing securities provided by the Stock Exchange and its membership was being used as a cheap method for selling new securities, bypassing the services—and costs—of merchant banks and other issuing houses. It was even reported in the 1930s that brokers were purchasing stocks and shares in bulk from either the companies themselves or from an issuing house and then selling them on to their clients or to other brokers on the floor of the Stock Exchange for a small premium. The estimate made in 1935 was that whereas the cost of an introduction or placing amounted to between $\frac{1}{4}$ and $\frac{1}{2}$ per cent of the sum raised, the average for a public issue was $3\frac{1}{2}$ per cent, and that could be much higher for a speculative issue that the public had to be persuaded to support.[84]

... in issues of comparatively small amount, the cost of a public prospectus or offer to sale, if not prohibitive, is a very serious charge. While underwriting, commissions, brokerage and some other expenses are automatically adjusted to the amount of the issue, being fixed percentages, other expenses, particularly advertising are not so easily adjusted

was the Stock Exchange's own verdict in July 1935.[85] They contrasted a minimum of £5,000 on advertising alone for a public offer for sale with £600 necessary for the advertisements necessary to meet the permission to deal requirements. Unfortunately, the Stock Exchange were also aware that the less publicity involved in a new issue the more open to abuse it was, either by excluding investors from an attractive offering or persuading others to subscribe without a full knowledge of the risks involved. The solution was, again, to tighten up on the regulations regarding placings and introductions though that might mean that small issues could become prohibitively expensive. Again, without actually introducing new regulations the emphasis was changed so that it became more difficult to obtain permission for a stock to be dealt on the Stock Exchange unless a prospectus had been produced or a public offer for sale had been made. Even where a placing or introduction was accepted in their place, the brokers involved had to be sure that the securities were as widely distributed as possible.

Consequently, though the Stock Exchange appeared to respond little to the abuses exposed by the Hatry scandal of the late 1920s, there was a noticeable shift in attitude. Increasingly the Stock Exchange saw itself not simply as a market for securities—any securities—but a guardian of quality as well. Thus it tried to eliminate those new issues to which there was attached the greatest risks, such as small mining companies at the development stage or manufacturing companies using untried technologies or producing novel products. It also limited access to the cheapest ways of raising capital, namely a placing or introduction, as these involved the greatest possible abuses. As a result the service that the Stock Exchange and its members could offer to the capital market did lose some of its vitality in the 1930s as it was less easy for brokers to utilize the floor of the Stock Exchange as a way of disposing of new securities.[86]

At the same time the merchant banks, recognizing that much of their international business had been lost, turned to domestic finance in the 1930s. This was not to say that the brokers lost out entirely. In 1937 there were 230 public issues in London handled by 109 finance houses, of which 77 per cent were for £100,000 or over. In contrast, in the same year, there were also 237 placings or introductions, handled by 92 stockbrokers, with only 53 per cent being for £100,000 or over. Clearly, there remained a rough division of responsibility within the capital market with the London stockbrokers tending to provide a service for the smaller issues. Even within that there was a division. A large and well-connected firm like Cazenoves was able to handle the larger issues, with five of the 16 they were involved with being over £0.5m. each in 1937. In contrast the brokers Seymour, Pierce and Company specialized in the smallest of issues with most of the 25 that they handled being for £50,000 and under. Making up the middle ground were Zorn and Leigh-Hunt who were involved with 12 issues, none being larger than £250,000. Consequently, when the stockbrokers are included among those handling new issues—whether public or private—in London in the 1930s, it is fairly evident that a considerable diversity existed in the services they offered, whether by size or type.[87]

Clearly, between the wars many members of the London Stock Exchange moved quickly to exploit the new opportunities that were now available in the capital market. Though they faced strong competition from both provincial brokers and new finance houses in London, they had established

---

[86] Roberts, *Schroders*, 264, 389; P. L. Cottrell, 'The Domestic Commercial Banks and the City of London, 1870–1939', in Y. Cassis (ed.), *Finance and the Financiers in European History, 1880–1960* (Cambridge 1992), 57; Collins, *Money and Banking*, 221; Burk, *Morgan Grenfell*, 91, 162; Ellinger, *The City*, 287, 300–1; MacMillan Committee, *Minutes*, Q 2561.
[87] Kynaston, *Cazenove*, 145, 158; Ellinger, *The City*, 287, 300–1; Morton, *British Finance*, 302.

for themselves a more important role in the capital market than they had possessed before 1914. However, the worsening prospects for overseas loans in the 1930s, coming after an already difficult period in the 1920s, increasingly diverted established merchant banks towards the domestic scene. During the 1930s these merchant banks, including ex-stockbrokers like Helbert Wagg, did become a serious threat to the type of new issue business undertaken by stockbrokers. It was difficult for stockbrokers to meet this competition directly as they also co-operated with the merchant banks in providing the retail distribution networks for issues. This was a business the brokers did not want to lose because of the commission income it generated, and so they had to choose between competing with merchant banks for business, and so lose all distribution income, or relinquish the handling of new issues in order to retain the revenue from commissions paid on the securities they sold to their clients. With the Stock Exchange refusing admission to any whose business was not wholly broking or jobbing, it was not possible, at this time, to create the integrated firms which circumstances were encouraging. Where these did exist they were formed outside the Stock Exchange, and so not subject to the monitoring that that institution would have provided. This was unfortunate for the potential for abuse was much greater where the same firm both gained financially from a successful new issue and was responsible for advising clients on the merits of new issues.

However, though many members of the Stock Exchange did become actively involved in the new issue business between the wars, including the promotion of companies, their prime function as a collective body was to provide a market for securities once issued. As in the past, by continuing to provide a market for securities it was easier to persuade investors to purchase new securities and thus facilitate the finance of long-term projects. As F. Hyde, Managing Director of the Midland Bank, observed in 1930:

We cannot lend our money direct for capital purposes, but we can lend our money on a *marketable* share. The effect of lending money on a *marketable* share may be that we are finding money for capital purposes that we would not find in the shape of a capital advance.[88]

The growing sophistication of, and specialization within, the British financial system not only allowed the banker to lend long-term but encouraged him to do so, safe in the knowledge that the underlying asset, in the form of a share or debenture, could be realized at will via the Stock Exchange. German bankers, faced with a much smaller and less active stock exchange, were envious of their British counterparts, and were worried by the risks direct participation in industry exposed them to because they did not possess such an easy alternative for employing their deposits. During

---

[88] MacMillan Committee, *Minutes*, Q 913 of QQ 870–90.

the questioning of the MacMillan Committee Jakob Goldschmidt, of the Darmstadter und National bank, was asked by the Chairman, 'Do I understand that the German banker, like the English banker, does not like to have his money tied up permanently in industry?' To which he replied, 'No, the German banker dislikes that as much as any banker anywhere else in the world.'[89] While many in Britain looked with envy on the German banking system in the 1920s because of its close connections with industry, the Germans themselves were well aware of the necessities which had forced such actions upon them and the problems it caused by locking up funds that could be withdrawn at short notice by depositors in unrealizable assets.

However, the securities that were ideal for such collateral purposes were not now those issued by business but that created by the British government to finance the war. Whereas in 1913 quoted British government securities totalled £1bn., or 9 per cent of all quoted securities, by 1920 the total had risen to £5.4bn. and the proportion to 32.6 per cent. With conversions of short- into long-term debt the amount rose to £6.5bn. in 1933 and £6.9bn. in 1939, keeping its proportion at around a third for the entire inter-war years. Generally, the result of the war had been to transform the weight of UK government issues among the securities traded in London at the expense of both foreign government and home and overseas corporate securities. These still commanded a presence on the London Stock Exchange but a much diminished one, and one that was seriously overrepresented on the official list in the case of foreign governments and American railroads.[90] (See Tables 5.1 and 5.2.)

In the 1920s the London Stock Exchange did try to recover its position as the premier international market for securities. In 1922 it was noted that:

Though Paris, New York, Amsterdam and Berlin are rightly considered International markets, London has at all times been a cosmopolitan one, and has consequently been used by all financial centres as a Clearing House.[91]

However, with the repatriation of American securities to New York, and the growing competition from that centre in foreign securities generally, especially government issues, London risked losing that status in the 1920s. The nominal value of foreign government bonds quoted did rise in the 1920s but the main expansion in this area was in colonial government debt. This generated less activity being almost entirely held by British investors, and so little traded between exchanges. Instead, the London Stock Exchange offered a home to a large variety of foreign corporate securities, such as Indian industrial and commercial enterprises and companies operating in tea, rubber, oil, and mining from throughout the world.[92]

[89] MacMillan Committee, *Minutes*, Q 7285 of QQ 7283–4, Q 6760.
[90] *Stock Exchange Yearbook for 1919*, 23; LSE: Special Subcommittee, Supplementary List, 27 Feb. 1931.
[91] LSE: General Purposes, 29 Mar. 1922.
[92] Ibid., 29 Nov. 1920, 16 May 1922, 15 Oct. 1923, 24 Oct. 1927, 20 Feb. 1928.

It was during the 1920s that the Stock Exchange began to compete vigorously for the business in tea and rubber company shares much of which had been lost to outside brokers before 1914, particularly with the establishment of the Mincing Lane Exchange in 1909. This was despite the fact that many of the companies were small, generating little turnover in the shares that they issued.[93] One firm especially active in developing the market in tea shares, for instance, was de Zoete & Gorton, having lost much of their pre-war business in American railways. As they explained in October 1923,

For many years business was entirely a matter of negotiation; jobbing in the ordinary way was almost impossible. Even today we estimate that out of about 200 companies which we follow closely, there is only a market in about 20 per cent; and an occasional market in another 20 per cent; dealing in the remaining 60 per cent is entirely a matter of negotiation; and in many cases it is only possible with the assistance of our clients.

We believe that the aid we have thus afforded has been largely responsible for the development which has taken place in dealing in Tea Shares in the House, and it has enabled other brokers to compete successfully with Mincing Lane, and created the demand for a wider jobbing practice, which is likely in the course of a few years to finally establish the Stock Exchange as the centre of this business.[94]

It was not only in overseas corporate securities that the London Stock Exchange tried to offer attractive market opportunities. Despite the competition from the well-established provincial stock exchanges, the London Stock Exchange was equally hospitable to domestic industrial and commercial concerns in the 1920s. In fact one of the complaints after the Hatry scandal and subsequent collapse in 1929 was that the Stock Exchange had been too free in granting such facilities to companies whose prospects and promoters were of a dubious nature. Certainly, a petition from 109 members claimed that

The London market provides facilities for free dealing in securities unequalled by those of any other centre in the world.[95]

Clearly in the 1920s one of the great growth areas for the London Stock Exchange was the securities of British manufacturing companies. One of the few barriers it began to impose in the 1920s was an attempt to force companies, whose securities it quoted, to maintain transfer offices in London as the lack of such a facility delayed the settlement of sales and purchases. As early as 1920 it was discovered that 302 companies were in this position, being mainly Northern or Scottish industrials—80 breweries and distilleries, 56 iron, coal, and steel companies, and 109 in the miscellaneous category.[96]

[93] Ibid., 29 Nov. 1920, 16 May 1922, 15 Oct. 1923, 24 Oct. 1927, 20 Feb. 1928.
[94] Ibid., 15 Oct. 1923.    [95] Ibid., 29 Oct. 1923.
[96] Ibid., 11 Feb. 1920, 8 Oct. 1928; LSE: Settlement Department, 8 Sept. 1927, 19 June 1928, 15 Sept. 1925, 8 Dec. 1925.

Though it was made more difficult to gain a Stock Exchange quotation for a security after the war than before, and though 'Permissions to Deal' had to be applied for before a security could be traded, neither of these precautions seemed to have imposed onerous conditions on the applicants. As it was explained in November 1930,

Trading facilities are freely granted to any reputable concern and an official quotation is optional . . .[97]

A proposal at that time to charge a fee to companies requesting permission to have their securities traded on the Stock Exchange was dropped because it might encourage smaller undertakings to not proceed. In fact the Stock Exchange had created, immediately after the First World War, a supplementary list of securities which were not officially quoted but for whom permission to deal had been given. The securities of the Hydro & Electric Securities Corporation, for example, were never officially quoted on the London Stock Exchange but, nevertheless, were very actively traded at times during the 1920s. Clearly, it was not the lack of recognition within the Stock Exchange that prevented a market developing there for particular securities, but more the opportunities that were available to members and their ability to grasp them. Swedish shares for example, in which there was some activity in London in the late 1920s, were dealt in outside because of the finer prices obtainable there, to the disappointment of the Stock Exchange.[98]

Consequently, during the 1920s the Stock Exchange exhibited a willingness to quote any securities which offered the prospect of generating good business for its members. If those prospects were limited the securities could be granted a simple permission to deal with the ability to gravitate to a full quotation if turnover justified it. As it was, between 1926 and 1930 a total of 7,696 securities, or over 1,400 a year were granted permission to deal, of which 42 per cent had a value of under £50,000, and 85 per cent were less than £0.5m. In contrast, of the 3,633 securities granted an official quotation over the period, 68 per cent were for amounts greater than £50,000, with most of those that were less than £50,000 being conversions of existing issues rather than new issues. Through the use of the 'Permission to Deal' facility the London Stock Exchange offered a ready market for very small new issues indeed, while 'even among those granted an official quotation there existed many for quite a small sums'. (Table 6.2.)

By no means was the London Stock Exchange only a market for large and/or active issues, whether home or overseas, in the 1920s. This description of how business was done in an inactive security in 1928 indicates the use to which the market was put.

[97] LSE: General Purposes, Non-Permanent, 26 Nov. 1930.
[98] H. Wincott, *The Stock Exchange* (London 1946), 88; LSE: General Purposes, 9 Aug. 1929; LSE: General Purposes, Non-Permanent, 27 Nov. 1930.

## Table 6.2. London Stock Exchange: Applications to trade securities, 1926–1930

### (a) Permission to Deal

| Year | Total No. | No par value No. | No par value % | <£50,000 No. | <£50,000 % | £50,000–£500,000 No. | £50,000–£500,000 % | £500,000+ No. | £500,000+ % |
|---|---|---|---|---|---|---|---|---|---|
| 1926 | 1,133 | — | — | 524 | 46 | 458 | 40 | 151 | 13 |
| 1927 | 1,360 | — | — | 597 | 44 | 606 | 45 | 157 | 12 |
| 1928 | 1,965 | 83 | 4 | 754 | 38 | 913 | 47 | 215 | 11 |
| 1929 | 1,495 | 40 | 3 | 606 | 41 | 628 | 42 | 221 | 15 |
| 1930 | 1,143 | 26 | 2 | 501 | 44 | 425 | 37 | 191 | 17 |
| TOTAL | 7,096 | 149 | 2 | 2,982 | 42 | 3,030 | 43 | 935 | 13 |

### (b) Official quotation

| Year | Total | | | <£50,000 | | | £50,000–£500,000 | | | £500,000+ | | |
|---|---|---|---|---|---|---|---|---|---|---|---|---|
| | Total | New | Conversions | Total | New | Conversions | Total | New | Conversions | Total | New | Conversions |
| 1926 | 578 | 216 | 362 | 144(25%) | 4 | 140 | 300(52%) | 112 | 188 | 134(23%) | 100 | 34 |
| 1927 | 654 | 257 | 397 | 156(24%) | 2 | 154 | 308(47%) | 121 | 187 | 190(29%) | 134 | 56 |
| 1928 | 848 | 230 | 618 | 292(34%) | 1 | 291 | 377(34%) | 114 | 263 | 179(21%) | 115 | 64 |
| 1929 | 848 | 228 | 620 | 294(35%) | 1 | 293 | 358(42%) | 116 | 242 | 196(23%) | 111 | 85 |
| 1930 | 705 | 183 | 522 | 242(34%) | 0 | 242 | 315(45%) | 94 | 221 | 148(21%) | 89 | 59 |
| TOTAL | 3,633 | 1,114 | 2,519 | 1,128(31%) | 8 | 1,120 | 1,658(45%) | 557 | 1,101 | 847(23%) | 549 | 298 |

### (c) Total (excluding conversions and no par value)

| Year | Total | | | <£50,000 | | | £50,000–£500,000 | | | £500,000+ | | |
|---|---|---|---|---|---|---|---|---|---|---|---|---|
| | Total | Deal | Quotation | Total | Deal | Quotation | Total | Deal | Quotation | Total | Deal | Quotation |
| 1926 | 1,349 | 1,133 | 216 | 528 | 524 | 4 | 570 | 458 | 112 | 251 | 151 | 100 |
| 1927 | 1,617 | 1,360 | 257 | 599 | 597 | 2 | 727 | 606 | 121 | 291 | 157 | 134 |
| 1928 | 2,112 | 1,882 | 230 | 755 | 754 | 1 | 1,027 | 913 | 114 | 330 | 215 | 115 |
| 1929 | 1,683 | 1,455 | 228 | 607 | 606 | 1 | 744 | 628 | 116 | 332 | 221 | 111 |
| 1930 | 1,300 | 1,117 | 183 | 501 | 501 | 0 | 519 | 425 | 94 | 280 | 191 | 89 |
| TOTAL | 8,061 | 6,947 | 1,114 | 2,990 | 2,982 | 8 | 3,587 | 3,030 | 557 | 1,484 | 935 | 549 |

*Source:* LSE: Committee of a Non-Permanent Character, 24 Feb. 1931.

On the morning of Wednesday 22nd August at the request of Mr E. M. Wilkins (a fellow broker) I—C. C. Mitchell, a broker—went into the market to ascertain the price of British Safety Glass Shares. I went first to Richardson and Co. who said that they no longer dealt in them. I next went to Julian Joseph and Co. who said the market was almost nominal at 2/6—3/6 and that it would probably be necessary to approach the shop. I thereupon went to John Gibbs & Co., the brokers to the Company, and saw Mr R. H. Shelton. I said I had an enquiry in 1,000 shares and had been to the market which I found was difficult. Mr Shelton asked me whether I wanted to deal for cash or the account and said the prices were 2/—2/9d. for the account and 2/9—3/6d. for cash.[99]

With the Hatry scandal and the world-wide financial and monetary collapse between 1929 and 1931, interest in whole groups of securities suffered a severe decline. In particular, foreign government securities, having suffered numerous defaults, lost their appeal in London and were shunned by British investors., In absolute terms the nominal value of these securities actually declined in the 1930s, indicating a large de-listing as they ceased to be actively traded. Many other foreign securities suffered the same fate, with mining, tea, and rubber companies facing both a collapse of commodity prices and currency restrictions which made it impossible to remit dividends to British investors. It was not a Stock Exchange resistance to foreign government and corporate securities that accounted for their declining importance among quoted securities in the 1930s, but a fundamental disillusionment among investors with the prospects for such issues. Among the few foreign securities in which there was a revival of interest were American stocks and bonds, because of the strength of the dollar. However, though the Stock Exchange continued to offer a home to an American market an increasing proportion of the business flowed directly to New York where the overwhelming bulk of all such securities were quoted and traded. As the Stock Exchange itself accepted by 1938 American securities were '. . . really a New York market'. Where British investors continued to have a significant stake in foreign securities that remained attractive, as with South African and Australian gold-mining companies, the London Stock Exchange continued to provide a hospitable home for trading, and one that could compete actively with domestic operators in both these areas.[100]

Nevertheless, it was increasingly British securities that the London Stock Exchange catered for in the 1930s, for the activity in a miscellaneous collection of mining companies hardly compensated for the loss of both foreign government debts and US railroad stocks and bonds. However, this was little revealed by the nominal value of securities officially quoted by the Stock Exchange. What they reveal is the continued importance of British government debt, and the declining significance of the securities issued by

[99] LSE: General Purposes, 3 Sept. 1928.
[100] Ibid., 17 Oct. 1932, 31 May 1937, 26 July 1937, 14 Mar. 1937; ibid., 7 Nov. 1938; LSE: Settlement Department, 15 Mar. 1935, 3 June 1937.

foreign governments and American railroads. Whereas in 1913 British government debt was but 9 per cent of the total, compared to foreign governments at 28.0 per cent and US railroads at 15.4 per cent, by 1939 this
position had been reversed, for British government debt stood at 38.5 per
cent compared to foreign governments at 12.2 per cent and US railroads at
4.8 per cent. (See Tables 5.1 and 5.2.) In particular, the conversion of War
Loans onto a more permanent basis in June 1932 greatly increased the relative importance of the long-term securities issued by the British government and quoted on the London Stock Exchange. Whereas in 1929 the
National Debt held in private hands totalled £7.0bn., with only 28 per cent
having a maturity of 25 years or over, by 1933, though the total had
changed little—being £7.2bn.—now 57 per cent was for 25 years or greater.
Inevitably this gave a boost to that element of the Stock Exchange's business at the very time the defaults of foreign governments on payments, the
collapse of the US economy, and general financial and currency turmoil,
destroyed interest in whole categories of foreign securities.[101]

In fact the nominal value of quoted securities was, increasingly a less and
less reliable indicator of what the Stock Exchange was providing a market
for. A growing number of the securities traded were not officially quoted,
but simply given permission to deal and were placed on a Supplementary
List. By 1939 the nominal value of the securities on the Supplementary List
totalled £1.8bn., or 10 per cent of the value of those on the Official List.
Where the average value of each issue of securities was £3.2m. on the Official List that on the Supplementary List was only £0.4m. It was not just on
size that there was a difference between the Official and the Supplementary
Lists. British government debt, for example, was all officially quoted and
that comprised almost 40 per cent of that total. In contrast, a large number
of issues by mining and manufacturing companies were to be found only
on the Supplementary List. Where mining securities comprised only 0.4 per
cent of the Official List they totalled 18.4 per cent of the Supplementary
List. Similarly, commercial and industrial securities were 7.1 per cent of the
Official List but 20 per cent of the supplementary. Consequently, through
the facility of the Supplementary List the London Stock Exchange was continuing to provide a market for small, and often speculative, issues of securities both from home and abroad, though this would be unrecognized by
an examination of the Official List. (Tables 6.3 and 6.4.)

In addition, though nominal and market value of securities did bear a
close relationship in terms of the overall total, this was not true in individual categories. On the Official List, for example, whereas the nominal
value amounted to £17.7bn. in 1937 the market valuation was £19.5bn.,
or an excess of 10 per cent. In 1938 the margin was only 3 per cent in
favour of nominal, though in 1939 it had stretched to 6 per cent, still in

---

[101] Howson, *Domestic Monetary Management*, 88, 106, 161.

Table 6.3. London Stock Exchange: Nominal and market values of securities quoted on 24 March 1939, by number and amount (£m.)

| Class of security | Official List | | | Supplementary List | | | Total | | |
|---|---|---|---|---|---|---|---|---|---|
| | Number | Nominal | Market | Number | Nominal | Market | Number | Nominal | Market |
| British government | 60 | 6,922.5 | 6,598.4 | — | — | — | 60 | 6,922.5 | 6,598.4 |
| UK public bodies | 506 | 934.4 | 891.5 | 50 | 12.0 | 10.3 | 556 | 946.4 | 901.8 |
| TOTAL | 566 | 7,856.9 | 7,489.9 | 50 | 12.0 | 10.3 | 616 | 7,868.9 | 7,500.2 |
| Colonial governments | 157 | 859.9 | 817.8 | 3 | 1.4 | 1.4 | 160 | 861.3 | 819.2 |
| Foreign governments | 283 | 2,197.7 | 395.2 | 56 | 517.7 | 92.5 | 339 | 2,715.4 | 487.7 |
| Colonial/Foreign public bodies | 262 | 161.3 | 117.7 | 16 | 15.8 | 2.9 | 278 | 177.1 | 120.6 |
| TOTAL | 702 | 3,218.9 | 1,330.7 | 75 | 534.9 | 96.8 | 777 | 3,753.8 | 1,427.5 |
| UK railways | 67 | 1,140.3 | 605.4 | 20 | 10.6 | 8.2 | 87 | 1,150.9 | 613.6 |
| Indian railways | 46 | 136.5 | 133.7 | 1 | 0.1 | 0.1 | 47 | 136.6 | 133.8 |
| Imperial railways | 72 | 314.7 | 228.9 | 3 | 0.8 | 0.3 | 75 | 315.5 | 229.2 |
| American railways | 62 | 865.4 | 383.0 | 6 | 39.1 | 2.5 | 68 | 904.5 | 385.5 |
| Foreign railways | 204 | 637.3 | 132.0 | 13 | 2.0 | 1.0 | 217 | 639.3 | 133.0 |
| TOTAL | 451 | 3,094.2 | 1,483.0 | 43 | 52.6 | 12.1 | 484 | 3,146.8 | 1,495.1 |
| Banks and discount houses | 80 | 195.0 | 433.4 | 19 | 208.0 | 25.0 | 99 | 215.8 | 458.4 |
| Financial, land, and investment | 799 | 487.9 | 429.2 | 409 | 114.7 | 101.6 | 1,208 | 602.6 | 530.8 |
| Insurance | 63 | 36.3 | 326.4 | 15 | 3.0 | 12.8 | 78 | 39.3 | 339.2 |
| TOTAL | 942 | 719.2 | 1,189.0 | 443 | 138.5 | 139.4 | 1,385 | 857.7 | 1,328.4 |

| | | | | | | | | | |
|---|---|---|---|---|---|---|---|---|---|
| Canals and docks | 26 | 30.7 | 64.4 | 32 | 12.6 | 11.7 | 58 | 43.3 | 68.1 |
| Gas | 140 | 126.4 | 124.6 | 316 | 33.8 | 35.6 | 456 | 160.2 | 160.2 |
| Electric light/power | 184 | 218.5 | 326.0 | 63 | 45.4 | 81.4 | 247 | 263.9 | 407.4 |
| Telegraph and telephone | 34 | 441.4 | 686.3 | 12 | 42.4 | 59.0 | 46 | 483.8 | 745.3 |
| Tramways and omnibus | 71 | 59.6 | 58.1 | 38 | 20.5 | 26.5 | 109 | 80.1 | 84.6 |
| Waterworks | 73 | 28.5 | 34.5 | 141 | 7.9 | 10.0 | 214 | 36.4 | 44.5 |
| TOTAL | 528 | 905.1 | 1,293.9 | 602 | 162.6 | 224.2 | 1,130 | 1,067.7 | 1,518.1 |
| Commercial/Industrial | 1,568 | 1,279.5 | 2,470.7 | 1,893 | 356.9 | 395.7 | 3,461 | 1,636.4 | 2,866.4 |
| Breweries/Distilleries | 401 | 215.0 | 380.3 | 122 | 21.6 | 28.8 | 523 | 236.6 | 409.1 |
| Iron, coal, and steel | 207 | 306.2 | 431.4 | 167 | 81.4 | 72.2 | 374 | 387.6 | 503.6 |
| Shipping | 60 | 73.6 | 62.2 | 32 | 14.1 | 12.6 | 92 | 87.7 | 74.8 |
| TOTAL | 2,236 | 1,874.3 | 3,344.6 | 2,214 | 474.0 | 509.3 | 4,450 | 2,348.3 | 3,853.9 |
| Mines | 47 | 76.2 | 123.0 | 478 | 333.7 | 591.3 | 525 | 409.9 | 714.3 |
| Nitrate | 6 | 9.1 | 3.0 | — | — | — | 6 | 9.1 | 3.0 |
| Oil | 33 | 162.3 | 512.1 | 27 | 35.6 | 49.7 | 50 | 197.9 | 561.8 |
| Tea, coffee, rubber | 182 | 60.0 | 55.0 | 672 | 67.8 | 49.7 | 854 | 127.8 | 104.7 |
| TOTAL | 268 | 307.6 | 693.1 | 1,177 | 437.1 | 690.7 | 1,445 | 744.7 | 1,383.8 |
| TOTAL | 5,693 | 17,976.1 | 16,824.2 | 4,604 | 1,812.4 | 1,682.6 | 10,287 | 19,787.9 | 18,507 |
| No par value | — | — | (485.5)* | — | — | (69.3)* | — | — | (554.8) |

* Included in total.

Source: LSE: Committee for General Purposes, Annual Report, 24 Mar. 1939.

Table 6.4. London Stock Exchange: Nominal and market values of securities quoted on 24 March 1939 (%)

| Class of security | Official List | | Supplementary List | | Total | |
|---|---|---|---|---|---|---|
| | Nominal | Market | Nominal | Market | Nominal | Market |
| British government | 38.5 | 39.2 | — | — | 35.0 | 35.7 |
| UK public bodies | 5.2 | 5.3 | 0.7 | 0.6 | 4.8 | 4.9 |
| TOTAL | 43.7 | 44.5 | 0.7 | 0.6 | 39.8 | 40.5 |
| Colonial governments | 4.8 | 4.5 | 0.1 | 0.1 | 4.4 | 4.4 |
| Foreign government | 12.2 | 2.3 | 28.6 | 5.5 | 13.7 | 2.6 |
| Colonial/Foreign public bodies | 0.9 | 0.7 | 0.9 | 0.2 | 0.9 | 0.7 |
| TOTAL | 17.9 | 7.9 | 29.5 | 5.8 | 19.0 | 7.7 |
| UK railways | 6.3 | 3.6 | 0.6 | 0.5 | 5.8 | 3.3 |
| Indian railways | 0.8 | 0.8 | — | — | 0.7 | 0.7 |
| Imperial railways | 1.8 | 1.4 | — | — | 1.6 | 1.2 |
| American railways | 4.8 | 2.3 | 2.2 | 0.1 | 4.6 | 2.1 |
| Foreign railways | 3.5 | 0.8 | 0.1 | 0.1 | 3.2 | 0.7 |
| TOTAL | 17.2 | 8.8 | 2.9 | 0.7 | 15.9 | 8.1 |
| Banks and discount houses | 1.1 | 2.6 | 1.1 | 1.5 | 1.1 | 2.5 |
| Financial, land, and investment | 2.7 | 2.6 | 6.3 | 6.0 | 3.0 | 2.9 |
| Insurance | 0.2 | 1.9 | 0.2 | 0.8 | 0.2 | 1.8 |
| TOTAL | 4.0 | 7.1 | 7.6 | 8.3 | 4.3 | 7.2 |
| Canals and docks | 0.2 | 0.4 | 0.7 | 0.7 | 0.2 | 0.4 |
| Gas | 0.7 | 0.7 | 1.9 | 2.1 | 0.8 | 0.9 |
| Electric light/power | 1.2 | 1.9 | 2.5 | 4.8 | 1.3 | 2.2 |
| Telegraph and telephone | 2.5 | 4.0 | 2.3 | 3.5 | 2.4 | 4.0 |
| Tramways and omnibus | 0.3 | 0.3 | 1.1 | 1.6 | 0.4 | 0.5 |
| Waterworks | 0.2 | 0.2 | 0.4 | 0.6 | 0.2 | 0.2 |
| TOTAL | 5.0 | 7.7 | 9.0 | 13.3 | 5.4 | 8.2 |
| Commercial/ Industrial | 7.1 | 14.7 | 20.0 | 23.5 | 8.3 | 15.5 |
| Breweries/ Distilleries | 1.2 | 2.3 | 1.2 | 1.7 | 1.2 | 2.2 |
| Iron, coal, and steel | 1.7 | 2.6 | 4.5 | 4.3 | 2.0 | 2.7 |
| Shipping | 0.4 | 0.4 | 0.8 | 0.7 | 0.4 | 0.4 |
| TOTAL | 10.4 | 19.9 | 26.2 | 30.3 | 11.9 | 20.8 |
| Mines | 0.4 | 0.7 | 18.4 | 35.1 | 2.1 | 3.9 |
| Nitrate | 0.1 | — | — | — | — | — |
| Oil | 0.9 | 3.0 | 2.0 | 3.0 | 1.0 | 3.0 |
| Tea, coffee, rubber | 0.3 | 0.3 | 3.7 | 3.0 | 0.6 | 0.6 |
| TOTAL | 1.7 | 4.1 | 24.1 | 41.0 | 3.8 | 7.5 |

Source: As Table 6.3.

favour of the nominal, reflecting the increasing pessimism about world economic and political conditions. Even on the Supplementary List the relationship was reasonably close, despite the more volatile nature of many of the securities, with the market value being only 6 per cent greater in 1939. (Table 6.3.)

Within the individual categories however, the differences between nominal and market values could be enormous. On the Official List, for instance, the nominal value of foreign government debt stood at £2.2bn. in 1939 whereas the market placed a value of £0.4bn., or 82 per cent less. Similarly, the market valuations of both UK and US railways, on the Official List, was almost half the nominal value. The discrepancy was even greater in terms of foreign railways, where South American railways had difficulty both earning profits and then remitting any dividends to the British holders of their stocks and bonds. In contrast, on the Official List the market value of commercial and industrial securities in 1939, which would be mainly domestic, was almost twice the nominal value. The market could also spot prospects with the market value of the issues made by the various oil companies standing at over three times the nominal value or those by insurance companies at almost nine times the nominal value. Similar differences were to be found on the Supplementary List, where were to be found many securities issued by foreign governments and corporations that no longer commanded the value they had once held, as well as others that had now risen substantially in the market's estimation such as electric light and power, telecommunications, or breweries and distilleries, either because of future possibilities or the guaranteed demand for their product.

Inevitably, these differences between values give an altered picture of the securities that the Stock Exchange was catering for by the late 1930s, when the market's estimate is taken. Though the position of UK government debt remains virtually unchanged on the Official List that for foreign government securities drops from 17.9 per cent to 7.9 per cent while that for overseas railways shrinks from 10.9 per cent to 5.3 per cent. Within this the big gains are made by commercial and industrial companies of all kinds, whose share virtually doubles from 10.4 per cent to 19.9 per cent and resource-based companies, whose share more than doubles, though from only 1.7 per cent to 4.1 per cent. Smaller, but still impressive gains, are also made by the financial and utility sectors. Within the Supplementary List, the two categories of commercial and industrial (all components) and resource companies (mining, oil, and plantations) dominate in market terms, with more than three-quarters of the market value, while government and railway securities are of little consequence being, collectively, 7 per cent of the total. Consequently, where the market value of the securities traded on the London Stock Exchange is taken, and both the Official and Supplementary Lists are included, it is fairly clear that the London Stock Exchange had responded well to the changes forced upon it in the inter-war years. Inevitably British government debt dominated, as was to be expected because of the costs of the First World War, but now commercial and industrial securities, of all kinds, had replaced both the debts of overseas governments and railway stocks and bonds to become the second biggest category. (Tables 6.3 and 6.4.)

Nevertheless, there were definite suggestions that the Stock Exchange was becoming less responsive than it had previously been to those wishing to have their securities traded there. The Hatry scandal had made the Stock Exchange much more aware of the way the market it provided could be used to sell securities to the ill-informed small investor, without any proper safeguards being put in place. Especially in terms of a quotation and, to a lesser extent 'permission to deal', it scrutinized more carefully all applications and was more willing to reject. This was reinforced in the mid-1930s after it was found that member brokers, such as Mumford & Bicknell, had been involved in share-pushing exercises. That firm, for example, which was headed by Alfred Sharp, had persuaded clients to buy shares in Heidelberg Estates and Exploration company at £4 each, by suggesting that it was about to be taken over at £10 per share. This turned out to be false and the price then collapsed. Incidents like that, combined with the subsequent publicity and the governments own investigation in share-pushing, were forcing the Stock Exchange itself to police the new issue market more and more through its ability to grant or deny either a quotation or permission to deal. In many ways this was a new task for the Stock Exchange's own function, in terms of self-regulation, had been to police the behaviour of its own members in buying and selling already issued securities for themselves and their clients. This function could be stretched to include the problem of share-pushing, where existing securities were concerned, but it was a major step for the Stock Exchange to become the watchdog for the whole securities business. In the past the Stock Exchange in granting quotations for permission to deal, had focused on whether the subsequent market would be fair to all concerned—buyer, seller, broker, and jobber. Now they were expected to vet each application to see whether the value placed upon it by the vendors or issuers reflected its 'true' worth.[102] This they did not have the expertise to do with the consequence that they, probably, erred on the side of caution.

However, they were well aware of the fine line they had to tread. As they noted in February 1937, they did possess the power to police the new issue market

> ... by the withholding or withdrawing of permission to deal in securities which for one reason or another appear to be unfit for sale to the public and by furnishing information and advice to interested parties and the press to do something towards preventing the exploitation of the public by unscrupulous operations.

[102] LSE: General Purposes, 11 Nov. 1935; Share-Pushing, Report, 67.

At the same time they were also very keen to ensure that

... no step should be taken which would restrict the freedom of the markets in which a vast volume of business is done ...[103]

The London Stock Exchange were also aware that even though they could deny facilities to a new issue of securities they had no power over non-members, and so a market could develop either on a provincial stock exchange or among the outside firms in London. They thus allowed their own members, for example, to trade in securities not quoted or dealt in London as long as sales and purchases did not take place on the floor.[104] At times the refusal to quote or deal was dictated by outside forces, especially the government. Throughout the inter-war years the government exercised a major influence over the capital market through both the Bank of England and the Stock Exchange. During the conversion of the 5 per cent War Loan in 1931/2, for example, the government enforced a complete ban on foreign loans.[105] Generally, the Stock Exchange was fully co-operative, refusing to quote or list securities when so requested. However in 1937 they suspended all arrangements for new industrial issues because of a threatened new tax on dividends paid on ordinary shares by manufacturing companies. Until the details became clear the Stock Exchange refused to grant trading facilities for securities that might, suddenly, drop substantially in value.[106] In fact, the Stock Exchange came to the defence of manufacturing industry because it felt, at a time of hesitant recovery,

... the money required would be raised more equitably by a special tax spread equally over the profits of all trading concerns.

For the Stock Exchange, its position was clear.

The Stock Exchange as a body had no interest in any one particular industry. It depends on the prosperity of industry as a whole ...[107]

Clearly, by the 1930s the Stock Exchange saw its future more and more as a market for domestic corporate securities. However, it was not simply expected to provide this market, but also to police it for, otherwise, there was a strong possibility of government intervention, especially after the Hatry scandal. As a senior member of the Stock Exchange, Sir Herbert Ellissen, put it in 1935,

I entirely appreciate the importance of the freedom of markets, and I do not for a moment deny that the fewer the restrictions the greater the freedom, but I would suggest that it is possible to give too much weight to these considerations.

---

[103] LSE: General Purposes, 1 Feb. 1937.
[104] Ibid., 22 Oct. 1937, 1 Nov. 1937; LSE: Subcommittee on Country Brokers, 4 Apr. 1939.
[105] Balogh, *Financial Organization*, 268–9, 271–3.
[106] LSE: General Purposes, 27 Apr. 1937, 5 May 1937, 14 June 1937.
[107] Ibid., 5 May 1937.

Important as the freedom of market is, it is, I would suggest, nevertheless more important under modern conditions that the transaction of business in public securities should be conducted under strict regulation. This strict regulation, the Stock Exchange as at present organised, supplies, and any action which would tend to disrupt the organisation might lead to consequences in the way of state interference which it is very desirable to avoid.[108]

The Stock Exchange was thus obliged to respond to the mood of the time, and that mood was towards greater control over access to the market provided by the London Stock Exchange, for securities that involved a high degree of risk and uncertainty. Thus it was relatively easy to get a quotation, or at least permission to deal, for the issues of companies with an established record, while an unproven business found its access barred. In fact there were even moves in November 1937 to form a London curb market because of the difficulty of getting certain securities traded on the London Stock Exchange. Though this appeared to come to nothing it was illustrative of the greater supervision being exercised by the London Stock Exchange.[109]

One illustration of this greater caution was the refusal to quote units issued by unit trusts. Initially these unit trusts represented an investment in a fixed group of securities and so the ability to buy and sell such units would have been an advantage to both existing holders and potential purchasers. They were also aware that unit trusts offered a means of channelling individual purchases by numerous small investors into the type of large deal that its members were used to handling for wealthier investors or financial institutions. Recognizing that this was the case, especially as its own members were involved with unit trusts, the Stock Exchange deliberated for some time whether to provide a market for these new securities. They noted in 1936

The introduction into this country of the Fixed Trust brought before the investing public a new commodity capable of being offered in a very attractive form as an alternative to the methods of investment which it had hitherto employed. The public, not unnaturally, turned to those through whom it was accustomed to invest its resources, and it thus became necessary at an early stage that the Committee of the Stock Exchange should set itself to consider whether, and if so to what extent, and under what safeguards, the Stock Exchange should open its market to, and allow its members to take part in dealings in the new commodity.

Appropriate action was accordingly taken to investigate this aspect of the question, and the conclusion reached in the early part of the year 1934 was that, for the time being at any rate, it was not desirable to provide a market on the Stock Exchange for the Units and sub-units of Fixed Trusts, or to take any official cognisance of the movement. After this date, however, the Fixed Trust 'birth-rate' rose

---

[108] LSE: Subcommittee on Country Broking, 20 June 1935, cf. LSE: General Purposes, Non-Permanent, 11 July 1935.     [109] LSE: General Purposes, 15 Nov. 1937.

so steeply that the Stock Exchange felt itself constrained to make a further investigation of the position, mainly with a view to determining whether it lay in its power to guard the public from exploitation by affording a market restricted to the Units and sub-units of such Fixed Trusts as might conform to standards set up by the Stock Exchange for the protection of the investor.[110]

The outcome of this deliberation was a continued refusal to trade in such units because of the worry that the prices could be controlled and manipulated by the various managements of unit trusts. As a result a false market could be created reminiscent of the ones engineered by Hatry back in the late 1920s. Instead, the Stock Exchange looked to the government to regulate the unit trust movement before these new securities would be acceptable on its market. Behind this decision also lay a fear that the unit trust movement could compete with stockbrokers for business, as these trusts would be big enough to settle transactions between investors without putting the sales and purchases through the market. Instead, the unit trust movement solved its own problems, without the need to use the Stock Exchange, by converting to a flexible portfolio basis and being willing itself to sell or redeem units, at short notice, with a spread between the two prices. Essentially, unit trusts dealt in their own units and by the late 1930s they had established for themselves an important role in meeting the needs of the small investor. The Stock Exchange's caution in refusing their units a market had, in the end, lost them business and helped create a rival.[111]

By 1939 the *Stock Exchange Official Yearbook* listed 21,000 securities, known to British investors. These had been issued by 9,400 companies and 2,000 governmental authorities and agencies. Of these 21,000 securities some 12,400, or 59 per cent were quoted on either the London Stock Exchange or another in the British Isles. In fact only 5,693 or 27 per cent were quoted in London with another 4,604, or 22 per cent having been granted permission to be dealt in there, making a total of 10,297 or 49 per cent. On that measure the London Stock Exchange only provided a market for half the securities known in London.[112] However, though known to British investors many of these securities had their market overseas, as with the large number of dollar securities traded in New York. Similarly, very many of the issues were too small to warrant any kind of market presence, let alone in London. There did continue to exist, for example, numerous and active local stock exchanges whose role was to provide a market for securities that were closely held in a particular community or among groups of specialized investors.

More significant is the need to discover whether there were groups of securities that were denied a market on the London Stock Exchange and could have thrived if they had been provided with it. Certainly in the 1920s

---

[110] Ibid., 16 Mar. 1936, cf. 16 Dec. 1935, 30 Mar. 1936, 23 Apr. 1936, 16 Nov. 1936.
[111] Morgan and Thomas, *Stock Exchange*, 179; Gleeson, *People and Their Money*, 30.
[112] *Stock Exchange Official Yearbook for 1939* (London 1939), p. v.

ADRs appeared to be in the category while in the 1930s it was unit trust units. However, neither of these categories represented the ownership of securities issued by governments and companies themselves. Even with the caution that came after the scandals and collapses between 1929 and 1931, the London Stock Exchange appeared willing to grant either a quotation or permission to deal to almost any issue unless it was too small or closely held to justify a public market or too dubious to be worthy of a public forum. As evidence of this was the fact that, despite the willingness of banks to lend to manufacturing companies in the 1930s, it became increasingly more attractive for them to raise finance through an issue of shares. The average yield on industrial debentures, for instance, which had stood at 8.1 per cent in 1921 was a mere 3.8 per cent in 1935, reflecting the willingness of investors to purchase such securities and the attractiveness of the terms to the companies.[113]

As *The Economist* observed in September 1937

Before the war, the small industrial undertaking obtained a very large proportion of its finance without making a general appeal to the public. From choice or necessity, industrialists now deem it worth their while to turn family businesses into public companies with widely diffused shareholdings.[114]

As a result banks were forced to purchase low-yielding government debt with their otherwise idle deposits instead of advancing it to corporate customers at a better rate of return.

A growing number of new issues for small companies, which then found a market on the London Stock Exchange, hardly suggests an institution not responsive to the needs of the capital market. Certainly it took time for it to learn to discriminate between the fraudulent and the speculative but, at all times, it offered a welcome to virtually all new issues and a market for securities of all kinds. In contrast, the German financial system collapsed between the wars and had to be rescued by the state. In the 1920s small German businesses, for instance, were unable to obtain finance either from the banks or by making a public issue and so were starved of finance, while larger companies looked abroad. During the 1930s the whole financial system, including the securities market, became controlled by the government. In contrast in Britain, Ford was able to raise £4.5m. in 1931 through a new issue, despite the economic crisis, in order to finance its new Dagen-

---

[113] D. M. Ross, 'The Clearing Banks and Industry: New Perspectives on the Inter-war Years' in Van Helten and Cassis (eds.), *Capitalism in a Mature Economy*, 60–4; Collins, *Money and Banking*, 254–5; Thomas, *Finance of British Industry*, 44; Ellinger, *The City*, 161; F. Capie and M. Collins, *Have the Banks failed British Industry* (London 1992), 54; D. M. Ross, 'Bank Advances and Industrial Production in the United Kingdom During the Inter-war Years: A Red Herring?', in P. L. Cottrell, H. Lindgren, and G. A. Teichova (eds.), *European Industry and Banking Between the Wars: A Review of Bank–Industry Relations* (Leicester 1992), 191, 194, 197, 199. [114] *The Economist*, 11 Sept. 1937.

ham car plant. There was no need to internalize finance through mergers and amalgamations with individual and institutional investors increasingly willing to hold the securities of smaller—though not small—companies.[115]

In 1929, during the speculative boom, of the securities issued by British companies, 77 per cent were in the form of shares compared to 23 per cent as debentures, indicating a willingness of investors to accept a considerable risk in their investment, and the Stock Exchange to provide a market for those types of securities. In the wake of the scandal and collapse, shares fell to 44 per cent of the total while debentures grew to 56 per cent. Subsequently, investors recovered their willingness to accept risk so that by 1937 the ratio was, once again, 70 per cent shares to 30 per cent debentures. Clearly, there was no problem in obtaining a market for these shares on the London Stock Exchange for, otherwise, it would have been difficult, or even impossible, to issue them.[116]

The members of the London Stock Exchange possessed no special magic that would solve the financial problems of the British economy between the wars. War had left an enormous debt that had to be financed and a large burden of taxation that limited the funds available for investment. The result was to force considerable change in the ways the British economy and especially British commerce and industry, financed itself. New skills had to be learnt as with the evaluation of new issues for small enterprises that could be either speculative, fraudulent or both. Gradually these skills were learnt and, if the Hatry scandal had not coincided with the Wall Street crash, the consequences might have been less traumatic than they were. As it was, in the 1930s the London Stock Exchange appeared better able to balance caution and risk while still providing a ready market for an ever-widening range of securities. Few securities seeking to utilize the market available on the London Stock Exchange were excluded, and that market appeared able to judge, accurately, the worth of the securities that were being traded, certainly in terms of yield, prospects, and security. The Stock Exchange again showed itself as a dynamic institution able to shift towards the needs of both the domestic economy and still vibrant areas of the world economy, like mining and oil, in the same ways as it had cultivated US railroads in the past. Certainly, in terms of the capital market it is difficult to attribute blame to the Stock Exchange for any deficiency of finance. The Stock Exchange could not market securities that investors were unwilling to buy, such as issues by companies in declining industries. All it could do was to better police the market for those securities that investors

---

[115] Balderston, 'German Banking', 14, 21, 27, 28, 29, 32; Hannah, *Rise of the Corporate Economy*, 71, 216; S. J. Prais, *The Evolution of Giant Firms in Britain* (Cambridge 1976), 4, 116; Vallance, *Centre of the World*, 122; S. E. Thomas, *British Banks and the Finance of Industry* (London 1931), 117–18; Atkin, *British Overseas Investment*, 159, 162.

[116] Green and Ross, *A Business of National Importance*, 202; Morton, *British Finance*, 261, 302, 304, 316.

were interested in, and this it did once it learnt to cope with the new developments.

Overall, therefore, one can detect a major divide with the First World War in the contribution made by the Stock Exchange to the British economy. Before the war economic development was financed in a variety of distinct ways with the importance of the Stock Exchange steadily growing. Self-finance was commonplace in commerce, manufacturing, construction, agriculture, and numerous other activities, where the scale of operations was insufficient to justify the need for intermediation of any kind. The securities that were issued tended to capitalize assets already in existence, for reasons of convenience and flexibility, rather than to finance further development. Finance obtained through the issue of securities could be characterized largely as the prerogative of government and infrastructure at home and increasingly abroad, with the Stock Exchange acting to increase the demand for such securities by expanding the supply of funds available for investment.

With the war something of a change in direction on the Stock Exchange occurred because of the rapid rise in government debt, government borrowing, and the level of taxation, and the steep fall in the general profitability of British industry, reflecting the altered international environment. The war upset the delicate but slowly changing ways by which the various components of the economy were financed. In particular, the lower level of profits reduced the importance of accumulated reserves as a source of capital for industry at the very time when the government's requirements for both short- and long-term funding curtailed the Stock Exchange's ability to increase the supply of funds available for investment in securities. Some adjustment had to take place and it was overseas investment that was squeezed out in the end, adding further complications for the already depressed export industries like shipbuilding, coal-mining, and textiles.

Nevertheless, though the quality of the service provided by the Stock Exchange did deteriorate between the wars, because of the restrictive practices imposed by London, this was of marginal importance in terms of the provision of finance. Of far greater significance was the relative reduction in the supply of funds for investment because of low profitability, taxation, and London's diminished international role, and the unattractiveness of many of the available domestic investments. As W. L. Hichens observed, 'You cannot expect financial institutions to take interest in an industry which is being run at a loss. It is not reasonable.'[117]

---

[117] MacMillan Committee, *Minutes*, Q 7980. For market performance between the wars see C. Pratten, *The Stock Market* (Cambridge 1993), 2, 40, 194.

# 7

# New Beginnings: The Second World War, 1939–1945

## INSTITUTIONAL RESPONSE

Unlike the First World War the Second was long expected, with preparations for the conflict beginning years before its eventual outbreak. There was also an early realization that aerial bombing of major cities, like London, would be an immediate and serious feature of such a war. As early as July 1937 the London Stock Exchange held its first meeting on how to cope with attacks from the air while a practice session was held in April 1938. This type of practical planning widened in scope as the likelihood of war grew in the later 1930s. Confidential discussions were held with the Bank of England in 1938 on what the Stock Exchange should do as war became a certainty, such as the postponement of the fortnightly settlement. Consequently, when war did eventually arrive in September 1939 the London Stock Exchange had, in place, a set of plans agreed with the Treasury and the Bank of England, which covered the day-to-day operations of both the institution and the market.[1] This is not to say that either the Stock Exchange or its membership was fully prepared for war as there was always the expectation that it would not happen. As late as May 1939, at a meeting of the Trustees and Managers, the hope was expressed that,

. . . as the International situation is clearing up, we shall see better markets all round very soon.[2]

However, a month later they were back to making plans in the event of war.[3]

Consequently, when the Second War did break out the Stock Exchange was swift to act, well aware that if it did not, direct government control was a distinct possibility. As it was, war was so widely anticipated that there was nothing like the panic of August 1914. Brokers, jobbers, bankers,

---

[1] LSE: General Purposes, Minutes, 26 July 1937, 18 July 1938; LSE: Trustees and Managers, Minutes, 19 Apr. 1938, cf. E. Hennessy, *A Domestic History of the Bank of England, 1930–1960* (Cambridge 1992), 5, 10, 55, 60.
[2] LSE: Trustees and Managers, Minutes, 17 May 1939.  [3] Ibid., 21 June 1939.

and others had all reduced their commitments so that there were few out-standing obligations that needed settlement, such as a vast mass of secur-ities being used as collateral for call loans from banks.[4] The Settlement Department, for example, which cleared the transactions between members in actively traded securities reported a general lack of business over the year preceding the outbreak of war.[5] In response to the outbreak the London Stock Exchange was closed on 1 September 1939, with the settlement of the current fortnightly account being suspended until further notice. A week later—7 September—the Stock Exchange was reopened, as an outside market was already operating. All sales and purchases for the pre-war account had to be settled by 21 September. Also, when reopened, all trading was to be for cash and for immediate delivery. With government debt and associated stocks being subject to minimum prices, fortnightly account sus-pended, and continuations and options banned, it was hoped to avoid any panic selling or the build up of speculative positions especially sensitive to news of military successes or reverses.[6] In all there had been a smooth and swift transition from peacetime to wartime operation, with the gov-ernment rightly judging that it was better to have the Stock Exchange open, but operating on a restricted basis, than to outlaw the development of an uncontrolled street market. Clearly, lessons had been learnt from the First World War!

What really concerned the Stock Exchange itself, in the opening months of the war, was not the management of the securities market but the practicalities of its physical location. With the mass bombing of London expected the government was prepared to order evacuation as a precaution. Consequently, the Stock Exchange needed to find an alternative home for its operations if it was to continue in business. Many among its member-ship were already convinced that destruction in the City of London would be such as to make it impossible to operate from there.[7]

... a good many firms have already transferred a large amount of their records, books, stationery, etc. to their emergency addresses and have also made arrange-ments for the billeting of a skeleton staff at or near their emergency address

was the Stock Exchange's own assessment of the situation in September 1939.[8] By the beginning of November a total of 514 out of the 784 member firms, or 66 per cent, had established an emergency address.[9] The greater problem was to relocate the Stock Exchange itself as there was the firm belief that once bombing really began the existing building in the City

[4] LSE: General Purposes, 26 Apr. 1939.
[5] LSE: Subcommittee, Settlement Department, 14 June 1938, 13 Sept. 1938.
[6] LSE: General Purposes, 24 Aug. 1939, 5 Sept. 1939, 6 Sept. 1939; LSE: Subcommittee of a Non-Permanent Character, 3 May 1939, 24 Aug. 1939.
[7] LSE: General Purposes, 28 Aug. 1939, 30 Aug. 1939, 31 Aug. 1939, 29 Sept. 1939.
[8] LSE: Report of Subcommittee on Emergency Settlement of Bargains, Sept. 1939.
[9] LSE: Interim Report of Subcommittee on Emergency Clearing, 9 Nov. 1939.

would be uninhabitable because of the glass ceiling over the trading floor. The solution found was a move to the film studios at Denham and as early as June 1939 an option to lease had been taken.[10]

In planning the move to Denham the Stock Exchange intended to replicate there the trading-floor, with priority given to accommodating jobbers and their staff. Brokers were expected to make their own arrangements.[11] However, valuable as this planning was, it betrayed an ignorance of the fundamental needs of the members of the Stock Exchange, especially the brokers. Above all brokers needed to maintain regular, and even constant contact, with other members of the City's financial community, though the use of meetings, messengers, and the telephone. Unless the rest of the City also moved, and to an adjacent site, then there was little point in relocating to Denham because access to clients would be very difficult. Those members involved in the consols market, for example, made it clear that they had to remain close to the Bank of England and, if it stayed where it was, so would they.[12] By the beginning of October it was already apparent that any move to Denham would be hampered not only by a general 'lack of facilities' but the absence of 'speedy communication normally existing in the City'.[13] There was also no expectation that any improvement in communication between Denham and the City would take place because of the low priority accorded to the Stock Exchange by the government. Nevertheless, even as late as July 1940 preparations continued to be made for an eventual move to Denham, and the evacuation plans were not finally abandoned until the end of that year.

Evacuation of Stock Exchange Firms and Departments to premises in the Country is not practicable owing to the nature of our business which calls for close and constant touch between all parties[14]

was the conclusion eventually accepted in November 1940. In February of the following year the option on leasing Denham was terminated with the Stock Exchange and its members determined to continue operating in the City as long as possible, despite the dangers and inconvenience. Even the idea of setting up an Emergency Clearing Department at Denham was abandoned.[15] All the planning had been in vain. The Stock Exchange was such an integral part of the City of London that it could not function without constant interaction with the other components. It took the war to make all concerned recognize this fact.

[10] LSE: General Purposes, 30 Aug. 1939; LSE: Trustees and Managers, 21 June 1939, 4 Oct. 1939.

[11] LSE: Emergency Clearing, 9 Nov. 1939.

[12] LSE: Trustees and Managers, 1 Nov. 1939, 15 Nov. 1939; LSE: Emergency Clearing, 9 Nov. 1939.

[13] LSE: Trustees and Managers, 4 Oct. 1939.

[14] LSE: General Purposes, 11 Nov. 1940, cf. 29 July 1940.

[15] LSE: 'Denham' Memorandum, 21 Feb. 1941; LSE: Subcommittee, Rules and Regulations, 18 Apr. 1940.

Conditions in the City were not easy during the early years of the war due to the damage and disruption inflicted by regular air raids. In particular there was the ever-present threat of fire due to bombing, which could have destroyed the Stock Exchange building completely. Preventing such an outcome necessitated constant risk and vigilance, as the managers reported in September 1940.

As the enemy are now dropping incendiary bombs in the City it is more necessary that a careful watch must be kept on the roof and top floors of the Building, otherwise fires could start and gain hold before they were discovered. The only time when any discretion can be given is when aircraft are immediately overhead and shrapnel is falling, then cover should be taken in the Fireman's shelter which had been specially constructed for this purpose.[16]

This threat of total destruction continued right up to 1945 with the V2 rocket campaign. However, damage only closed the Stock Exchange from 16 until 24 September 1940. Even then trading was switched to the Settlement Room on 17 September so that only one day's business was lost. Consequently, despite the pre-war fears, the Stock Exchange was able to remain open virtually throughout the war, though with slightly reduced hours.[17] Nevertheless, wartime conditions did lessen members' dependence on the floor of the Stock Exchange as a forum for buying and selling securities. Staff shortages, air raids, and the disruption to travel arrangements, both to and from and within the City, led to a growth of inter-office trading via the telephone as a convenient and speedy means of communication. Rather than being discouraged by the Stock Exchange the resort to telephone trading was encouraged, as it lessened the risk that a large number of members be killed if the trading-floor received a direct hit. Their own view, expressed in October 1940, was that,

. . . telephone services provide the best, and indeed at present the only practicable means of continuing dealings during raids. They provide moreover, a means of communication and dealing which are familiar and are widely used by members under normal circumstances.[18]

The priority of the Stock Exchange in the Second World War was to keep the market open and operating throughout, whether that was to be on the trading-floor in London or elsewhere through telephone contact between members. If that could be achieved then there would be less opportunity for rival markets to become established, while those members and their staffs who remained active would provide a nucleus from which the Stock Exchange could grow again once peace came. They were forever conscious of the expertise and talent that had been lost during the First World War

[16] LSE: Trustees and Managers, 18 Sept. 1940.
[17] LSE: General Purposes, 6 Sept. 1939, 8 Sept. 1939, 16 Sept. 1940; LSE: Trustees and Managers, 11 Jan. 1945, LSE; General Purposes, 16 Oct. 1940, 28 Oct. 1940.
[18] Ibid., 3 Oct. 1940.

with the long months of closure and the altered way of operating. Though nothing could be done regarding skills in such market techniques as continuations and options, for example, there was a desire to retain individuals who possessed skills that would be needed after the war was over. The Settlement Department, for example, had been closed for eight years as a result of the First World War, and the skilled personnel that such operations required had been lost as a result. The Department was, again, closed at the outbreak of the Second World War, with the move to cash trading and immediate delivery, but now every effort was made to redeploy the staff as they would be needed again when peace came.[19] However, the Stock Exchange's ability to maintain the market, and the services its members provided, was severely constrained by the influence and control exercised by government throughout the Second World War.

Though the planning involved in the attempt to relocate the Stock Exchange proved fruitless, much more valuable was the working relationship established with the government, either directly through the Treasury or, indirectly, through the Bank of England. From the very outset of the Second World War the government took over the management and planning of the economy. Unlike the First World War there was never any thought of permitting the members of the Stock Exchange to continue to play a role in the international securities market while, domestically, the object was to remove any competition for the funds that were required to wage war successfully.[20] In many ways this was but an intensification of the co-operation that had been in existence since 1931, when sterling left the gold standard. In September 1939, on the outbreak of war, the Stock Exchange introduced a rule, that if the Treasury objected to any new issue, it would not be listed or quoted. This ceding of ultimate power to the Treasury was done voluntarily by the Stock Exchange and ensured that the government could prevent any serious competition for savings appearing for its 'tap' loans.[21] The Stock Exchange was well aware of its subsidiary position in the matter of new issues during the war, as this statement of September 1942 indicates.

The policy of the Treasury regarding new issues may be summarised very broadly by the statement that a new issue can only be sanctioned if it is in the National interest, and that in the placing of new securities all possible steps must be taken to avoid any check to the subscription to the Government loans.[22]

Thus, following on from more informal contacts in the 1930s the Stock Exchange quickly moved to a position where it actively co-operated with the government in implementing financial policy. By March 1942 they were reporting their satisfaction with the arrangement

[19] Ibid., 19 Oct. 1939, 8 Jan. 1940; LSE: Subcommittee on Settlement Dept., 27 Sept. 1939, 2 Apr. 1940, 3 Oct. 1940, 26 July 1951.
[20] M. Collins, *Money and Banking in the UK: A History* (London 1988), 317–21.
[21] LSE: General Purposes, 5 Sept. 1939, 6 May 1940, 19 July 1943, 24 Mar. 1944.
[22] Ibid., 2 Sept. 1942.

The Stock Exchange has settled down to a wartime routine which not only affords all essential facilities to the investing public but at the same time provides means for carrying out the policy of the Government in various important directions such as the control of the new capital issues.[23]

However, almost from that point onwards there was growing dissatisfaction among the Stock Exchange and its membership about the arrangements. Because the Stock Exchange was an organized and regulated market the activities of its members could be supervised and controlled, whereas those of non-members were not.[24] The Stock Exchange was not disputing that controls were necessary at a time when the government needed to mobilize all available funds for the war effort. They were also ready to co-operate in ensuring that government requirements were met and even assist in furthering government aims. Instead, the basis of their objection was a belief that they were being controlled while others were not.[25]

What the Stock Exchange wanted from the government, in return for its full co-operation, was the legal recognition that it alone constituted the securities market in Britain. Only brokers belonging to recognized institutions, like the London Stock Exchange, should be permitted to buy and sell securities on behalf of clients, along with a small number of licensed firms and individuals. This would require an Act of Parliament if a legal basis was to be given to the quasi-monopoly that the London Stock Exchange needed, if it was to supervise the securities market on behalf of the government and not lose out in the process. Such an act did exist but it had never become law. In 1939 the 'Prevention of Fraud (Investors) Act' had been passed but never implemented because of the outbreak of war. This act was designed to safeguard the public from the exploitation of unscrupulous brokers and company promoters who tried to sell them worthless securities, after a number of well-publicized cases in the 1930s.[26] However, the Stock Exchange recognized that such an act could also be used to eliminate competition from non-members, whether fraudulent or not, and so pressed in December 1943 for it to become law.

If the Prevention of Fraud Act had been brought into force the Treasury would have had ready to its hand an easy means of exercising its control over the outside market, because all dealers in stocks and shares outside the recognised Stock Exchanges would have had to become either licensed or exempted dealers and so would have been known and controllable.[27]

This did, eventually, bring a response from the government and the act became law in 1944.[28]

[23] LSE: General Purposes, *Annual Report*, 24 Mar. 1942.
[24] Ibid., 6 Dec. 1943.     [25] Ibid.
[26] A. Jenkins, *The Stock Exchange Story* (London 1973), 168; H. Janes, *de Zoete and Gorton: A History* (London 1963), 67.
[27] LSE: General Purposes, 6 Dec. 1943.     [28] Ibid., 6 Nov. 1944.

Clearly, towards the end of the Second World War the Treasury recognized that if the Stock Exchange was going to be used to control the securities market it had to be given greater power than it possessed through its own authority over its membership. The Prevention of Fraud Act was but one measure taken to restrict the degree of competition that the Stock Exchange faced as the activities of all unlicensed intermediaries, who were not members of a recognized stock exchange, could be declared illegal.[29] Increasingly, the Treasury was aware that it needed to control the entire securities market and was using the London Stock Exchange to achieve that. In turn this meant that the Stock Exchange was acquiring a degree of power over the securities market which it had never possessed in the past.[30]

Long before hostilities came to an end it was clear to the Stock Exchange that wartime controls would continue into the foreseeable futures. By December 1944 such a situation was accepted as inevitable by the Stock Exchange.[31] In fact, as the war drew to a close the degree of intervention increased. After hostile publicity concerning investors who had made substantial profits from selling a new issue of stock by General Electric, the Bank of England in February 1945 tried to impose a rule that those allotted such securities could not sell them until after six months had lapsed. The government was behind such action equating all such buying and selling as unnecessary speculation, and were keen to introduce measures that would prevent it. Though the Stock Exchange protested, pointing out that such a rule would discourage investment in new issues, they recognized that they would have to comply if the government pursued the matter. Nevertheless, after discussions with the Bank of England a compromise was reached. In return for not introducing the six-months rule the Stock Exchange agreed that all new issues of £100,000 would continue to be cleared with the Bank of England, which, in addition, now had the power to declare the new issue market closed, so preventing even issues of under £100,000 being made. A division of responsibility had emerged whereby the Bank of England, on behalf of the government, could determine the timing and amount of new issues—the queuing system—while the Stock Exchange was left to decide whether the securities were acceptable to the market—granting permission to deal.[32]

Thus, even before the Second World War had ended a post-war compromise had been reached regarding the relative power of the government and the Stock Exchange over the securities market. Though the Stock Exchange was officially recognized as the institution that exerted control over the market, and received the backing of the government in carrying out that function, it was with the government itself that ultimate power

[29] Ibid., 11 Apr. 1944.
[30] Ibid., 19 Feb. 1945, 26 Feb. 1945; 7 May 1945, 28 May 1945.
[31] Ibid., 3 July 1944; Hennessy, *Domestic History*, 102; J. Fforde, *The Bank of England and Public Policy, 1941–1958* (Cambridge 1992), 785.
[32] LSE: General Purposes, 18 Dec. 1944.

rested. Like the Bank of England the Stock Exchange was being turned into an arm of the state, no longer representing the interests of its members but ensuring that their activities conformed to the requirements of government. In return the Stock Exchange received the support of the government in maintaining its position against non-members, who might have been expected to establish a separate, and non-regulated, market. Consequently, the six years of warfare saw a significant shift of power over the securities market, in favour of the state and there was no expectation that this would diminish, let alone be reversed, when peace came. No matter what people in the City of London would have liked.

We have handed over for the total war our freedom with both hands to those who are running the war. We do not regret it, but we in the City of London wish to say very politely and very firmly that the time is shortly coming when we shall demand this freedom back again.

These were the challenging words of the Lord Mayor of London in March 1945.[33] By then it was far too late for the decisions had already been taken that peace would bring no change in the relationship.

One illustration of where the power lay in this relationship was the question of minimum prices. These had been imposed, at government request, on the outbreak of war, and covered government and related securities. Their aim was to prevent any wave of selling, on the receipt of adverse news from the military front, that could destabilize the financial system. However, the rule was only enforced on the market controlled by the London Stock Exchange, and so trading grew up outside, whenever the current price dropped below the minimum level set. Consequently, the Stock Exchange tried to have the rule on minimum prices removed but to no avail. In December 1943, for example, they were informed that the War Cabinet regarded minimum prices as an indispensable part of the machinery for financing the war. The minimum prices on government stock, quoted by the Stock Exchange, set the benchmark for further government borrowing, making it easier to offer a lower rate of interest than might be currently obtainable on existing debt in the outside, but unofficial market. It was not until after the end of the war that government permitted the Stock Exchange to abandon its rules on minimum prices and then only after further discussions with the Chancellor of the Exchequer.[34]

Though the government exerted an increasingly powerful influence during the war the Stock Exchange was left largely undisturbed in the regulation of its own membership. One of the main functions of the Stock Exchange was to ensure a level playing field for all its members in terms of equal access to information. Consequently, without any support from the government or the Bank of England, it tried to ensure that price-sensitive

---

[33] LSE: General Purposes, 19 Mar. 1945.
[34] Ibid., 5 Sept. 1939, 8 Nov. 1943, 13 Dec. 1943.

information, such as company results, were released simultaneously to all. During the war this did pose problems when communications were interrupted due to damage or military use. The South Durham Steel and Iron Company, for instance, informed the Newcastle Stock Exchange of its proposed dividend at 10.45 a.m. but the London Stock Exchange did not hear until 12.20 p.m. The result was a spate of selling orders from Newcastle to London as the dividend was lower than expected. Naturally the London Stock Exchange was concerned as its members had to honour their commitments to purchase the stock at the higher pre-announcement prices, and so would make losses on the transactions. However, these problems were inescapable under wartime conditions and the Stock Exchange tried hard to ensure that all such announcements were known immediately to all concerned.[35]

A similar but more serious incident, unrelated to the war, came to the Stock Exchange's notice in 1943. At the time it was common practice for popular newspapers and periodicals to include a weekly column where an expert 'tipped' particular securities for a rise or fall. One such columnist was Edward Gayler, the City editor of the *Sunday Dispatch*, who specialized in South American and cinema company shares. However, his activities went further than this. Along with James G. Hart, of the brokers Crews & Co., and R. M. Pearson, who was an attaché with the brokers Hurst-Brown & Buckmaster, he started to buy or sell the shares he was to tip, in advance of the article appearing in the newspaper. As the publication of the article would tend to cause the price to rise or fall, according to the tip given, they could reverse the deal, profiting from the difference. After a time other members of the Stock Exchange became suspicious of what was happening and brought it to the attention of the Stock Exchange authorities. When the practice was discovered the Stock Exchange treated the matter very seriously as it was creating regular losses for those brokers and jobbers with whom Gayler and his associates were dealing. James Hart was expelled from the Stock Exchange while John Ellert, also of Crews & Co. was suspended for five years after his involvement was discovered. However, nothing could be done about Edward Gayler, or R. M Pearson, as neither were members. Furthermore, the Stock Exchange then decided to prohibit any of members from acting as journalists in order to prevent any situation developing where a broker recommended a security in which they were already trading. Unfortunately, this affected reputable columnists, such as W. Landells, of E. B Savory & Co., who wrote regularly for the *Financial Times*.[36]

Clearly, the Stock Exchange treated very seriously any matter of insider trading, whether accidental or deliberate but had limited power to deal with

---

[35] Ibid., 9 Dec. 1940.
[36] Ibid., 27 May 1943; LSE: Subcommittee on Records, 11 May 1943, 8 Oct. 1943, 5 Nov. 1943, 9 Nov. 1943.

its consequences. It could only discipline those who were involved if they were also members of the Stock Exchange, for it had no jurisdiction over non-members. As long as such incidents were rare, and members could be warned about doing business with those involved, then the self-regulation powers possessed by the Stock Exchange were sufficient to expose and restrain the practice. Certainly, there appeared to be no interest from either the Treasury or the Bank of England in becoming involved in outlawing such practices. As it was the members of the Stock Exchange who suffered, because of the losses they made on the agreed sales and purchases, if no final buyer or vendor had been arranged, government could regard the matter as one it left the Stock Exchange to deal with.

It was not only the relationship between the government and the Stock Exchange that was altering during the Second World War for the balance of power within the Stock Exchange itself was also being resolved. Throughout its history there had been a tension within the Stock Exchange between the members—brokers and jobbers—who constituted the market and the proprietors who owned the building and controlled the services it provided. Under the pressure of wartime restrictions and uncertainties there were renewed moves by the members to take full control of the Stock Exchange not only as a market but also as an institution.[37] Certainly the timing was opportune for, as a business, the Stock Exchange was in serious trouble during the war. The Stock Exchange's income was dependent upon the annual fees paid by the membership, plus the entrance fees of new members, and both were considerably reduced. Few new members joined the Stock Exchange during the war years while the active membership shrunk to under half the pre-war total. Those members on military or other duties were permitted to suspend their membership at no cost, so depriving the Stock Exchange of a major source of income. This was at a time when running costs remained high, for as the Stock Exchange was open, it needed to be manned, heated, and serviced while bomb damage had to be repaired. For the year ending April 1941 the income of the Stock Exchange fell by £125,000 leaving only a margin of £6,163 after all expenditure had been met. No dividends were paid that year or throughout the war. In fact, such was the shortfall of income that the Stock Exchange began asking, in 1942, for all absent members to pay 10 guineas per annum for the privilege of retaining their membership.[38]

As the war drew to a close the Stock Exchange as a business faced a rather uncertain future. The existing building, completed before the First World War, was considered inadequate for modern purposes and needed replacing. However, it was difficult to justify such a large expenditure when there was no clear idea concerning the level of demand there would be for the Stock Exchange in the post-war years. The Trustees and Managers had

[37] LSE: General Purposes, 7 June 1943.
[38] LSE: Trustees and Managers, 17 Jan. 1940, 17 Apr. 1941, 21 Jan. 1942, 20 Apr. 1944.

reported to them, in April 1945, a survey conducted by the *Daily Express* that indicated that only 29 per cent of the public felt that the Stock Exchange performed a useful function, while 33 per cent were clear that it did not, leaving 38 per cent with no opinion. Even earlier there was a recognition that the dual structure of control needed to be unified if the Stock Exchange was to be represented by a single body that would argue its case both with the government and the public at large. It was acknowledged from the outset that unification of control involved risks. Under the dual structure there was a distinction between the activities of the members and the activities of the Stock Exchange as an institution. If the members became solely responsible for running the Stock Exchange then they could be asked, collectively, to accept responsibility for the actions of the membership.[39]

However, the membership chose to ignore that risk when the proprietors invited them, in 1942, to begin discussions on the unification of control. This resulted in the formation of the Council of the London Stock Exchange on 12 May 1943, which replaced both the Committee for General Purposes and the Committee of Trustees and Managers.[40] Such a move was driven not by administrative convenience or even resolving tensions between members and owners but by the need to present a united voice to government, especially in the future.

Conditions after the war will be subject to rapid political and financial changes, and the problems which will arise will be far-reaching, and your Board feel that a single body composed of the Board of the Trustees and Managers and Members of the Committee for General Purposes will, in the interest of the Stock Exchange, be better able to overcome the many difficulties which will be present.

This was the view expressed in April 1944.[41] The first meeting of the Council did not take place until 26 March 1945, and so unification was hardly driven by wartime conditions. Similarly, the whole question of the ownership of the Stock Exchange—members or outside investors—was left in abeyance until the war ended, despite the weakened state of the institution's finances.

## EFFECTS ON MEMBERSHIP

The impact of the Second World War on the London Stock Exchange was not confined to its relationship with government or the way it was run, but also extended to the activities of the members themselves. On the eve of the war an estimated 13,646 people working in the City of London were directly involved with the London Stock Exchange. Of these 4,053 (29 per

[39] Ibid., 28 May 1940, 24 Apr. 1945; LSE: *Annual Report*, 24 Mar. 1944.
[40] Ibid.; LSE: General Purposes, 26 Jan. 1944, 26 Mar. 1945; LSE: Conjoint Committee, 6 Oct. 1942.
[41] LSE: Trustees and Managers, 20 Apr. 1944.

cent) were members with a further 2,721 (19 per cent) being their clerks who were permitted access to the Stock Exchange (authorized—707; un-authorized—1,288; Settlement Room—726). This left c.7,000 (c.50 per cent) as office staff supporting the activities of the brokers and jobbers, such as messengers, typists, telephonists, account clerks, and the emerging number of calculating-machine operators. During the war the actual membership of the Stock Exchange fell by around 500 as did the number of clerks. However, this did not indicate the actual loss of personnel, for members could remain registered at no cost or for a small fee, while many clerks were also retained as nominal employees while doing military service. By March 1942, for example, 1,321 members and 1,261 clerks (authorized and unauthorized) were serving in the forces, and these levels were sustained until the end of the war. Thus, around a third of all members and over half of authorized/unauthorized clerks were absent from the City from the outbreak of hostilities in 1939 until some time after their cessation in 1945.[42]

This drain on personnel was not drawn from a cross-section of those engaged in stockbroking/jobbing but was predominantly young. The result was to leave an aged—and ageing—profession. In April 1941, for instance, 85 per cent of partners in broking and jobbing firms were aged 46 or over, along with 63 per cent of authorized clerks and 58 per cent of the office departmental heads. The only youthful component were the messengers where 55 per cent were 18 or under, valued for their physical ability to run errands around the City. Basically the war made it difficult for Stock Exchange firms to recruit younger staff who could then be trained in all the duties of stockbroking or jobbing, whether on the trading-floor or in the office.[43]

Those called upon for military duties were not only young but were also men. This created opportunities for women with Stock Exchange firms. Even before the war around 1,600 women (c.11 per cent) were already employed by brokers and jobbers. Surprisingly these numbers also dropped considerably on the outbreak of war, with only 609 (38 per cent) still remaining by June 1942, though that was a higher proportion than for the men (30 per cent). Inevitably, Stock Exchange firms found it easier to recruit women than men so that their numbers rose to 1,271 by June 1942, and comprised 21 per cent of total personnel. Most of these women, however, continued to be employed in the traditional roles of typists and telegraphists while all calculating-machine operators were female. In June 1941 no women had yet become heads of department, though that was to come, and few were employed as messengers. Certainly for Stock

---

[42] LSE: General Purposes, 24 Mar. 1942, 6 July 1942, 24 Mar. 1943, 24 Mar. 1944; LSE: Council Minutes, 9 Apr. 1945; LSE: Trustees and Managers, 16 Apr. 1940, 17 Apr. 1941, 23 Apr. 1942, 20 Apr. 1943, 25 Mar. 1944, 25 Mar. 1945.

[43] LSE: General Purposes, 11 Nov. 1940, 21 Apr. 1941, 22 Dec. 1941, 6 July 1942.

Exchange firms women became, relative to men, more numerous during the Second World War but their status hardly altered. They continued, for example, to be denied physical access to the Stock Exchange. This, automatically, prevented them becoming not only partners in broking and jobbing firms but even operating as authorized or unauthorized clerks. Miss Lilian Stanfield, who had been employed by the brokers Knight & Searle since 1919, had risen to the position of managing clerk in the office by September 1941, when she enquired about admission to the Stock Exchange. She was refused. The Stock Exchange would not even permit Miss Pamela Gull, the daughter of a member, to be registered as an attaché in November 1941, because that would make her a quasi-broker for she could share half the commission on the business she brought in, rather than be paid a salary as an employee.[44]

Certainly, there was little sign that women made any kind of a breakthrough in the Stock Exchange before 1945. Generally, both broking and jobbing firms rather marked time during the war. Numbers contracted and those becoming partners were largely drawn from the ranks of experienced authorized clerks, with the obvious alternatives of sons and nephews being in short supply due to military duties. E. H. Burgess Smith and Samuel Cann, who were senior paid staff with the broking firm Sebags, both became partners during the war. Those firms that would not look outside the family for new partners, such as Foster & Braithwaite, lost out as a result. Peter Kemp-Welch moved from Foster & Braithwaite to Cazenoves in 1945, taking important clients, like Equity and Law (insurance), Baillie Gifford (fund manager), and David Wills (private wealth) with him. There also continued to be the recruitment of partners with important skills and connections. J. A. Smith, for instance, joined de Zoete & Gorton in 1945, and brought in useful contacts with the bankers Smith Payne & Smith and M. Samuel & Co.[45]

Bombing and staff shortages had their effects on particular firms, as offices were destroyed and partners and employees called up for other duties. Vanderfelt and Company, for example, had 11 dealers on the trading floor prior to the war but were down to only two as early as November 1939. The problem was that the war did not effect all firms equally. Those like L. A. Seligman & Co., whose main business was option dealing, saw it disappear completely because it was banned as too speculative. Trading in foreign securities was also badly affected by the war as links with foreign

[44] Ibid., 29 Sept. 1941, 3 Nov. 1941, 6 July 1942.
[45] *The Stock Exchange Clerks' Provident Fund 1874–1974* (London 1974), 22; Janes, *de Zoete and Gorton*; W. J. Reader, *A House in the City: Foster & Braithwaite, 1825–1975* (London 1979), 179, 181; D. Kynaston, *Cazenove & Co.: A History* (London 1991), 180; A. Martin, *Cazenove & Company, 1785–1955* (London 1955), 12; D. Wainwright, *Government Broker: The Story of an Office and of Mullens and Company* (East Molesey 1990), 76, 138; D. Sebag-Montefiore, *The Story of Joseph Sebag & Co. and its Founding Families* (n.p. 1996), 19.

exchanges were cut and securities requisitioned. By May 1940 almost the entire American market was inactive while Edgar Phillips, who traded in West African mining stocks, suspended his membership in April 1940 as he was doing so little business. One firm of brokers, Wise & Burnell, reported that they actually lost £200 a month because of the lack of business, stating that they would have to resign if this continued. Conversely, those active in the gilt-edged market, like Mullens, or in industrial issues, such as Vanderfelt & Co., experienced a rising volume of business from early on in the war.[46] The brokers, Leon Brothers, noted in January 1940, that 'we, as a firm, are doing considerably more business than previous to the outbreak of the war, with a depleted staff to cope with the same'.[47] What Leon Brothers had lost as a result of the war was the family home of one of the partners, Bletchley Park, which became the home of the code-breakers. More generally, out of 617 member firms replying to a questionnaire about the state of business in November 1941, only 85 (14 per cent) reported any increase in turnover, since the beginning of the war, though this did average 42 per cent. Conversely 452 firms (73 per cent) reported a decrease, and this averaged 38 per cent.[48]

A solution quickly adopted was to share staff and offices so that the business which still continued was carried out by those available. The government's own broker, Mullens & Co., reported in October 1939 that

As a result of the war we have lost all our member dealers and authorised clerks, and Mr A. Sheriff of Messrs A. Sheriff and Company, has kindly offered his services temporarily to deal on our behalf.[49]

Such arrangements became increasingly commonplace as the war went on, with its differential impact on business, members, staff, and accommodation. With the partners of E. F. Bigood & Co. on active duty their business was taken over, on a temporary basis, by Laurence, Keen & Gardner while Vivian Gray & Co. did likewise for Burge & Co. Summing up the situation, as it stood in December 1941, the Stock Exchange observed that

Since the outbreak of war 91 firms have gone out of business or have been absorbed by others, and there are fifty-five partial amalgamations involving 100 other firms.[50]

By July 1942, of the 796 firms into which the membership of the Stock Exchange was divided before the war, 114 had disappeared completely through merger, while another 110 were co-operating on a temporary basis. Many of these temporary arrangements also became full mergers before the

---

[46] LSE: General Purposes, 2 Oct. 1939, 23 Oct. 1939, 13 Nov. 1939, 15 Apr. 1940, 20 May 1940, 9 Apr. 1945.
[47] LSE: Rules and Regulations, 31 Jan. 1940.
[48] LSE: General Purposes, 22 Dec. 1941.    [49] Ibid., 23 Oct. 1939.
[50] Ibid., 22 Dec. 1941.

Table 7.1. Brokers and jobbers, 1938/9–1945

| | 1938/9 | | | 1945 | | |
|---|---|---|---|---|---|---|
| | Total | Broker | Jobber | Total | Broker | Jobber |
| No. of firms | 800 | 466 | 344 | 656 | 402 | 254 |
| No. of partners | 2,892 | 1,765 | 1,127 | 2,338 | 1,486 | 852 |
| Partners per firm | 3.6 | 3.8 | 3.3 | 3.6 | 3.7 | 3.4 |
| No. of clerks | 3,739 | 2,447 | 1,292 | 3,194 | 2,132 | 1,062 |
| Members as authorized clerks | 902 | 630 | 272 | 896 | 653 | 243 |
| Members as unauthorized clerks | 1,291 | 818 | 473 | 1,070 | 641 | 429 |
| Authorized clerks | 725 | 467 | 258 | 478 | 338 | 140 |
| Unauthorized clerks | 1,291 | 818 | 473 | 1,070 | 641 | 429 |
| Settling-room clerks | 744 | 461 | 283 | 658 | 424 | 234 |
| Clerks per firm | 4.6 | 5.3 | 3.8 | 4.9 | 5.3 | 4.2 |
| TOTAL PARTNERS + CLERKS | 6,631 | 4,212 | 2,419 | 5,532 | 3,618 | 1,914 |
| TOTAL PER FIRM | 8.2 | 9.0 | 7.0 | 8.4 | 9.0 | 7.5 |

*Sources*:  LSE: Committee for General Purposes, *Annual Reports*, 24 Mar. 1942, 24 Mar. 1945.

end of the war, or shortly afterwards. R. Beale joined the brokers, James Capel & Co. in 1945 from Cruickshank & Co., which then disappeared.[51]

Overall, the number of separate firms operating on the Stock Exchange fell from 810 before the war to 656 by the end, or by 154 (19 per cent). The decline was greatest among the jobbers where the number of firms fell by 90 (26 per cent) compared to the drop among the brokers of 64 (14 per cent). Nevertheless, this did not represent any real consolidation because the number of active partners and staff also fell. In 1938/9, the average number of partners per stockbroking firm was 3.6 (broker—3.8; jobber—3.3). Each firm could call on the assistance of a further 4.6 clerks (broker—5.3; jobber—3.8) who were permitted entry to the Stock Exchange to help in trading and settlement. (Table 7.1.) In addition, with around 14,000 involved in stock-broking/jobbing at that time, this put the level of office support staff, such as messengers, account clerks, and typists, at around nine per firm. Thus, overall, the average Stock Exchange firm involved only 17 people before the war. With total numbers actively involved in stockbroking/jobbing during the war at half the pre-war level, the result was smaller not larger firms. The

[51] Ibid., 25 Sept. 1939, 6 July 1942; M. C. Reed, *A History of James Capel and Company*. (London 1975), 88.

6,052 partners and staff of 1942, for example, were distributed between c.670 firms, or an average of nine each, which was appreciably smaller than the pre-war number. Clearly, wartime conditions did not create a pressure towards larger firms, whether in broking or jobbing.

The overall reduction in personnel due to the war was accompanied by an overall reduction in the business to be transacted. Stock Exchange turnover appears to have peaked in 1936/7 and then fallen to half that level by 1938/9. With the outbreak of war turnover fell further, reaching half its pre-war level by 1940/1. It was only after that date that turnover began to pick up, through not returning to its 1930s peak until after the end of the war, and then only in nominal terms. The result was to make a career on the Stock Exchange an unattractive one for the duration of the war. Whereas in 1937 the cost of a nomination for membership reached a high of £1,975 by 1939 it could be had for as little as £120, and then £75 in 1940. Even by the end of the war the price of a nomination was from £200–£400.[52] This position reflected the limited profitability of member firms at this time, though the situation did recover some what towards the end of the war. One firm, Eliott Young & Co., reported in August 1941, that

. . . many firms, as indeed ours is, are carrying on, not for any immediate profit, but so that those partners and those of the staff who are serving may have a Business to return to when the war is over.[53]

It was reported that the stockbroking firm of Capels experienced its lowest income since the First World War in 1940/1, before an improvement began. Cazenove's profits, which stood at £57,139 in 1940 had more than tripled to £193,391 by 1944.[54]

Certainly the Stock Exchange itself saw 1942 as a turning point with business increasing from then onwards. They reported a more than doubling of turnover between March–May and September–November 1942.[55] However, as the war drew to a close uncertainty about what peacetime conditions would mean for the Stock Exchange did dampen growth.

Stock Exchange business, which had been active, tended to diminish in volume in spite of the Allied victories. This appeared to be due to uncertainties in regard to the effect on post-war industry of war taxation and the change-over to peace time production[56]

was the view expressed in March 1944. However, this proved unduly pessimistic for turnover in the six months prior to August 1944 was reported to be up by 25 per cent.[57]

[52] F. Paukert, 'The Value of Stock Exchange Transactions in Non-Government Securities, 1911–1959, *Economica*, 28 (1962/3), 304; LSE: Trustees and Managers, 2 Aug. 1939; H. Wincott, *The Stock Exchange* (London 1946), 32; LSE: Council Minutes, 29 Aug. 1960.
[53] LSE: General Purposes, 18 Aug. 1941.
[54] Reader, *Foster & Braithwaite*, 177; Reed, *Capel and Company*, 87; Kynaston, *Cazenove*, 174.
[55] LSE: General Purposes, 19 July 1943.      [56] LSE: *Annual Report*, 24 Mar. 1944.
[57] LSE: General Purposes, 21 Aug. 1944.

Nevertheless, despite this welcome revival of business from midway through the Second World War, most members did continue to experience financial difficulties. Costs remained high or even rose, though overall personnel numbers fell. There was a desire to retain skilled staff absent on military duty as well as an obligation to pay similarly inactive partners some income from their own business. At the same time the move to a cash basis for trading and the suspension of centralized clearing greatly increased transaction costs. Each deal had now to be accompanied by either a payment or the delivery of the appropriate securities. Government regulations also greatly increased the amount of clerical work associated with each transaction, to ensure that all restrictions were complied with, such as control on foreign exchange or trading with the enemy. One estimate for November 1941 suggested that the average clerical time taken to arrange the completion of a sale or purchase had risen from 15 minutes before the war to 41 days, or a staggering 1,312-fold increase.[58]

Whereas before the war it was estimated the costs incurred by a broker averaged around one-third of commission income, by the end they were felt to be running at between 40 and 45 per cent. Only those brokers whose main business was in government debt had not seen an increase because the growth in turnover had kept pace with the rise in costs.[59] In particular there was a general feeling, by the end of the war, '. . . that small accounts are not very profitable . . .'[60] Jobbers could respond to these rising costs by widening the margin between the buying and selling prices they quoted and this they began doing from the very outbreak of war.[61] For brokers the obvious response was to increase the fixed rates of commission, which were binding on all members. However, this was not an easy matter for it could easily be interpreted as an attempt to profit from wartime conditions and increasing prices. The Stock Exchange had never enjoyed a good press and there was every indication that nothing had changed during the war. There was also the worry that any increase in charges would have to be greatest on that business done for small private investors, which could provoke the greatest publicity. The Stock Exchange itself faced problems in altering the fixed scale of commission for it reflected a compromise between those members who regarded it as too low and those who felt that it was excessive.[62] The solution picked on was to review the whole question of rebates for these tended to be confined to trade customers like banks and provincial brokers. Even before the war there had been agitation to have rebates restricted, and that demand was intensified after the outbreak of hostilities. One of the leaders of that campaign was the broker J. B. Braithwaite who made his position clear in February 1940:

[58] Ibid., 9 Oct. 1939, 16 Oct. 1939, 22 Dec. 1941; Hennessy, *Domestic History*, 103, 104.
[59] LSE: General Purposes 5 Feb. 1945.
[60] Ibid., 27 Aug. 1945.   [61] Ibid., 16 Oct. 1939.
[62] Ibid., 2 Oct. 1939, 7 Dec. 1942, 27 Aug. 1945; LSE: Subcommittee on Country Jobbing, 6 Feb. 1940, 27 Feb. 1940.

I believe that we should in any case have been forced before long to make such reductions as these, on account of steadily rising expenses and taxation. But war conditions present us with a unique opportunity of putting them over now, with the minimum of criticism and friction. We cannot raise our charges to the public to meet these conditions, as is being done on every hand by other businesses and industries, but we can, and I think that in the interest of our members that we must, achieve a similar end by the internal economy of reducing our rebates to agents.[63]

Despite the pressing need to raise income, and the forceful campaign directing attention to the rebates, voices were raised pointing out that business could be lost. One such was Walter B. Morrison, whose broking firm did a large country business. As he stated, earlier in the same month,

A good many years ago the committee did not hesitate to prohibit 'shunting' and destroy business connections which were very extensive and had taken years to build up.[64]

By May 1940 there had been a general tightening up of the rebate scheme. Only registered agents were eligible and there were to be carefully vetted by the Stock Exchange. Banks, remisiers (foreign agents), attachés (domestic agents), and clerks in broking and jobbing firms were all deemed acceptable plus a general list of solicitors, accountants, finance houses, investment trusts, and others. This list was regarded with suspicion by many brokers who saw it as a means through which fellow members could offer a discount service to favoured clients, in contravention of the agreed rate of charges. The proposal in May 1940 was to reduce the rebate to one-third for all agents. This was felt to be an equitable redistribution of the increased costs caused by the war.[65] As in the past the banks immediately objected to any reduction. However, after discussions the banks agreed to accept a rebate of one-third, along with the remisiers, attachés, and clerks. This was on condition that all other agents would receive a rebate of only one-quarter, which gave the banks a competitive advantage nation-wide over provincial brokers, lawyers, and accountants as well as other non-member financial intermediaries in London.[66]

These new rules on rebates came into force on 1 June 1941. Having reduced the level of rebate the Stock Exchange appeared less willing to restrict substantially those eligible for them. In 1944 the General Register of Agents, which excluded banks and brokers, still contained 3,772 names of whom the greatest number were solicitors—2,696 (71 per cent)—followed by accountants—476 (13 per cent)—and these were drawn from throughout the British Isles.[67] Without a branch network of their own, London brokers continued to rely heavily on other agents and financial

[63] LSE: Country Jobbing, 27 Feb. 1940.      [64] Ibid., 6 Feb. 1940.
[65] LSE: General Purposes, 6 May 1940; LSE: Country Jobbing, 9 Apr. 1940, 11 Apr. 1940.
[66] LSE: General Purposes, 28 Jan. 1941.      [67] Ibid., 28 Apr. 1941, 24 Mar. 1944.

intermediaries to generate the sales and purchases they handled. As such rebates remained an important means of attracting business

... the privileges of Agency should be accorded only to persons and firms who, by reason of their professional standing or habitual practice, are able to render to the Stock Exchange services of value in return for the rebates they receive

was the Stock Exchange's own frank assessment of the situation in January 1941.[68] Conversely, there was a reluctance to permit rebates to those who might be direct competitors. Thus rebates were allowed to members of provincial stock exchanges but not to those who belonged to the Mincing Lane Tea and Rubber Brokers' Exchange in London. The large clearing banks could demand a one-third rebate, because of the aggregate amount of their business, while the finance house, Dawnay Day & Co., was only given a one-quarter rebate, because it was much smaller in size. Basically, large institutional, and even individual clients, could get business done at a discount if there was enough of it, and this helped to keep clients loyal.[69]

## COMPETITION

Nevertheless, the reduction in rebates did put a strain on the relationship many brokers had established with City banks and finance houses over the years. By denying merchant banks and others membership of the London Stock Exchange, firms such as these, involved in large sales and purchase of securities on a regular basis, tended to channel it through one or two brokers whom they trusted. In return these brokers offered preferential rates which kept such customers loyal. It was well known that the brokers L. Messel & Company acted for Kleinwort Sons & Co., H. Carlebach & Co., for Crédit Lyonnais, and J. Sebag & Co. for the Swiss Bank Corporation. Naturally, firms such as these resented the reduction in rebate and were less inclined to put business through their broker, if it could be avoided. One attaché, R. de Watteville, was driven to complain by 1944 that the reduction in rebate, combined with the rising cost of living and heavy taxation, was making his business unremunerative. He had been active since 1923, using his Swiss connections to bring sales and purchases to London.[70]

In an even worse position were those North American brokerage houses who had remained in London despite the bombing and the restrictions. These were regarded as direct competitors for Stock Exchange business in dollar securities or for North American clients and so were denied, officially at least, any rebate on commission. By stopping them obtaining a discount on any sales and purchases undertaken by members of the London Stock

---

[68] Ibid., 28 Jan. 1941.    [69] Ibid., 13 June 1941, 16 July 1941, 27 Oct. 1941.
[70] Ibid., 29 Jan. 1940, 24 Apr. 1944.

Exchange it was hoped to hamper their business sufficiently to drive them out of London. Instead, according to David Yassukovich of White, Weld & Co., the result was that these firms increasingly bypassed the London Stock Exchange completely, dealing directly in North American stock exchanges and with British clients. By 1944 there were five New York brokerage houses in London—Baker, Weeks & Harden; Carl M. Loeb; Rhoades & Co.; Merrill Lynch; and White Weld & Co.—as well as A. E. Ames & Co. of Toronto. These firms increasingly constituted not only the market in North American securities for British investors, but also the conduit through which investors from the United States could purchase stocks and shares traded in London. These included issues from all over the world, such as South African gold-mining securities.[71]

What the London Stock Exchange had tried to do was to channel such business not through brokers with branches in different centres, but via the local membership of stock exchanges from around the world. As early as September 1941, in the wake of reduction in rebates, the entire membership of 23 foreign stock exchanges were recognized as eligible for the one-third discount on commission. Included were not only large and long-established stock exchanges like Toronto, Melbourne, Bombay, and Johannesburg but also such organizations as the Colombo Brokers Association (Ceylon) and the Malaya Share-Brokers' Association. However, stock exchanges from the United States were left out of these uniform reciprocal arrangements. It was recognized that it was US brokers who were providing the keenest competition for London in global securities trading, and so members of the Stock Exchange had to be left to make their own arrangements with counterparts across the Atlantic, especially in New York. Members of the London Stock Exchange who still undertook arbitrage continued to be permitted to disregard certain of the rules. For example, it was accepted that jobbers needed to maintain direct contacts overseas, such as with members of other stock exchanges, and that brokers could make markets for foreign clients, if an active two-way market was to be sustained. It was also recognized that the minimum commission rules, including rebates, were not appropriate for arbitrage business where the parties on each stock exchange traded in concert, collectively sharing any profits or losses that resulted. Despite the willingness to make some allowance for the peculiar nature of foreign business, the Stock Exchange remained conscious that it could result in a seepage of sales and purchases to other markets, where the commission charges were lower. As a result the rules concerning both minimum commission/rebates and dual capacity were gradually tightened up, with the element of discretion being reduced on every occasion.[72]

Generally, the level of foreign business—and thus foreign contact—was

[71] LSE: General Purposes, 21 Feb. 1944, 19 June 1944.
[72] Ibid., 5 Aug. 1941, 8 Sept. 1941, 11 Oct. 1941, 21 Feb. 1944; LSE: Country Jobbing, 3 Jan. 1940.

greatly reduced during the Second World War. Trading with the enemy was prohibited and so contact with all those countries controlled by those with whom Britain was at war was impossible. This meant, virtually, all of continental Europe. At the same time exchange and other controls greatly restricted trading in securities with the rest of the world, including the United States. Increasingly, it was only sales that were possible, for purchases required the use of foreign currencies for payment, and this was not permitted. Even access to communication was difficult throughout the war, as priority was given to military and official use. Finally, Britain's own stock of foreign securities, especially those from North America, was considerably reduced in the course of the war, making it difficult to generate any two-way trading in mutually held stocks. By August 1940 negotiable foreign securities worth £1.3bn. had been collected by the Bank of England and shipped to Canada for safe-keeping. Much was then sold by the government with disposals totalling £1.1bn.[73] Consequently, though the presence of New York brokerage houses in London was regarded as a threat by the Stock Exchange, the area and type of business they were engaged in was now of marginal significance. The American market had ceased to exist and the transatlantic trading of securities was of little importance.

Instead it was the market for domestic securities that was of major concern and this affected the London Stock Exchange's relationship with other financial intermediaries in Britain. The scale of commission charges and the system of rebates was designed to ensure, simultaneously, that the members of the London Stock Exchange captured as much of the available business as possible and received as a high an income as possible. The higher the charges, and the less the rebate, the more those clients who had much business to transact would seek alternatives. Conversely, the lower the charges the less income each sale or purchase would generate. The secret was to devise a scale that would maximize both, which was the position when charges were left to each broker and his negotiations with individual clients. Certain business was lost to the Stock Exchange because the scale of charges, even with a discount, were pitched at too high a level. The jobbers, Wedd Jefferson & Co., observed in 1944 that little of the trading in the short-term debt (under two years) issued by the government was handled by members of the Stock Exchange, because the commission rate of 1/8th per cent was too high for this type of business. Instead it was extensively traded outside the Stock Exchange by banks, discount houses, and others, so depriving jobbers like themselves of business.[74]

<hr />

[73] LSE: General Purposes, 29 Feb. 1940, 8 Apr. 1940, 15 Apr. 1940, 20 May 1940, 19 Aug. 1940, 13 Jan. 1941, 11 Sept. 1944; Fforde, *Bank of England*, 785; Hennessy, *Domestic History*, 98; Bank of England, *United Kingdom Overseas Investments 1938–1948* (London 1950), 4, 6–9.

[74] LSE: General Purposes 20 Mar. 1944.

The Stock Exchange continued to perceive, as its greatest threat, the activities of the members of the provincial stock exchanges, especially those who operated in dual capacity as both dealers and brokers.

Advertising Jobbers maintain what amounts to an organisation for attracting, intercepting and marrying business before it reaches London, with the inevitable consequence of weakening the structure and liquidity of our markets. Hitherto we have given every assistance to these firms, both by according them our most favourable commission terms, and by allowing them direct access to our markets, so that they can keep in constant touch with every change of price here, and even with the variations in price between different Jobbers, thus enabling them to compete most effectively with us.[75]

This was how the London Stock Exchange viewed the position in May 1940, reflecting a widespread feeling that they were being exploited by the provincial stock exchanges. Such was the strength of feeling that there was a move to deny provincial brokers any rebates on commission.[76] Despite this rivalry the common problems experienced by all stock exchanges, with the outbreak of war, gradually brought them closer together. At the same time as the London Stock Exchange was venting its feelings over provincial competition, Horace Richmond, Secretary of the Council of Associated Stock Exchanges, was asking for co-operation in forcing up the rate of commission on government debt, because

It appears to be the object of the Government to adopt all means which will make it difficult for investors to interest themselves in anything but Government loans, and if this is a correct interpretation of the intentions of the Government it is considered that it will seriously affect the position of all stockbrokers throughout the country.[77]

However, the London Stock Exchange refused the request, worried about any public backlash over such an unpatriotic action. They also turned down the provincial stock exchanges long-standing demand to end rebates to banks and favour provincial brokers instead.

Nevertheless, throughout 1940 the London Stock Exchange was conducting a thorough review of its relationship with the provincial stock exchanges, trying to identify what practices it wanted stopped and what it would concede in return. Naturally enough this investigation focused on country jobbing, which had posed a growing threat to the London Stock Exchange's dominance of the domestic securities market over the inter-war years. Even its own members, like the brokers Vickers da Costa & Co., did an extensive business with the provincial jobbing firm of J. W. Nicholson & Co. in Sheffield.[78] Eventually, on 28 January 1941 the following review

[75] LSE: General Purposes, 6 May 1940.
[76] Ibid., 18 Dec. 1939, 5 Feb. 1940, 6 May 1940.
[77] Ibid., 6 May 1940.     [78] Ibid., 14 July 1941.

and report was presented to the Committee for General Purposes for consideration:

Country Jobbing is a development that has grown up mainly during the last twenty years. Apart from the jobbing that takes place, in greater or lesser degree, in all provincial centres in the securities of concerns locally domiciled, Country Jobbing is of two kinds. The older established of these is a survival and modification of the practice originally called 'shunting', when the London Jobbers and the provincial markets were in direct contact with each other. This direct contact was abolished about 30 years ago, but contact is still maintained through the medium of brokers specialising in country business, who maintain direct private telephone lines or teleprinters to members of the provincial exchanges, who, similarly, specialise in London and inter-market business. These London specialists are now known as shunters, having inherited or taken over the title from the jobbing firms who were the original shunters.

This modified form of shunting, as carried on now between a London broker and member of a provincial exchange, is a normal and recognised activity. The function of the London broker is to supply the closest market quotations to his correspondent in the country, who, sometimes with the help of other similar inter-market connections, makes prices based there to the members of his exchange. This practice serves to project the facilities of the London jobbing market onto the trading floors of the provincial exchanges and so helps to unify and bind together the dealing machinery of our profession as a whole. The prices made in the provinces by the shunting organisations are, of course, based upon London, which possesses the only true and the only ultimate market in stocks and shares. If there were no shunting much of business secured in this way would no doubt have to come to London through other but slower channels, and on a basis perhaps more profitable to London, but speed and flexibility are always highly important factors in stock exchange dealings and shunting is freely recognised as a legitimate and useful part of our machinery.

The second kind of country jobbing has a different object in view. Instead of providing, for the floor of a single exchange, a service of inter-market prices in all securities, the firms engaged in this type of business specialise in lists of securities most actively dealt in, varying these lists from time to time as interest shifts from one group of securities to another, and seeking, by a wide publication of the lists and prices of the stocks they deal in, to attract business in these stocks from all the provincial exchanges and from brokers all over the country. As with shunting, the prices made by these firms are based upon London, and must be kept constantly in step with fluctuations in London if they are to attract business. The object however, is not to pass on to London the business that is collected but, on the contrary, to attract a volume of business so considerable that much may be 'married' at a jobbing turn, balances only of stock that cannot be so 'married' or otherwise disposed of, being undone on the London market.

This kind of Country Jobbing has both advantages and disadvantages from the point of view of the provincial exchanges. From the London point of view it is a harmful activity because it is designed to intercept and keep away from London business that otherwise would come there. If carried to an extreme this kind of jobbing would seriously undermine and weaken the London jobbing market, by diminishing its volume and its liquidity, and since the London jobbing market is the foundation upon which the whole edifice of our profession throughout the United Kingdom is built up, anything that tends to weaken it must be detrimental to the interests both of the London and provincial exchanges.

Whilst London in fact possesses the only real and ultimate market in stocks and shares, it does not claim any right to a monopoly of jobbing. If genuine jobbing markets, standing entirely on their own feet, and independent of London, could be established in one or more of the provincial exchanges such a development might be in the interests of the public. No exception even can be taken to the so-called jobbing described in the preceding paragraphs, detrimental though it is to London, provided that it is built up and carried on within the rules and etiquette of our profession, but London cannot be expected to provide facilities for business of this type which are organised not in co-operation but in competition with the London market.[79]

Encapsulated in the above was the London Stock Exchange's belief that it alone provided a ready market for securities in Britain and that non-members were essentially parasitic, living off the prices that it generated. Where non-members could be seen as providing an important channel of business for members of the Stock Exchange, then the competition they also represented could be accepted. Conversely, where non-members contributed little or nothing to the activities of the Stock Exchange, but drew business away instead, rules and regulations would be introduced and policed that made it difficult for them to do so. As the report went on to say,

. . . the proposals for regulating Country Jobbing are designed to confine facilities for direct access to our market to provincial firms who carry on recognised shunting activities or who do not engage in jobbing, other than in securities of a purely local nature.[80]

Attempts had already been made to prevent country jobbers gaining access to current prices on the Stock Exchange through restricting the use they made of direct telephone lines to members. Though this policy was to be persevered with, it was not especially practicable as it also interfered with the regular, and acceptable, contact that London Stock Exchange brokers maintained with fellow brokers in the provinces. Instead, the only realistic way forward was to enlist the co-operation of the provincial stock exchanges themselves. To do this the provincial stock exchanges had to be persuaded to take action against their members who operated as country jobbers, through threats and bribes from London.[81]

The London Stock Exchange then offered rebates on commission charges to the provincial stock exchanges which put them on a par with banks and better-placed than other agents. In return the provincial stock exchanges agreed to ban any of their members who operated as both brokers and

[79] LSE: General Purposes, 28 Jan. 1941.     [80] Ibid.
[81] Ibid.; LSE: Country Jobbing, 19 Mar. 1940, 20 Mar. 1940.

jobbers. Firms like J. W. Nicholson, of the Sheffield Stock Exchange, responded to this decision by splitting themselves into two separate firms, with one operating as a broker and the other a jobber. This met the spirit of the decisions but clearly evaded its intention, for the two firms continued to trade as one.[82] Gradually the London Stock Exchange had to accept the fact that country jobbing had not been eliminated through the agreement with the provincial stock exchanges. Nicholsons continued in business with around 900 clients spread throughout the country.

> No other firm in London or the Provinces (with the exception of Wheelock of Malvern) has acquired a clientele in this way, and it is the fact of the existence of this all-embracing connection with the clearing-house jobbing technique, that not only makes the Nicholson firm so dangerous in sapping away the strength of our jobbing market, but that also puts it in a class by itself, not comparable with any other business in London,

was the Stock Exchange's realistic observation of the situation in August 1942.[83] This provoked the further measure, in September, that members of the London Stock Exchange were banned from contacting non-member jobbers. However, this was impossible to police. By then the London and provincial stock exchanges had already set up a joint committee to resolve difficult issues, such as country jobbing, and this started meeting from June 1942. There were even suggestions in October 1942 of a move towards unifying all stock exchanges, but discussion on this was postponed until London dealt with its own dual control structure.[84]

However, willing as the provincial stock exchanges were to cooperate with London they were unwilling to take any firm action over country jobbers like Nicholsons unless they got what they wanted, which was direct access to London jobbers. Without that, provincial brokers would always experience stiff competition from banks. Local branches of national banks could send orders to London brokers and have them carried out at the same cost as a provincial broker, and could thus make the same charge to a customer. This made banks very competitive in handling transactions in national securities as their large branch networks could feed the business of their customers directly to London brokers rather than through a provincial stockbroker. However, the London Stock Exchange was reluctant to allow direct access as this would bypass its broking membership, many of whom gained a significant commission income from country orders via provincial brokers and bank branches. At the same time, if provincial brokers were given direct access to jobbers then

---

[82] LSE: General Purposes, 28 Apr. 1941, 13 June 1941, 28 Nov. 1941, 15 Dec. 1941, 21 May 1942.

[83] Ibid., 4 Aug. 1942.

[84] Ibid., 23 Feb. 1942, 24 Mar. 1942, 18 May 1942, 14 Sept. 1942; LSE: Joint Advisory Committee on Stock Exchanges, 25 Sept. 1942; LSE: Conjoint Committee, 6 Oct. 1942.

it would be difficult to deny other financial intermediaries, like the banks themselves.[85]

Consequently, though the provincial stock exchanges co-operated with the London Stock Exchange over country jobbing, so preserving its goodwill and the rebate on commissions, Nicholsons continued to operate successfully. In 1943, for example, it was discovered that Nicholsons had established a private telephone line to Gurney & Sons, members of the Bradford Stock Exchange, who, in turn, had a private line to the London Stock Exchange. Action was then taken to discontinue these connections but it was clear that Nicholsons could generate so much business for members of the London Stock Exchange, and provided such a valuable service, for members of provincial stock exchanges, that it was impossible to stop them operating.[86] Until the London Stock Exchange was willing to grant provincial brokers direct access to its trading-floor it would also continue to face competition from country jobbers. The developments in communications technology allowed a jobber to make a market in a select group of securities for members of all stock exchanges. As R. H. Lovett, in Bournemouth, noted in 1943, 'Twenty years ago a floor was everything, but development of telephonic communication had altered the entire system of conducting a jobbing system.'[87] With the large customer base that the combined membership of the provincial stock exchanges gave them, these country jobbers came to rival the London dealers, and attract business from London brokers, especially in industrial and insurance securities.[88]

As it was, problems with the telephone service during the war did reduce the competition from the country jobbers. Requisitioning of lines for offiicial and military use, combined with bomb damage made the telephone an unreliable, and often unavailable, form of communication. Naturally this affected the members of the London Stock Exchange itself as it was difficult for them to maintain contact with clients distant from London. The number of direct lines between London brokers and members of the provincial stock exchanges, was more than halved due to the war. The actual number fell from 99 in July 1939 to 53 in May 1941, for example. This forced the members of the London Stock Exchange back upon the telegraph, but even the use of that was considerably circumscribed by military controls.[89]

Communications between London and Belfast were largely dependent upon telegrams subject to rigid censorship, which involved such delays that replies could rarely be received within business hours,

[85] LSE: Joint Advisory Committee, 3 May 1942, 9 June 1942, 25 Sept. 1942, 23 July 1943; LSE: General Purposes, 6 May 1940, 14 Sept. 1942.

[86] Ibid., 25 Aug. 1943, 18 Oct. 1943.

[87] LSE: Joint Advisory Committee, 18 June 1943.     [88] Ibid., 25 Sept. 1942.

[89] LSE: General Purposes, 18 Nov. 1940, 8 May 1944; J. Hinshelwood (GPO) to R. B. Pearson (London Stock Exchange) 31 July 1941; Analysis of Direct Lines to Country Exchanges, May 1941; LSE: Conjoint Committee, 19 Aug. 1941, 28 Aug. 1941.

was the reported state of affairs on one important route in September 1941.[90] However, most of the business of the London Stock Exchange originated in London itself, and so more extensive use could be made of messengers and the trading-floor. In contrast, country jobbers were heavily reliant upon the telephone and the teleprinter, both to keep in touch with London prices and maintain contact with customers. Consequently, the effects of wartime communications difficulties bore much more heavily upon them.[91]

Nevertheless, the Second World War saw a continuation of the pre-war trend where the London Stock Exchange's command over the securities market, at home and abroad, continued to be slowly eroded by outside competition, in the form of foreign banks and brokerage firms, London discount houses, and country jobbers. It was also being bypassed in other ways during the war. At the outbreak of the Second World War the UK National Debt stood at £7.1bn. By the end of the war in 1945 this had risen to £21.1bn. A tripling in the size of the government's debt should have represented a massive increase in the business handled by the members of the London Stock Exchange. However, it did not, for much was of a temporary nature.[92]

To a large extent the government was bypassing the Stock Exchange by tailoring its products to appeal directly to the public and to banks and other financial institutions, and so tap savings at source.[93] There did continue to be an active secondary market in government debt, in the permanent and longer-dated issues, but the move to a cash basis greatly diminished its attractions. With no fortnightly settlement or options all securities bought had to be delivered and paid for. Thus money could not be lent to brokers and jobbers to employ, directly or indirectly, in holding easily marketable securities, like government debt, from account to account. The brokers, Heseltine, Powell & Co., for example, closed down their money-broking operations during the Second World War. Banks and others found it easier and cheaper to hold short-term government paper, renewing or redeeming when it became due.[94]

Even when members tried to revive account trading unofficially, by taking advantage of the inevitable delays in arranging payment or delivery due to wartime disruption, the Stock Exchange took action to prevent it happening.

. . . Stock Exchanges which have many hostile critics in the political world, are being closely watched, and we believe it is desirable, in view of the very possible renewal

[90] Ibid., 17 Sept. 1942.

[91] W. A. Thomas, *The Stock Exchanges of Ireland* (Liverpool 1986), 225.

[92] B. R. Mitchell, *British Historical Statistics* (Cambridge 1988), 602–3.

[93] LSE: General Purposes, *Annual Reports*, 24 Mar. 1939, 3 Apr. 1945; E. V. Morgan and W. A. Thomas, *The Stock Exchange: Its History and Functions* (London, 2nd edn. 1967), 196.

[94] LSE: General Purposes, 6 July 1942, 21 Sept. 1942; LSE: Rules and Regulations, 29 Apr. 1942; P. G. Warren, *Heseltine, Powell & Co: One Hundred Years of Stockbroking, 1851–1951* (London 1951), 24.

of market activity as the war progresses, to take steps to discourage speculation if it should show a tendency to arise, and to demonstrate to the outside world that we do discourage it and have taken definite action to that end.

This was the Stock Exchange's justification, in December 1942, for continuing to enforce the ban on account trading.[95] Short-term operations in securities were regarded by the public as valueless speculation rather than a means whereby temporarily idle funds could be remuneratively and safely employed. Consequently, the Stock Exchange did not want to attract attention to such activities during the war when it might result in even tighter control, though the outcome was that those with such funds to employ looked elsewhere. The loss of business in the gilt-edged market, to the non-member discount houses and banks, did concern the Stock Exchange but they were even more worried about any government controls that might be introduced if speculation was allowed to revive.[96]

Thus, though the vast growth in government debt should have produced a great increase in business for the members of the London Stock Exchange, the regulations under which they operated during wartime, the nature of the securities issued, and the competition from other financial intermediaries, produced little real gain. The government's own broker, Mullens, which should have benefited, had to be virtually restarted after the war, for example.[97] There was little by way of compensation to be found elsewhere in the capital market, for the Stock Exchange's ability to introduce new securities was strictly controlled by the government. From the very onset of war the Stock Exchange accepted, voluntarily, supervision from the Treasury over any new issues requesting a quotation or permission to be traded. Naturally enough the Treasury's priority was the finance of the government's military and civilian war effort. Over the five-year period 1941–5, for example, the London Stock Exchange granted an official quotation or permission to deal to securities with a nominal amount of £2.5bn. Of this, those issued by the British government totalled £2.1bn. (86 per cent). Furthermore, of the non-government securities amounting to £345m. some £313m. (91 per cent) was simply the replacement of existing issues of stocks and shares without any new funds being raised. The period 1941–5 saw only £32.4m. of new non-government securities being given a market on the London Stock Exchange, or a mere 1.5 per cent of the amount of UK government issues.[98]

For the London Stock Exchange the problem was not just that few non-government securities were being created but those that were did not involve the London Stock Exchange. Due to Treasury controls, members of

[95] LSE: General Purposes, 7 Dec. 1942.

[96] Ibid., 11 Jan. 1943, 19 July 1943, 11 Nov. 1943, 19 Mar. 1945, 17 Dec. 1945.

[97] Wainwright, *Mullens*, 76, Morgan and Thomas, *The Stock Exchange*, 229; Wincott, *The Stock Exchange*, 64, 117, 120–1.

[98] LSE: General Purposes, 21 Sept. 1942, 24 Mar. 1944; ibid., *Annual Reports*, 1940–5.

the Stock Exchange were prohibited from handling unapproved issues while the Stock Exchange was not allowed to provide them with a market. By September 1942 the Stock Exchange was driven to complain, pointing out to the Treasury:

For the placing of issues of the highest class, the Stock Exchange has developed a system which works satisfactorily as an alternative to the publication of an offer through the press. The brokers who handle such issues have learnt by experience the type of investor with whom stock can best be placed; the amount of stock which it is wise to offer to each, and the extent to which the market can best be used for the transaction of the business. . . .

If brokers are to be debarred from the exercise of their knowledge and experience in the placing of securities for the companies for whom they act the gradual development of an outside and uncontrolled market both for the original placing and subsequent transactions in securities is a danger which cannot be ignored.[99]

Basically what the Stock Exchange had begun to complain about was the discrimination under which they operated and the consequences it had both for themselves and the government. The Treasury's controls certainly stopped the involvement of the Stock Exchange and its membership in non-approved issues but it did not prevent such issues being made privately. As the Stock Exchange went on to say:

The issue is confined to a very small circle of large institutional investors, and the price received by the Company may be, through lack of competition, thereby depressed. The public can only participate later at an advanced price.[100]

Backing up this complaint was the evidence that between seven December 1939 and nine July 1943 the Treasury had refused it permission to make a market in the issues of 29 different companies—18 British and 11 foreign. One of these was an attempt by Scottish Brewers to issue £2,520,000 in shares, split equally between preference and ordinary. As a substitute that company raised £670,000 through a private issue.[101]

By the end of 1943, having failed to get any response from the government, the Stock Exchange was driven to complain not only about the discrimination they experienced but the ineptitude of Treasury control over new issues. While the Stock Exchange and its members were prevented from participating in non-approved issues, no action was taken when such issues were made, so competing with the government's own desire to eliminate competition for its own securities. In December 1943 the Stock Exchange expressed itself in full accord with government aims and sought to support them.

The Stock Exchange recognises fully the necessity for Treasury control both for the successful prosecution of the war and as a pre-requisite for post-war reconstruction.

---

[99] LSE: General Purposes, 21 Sept. 1942.   [100] Ibid.   [101] Ibid., 19 July 1943.

It believes itself to be an essential part of the National financial machinery and it desires to work with the other parts of that machinery and in harmony with the intention and direction of the whole. It desires to place at the disposal of the Treasury its unique knowledge of every aspect of the business of dealing in stocks and shares, and its peculiar ability to advise upon the practical effects that new policies have produced or are likely to produce.

It then went on to point out that the system in place was not delivering the control that the government wanted.

The capital market is controlled by the Treasury through its Advisory Committee and by agreement gives to the Treasury complete control over all Stock Exchange markets, but it leaves wholly uncontrolled the very large and powerful, but mainly non-professional markets that are outside the Stock Exchange jurisdiction. The principal constituents of these outside markets are the Banks, the Insurance Companies, the Investment Trust Companies, the Acceptance Houses, the Finance and Issuing Houses, the Association of Stock and Share Dealers, the Mincing Lane Tea and Rubber Brokers' Association, and the large number of 'Somerset' House and other outside stock and Sharebrokers up and down the country.

The Stock Exchange then pointed out the consequences of this lax control which targeted only one component of the capital market.

The effect of leaving this large outside market uncontrolled is naturally to drive into it that very business that the Treasury thinks it is against the national interest to permit. This is in fact happening, and it is likely to increase . . . we are aware of transactions in the outside market in lines of stock which the Treasury has refused to sanction or which may not even have been submitted to it, at prices below those that our members would have been willing to give. In fact there are already present the principal characteristics of a black market.[102]

Faced with mounting evidence that controls which only applied to the Stock Exchange were being increasingly evaded by non-members, and thus affecting the goverment's own fund-raising activities, the Treasury did, eventually, respond to the Stock Exchange's pleading. During 1944 Treasury control on issues of under £100,000 were removed while, at the same time action was taken to ensure that non-approved issues could not be made outside the Stock Exchange. These non-approved issues were referred to as 'grey market' securities and were defined as those that did not possess both Stock Exchange and Treasury permission to be traded on the Stock Exchange.[103] Clearly, the Treasury and the Stock Exchange were acting in concert to ensure effective control over the capital market, with exclusive access for the government when it required it. However, there was a cost attached to the support that the Stock Exchange was being given by the government in its efforts to restrict the ability of non-members to compete with it. It made the Stock Exchange very susceptible to political influence

---

[102] LSE: General Purposes, 6 Dec. 1943.      [103] Ibid., 11 Apr. 1944, 3 July 1944.

when its activities provoked hostile public opinion. This appeared in the case of the placing system, which had been used very successfully in the inter-war years as a cheap way of selling small issues of corporate securities to the investing public.

Small issues could not justify the costs of a prospectus or advertising and attendant charges. Instead a broker assembled a small syndicate of investors and intermediaries who would buy the entire issue at a discount, either for themselves or to retail to others. Jobbers, for example, would be involved at the outset as they could, gradually, unload their holdings on the market, selling to other brokers who recommended the stock to their clients. Certain brokers were extensively involved in handling placings, and continued to be so during the war, when permitted to do so. Between September 1939 and July 1945, Cazenoves handled 47 such issues, being one of the leaders in the field. Other brokers involved were Hoare & Co. (27), Myers & Co. (12), Laing & Cruickshank (11), and Rowe & Swan (10). The problem was that placings were, by their very nature, semi-private affairs, with only the members of the syndicate involved at the outset. Consequently, when a new issue was especially successful, with the price rising to an early premium, those who had not been invited to participate complained. A particularly successful placing of General Electric stock, early in 1945, provoked widespread public criticism because those involved were able to make quick profits by selling the shares they had taken—stagging a new issue. Such was the outcry produced that the Bank of England proposed a rule that those who were allotted shares through a placing would have to hold them for six months before being permitted to sell. Though this particular measure was dropped it was symptomatic of the fact that not only was the Stock Exchange's participation in the capital market dependent upon the Treasury but also the very practices it followed were open to scrutiny and control. The result was growing competition from non-members who were not subject to the same degree of supervision. Merchant banks, for example, were looking for alternative sources of business now that the foreign issue business was dead. Morgan Grenfell absorbed the small issue house of Cull & Co. towards the end of the war as a means of entering the new issue market for corporate securities.[104]

However, it was the Stock Exchange itself that was responsible for the continuing failure to cater for small investors. One of the members of the Stock Exchange, Crews & Co., had been among the pioneers of unit trusts in the 1930s, especially those involving the securities of rubber plantations, tin, and gold-mines. By their very nature these securities were very speculative, which meant that the valuation placed on the unit trust's portfolio was both a matter of judgement and very volatile. As these types of unit trusts were being marketed as investment vehicles for small investors by

[104] Ibid., 17 Apr. 1944, 25 Sept. 1944, 19 Feb. 1945, 26 Feb. 1945, 25 May 1945; Kynaston, *Cazenove*, 166, 168, 173.

Crews & Co., there was a strong feeling that the whole operation was bring-ing the Stock Exchange into disrepute. The result was that the Stock Exchange banned the partners of stockbroking firms from being directors of unit trusts or even from managing such organizations from their own office. Laudable as this was it did mean that the Stock Exchange was pre-venting its membership from being directly involved in a means through which small investors could purchase a spread of securities and so reduce the risks. Crews & Co., and another broker, Grieveson Grant & Co., were forced to sell their holdings in unit trust management companies as a con-sequence of these rules being introduced.[105]

Generally, over the duration of the war the nominal value of all secur-ities quoted and listed on the London Stock Exchange rose by £2.3bn. (+ 2 per cent). This consisted of a rise of £3bn. (+ 17 per cent) in officially quoted securities, where UK government stock was to be found, and a fall of £0.7bn. (– 39 per cent) in the Supplementary List, where smaller corpo-rate securities were to be found. However, the greatest decrease in the secu-rities for which London provided a market were in those issued overseas, by foreign and colonial governments and corporations. The nominal amount of foreign and colonial government debt, traded in London, fell by £0.9bn. during the war, and that of overseas railways fell by a similar amount. The collapse of the nominal value of a sector like telegraph and telephone, which had been of growing importance before the war, was due to the disappearance of securities belonging to companies operating over-seas, such as in North and South America. This was all part of the gover-ment's massive disposal of foreign securities in order to provide vital foreign exchange for the war effort. These included not only all available dollar securities, with compensation based on the prevailing New York price, but any that foreign investors would buy, such as those issued by Latin Amer-ican utilities, South African gold-mines and Malayan rubber plantations. At the outbreak of the Second World War, for example, British investors still held 51.8 per cent of the common stock of the Canadian Pacific Railway compared to only 18.9 per cent in Canada, 22.9 per cent in the USA, and 6.5 per cent elsewhere. As a result of government disposals and private sales, trading ceased in numerous foreign securities once actively bought and sold on the London Stock Exchange. The American market, for instance, finally ceased to exist. The few holdings of foreign securities that still existed in London were those belonging to foreign nationals, such as Belgians, Dutch, French, or Norwegian refugees. They were caught up in the attempt by the Bank of England to prevent German sales of securities stolen from such groups as Jewish bankers in Amsterdam.[106]

---

[105] LSE: General Purposes, 11 Dec. 1939, 8 Jan. 1940, 8 Feb. 1940, 6 Dec. 1943.
[106] Collins, *Money and Banking*, 326; J. Attali, *A Man of Influence: Sir Siegmund Warburg 1902–1982* (London 1986), 155; LSE: Non-Permanent, 28 Aug. 1939, 20 Sept. 1939, 28 Sept. 1939, 8 Apr. 1940; LSE: General Purposes, 29 Feb. 1940, 8 Apr. 1940, 20 May 1940; LSE: Rules and Regulations, 29 Apr. 1942; Warren, *Heseltine, Powell & Co.*, 24.

In terms of domestic securities the few new issues permitted to industrial and commercial companies were completely insufficient to compensate for the inevitable disappearance of others due to redemption, take-over, or bankruptcy. Overall, the result of the Second World War for the nominal value of securities, quoted and listed by the London Stock Exchange, was a massive rise in UK government debt of £4.9bn. (+ 71 per cent) and decline or stagnation in all other categories, ranging from a drop of £0.9bn. (– 24 per cent) in foreign government debt, £0.9bn. (– 45 per cent) in foreign railway stocks and bonds, and £0.5bn. in utilities (– 43 per cent) to falls of only £0.1bn. in commercial and industrial (– 6 per cent) and mining and agriculture (– 13 per cent) (Table 7.2). As a consequence UK government debt, which already comprised 35 per cent of the nominal value of all securities quoted and listed in 1939, saw its share rise to 54 per cent in 1945. In contrast foreign governments declined from 19 per cent (1939) to 13 per cent (1945), foreign railways from 16 to 10 per cent, utilities from 5 to 3 per cent, commercial and industrial from 12 to 10 per cent, and mining and agriculture from 4 to 3 per cent (Table 7.3). Everything other than UK government debt either declined substantially or stood still during the Second World War as the market provided by the London Stock Exchange and its membership was turned into an adjunct for financing the country's drive for military victory.

However, in terms of market value there were significant changes. Inevitably, the very weight of issues by the UK government pushed their share of the total up. Rising from 36 per cent in 1939 to 40 per cent in 1945. This growth, though, was only a little more than the rise in the nominal amount, and was easily outshone by the growing value attached to UK corporate stocks. The market value of UK railways rose by £0.3bn. (41 per cent) over the 1939–45 period while that of commercial and industrial enterprises grew by £0.9bn. (24 per cent) even though the nominal amount hardly changed (Table 7.3). Domestically, though investors were absorbing the huge increase in debt created by the government, their preferences were pushing up the market value of those domestic corporate issues that were available to them. With the yield on consols pegged at 2 per cent, and interest rates in the discount market running at 1 per cent per annum, it was easy enough for the government to attract savings into the securities it was creating. Nevertheless, there were investors wary of the permanence of those interest rates, and well aware that any general rise would be accompanied by a fall in the market value of the goverment's own debt. Consequently, they chose to invest some of the savings left to them, after a 50 per cent basic rate of income tax, in UK equities as companies could push up earnings and so maintain yields in real terms.[107] With few such issues being made during the war, those that did exist attracted increasing demand—hence rising prices. A similar

[107] Mitchell, *British Historical Statistics*, 645, 682, 684–5, 703.

Table 7.2. London Stock Exchange: Nominal and market values of securities quoted on 24 March 1939 and 3 April 1945, by number and amount (£m.)

| Class of security | Change in nominal total | Official List | | | | | |
|---|---|---|---|---|---|---|---|
| | | Number | | Nominal | | Market | |
| | | 1939 | 1945 | 1939 | 1945 | 1939 | 1945 |
| British government | + 14,941.4 | 60 | 55 | 6,922.5 | 11,863.9 | 6,598.4 | 12,168.0 |
| UK public bodies | − 35.8 | 506 | 466 | 934.4 | 903.7 | 891.5 | 922.0 |
| TOTAL | + 4,905.6 | 566 | 521 | 7,856.9 | 12,767.6 | 7,489.9 | 13,090 |
| Colonial governments | − 214.9 | 157 | 119 | 859.9 | 646.4 | 817.8 | 664.6 |
| Foreign governments | − 672.2 | 283 | 216 | 2,197.7 | 1,923.9 | 395.2 | 263.7 |
| Colonial/Foreign public bodies | − 29.7 | 262 | 196 | 161.3 | 138.7 | 117.7 | 100.4 |
| TOTAL | − 916.8 | 702 | 531 | 3,218.9 | 2,709.0 | 1,330.7 | 1,028.7 |
| UK railways | + 0.4 | 67 | 67 | 1,140.3 | 1,147.6 | 605.4 | 863.1 |
| Indian railways | − 49.5 | 46 | 19 | 136.5 | 87.0 | 133.7 | 87.2 |
| Imperial railways | − 119.0 | 72 | 34 | 314.7 | 195.9 | 228.9 | 154.7 |
| American railways | − 686.2 | 62 | 23 | 865.4 | 211.4 | 383.0 | 59.5 |
| Foreign railways | − 43.0 | 204 | 178 | 637.3 | 594.1 | 132.0 | 143.3 |
| TOTAL | − 897.6 | 451 | 321 | 3,094.2 | 2,236 | 1,483.0 | 1,307.8 |
| Banks and discount houses | − 5.5 | 80 | 73 | 195.0 | 192.1 | 433.4 | 512.8 |
| Financial, land, and investment | − 11.6 | 799 | 827 | 487.9 | 494.8 | 429.2 | 513.0 |
| Insurance | + 1.5 | 63 | 60 | 36.3 | 38.1 | 326.4 | 358.6 |
| TOTAL | − 15.6 | 942 | 960 | 719.2 | 725.0 | 1,189.0 | 1,384.4 |
| Canals and docks | + 1.0 | 26 | 27 | 30.7 | 30.8 | 64.4 | 128.3 |
| Gas | + 1.7 | 140 | 140 | 126.4 | 132.4 | 124.6 | 141.9 |
| Electric light/power | − 31.1 | 184 | 184 | 218.5 | 220.7 | 326.0 | 331.7 |
| Telegraph and telephone | − 429.1 | 34 | 28 | 441.4 | 44.3 | 686.3 | 87.6 |
| Tramways and omnibus | − 6.4 | 71 | 70 | 59.6 | 59.6 | 58.1 | 104.4 |
| Waterworks | + 2.9 | 73 | 75 | 28.5 | 31.5 | 34.5 | 41.6 |
| TOTAL | − 461.0 | 528 | 524 | 905.1 | 519.3 | 1,293.9 | 835.5 |
| Commercial/Industrial | − 42.2 | 1,568 | 1,553 | 1,279.5 | 1,283.6 | 2,470.7 | 3,150.7 |
| Breweries/Distilleries | + 0.2 | 401 | 379 | 215.0 | 211.1 | 380.3 | 501.0 |
| Iron, coal, and steel | − 76.0 | 207 | 209 | 306.2 | 252.7 | 431.4 | 385.3 |
| Shipping | − 11.1 | 60 | 57 | 73.6 | 65.7 | 62.2 | 89.3 |
| TOTAL | − 128.4 | 2,236 | 2,198 | 1,874.3 | 1,813.1 | 3,344.6 | 4,126.3 |
| Mines | − 76.0 | 47 | 41 | 76.2 | 44.4 | 123.0 | 143.2 |
| Nitrate | − 2.6 | 6 | 6 | 9.1 | 6.5 | 3.0 | 4.5 |
| Oil | − 11.9 | 33 | 32 | 162.3 | 160.3 | 512.1 | 568.6 |
| Tea, coffee, rubber | − 3.0 | 182 | 177 | 60.0 | 58.7 | 55.0 | 64.7 |
| TOTAL | − 93.5 | 268 | 256 | 307.6 | 269.9 | 693.1 | 781.0 |
| TOTAL | + 2,392.7 | 5,693 | 5,311 | 17,976.1 | 21,039.9 | 16,824.2 | 22,808.6 |
| No par value | — | — | | — | | (£485.5)* | (£254.9) |

* Included in total.

*Sources*: LSE: Committee for General Purposes, *Annual Reports*, 24 Mar. 1939, 3 Apr. 1945.

| Supplementary List | | | | | | Total | | | | | |
|---|---|---|---|---|---|---|---|---|---|---|---|
| Number | | Nominal | | Market | | Number | | Nominal | | Market | |
| 1939 | 1945 | 1939 | 1945 | 1939 | 1945 | 1939 | 1945 | 1939 | 1945 | 1939 | 1945 |
| — | — | — | — | — | — | 60 | 55 | 6,922.5 | | 6,598.4 | 12,168.0 |
| 50 | 30 | 12.0 | 6.9 | 10.3 | 2.9 | 556 | 496 | 946.4 | 910.0 | 901.8 | 942.9 |
| 50 | 30 | 12.0 | 6.9 | 10.3 | 2.9 | 616 | 551 | 7,868.9 | 12,774.5 | 7,500.2 | 13,092.9 |
| 3 | — | 1.4 | — | 1.4 | — | 160 | 119 | 861.3 | 646.4 | 819.2 | 664.6 |
| 56 | 46 | 517.7 | 119.3 | 92.5 | 23.3 | 339 | 262 | 2,715.4 | 2,043.2 | 487.7 | 287.0 |
| 16 | 11 | 15.8 | 8.7 | 2.9 | 0.7 | 278 | 207 | 177.1 | 147.4 | 120.6 | 101.1 |
| 75 | 57 | 534.9 | 128.0 | 96.8 | 24.0 | 777 | 588 | 3,753.8 | 2,837.0 | 1,427.5 | 1,052.7 |
| 20 | 20 | 10.6 | 3.7 | 8.2 | 0.9 | 87 | 87 | 1,150.9 | 1,151.3 | 613.6 | 864.0 |
| 1 | 1 | 0.1 | 0.1 | 0.1 | 0.1 | 47 | 20 | 136.6 | 87.1 | 133.8 | 87.3 |
| 3 | 3 | 0.8 | 0.6 | 0.3 | — | 75 | 37 | 315.5 | 196.5 | 229.2 | 154.7 |
| 6 | 6 | 39.1 | 6.9 | 2.5 | 7.5 | 68 | 29 | 904.5 | 218.3 | 385.5 | 67.0 |
| 13 | 14 | 2.0 | 1.9 | 1.0 | 1.8 | 217 | 192 | 639.3 | 596.0 | 133.0 | 145.1 |
| 43 | 44 | 52.6 | 13.2 | 12.1 | 10.3 | 484 | 365 | 3,146.8 | 2,249.2 | 1,495.1 | 1,318.1 |
| 19 | 17 | 208.0 | 18.2 | 25.0 | 22.2 | 99 | 90 | 215.8 | 210.3 | 458.4 | 535.0 |
| 409 | 370 | 114.7 | 96.2 | 101.6 | 104.3 | 1,208 | 1,197 | 602.6 | 591.0 | 530.8 | 617.3 |
| 15 | 12 | 3.0 | 2.7 | 12.8 | 13.4 | 78 | 72 | 39.3 | 40.8 | 339.2 | 372.0 |
| 443 | 399 | 138.5 | 117.1 | 139.4 | 139.9 | 1,385 | 1,359 | 857.7 | 842.1 | 1,328.4 | 1,524.3 |
| 32 | 29 | 12.6 | 13.5 | 11.7 | 33.5 | 58 | 56 | 43.3 | 44.3 | 68.1 | 161.8 |
| 316 | 286 | 33.8 | 29.5 | 35.6 | 30.7 | 456 | 426 | 160.2 | 161.9 | 160.2 | 172.6 |
| 63 | 42 | 45.4 | 12.1 | 81.4 | 20.4 | 247 | 226 | 263.9 | 232.8 | 407.4 | 352.1 |
| 12 | 8 | 42.4 | 10.4 | 59.0 | 15.2 | 46 | 36 | 483.8 | 54.7 | 745.3 | 102.8 |
| 38 | 32 | 20.5 | 14.1 | 26.5 | 34.9 | 109 | 102 | 80.1 | 73.7 | 84.6 | 139.3 |
| 141 | 143 | 7.9 | 7.8 | 10.0 | 9.7 | 214 | 218 | 36.4 | 39.3 | 44.5 | 51.3 |
| 602 | 540 | 162.6 | 87.4 | 224.2 | 144.4 | 1,130 | 1,064 | 1,067.7 | 606.7 | 1,518.1 | 979.9 |
| 1,893 | 1,833 | 356.9 | 311.3 | 395.7 | 526.5 | 3,461 | 3,386 | 1,636.4 | 1,594.9 | 2,866.4 | 3,677.2 |
| 122 | 124 | 21.6 | 25.7 | 28.8 | 41.5 | 523 | 503 | 236.6 | 236.8 | 409.1 | 565.9 |
| 167 | 145 | 81.4 | 58.9 | 72.2 | 64.9 | 374 | 354 | 387.6 | 311.6 | 503.6 | 450.2 |
| 32 | 26 | 14.1 | 10.9 | 12.6 | 18.9 | 92 | 83 | 87.7 | 76.6 | 74.8 | 108.2 |
| 2,214 | 2,128 | 474.0 | 406.8 | 509.3 | 651.8 | 4,450 | 4,326 | 2,348.3 | 2,219.0 | 3,853.9 | 4,778.1 |
| 478 | 418 | 333.7 | 289.5 | 591.3 | 741.9 | 525 | 459 | 409.9 | 333.9 | 714.3 | 885.1 |
| — | — | — | — | — | — | 6 | 6 | 9.1 | 6.5 | 3.0 | 4.5 |
| 27 | 24 | 35.6 | 25.7 | 49.7 | 51.4 | 50 | 56 | 197.9 | 186.0 | 561.8 | 620.1 |
| 672 | 671 | 67.8 | 66.1 | 49.7 | 52.8 | 854 | 848 | 127.8 | 124.8 | 104.7 | 117.5 |
| 1,177 | 1,113 | 437.1 | 381.3 | 690.7 | 846.1 | 1,445 | 1,369 | 744.7 | 651.2 | 1,383.8 | 1,627.1 |
| 4,604 | 4,311 | 1,812.4 | 1,140.7 | 1,682.6 | 1,898.4 | 10,287 | 9,622 | 19,787 | 22,180 | 18,507 | 24,701 |
| — | — | — | — | (£69.3)* | (£73.0) | — | — | — | — | (£554.8) | (327.8) |

Table 7.3. London Stock Exchange: Nominal and market values of securities quoted on 24 March 1939 and 3 April 1945 (%)

| Class of security | Official List | | | | Supplementary List | | | | Total | | | |
| --- | --- | --- | --- | --- | --- | --- | --- | --- | --- | --- | --- | --- |
| | Nominal | | Market | | Nominal | | Market | | Nominal | | Market | |
| | 1939 | 1945 | 1939 | 1945 | 1939 | 1945 | 1939 | 1945 | 1939 | 1945 | 1939 | 1945 |
| British government | 38.5 | 56.4 | 39.2 | 53.3 | — | — | — | — | 35.0 | 53.5 | 35.7 | 49.3 |
| UK public bodies | 5.2 | 4.3 | 5.3 | 4.0 | 0.7 | 0.6 | 0.6 | 0.2 | 4.8 | 4.1 | 4.9 | 3.8 |
| TOTAL | 43.7 | 60.7 | 44.5 | 57.4 | 0.7 | 0.6 | 0.6 | 0.2 | 39.8 | 57.6 | 40.5 | 53.0 |
| Colonial governments | 4.8 | 3.1 | 4.5 | 2.9 | 0.1 | — | 0.1 | — | 4.4 | 2.9 | 4.4 | 2.7 |
| Foreign government | 12.2 | 9.1 | 2.3 | 1.2 | 28.6 | 10.5 | 5.5 | 1.2 | 13.7 | 9.2 | 2.6 | 1.2 |
| Colonial/Foreign public bodies | 0.9 | 0.7 | 0.7 | 0.4 | 0.9 | 0.8 | 0.2 | — | 0.9 | 0.7 | 0.7 | 0.4 |
| TOTAL | 17.9 | 12.9 | 7.9 | 4.5 | 29.5 | 11.2 | 5.8 | 1.3 | 19.0 | 12.8 | 7.7 | 4.3 |
| UK railways | 6.3 | 5.5 | 3.6 | 3.8 | 0.6 | 0.3 | 0.5 | 0.1 | 5.8 | 5.2 | 3.3 | 3.5 |
| Indian railways | 0.8 | 0.4 | 0.8 | 0.4 | — | — | — | — | 0.7 | 0.4 | 0.7 | 0.4 |
| Imperial railways | 1.8 | 0.9 | 1.4 | 0.7 | — | 0.1 | — | — | 1.6 | 0.9 | 1.2 | 0.6 |
| American railways | 4.8 | 1.0 | 2.3 | 0.3 | 2.2 | 0.6 | 0.1 | 0.4 | 4.6 | 1.0 | 2.1 | 0.3 |
| Foreign railways | 3.5 | 2.8 | 0.8 | 0.6 | 0.1 | 0.2 | 0.1 | 0.1 | 3.2 | 2.7 | 0.7 | 0.6 |
| TOTAL | 17.2 | 10.6 | 8.8 | 5.7 | 2.9 | 1.2 | 0.7 | 0.5 | 15.9 | 10.1 | 8.1 | 5.3 |
| Banks and discount houses | 1.1 | 0.9 | 2.6 | 2.3 | 1.1 | 1.6 | 1.5 | 1.2 | 1.1 | 1.0 | 2.5 | 2.2 |
| Financial, land, and investment | 2.7 | 2.4 | 2.6 | 2.3 | 6.3 | 8.4 | 6.0 | 5.5 | 3.0 | 2.7 | 2.9 | 2.5 |
| Insurance | 0.2 | 0.2 | 1.9 | 1.6 | 0.2 | 0.2 | 0.8 | 0.7 | 0.2 | 0.2 | 1.8 | 1.5 |
| TOTAL | 4.0 | 3.5 | 7.1 | 6.1 | 7.6 | 10.3 | 8.3 | 7.4 | 4.3 | 3.8 | 7.2 | 6.2 |

| | | | | | | | | | | | | |
|---|---|---|---|---|---|---|---|---|---|---|---|---|
| Canals and docks | 0.2 | 0.2 | 0.4 | 0.6 | 0.7 | 1.2 | 0.7 | 1.8 | 0.2 | 0.2 | 0.4 | 0.7 |
| Gas | 0.7 | 0.6 | 0.7 | 0.6 | 1.9 | 2.6 | 2.1 | 1.6 | 0.8 | 0.7 | 0.9 | 0.7 |
| Electric light/power | 1.2 | 1.1 | 1.9 | 1.5 | 2.5 | 1.1 | 4.8 | 1.1 | 1.3 | 1.1 | 2.2 | 1.4 |
| Telegraph and telephone | 2.5 | 0.2 | 4.0 | 0.4 | 2.3 | 0.9 | 3.5 | 0.8 | 2.4 | 0.3 | 4.0 | 0.4 |
| Tramways and omnibus | 0.3 | 0.3 | 0.3 | 0.5 | 1.1 | 1.2 | 1.6 | 1.8 | 0.4 | 0.3 | 0.5 | 0.6 |
| Waterworks | 0.2 | 0.2 | 0.2 | 0.2 | 0.4 | 0.7 | 0.6 | 0.5 | 0.2 | 0.2 | 0.2 | 0.2 |
| TOTAL | 5.0 | 2.5 | 7.7 | 3.7 | 9.0 | 7.7 | 13.3 | 7.6 | 5.4 | 2.7 | 8.2 | 4.0 |
| Commercial/Industrial | 7.1 | 6.1 | 14.7 | 13.8 | 20.0 | 27.3 | 23.5 | 27.8 | 8.3 | 7.2 | 15.5 | 14.9 |
| Breweries/Distilleries | 1.2 | 1.0 | 2.3 | 2.2 | 1.2 | 2.3 | 1.7 | 2.2 | 1.2 | 1.1 | 2.2 | 2.3 |
| Iron, coal, and steel | 1.7 | 1.2 | 2.6 | 1.7 | 4.5 | 5.2 | 4.3 | 3.4 | 2.0 | 1.4 | 2.7 | 1.8 |
| Shipping | 0.4 | 0.3 | 0.4 | 0.4 | 0.8 | 1.0 | 0.7 | 1.0 | 0.4 | 0.4 | 0.4 | 0.4 |
| TOTAL | 10.4 | 8.6 | 19.9 | 18.1 | 26.2 | 35.7 | 30.3 | 34.4 | 11.9 | 10.0 | 20.8 | 19.3 |
| Mines | 0.4 | 0.2 | 0.7 | 0.6 | 18.4 | 25.4 | 35.1 | 39.2 | 2.1 | 1.5 | 3.9 | 3.6 |
| Nitrate | 0.1 | — | — | — | — | — | — | — | — | — | — | — |
| Oil | 0.9 | 0.8 | 3.0 | 2.5 | 2.0 | 2.3 | 3.0 | 2.7 | 1.0 | 0.8 | 3.0 | 2.5 |
| Tea, coffee, rubber | 0.3 | 0.3 | 0.3 | 0.3 | 3.7 | 5.8 | 3.0 | 2.8 | 0.6 | 0.6 | 0.6 | 0.5 |
| TOTAL | 1.7 | 1.3 | 4.1 | 3.4 | 24.1 | 33.4 | 41.0 | 44.7 | 3.8 | 2.9 | 7.5 | 6.6 |

*Source:* As Table 7.2.

situation also existed in terms of foreign securities. The market had already discounted the value of many foreign government securities before the war, as there was little prospect that interest would ever be paid or the debt would be redeemed, as with that of Russia. Consequently, during the war the main source of the decline in market values was not any change in sentiment but the delisting of foreign securities as they were requisitioned and sold by the government. One of the few categories of overseas securities still actively traded in London at this time were the shares of mining and plantation companies. Though their nominal amount fell, the market value rose by £0.2bn. (+ 18 per cent) as investors looked to the security provided by companies that produced minerals, oil, tea, and rubber (Table 7.2).

In many ways the London Stock Exchange marked time during the Second World War. Its involvement in the global securities market ceased due to the requisitioning of foreign securities and foreign exchange controls. Its position within the domestic securities market was eroded further by the provincial stock exchanges and non-member financial institutions through government restrictions and its own policy on commission rates. Nothing was resolved concerning its relationship with non-members who also operated in the securities market. As an institution the merger of the two controlling committees, representing the members and the proprietors, into a single council placed power wholly in the hands of the members. For the members themselves little changed as those too old or medically unfit tried to keep the business going as before. Though a few more senior staff advanced to partner level than was normal, few other groups made much progress, including women. Member firms, whether broker or jobber, remained small and personal, bound by kinship, class, religion, or experience. What really did change was the relationship between the Stock Exchange and the government. At the outbreak of war a working relationship already existed, having been established during the First World War and then the 1931 crisis. By the end of the war the Stock Exchange had become, almost, an administrative arm of the government in exercising supervision over the securities market. In return for this loss of independence the Stock Exchange sought, and, to an extent, received towards the end of the war government support against competitors in the securities market. An implicit contract had been formed between the Stock Exchange and the government. The government needed the Stock Exchange as a means of controlling the securities market both during the war and into peacetime. Thus, the government needed to bolster the power of the Stock Exchange within the securities market if it was to maintain this control. Consequently, the Stock Exchange was responsive to the requests of government for, by doing so, its power over the securities market was reinforced, while the government was responsive to the needs of the Stock Exchange because that was how it controlled the market. This was not a position sought by either side but it evolved into a working relationship during the Second World War, coming after the experiences of the First World War and the more regulated environment developed between the wars, especially in the 1930s.

# 8

# Recovery and Crisis: 1945–1949

## GOVERNMENT CONTROL

As the Second World War drew to a close in 1945 the London Stock Exchange was faced with one certainty amongst a sea of uncertainty. That certainty was that the controls and restrictions put in place since 1939 would not be rapidly dismantled. There was even the strong possibility that they would become a permanent feature of its peacetime operations. Faced with this certainty of government involvement in its activities the Stock Exchange had to devise a strategy that would allow it to both survive and prosper, under circumstances that were likely to be far removed from the conditions of the 1930s, and even more remote from those of before 1914, when it had been left, almost undisturbed, to manage its own affairs. If the strategy failed the result could be direct Treasury supervision over the securities market, bypassing the Stock Exchange completely, or even the nationalization of the institution itself, with its elected officials replaced by government appointments. Such was the fate that did befall the Bank of England in 1946, after the Labour Party won the 1945 election. Having experienced Treasury intervention in the securities market during the war, and protested about the resulting mismanagement and bias, this was not an outcome that the membership of the Stock Exchange wanted. Consequently, the decisions taken by the Stock Exchange in those post-war years were heavily conditioned by the need to maintain the goodwill of the government.

Consequently, though the ending of the war brought immediate calls from among the members to return to a peacetime mode of operation, the steps taken were slow and halting. Each move had to be negoti-ated with the government, either the Treasury or later the Bank of England, with due regard being paid to hostile public opinion. The London Stock Exchange had neither complete control over the securities market nor was it master of its own affairs, and so had to proceed cautiously if it was to retain what authority it still possessed. It was also not at all clear what the role of the London securities market was to be. The whole-sale disposal of a large proportion of Britain's holdings of foreign securities, combined with the great increase in the wealth of the American investor, had placed New York at the centre of what remained of the international securities market. Domestically, the provincial stock exchanges remained potent competitors in the field of corporate stocks and shares, as no solution had been found to the threat posed by country jobbers. Even in the realm of UK government debt the discount houses had emerged as rival dealers, serving major institutional investors like the banks. With a socialist government in power there was the whole question of whether there was a role for a securities market at all, as alternative ways of financing economic activity could be resorted to. The state itself had direct access to the nation's savings through taxation while financial institutions, like the banks and insurance companies, had become accustomed to buying and holding government debt directly during the war. The London Stock Exchange in 1945 was faced with fighting not only for its own survival but the preservation of the securities market, which was its only reason to exist.[1]

As early as March 1945 the Stock Exchange approached the Treasury, seeking an end to the cash basis of trading adopted since the beginning of the war. The Stock Exchange was well aware that only the restoration of the established trading techniques would allow its members to compete effectively against non-members, who were unhindered by the costs and restrictions that membership involved. In particular, the return of fortnightly accounts, contangos, and options would permit members to trade on trust, and thus avoid the need for large capitals or credit lines, as possessed by banks and other financial institutions. However, it was not until December 1945 when agreement, in principle, had been obtained from the Treasury, that preparations for account training could begin. Even then the Treasury wanted to be satisfied that the Stock Exchange had systems in place to handle the settlement of transactions and had introduced safeguards that would prevent trading for the account being used for speculative purposes. The government was worried that stock exchange speculation could be a disruptive influence on both exchange and interest rate levels in the rather fragile post-war economy. They also had a vested interest in delaying the reintroduction of the fortnightly settlement because it was not necessary for their own stocks. The Bank of England provided special certification facilities so that the ownership of government debt could be transferred on a daily basis, matching the requirement for cash payment. This made the National Debt a more attractive investment than other securities for those employing funds that were only available on a short-term basis.[2]

As it was, the Stock Exchange did take some time to re-establish the Settlement Department, which was considered essential if transactions in

---

[1] For the general picture see F. Capie, 'The Evolution of Financial Institutions and Markets in the United Kingdom in the Twentieth Century: The Domestic Economy', in G. D. Feldman, U. Olssen, M. Bordo, and Y. Cassis (eds.), *The Evolution of Modern Financial Institutions in the Twentieth Century* (Milan 1994), 33.

[2] LSE: Council, 19 Mar. 1945, 17 Dec. 1945, 8 July 1946.

actively traded securities were to be cleared, so that only residual payments and deliveries were required at the end of the account. This department had been closed down at the onset of war, when trading moved onto a cash basis. Though efforts had been made to retain the skilled staff this had not been particularly successful, and so new staff had to be recruited and trained. Also, the rooms they used had not been maintained, let alone updated, and that had to be remedied at a time of material and labour shortages. As it was the Settlement Department was not fully operational until January 1947, and some time after that before its performance was considered satisfactory. By then the fortnightly account had already been reintroduced.[3]

It had taken the Stock Exchange almost the whole of 1946 to persuade the Treasury that they had made adequate preparations for the introduction of the account, and to justify the need for this practice within their trading system. Finally, in July 1946, with the support of the Bank of England, they tried to persuade the Treasury to permit the reintroduction of accounts because of their proven convenience.

Prior to the outbreak of war in September 1939 it was the normal and traditional practice of the Stock Exchange (broken only by the war period of 1914–1918) to conduct its business on a system of fortnightly settlements or 'Accounts accompanied by facilities (known as contangos) for the continuation of bargains from Account to Account, and by option dealing.

This system goes back beyond the memory of any now living and it has been upheld by the general consensus of opinion and experience that when business is active fortnightly 'Accounts' are more orderly, more economical of manpower and more efficient than daily (or, as they are called, 'cash') settlements.

The established custom was then contrasted with the current position.

'Cash' settlement means, strictly, settlement on the day following the bargain. This is possible in British government stocks, for which the Bank of England provides special certificate facilities available to the market, and in bearer securities which pass by delivery. In the case, however, of other registered stocks and shares, which represent a very high percentage of Stock Exchange transactions, whilst delivery on the day following the bargain could be possible in very exceptional circumstances, it is generally speaking quite impossible, and in practice it has been found necessary to allow a period of five days for the passing of the purchaser's name, which is only the first step in the process of the preparation, transmission, signature and certification (if necessary) of the deed of transfer, which leads finally to the registration in the company's books of the purchaser's title.

It follows from these conditions that every day is a settlement day but a settlement day for liabilities of which neither the incidence nor the amount can possibly be predicted. With the greatly increased volume of business that has now to be dealt with, it is physically impossible for the system to work efficiently and disorder and

[3] LSE: Subcommittee, Settlement Dept., 21 Nov. 1946, 27 Mar. 1947; LSE: Council 23 Sept. 1946.

lack of control are unavoidable; the strain on manpower is very great and speculators are able to obtain a longer 'run'—sometimes a much longer run—than they can under a system of regular periodic settlements. The strain is now being felt also in the offices of many companies whose securities are actively dealt in and where work would be eased under periodic settlements through the elimination of many intermediate transactions.

Within these arguments the Stock Exchange was forced to abandon the possibility of restoring contangos and options in the face of a government that regarded them simply as speculative devices, possessing not even administrative convenience. Consequently, they were separated from the system of fortnightly accounts and attributed to a now bygone era of the Stock Exchange's past.

Contangos and options had their legitimate uses and performed a valuable function, especially in an international market such as London was at that time; but they could also be used, and were used, as vehicles for speculation.

Instead, what was proposed was a compromise whereby the fortnightly account would be restored but not continuations or options so that all transactions had to be settled within that period and could not be continued for longer.

To meet these conditions the Stock Exchange does not propose a reversion to the old system. It proposes instead a new system of Fortnightly *Cash* Settlements, without continuation facilities or options, and with a prohibition upon dealing for a future 'Account' before it has actually commenced: the recent change in commissions charges (suspension of the rule permitting commission to be charged only once if the same security was bought and sold within 28 days) would be retained as an extra deterrent to speculation. Gilt-edged securities would continue to be dealt in for cash, as they have been since 1914.

The effect of this would be to take advantage of those features of the old system that were conducive to order and efficiency, and to economy of labour, and to eliminate those that were favourable to speculation.

Eventually this pleading from the Stock Exchange, supported by the Bank of England, convinced a reluctant government to permit a resumption of account trading from 11 December 1946.[4]

It was not until January 1949 that the Stock Exchange raised with the Bank of England, which was now acting as the Treasury's agent in the City of London, the possibility of restoring contangos. Without the ability to extend transactions longer than a fortnight the members of the Stock Exchange were finding it difficult to compete with the better capitalized and better connected discount houses in the gilt-edged market. After a meeting with the Deputy Governor of the Bank of England it was agreed to explore ways by which contangos could be reintroduced in an acceptable form.

⁴ Ibid., 8 July 1946, cf. 23 Sept. 1946.

After further pressure from the Stock Exchange in March 1949 it was agreed that contangos could be reintroduced in April, but only if the Stock Exchange itself guaranteed that they would not be used for speculative purposes. However, the Bank of England made it clear that it was completely opposed to the reintroduction of options, because of their use in the build-up of a large speculative position, which could collapse with serious ramifications for the whole financial position. Having achieved the reintroduction of contangos the Stock Exchange decided to drop any request for the resumption of options for the moment.[5]

## INSTITUTIONAL CHANGE

What was slowly emerging was an arrangement whereby the Stock Exchange was entrusted with the responsible management of the securities market within a framework set by the Bank of England but determined, ultimately by the Treasury and the government in the light of national requirements and political perceptions. As the Bank of England made clear to the Stock Exchange, in November 1946 '. . . the market must resign itself to some general control over security movements for some time to come'.[6] Within that, the more responsibly the Stock Exchange behaved the more likely it was to be allowed to restore market practices, because it could be trusted to police their use and limit their abuse. However, there were limits to that trust. The Stock Exchange tried again, later in 1949, to seek the reintroduction of options but faced with a government grappling with international financial difficulties, leading to devaluation in September, they achieved nothing. Preventing the Stock Exchange reintroducing options and devices for forward trading, did not prevent them appearing. Non-members were not bound by the Stock Exchange's rules and so they could respond to the financial market's needs for safeguards against future movements in the prices of securities, influenced by exchange and interest rate fluctuations. When the Stock Exchange, for example, was closed temporarily, in the wake of devaluation, business switched to the street, City offices, and the greater use of the telephone. Nevertheless, because such trading was unofficial and the instruments used were not recognized, it received little publicity and so could be ignored by the government, Treasury, and Bank of England. As Robert Hall, economic adviser to the government at the time, noted in his diary in November 1949, 'The Stock Exchange is mad anyway and I don't think we should take any notice of them.'[7]

[5] LSE: Council, 10 Jan. 1949, 24 Jan. 1949, 31 Jan. 1949, 21 Mar. 1949, 4 Apr. 1949, 11 Apr. 1949, 19 Apr. 1949.
[6] Ibid., 4 Nov. 1946.
[7] Sir Robert Hall, 16 Nov. 1949, in A. Cairncross (ed.), *The Robert Hall Diaries* (London 1989), 96; LSE: Council, 8 Aug. 1949, 5 Sept. 1949, 19 Sept. 1949, 26 Sept. 1949, 31 Oct. 1949.

Unfortunately for the Stock Exchange ignoring such business was to its dis-advantage as it prompted the growth of an alternative market place.

During the war the Stock Exchange had consolidated control in the Council, which represented the views of the members. This still left the question of ownership for the Stock Exchange as a business was still controlled in 1945 by 3,710 shareholders, or proprietors. Though these proprietors had no power over the Stock Exchange as an institution they did own the building it occupied and were responsible for its main-tenance and servicing. Naturally, with the post-war uncertainty facing the Stock Exchange as a market place there was a reluctance among the proprietors to invest further in the building or improve the facil-ities and services it offered. As a result negotiations began to buy out the proprietors and convert the Stock Exchange into a member-owned institution, which was a long-desired objective. As the volume of busi-ness transacted on the Stock Exchange picked up after the war, sufficient confidence was built up among the membership to justify an offer to the proprietors. In February 1947 a scheme was formulated by Sir Edward Cripps and Mr H. L. Urling Clark, Chairman of the Stock Exchange which offered to convert the 20,000 outstanding shares into 40,000 4 per cent annuities, redeemable on 1 March 1953, later extended to 1958.

The valuation put on the Stock Exchange, as a building and a business, was thus £4m. and the membership accepted the commitment to provide £160,000 per annum to meet the interest charge on the annuities. All non-members were to surrender their shares and accept annuities by March 1948. There were still 3,700 shares (18.5 per cent of the total) held by non-members at this time. One share in the Stock Exchange was to be issued to each member of the Stock Exchange but these were to have no value and had to be surrendered without compensation when membership stopped. As such they were little more than membership certificates. When this scheme was put to the vote in November 1947 a total of 2,436 proprietors voted for it (84 per cent) and 454 (16 per cent) against, which was well in excess of the 75 per cent majority required from those voting. This was not surprising as the proprietors had experienced lean times during the war and could have had little optimism for the future. Nevertheless one proprietor did speak out against the terms offered, namely F. J. Shepherd, of P. N. Kemp-Gee & Co., who had been a shareholder since 1906. He regarded the whole scheme as one of confiscation, with the proprietors being denied any prospect of sharing in the future value of the institution they owned.[8]

However, as most shares were owned by existing members (81.5 per cent)

---

[8] LSE: Trustees and Managers, 25 Mar. 1945; 12 Feb. 1947, 22 Mar. 1947, 19 Nov. 1947, 30 Dec. 1947; Proposal for Re-organization and Consequential Alterations in the Deed of Settlements, 3 Mar. 1947.

they were more concerned with establishing total control over the Stock Exchange, which ownership would give them. They could then present a united front, especially in dealing with the government. The Chairman of the Stock Exchange, H. L. Urling Clark, expressed the prevailing sentiment in November 1947, when he said

Our main object in the Stock Exchange is not to make profits out of the building and the services rendered to the members. It is to enable us to carry on our own business.[9]

Henceforth, the membership of the Stock Exchange would be free of the influence of those whose interests lay in the present and future profits it generated as a business. The Committee for General Purposes and the Trustees and Management Committee were finally wound up on 8 March 1948, when all residual business was complete.[10] Instead, outside intervention was now coming from the government, either directly or via the Bank of England, and that would be responded to solely by the Council and its chairman, for

The Council shall control the affairs and the transaction of business in the Stock Exchange, and manage and administer the property, moneys, funds and assets of the undertaking,

according to the Council's own ruling in 1947.[11] Whatever the defects of dual control it had moderated the desire of the members to organize the Stock Exchange solely for their own benefit. This had maintained the market provided by the London Stock Exchange as a relatively open and flexible one, responsive to the needs of buyers and sellers of securities and the intermediaries that served them, though this influence had been waning between the wars. The question for the future was whether the government, through the Bank of England as its agent, could accomplish the same balancing act between serving the interests of the members who provided the market and the non-members, both individual and institutional, who used it.

When the members made the agreement buying out the proprietors, Stock Exchange business was picking up. Turnover in non-government securities had risen from an estimated £553m. in 1944/5 to £788m. in 1945/6 and then to £1,449m., or almost triple the wartime level. However, that was the post-war peak for business then began a steady decline, dropping to £1,185m. in 1947/8, £799m. in 1948/9, and £631m. in 1949/50, for non-government securities, or almost back to the wartime level. By January 1949 the Stock Exchange itself was of the opinion that the volume of business was down to about half the level of two years before. Their own estimate of the number of transactions indicate a fall from 117,594

---

[9] LSE: Trustees and Managers, 19 Nov. 1947.
[10] LSE: Council, 8 Mar. 1948.    [11] Ibid., 17 Feb. 1947.

in 1947 to 88,947 in 1948 and 75,822 in 1949, or a drop of 36 per cent.[12] With this precipitate collapse in turnover the attractions of a business career in the Stock Exchange were increasingly limited after 1947.

Nevertheless membership did rise from 3,588 in 1945 to 4,063 in 1949, producing an increase in income for the Stock Exchange, both through the fees paid by new members and the regular subscriptions. However, this rise in membership was more than matched by the declining numbers of authorized and unauthorized clerks. These dropped from 1,567 in 1945 to 1,025 in 1949, suggesting a switch between employing clerks, paid a regular salary to conduct business on the floor of the Stock Exchange, to the use of members, on a commission basis, instead. Such an action was a rational response by member firms, to declining business in the late 1940s. (Table 8.1.) Consequently, once the post-war boom was over the number of members and their clerks paying for admission to the Stock Exchange began to fall away, producing a crisis for the Stock Exchange as it was committed to a fixed payment of £160,000 per annum to the annuity holders, as well as meeting all the running and maintenance costs of the building. By the end of 1948 the Council of the Stock Exchange was forced to recognize that action to either increase income or reduce expenditure or both, was an urgent necessity.

The Revenue before the War provided a dividend of some £12 per share and a good balance to carry forward after making the necessary appropriations. But now, whilst the income is being maintained, the expenses have increased abnormally, due to the higher costs and taxation.[13]

The crisis was not due to rising taxation, wages, and expenses after the war for the government did maintain fairly strict direct and indirect controls over the economy. It lay with the difficulty of matching income and expenditure. One problem was that as a member-owned institution the membership expected a higher degree of service and lower charges than in the days when the Stock Exchange was run for profit. The Settlement Department, for instance, was not expected to generate an income from those using it, only to break even and so not be a burden on those who did not use it. However, as the volume of transactions fell so did its ability to break even, as its staff and office costs remained the same. By 1948 and 1949 the number of transactions cleared had fallen, from the post-war peak of 1.6m. per annum in 1947, to only 1.3m., and this was far short of the pre-war level of 3m. Towards the end of 1948 many members were questioning the need for a Settlement Department believing they could process transactions more cheaply themselves. This was espe-

---

[12] F. Paukert, 'The Value of Stock Exchange Transactions in Non-Government Securities, 1911–1959', *Economica*, 28 (1962/3), 304; LSE: Council, 25 Oct. 1948, 31 Jan. 1949, 30 Jan. 1950; LSE: Settlement Dept., 4 Nov. 1948, 25 Mar. 1949.

[13] LSE: Council, 22 Dec. 1948.

cially true of the firms with more extensive office staff. Agitation thus grew to close down the Settlement Department as a cost-saving exercise. If its charges could not be reduced the membership would cease to use it and closure was inevitable, as the Settlement Department itself recognized in November 1948[14]

There is little doubt that under the present conditions of business (2 per cent stamp duty, no contangos and nationalisation of securities) the pre-war turnover in the Department (3,000,000 items) is unlikely to be regained and if the Department is to survive to be available if business increases it must be made cheap.[15]

That month the decision was taken to subsidize the Settlement Department by forgoing the rent it paid (£4,150 per annum) for the space it occupied in the Stock Exchange, and by meeting part of its running costs (up to £12,000 per annum) from central funds. By 1950 this direct subsidy totalled £20,836, allowing the charges to be reduced which both encouraged use and reduced criticism. However, it also meant that the Stock Exchange was subsidizing a service used largely by the smaller member firms from the fees paid by all.[16]

What was happening with the Settlement Department was the beginning of a process where the Stock Exchange itself began to provide a growing range of services for its membership, in addition to the trading-floor where securities could be bought and sold. One such facility was the centralized delivery and payment of registered stocks between members. Traditionally this had been done by the use of messengers, who went round brokers' offices in the city. As members had to maintain offices close to the Stock Exchange, the distance travelled by these messengers was limited, though wartime destruction and post-war building controls did make it difficult to maintain this physical proximity. Consequently, as early as November 1947 moves were begun to establish a central transfer and payment office, which became operational on 3 August 1948.[17]

Consequently, as a member-owned institution it was difficult for the Stock Exchange to reduce its costs by dispensing with some of the services it provided, or ensure that the changes made covered all the costs. There was always going to be a group of members with a vested interest in preserving the status quo and had the power to do so as the Council was a fully elected body. In the past the services the Stock Exchange provided were under the control of the Trustees and Managers, which represented the proprietors not the members, though they did have an influence. Rather than reduce the services in the face of rising costs and declining business the pressure from the members was to extend the facilities but reduce the charges.

[14] LSE: Council, 29 Nov. 1948; LSE: Settlement Dept., 26 July 1951.
[15] Ibid., 4 Nov. 1948.
[16] Ibid., 25 Nov. 1948, 26 July 1951.
[17] LSE: Council, 28 Jan. 1946, 3 Nov. 1947, 3 Aug. 1948, 20 Sept. 1948; R. Hartley, *No Mean City: A Guide to the Economic City of London* (London 1967), 108.

Table 8.1. London Stock Exchange: Members and clerks (authorized and unauthorized), 1945–1950

|  | 1945 | 1946 | 1947 | 1948 | 1949 | 1950 |
|---|---|---|---|---|---|---|
| Members: Total | 3,558 | 3,645 | 3,838 | 3,948 | 4,063 | 4,050 |
| as authorized clerks | 883 | 906 | 978 | 969 | 1,033 | 1,020 |
| as unauthorized clerks | 90 | 108 | 119 | 124 | 153 | 142 |
| Clerks: Total | 2,225 | 2,126 | 1,961 | 1,868 | 1,697 | 1,539 |
| authorized clerks | 480 | 454 | 383 | 344 | 272 | 256 |
| unauthorized clerks | 1,087 | 1,014 | 896 | 839 | 752 | 646 |
| Settling-Room clerks | 658 | 658 | 682 | 685 | 672 | 637 |
| OVERALL TOTALS | 5,783 | 5,771 | 5,800 | 5,816 | 5,760 | 5,589 |

Source: London Stock Exchange: Annual Reports, 24 Mar. 1945–24 Mar. 1950.

It was also very difficult for the Stock Exchange to increase its income as the membership would oppose both any increase in fees and an expansion in numbers. The former would increase their costs at a time when business was in decline while the latter would create more competitors for that business which was still being done. Nevertheless, the Stock Exchange was forced to suggest in November 1948 that annual subscription fees should be raised by 25 per cent for members and 50 per cent for clerks. There appeared no other way out of this crisis. Naturally enough these large increases met strong resistance from among the membership at this time.

Such was the power of the members that the Council backed down, agreeing in February 1949 to meet the revenue shortfall through a substantial rise in the entrance fee. A new member would, in future, pay a joining fee of £1,100 though that could be reduced by up to half depending on the time spent as a clerk.[18] However, this was hardly a solution as the Stock Exchange was not attracting many new members, and an increase in the entrance fee would discourage potential applicants. Between 1949 and 1950 the number of members actually fell by 13. (Table 8.1.) As it was impossible to either reduce costs or raise membership fees, and higher entrance fees were little more than a risky short-term measure, the Stock Exchange began looking seriously at additional sources of income. One suggestion came from the member firm of Goff & Goff, who proposed that the Stock Exchange charge companies for quoting their securities. In the past the Stock Exchange had been wary of such moves as high entrance fees and quotation charges because it might encourage the appearance of rival exchanges, and thus undermine the value of the Stock

[18] LSE: Council, 22 Nov. 1948, 28 Feb. 1949.

Exchange as a business. However, with the Stock Exchange now run for the benefit of the membership, and its position in the securities market safeguarded through the relationship with the government, it was possible to take such risks as these. With the Prevention of Fraud Act it was difficult for non-member brokers and jobbers to operate in London, and with the Bank of England supervising any nascent 'grey' market for securities, it was difficult for a rival stock exchange to emerge in the post-war years. Thus, it was agreed to start charging for a quotation from March 1949. The Stock Exchange also began to explore, with the Inland Revenue, the question of whether its income was exempt from taxation as a mutual organization.[19]

It is clear that the final ending of outside ownership and dual control did have major implications for the Stock Exchange. The change made it much more difficult to both resist the demands of members for improved services at lower charges and to impose higher annual fees on the membership. This created a search for alternative sources of income that would provoke less hostility and these were found through charging more to those who wanted to become members or companies who needed a market for their securities. In turn, these costs imposed on non-members were only enforceable because of the position now occupied by the Stock Exchange within the securities market. That position had emerged during the war when the government used the organization and regulatory power of the Stock Exchange to control the securities market and continued to do that, via the Bank of England, in peacetime. In return for the co-operation it gave government, both during the war and thereafter, the Stock Exchange was able to bolster its position with the securities market through legislative and regulatory controls on potential competitors. Though it was by no means a monopoly the London Stock Exchange now possessed greater control over the British securities market than it had ever had in the past, and it derived this power less from competitive power of its members, and more from the evolving relationship it had with the Bank of England, the Treasury and, finally, the government itself.

One consequence of the position that the Stock Exchange now found itself in was the growing pressure on it to accept greater responsibility for the actions of those it admitted as members. There were growing demands from the public that the Stock Exchange should guarantee that its members would be financially sound and operate to the highest standards. Where this was not the case the public could expect to be compensated. Traditionally the Stock Exchange's primary role was to enforce market discipline between members, involving payment and delivery, so creating a climate of trust that was conducive to business. Those members who broke specific rules could be punished in a variety of ways, with expulsion being the ultimate

---

[19] LSE: Council, 3 May 1948, 28 Feb. 1949; LSE: Committee on Quotations, Charges for Quotation, 17 Mar. 1949, 21 Nov. 1949.

penalty. A member who defaulted on a deal would, inevitably, be expelled, indicating the severity of that crime in a market where trust was all-important. A member whose general conduct gave cause for concern would not be censured or expelled but could fail to gain re-election, which took place annually. Such a decision was not taken easily, however. One such case was that of Ernest Strangeman, whose re-election in March 1946 raised numerous objections. One such was from E. Cunningham, on the grounds that

He is continually collecting cigarette-ends from the tins at the inside doors of the House, rummaging the waste-paper baskets for newspapers or anything he may desire, picking up cigarette-ends at two local railway stations . . . he is dirty, his clothes disgusting and he smells horribly.[20]

Hardly the image of the respectable stockbroker but it was not until the March of 1947 that his membership was not renewed.

The problem the Stock Exchange faced was that its jurisdiction covered the dealings between members, and so the Strangeman case was a legitimate one, but did not cover the relationship between member and non-member, as long as it did not contravene the rules and regulations laid down. This they were all aware of, recognizing in March 1947 that

The disciplinary rules of the Stock Exchange are few and simple, they do no more than clothe the Council with authority to inflict penalties of expulsion, suspension or censure, on their members in certain more or less clearly defined circumstances. They give no indication as to how allegations of the existence of such circumstances are to be brought to the notice of the Council, or how when so brought, the Council is to satisfy itself that such allegations are or are not well founded. No attempt has ever been made to assimilate the proceedings in these cases to those of a legal tribunal.[21]

Nevertheless, the expectation continued to grow that clients of stockbrokers could seek redress from the Stock Exchange itself for any fraud or incompetence they experienced. At the very least investors could expect the Stock Exchange to punish such members while there was also the hope of compensation.

In the late 1940s individual investors increasingly complained to the Stock Exchange about losses suffered at the hands of dishonest stockbrokers. One such in 1947 was George King, a film producer, who dealt through K. H. S Fox. Fox was a half-commission man with the broking firm of Roy Marshall & Co. He had known King for a number of years and obtained £500 from him to invest. Fox then speculated with this money and lost it all. When this was uncovered he resigned from the Stock Exchange.[22] A more serious case was brought to the Stock Exchange's

---

[20] LSE: Council, 4 Mar. 1946, cf. 24 Mar. 1947.
[21] Ibid., 10 Mar. 1947.    [22] Ibid., 3 Nov. 1947.

attention in 1948 by Geoffrey Taylor, an investor from Leatherhead in Surrey. Taylor possessed an extensive portfolio of South African gold-mining shares and UK industrials, and dealt by telephone through the broking firm of Bernard A. Cahill & Co. Cahill's, however, sold securities they were holding on Taylor's behalf, and used the money for speculation on their own account. Unfortunately these turned out disastrously and so they could not replace the securities when Taylor requested them. It turned out that a number of other clients had money and securities used in this way, with the missing amount totalling £16,000. However, the two partners—Bernard Cahill and L. C. E Bellingham—had placed only £1,000 each in the firm, and a mere £500 in assets could be realized to repay clients. In the end the clients agreed to accept £12,000 in compensation, which was provided from the private assets of the partners and their sureties. In the light of this case the Stock Exchange ordered an inquiry into the costs and feasibility of a compensation fund.[23]

Even before the Second World War moves in that direction were made, though nothing had come of it. However, in the aftermath of the Second World War the pressure became irresistible. By then the Stock Exchange was so closely identified with its membership, in the eyes of the public, that any wrongdoing by the brokers undermined the authority of the institution. There was also the possibility that if the Stock Exchange failed to act itself, it would not be long before the government did.[24] Action along these lines was further encouraged in January 1949 when another investor, H. E. Simpkins, complained. He had lost money when his broker defaulted and regarded the Stock Exchange as responsible because it had failed to ensure the financial health of its members. He also accused the Stock Exchange of having no mechanism in place to compensate clients like himself when they were let down by their brokers.[25] If the Stock Exchange did establish a compensation fund, and monitor the financial standing of members, it would have the double effect of reducing criticism and differentiating their members from non-members. Consequently, a compensation fund was seen to have increasing attractions. The Stock Exchange also calculated that the cost of compensation would not be high, if spread among the membership as a whole. It was calculated that over the year 1923–39 the Stock Exchange would have had to have pay out a total of £104,037 as compensation, or only £6,119 per annum. Thus the problem was not a serious one though individual cases generated a great deal of public interest. A levy of 2 guineas per member, including both brokers and jobbers, would generate an income

[23] LSE: Council, 5 Oct. 1948, 25 Oct. 1948, 8 Nov. 1948.
[24] LSE: Interim Report of the Committee Appointed to Consider the Need for Establishing a Guarantee Fund, 19 May 1949.
[25] LSE: Council, 3 Jan. 1949.

of c.£8,600 per annum and so more than cover the average level of compensation. In the light of these estimates, and the need to be seen to be taking action, the Stock Exchange set up a Guarantee Fund on 25 March 1950.[26]

The existence of this collective guarantee of the financial probity of its members meant, inevitably, that greater care had to be exercised over those who were admitted to the Stock Exchange. Members had not only to be able to trust each other as they bought and sold securities but they were now responsible for their actions outside the Stock Exchange, if this involved any fraudulent or negligent behaviour regarding clients. Consequently, in addition to greater scrutiny of prospective entrants, increased sureties were demanded from new members. Three sureties of £500 each were now required though this was reduced to two of £300 each for those with four years experience as a clerk. As these sureties could only be provided by other members of the Stock Exchange, there was an increasing tendency to favour as new members those who were known and trusted such as relatives, friends, business associates, and clerks of long standing. Though compensating the clients of brokers for losses, that were not of their own making, was a laudable action, it did encourage the Stock Exchange to be more wary of admitting to membership those whose actions might have financial implications for all.[27]

As it was there was a hardly a large demand for Stock Exchange membership in the late 1940s, apart from those already in the business, such as clerks, or connected through family and friends. By 1950 a nomination could be brought for as little as £5. Some existing members left to pursue other careers. Jonathan Backhouse left the stockbroking firm of Read, Hurst, Bran & Co. in 1950 to join the merchant bankers, Schroders. Those members who did remain sought ways to reduce costs and increase income, in order to stay in business.[28] Some of course did not survive. One firm that failed in the late 1940s were the brokers, Egerton, Jones & Simpson. They gave as the reason for their demise, '. . . declining business over the last four to five years with no corresponding cut in office expenses. Certain bad debts had precipitated the failure.'[29] Those firms that did survive could only do so by reducing their expenses and seeking new sources of revenue. The switch away from salaried employers to using fellow members as

[26] Ibid., 2 Aug. 1948, 27 Feb. 1959, 2 Mar. 1950, 6 Mar. 1950; LSE: Compensation Fund Committee, Report and Recommendation, 27 Feb. 1950.

[27] LSE: Council, 23 May 1949.

[28] A. Gleeson, People and Their Money: 50 Years of Private Investment (M & G Group), 52; The Stock Exchange Clerks' Provident Fund Centenary 1874–1947 (London 1974), 22; R. Roberts, Schroders: Merchants & Bankers (London 1992), 317; R. Coopey and D. Clarke, 3i: Fifty Years of Investing in Industry (Oxford 1995), 30.

[29] LSE: Subcommittee on Readmission of Defaulters, 6 July 1950, cf. 13 July 1950, 9 Nov. 1950.

half-commission men was but one way to reduce the burden of fixed out-goings when income was in decline. (Table 8.1.)

A more radical solution would have been amalgamation among the members to create larger firms of brokers and jobbers. Larger firms could economize on such areas of expenditure as accommodation, membership fees, back-office staff, messengers, and equipment. It was a policy advo-cated by one firm of brokers, S. C. Maguire & Co., in 1947. 'Both on the Stock Exchange and elsewhere there has of late years been a steady ten-dency towards larger units of industry . . .'[30] However, the Stock Exchange continued to restrict the number of partners each firm could have and the number of authorized and unauthorized clerks that each member could employ on the trading floor. As a result brokerage firms like Cazenoves and Mullens expanded little in size during the late 1940s, with the number of partners remaining constant.[31] To a firm like S. C. Maguire & Co. this was considered unfortunate: '. . . we feel it is perhaps a disadvantage to the Stock Exchange that the growth amongst outside Financial Houses should proceed faster than our own.'[32] The Stock Exchange was preventing the cre-ation of large and well-capitalized member firms that would be the rival of non-members such as the investment banks. Consolidation was taking place but it was happening slowly. In 1945 the membership of the Stock Exchange was divided into 656 firms, (5.4 per firm) whereas by 1950 there were still 551 firms (7.4 per firm). Among those were a few large ones, like Cazen-oves with 18 partners in 1950, but many consisted of one or two partners, few staff, and little capital. However, each member had a vote and thus the smaller firms could block any attempts by the larger to remove obstacles to their growth.[33] A number of firms did become corporate members at this time, such as Cazenoves in 1946 and Mullens in 1949, but this was for tax reasons. The company and the partnership had to be identical and all had to be members of the Stock Exchange, precluding outside investors from participating. A company could build up reserves out of income, without that income being taxed, whereas a partnership could not.[34]

Similarly, the Stock Exchange continued to forbid members from estab-lishing operations outside London, even though this was requested in 1948 for tax purposes. If shares were registered as owned in the UK tax had to be paid on the dividends. The brokers Vickers da Costa wanted to set up a company in South Africa which would act as the nominal owner

[30] LSE: Council, 3 Mar. 1947.

[31] A. Martin, *Cazenove & Company, 1785–1955* (London 1955), 12; D. Wainwright, *Gov-ernment Broker: The Story of an Office and of Mullens and Company* (East Molesey 1990), 138.                                                                      [32] LSE: Council, 3 Mar. 1947.

[33] J. H. Dunning and E. V. Morgan, *An Economic Study of the City of London* (London 1971), 300.

[34] Martin, *Cazenoves*, 10–11; D. Kynaston, *Cazenove & Co.: A History* (London 1991), 170; Wainwright, *Mullens*, 77; LSE: Council, 21 Jan. 1946, 11 Oct. 1948.

of the shares that it traded between London and Johannesburg. Thus the domicile of the shares would remain outside the UK and so tax would be avoided. However, the Stock Exchange would not permit such a move, making it difficult for their members to compete against the banks and other finance houses that did operate in different countries. Again, the rules of the Stock Exchange were preventing the evolution of large firms that could both economize on costs and generate additional business against outside competition.

A number of member firms did develop additional lines of business, to compensate for the declining volume of sales and purchases on the Stock Exchange. The larger firms with a tradition of involvement in new issues sought to expand that activity, as did Cazenoves and Panmure Gordon. Others, like James Capel, sought to provide stockbroking services for the institutional investor, which was also the direction followed by Phillips & Drew and by Mullens. The problem was that in both new issues and financial services generally, there was growing competition. Merchant banks, for example, recognizing that the foreign loans business was now dead, switched to handling issues for British industrial and commercial companies. There were also a number of relative newcomers who saw opportunities in handling domestic new issues and giving investment advice, such as Sir Siegmund Warburg, Harley Drayton, and Kit Dawnay. Consequently, there was only limited scope for brokers and jobbers, outside their traditional areas of activity. The delay in restoring contangos and options greatly restricted money-broking while exchange controls and the disposal of overseas securities greatly reduced arbitrage. As a result many brokers were driven to rely heavily on the commission income generated by the activities of individual and institutional clients, which then flowed through to activity on the trading-floor from which jobbers could earn an income.[35] A broker such as Heseltine, Powell & Co., who had once conducted extensive arbitrage and money-broking operations now '. . . relied very largely on its ordinary commission business to provide its revenue, the American and Contango Operations having almost ceased'.[36] The result was, inevitably, to focus attention on the scale of commission charges, once the post-war boom died away. However, altering or increasing the level of commission charged was not an easy matter. There was general agreement that the least remunerative business were sales and purchases for small investors, but

[35] Kynaston, *Cazenove*, 186, 192, 198, 200; M. C. Reed, *A History of James Capel and Company* (London 1975), 92; Wainwright, *Mullens*, 91; J. Atttali, *A Man of Influence: Sir Siegmund Warburg, 1902–1982* (London 1986), 184–5; S. D. Chapman, *Raphael Bicentenary, 1787–1987* (London 1987), 44; B. H. D. MacDermot, *Panmure Gordon & Company, 1876–1976: A Century of Stockbroking* (London 1976), 59–60; W. J. Reader and D. Kynaston, *Professional Stockbrokers: A History of Phillips & Drew* (London 1998), 34.
[36] P. G. Warren, *Heseltine, Powell and Company: One Hundred Years of Stockbroking, 1851–1951* (London 1951), 28.

it was felt to be impossible to increase charges here without risking a public outcry and government controls. Instead, attention focused once again on the question of the discounts available to particular clients. This issue was raised as early as September 1947.[37] R. J. Lumsden, the Chairman of the Stock Exchange, probably echoed in June 1947 a growing view of many members that they had the power to impose their charges upon the investing public.

In reviewing the whole question of the proper division of commission between the Stock Exchange and its agents it must be remembered that it is not merely a question of assessing the respective amounts of work done, or the value of the introduction, or of the bearing of credit risks. The most important factor to be considered and one which is frequently overlooked is that the Stock Exchange alone provides not only the professional skill and in the main the statistical and advisory services upon which so much business depends nowadays, but in addition, exclusively, provides the central and indispensable factor in every transaction, namely, the jobbing market, without which, and without reference to which, no transaction in quoted securities can take place either inside or outside the exchange.

This made the question one of using rebates to target very specific clients who might not otherwise use the Stock Exchange.
    As Lumsden continued,

... there is case for making rebates of commission upon business which would in any case have to come to the Stock Exchange ... rebates should only be made to agents who, in the main, create business that would not otherwise be done.[38]

The result of these moves was a doubling in August 1947 of the level (from £2,500 to £5,000) above which some discretion on charges could be exercised and restrictions on the number registered as eligible for discounts. Behind all this was a continuing attack on any rebates for solicitors and accountants, who were felt to be sharing a commission which should all go to the stockbroker. However, many small broking firms had long-established links with particular solicitors and accountants, which produced a steady stream of business as investors financial affairs changed from year to year. These small brokers were worried that, without the rebate, the banks would capture most of this business, and then channel it through a small number of large brokers.[39] One broking firm, McAnally, Inglis & Littlejohn, complained in December 1947 that restricting the rebate to banks alone would cause '... a loss of 20 per cent of its business, and a

[37] LSE: General Purposes, 27 Aug. 1945, 9 Sept. 1946, 10 Feb. 1947.
[38] LSE: Council, 30 June 1947.
[39] Ibid., 18 Aug. 1947, 29 Sept. 1947, 1 Dec. 1947, 22 Dec. 1947.

breach of associations built up over many years.'[40] Nevertheless, faced with a continuing decline in the volume of business the Stock Exchange decided that only banks and provincial brokers would be eligible for discounts. At a stroke this would remove almost 5,000 clients of stockbrokers who had, traditionally, been given a share of the commission that their business generated. Prominent amongst these were 3,141 solicitors and 700 accountants located throughout the British Isles. These new restrictions were to come into force on 1 January 1949.[41] In many ways this was a risky strategy for the London Stock Exchange. Without a branch network its brokers lacked direct contact with those numerous investors who did not live in London and the vicinity. For individual investors it was still believed in 1948 that those desiring to use a London broker should obtain an introduction '. . . through personal sources such as an introduction by a friend'.[42] The car did extend the reach of the London broker with one, John Williams, regularly using it to visit those of his clients '. . . who, for various reasons, have been unable to come to my office to discuss business matters',[43] though this was being hampered by petrol rationing in 1949. Those brokers whose business involved direct contact with individual investors resident in the London area, either permanently or temporarily, pressed for an end to the sharing of commission of any kind, as this allowed other agents, such as solicitors, accountants, and banks to compete with them on price.

Such brokers appeared to be numerous among the membership, generating for themselves a reasonable income from serving the wealthy individuals who still resided in the London area. They were backed by the small jobbers who relied on numerous small buy and sell orders to make a profit and balance their positions. Conversely, there also existed among the membership many brokers whose business relied heavily on agents such as solicitors and accountants, resident in both London and the country at large. Without the right to share commissions these brokers would lack the ability to reward those who gave them their custom. The business from one large firm of solicitors, Ellis Peirs & Co., generated £6,927 in gross commission in 1947, for example, and this had grown substantially over the years. As that firm of solicitors explained

We have some 700 Trusts ranging from £100,000 a year income and millions of capital down to those of smaller trusts where the question of income and capital are of vital importance to the beneficiaries . . . In a large number of cases the clients rely on and follow our advice as to changes in investments and in many cases where one or other of the partners in this firm are Trustees or Attorneys we carry out changes of investments without reference to anyone else.[44]

[40] Ibid., 29 Dec. 1947.    [41] Ibid., 21 Apr. 1947, 16 Feb. 1948.
[42] Ibid., 1 Nov. 1948.    [43] Ibid., 15 Aug. 1949.    [44] Ibid., 21 June 1948.

If they had to charge their clients full commission when securities were bought and sold, and then add an excess for their services, they would lose the trust business to banks who could obtain an income via the rebate they were still to be allowed. Thus those brokers doing a large business for solicitors could expect to lose it to those acting for the banks.

The same was also true for those brokers acting for assorted finance houses, for they were also to be excluded. One such firm were the accountants, Everett, Chettle & Co., who both advised individual clients and managed three investment trusts. In 1947 they had paid £7,450 in gross commission to members of the London Stock Exchange. As they explained,

We have for some twenty years made a practice of advising clients in regard to their investments and in recent years our investment connection has increased so that it now extends to cover individuals and companies for whom we do not act as accountants. In the case of many of our larger accounts we have complete discretion as to the purchase or sale or switching of investments and in practice the client in these cases is only advised after the transactions have been carried out.[45]

Again, their expectation was that, if they had to levy an extra charge on their clients for the sale and purchase of securities they would lose the business to the banks, and thus to those brokers favoured by the banks. Both the solicitors and the accountants also pointed out that they were not simply competing with brokers, and thus gaining a share of the commission without doing anything for it. It was not only that they had the direct contacts with specific investors but also that they were providing a valuable legal and/or investment service that was necessary in a financial world made increasingly complex by taxation, exchange controls, and other legal requirements. Ellis Peirs & Co. claimed their Trust Department cost them £2,500 a year to run while Everett, Chettle & Co. indicated that

At present one of our partners devotes considerable time in and out of the office to reading and research on financial and economic matters likely to effect stock exchange values, apart from studying Company reports and statistics in the usual way.[46]

Solicitors and accountants did not feel that they were simply passing on the business of their clients to stockbrokers and getting a share of the commission for no work. Instead they pointed out that many of the sales and purchases were the product of their own advice and research, and so they were entitled to a share of the commission they produced. So annoyed were they that in June 1948 W. Mackenzie Smith, President of the Law Society, threatened the Stock Exchange that if their members were excluded from sharing commission they would channel all their business through the banks so that brokers would receive no benefit from the move.[47]

However, the Stock Exchange was impervious to these threats and pressed on with its intention to remove rebates from all but the banks. The

[45] LES: Council, 12 Apr. 1948.    [46] Ibid., 21 June 1948.    [47] Ibid., 7 June 1948.

protests of 26 of the major stockbroking firms, like W. Greenwell & Co., Govett, Sons & Co., and Kitcat & Aitken, were also ignored. They had used the ability to share commission as a way of reducing the charges made to important clients like London finance houses and investment companies. As a result they could remain competitive against non-members, such as New York brokerage firms or European banks. However, if the right to rebate was removed they would have to charge the full commission, which could be detrimental to their business. Eventually, in 1948, 1,667 members (42 per cent of the total) signed a petition, protesting against the proposed rules on rebates. This was organized by Christopher Arnold-Forster of Laurence, Keen & Gardner. However, it was ignored.[48] It was not until the major British banks—commercial and merchant—themselves joined in the protest against the ending of rebates that the Stock Exchange began to reconsider its policy. The banks started to oppose the change when they realized that, though they themselves would retain the privilege of a rebate, their trustee departments would not, and that was where much of their stock exchange business was generated. American and foreign banks in London were already annoyed because they were to receive only a rebate of a quarter while the British banks were to get one-third returned.[49]

The matter reached a head in November 1948 when the clearing banks made it clear to the Stock Exchange that if their trustee departments were excluded from receiving a rebate then they would increase the charges they made to stockbrokers for banking services. This then led the Governor of the Bank of England to intervene, calling a meeting of the banks and the Stock Exchange. The outcome of this meeting was that the Stock Exchange postponed the introduction of the new rebate scheme until 1 April 1949; and the banks agreed to defer the new bank charges until that date. Once the Stock Exchange not only started to lose the support of the clearing banks in its proposed revision of its rebate scheme, but faced their outright opposition, it became very difficult to proceed with the scheme. The main source of Stock Exchange business were the major British banks followed by overseas banks in London and British merchant banks, and this was reflected in the fact that these would retain the right to a rebate.[50] As the brokers J. & A. Scrimgeour put it,

... the sole justification for returning one-third commission rather than one-quarter commission to the Banks, was that the members of the British Bankers Association form a geographically widespread and financially comprehensive service to hundreds of small clients throughout the country. This is of inestimable assistance to members of the Stock Exchange, who even if they were prepared to undertake this work, would not under present conditions have the facilities to do so.[51]

[48] Ibid., 3 May 1948, 10 May 1948, 5 July 1948.
[49] Ibid., 7 June 1948, 30 Aug. 1948, 27 Sept. 1948, 25 Nov. 1948.
[50] Ibid., 1 Nov. 1948, 8 Nov. 1948, 15 Nov. 1948, 25 Nov. 1948, 13 Dec. 1948.
[51] Ibid., 27 Sept. 1948.

Eventually, after a ballot of members, the Stock Exchange dropped the whole idea of revising the rebate scheme in January 1949. Solicitors, accountants, and others continued to receive the privileges of a rebate. Their numbers were also as large as ever in 1949 so any attempt to curb the rebate scheme in that way had also failed. Faced with the opposition of virtually the whole City of London the Stock Exchange was unable to force through any revision of its charges which forced those who used its services to pay more. It could resist the pressure from casual users like solicitors and accountants, but not the power of the banks. Collectively, the banks generated a vast volume of sales and purchases, and they could enlist the support of the Bank of England and threaten serious retaliation. In the end they forced the Stock Exchange to abandon the change before it was ever introduced. Of course, the problem did not go away for brokers continued to face, in the late 1940s, a situation of falling business and rising costs, which had to be tackled in some way.[52] The brokers Penn & Crosthwaite probably voiced the views of many when they complained in September 1949 that

Stockbrokers are working on a 1911 scale of commissions and with 1949 expenses. Fortunately, they have been enabled to do this over the last 38 years by a steady increase in investors of the medium-class, and also the increase in the number of securities dealt in. This position has now changed in that the funds of the medium-sized investor are becoming less, and nationalisation is taking out of the list of securities a large number of those which where the favourites of investment brokers.[53]

By the end of the 1940s it was not only the Stock Exchange that faced a crisis, caught between rising costs and stagnant or falling revenue, for most of its membership were in the same predicament. Unfortunately, any of the options open to them to solve these problems were found impossible to implement. As a member-owned institution the Stock Exchange was driven to provide improved services, and so could not reduce its expenses, while it was unable to charge more for membership. Members were unable to reduce their own costs as the rules made the creation of large firms impossible, especially any attempt to create wide-ranging organizations including both broking and jobbing, let alone investment banking. Politically, any increase in commission rates for the small investor was impossible while large users of the Stock Exchange, like the banks, had the power to prevent any rise in their charges, either directly or through limitations on discounting. Though the immediate post-war years had seen a recovery in the fortunes of the Stock Exchange and its members, that proved to be only temporary, for the late 1940s witnessed a serious collapse in business. With growing competition from non-members, whether merchant banks or country

<hr>

[52] LSE: Council, 24 Jan. 1949, 5 Sept. 1949.  [53] Ibid., 12 Sept. 1949.

jobbers, the Stock Exchange and its members faced a bleak future as they approached 1950.

Towards the end of the Second World War both the London and provincial stock exchanges had been working towards a possible merger. This would have created one organization controlling the entire British securities market, and presenting a united front to the government and other financial institutions. The stumbling block to achieving this end continued to be the London Stock Exchange's unwillingness to concede direct access to London jobbers for provincial brokers. What London proposed was that jobbers could only deal directly with members of their own stock exchange, and so provide a market in local securities. Such a move would eliminate the competition London experienced from country jobbers. Country jobbers could only survive on the collective business of provincial stockbrokers, which was made possible by the telephone. London would not provide non-London brokers with a substitute to country jobbing in the form of the ability to deal directly with a London jobber.[54] As J. J. Ross, an Edinburgh broker, put it in July 1946, 'If he dealt in London he paid half commission and the jobbers turn, and if in the country it was done free of commission and only the jobbers turn was paid.'[55]

London was also unwilling to fully liberalize the use of telephone and teleprinter links between London and the provinces as this might also encourage competition from non-members, based on a immediate access to current London prices. In the end the whole scheme, for affiliation with the provincial stock exchanges, was dropped in October 1946. The more concessions that London was forced to make regarding direct access to its market, the more opposition built up in London from among the membership to any kind of arrangement. There were, simply, too many brokers in London who felt that exclusive access to London jobbers was vital in maintaining the business they did and the charge they could make for it. In this they were supported by numerous individual jobbers who serviced them and did not want increased competition from large jobbing firms, in London or outside, or to have their margins squeezed through the power of large broking firms. Too many members saw the status quo as providing some security at a time when the whole future of the Stock Exchange, and the services its members provided, was in doubt.[56]

[54] W. A. Thomas, *The Provincial Stock Exchanges* (London 1973), 245–6, 316; W. A. Thomas, *The Stock Exchange of Ireland* (Liverpool 1986), 227; Reed, *Capel and Company*, 90–2; Chapman, *Raphael Bicentenary*, 44; Kynaston, *Cazenove*, 191–5; Wainwright, *Mullens*, 82, 91; W. J. Reader, *A House in the City: A Study of the City and of the Stock Exchange Based on the Records of Foster & Braithwaite, 1825–1975* (London 1979), 177; Proposals for the Affiliation of the Country Exchanges to the London Stock Exchange, 16 May 1946; Joint Advisory Committee on Stock Exchanges, 7 Dec. 1945, 17 June 1946; LSE: Council, 11 June 1946, 22 July 1946.

[55] Joint Advisory Committee on Stock Exchanges, 26 July 1946.

[56] LSE: Council, 14 Oct. 1946.

Nevertheless, the London Stock Exchange was powerless to prevent the growing links between London and the provinces that the telephone and teleprinter links provided. It was in the interests of the larger London brokers, such as Cazenoves and Capel-Cure, to have such links because it generated much business for them, and so they met most of the charges involved. Thus, as soon as they were able, brokers such as these invested in direct teleprinter lines to the offices of brokers in such provincial centres as Liverpool and Birmingham.[57] Without the instantaneous contact these lines gave it would be difficult for London brokers, and thus the London market, to provide the nation-wide service that was increasingly required. Nationalization had removed many of the local specialities that had sustained activity on the provincial stock exchanges, as with railways, coal and steel, gas and electricity, while institutional and other investors sought substitutes among the securities of domestic commercial and industrial companies for those overseas stocks and bonds lost during and after the war. Thus, more than ever, the London broker was in an ideal position to provide the central element within an integrated national securities market, despatching and receiving orders from provincial contacts as well as tapping into the market provided by London jobbers. At any one time the London securities market could offer a greater variety of securities than any other British market while the volume of daily transactions made it easier to buy and sell there than anywhere else. Nevertheless, the failure to integrate the provincial brokers into this market allowed country jobbers to survive by providing a market in a restricted range of securities, especially industrials, popular among investors outside London, though also attractive to those in London.[58]

Consequently, though fundamental forces in terms of communications, investor preference, and nationalization favoured the London Stock Exchange in the late 1940s, a refusal to widen the scope of the institution by incorporating the non-London brokers, prevented it from taking full advantage of these forces. As a result London was forced to share the domestic securities market with its domestic counterparts. Internationally, the problem lay mainly in the realm of the wholesale disposal of foreign securities and the continuance of exchange controls. Even after the war had ended British investors continued to sell foreign securities. Investors, both individual and institutional, in such countries as Canada, Australia, New Zealand, and South Africa, had grown relatively wealthier than their British equivalents during the Second World War and, increasingly, directed their savings into acquiring domestic assets once monopolized by the British. The Mount Lyell mining and railway company, for example, was an Australian concern which, in 1910 was 77.7 per cent owned by British investors. By

[57] LSE: Council, 28 Jan. 1946, 11 Feb. 1946, 18 Feb. 1946.
[58] Thomas, *Provincial Stock Exchanges*, 245–6, 316; Thomas, *Stock Exchanges of Ireland*, 196, 246.

1920 the proportion British-held had fallen slightly to 72.5 per cent but then began a dramatic increase in Australian purchasing, which pushed the British share down to 34.4 per cent in 1930 and 22.7 per cent in 1940, reaching 14.7 per cent in 1950.

Even where there were not domestic investors ready to purchase British holdings, as in much of Asia, Africa, and Latin America, American investors were often ready to acquire such securities, especially where they were in resource-based companies such as South African gold-mining and Malayan rubber plantations, or Latin American utilities. Nationalization was also common abroad with the Argentine government buying its own railway network in 1948 for £150m. (nominal value £248m.). The sale of these foreign securities was also not being matched by the purchase of others, as foreign exchange controls made it impossible for investors to reinvest abroad, as in Western Europe where there were growing opportunities in the post-war years. The overseas holdings of British investors fell by an estimated £1.2bn. over the 1938–46 period, and then by a further £0.4bn. by 1948.[59]

Clearly, the disposal of foreign holdings, and exchange controls, led to a major fall in the overseas securities held by British investors. However, much of the Stock Exchange's trading in foreign securities was not on behalf of British investors, but foreign investors, who used London because of the market it provided and the skills of the brokers and jobbers involved. In the aftermath of wartime restrictions the Stock Exchange tried to rebuild this business, formalizing links with overseas exchanges. International business generally, and arbitrage in particular, did pick up. In March 1947, for example, there were 39 member firms conducting arbitrage with 90 correspondents abroad and this had risen to 49 firms and 118 correspondents by March 1950. However, exchange controls were a continuing problem for those members conducting an international business for, by its very nature, it involved the need to make payments abroad which, in the short run, could not always be matched by receipts. The government, under the Exchange Control Act of 1947, had tried to make the controls more responsive to the needs of those doing an international business by agreeing that their activities would be supervised by the Stock Exchange's own Share and Loan Department and not directly by the Treasury. The assumption was that the Stock Exchange better understood the needs of the business. Nevertheless, the controls still remained and only jobbers, not brokers, were covered by the Stock Exchange's own system of supervision.[60]

[59] LSE: General Purposes, 8 Oct. 1945, 14 Jan. 1946; LSE: Council, 18 Feb. 1946, 4 Mar. 1946, 26 June 1950; Bank of England, *United Kingdom Overseas Investments, 1938 to 1948* (London 1950), 4–6; W. T. C. King, *The Stock Exchange* (London 1954, 2nd edn.), 50; Roberts, *Schroders*, 312.

[60] LSE: Council, 11 Feb. 1946, 18 Feb. 1946, 4 Mar. 1946, 22 Mar. 1946, 31 Mar. 1947, 11 Aug. 1947, 15 Mar. 1948, 24 Mar. 1950.

Certainly, towards the end of 1948 those members conducting an international business were finding that they were being increasingly bypassed because of the way exchange controls were implemented. These included such major participants as Straus Turnbull & Co. and R. Raphael & Sons. According to them,

Much business between foreign centres has hitherto been transacted through London, because of the particular financial 'know how' existing here, and this has naturally contributed substantially to our invisible exports. With the increasing restrictions in London, more and more of this business is done direct between various foreign centres, the only form of payment made to London being the expression of thanks for explanations and assistance given in conducting the business. It is only too obvious that once these contacts have been fully established the business will, in future, always be conducted through these channels, resulting in a permanent loss to the City.[61]

In order to prevent any drain of foreign currency the government insisted that the proceeds of any disposal of foreign securities be reinvested in gilt-edged securities. This was not what many foreign holders of such securities wanted and, unlike British investors, they could avoid it happening to them by directing their transactions away from London. It was reported that European holders of sterling securities were selling them in New York, as they could invest the dollars so obtained in any securities they wanted. Thus not only did this result in a loss of business to members of the Stock Exchange, estimated at 4 per cent of the value of each transaction, but it also created pressure on the foreign exchange reserves as interest on these securities had now to be paid out in dollars not European currencies. However, the Treasury was unwilling to relent because of the existing pressure on sterling.

The London Stock Exchange itself became increasingly restrictive on what international business it permitted its members to transact. As in the case of provincial brokers and jobbers there was an increasing suspicion that these members dealing with foreign banks and brokerage houses were responsible for a seepage of business away from the Stock Exchange, as investors sought to avoid the fixed commission charges. The result, in May 1948, was to tighten up further the rules on jobbers dealing with non-members and brokers making prices. Both activities were outlawed for domestic business but had been permitted, under certain conditions, for international transactions, as it was recognized that it was necessary if bargains were to be matched.[62]

The case of the 'mock' dollar also indicates an unwillingness by the Stock Exchange to modify its practices in order to accommodate the changing requirements of the international business in securities. Conventionally US

---

[61] LSE: Council, 9 Aug. 1948.    [62] Ibid., 18 May 1948, 30 May 1949.

and Canadian Securities were quoted in dollars at an exchange rate of 5 dollars to the pound. This had always required conversion so as to obtain the precise equivalent at prevailing exchange rates, but was now even more complex because of the premium on the dollar/pound exchange rate. J. L. Thorman, of Myers & Co., requested the Stock Exchange to consider quoting all North American securities in sterling so as to make their prices clear to investors, and he supported his case by showing the complexity of the current situation.

At present we get, for example, US Steel quoted in New York at $22 5/8; to find the price in London we multiply by 5/4.025 × 135/100 and then, to find the cost of 100 shares, we have to multiply the price by 100 and divide by 5. Most of this could be avoided by dealing directly in sterling prices. Thus for US Steel, if NY price is 22 5/8 and the security Exchange rate is $2.98 to the £ ( = premium of 35%) then the sterling price is simply $22 5/8/2.98 or £7.16.6d per share.
    The public would then know exactly what they were paying for a share, instead of having to go through a complex series of calculations introducing a currency which has no real existence at all.[63]

This suggestion was rejected as a result of opposition from most of those dealing in US securities. The very complexity of the transactions gave them an advantage in maintaining control over what little remained of the American market on the London Stock Exchange. A similar request for change in December 1949, from James Capel & Co., was also rejected. By then the devaluation of the pound had brought the premium on the dollar/pound exchange rate down to 14 per cent. General Motors was quoted at $66 in New York but cost £26.87 in London, even though an exchange rate of $2.80 to the pound should have meant a price of £23.57.[64]
    Consequently, though the operation of exchange controls was an important influence on transactions in the global securities market bypassing London, the Stock Exchange's own attitude also contributed. By the late 1940s it was so committed to defending its own practices and charges to prevent any loss of business, that it failed to seize the opportunities that a more liberal attitude could bring. Consequently, it was New York brokerage houses and European banks that increasingly conducted the international business that was being done in London. Financial firms and institutions like these possessed the contacts abroad and so could internalize transactions so that they took place between the clients of their various branches, with London a convenient intermediary position.[65] Transactions in foreign securities between investors world-wide still needed to take place but they did not need to take place in London, let alone the London Stock Exchange.

[63] Ibid., 29 Aug. 1949.     [64] Ibid., 28 Dec. 1949.     [65] Ibid., 30 May 1949.

## DECLINING IMPORTANCE

This inability by the London Stock Exchange to capitalize on its established position in domestic and international securities was symptomatic of a general failure by the Exchange and its membership in the post-war years. The Stock Exchange's response to competition, driven largely by the influence of the smaller brokers and jobbers, was to become ever more restrictive. For example, by 1949 it was clear that the Stock Exchange and its membership was being bypassed by the largest institutional investors who, because of their size, were able to match buying and selling orders internally. Such was their success in this that they attracted the custom of brokers looking to buy and sell on behalf of their clients. Consequently, jobbers lobbied the Council of the Stock Exchange to put more pressure on brokers, forcing them to put their orders through the Stock Exchange and not to outside houses.[66] As a result, the Stock Exchange reminded its membership, in December 1949, that

The provision that business may not be done outside the House unless it has first been offered in the market on the same terms as those on which it is proposed to deal with the non-member, was laid down in 1944 specifically for protection of the market against the diversion outside the House of business capable of being transacted in the market.[67]

It was this tension between brokers and jobbers that also restricted the growth of larger firms. Jobbers were worried that if brokers became larger and larger, they could settle more bargains between clients without using a jobber. Conversely, brokers were worried that, if they had to deal with a few large jobbing firms, the margin between the buy/sell prices they would be offered would grow, encouraging clients, especially institutions, to bypass the Stock Exchange entirely.

As it was, the members of the Stock Exchange continued to face strong competition in the trading of short-dated government debt.[68] Traditionally, many of the transactions on the London Stock Exchange had emanated from the money market, as temporarily available funds were used to buy government debt. Unfortunately for the Stock Exchange the ending of account trading during the war, and then the delayed resumption of continuations and options, removed a number of major trading devices members had used to compete in these money-market transactions. Without these trading devices the jobbers lack of capital, due to the restriction on raising funds outside the partnership, made it difficult for them to compete against the discount houses and merchant banks, who did not suffer from any such prohibition.[69]

---

[66] LSE: Council, 10 Jan. 1949, 2 Aug. 1949.     [67] Ibid., 12 Dec. 1949.
[68] Ibid., 8 Aug. 1949, 31 Oct. 1949; Roberts, *Schroders*, 395.
[69] H. Wincott, *The Stock Exchange* (London 1946), 64, 117, 120–1, 123; F. W. Hirst, *The Stock Exchange: A Short Study of Investment and Speculation* (London 1948), 210; King,

By the late 1940s, such was the decline in turnover on the London Stock Exchange, that it was having increasing trouble competing against the discount houses and merchant banks in the most actively traded areas of the gilt-edged market, where the ability to buy and sell large amounts quickly was the principal requirement for those trading on temporarily available funds. As the Stock Exchange itself recognized in January 1949:

This decline in business has produced a situation of real gravity, not so much because of its effect upon individual firms, unfortunate though this may be, but because of its effect in decreasing the liquidity of markets and narrowing the freedom of dealing on the Stock Exchange.[70]

The Stock Exchange blamed its difficulties on the restrictions it was forced to operate under, especially the failure to reintroduce continuations and options, compounded by the doubling of the transfer stamp duty in August 1947. Certainly, the number of bargains did drop substantially after the introduction of stamp duty, being down from an average of 10,921 (March–July 1947) to 7,648 (August–December 1947).[71]

Whereas a 2 per cent transfer duty was bearable when securities were bought and sold only intermittently, it was a considerable burden on short-dated stock as there was much less time available in which the costs of the tax could be recouped through appreciation in value. Clearly the stamp duty increase did limit the use of securities for money-market purposes, switching attention to Treasury Bills and other short-term instruments not traded on the Stock Exchange. Nevertheless, jobbers continued to retain their 10s. stamp duty concession, which allowed them to buy and sell securities without paying the 2 per cent stamp duty, if the transaction was completed within a short period.[72] More important for the Stock Exchange was its regulations which prevented its members reaching the size and obtaining the capital that money market transactions now demanded, with the restrictions on options and contangos. This created opportunities for non-members, which the discount houses, in particular, were quick to seize. They were already larger and better capitalized than the jobbers and could cope with the effects of heavy personal taxation by converting into companies and seeking outside funding. All the jobbers could do was to try and shelter their income in good years as reserves. Even by 1945, five of all the 11 discount houses were public companies. High taxation and government controls had become established facts in post-war Britain and the discount

*The Stock Exchange*, 77; W. T. C. King, 'The London Discount Market', 24–7, and D. Sachs, 'Survey of the Financial Institutions of the City of London', 86–7, in Institute of Bankers, *Current Financial Problems and the City of London* (London 1949).

[70] LSE: Council, 31 Jan. 1949.
[71] Ibid., 30 June 1947, 13 Oct. 1947, 31 Jan. 1949.
[72] Ibid., 30 June 1947, 15 Dec. 1947; E. Nevin and E. W. Davis, *The London Clearing Banks* (London 1970), 174; W. T. C. King, 'The Markets Changing Role', in the Institute of Bankers, *The London Discount Market Today* (London 1962), 9.

houses were better able to adjust their structure to the consequences than the members of the Stock Exchange, bound as they were by rules that both limited the number of partners and prohibited the raising of outside capital.[73]

The same difficulties also beset the members of the Stock Exchange in their operations in the capital market. Realizing that the days had gone when they could prosper by handling only large issues for governments, railways, and major companies at home and abroad, the London merchant banks turned their attention, increasingly, to what was left. This was in the field of issues of securities for often medium-sized domestic companies operating in the field of industry and commerce. Though a few merchant banks and others had taken up this business in the inter-war years, including ex-stockbrokers like Helbert Wagg; much of this was undertaken by members of the London Stock Exchange. Firms like Cazenoves had made something of a speciality of such new issues in the 1930s, and continued to be involved in the 1940s. However, with the growing involvement of the larger and better capitalized merchant banks, stockbroking firms found it increasingly difficult to compete.[74] As the brokers Fielding, Son & Macleod explained in November 1946,

... no Stock Exchange firm ever has been, is now, or ever will be, equipped with the same detailed and experienced research organisation as that maintained by the reputable Issuing Houses.[75]

With the Companies Act of 1948 the handling of new issues was made more complex, which benefited the merchant banks as they were already of a size that allowed them to employ the skilled and experienced staff required. In 1950, for example, the merchant bank Morgan Grenfell employed 105 people, had a paid-up capital of £1.5m., and generated profits of £0.5m. per annum. As with the discount houses the merchant banks increasingly converted into companies, giving them access to outside capital.[76] The result was a changing relationship between brokers and merchant banks. Those members that wanted to continue developing a business as a new issue house for British companies left the Stock Exchange.

[73] W. M. Scammell, The London Discount Market (London 1968), 42, 222, 227; G. A. Fletcher, The Discount Houses in London: Principles, Operations and Change (London 1976), 52, 59, 61, 64; H. C. Cowen, 'The London Stock Exchange and Investment', in Institute of Bankers, Current Financial Problems, 34–5, 245–6, 253, 256.

[74] Kynaston, Cazenove, 186, 192; W. A. Thomas, The Finance of British Industry, 1918-1976 (London 1978), 177–8; Attali, Sir Siegmund Warburg, 184–5, 192; W. L. Fraser, All to the Good (London 1963), 230; J. McCartney-Fulgate, 'Merchant and Other Banking Houses', in Institute of Bankers, The City of London as a Centre of International Trade and Finance (London 1961), 95.

[75] LSE: Council, 11 Nov. 1946.

[76] Kynaston, Cazenove, 195; K. Burk, Morgan Grenfell, 1838–1988: The Biography of a Merchant Bank (Oxford 1989), 272, 283; Roberts, Schroders, 319.

Henry Ansbacher & Co., for instance, had built up a strong following in industrial securities, both as an issuer and as a broker, but ceased to be members of the Stock Exchange by August 1949. They had found it easier to operate outside, freed from the limitations imposed by the Stock Exchange.[77] Even the Industrial and Commercial Finance Corporation (ICFC), set up in 1945 under government pressure, appointed an ex-stockbroker William Piercy as its head because of his experience in handling new issues. Its role was to bypass the new issue market and provide direct financial support for medium-sized companies.[78] Those stockbrokers who remained members of the Stock Exchange, and retained an involvement with new issues, did so increasingly as agents of the merchant banks, not as independent finance houses. The merchant banks valued stockbrokers because of their ability to distribute new issues directly to their clients or to other investors through fellow brokers and jobbers. The government had felt it necessary to bridge the supposed gap in the funding of medium-sized domestic companies (the MacMillan Gap) with the creation of both the ICFC and the Finance Corporation for Industry (FCI) after the Second World War. However, the replacement of stockbrokers as issuing houses by merchant banks was an illustration of both the ease by which other intermediaries entered the field and the competitive nature of the business they were involved in. The rules of the Stock Exchange prevented stockbroking firms responding to the growing post-war conversion of private companies into public concerns, and their raising of additional capital through new issues, and so their place was taken by others.[79]

Members of the Stock Exchange had the choice of either co-operating or competing with the merchant banks and, as Fielding, Son & Macleod put it in November 1946, competition could have disastrous consequences.

'Institutional investment' seems likely to prove an increasingly progressive factor in the matter of providing fresh money for new issues and it would not be a difficult matter in a number of cases to short-circuit the Stock Exchange entirely.[80]

It was better to retain at least part of the business than refuse to co-operate with the merchant banks and, very probably, lose it all, including not only the initial distribution of securities to clients but subsequent trading.

In one sense it was easier for the Stock Exchange if its own members were not directly involved in new issues, because it was increasingly

[77] LSE: General Purposes, 20 Aug. 1945; LSE: Council, 11 Feb. 1946, 15 Aug. 1949.

[78] Coopey and Clarke, *3i: Fifty Years Investing in Industry*, 30; Thomas, *Finance of British Industry*, 148, 177–8, 278; J. Kinross, *Fifty Years in the City: Financing Small Business* (London 1982), 116–19, 122, 138, 151.

[79] Kynaston, *Cazenove*, 198–9, 200, 204; MacDermot, *Panmure Gordon & Co.*, 58–62.

[80] LSE: Council, 11 Nov. 1946.

expected to police the market. The government itself, through its Capital Issues Committee continued to regulate the flow of new issues onto the market, as it had done during the war. As Wincott noted in 1946

Already the Government has laid down a list of priorities for new capital issues, favouring the export trades, housing, rehabilitation and holiday ventures, for example. All proposals to raise a new capital above a limit of £50,000 in any one year must have official approval, and official approval will not be given at the present time for projects deemed to be a luxury or non-essential character.[81]

Investment trusts were prohibited from raising any new funds until 1953, while Lloyds Bank, was informed in the late 1940s that it would not be permitted to raise any extra capital. Generally, through a high rate of taxation, dividend restraint, and exchange controls, the government was in a position to dictate both the amount and nature of investment taking place in the post-war years. Between 1945 and 1950 the government's own debt rose by £3.8bn., of which 37 per cent was raised externally, whereas corporate new issues grew by only £0.8bn., and 83 per cent of that was for domestic purposes. The investments of institutions, like banks and insurance companies, were dominated in the post-war years by government debt as ever-more corporate securities disappeared through nationalization. Whereas in 1936 UK life assurance companies had 22 per cent of their assets (totalling £1.7bn.) in UK government securities and 34 per cent in corporate securities, by 1948 the assets (totalling £2.7bn.) were now distributed as to 40 per cent UK government and 28 per cent corporate securities.[82]

With this system of government control what the Stock Exchange was left with was the supervision of the quality of the issues being made. Under pressure from the government, and responding to public pressure arising from new issues that appreciated or depreciated quickly after issue, the Stock Exchange did tighten up its requirements for a listing or quotation. As early as February 1946 they had begun a process whereby permission for a 'placing' was more difficult to obtain.[83] Though conscious that it was desirable to keep down the costs of a new issue, and thus make the Stock Exchange attractive to those of small amount, there was also the problem that it was with these small issues, made away from the public gaze and without a prospectus, that the greatest abuses had occurred. Investors either

[81] Wincott, The Stock Exchange, 151; Roberts, Schroders, 325.

[82] J. R. Winton, Lloyds Bank, 1918–1969 (Oxford 1982), 114; Roberts, Schroders, 325; F. W. Paish, Business Finance (London 1961, 2nd edn.); N. Macrae, The London Capital Market: Its Structure, Strains and Management (London 1955), 173, 177; J. Johnston and G. W. Murphy, 'The Growth of Life Assurance in UK since 1880', Manchester School of Economic and Social Studies, 25 (1957), 155; M. Collins, Money and Banking in the UK: A History (London 1988), 327–8; LSE: Council, 16 June 1947; data from B. R. Mitchell, British Historical Statistics (Cambridge 1988).

[83] LSE: Council, 4 Feb. 1946.

felt cheated because they had not been allowed to participate in an issue that went to an immediate premium or because they had been sold securities that fell greatly in value.

There have been a number of placings in the past which have given the Council great concern. This has been particularly applicable during the war when public offers were not permitted. As a result, securities have been introduced to the Stock Exchange under conditions which have created wide dissatisfaction, and which have attracted undeserved criticism of the Stock Exchange.

Such was the reflective view of the Stock Exchange in March 1946. The response was to develop a clear distinction between an 'introduction' and a 'placing'. An 'introduction' was when there was no immediate intention to sell shares to investors, rather a desire to establish a market through which existing shareholders might wish to dispose of part of their holdings in the future. In contrast, a 'placing' had the express purpose of selling new or existing shares to investors through the creation of an active market on the floor of the Stock Exchange. In future this was to become more difficult, taking the form of the issue of a prospectus, for new shares, or an offer for sale, if existing shares.[84] Initially, at least, the Stock Exchange remained fairly liberal in granting quotations to securities once issued, stating in July 1947 that

. . . they did not normally concern themselves with the merits of an issue—with questions of price, capital structure and so forth—but they did require that there should be full and clear disclosure of all material facts.[85]

Where full disclosure was not made, and the fact discovered, quotations could be, and were, refused, as in the case of the Stanhope Steamship Company, for which Cazenoves were brokers. They were even willing to grant quotations to the units of unit trusts, as proper safeguards were now felt to be in existence. South African mining securities, traded in Johannesburg, were also quoted from July 1949 onwards without further scrutiny, because the Johannesburg Stock Exchange was now much stricter in scrutinizing new issues. By the late 1940s the serious decline in turnover was encouraging the London Stock Exchange to pursue any market which had the prospects of reviving business for its members.[86] Nevertheless, the Stock Exchange had to be careful in the securities it permitted to be traded on its floor, for the investing public increasingly regarded it as the regulatory authority to which complaints could be made regarding any misdeed by a company. In 1949, for example, one investor, Brenda Clarke, complained to the Stock Exchange that she had bought shares in a company called Specialloids, after it had made an optimistic forecast and paid an interim dividend, whereas one month later it

[84] Ibid., 25 Mar. 1946.   [85] Ibid., 8 July 1947.
[86] Ibid., 21 July 1947, 9 Feb. 1948, 18 May 1948, 20 Mar. 1949.

had passed the dividend on the preference shares. Though the Stock Exchange took no action on this matter it was increasingly placed in the position of not only regulating the behaviour of its members between themselves, and then between member and client, but also the relationship between the companies whose securities it quoted and the investors who bought and sold them.[87]

However, many of these areas lay outside any jurisdiction that the Stock Exchange possessed. It could police its own members through fines or expulsion. It could police companies through preventing their securities being traded. Both these actions could drive business into outside markets as non- (even ex-) members traded securities that the Stock Exchange did not, or refused to, list or quote. An illustration of the limit of its power was in the growing problem of insider trading. The Stock Exchange took pains to monitor the activities of those members who were permitted to write for newspapers, journals, and agencies like Reuters. H. C. Cowen (of F. C. Simon & Co.) wrote for the *Financial Times* as Lex while E. A. Grant (of Grieveson, Grant & Co.) wrote under the name of Austin Friars for such periodicals as *The Economist, Investors' Chronicle*, and *Banker*. In all there were some 30 members who contributed regularly to the various publications.[88] In the case of non-members, however, they were powerless to act. One such case was that of shares in greyhound-racing tracks. On 16 March 1949 the chairman of the companies owning these was informed by the Home Secretary that the wartime ban on mid-week dog racing was to be relaxed. To anticipate for this happening the companies were given time to prepare, in advance of the announcement. Aware of the fact that the extra business would push up the share price some of the chairmen, particularly W. J. Cearns of South London Greyhound Racecourses and Southend Stadium Ltd., bought shares and then sold them for a profit after the announcement was made. The Stock Exchange investigated the unusual share activity but was powerless to act. In cases such as these it normally lodged a complaint with the chairman of the company involved, so that the employee could be disciplined! As it was the principal losers were jobbers who had agreed to sell shares in expectation of buying them in the market, but were caught by the price rise.[89]

In the late 1940s nationalization at home and abroad removed whole categories of securities from those traded on the London Stock Exchange. British railways simply disappeared as an important and distinct category. Electricity and gas suffered a similar fate as did coal-mining. Similarly many foreign securities were either sold off voluntarily or nationalized,

[87] LSE: Council, 10 Jan. 1949; Hirst, *The Stock Exchange*, 212–13; King, *The Stock Exchange*, 85–7.
[88] LSE: Council, 22 Mar. 1949.     [89] Ibid., 19 Apr. 1949.

like Argentine railways. In their place investors were issued with ever-more government stock, or could reinvest the proceeds among domestic corporate issues. However, controls over issues by British companies and the virtual prohibition on the issue or purchase of foreign securities, restricted the full replacement of these lost securities with similar ones. These made the members of the Stock Exchange ever-more dependent upon trading in UK government debt for their livelihood. In 1950 around half of all quoted securities, whether nominal, or market value, consisted of UK government debt. Much of the foreign securities quoted, whether government or corporate, generated little activity as few were still owned by British investors. The one growth area was domestic corporate stocks whose market value almost doubled between 1945 and 1950. (Tables 8.2 and 8.3.) An estimate for 1949 suggested that turnover on the London Stock Exchange comprised 85 per cent UK government stock compared to 15 per cent in non-government securities. In the early post-war years nation-alization and the sale of foreign assets had generated much business, as investors reinvested the proceeds, for not all wished to retain the government debt they had received. However, by the late 1940s that stimulus to business had largely faded away leaving brokers and jobbers with a much restricted market.[90] At the same time the high rates of personal taxation, combined with dividend and other controls, greatly restricted the funds available to private investors. Instead it was the institutions, such as the banks and insurance companies, that were increasingly important among the investment community.[91]

Consequently, by the end of the 1940s the London Stock Exchange had not only failed to recover much of its pre-war role in the securities market, but the position it did occupy was being undermined either through government controls and intervention or competition from non-members. In its place the London Stock Exchange was establishing a role for itself as the regulatory body for the securities market, supported in this task by the Bank of England and the Treasury. However, in this it occupied a very weak position as the government had little regard for the role it performed, and there was always the possibility that they would be replaced with direct controls. In addition, the declining turnover experienced in the late 1940s was undermining the very survival of the Stock Exchange. As a result of buying out the proprietors in 1947 the Stock Exchange had committed itself to an annual expenditure of £160,000 per annum over and above the yearly running costs. Caught between an inability to reduce expenditure , because of the needs of the members, and increase income, because of the resistance of the members, the Stock Exchange

---

[90] Macrae, *London Capital Market*, 53; Paukert, 'Stock Exchange Transactions in Non-government Securities', 304; LSE: Council, 23 Jan. 1950.

[91] Gleeson, *People and Their Money*, 52, 54; LSE: Council, 12 Sept. 1949.

Table 8.2. London Stock Exchange: Nominal and market values of securities quoted in 1945 and 1950 (£m.)

| Category of security | Nominal value | | | Market value | | |
|---|---|---|---|---|---|---|
| | 1945 | 1950 | Difference | 1945 | 1950 | Difference |
| British government | 11,863.9 | 14,668.1 | + 2,804.2 | 12,168.0 | 13,758.2 | + 1,590.2 |
| UK public bodies | 910.6 | 574.2 | − 336.4 | 942.9 | 534.5 | − 408.4 |
| TOTAL | 12,774.5 | 15,242.3 | + 2,467.8 | 13,092.9 | 14,292.7 | + 1,199.8 |
| Colonial governments | 646.4 | 591.2 | − 55.2 | 664.6 | 566.7 | − 97.9 |
| Foreign governments | 2,043.2 | 1,881.5 | − 161.7 | 287.0 | 207.0 | − 80.0 |
| Colonial/Foreign public bodies | 147.4 | 109.2 | 38.2 | 101.1 | 73.5 | − 27.6 |
| TOTAL | 2,837.0 | 2,581.9 | 255.1 | 1,052.7 | 847.2 | − 205.5 |
| UK railways | 1,151.3 | 20.3 | − 1,131.0 | 864.0 | 10.3 | − 853.7 |
| Indian railways | 87.1 | 45.1 | − 42.0 | 87.3 | 43.7 | − 43.6 |
| Imperial railways | 196.5 | 171.1 | − 25.4 | 154.7 | 163.0 | + 8.3 |
| American railways | 218.3 | 181.2 | − 37.1 | 67.0 | 88.6 | + 21.6 |
| Foreign railways | 596.0 | 124.5 | − 471.5 | 145.1 | 37.6 | − 107.5 |
| TOTAL | 2,249.2 | 542.2 | − 1,707.0 | 1,318.1 | 343.2 | − 974.9 |
| Banks and discount houses | 210.3 | 210.0 | − 0.3 | 535.0 | 599.1 | + 64.1 |
| Financial, land, and investment | 591.0 | 619.5 | + 28.5 | 617.3 | 709.4 | + 92.1 |
| Insurance | 40.8 | 43.0 | + 2.2 | 372.0 | 362.6 | − 9.4 |
| TOTAL | 842.1 | 872.5 | + 30.4 | 1,542.3 | 1,671.1 | + 146.8 |
| Canals and docks | 44.3 | 25.1 | − 19.2 | 161.8 | 112.6 | − 49.2 |
| Gas | 161.9 | 23.9 | − 138.0 | 172.8 | 20.2 | − 152.6 |
| Electric light/power | 232.8 | 56.8 | − 176.0 | 352.1 | 94.3 | − 257.8 |
| Telegraph and telephone | 54.7 | 52.4 | − 2.3 | 102.8 | 110.9 | + 8.1 |
| Tramways and omnibus | 73.7 | 66.0 | − 7.7 | 139.3 | 149.1 | + 9.8 |
| Waterworks | 39.3 | 42.9 | + 3.6 | 51.3 | 46.5 | − 4.8 |
| TOTAL | 606.7 | 267.1 | − 339.6 | 979.9 | 533.6 | − 446.3 |
| Commercial/Industrial | 1,594.9 | 2,018.5 | + 423.6 | 3,677.2 | 4,097.9 | + 420.7 |
| Breweries/Distilleries | 236.8 | 274.7 | + 37.9 | 565.9 | 535.6 | + 30.3 |
| Iron, coal, and steel | 311.6 | 341.9 | + 30.3 | 540.2 | 544.8 | + 94.6 |
| Shipping | 76.6 | 82.2 | + 5.6 | 108.2 | 117.0 | + 8.8 |
| TOTAL | 2,219.9 | 2,717.3 | + 498.2 | 4,778.1 | 5,295.3 | + 517.2 |
| Mines | 340.4 | 369.0 | + 28.6 | 889.6 | 1,327.9 | + 438.3 |
| Oil | 186.0 | 223.7 | + 37.7 | 620.0 | 652.8 | + 32.8 |
| Tea, coffee, rubber | 124.8 | 128.8 | + 4.0 | 117.5 | 98.8 | − 18.7 |
| TOTAL | 651.2 | 721.5 | + 70.3 | 1,627.1 | 2,079.5 | + 452.4 |
| TOTAL | 22,180.6 | 22,944.8 | + 764.2 | 24,701.0 | 25,062.6* | + 361.6 |

* Includes £603.3m., being the market value of shares of no par value (conversion at $5 = £1 when required).

Sources: London Stock Exchange: Committee for General Purposes, *Annual Report* 3 April 1945; *Stock Exchange Official Yearbook*, 1952, 1,791.

Table 8.3. London Stock Exchange: Nominal and market values of securities quoted in 1945 and 1950 (%)

| Category of security | Nominal value | | | Market value | | |
|---|---|---|---|---|---|---|
| | 1945 | 1950 | Difference | 1945 | 1950 | Difference |
| British government | 53.5 | 63.9 | + 10.4 | 49.3 | 54.9 | + 5.6 |
| UK public bodies | 4.1 | 2.5 | − 1.6 | 3.8 | 2.1 | − 1.7 |
| TOTAL | 57.6 | 66.4 | + 8.8 | 53.0 | 57.0 | + 4.0 |
| Colonial governments | 2.9 | 2.6 | − 0.3 | 2.7 | 2.3 | − 0.4 |
| Foreign governments | 9.2 | 8.2 | − 1.0 | 1.2 | 0.8 | − 0.4 |
| Colonial/Foreign public bodies | 0.7 | 0.5 | − 0.2 | 0.4 | 0.3 | − 0.1 |
| TOTAL | 12.8 | 11.3 | − 1.5 | 4.3 | 3.4 | − 0.9 |
| UK railways | 5.2 | 0.1 | − 5.1 | 3.5 | = | − 3.5 |
| Indian railways | 0.4 | 0.2 | − 0.2 | 0.4 | 0.2 | − 0.2 |
| Imperial railways | 0.9 | 0.7 | − 0.2 | 0.6 | 0.7 | + 0.1 |
| American railways | 1.0 | 0.8 | − 0.2 | 0.3 | 0.4 | + 0.1 |
| Foreign railways | 2.7 | 0.5 | − 2.2 | 0.6 | 0.2 | − 0.4 |
| TOTAL | 10.1 | 2.4 | − 7.7 | 5.3 | 1.4 | − 3.9 |
| Banks and discount houses | 1.0 | 0.9 | − 0.1 | 2.2 | 2.4 | + 0.2 |
| Financial, land, and investment | 2.7 | 2.7 | = | 2.5 | 2.8 | + 0.3 |
| Insurance | 0.2 | 0.2 | = | 1.5 | 1.4 | − 0.1 |
| TOTAL | 3.8 | 3.8 | = | 6.2 | 6.7 | + 0.5 |
| Canals and docks | 0.2 | 0.1 | − 0.1 | 0.7 | 0.4 | − 0.3 |
| Gas | 0.7 | 0.1 | − 0.6 | 0.7 | 0.1 | − 0.6 |
| Electric light/power | 1.1 | 0.2 | − 0.9 | 1.4 | 0.4 | − 1.0 |
| Telegraph and telephone | 0.3 | 0.2 | − 0.1 | 0.4 | 0.4 | = |
| Tramways and omnibus | 0.3 | 0.3 | = | 0.6 | 0.6 | = |
| Waterworks | 0.2 | 0.2 | = | 0.2 | 0.2 | = |
| TOTAL | 2.7 | 1.2 | − 1.5 | 4.0 | 2.1 | − 1.9 |
| Commercial/ Industrial | 7.2 | 8.8 | + 1.6 | 14.9 | 16.4 | + 1.5 |
| Breweries/Distilleries | 1.1 | 1.2 | + 0.1 | 2.3 | 2.1 | − 0.2 |
| Iron, coal, and steel | 1.4 | 1.5 | + 0.1 | 1.8 | 2.2 | + 0.4 |
| Shipping | 0.4 | 0.4 | = | 0.4 | 0.5 | + 0.1 |
| TOTAL | 10.0 | 11.8 | + 1.8 | 19.3 | 21.1 | + 1.8 |
| Mines | 1.5 | 1.6 | + 0.1 | 3.6 | 5.3 | + 1.7 |
| Oil | 0.8 | 1.0 | + 0.2 | 2.5 | 2.6 | + 0.1 |
| Tea, coffee, rubber | 0.6 | 0.6 | = | 0.5 | 0.4 | − 0.1 |
| TOTAL | 2.9 | 3.1 | + 0.2 | 6.6 | 8.3 | + 1.7 |

*Sources*: As Table 8.2.

was heading for financial ruin. Try as it might to solve these problems no solution had been found by the end of the 1940s. As the London Stock Exchange moved into the second half of the twentieth century, the outlook for itself as an institution and the business of its members, must have appeared bleak indeed.[92]

[92] LSE: Council, 21 Mar. 1949; Scammell, *The London Discount Market*, 42; King, 'The Market's Changing Role', 9; Cowen, 'The London Stock Exchange and Investment', 34–5.

## 9

# *Drifting Towards Oblivion,*
# *1950–1959*

There could have been little confidence on the London Stock Exchange in 1950 that it had much of a future. As an institution its income was static, its costs were rising, and its fixed expenditure substantial. Membership was not attractive to the younger generation and was beginning to fall, as death and retirement took its toll. As a market many of its most actively traded securities had been sold to foreign investors or governments, while nationalization at home had removed whole railways, utilities, and coal. In the immediate post-war years all this had been hidden by the turnover generated by the reinvestment of the proceeds from overseas sales and nationalization, but this had now largely run its course. Instead, the London Stock Exchange was forced to compete for much of the business that still existed with both provincial brokers and London finance houses. Neither of these groups were governed by the same regulations that limited the room for manœuvre available to Stock Exchange members. Even the role the Stock Exchange had developed for itself, as the government's regulatory authority for the securities market, was none too secure. Operational control over the financial markets was vested in the Bank of England, with the Stock Exchange being but a small component. As long as the Stock Exchange carried out the wishes of the government, as transmitted by the Bank of England, it could retain a role for itself within the emerging apparatus of a managed economy. If it failed to deliver there was the unstated but ever-present threat that it would be bypassed by direct supervision from the Bank of England or a government appointed supervisory body.

Nevertheless, when those running the Stock Exchange in 1950 looked back, rather than forward, they took comfort in what they had achieved. Despite world wars, global economic collapse, and a socialist government, the Stock Exchange had not only survived but retained its independence, and this had required considerable change in the way it, as an institution, and its membership, operated. Too often survival is taken for granted but to many in the Stock Exchange in the early 1950s it was regarded as something of a miracle. One such was Sir Herbert Ellissen, who had been a

member of the Committee of General Purposes, and the Council that succeeded it, from 1910 to 1916 and again from 1929 to 1952. On his retirement in 1952 he addressed the then Chairman of the Council, John
Braithwaite, with these words

The long period of years covered by my membership of the Committee for General
Purposes and the Council have been full of incident beginning with the introduction of Commission Rules in 1909 and ending (for me) with the setting up of the
Compensation Fund and including the emergency regulations dealing with the outbreak of two world wars . . . Between the days of Sir Robert Inglis [Chairman pre-
First World War] to yourself, sir, there lie four decades of unquiet years which might
well have daunted any less vigorous a community, but the House has been able to
turn them to good account and I feel emerges from them more competent and more
respected than at any time in its long and colourful history.[1]

Clearly to someone like Sir Herbert Ellissen the Stock Exchange was to be
congratulated on its very survival rather than criticized for what it had
failed to achieve.

Nevertheless, despite such a euology from a retiring member, the Stock
Exchange had to take action if it was to solve its own internal problems,
as well as preserve an important role for itself within the post-war financial system. As a priority it had to find ways of either cutting expenditure
or generating income or both, if it was not to face bankruptcy, by being
unable to pay the interest on the annuities it had issued when buying out
the proprietors. The introduction of a charge for quoting securities was
beginning to generate significant income by the early 1950s. For 1953 the
Stock Exchange received over £105,000 from quotation fees. As no fees
were charged for government and related stocks, whether British or colonial, this was basically a charge levied on companies that wanted a public
market for their securities.[2] In addition, after prolonged discussions with
the Inland Revenue the Stock Exchange managed to convince them in 1952
that they were now a mutual organization rather than a business. This
greatly reduced their liability for taxation, as mutual status meant that no
tax was paid on the excess of income over expenses. The saving for the
Stock Exchange was estimated at £250,349 for the period between 1948
and 1952, which they could now reclaim. Despite occasional attacks by the
Inland Revenue on this mutual status in the 1950s the Stock Exchange
managed to preserve the favourable tax status it had acquired.[3] Consequently, the Stock Exchange was able to remedy its financial problems
without tackling the fundamental dilemma it faced, namely the difficulty of
passing on to its members the full costs of the services they enjoyed.

The expenses of the Stock Exchange continued to grow in the 1950s as

[1] LSE: Council, 5 May 1952.
[2] *Stock Exchange Official Yearbook* (London 1951), 1481, LSE: Council, 7 Dec. 1953.
[3] Ibid., 26 June 1950, 24 Mar. 1952, 7 Dec. 1953, 30 Jan. 1956.

wages and prices slowly but inexorably rose. Most of the costs incurred in the running of the Stock Exchange had to be financed out of the subscriptions paid by the membership, supplemented by other sources of income such as quotation fees.[4] The Settlement Department, for example, could not be made to pay. If the charges were increased to cover costs then the larger firms would simply not use it and the smaller firms would complain. Thus an annual subsidy was required, despite investment in mechanization, so as to reduce the rise in labour costs. Between 1949 and 1958 this subsidy totalled £146,000 having risen from £8,000 per annum in 1949 to £34,021 per annum in 1958. In 1949 Hollerith punched-card equipment was purchased for £7,160 plus annual running expenses of £2,500, in a bid to reduce costs substantially. Generally, by the end of the 1950s the computerization of clerical duties was seen to be the only solution to escalating labour costs. In 1959 rental charges of £18,575 per annum were being paid to International Computers and Tabulators for equipment.[5]

Consequently, throughout much of the 1950s the Stock Exchange was never in a position to undertake the major rebuilding that had been deemed necessary at the end of the Second World War. Refurbishment and minor alterations had to suffice instead. However, by 1958 plans were being formulated to replace the existing building with a new one costing c.£4.5m. This project was expected to take place in 20 years time. To this end an increase in members' subscriptions was required if a sufficient capital sum was to be made available. Inevitably this provoked considerable opposition both to the plans themselves and to any increase in membership fees. This made it very difficult for the Stock Exchange to do any more than respond to the current requirements of the membership. Nevertheless as turnover gradually picked up in the late 1950s and confidence in the future of the Stock Exchange grew, plans for rebuilding began to achieve an unstoppable momentum. By then the income from quotation fees, allied to the tax savings, was beginning to generate a growing surplus that could be applied to the construction of a new Stock Exchange, without a substantial increase in the subscription fee.[6]

Central to the very survival of the Stock Exchange in the 1950s, and any progress it was to make, was its relationship with the government of the day. This was now conducted, almost exclusively, through meetings between the Chairman of the Stock Exchange and the Governor of the Bank of England, rather than direct contact with either the Treasury or the Chancellor of the Exchequer as had existed earlier in the century. This was all part of the informal control exercised over the City of London by the government, either directly or indirectly. The Chairman of the Stock Exchange,

[4] Ibid., 19 Mar. 1951, 21 May 1951, 20 Feb. 1956.
[5] Ibid., 12 Dec. 1955, 7 July 1958, 29 Sept. 1958, 23 Feb. 1959, 9 Mar. 1959, 16 Mar. 1959, 13 July 1959.
[6] Ibid., 23 Jan. 1956, 20 Jan. 1958, 10 Feb. 1958, 24 Feb. 1958, 29 June 1959.

John Braithwaite, informed Council in October 1950 how the arrangement worked.

The advice we receive is not by way of a formal approval or disapproval of the step we contemplate, but is merely a verbal expression of opinion that they see nothing to object to in the course we propose; or that they think we should be well advised not to press a particular matter at a particular time.

He went on to add, contrasting experience in London with that in New York and Johannesburg, that,

. . . this informal control, if it is operated reasonably, as it has been hitherto, is infinitely to be preferred to formal or statutory control.[7]

Though this informal control might appear a more flexible arrangement than direct intervention, backed by the power of the law, it also had major disadvantages. The principal one was that it encouraged a high degree of caution. The merest expression of disapproval from the Bank of England, whether acting on its own or on behalf of the Treasury, was sufficient to discourage the Stock Exchange from pressing ahead with any contemplated changes. There was always the implied threat that if the Stock Exchange did not comply then statutory control would be introduced and that would be much more restrictive.

Braithwaite explained all this to the Council in May 1953:

My talk with the Governor last week, which as I said was informal and off the record, was directed on my side to confirming in my mind that the Governor and I had the same ideas as to the relations between the Stock Exchange and the Bank and the Treasury: and I was glad to find that that was so, though I was pretty confident of it. The Bank claims no jurisdiction or authority over the Stock Exchange, and would not accept any such responsibility even if we wished them to do so; and that, I am sure, goes equally for the Treasury, since the Bank is a branch of the Treasury and advises the Treasury on City matters. But The Bank will always offer their advice when we ask for it, and will give us all the help and co-operation they can, in the same way that *they* seek and receive *our* co-operation with them over many matters.

I believe it is true that the relations between the Stock Exchange and the Bank have been growing in closeness and cordiality for many years and have never been better or more friendly than they are now, and it is manifestly most desirable that this should be so. These relations are one of the most valuable assets of the Stock Exchange and are one of our best defences against Government interference. Nevertheless, our independence remains, and I hope we shall never surrender it voluntarily or without sufficient cause. I can perfectly well envisage the Stock Exchange acting against the opinion of the Bank, but it would, in my view, have to be on a matter either of small importance, in which case we should be unlikely to have asked advice, or of very major importance and upon very strong and sure grounds.[8]

---

[7] LSE: Council, 30 Oct. 1950.  [8] Ibid., 11 May 1953.

Consequently, the government via the Bank of England, was able to influence the operation of the Stock Exchange in the 1950s without the need for either statutory controls or even written directives. Instead, it could take place via informal and unrecorded meetings, with the implication being ever-present that if the Stock Exchange did not co-operate the relationship would become both statutory and formal.

This had the effect of making the Stock Exchange a much more conservative institution in the 1950s than it had ever been in the past, as that was perceived to be the best way of preserving its existence. The other disadvantage was that the arrangement placed great power in the hands of the Chairman of the Stock Exchange as it was through him that the relationship existed. As the content of these meetings were secret it was difficult for the members of the Stock Exchange, even those on the Council, to question the decisions reached and the reasons behind them. Braithwaite firmly told the Council in 1950,

... the relations of the Stock Exchange with the Bank and the Treasury are highly confidential, and it would be unfortunate in the highest degree if these matters were discussed on the floor of the House, and still more if any reference to them were to find its way into the Press.[9]

In the course of the 1950s Braithwaite, who was Chairman of Council throughout the years 1949–59, increasingly acquired a position within the Stock Exchange more akin to that of a full-time chief executive rather than the elected representative of the membership. Though he was not paid a salary as Chairman, still being a partner in the family stockbroking firm, he did receive increasing privileges. Secretarial support, for example, was expanded for all Council members while the Chairman was given an official car and chauffeur in 1954. This came to include a number of cars, including a Rolls-Royce. A small detached house in Lewisham was even purchased in 1956 for £3,100, to accommodate both the chauffeur and the car. Braithwaite received official recognition for the role he was performing, with a knighthood in 1953.[10]

During the 1950s, with Braithwaite as Chairman, the model being followed was that of the Bank of England. In exchange for direct access to the Governor of the Bank of England, and thus the ear of the government, the Stock Exchange was expected to conduct itself in a way that met government approval and fitted in with the direction of financial and monetary policy. Prompting acquiescence to the wishes of the Bank and the government was the belief that the Stock Exchange continued to be poorly regarded in the country at large and only good behaviour would prevent a greater degree of political interference than they already experienced. The

[9] Ibid., 30 Oct. 1950.
[10] Ibid., 1 July 1953, 30 Aug. 1954, 24 Sept. 1956, 2 June 1958, 16 Nov. 1959. W. J. Reader, *A House in the City: Foster & Braithwaite, 1825–1975* (London 1979), 171, 175.

devaluation of 1949, for example, had resulted in an attack on the City generally, and the Stock Exchange in particular, by Hugh Dalton, the Chancellor of the Exchequer, as he sought to divert attention from his government's own handling of the economy.[11] The Stock Exchange's response was to try and make their activities more accessible to the public, and explain the role they performed. To this end they decided to construct a public gallery, costing £2,500, and provide between £10,000 and £15,000 for a film on the Stock Exchange.[12] It was clear to the Stock Exchange that they were faced with the

... necessity of putting the House into a state of defence against political attack, which can best be done by making the importance and the magnitude of its work very much more widely known, understood and appreciated than at present.[13]

Furthermore, the advertising agency J. Walter Thompson were employed on a regular retainer to improve the image of the Stock Exchange. As it was, the request to the Ministry of Works to build a spectator's gallery was refused in 1952 because labour and material were required for the government's own projects, especially rearmament. It was not until 1953 that work could commence, with the gallery opening on 16 November of that year. By then the cost had more than doubled, to £5,540.[14]

Despite these efforts the image of the Stock Exchange as either irrelevant or a centre of harmful speculation continued to persist in the 1950s. J. A. Hunter, of the brokers Messel & Company, expressed his fears as late as May 1957, stating that 'We believe that the Stock Exchange would be in jeopardy should a Socialist Government, antagonistic to the City, be returned.' At the very least direct control was to be expected. These fears over the Stock Exchange's public profile, and worries over government intervention, had a major influence on the trading practices that the Council of the Stock Exchange were willing to countenance. This can be seen clearly in the struggle that took place over the reintroduction of options, which had been banned on the Stock Exchange, under government direction, since the outbreak of the Second World War. In May 1951 a campaign to restore the use of options was begun by Gerard Baily (of Weddle, Beck, Baily & Co.) who had traded in options since before the First World War. He maintained that options were highly technical devices of immense value to the market.

Options have been utilised for years by the Public as an insurance over a period to cover emergencies in order to protect their shareholdings, and this form of dealing is greatly appreciated by Jobbers desirous of protecting their books either way, thereby helping the creation of free and liquid markets, not only in dealing, but in contangos.

[11] LSE: Council, 16 Jan. 1950, 23 Jan. 1950.
[12] Ibid., 24 Apr. 1950.      [13] Ibid., 15 May 1951.      [14] Ibid., 20 May 1957.

Rather than being regarded as contributing to the buildup of speculative positions, with all the risks that involved, he suggested that options were '. . . similar to a premium demanded by an insurance office against any form of risk for a period'.[15] With options remaining banned on the Stock Exchange, the business flourished outside, being conducted by other financial intermediaries in London, Paris, and Johannesburg.

This request from Baily for a restoration of option trading was refused by the Council, unwilling to upset the Bank of England, and thus the government, by introducing what was generally regarded as a vehicle for speculation. However, many members were reluctant to accept the Council's decisions as final, especially with the election of a Conservative government in 1951. Consequently, in April 1952 142 jobbers petitioned for the resumption of option dealing, as it was '. . . a natural and efficient method of protecting positions, especially in times of uncertainty'. They also felt options would increase the volume of business and improve liquidity. Council ignored their request and so they went directly to the Bank of England, in order to explain the beneficial role played by options.[16] This approach failed, with the Chairman of Council, John Braithwaite, stating in May 1953 that, after soundings among the members, he had come to the opinion that

. . . there is no strong demand for options from either Jobbers or Brokers, and no claim is put forward that they are even an important part of our market machinery.[17]

The members of the Stock Exchange had been denied options for so long that most had got out of the habit of using them, especially when their normal business was the regular buying and selling on behalf of long-term private or institutional investors. Those members that did make use of options resorted to the alternatives provided by outside firms, so that the only serious agitation for their restoration was from those members who had traded in options in the past and wanted to do so again.

Under these circumstances Braithwaite was very reluctant to permit members of the Stock Exchange to provide or trade options, because of their strong association with speculation. If uncontrolled speculation took place, resulting in a major crash in which investors lost heavily, Braithwaite was convinced that the Stock Exchange would lose its independence. In his own words

I have also always in mind the major policy of defending the Stock Exchange against the attempt that is sure to be made sooner of later to bring it under Government control.[18]

---

[15] Ibid., 21 May 1951, cf. 30 July 1951, 28 Apr. 1952, 1 Dec. 1952, 26 Jan. 1953, 26 Oct. 1953, 12 Aug. 1957.

[16] Ibid., 2 July 1951, 21 Apr. 1952, 12 Dec. 1953.

[17] Ibid., 11 May 1953.     [18] Ibid.

Braithwaite's aim was to minimize any negative publicity that the Stock Exchange might suffer as this could prompt a public reaction which would then be taken up in Parliament, leading to direct intervention. At the same time a positive image of the Stock Exchange was to be projected through the opening of the public gallery and a co-ordinated advertising campaign. The result of this would be to remove any pressure on the government to act, or be seen to be acting, to control the operation of the Stock Exchange. As he, personally, saw little value in options, dealing mainly for investment clients, he was reluctant to risk this strategy by reintroducing them or use his relationship with the Bank of England to persuade it of their value.

On this matter of option dealing, whilst I did not formally seek the Governor's advice, the interview being off the record, I was left in no doubt that his advice, if asked, would be definitely against the restoration of options, because he feels very much as I have expressed to you for myself, that no advantages would accrue to the Stock Exchange that would at all counterbalance the adverse political repercussions that he thinks would be set up.[19]

As a consequence Council backed Braithwaite and blocked moves among membership for a return of options.

Nevertheless, this decision failed to silence that small group who wanted to bring back options, for they were very unhappy at being prevented from undertaking a traditional activity of members of the Stock Exchange. One was Graham Greenwell, who advocated ignoring the views of the Bank of England and persuading the public that options made a valuable contribution to the securities market. In particular, he was incensed because,

The Council should not encourage or permit a majority to interfere with the rights of a minority to do specialized business merely on the grounds that only a minority are interested. This attitude would drive out of the House not only option business but arbitrage and new issue business.[20]

However, as all these activities were undertaken by selected groups of members, rather than generally, he was unable to muster sufficient support, at that time, to challenge the decisions made by the Council. Clearly the Stock Exchange was running the risk that in seeking to placate public opinion and maintain the goodwill of the government it was restricting the business that its members could do, to the advantage of non-members.

The question of options would not go away despite the opposition of the Chairman, Council, the Bank of England, the Treasury and the government to their reappearance. In May 1954 11 firms including Ricardo Issacs & Bray, Berger & Gosschalk, and Medwin & Lowry, again petitioned for the restoration of options.

The reintroduction of Option dealing would gradually restore the London Stock Exchange the pre-eminence which it up to 1939 occupied with Stock Exchanges

[19] LSE: Council, 11 May 1953.    [20] Ibid., 26 May 1953.

abroad, including New York, Paris, Johannesburg, where option dealing continues to function.[21]

This request met the strong opposition of Braithwaite, who warned, yet again, of the possible consequences, though he now conceded that the Bank of England would not block such a move,

I am able to say that if we restore option dealing there will be no comment from the Bank, but it remains the Governors' opinion that on balance we should be best advised in our own interests to leave things as they are. That is an opinion upon which we can each place our own value, but, apart from its own importance, it may well be a pointer to the probable reaction of the City generally. The relations between the Stock Exchange and the Bank of England (and for that matter with the Chancellor of the Exchequer also) have never been closer or more cordial than they are to-day. The value of that to us can hardly be overstated. It is our strongest defence against Government interference, which is no issue now, but may be a very live issue under another Labour Government, with the precedents of New York and Johannesburg ready to their hands. With regard to the public we may need to consider whether, if we restore options, we may not be undoing something of the increased prestige and public regard that we have gained in recent years.[22]

This time there was a vote in Council on the issue with 18 voting against the restoration and only seven for, with three abstaining. Another battle to restore fully the pre-war trading system had been lost.

It was not until May 1957 that the question of options resurfaced, with six firms wanting the issue discussed. These included some of the major jobbers, such as Akroyd & Smithers and Durlacher Godson & Co., as well as influential brokers like L. A. Seligman & Co. and Leon Brothers. The arguments then raged in Council. As before they focused on the balance between what options contributed to Stock Exchange business and the political risk of reintroducing them. When a vote came in November 1951, Council decided against the restoration of options by a majority of 16 to 11. However, this time the pressure for restoration did not die away, but continued to mount.[23] By April 1958, after a petition by 58 Members, Council was forced to convene an extraordinary general meeting of the entire Stock Exchange to discuss the following motion,

That the volume of Stock Exchange business having decreased considerably throughout the past year, it has become imperative to remove the war-time restriction placed on Option Dealing, and restore facilities for transacting this form of business forthwith.[24]

As business languished in the 1950s members of the Stock Exchange were more willing to reintroduce pre-war practices in the hope that they might stimulate turnover, even if they did carry the risk of political repercussions.

[21] Ibid., 24 May 1954.     [22] Ibid., 19 July 1954.
[23] Ibid., 13 May 1957, 21 Oct. 1957, 11 Nov. 1957.     [24] Ibid., 29 Apr. 1958.

When the issue was put to a vote of the entire membership in May 1958 the result was a majority of 1,485 for restoring options against 766. Council had been defeated, option dealing was to be restored, and members had decided to ignore the wishes of the Bank of England, the government, and public opinion.[25]

Consequently, after an absence of 19 years members of the Stock Exchange were, once again, able to provide and deal in options. What the struggle to restore this facility indicates is the extent to which permissible trading practices on the London Stock Exchange were conditioned by the real or perceived wishes of the Bank of England. That, in turn, was determined by the economic and political agenda of the government of the day. Instead of Stock Exchange practices being driven by the evolving demands of the market, and the desire to maintain a disciplined trading environment, in the 1950s they were determined by outside agencies concerned with their own interests. As a result the ability of the London Stock Exchange to respond to the needs of the market was severely curtailed by the environment within which it operated, though no direct or statutory control was ever exercised. Without formal recognition or authority the Council of the London Stock Exchange had been transformed into an executive arm of the government, rather than the presiding body whose functions were to police and facilitate the business of its members. It was only towards the end of the 1950s, especially with the departure of John Braithwaite as Chairman, that the Council of the Stock Exchange began to examine the role it performed. As a result of that examination six functions emerged, namely:

1. Maintenance of a free market where the public could deal quickly, easily, and at a minimum cost.
2. Protection of the public by controlling securities allowed to be quoted.
3. Compensation fund for the public.
4. Administer rules and ajudicate disputes.
5. Promote the Stock Exchange.
6. Plan for the future.

Though the public service function was ranked more highly than the discipline of the members, providing a securities market was, again, at the top of the list of priorities.[26] The victory achieved by the members in bringing back options had wider implications in that it indicated the beginning of a re-evaluation of what the Stock Exchange was for. Out of that came the discovery that the Stock Exchange was not an institution like the nationalized Bank of England but a market place that only existed to serve the interests of its members.

Nevertheless, though the Stock Exchange began to rediscover its primary role towards the end of the 1950s the government, through the Bank of

[25] LSE: Council, 27 May 1958, 21 July 1958, 13 Oct. 1958, 3 Nov. 1958.
[26] Ibid., 9 Mar. 1959.

England, continued to use it as a means of policing any activities regarding securities. For example, the Inland Revenue discovered that companies were able to establish, for themselves, artificial losses in their investments in securities, against which they could claim tax relief. By buying government securities, or the issues of nationalized industries, including the right to the interest payment ('cum div'), and then selling it immediately without that right ('ex div'), a company could report a loss on its investment, even though that loss was equivalent to the interest payment it received. This could all be undertaken without risk as the purchase and sale could be done simultaneously. These transactions had reached such a scale by August 1956 that the government put pressure on the Stock Exchange to make the practice more difficult. Further changes to Stock Exchange practices were made in 1957, when the Inland Revenue discovered that by buying stock 'cum div', and selling it 'ex div', the tax paid on the dividend could be reclaimed even though it was never paid. These operations were referred to as 'bond washing' with Braithwaite, in August 1957, referring to them as '. . . a scandal', observing that '. . . note of them is being taken in Parliament . . .'[27]

The problem the Stock Exchange faced was that when it placed restrictions on its members abilities to conduct such operations, they simply shifted into the hands of non-members. The jobbers, Bruce and Hinton, were quick to inform the Stock Exchange that a result of the new rules would be that '. . . a lot of business which normally comes through the Stock Exchange will now go through the lesser known Merchant Banking Houses.' The Inland Revenue was expecting the Stock Exchange to stop such abuses as bond washing, rather than adjusting the right of tax relief and tax refunds or being more rigorous in its own investigations. Where the Stock Exchange complied, but it remained possible to buy and sell stock 'cum' and 'ex div', then the business was now done elsewhere. At the same time the Stock Exchange's own tightening up of its regulations interfered with the normal business of the market, for money had traditionally been employed temporarily in the holding of securities. Bruce and Hinton gave one example:

Most jobbers realize that the Discount Market frequently buys stock that is full of accrued interest 2 or 3 weeks before it goes ex dividend taking the dividend when it sells, having also taken a market risk during that period. This we have always considered to be legitimate business . . .

The new rules would make such operations more difficult and involve more bureaucratic form-filling. Though the Stock Exchange did not monopolize the securities market they were being treated as if they did, with their members being prevented from doing business not denied to others. It was

[27] Ibid., 7 Aug. 1956, 6 May 1957, 27 May 1957, 9 Aug. 1957, 12 Aug. 1957.

only with the Finance Act of 1959 that general restrictions were imposed in an attempt to stop bond washing.[28]

During the 1950s the Stock Exchange appears to have gained little from this willingness to comply with the government's wishes, apart from tax relief as a mutual organization and a freedom from direct control or intervention. Throughout the 1950s, for example, the Stock Exchange lobbied successive Chancellors of the Exchequer for a reduction in the stamp duty on transfers of securities. This had been raised to 2 per cent under the post-war Labour government, and was considered especially onerous on short-dated issues for which there was little time to recover the tax paid through the income resulting.[29] With an incoming Conservative government the Stock Exchange made a case for a reduction in stamp duty, both to help the operation of the market and to bring international business to London

Previously institutions interested in particular stocks or groups of stocks would freely enter the market on a fall, or supply stock on a rise, and this, as well as assisting the market generally, helped also to reduce the extremes of price movements. The 2 per cent stamp duty makes these operations too expensive and so deprives the market of this support. The 2 per cent stamp duty . . . is driving business away, and, instead of being attracted to London, New York, Paris and Switzerland, all now, for example, deal direct with Johannesburg in South African mining shares, and in diamond and copper stocks.[30]

However, this brought no response from a government conscious of the need to retain all sources of revenue, and of the benefits conferred on its own capital-raising powers by the freedom from stamp duty enjoyed by the stock issued by British and dominion governments, municipalities, and public boards.

Despite the rebuff the Stock Exchange continued to bring to the government's attention the adverse consequences that the high rate of stamp duty was having. In 1956 they went so far as to suggest differential rates with a 1 per cent duty for fixed interest bearing securities while leaving equities at 2 per cent. This would make debentures issued by companies more competitive with government debt and thus assist in the financing of investment. By then their pleading had taken on a more strident tone, suggesting that the tax was positively harmful for the British economy.

A duty of 2 per cent is the highest tax in the world on the movement of securities, and constitutes a formidable barrier to the flow of American, Canadian and overseas funds to the London market, which might do much to strengthen the exchange position of sterling. It is a measure directly in restraint of Trade . . . In view of the declared policy of the Government to stimulate savings and to encourage the development of a property-owning and share-owning democracy, it is most desirable that

[28] LSE: Council, 19 Aug. 1957, 26 Aug. 1957, 17 Aug. 1959.
[29] Ibid., 13 Nov. 1950, 4 Dec. 1950.     [30] Ibid., 7 Jan. 1952.

investment in industry should not be discouraged. The 2 per cent duty is a serious obstacle to all investment and especially to the investment of small amounts. It is a discouragement to a potential investor, when a large proportion of the first year's net interest on a first class fixed interest investment is taken away by this Tax.[31]

As in the past this request for a reduction in stamp duty was ignored. It is fairly clear that in 1950s the Conservative government, like its Labour predecessor, paid little attention to the views or interests of the Stock Exchange, being more concerned with the health of the economy, the balance of payments and the state of public finances. It was pointed out in 1959 that the restrictions being placed by the government on sale and repurchase agreements, in order to stop bond washing, could undermine the arbitrage business that had built up during the 1950s. However, the government's priority was its tax revenues not the support of an international business it neither welcomed nor understood. If the position of the Stock Exchange is at all representative of that of the City as a whole in the 1950s, it is difficult to detect that it had much influence over government. It was the converse that was the case, with the Stock Exchange forever conscious of the need to please government or risk direct intervention.[32]

## POLICING THE MEMBERS

However, though acting as the Bank of England's regulator of the securities market absorbed much of the administrative time of chairman, Council and staff of the Stock Exchange, it continued to have to perform its traditional functions of protecting and policing the day-to-day activities of its members. Controlling the dissemination of price-sensitive information, for example, became a steadily more serious issue during the 1950s, with little sympathy for the Stock Exchange's position from either the government or the public. It was not in the interests of the Stock Exchange membership as a whole if a few gained advance or exclusive access to information that could influence the prices of stocks and shares. As jobbers, in particular, frequently sold in the expectation of being able to deliver through subsequent purchases, any sudden increase in prices would leave them exposed to large losses. Similarly, those brokers who advised clients to purchase before a sudden price fall could lose custom especially if other brokers appeared better able to predict the future. One such incident was the raising

---

[31] Ibid., 30 Jan. 1956, cf. 12 Jan. 1953, 23 Jan. 1956, 9 Dec. 1957.
[32] D. Wainwright, *Government Broker: The Story of an Office and of Mullens and Company* (East Molesey 1990), 84–7; D. Cairncross, 'The Bank of England: Relationships with the Government, the Civil Service and Parliament', in G. Toniolo (ed.), *Central Banks' Independence in Historical Perspective* (Berlin 1988), 54; LSE: Council, 22 June 1959, 17 Aug. 1959; R. Roberts, 'The City of London as a Financial Centre in the Era of Depression, the Second World War and Post-war Official Controls', in A. Gorst, L. Johnman, and G. W. S. Lucas (eds.), *Contemporary British History, 1931–1961* (London 1991), 62–3; E. Hennessy, *A Domestic History of the Bank of England, 1930–1960* (Cambridge 1992), 118–19.

of the Bank rate from 5 per cent to 7 per cent on 19 September 1957, for this caused large losses to holders of stock, and led to a government enquiry to establish whether the information had been leaked beforehand. Clearly the assumption was that the members of the Stock Exchange were profiting at the investors' expense by having access to information denied the public, and so being able to sell and then buy back at a profit. However, the problem was the government's, as it was the potential source of any information not the Stock Exchange where such securities were traded. Nevertheless, it was the Stock Exchange that was portrayed as the villain not the victim in these cases of insider trading, even though the Bank Rate Tribunal set up to investigate the 1957 incident, could find no evidence for this.[33]

The Stock Exchange was always keen to eradicate insider trading and conducted its own internal investigations in order to discover who was benefiting. One such case was in 1958 when it was noticed, through questioning brokers, that a particular investor—E. Gainley—was regularly buying shares in advance of them being tipped by the *Stock Exchange Gazette*. However, there was nothing that the Stock Exchange itself could do to stop Gainley's activities, apart from informing the journal, as what he was doing was not illegal. This case was followed by one in 1959 when evidence was uncovered of dealings in shares prior to them being tipped by a stockbroker in the *Investors' Chronicle*. Here a stockbroker was implicated. A. S. Keats, a partner in Walker, Cripps & Co., was in the habit of meeting a printer in a bar in Worwood Street. This Mr Land was employed by St Clements Press, who printed the *Investors' Chronicle*, and so had advance information about which shares were to tipped. Also involved were two investors—a Mr Seaman who was a publican and Mr G. Lewis, a café proprietor, for whom Keats acted. It was decided to inform the editor of the *Investors' Chronicle*, in the expectation that they would take action. The problems of tip sheets was a long-standing one with the Stock Exchange maintaining a list of its members and their clerks attached to newspapers and magazines. Where abuses occurred it could be tackled by contacting the printers and publishers, as they had a vested interest in maintaining the confidentiality of their magazines and newspapers until publication.[34]

More difficult was the leakage of information regarding takeover bids. There were a growing number of these and, clearly, some of those involved profited from their knowledge by buying shares in the market in advance of announcement. The result was to cause losses to particular jobbers and brokers. This provoked a number of disputes between members as some were suspected of being party to building upon advantageous positions before an announcement was made. As it was often the directors of the companies concerned that were involved it was difficult for the Stock

<hr>

[33] LSE: Council, 20 May 1957.    [34] Ibid., 31 Mar. 1959.

Exchange to seek their help in stamping out the activity. Also it was not easy to identify the particular individuals concerned, as in the case of the takeover of the British Bank of the Middle East by the Hong Kong and Shanghai Bank in 1959. Unfortunately for the Stock Exchange the government was unwilling to take any action to stamp out the practice. Instead, Members of Parliament, such as Ted Leather, blamed the Stock Exchange, which was a view that reflected popular opinion. The argument was that without the market provided by the Stock Exchange, and the co-operation of the membership, then it would not have been possible for individuals to profit from the knowledge that they possessed. Consequently, the Stock Exchange was expected to prevent such practices taking place.[35] In response, one member, Patrick Fleming, was driven to write to Ted Leather making the point that

If you yourself, hold shares in a company and get advance information that the company is bust and sell your shares before the news leaks out, it is your conduct which should be called in question, and not that of the SE.[36]

As it was, the whole matter was beyond the control of the Stock Exchange acting alone but too complicated for the government to tackle.

However, the limitations faced by the Stock Exchange were only partly the responsibility of the government. As the cases of both options and bond washing also indicate there was a willingness by the chairman and Council to pursue more restrictive policies than in the pre-war era. The Stock Exchange was simply reluctant to re-establish the more fast-moving and risky type of business that had been so prevalent in the past. In particular the 1950s were characterized by the dominant influence of the likes of John Braithwaite, who reflected the interests and attitudes of those brokers who served a well-established investment clientele, both private and institutional. Such brokers, along with the small jobbers who served them, were among the majority of the membership and so they had the power to determine the direction that the Stock Exchange was taking. Their power had never been so unrestricted and they used it to ensure that the interests of the Stock Exchange were their interests. J. A. Hunter represented the views of the large brokers and he was well aware of the power struggle that was taking place.

Any major change which may be proposed tends to be opposed by a considerable number of the Stock Exchange membership because of the fear that over the shorter term, it may affect their livelihood although, over the longer term, it may be well admitted to be of the general good.[37]

In the past the proprietors had acted to curb the excesses of the members, conscious that too many restrictions might lead to the creation of a rival

[35] Ibid., 6 Dec. 1954, Wainwright, *Mullens*, 91.
[36] LSE: Council, 24 Nov. 1958, 25 May 1959, 6 July 1959, 4 Jan. 1960.
[37] Ibid., 26 Oct. 1959, 23 Nov. 1959, 11 Dec. 1959.

exchange. However, the proprietors had been bought out and it was in the self-interest of the government to bolster the authority of the Stock Exchange, against any competition, as that was how it tried to regulate the securities market. At the same time many of those who might have challenged the restrictions in trading being introduced in the 1950s were unaffected by them, because they were not eligible for membership of the Stock Exchange. It was in the 1950s that the Stock Exchange first really operated as an insiders' club. Even then, by the end of the 1950s there was growing concern among certain of the members that the Stock Exchange's rules and regulations were threatening the very business that it was meant to promote. One who expressed his worries was the long-serving member Charles Dreyfus, of Greener, Dreyfus & Co., who wrote to the Council in March 1959:

Like most traders and professions we are a mass of restrictive practices to which we are accustomed and find highly attractive. . . . But we have to justify these practices perhaps openly against criticism and certainly unobtrusively against the silent economic forces which can result in big transactions bypassing the Stock Exchange because it is too expensive. Members of the Stock Exchange earn their keep socially by negotiating purchases and sales and acting as temporary buffers when they go long or short of stock.[38]

In as diplomatic way as possible Dreyfus was trying to remind the Council that they had to tread a careful line between the regulations necessary to produce an orderly market and the freedom necessary for those in the market place to conduct their business against the competition of non-members. Getting the balance right in the 1950s was greatly complicated by the intervention of the government that had an agenda of its own. Unfortunately, there is also the distinct impression that in the 1950s the Stock Exchange was much keener to maintain the goodwill of the government and the Bank of England, and through that preserve its importance, than to ensure that the market it provided remained competitive against that offered by non-members.

However, for most of the 1950s the members were, generally, content to accept the restrictive and conservative policies that were being pursued. For a start many of those who became members at that time were self-selected being known to existing members through family relationships and friends. The partners in Mullens, for example, were recognized as a fairly close-knit group at this time, being drawn from the sons and nephews of previous partners or other close family contacts. Commonplace was the practice in the broking firm, Sebags, where each partner had the right to nominate a son to the partnership and, in Foster & Braithwaite, with every new partner in the 1950s being related to an existing partner. Nevertheless, there were firms like Phillips & Drew where recruitment was simply on merit as Sidney

[38] LSE: Council, 28 Dec. 1959.

Perry, the controlling partner, had no children. Frederick Menzler, who had been recruited from London Transport, began a policy of recruiting Oxbridge graduates in the 1950s. However, an entrance fee of 1,000 guineas, plus an annual subscription of 105 guineas, was a serious obstacle to membership especially at a time when the prospects of a Stock Exchange career were considered poor and uncertain. This discouraged those who knew little about the Stock Exchange, and were not confident that such expenditure would generate an income to justify it.[39]

George Nissen, who joined the brokers Pember & Boyle in 1953, having been at school with the son of a partner, remembered that 'The Stock Exchange was politically out of favour and rather beleaguered and not looked on as a place of much excitement. There was talk of nationalizing it, which was a crazy idea.'[40] Among those who did become members at this time through connections, a number left to seek careers elsewhere. Tony Waley whose father was a very successful broker, and two uncles were jobbers, joined Sebags but left after a couple of years to become a second-hand bookseller in Reigate.[41] The lack of attractions of the Stock Exchange for most of the decade was reflected in the price of nominations, which became worthless in the early 1950s, with over 50 per cent being unsold between 1951 and 1953. One was sold for £10 in May 1951 and another for £50 in March 1954. It was not until the late 1950s that membership of the Stock Exchange again became attractive, with a nomination selling for around £2,000 in 1959. By then membership had fallen to 3,497 in December 1959 compared to 4,050 in March 1950, or a drop of almost 14 per cent during the course of a decade.[42]

Though the Stock Exchange had a notional ceiling of 4,000 on membership this fall was not due to any deliberate curtailment but a lack of demand, with nominations to be had for almost nothing for much of the 1950s. Only women and foreigners were deliberately excluded, along with those who had not served their country during the war. Considering the cost of admission and the prospects held out few were enticed to join. Those who did were largely clerks. As early as 1951 over three-quarters of the members had served four or more years as clerks and that became the normal practice thereafter, especially as clerks could join for 500 guineas.[43] Instead of a career on the Stock Exchange being exclusive because of

[39] Wainwright, Mullens, 92; D. Sebag-Montefiore, The Story of Joseph Sebag & Co. and its Founding Families (n.p. 1996), 21; Reader, Foster & Braithwaite, 181; W. T. C. King, The Stock Exchange (London 1954, 2nd edn.), 40–2; C. Courtney and P. Thompson, City Lives: The Changing Voices of British Finance (London 1996), 21, 38; LSE: Council, 21 May 1954; W. J. Reader and D. Kynaston, Phillips & Drew: Professionals in the City (London 1998), 42.
[40] Courtney and Thompson, City Lives, 38.    [41] Sebag-Montefiore, Sebag & Co., 21.
[42] LSE: Council, 24 Apr. 1950, 19 Mar. 1951, 30 Apr. 1951, 7 May 1951, 3 Nov. 1952, 6 Jan. 1958, 2 Nov. 1959, 14 Dec. 1959.
[43] Ibid., 22 Jan. 1951, 31 Dec. 1956; The Stock Exchange Clerks' Provident Fund Centenary, 1874–1974 (London 1971), 22.

barriers to entry in the 1950s, the problem was that it was unattractive to those who were not already in the business, either by working for a broker or jobber or through family connections.

Nevertheless, the need to bring in others, because of their skills and/or connections remained strong, forcing firms to look beyond trained clerks and family members. There were still half-commission men around in the 1950s who could gravitate to partnership level if they generated sufficient business. One still operating was Herbert Harris, who was an attaché with Harley & Co. He had built up a clientele of over 90 people in the course of 35 years, since he left the army in 1921. As he said himself, 'I have never touted for clients, they have come to me by recommendation one to another. I am still dealing for men, and their families, who served with me in 1914–20'.[44] The brokers, Sebags, for example, continued to recruit those who could bring in business through their links with wealthy individuals or with financial institutions.[45] In an attempt in 1955 to analyse what a successful stockbroker required, the Stock Exchange itself came up with 'judgment, experience, a sense of timing, and a "nose"'. It then concluded that 'A man may be born with, or acquire, the first. Time and his elders will provide him with the second', but went on to state that 'Even if teachers could be found it is doubtful whether the last two qualities could be learnt'.[46]

There also continued to be openings for those who proved themselves to be skilled traders in securities. George Nissen, for example, spent some time on the floor of the Stock Exchange in the 1950s and later recollected the environment that existed there

There were certainly plenty of old public-schoolboys on the floor of the Stock Exchange, but there were plenty who were not. It was a very equal kind of community, the floor community, which was quite different from the actual offices. The qualifications for a good dealer in the Stock Exchange were in a way the qualifications of a really good barrow-boy. You had to be very quick, you had to have a good personality—not necessarily a very pleasant personality, but you had to have the ability to get on with people. There was always a way into a partnership at Pember and Boyle through the dealing side.[47]

A private client stockbroking firm needed partners who could develop close working relationships with clients, and that required a particular type of person, often with a public school background. Conversely, there were firms, both brokers and jobbers, who undertook a lot of dealing, and for that a different type of person was needed. They might have a public school background and possess family connections with existing members but,

[44] LSE: Council, 12 Dec. 1955.
[45] Sebag-Montefiore, *Sebag & Co.*, 21, 30, 45–7; D. Kynaston, *Cazenove & Co.: A History* (London 1991), 214–15, Wainwright, *Mullens*, 84, 91–4.
[46] LSE: Council, 17 Oct. 1955.          [47] Courtney and Thompson, *City Lives*, 76–7.

above all, they had to be able to trade successfully. If they could not, the firm would lose both money and clients.

Also in the 1950s there was a growing need for recruits who possessed detailed and specialist knowledge regarding particular types of securities. Investors, both individual and institutional, looked to stockbrokers not only for the ability to buy and sell securities on commission but to advise on the relative merits of the different ones available. Capels in 1957, for instance, had 10 partners and each had a particular area of specialization, ranging from Australian mining shares to the securities of British investment trusts. W. I. Carr, Sons & Co. went so far as to employ an American, Herbert Gumprecht, in 1956 in order to cultivate a two-way trade in North American securities for British investors and British securities for North American investors. This specialization did not need to be geographic or by different types of securities for it also affected the legal and fiscal environment that now affected the world of investment. Cazenoves, for example, employed a chartered accountant in 1954 in order to advise on the tax efficiency of investments, while Phillips & Drew had a team of financial specialists who could advise institutional clients on gilt-switching in order to improve yields.[48]

Clearly the Stock Exchange continued to offer a wide variety of openings in the 1950s not all of which could be filled by those who entered through family connections or long apprenticeships as clerks. The problem in the 1950s was that it could not always get them. In 1957 one member reported that '. . . good dealers are extremely difficult to find'.[49] The very fact that membership fell over the decade suggests that the Stock Exchange was facing problems of recruitment in the 1950s or creating them for itself. Especially in the first half of the 1950s many among the existing membership were struggling to make a living for themselves, let alone offer attractive opportunities to newcomers. Though somewhat tongue in cheek this objection in 1953, by the partners in Francis, How & Lownders, to the proposed public gallery, paints a picture of a rather moribund market populated by bored and idle people.

We cannot think that the interests of the Stock Exchange will be advanced if we are to allow the public to see the rather schoolboyish activities of certain dealers in the matter of throwing paper balls, flying paper airplanes and darts, and occasional ragging. Nor can we think our interests will be served by the spectacle of members draped in undignified attitudes on the benches more or less asleep. These things could and would be used against us politically. In addition, we think some members would have a hard task explaining to their wives what a really hard day in the City means if their spouses were allowed to go into the gallery and see for themselves.[50]

---

[48] M. C. Reed, *A History of James Capel and Company* (London 1975), 94–5; Kynaston, *Cazenove*, 198, 224; LSE: Council, 24 Sept. 1956; ibid., 2 Feb. 1953; Reader and Kynaston, *Phillips & Drew*, 34, 52.
[49] LSE: Council, 29 Apr. 1957.     [50] Ibid., 2 Feb. 1953.

There is the distinct impression that the Stock Exchange was not an attractive career for much of the 1950s. In June 1953 Simons & MacClymont were reported as reducing staff and curtailing expenditure, because '. . . conditions have been extremely difficult on the Stock Exchange for a long time'.[51] George Perry, a member, was one of those made redundant and he became an insurance agent. When business did begin to pick up from the mid-1950s it co-incided with a growing caution in the Stock Exchange over whom to accept as new members. There had always been a resistance to newcomers on the Stock Exchange among the long-established members, and this continued in the 1950s. This reflected the inevitable tension between the different groups involved, ranging from the private client stockbroker moving in the circles of the established and the wealthy to the dealer whose income depended upon his ability to buy and sell at a profit. An example of this tension came to the fore in 1954 with a growing number of complaints from partners in old-established broking firms regarding the behaviour of certain of the clerks. Basil Giles, of Giles & Overbury, was one who wrote saying, 'I am naturally jealous of the good reputation of the Stock Exchange and the behaviour of the young male and female hooligans, to say nothing of their appearance, employed by some members fills me and others with disgust'.[52] This was at the height of the 'Teddy boy' craze and it affected the youth of the Stock Exchange as much as the population generally, to the annoyance of many older members. Such behaviour was no stranger to the Stock Exchange and it proved powerless at controlling it for Basil Giles was still complaining in 1958.

However, this social resistance was combined in the 1950s with a desire to impose a quantitative limit so that there would be sufficient business for all members to be guaranteed a decent income. This was seen in the reluctance to revive the nominations that had lapsed during the lean years even though numbers were well under 4,000.[53] Furthermore this quantitative limit was then combined with greater qualitative checks, with the growing realization that the membership, collectively, were responsible for the losses incurred by members' clients if due to fraud or negligence. This arose with the introduction of the Compensation Fund in March 1950. Therefore, by December 1953 a requirement had been introduced that from 1954/5 onwards every member had to have their annual accounts prepared by an independent accountant. Further large losses, which had to be met from the Compensation Fund, led to the introduction of both external audits for member firms, which allowed the Stock Exchange to monitor their activities, and a requirement that new members would be fully trained in such basics as keeping accounts and company law. Especially after the failure of Barnyard, Lacey & Co. in 1957 there was general feeling that it was ne-

---

[51] LSE: Council, 8 June 1953, cf. 5 Apr. 1954.
[52] Ibid., 27 Sept. 1954, cf. 22 Sept. 1958.
[53] Ibid., 29 Nov. 1954, 13 Dec. 1954, 14 Dec. 1959.

cessary to not only monitor but police the operations of individual members. Barnyard, Lacey & Co. had failed with liabilities of £144,090 but assets of only £28,866, leaving the Compensation Fund to find £115,224. Of these liabilities £100,410 was due to clients, some of whose securities had been sold without their knowledge. The Compensation Fund had become a charge on the Stock Exchange as an institution rather than a separate levy on the membership. Though audits and training were introduced to safeguard the membership and protect the investor, they also reflected the increased power of the Stock Exchange over both the admission of new members and the activities they conducted.[54]

In 1955 the attaché Herbert Harris, was removed from the list of those entitled to a share of commission due to complaints by one of his clients, a Miss Herbert. She alleged he was making excessive charges.[55] More difficult to police was the practice of churning that Mrs C. V. Holder brought before the Council. Her investments were managed by the broker S. R. Channon, originally of James Watson & Co., and then Channon & Co. The portfolio was worth £16,300 in 1950, but only £6,847 by 1959. During the 1950s, sales of £235,046 and purchases of £235,501 had been made, as the portfolio was switched from government stock into mining shares. This generated a large commission income for Channon. As the accountants Peat, Marwick, Mitchell & Co. reported:

The most notable feature of the account is the large number of transactions where stocks have been sold and bought for the account, at a loss to Mrs Holder . . . Mrs Holder may well be surprised that so many transactions should have not produced more satisfactory results.[56]

Unfortunately for Mrs Holder she had given Channon full discretion in the handling of her investments and no crime had been committed, as every transaction and security was accounted for. Thus the Stock Exchange could do nothing, through it was obviously worried about such practices.

During the 1950s the Stock Exchange grew in authority, bolstering its relationship with the Bank of England and the government through greater control over its own membership. All members and their clerks had to wear badges on the trading-floor in 1959, for example.[57] In turn, the power possessed by the Stock Exchange was used, more and more, by the small stockbroking firms to both resist the changes that were threatening them, and to create an environment that benefited them. Though membership fell in the 1950s the decline was almost entirely among the jobbers, with the number of brokers remaining roughly constant. In 1950 there were 2,660 brokers (72 per cent) and 1,034 jobbers (28 per cent) among the active membership while in 1959 there were still 2,594 brokers (78 per cent) but only 719 jobbers (22 per cent). Thus a rising proportion of the membership were

[54] Ibid., 6 Mar. 1950, 7 Jan. 1952, 7 Dec. 1953, 24 June 1957, 19 Aug. 1957, 31 Mar. 1958, 8 Apr. 1958.
[55] Ibid., 12 Dec. 1955.    [56] Ibid., 14 Jan. 1960.    [57] Ibid., 19 May 1959.

brokers and they all had votes.[58] Some of these brokers were members in little more than name, having joined long before the introduction of the 1,000 guineas entrance fee. With nominations having little resale value they were also not inclined to leave. One such was Moss Isaacs. He was 86 years old in 1955, having been a member for 65 years, and did enough business to pay his subscription, meet his daily expenses, and generate a profit of c.£80 per annum. Similarly, the half-commission man Herbert Harris, was generating an income of about £650 per annum from his 90 clients, after meeting all expenses. Consequently, it was still possible to generate an adequate income as a private client broker in the 1950s, and these collectively, possessed an enormous power and influence within the Stock Exchange.[59]

In addition, though the number of separate firms in the Stock Exchange did fall in the 1950s, dropping from 483 in 1954 to 418 in 1959, small firms continued to dominate the membership. Stock Exchange rules continued to restrict both the number of partners in a firm and the number of clerks it could employ on the floor. When Montagu, Stanley & Co. merged with Shaw Loebl & Co. in 1953 they exceeded the number of authorized clerks permitted under Stock Exchange rules. They then requested that such rules be relaxed but the Stock Exchange would not agree. As a result larger firms had limited scope for enjoying economies of scale that would allow them to compete more aggressively against the smaller members. Generally the rules were explicitly designed to limit any advantage enjoyed by larger firms. For example, attempts to have advertising permitted so as to stimulate new business were rejected as it would, obviously, benefit the larger brokers rather than the smaller. This was despite the fact that it was recognized that stockbrokers needed to find new ways of gaining clients, other than through personal introduction. Again, though signs of competition between stockbroking firms were evident in the 1950s, attempts were made to try and suppress them, again to the disadvantage of the larger firms. Capels, when trying to expand by poaching clients from the smaller firms were warned off by the Council in 1955. As a consequence, the average stockbroking firm in 1959 had only six partners plus a further five clerks, including members who were permitted access to the floor. The average jobbing firm was even smaller with only five partners and four clerks. Firms like Capels and Cazenoves, with anything between 10 and 18 partners were among the giants at this time. Mullens, the government's own broker had eight partners in 1950 and nine in 1960. Phillips & Drew, with 11 partners and 150 staff in 1960, was one of the giants of the Stock Exchange.[60]

Numerically, the small broking firm could exert a powerful influence on

[58] LSE: Council, 3 Nov. 1952, 3 Mar. 1958, 5 Jan. 1959.

[59] Ibid., 31 Jan. 1955, 12 Dec. 1955.

[60] Ibid., 13 Feb. 1950, 9 Mar. 1953, 21 Dec. 1953, 11 July 1955, 19 Dec. 1955, 5 Nov. 1956, 4 Apr. 1959; King, *The Stock Exchange*, 43; Kynaston, *Cazenove*, 218; Reed, *Capel and Company*, 92; Wainwright, *Mullens*, 94, 138; Reader and Kynaston, *Phillips & Drew*, 72.

the direction followed by the London Stock Exchange, even though the larger brokers and jobbers undertook most of the business. This was especially true where these firms largely acted for institutional clients as these were of growing importance in the 1950s. The brokers, Green & Co. acted for 50 institutional clients in 1958, for example. Typical of the type of orders these firms handled was the business done by the brokers Northcote & Co. in 1956. In the October of that year they bought and sold nationalized industry stock totalling £2.5m. for only 7 clients and that was followed by business worth £3.3m. in December for the same clients. In turn this was handled by the larger jobbers. Between October and December 1956 the jobbers Francis & Praed handled transactions totalling £15.5m. in nationalized industry stocks.[61] Thus, though brokers were faced with a low level of business for much of the 1950s it was the small firms with largely private client operations that suffered most. Turnover on the Stock Exchange declined until 1952/3 before beginning a hesitant recovery, which did not develop full momentum until the end of the 1950s.[62] At the beginning of the 1950s stockbroking was facing a crisis, as was made clear in July 1952.

The cost of conducting Stock Exchange business has . . . been rising steadily, and in the last few years has increased very sharply. Salaries, telephone charges, office expenses, and, with many firms, mechanisation costs, have all risen, and at the same time modern conditions very properly require an increasingly high standard of statistical and informatory service for the public. Much has been done in the way of reorganization, amalgamation of firms, etc; but a problem remains of real difficulty and even hardship for many firms, both in London and the provinces.[63]

Inevitably, this focused attention, once again, upon both the individual rates of commission charged and the question of rebates. As a result there was a mounting campaign to increase the commission rates and reduce the rebates. Specific proposals included an increase on the commission charged for dealings in gilt-edged stock from $\frac{1}{4}$ to $\frac{3}{8}$ per cent and a reduction in rebates, bringing banks down to 25 per cent and all others to 20 per cent.[64] Again, it was the rebates to banks that proved the most contentious issue, and it was dropped, because of their importance, as was recognized in 1952

The Joint Stock Banks, with their thousand branches spread over every city, town and almost every village in the country, draw to the Stock Exchange a very large business, much of which would not otherwise come here. This they distribute very widely amongst our broking firms (and amongst provincial brokers also) and it forms a substantial proportion of the business of all Stock Exchanges. The Joint Stock Banks, in addition to their agency business, bring to the Stock Exchange a

[61] LSE: Council, 8 Apr. 1957, 15 Dec. 1958.
[62] Ibid., 9 Dec. 1957, 29 Apr. 1958, 16 May 1959, 19 Oct. 1959; F. Paukert, 'The Value of Stock Exchange Transactions in Non-Government Securities, 1911–1959', *Economica*, 28 (1962/3), 304.
[63] LSE: Council, 28 July 1952.　　[64] Ibid., 21 Apr. 1952, 28 July 1952, 18 Aug. 1952.

very large business on their own account, the commission upon which, although the transactions are carried out by comparatively few firms, is also spread very widely over our broking firms.[65]

Other groups, such as the merchant banks, could not exert the influence possessed by the joint-stock banks and so they had to accept a reduced rebate. The specific increases in gilt-edged securities and bearer bonds were also pushed through by November 1952.[66]

The result of these increases in rates and reduction of rebates was to encourage institutional investors to seek ways of buying and selling without using the Stock Exchange. The Post Office, for example, offered favourable rates for small transactions in gilt-edged stock, because of the special privileges given to the government broker, and the Stock Exchange was unwilling to interfere with this. For bearer securities the increase in commission charges caused an appreciable drop in turnover as business was driven abroad. However, the Stock Exchange was reluctant to reverse the increase as most members were pleased. One firm, E. A. S. Oldham, reported a 20–25 per cent increase in commission income by February 1953, with the amount returned by way of rebate remaining static.[67] It was quite clear that the Stock Exchange saw its future in satisfying the investment needs of the British public, both directly and indirectly, and this meant that it could not risk alienating the banks as they possessed the retail network which channelled orders to London. Though rebates were granted to other groups, such as the merchant banks and agents at home and abroad, they were considered of secondary importance.

Those firms that handled large institutional orders continued to bend the commission rules in order to retain such business. The Stock Exchange was willing to accept such practices as long as they did not absolutely flout the rules. Though small brokers could press for absolute adherence to the commission rules the Council of the Stock Exchange were aware of the feelings elsewhere in the City that its scale of charges was considered too high, and was willing to allow a level of discretion to its members in order to deflect criticism.[68] Phillips & Drew, for example, were brokers with a large institutional business and they reported in 1957 that

we transact a considerable number of bargains in the Home Corporation and Dominion and Colonial Markets where it frequently happens that an order of £50,000 may be executed in parts over a few days when to deal in one day is impossible.[69]

Orders of £50,000 and over qualified for a reduced rate of commission and they contended that if the cumulative total for one client came to that, then it was eligible. By modifying the rules in that way they were able to offer regular discounts to institutional clients on all their business.

[65] LSE: Council, 15 Sept. 1952.     [66] Ibid., 13 Oct. 1952, 10 Nov. 1952.
[67] Ibid., 22 Sept. 1952, 26 Jan. 1953, 16 Feb. 1953.
[68] Ibid., 1 Feb. 1954, 1 Mar. 1954, 3 Sept. 1956.     [69] Ibid., 14 Jan. 1957.

Conversely, there was a general feeling that the commission rate on small deals was too low, because of the costs involved. Here the Stock Exchange was in a dilemma. Politically the Stock Exchange wanted to be seen to cultivate the small investor but it was incapable of devising a strategy that would both generate business and make it profitable. Stockbroking firms remained too small to provide a service that would handle a large number of small transactions cheaply and quickly. Instead they left that to the banks, which possessed the retail operations, while they concentrated on meeting the needs of wealthy individuals and financial institutions. Thus, though statements were made indicating the Stock Exchange's concern for the small investor the only practical help offered was to resist the calls to raise the commission rates on such deals.[70] The brokers Sutherland, Pershouse & Co. made the case for an increase in the minimum level of commission charges in 1957

Nearly all brokers are called on to execute a vast number of small orders and the fact that many of these are received from banks, solicitors, and other agents reduces the net commission receivable and we contend that most small bargains are not only unprofitable but actually incur a loss. We are fully alive to the desirability of encouraging the small investor but his business, which often involves considerable service should at least pay for itself.[71]

The problem with any fixed scale of charges was that it was set too low for some deals and too high for others. Thus the members of the Stock Exchange felt they were losing money on small deals, because the rates there were too low, while they were losing business on the large deals, as the rates there were too high. However, there was a great reluctance to alter, radically, the system of fixed commission rates, and the discounts available, that had been built up over the years. For example, it was through the profits made on the larger deals that brokers were able to subsidize the losses on the small deals. In 1959 it was estimated that 20 per cent of all sales and purchases were for £100 or less but it remained important that these continued to be carried out because, '. . . one of the principal functions of stockbrokers is the giving of personal advice on matters of investment to all categories of the investing public'.[72] As long as the Stock Exchange was seen to be serving the investing public directly it could portray itself as an important part of the financial system in terms that could be generally understood. If it ceased to do that, because of its charges, it would lose what public understanding it had.

However, in the 1950s change was vital if the members of the Stock Exchange were going to continue serving the investing public, for that public was itself altering. Affluence and taxation in particular were simultaneously widening the number of investors but contracting those that were

[70] Ibid., 12 Sept. 1955, 19 Mar. 1956, 14 May 1956, 26 Aug. 1957.
[71] Ibid., 14 Oct. 1957.    [72] Ibid., 9 Mar. 1959.

seriously wealthy. As the brokers H. & R. Wagner, explained in December 1957, this had implications for the Stock Exchange

... when most clients were wealthy ... occasional small bargains were carried out for them as part of the normal service. Owing to the great changes which have taken place in the distribution of wealth in the country there has been a large increase in the number of small bargains for investors who have not the wealth for large bargains.[73]

This point was then taken up in February 1958 by another firm of brokers, Weddle, Beck & Co.

In the previous decade Brokers relied upon the middle and upper classes for the bulk of their business. Today, with onerous taxation and depleted incomes, this type of business is much reduced and money is now spread more widely and in smaller parcels amongst the class of people who know little or nothing of the Stock Exchange.[74]

This new investing public required a different kind of service from the exclusive and personal contact that had characterized the broker/client relationship of the past. In turn that meant the emergence of a different kind of stockbroking firm. If charges were not be increased and, ideally, lowered, brokers had to reduce the cost of each transaction by increasing their turnover and decreasing their expenses. Increasing turnover was already difficult because of the ban on advertising, the restriction on competition, the uniform scale of charges, and the inflexibility of the commission rate regime. Stock Exchange rules also reduced, considerably, any advantage to be gained from mergers and the creation of large firms as the volume of business was restricted by the number of partners and clerks permitted. One solution would have been the creation of firms that integrated stockbroking into the provision of other financial services, such as banking and insurance, but that course of action was precluded by the Stock Exchange's rules on the outside activities of members and those they were associated with. Though that rule had originated as a means of reducing the level of exposure to risk and loss faced by the membership as a whole, it was increasingly used as a way of excluding competitors from the Stock Exchange. Members, for example, were forbidden to be directors of unit trusts as they were still regarded as competitors. Reginald Baxter, for example, had to resign from the Stock Exchange when he formed in 1950 the Overseas American Finance Company, as this traded extensively in securities.[75]

Under the rules of the Stock Exchange it was also impossible to create a nation-wide stockbroking firm as no member was allowed to join another stock exchange or even maintain a branch office outside London. This even extended to membership of other types of exchanges, so stopping the cre-

[73] LSE: Council, 9 Dec. 1957.     [74] Ibid., 10 Feb. 1958.
[75] Ibid., 18 Feb. 1957, 15 June 1959.

ation of broking firms that could trade in commodities as well as securities or also covered insurance with the Lloyds market. J. Sproat Williamson, for instance, wanted to become a member of the Corn Exchange, as that was where he had good connections since 1927 and where he did most of his business. Membership would allow him to '... meet my friends and clients and do what Stock Exchange business I can find there'. His request was refused. Similarly, the brokers Brown, Bliss & Co. were refused permission for their clerk, D. J. Branch, to become a member of the Baltic Exchange. This was despite the fact that their firm had long-standing connections with the Baltic Exchange through the Branch family.

Our firm has been dealing for more than thirty years with many of the leading member firms and individual member firms and individual members of the Baltic Exchange. During post-war years due to the efforts of the late J. C. Branch and more recently his son, commissions received by our firm from this source have ranged up to £15,000 per annum ... During the last eighteen months Mr D. J. Branch has visited the Baltic Exchange daily and as he has had access to the Stock Exchange markets he has been in a position to deal and advise his clients on market conditions etc. far more advantageously than would have been the case through a third party. Quite apart from the service given, which we believe is greatly appreciated by his clients, we would find it very difficult under normal market conditions, to replace Mr Branch with another dealer, bearing in mind the special knowledge and requirements of clients in this case.[76]

Despite the plea, and the evidence of the business generated, the Stock Exchange refused to sanction dual membership. It was conscious that failure in one exchange would make an impact on the other while it was also aware that a rival market could always develop elsewhere, if another exchange permitted trading in securities under less onerous rules and regulations.

Consequently, the creation of large stockbroking firms, whether integrated with allied activities or not, was simply not possible under Stock Exchange rules in the 1950s. Any pressure for change was resisted by the small broking firms whose business would be threatened by such moves. Instead, limited steps were taken to reduce the expenses of operation, such as the movement of offices, notably back offices, from the area immediately around the Stock Exchange. Spencer Thornton & Co., for example, resited their clerks in an office in Peckham in 1954, because of '... the prohibitive cost of a short lease of even moderate office accommodation in the City'.[77]

For the same reasons Vickers da Costa were relocating their main office to premises in King William Street in 1955. In keeping with the times some members set up separate service companies that would provide them with office accommodation and staff. As companies they received a more favourable tax treatment than individuals, without having to go to the length

[76] Ibid., 20 May 1957, 18 Nov. 1957.    [77] Ibid., 4 Oct. 1954, cf. 23 May 1955.

of incorporating the whole firm, which some of the larger partnerships had done. Also, by the end of the 1950s office mechanization was being adopted as a way of reducing expenses, especially of clerical staff. The jobbers, Durlachers, installed computers in the late 1950s for example.[78]

During the 1950s it was clear that the Stock Exchange was failing to capture the business of the small investor while it was suffering from the demise of its traditional clients, the large investors. However, the savings of the nation were also falling into the hands of the institutions to a greater and greater extent, and these included not only the joint-stock banks but a growing variety of merchant banks, finance houses, investment and unit trusts, and insurance companies. The Stock Exchange, itself, observed in 1957 that

... the traditional private investor had become less important, and small savings were canalized through the Insurance companies and Pension Funds, whose dealings dominated most markets and most issues.[79]

Some of the larger and better connected of the stockbroking firms capitalized on these changes by developing ever closer connections with particular financial institutions. Firms like Capels, Cazenoves, Phillips & Drew, and Sebags, prospered from such contacts. Phillips & Drew's net profit doubled during the 1950s, from £89,591 in 1950/1 to £160,593 in 1958/9. They invested in the qualified staffs necessary not only to buy and sell securities but to feed their clients with expert knowledge on the state of the market and the merits of individual securities. By 1957, for example, Capels had a staff of 70 and it was continuing to grow, despite the restrictions imposed by the Stock Exchange on partners and authorized/unauthorized clerks.[80] These larger firms recruited from among the existing membership, offering better prospects and a safer source of income than private client stockbroking. One member who moved was Dundas Hamilton. Despite becoming a partner in his father's firm, Carroll & Co., in 1948 he left it in the early 1950s to join Fielding, Son & Macleod. This was a much bigger firm with strong institutional links. Both the firm and its business grew in the 1950s. They started a pension fund department in 1954. In 1958 it merged with another broker, Newson-Smith & Co., to form Fielding, Newson-Smith.[81] The impression is given of considerable movement between firms in the 1950s with those handling an institutional business growing while those with a predominately private client business declined. The Stock Exchange noted in December 1958 that

---

[78] LSE: Council, 12 Mar. 1956, 30 Apr. 1956, 15 Oct. 1956, 18 Feb. 1957, 4 Dec. 1959; Courtney and Thompson, *City Lives*, 205.

[79] LSE: Council, 9 Dec. 1957, cf. 20 Oct. 1950.

[80] Ibid., 15 Dec. 1958; Reed, *Capel and Company*, 91-3; Kynaston, *Cazenove*, 231; Sebag-Montefiore, *Sebag & Co.*, 45; Reader and Kynaston, *Phillips & Drew*, 45.

[81] Courtney and Thompson, *City Lives*, 63.

. . . a substantial number of members and clerks move from one firm to another in the course of each year.[82]

Nevertheless, these expanding firms remained a distinct minority in the 1950s and so their views on more competitive charges and practices were largely ignored. In particular, members of the Stock Exchange found it difficult to compete with non-members, such as the merchant banks, because of a shortage of capital. In the past that had not been a major problem. Low taxation had allowed brokers and jobbers to reinvest their profits so as to build up a solid capital base over time, perpetuated by the family structure of many of the firms. However, heavy post-war taxation, allied to a prolonged depression in stock exchange business in the late 1940s/early 1950s, greatly diminished the ability of self-finance to provide the capital required. The Stock Exchange was aware of the problem as early as January 1951,

In the past members, out of their current earnings, could accumulate capital for their business and provide savings for their retirement. For some appreciable time this has not been possible owing to the high rates of taxation and the incidence of the previous year basis of assessment, which does not permit the averaging of good years with bad.[83]

At that stage greater tax efficiency, as with the adoption of the corporate form, was felt to be solution. Hence the reason it was taken up by the likes of de Zoete & Gorton. Even when that course had been followed some of the larger firms still lacked the capital reserves necessary to finance the level of business they were doing, especially in competition with non-members. Merchants banks, investment trusts, discount houses, and others increasingly converted into joint-stock companies at this time, raising capital from outside investors. In 1953 the Bentworth Trust, for example, had two subsidiaries both competing with Stock Exchange members in the issuing and trading in securities, and they were one among many.[84]

Consequently, there was a growing demand from a few members to be allowed to raise additional capital from among non-members. Brokers were less affected as most bought and sold on commission, and did not require a large capital to finance market operations. In contrast, jobbers were often in a position where they had to carry securities until they sold them at a favourable price.[85] L. C. Denza, a partner in the jobbers Paul E. Shaw & Co., explained the predicament they faced after the Second World War.

Although taxation remained relatively high after Word War I, it was nevertheless still possible to save important sums of money out of income until the approach of World War II (say 1937/8). Since then the very high scale of taxation has made considerable savings out of income no longer possible, and as a result the capital

[82] LSE: Council, 15 Dec. 1958.   [83] Ibid., 22 Jan. 1951.
[84] Ibid., 18 May 1953, 12 Sept. 1955, 15 Oct. 1956.
[85] Ibid., 21 May 1951, 17 Dec. 1956.

resources of the jobbing fraternity as a whole have progressively diminished. It can moreover be asserted quite definitely that this process will continue at an accelerating pace unless measures are taken to deal with the situation. High taxation has obviously come to stay for a long while.

He went on to add that by the early 1950s the problem had become very serious. The older jobbers, who had accumulated capital before the Second World War, were beginning to retire, and their places were being taken by younger dealers who had not been able to build up sufficient capital for the requirements of the market. At the same time the risks of operating without sufficient capital were a serious deterrent to those contemplating setting up on their own or becoming partners in a jobbing firm. The foreign market had attracted no new jobbing firms since 1950, despite experiencing a growth in business. Denza concluded that

The experience needed by a dealer assuming the responsibility for running an important 'book' is very considerable and takes a good many years to acquire. We are already very short of younger men.

Accordingly, Denza was of the opinion that there was a crisis on the Stock Exchange in 1952 as the jobbing capacity was inadequate

A careful analysis of the number of firms actively engaged in jobbing and running a book on a sufficient scale to help to constitute a market has recently been computed at hardly more than 60—although of course some of them are engaged in more than one market. It will hardly be disputed that this number is barely sufficient for present-day requirements, if the present system is to continue. When markets are difficult and particularly when they are falling, dealings in many securities frequently become virtually impossible in other than small amounts. This discourages many clients from placing large orders, and must increase the tendency for business in big amounts to be transacted outside the House.[86]

This analysis and judgement by Denza was accepted by the Council of the Stock Exchange, which then sought ways of introducing outside capital into jobbers' firms but without changing the individual nature of the membership. Various suggestions were made, including copying the European practice where banks were admitted as members. However, none was acceptable to the membership as a whole, worried about the influence possessed by those who provided the capital, such as the large financial institutions. The problem was that if financial institutions gained control over the jobbers how could the member brokers retain exclusive access to the dealing service they provided.[87]

Therefore no action was taken. By the beginning of 1956 the situation had become even more serious.

Notwithstanding the greater activity which prevailed during the past year the jobbing market of the Stock Exchange has continued to contract. A further 6 firms

---

[86] LSE: Council, 1 Dec. 1952.    [87] Ibid., 16 Mar. 1953.

have gone out of business, reducing the total number from 238 (the figure as at 1 August 1947) to 134, a reduction of 104 firms, or 43 per cent.[88]

Again, no action followed. By March 1957 the problems of the jobbing system were being described as '. . . disturbing . . .' with brokers such as J. A. Hunter (of L. Messel & Company) expressing worries about the situation, blaming it on the high costs of doing business on the Stock Exchange.[89] These views were ignored as was that of E. L. Taylor, of the jobbers Hadow & Turner, who wrote to highlight the situation in July 1958.

It is plainly observable that there has been a steady and marked diminution in the number of jobbing firms with sufficient capital resources to entertain large transactions and for business of this character to bypass the House, although the basis of this business in on Stock Exchange prices.[90]

His only suggestion was the introduction of a system of minimum turns, equivalent to minimum commission rates, but this would hardly have met the competition from non-member dealers that was building up over the decade. When it was discovered that one firm of jobbers, Francis Egerton & Co., had obtained capital from the brokers Straus Turnbull & Co., this was deemed to be against the rules of the Stock Exchange. Both firms were banned from the Stock Exchange for six months, which effectively ended the career of the Egerton partner involved, namely Berthold Mendelssohn who was 80 years old and had been a member for 47 years.[91]

In fact, the Stock Exchange's only response to the gradual demise of the jobbing system was to introduce, late in the day, further regulations forcing brokers to bring more of their business to the floor. All this did was restrict the freedom of brokers to operate, disadvantaging them against non-members, without aiding the jobbers. The problem was that the telephone was making it easier and easier for brokers to contact each other directly or large institutional holders or non-member dealers, like the North American brokerage houses, to try and match sales and purchases, without ever bringing the business to the Stock Exchange.[92] By November 1958 the Stock Exchange was forced to recognize that,

. . . a fundamental change in the transaction of Stock Exchange business has taken place due to the considerable number of deals which are negotiated by Brokers between non-members and which only reach the Jobber on put through terms. This fundamental change has been brought about largely by the growth in importance of institutional clients.[93]

Brokers were now sending their clerks to the floor of the Stock Exchange to conduct the sales and purchases that they could not do from the office. The result of this was the emergence of a number of large jobbing firms

---

[88] Ibid., 23 Jan. 1956.     [89] Ibid., 18 Mar. 1957, 20 May 1957.
[90] Ibid., 28 July 1958, cf. 25 Aug. 1958.     [91] Ibid., 27 July 1959.
[92] Ibid., 9 June 1955, 23 July 1956.     [93] Ibid., 24 Feb. 1958.

that did possess the capacity to both compete with outside dealers and provide the telephone service that brokers now required. One such was F. & N. Durlacher, which took over Deacon Godson in 1953 and A. L. Gooday in 1958, so extending its dealing in industrial securities into textiles, engineering, and motor vehicles. Another was Wedd Jefferson which took over Hopkins & Giles in 1957, so consolidating its already strong position in gilt-edged stocks.[94]

With brokers in the ascendancy in the Stock Exchange the Council was reluctant to introduce measures forcing greater use of the jobbers as this could, in turn, result in investors bypassing the members who were brokers, because of the poorer service they provided. Nevertheless, the predicament faced by the smaller jobbers did lead the Stock Exchange to introduce a rule discouraging brokers from matching deals in their own offices. Instead the deal had to be passed through a jobber. For the brokers that complied it increased their charges, which they passed on to their clients, making them less competitive. For others such a rule encouraged evasion as it was difficult for the Stock Exchange to police what was happening in brokers' offices or via the telephone.[95] The dilemma the Stock Exchange faced was that it was unable to force brokers to buy and sell only through the jobbers as that would undermine their ability to compete with non-members, such as the provincial brokers or the North American brokers operating in London. Conversely, if the Stock Exchange did not help the jobbers one of the main advantages possessed by the brokers, in the shape of exclusive access to the trading-floor, would be worth little, exposing them to the full competition of non-members unencumbered with the costs and restrictions that came with the membership. Charles Dreyfus warned in 1959 that 'perhaps one day the Pru will ring up the Pension Fund instead of Throgmorton Street', envisaging an end of the intermediary function of not only jobbers but brokers.[96]

In the end the Stock Exchange did nothing substantial, as any real solution would have involved a radical restructuring of the structure of jobbers and their relationship to brokers. Instead, it left jobbers to cope with the problem themselves not only largely unaided by the Stock Exchange but hampered by the rules under which they had to operate. The result was that outside competition grew and brokers increasingly turned to others when it came to closer pricing and large volumes. In response a process of consolidation took place among the jobbers with the remaining firms trying to survive by taking control of particular sectors of the market or spreading themselves over a widening range of securities. The result was that the market provided on the floor of the Stock Exchange became a less competitive one as more and more trading took place on the telephone. This

[94] LSE: Council, 24 Feb. 1958. *Wedd, Durlacher Mordaunt & Co., Members of the Stock Exchange, London* (n.p. 1984).
[95] LSE: Council, 31 Mar. 1959.  [96] Ibid., 2 Nov. 1959.

was not inevitable in the 1950s for the trading-floor still possessed many advantages over the telephone contact, as was reported to the Stock Exchange in 1959 by Blackwell & Co.:

Inter-office dealings suffer from the disadvantage that during periods of intense activity communications become choked and we have noticed recently that Brokers have found it quicker to come in person to our office than to telephone. This is despite the fact that our telephone system is the most modern and efficient that the G. P. O. can at present provide, and we can see no immediate improvement in that direction.[97]

Though the growth of large institutional holders of securities, and the use of the telephone, did facilitate the direct matching of sales and purchases between investors, or the use of only brokers as intermediaries, the trading-floor provided by the Stock Exchange remained of major importance. Institutions did not want to deal directly with each other, because of what it revealed, while the telephone system lacked the capacity and the flexibility to cope with a multitude of users trying to contact each other at the same time in active markets. It best served the broker or investor trying to negotiate a particular deal.

## Growing Competition

Where the Stock Exchange was more active was in trying to close outsider access to its market and the seepage of business to non-members. Restructuring and reorganizing the market was not a priority of the Stock Exchange in the 1950s. A Planning Committee was not formed until December 1957. Rather the Stock Exchange's priority was to defend its domestic business against competition and maintain current practices.

Inevitably this brought the London Stock Exchange into conflict with its provincial counterparts. As early as April 1950 the provincial stock exchanges were informed that

Without the London jobbing system there would be no shunting system on your floors, and your exchanges would be no more than associations of stockbrokers, without a market such as you now have through the operation of shunting.[98]

Shunting was carried on by means of private telephone circuits connecting the office of a London broker with brokers' offices in the major provincial cities. However, by means of the omnibus circuits that were coming into use, telephone networks were being established that not only linked London with provincial brokers but the provincial exchanges with each other, being fed all the time with current prices on the floor of the London Stock Exchange. Based on these prices provincial brokers could buy and sell between each other, and so deprive London of business it had once done. These omnibus circuits had

---

[97] Ibid., 31 Mar. 1959, 7 Sept. 1959.     [98] Ibid., 17 Apr. 1950.

. . . the effect of making Manchester, Liverpool and Birmingham, to a considerable extent, one floor, and so increasing again the volume of business that is done largely upon the back of London, but which is kept away from London.[99]

Naturally enough the London Stock Exchange wanted to retain these direct links between London and provincial brokers, as it both brought business to London and helped settle transactions in local industrials. However, London also wanted to stop the provincial exchanges developing a collective independence through omnibus circuits which would allow them to challenge the market provided by London in particular groups of securities. Edward Notman, of the Edinburgh Stock Exchange, made it clear that any restrictive measures by London would be resisted by the provincial stock exchanges, and could lead to even more business bypassing London than was currently the case. At that stage the London Stock Exchange decided to leave matters as they stood and the competition from the provinces continued to grow in the early 1950s. London was even forced in 1952 to lower the rates of commission charged for transactions with provincial brokers in order to prevent the loss of even more business. London was also trying to prevent the spread of omnibus circuits as these fostered the growth of rivals to its own market in particular securities. The London brokers, Moy, Davies, Smith, Vandervell & Co., for example, maintained an active market in Northern iron and steel companies through a link with the Sheffield brokers, Christopher Barber & Sons. In 1954 they wanted to extend the connection to H. E. Rensburg & Co. (Liverpool), F. W. Staveacre & Co. (Manchester), and Smith, Keen, Barnet & Co. (Birmingham). This request was refused because of fears that it would divert business from London.[100]

The problem London faced was that the diminishing number of jobbers and the improvements in communications during the 1950s were removing the influence once exerted by a physical presence on the floor of the Stock Exchange. Though that was still important more and more business was now conducted on an office-to-office basis using the telephone. At the same time the improvement of links between those trading on the floor of the Stock Exchange and their offices was making it possible to broadcast current prices further and further afield. In 1954 brokers and jobbers still had to queue at the telephone boxes in the Stock Exchange in order to make local calls. Conversely, by 1957 discussions were underway that would have allowed the installation of closed circuit TV links between members' offices and their own telephone boxes in the Stock Exchange. That was fairly uncontentious as it merely improved an existing voice link. More contentious was the move in 1958 to permit members direct access to outside

[99] LSE: Council, 15 May 1950, 29 Sept. 1952, 11 Jan. 1954.
[100] Ibid., 17 May 1954, 7 Jan. 1957, 4 Mar. 1957, 28 July 1958, 18 Aug. 1958, 22 Sept. 1958, 6 Apr. 1959, 6 July 1959, 22 Feb. 1960.

telephone lines from the floor itself. If introduced these telephones would also allow brokers to maintain direct contact with clients from the floor of the Stock Exchange, relaying prices and taking orders as the market unfolded. As these telephones would also be placed on jobber's pitches it would allow them to buy and sell simultaneously on the floor of the Stock Exchange and outside.

Despite a survey that indicated jobbers were opposed and brokers were in favour, the Stock Exchange decided to provide direct outside lines for any member that wanted the service. As jobbers were forbidden under the rules from dealing with non-members, the facility was of limited use to them, whereas it would allow brokers to quote price changes to important clients and provincial brokers, as they were taking place on the floor of the Stock Exchange, without even the delay of being routed via their office. During 1959 the possibility of computerized displays of market prices on the floor of the Stock Exchange and in brokers' offices was raised, as the technology was available. By February 1960 EMI had been commissioned to provide an electronic quotation service.[101] As a consequence, it was becoming impossible to confine current prices on the floor of the Stock Exchange to those actually there, or even in the offices of the members. Once known these prices could be quickly broadcast, via omnibus circuits and teleprinters, and it was in the interests of brokers to do so as orders might result. If a broker matched a sale and purchase himself, without going through a jobber, then only one commission could be charged. Where this involved large and regular clients like provincial brokers or financial institutions, this offered scope for rebating commission, and so encouraged business to come to London.

Essentially, the existence of rapid communications networks were allowing brokers to bypass the jobbers as more transactions could be settled on a bilateral basis, as between the members of the separate stock exchanges. By May 1958 the Planning Committee of the London Stock Exchange saw as inevitable the creation of an integrated stockbroking profession within the UK, as a result of these developments. This would involve common standards and policies, the elimination of duplicated facilities, and the ending of the competition between London and provincial brokers. This could be achieved through London extending membership to country brokers, creating in the process national stockbroking firms offering a low-cost service to investors. However, such a radical move would destroy the autonomy of each individual stock exchange, as well as give provincial brokers direct access to the London market. This course of action was too radical for the 1950s and so it was not pursued actively at the time.[102] Instead, an uneasy relationship between the London and provincial stock exchanges remained. London brokers needed their provincial counterparts both as agents feeding

---

[101] Ibid., 7 Sept. 1959.    [102] Ibid., 12 May 1958; Kynaston, *Cazenove*, 214.

them business and as supplementary markets where securities of largely local interest could be bought and sold. Conversely, the provincial brokers needed London because of the range and liquidity of its market and as a source of authoritative pricing for most securities. As the same time the London Stock Exchange tried to restrict the members of the provincial markets to dealing only in their own local securities, while the country brokers sought ways of bypassing London, keeping more of the business that passed through their hands to themselves, which modern communications increasingly allowed them to do, as they could operate collectively as a group.

In many ways the trends were against the survival of the provincial stock exchanges because nationalization on the one hand, and mergers creating large national firms on the other, removed the individuality of local markets. This meant that the provincial stock exchanges had to compete more and more with London for what business there was. This they were able to do because of the restrictions and charges imposed by the London Stock Exchange. The telephone could bring business as easily to London as take it away, and country jobbers like Carr Workman in Belfast or Nicholsons in Sheffield remained active.[103] In addition, the growing importance of large institutional investors, like the insurance companies and pension fund managers, meant that a high proportion of securities were in relatively few hands. By 1954, for example, the life assurance companies had assets valued at £4.1bn., of which 29 per cent was in government debt and another 35 per cent in corporate securities. Altogether it was estimated that insurance companies held 10 per cent of all securities quoted on the Stock Exchange in 1953. Instead of routeing orders via jobbers, brokers could approach these institutional investors directly with offers to purchase or sell, so bypassing the jobbers and avoiding paying their 'turn', or difference between a buy and sell price. Conversely, these institutions tended to direct most of their business into the hands of the largest brokers, with their specialist staffs, who could offer the service they wanted, especially as fixed commission meant the charges were the same regardless. The broker, L. Messel & Company, had a member of staff from the Edinburgh-based funds managers, the British Assets Trust, with them for two months so as to develop a strong working relationship. Consequently in the 1950s the continuing developments in telecommunications meant that the provincial brokers were able to bypass the London market to a greater degree than before while the growing institutional nature of investment meant that investors themselves were becoming more powerful, and more able to bypass the jobbers. Though the London Stock Exchange still commanded the domestic securities market it had no monopoly, facing increasing competition both nationally and in London. Nationally there were still 23

---

[103] W. A. Thomas, *The Provisional Stock Exchanges* (London 1973), 241, 245–6, 261, 317–18; W. A. Thomas, *The Stock Exchanges of Ireland* (Liverpool 1986), 227, 246.

provincial stock exchanges, plus brokers who were members of none. In London the discount houses, for example, with their greater capital and better banking connections were real rivals to the Stock Exchange in the trading of shorterdated government debt.[104]

The situation was much the same internationally. Despite exchange controls there was a revival of interest among investors in the 1950s in overseas securities. In particular, institutional investors were keen to diversify away from the heavy commitment to government debt that the Second World War, and post-war nationalizations, had created. This was all in the form of fixed interest securities denominated in sterling, and thus susceptible to depreciation in value due to both inflation and devaluation. As early as 1950 there was a growing interest in South African and Australian securities among insurance companies and investment trusts. Being in the sterling area this did not involve the difficulties of North American investments, though these also attracted growing interest.[105] However, there was no guarantee that that business would flow via the London Stock Exchange, though institutional links were developed in the 1950s. Throughout that decade the London Stock Exchange formally recognized other stock exchanges abroad, and even helped in their establishment as in the countries of the Commonwealth. However, integration of stock exchanges at an international level was especially difficult at a time when the movement of money, capital, or securities between countries was heavily regulated. There was also the question of the different ways that stock exchanges were organized in each country, regarding the admission of banks and the rules covering trading. Closer co-operation between the various European stock exchanges, as initiated from Paris, was clearly a desirable goal in the 1950s but rendered impractical because of widely divergent national and institutional priorities and institutional regulations. [106]

The moves towards closer integration was coming at the level of the firm rather than the institution. The growing interest in Australian securities, for example, led to institutional investors establishing direct links with Australian brokers. For North American securities there was the long-standing presence of US and Canadian brokerage houses in London though this had been reduced during the Second World War. In the 1950s their numbers built up again and it was they who conducted much of the investment in dollar securities for British investors, rather than the brokers and jobbers who were members of the London Stock Exchange. Even London brokers

[104] J. Johnstone and G. W. Murphy, 'The Growth of Life Assurance in UK since 1880', *Economic and Social Studies*, 25 (1957), 154–5; W. King, 'The Market's Changing Role', 11–14, and H. F. Goodson, 'The Functioning of the London Discount Houses', 18–19, in Institute of Bankers, *The London Discount Market Today* (London 1962); W. M. Scammell, *The London Discount Market* (London 1968), 48, 221, 227; G. A. Fletcher, *The Discount Houses in London: Principles, Operations and Change* (London 1976), 40, 55, 61; LSE: Council, 12 Mar. 1956, 14 Nov. 1957.

[105] Ibid., 30 Jan. 1950, 30 Oct. 1950, 17 Dec. 1956.

[106] Ibid., 14 Sept. 1953, 28 Dec. 1954, 25 Mar. 1957, 9 Nov. 1959, 28 Dec. 1959.

were preferring to place clients' orders with the US and Canadian firms in London rather than through jobbers in the American market, because they offered a better service and keener prices. At the same time a deal with these firms generated commission for a broker while sale or purchase with a jobber did not.[107] Individual brokers also established contacts overseas through which sales and purchases could be made. Dix & Maurice in London trained J. Gissing, of the Sydney brokers C. B. Quinan & Cox, for four months in 1956 while in the previous year Cazenoves had formed a link with the New York brokers, Kidder Peabody. This involved the New York firm opening a London branch in Cazenoves' office. There was even co-operation between brokers to develop new markets in foreign securities. In 1959 four brokers—Norris Oakley Brothers, Panmure Gordon & Co., L. Messel & Company, and Zorn & Leigh Hunt, set up a joint operation to try and develop an interest in European securities.[108]

However, these moves at an individual level received little support from the Stock Exchange as most members were worried that it would lead to a seepage of business abroad, rather than generating extra turnover for London. There was thus a reluctance to modify the Stock Exchanges rules, practices, or charges to allow for the particular needs of those who were trying to revive the international dimension of the market. Quite the reverse was often the case, with any international connection being viewed by most members as a device used by a few to evade the charges and restrictions imposed by the Stock Exchange. I. J. Alberg & Co. received little help in trying to revive their continental European business in the early 1950s, for example, as it would have involved them making extra payments to their Paris agent, Gaston Weiner.

Mr Gaston Wiener has been our representative in Paris for the whole of France for over thirty years and represented the firm we succeeded previous to that. During all this time he played his part in building up a valuable connection which was, of course, for the time being destroyed by the war and consequent restrictions. There is evidence that Continental business is reviving to a limited extent and with the removal of further restrictions may again become active, and our representative, who has continued all these years to be registered with the Stock Exchange, now wishes to reopen his Paris office and resume his former activities in so far as that is possible.[109]

This reluctance by the London Stock Exchange to meet the needs of those doing an international business was unfortunate. The exodus of bankers and brokers from continental Europe, especially Jews from Germany, both in the 1930s and 1940s, had established a wealth of expertise and connections in London through which such business could be conducted. One such

---

[107] LSE: Council, 30 Oct. 1950, 3 Mar. 1958, 12 May 1958.
[108] Ibid., 17 Sept. 1956, 6 Apr. 1959; Kynaston, *Cazenove*, 225.
[109] LSE: Council, 9 Apr. 1951.

person was Hans Schlesinger. He had trained with a merchant bank, spending some time on the Berlin Stock Exchange, before settling in London in 1936. By 1938 he was co-operating with the Stock Exchange member S. P. Angel to transact business for German clients. As he said himself, when he joined the Stock Exchange in 1953

I have been able to bring to the London Stock Exchange a substantial amount of business from important Foreign Banks, which, but for my efforts, might have bypassed London.[110]

Consequently, there existed both the talent and the connnections necessary to revive London's international role, despite the restrictions imposed by the government, but it was the Stock Exchange's own rules and regulations that prevented it from participating fully in this revival.

As foreign banks, North American brokerage firms, and British finance houses all used London as a base for international securities transactions in the 1950s, it is clear that it was the Stock Exchange's own rules that stopped its members from participating to the extent they wished. For example, the Bank of England permitted foreign residents to sell one security and reinvest in another, or transfer the securities to another foreign resident, without having to be bound by British foreign exchange controls, which required conversion of any dollars received into sterling. By 1952 it was reported that

... it is now common practice for stock to be sold from one foreign resident to another in dollars and the buyer sells the stock on the Stock Exchange, reinvesting the proceed in some other security he wants, or which he can arbitrage. This is excellent business for the Stock Exchange, but competition from outside firms is keen.[111]

Consequently, those members conducting the business wanted permission to reduce the commission they charged so as to compete more effectively with the non-members. They were refused as the Stock Exchange was determined to preserve the fixed rate regime and regarded any concessions as undermining it. Those engaged in the buying and selling of foreign securities complained throughout the 1950s that the high commission rates charged were driving the business into the hands of non-members, but as they were very much a minority in the Stock Exchange they were unable to obtain any concessions or relaxations.[112]

It was not just the minimum rates that members had to charge which lost them business in foreign securities. The necessity for brokers to try their own market first also lost them valuable time, in competition with non-members, especially the London based US brokers who could give an almost immediate response by contacting New York directly. For institutions that

---

[110] Ibid., 21 Dec. 1953.    [111] Ibid., 5 Aug. 1952.
[112] Ibid., 31 Jan. 1955, 25 Apr. 1955.

wanted to complete deals quickly this led to them bypassing members of the Stock Exchange in favour of the foreign banks and brokers in London. Even the Stock Exchange's requirement to fill in a form and await authorization, for a transaction involving dollar exchange, caused delays that were sufficient to lose brokers such as Stocken & Concannon, the business. However, in its role as the Bank of England's supervisory agent for the securities market, the Stock Exchange was unwilling to abandoned such formfilling, though it did agree to create a faster service for urgent business.[113] The Stock Exchange was also unwilling to change the practice of quoting American securities in terms of the Stock Exchange dollar ($1 = 4s.), despite the fact that this gave a totally false impression of the price of these securities. A number of members wanted, in 1958, to move to either quoting in dollars at the current exchange rate, or convert the prices into their sterling equivalents. This would make it easier for brokers to compare the prices quoted by jobbers inside the Stock Exchange with those of outside dealers. However, the Stock Exchange was '. . . not prepared to interfere with existing practice . . .' because

The market expressed the unanimous view in the strongest possible terms that they did not wish to abandon their long-standing practice of quoting these shares in the Stock Exchange dollar. They were of the opinion that to alter the present basis would mean the loss of the international market to London, would lead to chaos in dealings and they were not even prepared to countenance dealing in sterling prices for an experimental period.[114]

Naturally enough there was no sympathy in 1959 when those brokers and jobbers dealing in international securities wanted to extend the Stock Exchange hours to the pre-war time of 4 o'clock, rather than the current 3.30 p.m. This would give them more opportunity to transact American business, as the New York Stock Exchange opened at 3.00 p.m. UK time. Instead, they were recommended to form a 'street' market in one of the Courts, as in the past.[115]

Towards the end of the 1950s there was a growing exasperation with the Stock Exchange from those members who were most involved in the international securities business, though the government did not escape blame. One member who voiced his complaints was H. A. G. Vanderfelt, whose firm had long been involved in trading gold-mining securities between London and other financial centres. He recollected in 1959 that '. . . when I first joined the Stock Exchange in 1922, my firm had, what today could only be described as a fantastic turnover with Paris and other continental Centres.' He then went on to indicate that, once again, 'International business is expanding and we should do everything we can to encourage this

---

[113] LSE: Council, 4 Apr. 1955, 25 Apr. 1955, 9 May 1955, 15 Oct. 1956.
[114] Ibid., 8 Sept. 1958, cf. 18 Aug. 1958, 15 Sept. 1958.
[115] Ibid., 17 Nov. 1958, 2 Nov. 1959, 9 Nov. 1959.

expansion.' But added that 'Those of us who do such business, realize more than most people how frequently London is now bypassed because of our stamp-duty and outmoded methods.' In particular, he referred to the length of delays that occurred when sales and purchases were made in London, which forced up his costs and encouraged clients to use other markets. A beneficiary of this was the Johannesburg Stock Exchange which was supplanting London as the major market for gold-mining shares.

I know for a fact how much business London loses at the moment, because I see our Agents' figures when I go to South Africa each year. Their profits are now three to four times what they were two years ago. This is due to the direct receipt by them of orders from American and most Continental Centres,

was Vanderfelt's observation.[116] South African gold-mining shares were one of the few international markets that the London Stock Exchange continued to possess in the 1950s. However, the Stock Exchange's own charges and practices were leading to its decline. The Exchange had already lost its position in such markets as American securities by the early 1950s. 'There can be no doubt that the majority of institutional business in American securities passes direct between the institutions and American Houses.'[117] By the late 1950s the same was happening in South African securities, with New York and Johannesburg being the gainers in each case. At the same time the London Stock Exchange was failing to develop alternative international markets in the way it had between the wars. Then it had tried hard to cultivate markets in South African, Indian, and Far Eastern securities, to compensate for the greatly diminished American market. In the 1950s there were possibilities in continental Europe and Japan but little effort was made in that direction. The lack of flexibility on commission charges for both European remisiers and Japanese banks, for example, did little to encourage them to direct business to London, faced as they were with the additional burdens of taxation and exchange controls.[118]

Inevitably, the Stock Exchange's lack of concern over the fate of the once important international business, spilled over into outright hostility towards international arbitrage. To a growing extent arbitrage was regarded as a loophole in the Stock Exchange's charges and regulations, which had to be closed. In arbitrage jobbers were permitted to deal directly with non-members, while brokers did not have to follow the minimum commission rules. Beginning in 1953, when turnover on the Stock Exchange was at a low level, the privileges of the arbitrageurs began to be further undermined. It was almost as if arbitrage was being blamed for diverting business away from the Stock Exchange, because every sale or purchase in London had to be matched by a reverse deal on a foreign stock exchange. As it was the

[116] Ibid., 8 June 1959.     [117] Ibid., 29 June 1953.
[118] Ibid., 29 June 1953, 17 Jan. 1955.

first attack was to prevent jobbers from conducting arbitrage in anything other than the securities they already made markets in. Arbitrage was permissible in those as it helped jobbers respond to the sales and purchases on the floor of the Stock Exchange, through corresponding purchases and sales elsewhere, and so maintain liquid markets. The restriction reduced the flexibility of the jobbers to changing market requirements as it restricted the range of securities they could now trade in. Nevertheless, despite opposition the restriction was imposed on the jobbers.[119] At the same time the arbitrage operations of brokers was attacked by an attempt to outlaw joint-account operations. In joint-account arbitrage the broker shared profits and losses with the non-member and did not charge commission. This was justified by the fact that if commission was charged most arbitrage would not be profitable, as the margin between sale and purchase price was so low, and could only be justified by the volume of business. However, joint-account trading was seen to offer a way of evading the minimum commission rules because the broker was not charging the non-member. Consequently, the Stock Exchange introduced a rule that commission must be charged, either by the member or by the non-member for whom he was acting. As much arbitrage involved no clients, with members of the London Stock Exchange co-operating with members of foreign stock exchanges, to profit from any price difference that appeared between their two markets, such a rule would drive the business out of the Stock Exchange.[120] Cazenoves did point this out to the Stock Exchange

We were concerned last year in selling South African securities totalling in all a huge sum of money. This we were able to do to the satisfaction of our clients, and with considerable advantage to our correspondents in South Africa and ourselves, in face of intense opposition and competition from outside finance houses, who used every artifice to secure the business. If the proposed amendments had been in force when discussions regarding this business were taking place we should have had no other option, in the best interests of our clients and for the maintenance of their goodwill, but to advise them that their cheapest method of procedure would be to deal direct with South Africa or through an outside finance house who could have dealt either in London, Paris, or Johannesburg, for the most part untrammelled by the rules of the London Stock Exchange[121]

However, the Stock Exchange was willing to accept the loss of international business in order to preserve the policy that all clients must pay the minimum commission charges. This was considered vital for the survival of the brokers, most of whose income was generated by handling sales and purchases of domestic securities. Consequently, the intensity of the campaign against arbitrage did not abate, but sought other targets. As there was no time overlap between trading in London and Singapore it was ques-

[119] LSE: Council, 22 June 1953.   [120] Ibid., 29 June 1953.
[121] Ibid., 6 July 1953.

tioned whether this was arbitrage or not. If it was not arbitrage, jobbers would be forbidden to trade with non-members and brokers would have to charge commission to brokers in Singapore. More generally attempts were made to limit those with whom arbitrage could be conducted and the securities that could be traded. Successful arbitrage needed flexibility, for it was not always possible to close a deal unless other correspondents and other securities were included, and it was the flexibility that was continually undermined in the 1950s. [122]

Throughout the 1950s the London Stock Exchange concern was not to promote arbitrage as a means of increasing its international role but to ensure that it was not being used as a way of evading the rules on dual capacity and fixed commissions. This led the Stock Exchange to define permissible arbitrage in very narrow terms, as in 1957.

Arbitrage is defined as the business of buying and selling a security as a Principal in one centre with the intent of reversing such transaction in a centre in a country different from that in which the original transaction has taken place in order to profit from price differences between such centres and which business is not casual but contains the element of continuity. It is therefore essential that there is a market in the security in both centres independently.[123]

Ideally arbitrage would be conducted between the members of two stock exchanges only dealing in securities commanding an active international market, and exposing themselves to minimal risk as a purchase in one centre was instantly reversed with an equivalent sale in the other.

However, the reality was somewhat different as Vickers da Costa & Co. tried to explain in 1958.

Nearly all arbitrage business involves a risk or a series of risks covering time, security price changes, and currency rate fluctuations. In addition there are bull and bear positions, the actual physical location of the security concerned, credit facilities and cost thereof. All these factors enter into the decisions as to whether a particular arbitrage proposition looks attractive or not, and certainly account for why competitors in the same business sometimes appear to be doing business on different terms.[124]

The problem was that the profits they made from arbitrage were not sufficient to justify the risks they took because of the costs involved and the restrictions under which they operated, as members of the Stock Exchange. As it was the Stock Exchange was unsympathetic to the position of those brokers and jobbers who engaged in arbitrage while the government continued to regard it as a form of international speculation that undermined exchange controls.

Therefore, in the 1950s the London Stock Exchange tended to adopt an insular attitude towards the international securities market, concentrating

---

[122] Ibid., 10 Aug. 1953, 17 Aug. 1953.   [123] Ibid., 28 Jan. 1957.
[124] Ibid., 17 Nov. 1958, cf. 11 May 1959, 1 June 1959, 22 June 1959.

upon preserving its position in the market for domestic securities and handling the sales and purchases of British investors, whether individual or institutional. Little attention was paid to the damaging consequences of its regulations and charges for its position within the global securities market. International business was simply not regarded as being especially important with trading increasingly confined to the national stock exchanges that were reviving or appearing in the 1950s. Consequently, this could be safely neglected, or even restricted, if it posed a threat to the domestic securities business by undermining the twin principles of single capacity and fixed commission rates. Thus the loss of trading in such areas as American and South African securities was both an inevitable and necessary sacrifice if control over the domestic market was to be preserved. The result was that the London Stock Exchange was failing to participate in the revival of international trading of securities. Though much took place in London, it was outside the London Stock Exchange.[125] This neglect and hostility towards the international market was beginning to appear a dangerous mistake even by the end of the 1950s. In June 1959 the brokers Straus Turnbull & Co., reported that, 'An increasing number of securities which are dealt in on the London Stock Exchange are also being traded on overseas Stock Exchanges.'[126] By then the separate international market that had developed in the late 1950s was beginning to invade the territory of the London Stock Exchange itself.

## MONEY AND CAPITAL

The London Stock Exchange also lost most of what remained of its role in the money market in the 1950s. Traditionally brokers and jobbers had borrowed temporarily idle money from diverse individuals and companies, but especially financial institutions, and employed it to advantage by buying and holding higher yielding securities. This they did either themselves or by lending to others on the Stock Exchange who did. There were even members that specialized in such activities, known as money brokers. In 1950 Cazenove & Co., Laurie Milbank & Co., and Sheppards & Co. were three of the largest. Cazenoves made between £100,000 and £200,000 on its money-broking operations in the 1950s. They were conduits through which the banks lent money to members of the Stock Exchange, with jobbers as the major players. The securities purchased were used as collateral with a 5 per cent margin on gilt-edged stocks. These money brokers also lent stock, in return for a fee, which they obtained from large holders, such as the financial institutions. They could also arrange the temporary swapping of securities to meet the changing demands of the market place, with a 5 per cent margin being a regular requirement. With £52,500 3.5 per cent Conversion

---

[125] P. Einzig, *The Euro-Bond Market* (Oxford 1970), 23.
[126] LSE: Council, 8 June 1959.

Loan as collateral, for example, a jobber could borrow £50,000 3.5 per cent War Loan. By operations of this kind the market was kept supplied with both the credit and the securities that were necessary if the equilibrium between supply and demand was to be maintained, across all the variables of time, type, and quantities. In the process the jobbers profited from the turn on every deal, the brokers from the commission they charged, and the outside financial institutions from the temporary employment of either money or stock.[127] However, such a situation depended on the existence of markets where securities could be quickly bought and sold in large quantities, allowing for money to be employed or released and switches between stocks made.

Unfortunately, it was this dimension of the Stock Exchange's activities that had been most damaged in the 1940s, both by the war and post-war policies of economic management. The continuous turnover of securities was equated in the eyes of most, and certainly among politicians and civil servants, as speculation that threatened the stability of the economy. Thus, measures to prevent it were considered to have no adverse consequences on the economy and could be positively beneficial. Consequently, even after fortnightly accounts and continuations had been reintroduced in the late 1940s, they remained ringed by restrictions. Continuations, for example, were only permissible between brokers and jobbers, on the grounds that longer than a fortnight might be required before a jobber could deliver the securities he had committed himself to. However, as many deals were also made between brokers, being denied access to this facility limited the role they could play. It was not until May 1953 that broker-to-broker contangos were permitted once again, allowing brokers more opportunities to employ borrowed funds in the market. By the end of September 1954 continuations open with jobbers totalled £9.8m. while those between brokers came to £2.2m.[128]

Even then, however, the absence of options freely available in the Stock Exchange continued to impair the operation of the markets. It was only in the most heavily traded of securities, such as gilt-edged, that there existed truly liquid markets where any amount could be bought and sold at short notice, with little fluctuation in price. Turnover in the gilt-edged market was estimated at £30m. per day in 1957 or £7.8bn. per annum. Without options, which jobbers could use to try and cover their more exposed positions, they were reluctant to buy or sell without a great deal of confidence that they could reverse the deal fairly quickly.[129] As one firm of brokers, McNally, Montgomery & Co., noted in December 1956:

[127] Ibid., 8 May 1950, 30 Jan. 1956; Kynaston, *Cazenove*, 219.
[128] LSE: Council, 8 Jan. 1951, 15 Jan. 1951, 5 May 1952, 26 May 1953, 11 Oct. 1954.
[129] Ibid., 21 May 1951, 27 Aug. 1951, 21 Apr. 1952, 5 May 1952, 6 Jan. 1958, 21 July 1958.

There are a large number of stocks in these days, such as Investment Trust issues, water company stocks, or the shares of smaller industrial companies, to instance only a few, where the chance of completing an order of a value of say £10,000 within the stated period (56 days) is probably very small.[130]

This precluded their use for money-market operations as there could be no guarantee that the stock could be sold if a loan had to be repaid.

When options were again permitted in 1958 the Stock Exchange continued to limit their value by restricting their use to members alone, even though this was not required by the Bank of England. Firms such as Leon Brothers and L. A. Seligman & Co. referred to these restrictions as '. . . crippling . . .', faced as they were with circumstances which made option dealing difficult normally.

Conditions for option dealers today are far more difficult than before the war, markets are much narrower, Contango facilities are very limited and the stamp duty is double what it was.[131]

These charges and conditions conspired to increase both the risks and the costs involved in large-scale but short-term purchases and sales, and thus reduced the role played by quoted securities in the money market. A year later Sternberg Brothers, who were large option dealers, were finding that the inability to undo an option with a financial institution or mining finance house, because these were non-members, was severely restricting their business. The Stock Exchange would not alter its rules. Some brokers, such as Morton Brothers, even took to placing clients' money on deposit with building societies rather than employing it on the Stock Exchange.[132] The restrictions on dealing in bonds, introduced by the Stock Exchange and then the government, from 1957 onwards, in order to prevent bond washing, further impaired the ability to use securities as homes for temporarily idle funds.[133] Consequently, the contribution that the London Stock Exchange could make to the operation of the money market in the 1950s was greatly reduced through a combination of the Stock Exchange's own charges and restrictions, and government controls.

It was not that there was no longer any demand for the facilities once provided by the Stock Exchange. Banks and other financial institutions in London continued to seek ways of employing large sums of money in remunerative but temporary ways. The Stock Exchange itself noted in 1957 that

The main classes of investors in the gilt-edged market are the Clearing Banks, Trustee Savings Banks, Industrial companies, Lloyd's Underwriters and the Discount Market, who invest in relatively short-dated stocks . . .[134]

---

[130] LSE: Council, 10 Dec. 1956, cf. 14 Jan. 1957.
[131] Ibid., 13 Oct. 1958, cf. 21 July 1958, 3 Nov. 1958, 17 Nov. 1958.
[132] Ibid., 5 Apr. 1954, 11 May 1959; Wainwright, *Mullens*, 91.
[133] LSE: Council, 19 Aug. 1957, 26 Aug. 1957, 20 Jan. 1958.
[134] Ibid., 14 Oct. 1957.

Institutions such as these frequently possessed funds which they were reluctant to lend other than on a daily basis, as they could equally flow out again. In the past the members of the Stock Exchange had been large borrowers of such funds but the restrictions and changes under which they operated in the 1950s made them less able to make profitable use of short-term loans. Instead the merchant banks, and the London branches of foreign banks, stepped in to use these funds for dealing in a wide range of short-term financial instruments. These included Local Authority loans and an inter-bank money market. This was in addition to the well-established competition from the discount houses, with their commanding position in the Treasury Bill market. In 1958, for example, the London discount market was employing £1.6bn. not only in financing a portfolio of Treasury Bills (56 per cent) but also short-dated government stock (30 per cent). There thus developed in the 1950s an active market in short-dated securities outside the Stock Exchange, in which financial institutions could easily and profitably employ temporarily idle funds.[135]

The London Stock Exchange even discovered that this outside market was favoured by the Bank of England, acting on behalf of the government. As this market largely dealt in government debt, whether stocks or bills, the Bank of England was keen to ensure that it faced as little competition as possible, such as from a market inside the Stock Exchange involving industrial securities.[136] However, this was transformed into outright discrimination when the Bank of England began to charge jobbers more for borrowed money than discount houses, even though the collateral given was identical, being British government stocks. This policy was introduced after the crisis of September 1957 when the Bank rate was increased to 7 per cent, and had the effect of further undermining the already weakened market for short-dated government stock provided by the Stock Exchange. In December 1958 the 17 dealers in British government stock, including Wedd Jefferson, Akroyd & Smithers, and Francis Praed, made their predicament clear.

During the past 30 years the number of firms trading in our market has fallen by half, and the National Debt vastly increased to the present staggering figure. Even with the reduced capitals of the trading firms concerned, huge amounts of stock are turned over without unduly straining our resources, but the fact remains that to finance this turn-over the cost of borrowing is far too big an expense to set against the hoped for profit on these large transactions, many of them involving switching operations.[137]

[135] M. Collins, *Money and Banking in the UK: A History* (London 1988), 365, 371, 373; E. Nevin and E. W. Davis, *The London Clearing Banks* (London 1970), 174, 216; King, 'The Market's Changing Role', 11–12; E. A. Shaw, *The London Money Market* (London 1975), 32; Scammell, *The London Discount Market*, 35, 42, 48, 100; Fletcher, *The Discount Houses in London*, 55, 82, 87–8, 117, 148, 154–5.

[136] LSE: Council, 14 Oct. 1957, 9 Dec. 1957.

[137] Ibid., 15 Dec. 1958, cf. 6 Apr. 1959.

Consequently, the central place that the Stock Exchange had once occupied in the London money market hardly existed in the 1950s, for its was increasingly taken by the activities of merchant bankers, foreign bankers, and money brokers who did not suffer the restrictions of membership and could more easily evade government controls. At the same time the Bank of England gave its support to the activities of the discount houses, with whom it had a much closer working relationship than the jobbers of the London Stock Exchange.

It was also difficult for the members of the London Stock Exchange to play a role in the international money market, circumscribed as they were by government exchange controls on the one hand and regulations on the other that limited arbitrage operations and options.[138] Nevertheless, the scope for such involvement was there for London continued to trade securities which had an international market. Blackwell & Co. reported in 1958 that

We deal principally in stocks in which there is considerable international interest, and which are correspondingly affected by items of news or rumours relating to international affairs.

In particular they observed the importance of events in the United States upon the British prices of securities.

... after the opening of the New York Stock Exchange, the publication of American Stock Market prices has a considerable influence on quotations in the London Market.[139]

By virtue of its long trading and imperial past London was the market for a number of major companies with international appeal. One such company was Shell Transport and Trading which was traded between London and Paris, with a difference of 0.9 per cent sufficient to trigger matching sales and purchases.[140] The international transfer of the ownership of securities was still one element maintaining the equilibrium of exchange rates in the 1950s, but of small significance compared to the operations of government, central banks, and commercial banks.[141] Nevertheless, the London Stock Exchange did have a potential role to play in the international money market. In October 1947 the government had introduced a system of investment dollars to replace the wartime restrictions on the holding of dollars. There now developed on the Stock Exchange a market in the dollars that were obtained when US or foreign stocks were sold to American investors, because these dollars could now be used to buy dollar securities rather than surrendered to the government. What was

---

[138] LSE: Council, 9 Dec. 1957.     [139] Ibid., 17 Nov. 1959.     [140] Ibid., 1 June 1959.
[141] P. Einzig, *The History of Foreign Exchange* (London 1962), 302-3; P. Einzig, *A Textbook on Foreign Exchange* (London 1966), 1, 213; E. W. Clendenning, *The Euro-dollar Market* (Oxford 1970), 23.

created was a market in investment dollars which traded at a premium to ordinary dollars because of the investment use to which they could be put. As the market of the securities was on the floor of the London Stock Exchange, it was the brokers and jobbers there who took early control of this market. Unfortunately, they were not able to compete against the greater resources, expertise, and connections of the banks and so they lost this market in the 1950s.[142] However, even in the 1950s there were opportunities which members of the Stock Exchange were eager to exploit. Vickers da Costa observed in 1958 that

... following the much greater confidence in sterling *vis-à-vis* the dollar we have noticed an increasing tendency for cash balances and securities belonging to 'non-residents' clients to come to us for safe custody, whereas previously they were almost always held by American, Canadian and Swiss Banks.[143]

These holdings then led to business for the London Stock Exchange for, as the money was invested or required, securities were bought and sold. However, such operations for international clients could only be done by maintaining close links with members of foreign stock exchanges, and required the ability to spread option counterparties beyond the confines of the Stock Exchange membership. Unfortunately for Vickers da Costa the Stock Exchange was unwilling to relax its rules on either arbitrage or options, and so the business was being lost to merchant banks and other outside finance houses.

The value that the Stock Exchange possessed for the money market was an ability to employ idle balances remuneratively while retaining the ability to access them immediately. Added to this was a specific international dimension because securities were a means of moving funds spatially in response to constant fluctuations in exchange rates, interest rates, and other variables. Though internal and external government controls did limit the ability of the London Stock Exchange to provide the free and open facilities that the money market required in the 1950s, the very revival of such operations in London in the 1950s does not suggest that they were insurmountable obstacles. The appearance of parallel money markets and the activities of merchant banks, discount houses, and the branches of foreign banks in London indicate that there was a growing need for both domestic and international money-market facilities in the 1950s, despite the controls exerted by the central banks of the world. Consequently, the London Stock Exchange's failure to place itself once again at the centre of London money-market activities, must be accounted for by the restrictions imposed on its membership and the charges they were obliged to make. These restrictions ranged from the inability to obtain outside capital and form links with other financial institutions, at a time when both were important, to the

[142] Einzig, *The Euro-Bond Market*, 170–3, Einzig, *Textbook on Foreign Exchange*, 147.
[143] LSE: Council, 17 Nov. 1958, cf. 1 Dec. 1958, 22 June 1959.

controls placed on options, arbitrage, and dealing 'cum' and 'ex' dividend. At the same time fixed commission rates could not be made to fit the requirements of much money-market activity, involving as it did large volume transactions for small margins.[144]

Instead, the members of the Stock Exchange concentrated more and more on meeting the needs of longer-term investors. However, the members of the Stock Exchange were, at the same time, increasingly relegated to a minor role in the issuing of new securities by British companies. One problem was that the dominant purchasers of newly issued securities were no longer large numbers of individually wealthy people but those institutions handling the collective savings of the nation. Even in 1950 this situation was already clear to the Stock Exchange

Owing to the trend of present-day taxation it is no longer the private but the institutional investor who is the determinant in arriving at the terms of an issue. The public may, and often do contribute largely to the oversubscription of an attractive issue, but this is almost entirely due to the hope of securing tax-free profits: a loan, the terms of which are 'tight' attracts virtually no public subscriptions.[145]

The place of the private investor was taken increasingly by the financial institutions, and they were large enough to establish direct relationship with those handling new issues. Such institutions also favoured large issues as they neither wanted too much of a single issue of securities, which might be unsaleable, nor too many separate holdings, as that would be more complex to manage. The merchant banks were better able to handle these larger issues because of their greater capital base, and their spread and depth of skilled staff. Most stockbroking firms were unable to compete as they remained small in comparison to the merchant banks, which adopted, increasingly, the joint-stock form.[146] The result was that stockbroking firms largely lost their active involvement in the new issues market. This included some of the largest, such as Cazenoves. Instead, it was merchant banks like Schroders, Warburgs, and Morgan Grenfell, and ex-brokers such as Helbert Wagg and Ansbachers, that dominated the field, having recognized that exchange controls, and two costly wars, had destroyed their international business.[147]

What business the stockbrokers were left with centred on the small issues

[144] Witness the success of the Merchant Banks, cf. R. Roberts, *Schroders: Merchants & Bankers* (London 1992), 319, 324, 327, 337, 339, 341, 346.

[145] LSE: Council, 30 Oct. 1950.

[146] Ibid., 9 Dec. 1957, 15 Dec. 1958; W. D. Rubenstein, *Men of Property: The Very Wealthy in Britain Since the Industrial Revolution* (London 1981), 171, 188; Roberts, *Schroders*, 342–4, 406–41.

[147] K. Burk, *Morgan Grenfell, 1838–1988: The Biography of a Merchant Bank* (Oxford 1989), 171–8; J. Attali, *A Man of Influence: Sir Siegmund Warburg, 1902–1982* (London 1986), 192, 198, 201; W. L. Fraser, *All to the Good* (London 1963), 254; J. McCartney-Fulgate, 'Merchant and Other Banking Houses', in Institute of Bankers, *The City of London as a Centre of International Trade and Finance* (London 1961), 95.

of under £1m. that the merchant banks tended to neglect as unremunerative. Even there, however, the brokers faced competition from newer finance houses—the government sponsored agencies, namely the Industrial and Commercial Finance Corporation (ICFC) and the Finance Corporation for Industry (FCI). While FCI concentrated upon financing the steel industry in the 1950s, ICFC specialized in making loans to small businesses. Being headed by an ex-stockbroker, William Piercy, and including a mixture of other bankers and brokers, it competed directly with those stockbrokers who were still involved in the new issue business. In the 1950s, for example, ICFC underwrote new issues for such firms as Murphy Radio and Marley Tiles, with its investment portfolio growing from £19.3m. in 1950 to £35.7m. in 1959. By then one-quarter was directed towards small engineering firms.[148] Squeezed between the merchant banks and ICFC the openings available to brokers in the new issue business were severely curtailed in the 1950s. Nevertheless, certain firms continued to persevere, such as Panmure Gordon & Co., even though this brought them into conflict with the merchant banks who were also important clients. It was this conflict of interest that led Cazenoves to withdraw from handling new issues themselves, becoming sub-underwriters to the likes of Barings.[149]

However, opportunities did continue to appear for brokers to participate in the new issue business in the 1950s. Pidgeon & Stebbing for example, handled the placing of £1m. 5¼ per cent stock for Southend-on-Sea. They carried out the whole transaction for a fee of £2,500 and calculated that, when all other costs such as stamp duty, were added in, the Council paid £5.5 per cent per annum for its money over the 9.5-year life of the loan, which they regarded as an attractive rate in 1956.

Current mortgage rates are such as to emphasize the attraction of the above method of borrowing, and our advice to all our corporation clients is to place their name on the queue of borrowers with the Bank of England.[150]

As with many of the other innovations by members in the 1950s this one incurred the hostility of the Stock Exchange. In order to promote the business Pidgeon & Strebbing canvassed local authorities generally but some of these were clients of other brokers. This broke the rules on poaching and so was forbidden, preventing Pidgeon & Strebbing from advertising the service they offered.

That was not the only obstacle that the Stock Exchange placed in the way of its own membership playing an active role in the new issue business, though at least it remained exempt from any minimum commission

[148] R. Coopey and D. Clarke, 3i: Fifty Years Investing in Industry (Oxford 1955), 30, 37, 40, 43, 46, 397; J. Kinross, Fifty Years in the City: Financing Small Business (London 1982), 138, 151, 179, 192; LSE: Council, 9 Dec. 1957.
[149] Kynaston, Cazenove, 198–204; B. H. MacDermot, Panmure Gordon & Co: A Century of Stockbroking (London 1976), 59–62.                    [150] LSE: Council, 22 Oct. 1956.

rule.[151] The great advantage possessed by members of the Stock Exchange in new issue business was their ability to sell securities directly to their own clients and those of fellow brokers through a placing or introduction. In a placing, for example, the broker often contracted to buy the securities at a fixed price and then resold them, with a small margin added, to his own clients and, through a jobber on the floor of the Stock Exchange, to other brokers for their clients.

... placings, if they can be done fairly and properly, are the only reasonable method of bringing shares of new small companies to the public, when the cost of an 'offer for sale' is prohibitive.[152]

This was the Stock Exchange's own judgement in January 1960. The problem with both a placing and an introduction was that they excluded the general public from participation, as only the clients of the brokers involved had the opportunity to purchase. In addition the clients of the lead broker got the shares at a cheaper price than those of brokers who bought through the market, as they added on a small commission charge for their trouble, and the jobber took his turn. The lead broker made his profit from the margin between the price paid for the securities and the resale price. The great merit of the system was its extreme cheapness, which was derived from the established network of investors available to brokers via the floor of the Stock Exchange, as they cut out all advertising and related charges.

Unfortunately for the brokers involved the Stock Exchange increasingly took the view that all new issues must be made publicly, through a prospectus, so giving all investors the opportunity of subscribing. In December 1958 a rule was introduced whereby at least 25 per cent of an issue of shares and 20 per cent for fixed interest securities, had to be made available in the market at the time of a placing. This allowed the smaller brokers to obtain shares for their clients where in the past they had all been distributed among the clients of the larger brokers who undertook the issuing business either themselves or in association with the merchant banks. Gradually, in the 1950s brokers found it more and more difficult to make a placing or introduction on the floor of the Stock Exchange. They were recommended to pursue a public offer instead, even though it was recognized that this was the most expensive method. In 1955, for example, the request from W. Greenwell & Co. to place £10m. in debenture stock for British Oxygen was turned down. Introductions fared even less well being the method used for only 31 out of 1,115 issues quoted in 1957/8. It was only in February 1960 that the Stock Exchange, recognizing it was pricing itself out of the new issue market, raised the possibility of using an offer for sale by tender rather than a public issue. However, by then the damage was done. At the same time, the Stock Exchange increasingly recommended to

[151] LSE: Council, 15 Sept. 1952.     [152] Ibid., 11 Jan. 1960.

companies that any new issue had to be made to existing shareholders, before outside investors, like the large financial institutions. This might produce additional trading on the Stock Exchange as different investors bought or sold the new securities, but it did diminish the use of an intro-duction, through which additional quoted securities could be quickly, easily, and cheaply sold to investors.[153] Generally, in the 1950s the Stock Exchange lost the direct role it had once played in the new issue market. Similarly, though a number of stockbroking firms did become heavily involved in takeover bids, such as Behrens Trusted, it was again the merchant banks that made a speciality out of the business. Brokers benefited as they were used to buy shares in the market, so generating both commission income and jobbers' turns, but it was the merchant banks that formed the close relationships with the companies involved, and were thus entrusted with subsequent business, such as new issues, mergers or further takeovers.[154]

Though the capital market remained heavily regulated by the government in the 1950s that was not the reason for the lack of activity by brokers and jobbers in the field of new issues. The explanation for that lay in the com-petition that existed in the 1950s from a host of finance houses in London ranging from the quasi-government institution, the ICFC, to a range of old and new merchant banks. Faced with this the members of the Stock Exchange were at a competitive disadvantage because of the limitations they suffered on access to capital and the restrictions on the use of placings and introductions.[155]

The outcome for the Stock Exchange was that its membership became ever more reliant for their income on the market they provided for already issued securities rather than any contribution they made to the creation of these securities. In 1956 the Stock Exchange sought to explain its impor-tance by indicating the indirect role it played in the capital market.

The importance of the Stock Exchange lies in the fact that individuals and compa-nies will not normally and freely embark the results of their thrift in the capital market unless they are assured that the securities for which they exchange their money will be freely marketable, that is to say, these securities can, upon need, be easily exchanged again for money, even though it may be at a different price level. The Stock Exchange provides for the nation this machinery of exchange, which is essential to an efficient capital market, which in its turn, is essential to the

---

[153] Ibid., 30 Oct. 1950, 23 May 1955, 15 Dec. 1958, 13 July 1958, 4 Jan. 1960, 1 Feb. 1960.

[154] S. J. Prais, *The Evolution of Giant Firms in Britain* (Cambridge 1976), 41, 45–6, 87–91, 116, 123–4; L. Hannah, *The Rise of the Corporate Economy* (London 1976), 117, 216; LSE: Council, 10 Dec. 1956, 14 Jan. 1957, 14 Oct. 1957; L. Hannah and J. A. Kay, *Concentration in Modern Industry: Theory, Measurement and the UK Experience* (London 1977), 86; W. A. Thomas, *The Finance of British Industry, 1918–1976* (London 1978), 162, 173, 220–1, 230; G. Jones, *British Multinational Banking, 1830–1990* (Oxford 1993), 259.

[155] LSE: Council, 4 Dec. 1950; Roberts, *Schroders*, 325; Thomas, *Finance of British Indus-try*, 184, 199; J. R. Winton, *Lloyds Bank, 1918–1969* (Oxford 1982), 144, 160, 169.

expansion of the industry and commerce of the nation. . . . The existence of such a market facilitates the raising of fresh capital by governments and by industrial and other undertakings, and makes possible the realization of securities for the payment of estate duty and other taxation.[156]

Because of the costs and restrictions imposed by the Stock Exchange itself, combined with government controls and taxation, the contribution made by the market provided by the Stock Exchange to the economy rested upon the opportunities it gave to long-term holders to both move into and out of the market and switch between different securities. Self-finance, generated from reinvested profits, was the source of around 90 per cent of the funds used by even quoted companies in the 1950s, with most of the rest coming from bank borrowings rather than issues of securities. It was only at those times when the government restricted bank lending that companies turned to the issue of securities as an extra source of funds.[157]

The Stock Exchange itself was limiting the role it played, as a market for quoted securities for it was always conscious that it was now expected to exercise some control over the securities to which it granted a quotation or otherwise risk a public outcry for stricter government control, if specific stocks or shares proved worthless or fraudulent.

The Stock Exchange rigidly controls the granting of quotations on its market, and its requirements, which have to be observed by all concerns seeking a quotation, are stricter than those imposed by Company Law.[158]

Though a company without a trading record could be quoted that was now increasingly rare. The Stock Exchange opted for the more cautious policy that favoured established enterprises converting to the joint-stock form and selling shares to the investing public.[159] The result was to deny a market on the Stock Exchange to speculative new issues that had provided so much activity in the past, such as overseas mining ventures or new technology ventures.

In the end, the circumstances that came to the aid of the Stock Exchange, and generated a growing volume of business were the changing investment requirements of British investors, both institutional and individual. Two world wars had led to both a great increase in holdings of government stock and the wholesale disposal of overseas securities, both government and corporate. This was compounded by the nationalization programme of the post-war Labour government that created ever-more fixed interest debt. With persistent inflation in the 1950s, and a buildup of private savings

[156] LSE: Council, 30 Jan. 1956.

[157] Prais, *Giant Firms*, 9; Thomas, *Finance of British Industry*, 218, 310, 325; E. R. Shaw, *The London Money Market* (London 1975), 20; Scammell, *London Discount Market*, 83, 100, 227; N. Macrae, *The London Capital Market: Its Structure, Strains and Management* (London 1955), 99, 103, 105, 157; F. W. Paish, *Business Finance* (London 1961), 128, 134; LSE: Council, 30 Apr. 1951, 25 Mar. 1957, 14 Oct. 1957.

[158] Ibid., 30 Jan. 1956.      [159] Ibid., 4 Dec. 1959.

looking for investment, there was growing resistance to holding only fixed interest securities and a need to seek alternatives. Banks, building societies, and other financial institutions therefore began slowly to sell their huge holdings of government debt, using the proceeds to lend to industry, finance house purchase, or property investments. Within the securities market there was a decisive shift towards holdings of ordinary shares, where dividends could increase in line with inflation, and away from debentures paying a fixed return. In 1950 56 per cent of the company securities issued were in the form of debt compared to 36 per cent in ordinary shares. As early as 1955 the position had been reversed, with 65 per cent in ordinary shares, and this was the position throughout the second half of the 1950s.[160]

The Stock Exchange tried to explain what was happening to the government-appointed Radcliffe Enquiry in 1957:

Impetus was given to the movement away from low-yielding fixed interest securities by the shortage of capital and consumer goods, by the accompanying and persistent inflation, and by the determination of investors to adapt their policy as they could to a situation which attracted as well as threatened them. Meanwhile the traditional private investor had become less important, and small savings were canalised through the Insurance Companies and pension funds, whose dealings dominated most markets and most issues. The critical professional edge under which contemporary investment problems thus increasingly passed was more and more being brought to bear also on the portfolios of charities, schools and colleges and kindred public bodies. These, in growing numbers, together with many private trusts, sought and obtained relief from the rigid investment clauses and became sellers of gilt-edged securities. Prominent among those switching into equity stocks were the Church Commissioners, whose change of policy, widely publicized, was also widely copied.

The Stock Exchange put the blame for what was happening on the government's monetary policy which had the effect of discouraging investors from placing their savings in fixed interest securities, especially ones for long or indefinite periods. As the evidence to the Radcliffe committee continued:

For permanent investors in the gilt-edged market however, the many years of 2 per cent Bank rate and the long succession of 3 per cent issues had induced a feeling that 3 per cent was indeed a basic interest rate. The re-introduction in 1951 of the Bank rate as a monetary weapon, therefore, came as something of a shock, and many institutional funds had to revise their portfolios drastically. The first half of 1952 accordingly saw markets in which large quantities of undated and long-dated stocks were jettisoned in favour of those with medium short maturities. Although the market recovered in due course, undated stocks had lost their attraction, and the emphasis was mostly on stocks of middle date. So much was this the case that more than a year later the authorities took advantage of the improvement in the

[160] Prais, *Giant Firms*, 117; W. M. Clarke, *The City in the World Economy* (London 1965), 106, 111; Thomas, *Finance of British Industry*, 155, 277; Macrae, *London Capital Market*, 157; Paish, *Business Finance*, 134; Winton, *Lloyds Bank*, 162, LSE: Council, 14 Oct. 1957.

market to issue over a period of fifteen months a series of loans ranging (with one exception) over maturities between 1957 and 1969. Hardly, however, had this series been concluded that a new credit squeeze hit the market with Bank rate rising rapidly from 3 per cent to 5.5 per cent, and heavy selling was encountered. On this occasion the brunt of the selling fell on the middle-dated stocks which had so recently been put out by the Treasury. In the first six months of 1955, the investments of the Clearing Banks fell by £225m., and within eight months of their issue Exchequer 2 per cent 1960 had fallen 10 points to 90, and Funding 3 per cent 1966/8 by 20 points to 80. In fact, falls of this magnitude in newly-issued securities have, at least temporarily shaken the confidence of important investors, such as the books, and rendered more difficult the action of the Government itself.[161]

In the October of 1957 the Stock Exchange had already warned that the banks had become heavy sellers of gilt-edged securities over the last two years, worried as they were by the capital depreciation suffered when the underlying rate of interest was rising. At the same time the increased borrowing by both nationalized industries and local authorities, which they were now allowed to pursue independently of central government borrowing, was having an adverse effct on the entire market of fixed interest securities.

Local Authority loans have always been popular with the small investor, but it must be remembered that there is very seldom a great amount of money available for any one of these loans at a particular time, and also that they are now available in such large quantities that they affect not only Colonial borrowing but the Government Market as well. The Stock in the initial stages is often left in the hands either of the underwriters, or of the speculator commonly known as the 'stag', and which of these holds the stock initially depends upon the terms on which the stock has been offered and upon general market conditions—that is to say upon whether the issue has been a success or a failure[162]

Considering the growing awareness that inflation was now a permanent feature of the economy, there was an increasing reluctance among investors to accept fixed interest securities, but it was this that was made available to the market in growing quantities by central and local government and the nationalized industries. Even when colonial loans had been squeezed out, and foreign ones prohibited under exchange control regulations, there was still too much for the market to absorb. Hence the failure of the market value of government debt to match its nominal value. The nominal value of quoted UK government securities, for example, grew by £3.6bn. between 1950 and 1960 but the market value by a mere £0.6 bn. (Table 9.1) Essentially, in the 1950s the growth in the market for government securities was driven by the issues being made by the central and local authorities, and the nationalized industries, which was more and more reluctantly absorbed by the investing public, whether institutional and individual. In the process

[161] LSE: Council, 9 Dec. 1957.     [162] Ibid., 14 Oct. 1957.

Table 9.1. London Stock Exchange: Nominal and market values of securities quoted in 1950 and 1960 (£m.)

| Category of security | Nominal value | | | Market value | | |
|---|---|---|---|---|---|---|
| | 1950 | 1960 | Difference | 1950 | 1960 | Difference |
| British government | 14,668.1 | 18,259.9 | + 3,591.8 | 13,758.2 | 14,352.5 | + 594.3 |
| UK public bodies | 574.2 | 743.7 | + 169.5 | 534.5 | 619.9 | + 85.4 |
| TOTAL | 15,242.3 | 19,003.6 | + 3,761.3 | 14,292.7 | 14,972.4 | + 679.7 |
| Colonial governments | 591.2 | 815.8 | + 224.6 | 566.7 | 662.8 | + 96.1 |
| Foreign governments | 1,881.5 | 1,662.9 | − 218.6 | 207.0 | 204.1 | − 2.9 |
| Colonial/Foreign public bodies | 109.2 | 114.2 | + 5.0 | 73.5 | 79.3 | − 5.8 |
| TOTAL | 2,581.9 | 2,592.9 | + 11.0 | 847.2 | 946.2 | + 99.0 |
| UK railways | 20.3 | 4.1 | − 16.2 | 10.3 | 2.3 | − 8.0 |
| Indian railways | 45.1 | 1.7 | − 43.4 | 43.7 | 1.5 | − 42.2 |
| Imperial railways | 171.1 | 167.3 | − 3.8 | 163.0 | 189.6 | + 26.6 |
| American railways | 181.2 | 102.9 | − 78.3 | 88.6 | 66.1 | − 22.5 |
| Foreign railways | 124.5 | 90.0 | − 34.5 | 37.6 | 33.7 | − 3.9 |
| TOTAL | 542.2 | 366.0 | − 176.2 | 343.2 | 293.2 | − 50.0 |
| Banks and discount houses | 210.0 | 445.2 | + 235.2 | 599.1 | 1,216.9 | + 617.8 |
| Financial, land, and investment | 619.5 | 883.0 | + 263.5 | 709.4 | 2,219.1 | + 1,509.7 |
| Insurance | 43.0 | 107.3 | + 64.3 | 362.6 | 1,097.9 | + 735.3 |
| Property | — | 229.3 | + 229.3 | — | 517.0 | + 517.0 |
| TOTAL | 872.5 | 1,664.8 | + 792.3 | 1,671.1 | 5,050.9 | + 3,379.8 |
| Canals and docks | 25.1 | 27.2 | + 2.1 | 112.6 | 24.0 | − 88.6 |
| Gas | 23.9 | 19.0 | − 4.9 | 20.2 | 29.5 | + 9.3 |
| Electric light/ power | 56.8 | 59.2 | + 2.4 | 94.3 | 242.8 | + 148.5 |
| Telegraph/ telephone | 52.4 | 26.4 | − 26.0 | 110.9 | 61.7 | − 49.2 |
| Tramways/ omnibus | 66.0 | 78.2 | + 12.2 | 149.1 | 150.4 | + 1.3 |
| Waterworks | 42.9 | 83.7 | + 40.8 | 46.5 | 65.6 | + 19.1 |
| TOTAL | 267.1 | 293.7 | + 26.6 | 533.6 | 574.0 | + 40.4 |
| Commercial/ Industrial | 2,018.5 | 4,791.2 | + 2,772.7 | 4,097.9 | 15,207.9 | + 11,110.0 |
| Breweries/ Distilleries | 274.7 | 506.9 | 232.2 | 535.6 | 1,205.6 | + 670.0 |
| Iron, coal, and steel | 341.9 | 533.8 | 191.9 | 544.8 | 1,271.5 | + 726.7 |
| Shipping | 82.2 | 175.6 | + 93.4 | 117.0 | 287.8 | + 170.8 |
| TOTAL | 2,717.3 | 6,007.5 | + 3,290.2 | 5,295.3 | 17,912.8 | + 12,676.7 |

Table 9.1. (cont.)

| Category of security | Nominal value | | | Market value | | |
|---|---|---|---|---|---|---|
| | 1950 | 1960 | Difference | 1950 | 1960 | Difference |
| Mines | 369.0 | 560.3 | + 191.3 | 1,327.9 | 2,146.4 | + 818.5 |
| Oil | 223.7 | 671.6 | + 447.9 | 652.8 | 2,878.3 | + 2,225.5 |
| Tea, coffee, rubber | 128.8 | 128.2 | − 0.6 | 98.8 | 226.2 | + 127.4 |
| TOTAL | 721.5 | 1,360.1 | + 638.6 | 2,079.5 | 5,250.9 | + 3,171.4 |
| TOTAL | 22,944.8 | 31,288.6 | + 8,343.8 | 25,062.6 | 45,060.4 | + 19,997.8 |

*Sources*: Stock Exchange Official Yearbooks, 1952, 1,791, and 1960, 1,669.

government itself was driven to take steps to enhance the attractions of its securities by diminishing those of alternatives. Exchange controls already reduced opportunities to participate in foreign offerings to very low levels, while credit squeezes and other such devices at home limited the availability of corporate issues from time to time. The Bank of England still had to give permission for such issues in any case.[163]

Despite the efforts of the government and the Bank of England, investors increasingly turned to corporate securities as an alternative. These were not in the form of debentures or preference shares that had been popular in the past, but were in the form of ordinary shares or equities, as only these offered some insurance against inflation though not against poor management. In response to this demand, rather than as a means of raising extra capital, a growing number of businesses in Britain converted themselves into the joint-stock form and sold shares to investors. As institutional investors in particular preferred large issues from large companies, because of their liquidity, this process was accompanied by mergers, acquisitions, and takeovers. Between 1950 and 1960 the nominal value of the commercial, industrial, and allied securities quoted on the London Stock Exchange rose from £2.7bn. to £6.0bn., or more than doubling. Even more spectacular was the market value of these securities, which increased from £5.3bn. to £18.0bn., or more than tripling. Whereas in 1950 the market value of securities such as these had a premium of 121 per cent over their nominal value, by 1960 the premium had widened to 239 per cent. A similar phenomenon took place in the securities issued by resource-based companies, most notably those in South African gold-mining and international oil. The premium of the market value over the nominal value widened from 89 per cent in 1950 to 153 per cent. Symptomatic of the whole change was the creation of a new market on the Stock Exchange, namely property

[163] M. Collins, *Money and Banking in the UK: A History* (London 1988), 375, 424–5, 440, 449, 460, 462, 476; C. Pratten, *The Stock Market* (Cambridge 1993), 40, 75; J. J. Siegel, *Stocks for the Long Run: A Guide to Selecting Markets for Long-Term Growth* (Chicago 1994), 16, 18, 110.

**Table 9.2. London Stock Exchange: Nominal and market values of securities quoted in 1950 and 1960 (%)**

| Category of security | Nominal value | | | Market value | | |
|---|---|---|---|---|---|---|
| | 1950 | 1960 | Difference | 1950 | 1960 | Difference |
| British government | 63.9 | 58.4 | − 5.5 | 54.9 | 31.9 | − 23.0 |
| UK public bodies | 2.5 | 2.4 | − 0.1 | 2.1 | 1.4 | − 0.7 |
| TOTAL | 66.4 | 60.7 | − 5.7 | 57.0 | 33.2 | − 23.8 |
| Colonial governments | 2.6 | 2.6 | = | 2.3 | 1.5 | − 0.8 |
| Foreign governments | 8.2 | 5.3 | − 2.9 | 0.8 | 0.5 | − 0.3 |
| Colonial/Foreign public bodies | 0.5 | 0.4 | − 0.1 | 0.3 | 0.2 | − 0.1 |
| TOTAL | 11.3 | 8.3 | − 3.0 | 3.4 | 2.1 | − 1.3 |
| UK railways | 0.1 | — | − 0.1 | — | — | — |
| Indian railways | 0.2 | — | − 0.2 | 0.2 | — | − 0.2 |
| Imperial railways | 0.7 | 0.5 | − 0.2 | 0.7 | 0.4 | − 0.3 |
| American railways | 0.8 | 0.3 | − 0.5 | 0.4 | 0.1 | − 0.3 |
| Foreign railways | 0.5 | 0.3 | − 0.2 | 0.2 | 0.1 | − 0.1 |
| TOTAL | 2.4 | 1.2 | − 1.2 | 1.4 | 0.7 | − 0.7 |
| Banks and discount houses | 0.9 | 1.4 | + 0.5 | 2.4 | 2.7 | + 0.3 |
| Financial, land, and investment | 2.7 | 2.8 | + 0.1 | 2.8 | 4.9 | + 2.1 |
| Insurance | 0.2 | 0.3 | + 0.1 | 1.4 | 2.4 | + 1.0 |
| Property | — | 0.7 | + 0.7 | — | 1.1 | + 1.1 |
| TOTAL | 3.8 | 5.3 | + 1.5 | 6.7 | 11.2 | + 4.5 |
| Canals and docks | 0.1 | 0.1 | = | 0.4 | 0.1 | − 0.3 |
| Gas | 0.1 | 0.1 | = | 0.1 | 0.1 | = |
| Electric light/power | 0.2 | 0.2 | = | 0.4 | 0.5 | + 0.1 |
| Telegraph and telephone | 0.2 | 0.1 | − 0.1 | 0.4 | 0.1 | − 0.3 |
| Tramways and omnibus | 0.3 | 0.2 | − 0.1 | 0.6 | 0.3 | − 0.3 |
| Waterworks | 0.2 | 0.3 | + 0.1 | 0.2 | 0.1 | − 0.1 |
| TOTAL | 1.2 | 0.9 | − 0.3 | 2.1 | 1.3 | − 0.8 |
| Commercial/Industrial | 8.8 | 15.3 | + 6.5 | 16.4 | 33.8 | + 17.4 |
| Breweries/Distilleries | 1.2 | 1.6 | + 0.4 | 2.1 | 2.7 | + 0.6 |
| Iron, coal, and steel | 1.5 | 1.7 | + 0.2 | 2.2 | 2.8 | + 0.4 |
| Shipping | 0.4 | 0.6 | + 0.2 | 0.5 | 0.6 | + 0.1 |
| TOTAL | 11.8 | 19.2 | + 7.4 | 21.1 | 39.9 | 18.8 |
| Mines | 1.6 | 1.8 | + 0.2 | 5.3 | 4.8 | − 0.5 |
| Oil | 1.0 | 2.1 | + 1.1 | 2.6 | 6.4 | + 3.8 |
| Tea, coffee, rubber | 0.6 | 0.4 | − 0.2 | 0.4 | 0.5 | + 0.1 |
| TOTAL | 3.1 | 4.3 | + 1.2 | 8.3 | 11.7 | + 3.4 |

*Sources*: As Table 9.1.

companies, whose securities had a market value of £517m. by 1960. (Table 9.1)

Faced with this change all the Stock Exchange could do was respond by quoting the securities that were increasingly issued by the corporate sector in the 1950s. This it did, so providing them with the market they required. (Table 9.2.) In many ways this change was ideal for the London Stock Exchange of the 1950s. Buying and selling these securities did require greater negotiation than trading large amounts of fixed interest stock issued by, or backed by, the British government. Thus it would justify the minimum commission rates that brokers could demand and the wider turns that jobbers needed. The rising market value of these securities also generated increased commission for the brokers. Though the nominal value of securities quoted grew by £8.3bn. between 1950 and 1960, the market value increased by £20bn., and more and more of that was composed of corporate securities. (Tables 9.1 and 9.2). Consequently, without any planning or positioning the London Stock Exchange found a role for itself in the late 1950s as a market for domestic corporate securities, due to circumstances entirely beyond its own control or its own manufacture. Essentially, it had taken over the role once performed by the provincial exchanges and that was bound to lead to either greater competition or greater co-operation in the future. The London Stock Exchange may have been drifting towards oblivion in the 1950s, helped by its own unwillingness or inability to reorganize and reposition itself, but the rapid expansion of domestic securities, issued by a wide variety of British companies, rescued it from that fate. There was a growing need for a national market in industrial issues and that was what the London Stock Exchange was providing by the late 1950s. The London Stock Exchange had found a role despite itself.

# 10

# Failing to Adjust, 1960–1969

## RELATIONS WITH GOVERNMENT

The status quo had not been an option in the 1950s but the Stock Exchange had chosen it without disastrous consequences. It was even less of an option in the 1960s and there was no guarantee that, if it was chosen, the Stock Exchange would have a particularly promising future by the end of the decade. Membership continued to decline with the very heart of the market, in the shape of the jobbers, facing a difficult and uncertain future, as talent and capital drained away through retirement. Even brokers, with a more certain income from fixed commissions, found it difficult to recruit new staff and potential partners, while restrictions on size and capital left them vulnerable to outside competition. The Stock Exchange itself was increasingly in need of modernization as no major reconstruction had been undertaken since the end of the war. There was always the possibility of a change of government, reviving fears of nationalization and intervention. The structure of commission charges had to be adjusted in such a way that the institutions would continue to use the members of the Stock Exchange. Conflicts of interest between brokers and jobbers and between large and small firms had to be resolved without so alienating either party that they ceased to value membership and left.

During the 1960s the government rather than the market continued to be the major influence over the way London Stock Exchange developed. This was both in terms of general economic policy, which affected the environment within which the Stock Exchange operated, and of monetary and fiscal policies which had direct bearing on the activities of investors and borrowers as well as the membership itself. As in the past the Stock Exchange appeared largely unsuccessful in getting the government to take note of its particular requirements in an increasingly competitive world. The 2 per cent stamp duty on transactions, for example, was a long-standing annoyance to the Stock Exchange, convinced as they were that it cost them business, especially in competition with foreign stock exchanges where such a tax was either lower or non-existent. Consequently, almost on an annual basis, they lobbied the Chancellor of the Exchequer for a reduction, pointing out the damage it was causing. However as the government's own gilt-edged securities were exempt from stamp duty the Chancellor was little inclined to listen, even when made aware of the consequences for the market in terms of distortions and international competitiveness.[1]

However, it was not stamp duty alone that was diverting transactions in securities away from London. The desire by the Inland Revenue to ensure that no income escaped taxation was also having a detrimental effect on the London Stock Exchange's ability to conduct an international business, but the government was unwilling to make changes that would cost it revenue in the short run. As British securities were taxed at source, non-residents had to reclaim the tax paid, and this deterred many from doing so because of the time and expense involved. At the same time the Inland Revenue were starting to tax dividends on non-UK securities whenever they passed through the hands of a British resident, which often happened when London brokers and jobbers acted as intermediaries involving foreign investors. Again, the result of this excess of zeal was to drive the business away from London, much to the Stock Exchange's disgust. As it noted in November 1962:

such irritations as these, cumulatively and combined with others such as the 2 per cent stamp duty, slowly drive overseas investors elsewhere with their security business.[2]

Eventually, however, Stock Exchange pressure did pay off, for in April 1963 the government announced that stamp duty was to be halved, being reduced from 2 per cent to 1 per cent.[3]

However, this concession was being used by the government to soften opposition to a capital gains tax. This had been under discussion in 1961 when the idea of taxing the rising nominal value of securities was first raised. It provoked outright opposition from the Stock Exchange, who regarded it as politically motivated. In their view the government was keen to cultivate the popular support of the electorate by being seen to tax those who gained from rising share prices due to speculative surges, takeover bids, and under-priced new issues. Nevertheless, a capital gains tax was introduced in 1963. This tax ignored the fact that the underlying rise in share values was also due to inflation for the prices of securities were driven up as the purchasing power of money declined. The Stock Exchange were of the opinion that with a capital gains tax

the whole machinery of raising money for the government and for industry could be irretrievably damaged to the detriment, not merely of the Stock Exchange and the City, but of the whole business community upon which prosperity depends.[4]

Despite this warning, a Conservative government was willing to take this risk because of the extra revenue such a tax would raise as well as the ben-

---

[1] LSE: Council, 31 Oct. 1960, 14 Nov. 1960, 20 Feb. 1961.
[2] Ibid., 26 Nov. 1962, cf. 12 June 1961.
[3] Ibid., 6 May 1963.     [4] Ibid., 11 Dec. 1961, cf. 6 May 1963.

eficial political advantage. Despite the reduction in stamp duty, much business continued to bypass London because of the 1 per cent tax, especially on bearer bonds that commanded an international market.[5] In addition, the capital gains tax did have a depressing effect on stock exchange business for it was further extended in scope under the Labour government in 1965. In particular, it discouraged investors in long-dated fixed-interest stocks. The price of such stock fell when interest rates rose while, if interest rates fell, the price rose, but capital gains tax would have to be paid. The possibility of loss remained the same but now the post-tax profit to be made on a rise was less, so reducing the incentive to buy and sell such securities. By June 1965 the brokers J. & A. Scrimgeour estimated that the capital gains tax had reduced their turnover by 50 per cent. The Stock Exchange's own investigation in November 1965 suggested that turnover was down by over one-third, as investors were discouraged from selling securities because they would incur tax on the profits realized. However, the government was not willing to modify their tax regime in order to limit the damage being inflicted on the Stock Exchange. As with Conservative governments between 1951 and 1964. Repeated requests and suggestions were largely ignored by Labour governments between 1964 and 1970.[6]

In areas that really mattered to the Stock Exchange, such as taxation, there is little evidence to suggest that it made any difference whether Labour or the Conservatives were in power. It was not until August 1963 that the level of stamp duty was actually reduced, despite the fact that the Conservatives had been in power since 1951. Though it was the Labour government that developed the capital gains tax it had originated under the Conservatives before the 1964 election. As in the 1950s there is a total absence of evidence to indicate that the Stock Exchange was able to exert much influence on the government, even in those areas of most concern to it. The view of most members was summed up in a petition to the Stock Exchange in December 1962, signed by over 300 of them.

To face reality, we can look for hindrance, not help from the present government and it appears more than likely that they will be replaced by another which will be no more concerned than they for fostering markets.[7]

The Stock Exchange was well aware that if it did not work with the government it would lose what authority it had within the financial system. This co-operation did have its benefits with both the devaluation of November 1967 and the gold crisis of March 1968 passing off with little more than the brief closure of a day.[8] With the Bank of England now part of the machinery of government there was a steady flow of information and

[5] Ibid., 11 June 1964, 20 July 1964.
[6] Ibid., 14 Dec. 1964, 21 June 1965, 22 Nov. 1965, 31 Jan. 1966, 28 Nov. 1966, 30 Oct. 1967.
[7] Ibid., 24 Dec. 1962.
[8] Ibid., 31 Oct. 1966, 20 Nov. 1967, 15 Mar. 1968, 25 Mar. 1968, 9 June 1969.

consultation from the Treasury to the City of London, and the Stock Exchange being an integral part of the process. That did not mean that the Stock Exchange had much influence over government decision-making, but it did ensure that the damaging consequences of crises could be minimized by forward planning and co-ordinated action. In return the Stock Exchange had to deliver not only an orderly market place but also one responsive to the needs of government, as in the continuing battle to eliminate 'bond washing'. At all costs the Stock Exchange appeared determined to retain control over the securities market, and was willing to introduce and police restrictive regulations itself, in return for a freedom from direct outside control. Unfortunately, the result of this was that the Stock Exchange was an increasingly regulated market which was not always to the liking of those who used it, so encouraging them to trade outside where possible.[9]

In return for fulfilling this regulatory role the Stock Exchange did expect the government's support in its aim of trying to ensure that all buying and selling of securities passed through the hands of its members. In 1968, for example, the Stock Exchange wrote to the Inland Revenue

There is no doubt that transactions are taking place outside the Exchange on behalf of individuals and my Council consider that legislation should be introduced to ensure that all those permitted to deal in securities are treated uniformly, otherwise there exists an open invitation to bypass the recognized Stock Exchanges.[10]

However, the government was reluctant to go this far. It was relatively easy to exercise some degree of supervision and control over those in the securities market that belonged to the London Stock Exchange, because they were governed by the rules and regulations of that organization, and could be forced to abide by these by these through the threat of a fine, suspension or expulsion. To extend that level of authority to a miscellaneous group who dealt in securities on a regular or even occasional basis, and belonged to no such organization, was an entirely different matter. It would require an administrative arm staffed with people who understood the business and the introduction of sanctions to be used against those who broke the rules. Consequently, it was easier to ignore the activities of the non-members, unless they actually broke the law, and use the stock exchanges especially London, to monitor and police the bulk of transactions. The Stock Exchange, for example, towards the end of 1966 warned the Board of Trade that Investors Overseas Services was evading British safeguards on investment by operating through a subsidiary, International Life Insurance Company (UK). The Board of Trade dismissed the warnings but the Stock Exchange took what action it could. In May 1967 it refused permission for

---

[9] LSE: Council, 20 Sept. 1965, 18 Jan. 1966, 7 Feb. 1966, 4 Apr. 1966, 12 Apr. 1966, 18 Apr. 1966, 18 July 1966, 21 July 1969.
[10] Ibid., 19 Sept. 1968, cf. 11 Apr 1960.

its own members to act for Investors Overseas Services because of serious doubts about its activities.[11]

The beginning of the breakdown in this relationship where the government relied on the Stock Exchange to police the securities market began in the late 1960s. In July 1967 the Stock Exchange received an approach from the Monopolies Commission. This was in the nature of a preliminary enquiry regarding certain practices that could be regarded as being against the public interest. In particular, the Monopolies Commission wanted to discover what justification there was for restrictions on admission to the Stock Exchange, prohibition of outside activities, and the enforcement of a minimum commission regime.[12] Even with the enquiry by the Monopolies Commission there was no sign that there was to be any change in the postwar relationship between the Stock Exchange, the Bank of England, and the government. No link was drawn between the Stock Exchange's ability to maintain a range of restrictive practices and its semi-monopolistic control of the domestic securities market. The government of the day, whether Conservative or Labour appeared content in the 1960s for the Stock Exchange to regulate the securities market, either alone or with other City firms and institutions, without the need for statutory powers or official intervention. This had been so with bond washing and was also happening with the continuing problems over insider trading, which was creating more and more difficulties for all concerned, as takeover bids became more common in the 1960s. This concern came to a head, once again, in 1961 with the takeover of Odhams Press Ltd. by the Thomson organization. At the beginning of January 1961 four individuals closely involved in the proposed deal began to buy shares in Odhams. These were Sir Christopher Chancellor, Chairman of Odhams, J. M. Coltart, Managing Director of Thomson Newspapers, and P. Cookman and C. N. McQueen, directors of Scottish Television (a Thomson Company). At the end of January they started selling the shares at a premium of almost 50 per cent on the pre-bid price, leading to a number of complaints to the Stock Exchange from its members.

Lacking any kind of legislation or sanction, because the government regarded the matter as one to be dealt with by the market, all the Stock Exchange could do was pass the information their investigation revealed on to the chairmen of Odhams Press and Thomson Newspapers—the very people involved.[13] The Stock Exchange fully recognized its own limitations in taking action against those who used inside information to trade in a company's shares to their advantage. Responding to outside calls in 1964 for them to take action they made clear that

The leakage of information about public companies is primarily a matter for the Board concerned, who naturally must protect their shareholders' interest. The Stock

---

[11] Ibid., 12 Dec. 1966.    [12] Ibid., 10 July 1967.    [13] Ibid., 27 Feb. 1961.

Exchange is not in a position to prevent such leakages, or take any direct action to discourage them, or to initiate any proceedings against those responsible for them. The Council can only take evidence from its own members by requiring firms to disclose of all dealings in the relevant shares.[14]

It was not until 1966 that the Stock Exchange decided that time for concerted action had come. The Stock Exchange was being blamed for allowing individuals to profit from inside information but it could not solve the problem itself, try as it might through investigations and punishing its own members. The banks and issuing houses needed to be involved. This decision was prompted by an offer from Hawker Siddeley for Crompton Parkinson preference shares, which had been preceded by considerable buying in the market beforehand.[15]

The outcome of this approach by the Stock Exchange to the rest of the City was the formulation of a Takeover Code by August 1967. A small Takeover Panel, consisting of members from issuing and accepting Houses; the insurance, investment, and pension funds, the clearing banks, and the CBI, as well as the Stock Exchange, was to oversee the operation of the code. The Bank of England was then included on the recommendation of the chairman of the Stock Exchange, and the Takeover Panel was formally established in 1968. The only sanction the panel had available was a refusal to quote or a suspension of the existing quotation for company's shares on the Stock Exchange.[16] Again, the Stock Exchange was being expected to police a practice of which its members were the main victim. Because of the difficulty of discovering whether insider trading had actually taken place, as opposed to intelligent guesswork, and then the problem of how to punish those involved if a case could be proved, neither the government nor the rest of the City were keen or able to act. At least by the end of the 1960s considerable progress had been made in both putting in place an expected code of practice, against which an individual's actions could be judged, and widening concern about insider-trading practices beyond the Stock Exchange. This had all been driven by the Stock Exchange with its need to ensure all had equal access to information, so as not to expose its own members to market manipulation. In 1961, for example, it had already recommended to companies that all announcements be made during working hours, so that all concerned would know the situation immediately, and could take appropriate action.[17]

---

[14] LSE: Council, 15 June 1964.     [15] Ibid., 25 Dec. 1966.

[16] Ibid., 14 Aug. 1967, 21 Aug. 1967, 21 Apr. 1969. The impression is given that the formation of the Takeover Panel took place on the initiative of the Bank of England, whereas it was actually the Stock Exchange that was responsible. See R. Roberts, 'The Bank of England and the City', in R. Roberts and D. Kynaston (eds.), *The Bank of England: Money, Power and Influence 1694–1994* (Oxford 1995), 176; *Financial Times*, 27 Mar. 1998.

[17] LSE: Council: *Annual Report*, 24 Mar. 1962.

## RELATIONS WITH MEMBERS

That aim to create a level playing field, both for members and non-members, had been a long-standing one for the Stock Exchange. In the 1960s it was accompanied by an equal desire to ensure that all members possessed both the training and the capital so that they could play an active role in the market, but not pose a threat to others through the risks they ran and an inability to cover any losses that resulted. The existence of the Compensation Fund was exerting a growing influence on the Stock Exchange's policy on both the admission of new members and controlling the organization and behaviour of those already there. This was especially true as the losses covered were extended. Thus, greater and greater care was taken in vetting potential applicants leading to examinations in 1967. The result of this was the dropping of the annual renewal of membership, also in 1967, which had been an easy device for removing those considered unsatisfactory, after a brief sojourn in the Stock Exchange.[18] A more serious hurdle was a move against single-partner firms as it was discovered that these were disproportionately responsible for failures on the Stock Exchange. Thus in 1961 it was decided that all firms had to have a minimum of two partners, so making it difficult for individuals to become members. Those single-partner firms that were already in operation were allowed to continue but pressure was put on them to merge to form bigger units. The result of this policy was to make it difficult for the London Stock Exchange to accept as members many of the stockbrokers who operated in towns around London when they expressed an interest in joining in 1966. Most of these were small single-man firms as the amount of business they conducted was insufficient to justify a greater size, especially as the Stock Exchange's own regulations precluded the pursuit of any other occupation.[19]

Not only were the Stock Exchange's rules making it difficult for a single trader to join and operate but minimum capital requirements were also being introduced, again because of the Compensation Fund. Between 1950 and July 1967 a total of £1,068,508 had been paid out to claimants under the Compensation Fund but only £271,491 had been recouped from the estates of failed members, or a deficit of £797,017. Though the Compensation Fund's accumulated reserves had risen to £746,408 by then, the further potential losses did give the Stock Exchange every reason to investigate more closely the financial health of its members and act upon what it found.[20] From the very beginning of the 1960s the Stock Exchange began to scrutinize more carefully the balance sheets that members had to

[18] LSE: Council, 11 Apr. 1960, 24 Apr. 1961, 23 May 1961, 5 Mar. 1962, 2 May 1967, 9 Oct. 1967.
[19] Ibid., 5 June 1961, 16 Apr. 1962, 25 May 1966, 4 July 1966.
[20] Ibid., 10 July 1967.

maintain. After each major loss the level of scrutiny increased, with a tightening up on the records which each firm had to keep, regular auditing of the accounts, compulsory insurance against fraud by employees, and requirements on a minimum level of solvency. The failure of York, Green & Co. in 1961 and Cutbill & Co. in January 1966, with an estimated deficit of £150,000 and £225,000 respectively, each led to specific improvements in accounts that firms kept, and the Stock Exchange's monitoring of these through independent accountants. As early as August 1960 an investigation into the accounts of the broking firm of S. R. & G. H. Channon, had revealed net tangible assets of only £5,352, including office furniture. At the same time the firm had debts of £71,899 outstanding in the market against credits of only £57,634, or a deficit of £14,265.[21]

Out of these relvelations came the requirement that each stockbroking firm had to possess a minimum capital of £10,000 plus a further £5,000 for each partner if there were more than two. For jobbers the minimum was set higher at £15,000. Though some felt such requirements would bar '. . . those candidates with brains and other qualifications of merit. . . ' who did not possess the requisite capital, the Stock Exchange was more concerned with limiting the losses that all would, collectively, have to bear if a member with little capital failed.[22] Nevertheless, this was not a particularly large obstacle to membership because the cost of entry was not especially high. The entrance fee remained fixed at 1,000 guineas as did the annual subscription of 215 guineas. In addition a nomination had to be purchased and these fluctuated in value depending on the amount of business being conducted on the Stock Exchange. At the beginning of the 1960s the average price was around £1,400 but dropped to a low of £146 in 1967 before recovering to £928 in 1968. In contrast, it was estimated in 1969 that a seat on the New York Stock Exchange cost $200,000, plus an entrance fee of $7,500 and an annual subscription of $1,500.[23]

Consequently, in order to safeguard the institution and its membership, the Stock Exchange intervened to ensure that every firm had a minimal level of management and capital, which did have some limited implications for both the ease of entry and the freedom to operate. Conversely, the Stock Exchange remained antagonistic towards very large firms, despite the fact that in the 1960s this was being encouraged by the needs of the institutional investors and the complexities created by taxation. Already large firms, like the brokers Capels, became even larger in the 1960s, merging with Nathan & Rosselli in 1964. The combined firm had 19 partners and 300 staff in 1965, making it one of the biggest on the Stock Exchange, with a wide range of institutional clients such as banks, finance houses, money

[21] LSE: Council, 22 Feb. 1960, 18 July 1960, 26 Sept. 1960, 20 Dec. 1961, 29 Jan. 1962, 13 Apr. 1964, 7 Mar. 1966, 4 Apr. 1966, 22 Dec. 1969.
[22] Ibid., 5 June 1961.
[23] Ibid., 21 July 1961, 24 Dec. 1962, 22 June 1964, 21 Apr. 1969, 10 Nov. 1969.

brokers as well as private investors. In 1967 further growth took place when Clayton, Byng & Paget were absorbed, which brought in more private clients as well as a connection with solicitors. Stockbrokers were also trying to spread the source of their business so that they were not dependent upon any particular branch, and thus be vulnerable to a change of fashion. When Raphaels merged with Robinson & Glyn in 1967 they were attempting to add a volume business to an established clientele of wealthy investors. Even without mergers the larger firms were getting bigger in the 1960s, by recruiting from each other. In 1969 Cazenoves recruited Michael Richardson from Panmure Gordon, where he was already a partner. On his move he brought both the team he worked with and the clients they served. Mullens, which steered clear of mergers and diversification's because of is roles as the government broker, saw its partners rise from nine in 1960 to 11 in 1970, while Foster & Braithwaite began to offer partnerships to non-family members from 1968.

The same pattern of growth and amalgamation was also apparent among the jobbers. Between 1960 and 1968 Durlachers merged with Bone Oldham (1960), Bradford & Payne (1963), and Kitchen, Baker, Shaw (1965) so as to extend their dealing into such areas as breweries, steel-making, hotels, and racecourses. Eventually, in 1968 they merged with Wedd Jefferson which itself had taken over Hadow & Turner in 1962. Overall, whereas in 1960 there were 405 Stock Exchange firms with 2,431 partners, by 1970 the number of firms had almost halved to 223 while the number of partners was down by only 14 per cent at 2,038. As a result the ratio of partners to firms had risen from 6.0 in 1960 to 9.3 in 1970. The growth of scale was marked among both jobbers, where the number of partners per firm increased from 5.5 in 1960 to 8.8 in 1970, and stockbrokers, who witnessed a rise from 6.2 in 1960 to 9.4 in 1970.[24] Though the Stock Exchange recognized the process at work, and the reasons behind it, there was only a gradual reluctance to amend the rules so as to accommodate the larger firms, and even attempts to prevent it.

The Stock Exchange set a maximum to the number of clerks, authorized and unauthorized, that a firm could employ on the floor of the Stock Exchange. Firms had taken to evading the limitation by employing other members as their clerks. This had the result of boosting the membership by the inclusion of many who were little more than clerks, indicating both the

[24] M. C. Reed, *A History of James Capel and Company* (London 1975), 94–5, 97–9, 101; S. D. Chapman, *Raphael Bicentenary, 1787–1987* (London 1991), 269; D. Wainwright, *Government Broker: The Story of an office and of Mullens and Company* (East Molesey 1990), 138; W. J. Reader, *A House in the City: A Study of the City and of the Stock Exchange Based on the Records of Foster & Braithwaite, 1825–1975* (London 1979), 181; *Wedd, Durlacher, Mordaunt and Company, Members of the Stock Exchange, London* (n.p. 1984); D. Cobham, 'The Equity Market', in D. Cobham (ed.), *Markets and Dealers: The Economics of the London Financial Markets* (London 1992), 29; W. J. Reader and D. Kynaston, *Professional Stockbrokers: A History of Philips & Drew* (London 1998), 74.

ease and cheapness of admission for much of the post-war era. In 1962 this was changed so that the maximum of five clerks (two authorized/three unauthorized) was to include any members who were acting as clerks. As compensation the Stock Exchange would look sympathetically on any request from a firm to employ above the maximum. Nevertheless, the effect was to reduce the benefits that a firm could obtain from a larger scale of operation, by imposing a physical limit on the number of clerks it could employ to deal for it in the Stock Exchange. In the larger stock-broking firms the senior staff tended to remain in their offices, or visiting clients, in order to generate business. In turn, they employed clerical staff for such back-office duties as settling transactions and billing clients, along with dealing staff who bought and sold in the Stock Exchange and kept in touch with the market. Clearly, as the volume and variety of a firm's business grew, with an increasing number of partners, so did the requirement for staff in the office and on the trading-floor.[25] Thus as long as this restriction on the use of clerks on the trading-floor remained there was a limit to the size of a stockbroking and jobbing firm, but this restriction became less and less important as more business took place on the telephone from offices.[26] By November 1966 the Stock Exchange had come to recognize that,

In recent years there has been a growing tendency for small and medium-sized broking firms to amalgamate, probably to obtain the economies of scale so necessary to provide the services required by investors, particularly the Institutional Investors, who continue to assume an ever-increasing importance.[27]

Thus in 1967 the Stock Exchange removed any limit on the number of partners a Stock Exchange firm could have. The result was the creation of a number of even larger broking and jobbing firms. In 1969 Wedd Durlacher were the largest jobber, with 30 partners and a further 41 associated members, while Sheppards & Chase were the largest brokers in number of partners with 30, though Scrimgeour were bigger overall having 27 partners and 35 associated members. The era of the large firm had definitely arrived and it was beginning to change attitudes and policies on the Stock Exchange.[28]

One example of the change of attitude was on the question of advertising, which the Stock Exchange had remained resolutely opposed to from its very inception. It was not that the Stock Exchange did not approve of advertising or failed to recognize its ability to influence those to whom it was directed. During the 1960s the Stock Exchange itself commissioned an number of expensive advertising campaigns in an attempt to convince the public of the merits of the securities market in the face of hostile opinion. It was worried that if the public continued to regard the Stock Exchange

---

[25] LSE: Council, 5 June 1961, 19 Feb. 1962, 5 Mar. 1962, 22 July 1963.
[26] Ibid., 1 Oct. 1962, 28 Feb. 1966.   [27] Ibid., 21 Nov. 1966.
[28] Ibid., 31 July 1967, 13 Jan. 1969.

as either irrelevant or, even worse, positively harmful, being a centre of damaging speculation and insider trading, it could provoke outside intervention. Consequently, it was keen to persuade as many people as possible that the Stock Exchange played an essential and positive role in the machinery of finance. This was done through the viewing gallery and visitor centre, publicity in newspapers, and free information to schools, clubs, and other organizations, including the hire of specially made films.[29]

In contrast, individual members were not permitted to advertise as this would foster competition for clients, which the Stock Exchange was opposed to. Dundas Hamilton, for example, of Fielding, Newson, Smith & Co., was reprimanded in 1961 for enticing away the clients of other broking firms through circulating local authorities with the services his firm offered for the investment of superannuation funds. There was also the feeling that by not advertising Stock Exchange members differentiated themselves from those that did, who were regarded as little better than 'share pushers', trying to sell grossly overvalued securities to gullible investors. However, the increasing competition from both US brokerage houses and British and foreign banks, both of whom did advertise and were respected, began to undermine the Stock Exchange's outright opposition. Individual firms began to campaign for the right to publicize themselves in the way that non-member brokers and bankers did. The result was some minor relaxation in the rules in 1965, allowing newspapers to name the stockbroking firms whose research they were quoting. Advertising as such remained prohibited, though. The smaller firms were worried that it would increase their costs and expose them to competitive pressures, while some of the larger and more successful firms, such as Cazenove & Co., de Zoete & Gorton, L. Messell & Company, and Phillips & Drew, considered advertising unnecessary. It was only those firms in the middle, like Brewin, Scrutton & Son, who wanted to advertise in order to compete with merchant banks and unit trusts. By the end of the 1960s some members were, again, demanding the right to advertise in newspapers. Despite considerable support and an acceptance that the Stock Exchange had the right to vet any advertisement, the demand was again rejected. The Stock Exchange remained committed to limiting competition between members, and was suspicious of the consequences that unrestricted advertising could bring. There was also little incentive for members to conduct extensive advertising campaigns as the fixed commission regime meant that they could not compete on price by offering a cheap execution-only service.[30]

An even more powerful restraint on the growth of large firms was the insistence that all partners had to be members and that they could have no other occupation apart from broking and jobbing. This, effectively,

[29] LSE: Council, 4 Mar. 1963, 2 Sept. 1963, 15 June 1964; LSE: *Annual Reports*, 1962–4.
[30] LSE: Council, 27 Feb. 1961, 4 Mar. 1963, 15 July 1963, 7 Oct. 1963, 20 Sept. 1965, 4 Dec. 1967, 2 June 1969, 26 Oct. 1970; LSE: *Annual Report*, 24 Mar. 1968.

deprived Stock Exchange firms of the ability to obtain additional capital, in exchange for a share of the profits, or the opportunity to establish close alliances with others providing financial services. Both stockbroking and jobbing were becoming more capital-intensive in nature, at the very least because of the expensive nature of the equipment required. The brokers J. & A. Scrimgeour and Kitcat & Aitken, for example, set up a joint company in 1961 in order to share the use of an electronic computer which they required for record-keeping purposes, and these were already fairly large firms. In the 1960s computerization spread rapidly among the major brokers and jobbers, increasing the capital costs involved in the business.[31]

There was also the costs of accommodation with some firms being driven to locate further afield because of the rents charged for an office near the Stock Exchange and Bank of England. In 1962 Capel-Cure relocated to Cannon Street while, in 1961, MacNicol & Co. had moved their back-office facilities to Kingston in Surrey, concluding after a study of costs and recruitment of staff, that '. . . it is apparent that considerable benefits would be obtained if we were to take offices for this purpose outside the City of London'.[32] The ending of the restriction on the size of partnerships did allow firms to tap increased capital, through that provided by each partner. The problem here was that the capital required to support both broking and jobbing operations was tending to grow more rapidly than the ability of the partners to provide it. In the 1960s the imposition of the capital gains tax, on top of the already high level of income tax, increased the difficulty that jobbers and brokers experienced in building up a capital base through retained income and trading profits. Consequently, as older members retired, and drew out their capital it was not easy to replace it from the accumulated savings of those who took their place.[33]

If a broker or jobber wanted to expand his capital base, beyond that which the partners could provide, he had to borrow on a fixed interest basis. This involved a considerable risk because income could fluctuate greatly from year to year. The Stock Exchange itself became very worried about firms operating on such a highly geared basis, as revealed in some balance sheets. In 1967 it was noted that the broking firm of Lewis Altman & Co., with a net capital of only £16,000, were relying on a bank loan of £200,000 to finance purchases on behalf of the two partners and their clients. At least for broking firms their capital requirements could be largely met through the creation of larger units, as permitted in the late 1960s. The costs of equipment, offices, and staff could be spread over the earning capacity of numerous partners servicing a wide range of clients, while the capital available provided greater security for bank borrowings. The largest broking firms in 1969 had a minimum capital of £250,000, for example, though

---

[31] LSE: Council, 5 June 1961, cf. 17 Sept. 1962.
[32] Ibid., 10 July 1961, cf. 22 Jan. 1962.
[33] Ibid., 16 Mar. 1964, 7 Feb. 1966, 28 Nov. 1966, 2 Dec. 1968.

even this was regarded as inadequate by some.[34] Scrimgeours, with 27 partners felt that a capital of £1m. was necessary to support their operations
because '... broker firms are now being forced to borrow in order to
finance the settlement of their clients' business to an extent which could not
have been conceived ten years ago'.[35] They then pointed out that such
capital was not readily available from the partners because of the difficulty
of finding those who possessed both the necessary capital and the ability to
conduct a successful stockbroking business.

The problem was even more acute for jobbers, where the possibility of
finding dealers who both possessed the requisite capital, to allow them to
take and hold positions until the market changed, and the requisite ability,
so as to know when to trade successfully, was unlikely. As Geoffrey Hicks,
himself a dealer, noted in 1964: 'Jobbing appears to be rather like "book-
making" on a race-course, demanding certain qualities that can hardly be
taught.'[36] Thus, whereas the brokers could recruit those from wealthy families, for these also happened to possess useful connections, and so renew
their capital in that way, such a course was much less open to jobbers who
had to take talent wherever they found it. One solution to the shortage of
capital was to allow firms to recruit partners who would provide capital in
return for a share of the profits or losses, but not participate in the actual
business. Simple as this remedy was it created numerous complications,
which long delayed its implementation. There were those who were afraid
that if outside capital was introduced it would allow the creation of a few
very large broking and jobbing firms. These would then be able to drive
the smaller firms out of business. Brokers were also worried that if there
were only a few large jobbers then they could dictate prices in the markets.
Jobbers feared that large broking firms could match more sales and purchases internally, so bypassing them completely. Consequently, for a variety
of reasons there was considerable opposition to the idea of outside capital.
Nevertheless, the need to find some solution to the problem remained,
forcing the Stock Exchange to consider the idea of limited partnerships in
1964, as capital drained away through retirement.

Under this proposal outsiders could provide up to one-third of the capital
of a firm, with the members providing the rest. It was not until September
1965, that these limited partnerships were accepted by the membership as
a whole, and February 1966, before they could be proceeded with, which
was almost two years after the initial proposal. However, these limited partnerships were not a success for the simple reason that there were few individuals with the requisite wealth who were willing to risk it by investing
in either a stockbroker or jobber, especially with unlimited liability.[37] It

[34] Ibid., 20 Dec. 1961, 9 Jan. 1967, 13 Jan. 1969.
[35] Ibid., 3 Feb. 1969.    [36] Ibid., 24 Feb. 1964.
[37] Ibid., 30 Oct. 1961, 17 Sept. 1962, 21 Jan. 1963, 16 Mar. 1964, 4 Oct. 1965, 27 Nov.
1965, 7 Feb. 1966.

took the London Stock Exchange until 1969 to accept this fact, recognizing that

... the supply of unlimited liability capital seemed to be getting scarcer due to the success of various Government's policies relating to the redistribution of wealth and the prevention of accumulation of wealth.[38]

Such a late recognition of its own predicament is surprising because the Stock Exchange had long attributed the decline of the individual investor to the effects of taxation. Nevertheless, by 1969 the Stock Exchange had begun to consider allowing brokers and jobbers to operate as limited liability companies in order to make them attractive to those willing to invest risk capital.[39]

More fundamentally the Stock Exchange, throughout the 1960s, was unwilling to accept that the only realistic sources of capital were institutions, in particular financial institutions, because it regarded them as a threat to itself and its members. An overriding concern regarding the introduction of outside capital was that it would allow rival financial institutions, like the merchant banks or even foreign brokers, to gain a foothold in the Stock Exchange. That would then be a prelude to demands for full membership, exposing both brokers and jobbers to the competition of such large and well-capitalized companies as the commercial banks or the New York brokerage houses. The Stock Exchange made it a strict rule that no member could be associated with any company that, itself, bought and sold securities to any degree. Hence the ban on members being directors of unit trusts or similar financial concerns.[40]

Consequently, throughout the discussions on the introduction of limited partnerships it was made clear that banks, merchant banks, issuing houses, discount houses, insurance companies, investment trusts, and pension funds would not be eligible for participation. These, of course, were the very organizations that would have been the most likely to become involved as they had both the capital and knowledge to assess the risk, as well as a vested interest in forming closer links with brokers and jobbers. As it became clear that the scheme was failing to attract outside capital the prohibition on pension funds alone was removed in 1968. There was also to be no relaxation of the unlimited liability risk run by all members of the Stock Exchange whether they operated though a partnership, or a company that exactly replicated the partnership but enjoyed a more tax-efficient status. Even when the possibility of brokers and jobbers becoming limited liability companies was raised in 1969, there was no intention of allowing other financial institutions to become involved. The smaller brokers, for example, were worried that if a bank was allowed to take a share in a cor-

---

[38] LSE: Council, 13 Jan. 1969.     [39] Ibid., 13 Jan. 1969, 14 Apr. 1969.
[40] Ibid., 31 Oct. 1960, 25 Feb. 1963.

porate broking firm it would then direct all its business in that direction, to the detriment of all other brokers.[41]

Nevertheless, such opposition was no longer sufficient to stop such a move by the end of the 1960s, considering the pressing need for capital among many brokers and jobbers and the recognition that such connections already existed between brokers and financial institutions. Thus in June 1969 it was agreed that not only could brokers and jobbers incorporate themselves as limited liability firms but they could accept shareholdings from institutions. The Stock Exchange expressed sufficient confidence to believe that this would not lead to banks coming to dominate the whole business of buying and selling securities, reducing brokers and jobbers to minor and subsidiary rules, as was the case in continental Europe. As the 1970s approached the Stock Exchange had been forced to recognize that it had to permit some kind of relationship between its members and outside financial institutions if they were to find the capital that was increasingly required and develop the type of close relationships that the trade in securities now required. At this stage the Stock Exchange remained confident that any relationships that did develop would be on its terms and that it would continue to control the market-place, not the banks.[42]

However, in all this the Stock Exchange had failed, as in the 1950s, to address the fundamental difficulties faced by the jobbers that was driving them into extinction. Jobbing firms were undercapitalized compared to outside dealers. Non-members could raise additional finance by converting into joint-stock companies and selling shares to the investing public. Jobbers could not do this and the high levels of taxation made it difficult for the partners themselves to provide the funds required. As a result the number of partners in jobbing firms was steadily shrinking, falling from 760 in 1951 to 520 in 1961, or by 32 per cent, and those that remained were grouping themselves into larger and larger units. The number of firms fell from 179 to 89, over the same period, or by 50 per cent, and less than half these were considered to possess the capital necessary for their operations. However, further amalgamations were also not perceived as the solution because brokers found, increasingly, that the market in the less-traded securities was provided by only a few jobbers, so restricting competition and widening the margins between buy and sell prices. Even when formal mergers did not take place informal co-operation could result in the control of them being in the hands of one group. In turn this encouraged the use of non-member dealers such as the broker/jobbers belonging to the provincial stock exchanges or specialist London merchant banks, and mining-finance houses.[43]

[41] Ibid., 16 Mar. 1964, 24 Aug. 1964, 19 Feb. 1968, 8 July 1968, 13 Jan. 1969, 14 Apr. 1969, 27 May 1969.
[42] Ibid., 30 June 1969, cf. 2 June 1969, 22 Sept. 1969.
[43] Ibid., 23 Jan. 1961, 30 Oct. 1961.

The Stock Exchange was well aware of the dilemma it faced over jobbing but was incapable of responding to it because any decisive action would necessitate a radical change in the way it operated, and what it permitted jobbers to do. This was made clear to them in a lengthy memorandum by Douglas Eton, from the firm of Murton & Adams. He wrote in 1962, that:

> . . . the smaller firms are being eliminated and amalgamations and market partnerships are providing much larger and stronger trading units. If the jobbing system is to survive in its present free and uncontrolled condition, this process of rationalization must stop at exactly the right time, that is when the balance of power between Brokers and Jobbers is equal and the mutual interdependence is properly recognized on both sides. If rationalization goes beyond that point, then the Jobbing system will either die a natural death and be replaced by specialists, which process some regard as inevitable, or, be retained because it has established a virtual monopoly over the business that it does. This monopoly will in the end require a system of control every bit as complicated as the specialist system.

He went on to argue that this process of rationalization should be slowed down, so as to prevent it going too far. However, those jobbers who had responded to the situation with mergers and market partnerships, and so acquired some monopolistic positions in certain markets, were unwilling to accept any interventions that would increase competition as with, for example, the introduction of outside capital. Eton's other suggestion was a ban on roving jobbers who entered active markets and then moved on, once trading declined.[44] As it was, the Stock Exchange failed to respond to either suggestion. Any ban on roving jobbers would undermine the ability of the market as a whole to shift capacity to where it was required, while outside capital would bring in its wake, outside influence. How could jobbers be prevented from making prices to non-members when these non-members were shareholders? Consequently, the process of mergers and market partnerships continued, with the latter often leading to the former. Durlachers and Wedd Jefferson were already operating a joint-book before they merged to become one firm.[45]

However, by the mid-1960s even the device of merger and market partnership was failing to provide the level of capital required to maintain active markets. As had been noted in 1962:

The basis of the Jobbing System is that Jobbing Firms should, day in and day out be prepared to make prices in defined stocks to brokers. It is conceded that this is not always possible, but as long as they are prepared to buy and offer stock, as the case may be, they are under present conditions maintaining a market. It is essential that they should carry out this function daily and yearly.[46]

---

[44] LSE: Council, 13 Aug. 1962.     [45] Ibid., 27 Nov. 1965, 29 Nov. 1965.
[46] Ibid., 13 Aug. 1962.

Though jobbers were generating profits of £2m. per annum much of this was lost in taxation, leaving insufficient in the business to support the market, once salaries, office expenses, and interest had been paid. The introduction of limited partnerships had allowed the capital available to jobbers to grow from £4m. to £6.5m. between 1965 and 1966. However, if this risk capital was used to provide the average 5 per cent margin that banks insisted upon for loans with securities as collateral, it meant the market's capacity was no more then £130m. This was at a time when the market capitalization of quoted securities grew from £45bn. in 1960 to £107bn. in 1970.[47] (See Table 10.1.)

At last the Stock Exchange had to face up to the fact that there was a crisis in jobbing, which was likely to destroy the uniqueness of the system in London. In the bourses of continental Europe, and over-the-counter (OTC) markets in North America dual capacity firms operated, that both made markets and bought and sold for clients, as on the provincial stock exchanges. The London Stock Exchange was unwilling to accept this because of the inherent conflict of interest, and the loss of competitive advantage that their broker members enjoyed through exclusive access to jobbers. On the New York and American Stock Exchanges specialists operated but they only catered for the most active securities, leaving brokers without a ready market in the remainder. Though the markets in many securities in London were only nominal, the London Stock Exchange was unwilling to abandon one of its claims of providing a ready market in the widest range of securities. However, the current situation in London was leading towards the creation of only three or four large jobbing firms that would be profitable. This was not acceptable to the London Stock Exchange, because of the restricted choice that would be available to its broker-members.[48] Eventually in 1969 it was accepted that financial institutions could participate in jobbers, so allowing them to provide the markets inside the Stock Exchange that broker-members desired. However, so as to place a limit on the influence of the financial institutions it was ruled that 51 per cent of the shares in these new limited-liability jobbing companies must be held by members, with any single non-member restricted to a maximum holding of 10 per cent.[49]

Generally, what was happening was that the role to be played by jobbers was continuing to diminish in the 1960s. The growth of large stockbroking firms with a range of clients meant that they handled a significant proportion of all transactions coming to the Stock Exchange and so were able to match more of them internally. Also, outside the Stock Exchange the increasingly institutional nature of investment meant that fewer sales and purchases came to the market, because many transactions could be done

---

[47] Ibid., 3 Oct. 1966.
[48] Ibid., 6 Dec. 1965, 3 Oct. 1966, 24 Oct. 1966, 14 Nov. 1966.
[49] Ibid., 3 Oct. 1966, 13 Jan. 1969, 14 Apr. 1969, 21 Apr. 1969, 2 June 1969.

**Table 10.1. London Stock Exchange: Nominal and market values of securities quoted in 1960 and 1970 (£m.)**

| Category of security | Nominal value | | | Market value | | |
|---|---|---|---|---|---|---|
| | 1960 | 1970 | Difference | 1960 | 1970 | Difference |
| British government | 18,259.9 | 21,638.4 | + 3,3785.4 | 14,352.5 | 16,100.6 | + 1,748.1 |
| UK public bodies | 743.7 | 2,099.2 | + 1,355.5 | 619.9 | 1,710.4 | + 1,090.5 |
| TOTAL | 19,003.6 | 23,737.6 | + 4,734.0 | 14,972.4 | 17,811.0 | + 2,838.6 |
| Colonial governments | 815.8 | 735.5 | − 80.3 | 662.8 | 538.0 | − 124.8 |
| Foreign governments | 1,662.9 | 2,000.4 | + 337.5 | 204.1 | 1,403.0 | + 1,198.9 |
| Colonial/foreign public bodies | 114.2 | 117.4 | + 3.2 | 79.3 | 67.7 | − 11.6 |
| TOTAL | 2,592.9 | 2,853.3 | + 260.4 | 946.2 | 2,008.7 | + 1,062.5 |
| Banks/discount houses | 445.2 | 1,470.5 | + 1,025.3 | 1,216.9 | 6,054.3 | + 4,837.4 |
| Financial, land, and investment | 883.0 | 2,201.4 | + 1,318.4 | 2,219.1 | 5,755.3 | + 3,536.2 |
| Insurance | 107.3 | 383.3 | + 231.0 | 1,097.9 | 2,140.1 | + 1,042.2 |
| Property | 229.3 | 947.5 | + 718.2 | 517.0 | 1,758.3 | + 1,241.3 |
| TOTAL | 1,664.8 | 4,957.7 | + 3,292.9 | 5,050.9 | 15,708.0 | + 10,657.1 |
| Railways, trams, canals, docks | 471.4 | 472.2 | + 0.8 | 467.6 | 644.3 | + 176.7 |
| Gas, electricity, and water | 161.9 | 273.1 | + 111.2 | 337.9 | 329.1 | − 8.8 |
| Telegraph and telephone | 26.4 | 163.7 | + 137.3 | 61.7 | 1,722.3 | + 1,660.6 |
| TOTAL | 659.7 | 909.0 | + 249.3 | 867.2 | 2,695.7 | + 1,828.5 |
| Commercial/Industrial | 4,791.2 | 11,095.7 | + 6,304.5 | 15,207.9 | 54,737.5 | + 39,529.6 |
| Breweries/Distilleries | 506.9 | 1,192.6 | + 685.7 | 1,205.6 | 2,480.6 | + 1,275.0 |
| Iron, coal, and steel | 533.8 | 384.8 | − 149.0 | 1,271.5 | 1,368.2 | + 96.7 |
| Shipping | 175.6 | 219.3 | + 43.7 | 287.8 | 486.1 | + 198.3 |
| TOTAL | 6,007.5 | 12,892.4 | + 6,884.9 | 17,972.8 | 59,072.4 | + 41,099.6 |
| Mining | 560.3 | 891.1 | + 330.8 | 2,146.4 | 8,223.0 | 6,076.6 |
| Oil | 671.6 | 947.5 | + 275.9 | 2,878.3 | 1,758.3 | + 1,120.0 |
| Plantations | 128.2 | 129.3 | + 1.1 | 226.2 | 136.7 | − 89.5 |
| TOTAL | 1,360.1 | 1,967.9 | + 602.8 | 5,250.9 | 10,118.0 | + 4,867.1 |
| TOTAL | 31,288.6 | 47,317.9 | + 16,029.3 | 45,060.4 | 107,413.8 | + 62,353.4 |

*Source*: Stock Exchange Official Yearbooks, 1960 and 1970.

internally or through non-member jobbers, so saving on either jobber's turn, broker's commission, or both. Finally, the ability of non-member dealers, such as the discount houses and merchant banks, to raise additional capital, placed them in an advantageous competitive position compared to jobbers. What was developing, was a vicious circle in which jobbers were ceasing to make prices in securities with only a narrow market, and widening the turn in others, so encouraging brokers to undertake their own business or use non-member dealers. In turn, this encouraged existing jobbers to leave or merge, so shrinking the dealing community and further damaging the service provided.[50]

The result was that the number of jobbers fell from 22 per cent of the membership in 1960 to 13 per cent in 1970. Increasingly the London Stock Exchange was becoming a broker-only institution in which sales and purchases were matched not on the trading-floor but within offices or via the telephone. A smaller and smaller proportion of total transactions was passing through the hands of the jobbers with consequences for both their competitiveness and the market they provided. The problems were there for all to see as in this report written in 1966,

The general climate of business in the City has changed over the past twenty years, bringing much fiercer competition between brokers and greater concentration of business in the hands of institutions. Both these competing groups have exerted a severe pressure on the jobbers ... As a result ... the standard of ethics and practices in dealing has altered and deteriorated ... there has at times been too great competition between jobbers with the result that the number of jobbing firms has greatly declined. The Capital Gains Tax has curtailed the activities of the short-term operator. As a result, reduced turnover has made jobbing much more difficult with its consequent effect upon the investor's ability to deal. A considerable amount of business tends to be done outside the market although using the market as a basis for price and as a long stop, when the business cannot be done elsewhere ... It is a fallacy to believe that there should automatically be a close price at all times for all stocks dealt in by the jobbing system. Although one of the functions of a jobber is to create a market, he can only continue to do so to the extent that buyers and sellers in a stock do exist. Wide prices and an inability to deal in a stock only reflect a lack of potential dealers in that stock.[51]

But the Stock Exchange took no action until the very end of the 1960s. In the meantime the power of the brokers grew and grew. The priority for these brokers was to maintain their income, at a time of rising costs due to wage increases and office expenses. Despite economies, such as the relocation of offices and computerization, stockbrokers were faced therefore with a need to increase their income during the 1960s. This was especially the case in those years when turnover was low, as in 1961 and 1966, because their income was heavily dependent upon the volume of sales and purchases handled, while their staff and office costs were relatively fixed. In particular, the amount of paper work required in the 1960s increased enormously with the Stock Exchange's own demand for audited balance sheets and the government's taxation returns, especially for stamp duty and capital gains. At the same time clients expected more from their brokers by way of valuations and accounts suitable for tax purposes. One solution suggested

[50] Ibid., 1 May 1961, 7 Feb. 1966, 25 Nov. 1968, 21 Apr. 1969, 28 July 1969, 2 Sept. 1969, 1 Dec. 1969.      [51] Ibid., 7 Feb. 1966, 13 June 1966.

by the brokers Longman, Towsey & Co., was to reduce these expenses by sharing office and other facilities. The Stock Exchange itself vetoed that proposal because of the complexities it would create if one of the firm's involved failed.[52]

Another solution was to start charging for these additional services, like valuations and portfolio management. As a result a fixed scale of fees for services was introduced at the beginning of 1966, followed by the inevitable complaints that they was either too high or too low.[53] However, amalgamations and charges for particular services were only a partial remedy to the squeeze experienced by many brokers, with inflation pushing up their expenses but the level of charges fixed. The result was, once again, to put pressure on the Stock Exchange to revise upwards the rate of commission. In particular, there were constant complaints that the level of the minimum commission was so low as to make the business uneconomic.

This was despite a doubling of the minimum commission rate in 1960. Basically, many brokers wanted the minimum rate set at such a high level that the small investor, with under £100 to invest, would be encouraged to choose a savings scheme or a unit trust, and not invest via a stockbroker. This was business most members did not want but found it difficult to discourage through raising their charges, because the Stock Exchange considered that politically sensitive. Nevertheless, the minimum commission on small bargains was doubled from £1 to £2 in 1964. Despite that increase many brokers, even the large ones like Phillips & Drew and W. Greenwell & Co., considered that, at least, 70 per cent of the transactions they handled were for private clients and generated a fee of under £10 each. This made them unprofitable considering the transaction time and clerical work involved. However, with a Labour government in power there was an understandable reluctance to increase minimum commission rates yet again, and so the complaints were ignored.[54]

While there were complaints from members that the charges made for handling numerous small sales and purchases made the business unremunerative, there were also complaints that the rates on high volume business made the Stock Exchange uncompetitive. Here there was pressure to have the rates reduced. In particular, it was pointed out by brokers such as John Hunter (of L. Messel & Company) that the London Stock Exchange was losing the business in international securities because the commission charged was too high. Generally, there was outside pressure on the Stock Exchange to reduce its fixed charges on high volume business from the likes of the merchant banks and insurance companies. In turn that was supported

---

[52] LSE: Council, 23 Jan. 1961, 5 June 1961, 10 July 1961, 31 July 1961, 17 Sept. 1962, 21 Jan. 1963, 3 May 1965, 24 Oct. 1966, 8 Apr. 1969.

[53] Ibid., 9 Nov. 1964, 20 Dec. 1965, 21 Feb. 1966.

[54] Ibid., 12 Sept. 1960, 29 Apr. 1963, 29 July 1963, 8 June 1964, 27 July 1964, 22 Mar. 1965, 20 Nov. 1967.

by the large brokers who handled the sales and purchases for them, in the expectation that lower charges would be accompanied by an increased volume of business, so generating larger profits. The largest jobbers also supported any reduction in charges as bringing more transactions to their market, and thus creating more income for them. However, moves in direction of a reduction were then opposed by those who saw only a decreased revenue for themselves, especially the private client brokers and the smaller jobbers who could not handle the large orders coming from institutional investors. Consequently, any attempt to vary the scale of fixed commissions met with strong resistance throughout the 1960s, with the Council of the Stock Exchange reluctant to make more than minor changes.[55] In September 1963, for example, there was a request from insurance companies, as a group, to reduce the commission on transactions in gilt-edged securities. Though the Stock Exchange was willing to make a few small concessions it would not reduce the rate.

Although it is true that the volume of business in gilt-edged securities has been greatly increased in the last 15 years it is equally true that during this period not only has the cost of the service provided by the brokers increased many more times, but the service itself has been greatly expanded, with the availability of electronic computers etc. As a result the current level of the gilt-edged commissions relative to expenses is low compared with pre-war.[56]

However, after intervention by Mullens, the government broker, the commission on large transactions in gilt-edged, especially above £5m., was reduced in the November of that year. Even so, the insurance companies continued to press for further reductions. They wanted a 50 per cent reduction on deals over £250,000 but the Stock Exchange refused to concede this because it would encourage institutional investors to direct all business through one or few brokers, because of the lower rate on higher volume.[57] Brokers like Pember & Boyle, who did a large business in gilt-edged defended the rate because of the experience and effort it required to carry out large and successful deals in the market. They argued throughout the 1960s against any reduction on the rate charged, while R. Layton & Co., another firm of brokers, even wanted higher rates of commission for business in gilt-edged securities. The result was when institutional investors did obtain further reductions it was only through considerable pressure.[58]

Another area of contention between members and with users of the Stock Exchange were rebates. Those customers that generated a high volume of business, such as the insurance companies, were rewarded with low commission charges but no discounts. Those customers producing a regular

[55] Ibid., 29 Apr. 1963, 13 May 1963, 8 July 1963, 24 June 1963, 8 July 1963, 15 July 1963, 29 July 1963, 1 June 1964, 4 Nov. 1968.
[56] Ibid., 30 Sept. 1963.      [57] Ibid., 11 Nov. 1963, 6 Jan. 1964.
[58] Ibid., 18 Jan. 1964, 17 Feb. 1964, 6 Dec. 1965, 31 Jan. 1966, 2 May 1966, 28 Nov. 1966, 13 Mar. 1968, 10 June 1968, 21 Oct. 1968, 30 June 1969, 5 Jan. 1970.

stream of smaller business, such as the banks, paid higher rates of commission but gained through the rebates. This left those that did not fall into either of these categories to pay the full rate which also had to be big enough to cover the unremunerative business transacted for the minimum commission alone. Within this group there were those who felt cheated because they received neither a lower rate of commission nor a rebate, and considered themselves entitled to one or the other. In this they were supported by those brokers who were keen to keep their custom in competition with non-members.[59] This was especially the case with those who acted as agents for brokers on an occasional basis, bringing in the orders of customers when and where it arose.

However, the Stock Exchange made it clear that discretion was not permissible, as in this statement of September 1966:

> ... any advantage to be gained from permitting brokers to allocate Commission to Country Brokers or any other group of non-members would be more than offset by the disadvantages that would arise from the relaxation of a basic principle of the commission rules which prohibits members from sharing their commission with any non-members other than Registered Agents and then only to the extent permitted by the Rules.[60]

Despite attempts to control this register of agents it had continued to grow in the 1950s and 1960s. Between 1956 and 1966 the General Register, which covered solicitors and accountants (1966: 63 per cent solicitors, 26 per cent accountants), had increased from 5,436 to 6,994. In both years 58 per cent of those on the General Register were to be found in London, reflecting the proliferation of legal and financial services in the City. The rest were spread across the British Isles ranging from 5/6 per cent in Glasgow, 5 per cent in Manchester, 4/5 per cent in Birmingham, and 4 per cent in Liverpool through 1 per cent in such centres as Cardiff, Leeds, Nottingham, and Oldham. There were also the members of the Provincial Brokers' Stock Exchange who numbered 448 in 1956 and 616 in 1966, and they were spread throughout the smaller towns, especially in the South-East of England. In addition to the General Register there were registers of banks (130), remisiers (overseas representatives) (30), attachés (domestic agents) (80), and clerks (2,000), as well as retired associates (450).[61]

Though they had failed to cut the number of such agents the Stock Exchange had reduced the share of commission that they were entitled to on the business they brought to the brokers. This had the effect of reducing their incentive to both develop such business and then pass it on to

---

[59] LSE: Council, 2 May 1966, 16 May 1966, 9 Dec. 1968.

[60] Ibid., 19 Sept. 1966, cf. 29 July 1963.

[61] Ibid., 3 July 1961, 5 Mar. 1962, 12 Mar. 1962, 7 May 1962, 21 Mar. 1966, 17 Oct. 1966.

members of the London Stock Exchange.[62] In 1962 the London firm of Chartered accountants, J. Hilbert Grove & Co., complained that, '. . . if it were not for us, the majority of the business we bring the Stock Exchange would be done through the Banks'.[63] They asked for the right to receive a larger share of the commission that the broker charged the client. This was not accepted. The Stock Exchange granted large commercial banks a higher rebate available to other intermediaries, because of the power they were able to exert, both directly and via the Bank of England. Naturally this annoyed those entitled to only a lower rate or refused one altogether, as were the New York brokerage houses in London. In 1964 the Issuing Houses Association, representing the merchant banks, tried to get an improved deal for their members because of the amount of business they were generating for members of the Stock Exchange.

> . . . management of substantial funds is increasingly coming into the hands of professional managers (many of whom are members of this Association) who do a great deal of work and generate a great deal of business which is to the benefit of your members . . . these agents are wholly unremunerated for a great deal of this work and this has the inevitable effect of creating a tendency on the part of these Agents to deal elsewhere.[64]

Despite this request, and the threat to move business away, wherever possible, the Stock Exchange refused to grant any additional concessions to the merchant banks. The Stock Exchange was only willing to allow its members to rebate commission where it could be shown that it would create substantial additional business or prevent the diversion of existing business. They were not convinced that either would happen in the case of the merchant banks while they were also worried that any concessions to the merchant banks would allow them to gain a competitive edge over their own members in handling the sales and purchases of securities.

The Stock Exchange had an ambivalent attitude towards those who brought it business, regarding them as both rivals and allies. The small and medium-sized firms of stockbrokers saw solicitors, accountants, provincial brokers, and bank branches as all competing for the orders from the individual investor while the large stockbroking firms were worried about merchant banks developing ever closer relationships with the large financial institutions. However, towards the end of the 1960s there was a growing realization that the combination of fixed commissions and low rebates was losing the Stock Exchange business in the more competitive environment that existed.[65] The actual or potential loss of business coming from other intermediaries was forcing the Stock Exchange to recognize that agents did play an active role in bringing business to their members

[62] Ibid., 27 Nov. 1961, 16 July 1962.    [63] Ibid., 29 Oct. 1962.
[64] Ibid., 12 Oct. 1964, cf. 30 Nov. 1964.
[65] Ibid., 1 May 1967, 8 May 1967, 3 July 1967, 16 Dec. 1968.

and so they had a right to demand a share of the commission paid by brokers' clients.

It is now widely appreciated that institutions bringing business to the Stock Exchange often act on behalf of many different principals whose business they aggregate in order to obtain the maximum benefit from the commission concessions and the most satisfactory means of executing the business in the market.[66]

As a consequence the pattern of the past was to be reversed, with those agents who brought business to the Stock Exchange being more financially rewarded. The proposal put forward was that agents would be allowed to share commission on all the business they brought in, not just the first £2,500 limit which had been set to stop the likes of merchant banks and insurance companies receiving the double advantage of lower rates on high volume business and rebates on regular business. Inevitably this move provoked opposition from those brokers, such as Grieveson, Grant & Co. and Phillips & Drew, who saw in it a reduction in income and an increase in competition.

The existing rules about Agents' commission are based on sound commercial principles and recognition of the need to preserve a minimum commission structure within the Stock Exchange. Under the new rules Agents would have nearly all the advantages of Stock Exchange membership without a number of its most important disadvantages and responsibilities.

In fact, they felt the proposed changes to the amount of commission rebated to agents would

... put the banks in a position to charge an effective rate below the minimum, because Stock Exchange commission is just one of their sources of remuneration for financial services.[67]

The real concern was that the concessions being offered to maintain the loyalty of agents like lawyers and accountants would be used by the banks, both commercial and merchant, to offer a low-cost dealing service to their customers, subsidized by the other services they provided and in which they did not compete with members of the Stock Exchange. Here was the inevitable dilemma for any uniform fixed-price regime. The need to tailor it to fit all clients, under all circumstances, and at all times. Naturally, those members who saw no immediate gain for themselves in the proposals resisted them. Again, it was the small and medium-sized firms that felt they had most to lose.[68] Teather & Greenwood probably spoke for them when they argued in December 1968 that:

If the big firms that handle the large business reckon that lowering the cost of very large bargains will bring into the House business which is now effected outside, I

---

[66] LSE: Council, 10 June 1968.    [67] Ibid., 11 Nov 1968.
[68] Ibid., 2 Dec. 1968, 9 Dec. 1968.

am not one to argue the point; but I am sure that it is unwise, possibly suicidal, to reduce the amount of commission to be retained by brokers on medium-sized business.[69]

A medium-sized broker, such as Quilter & Atchley, with seven partners and four associates, numbered among its clients both banks and private investors. Between May and October 1968 it transacted 4,494 sales or purchases for banks, producing c.£30,000 in commission. However, they had to pass on 25 per cent of that to the banks. In contrast, their private client business produced a commission income of c.£50,000 over the same period and that was what they wanted to preserve, for if it was taken by the banks and then passed on to them they would again lose 25 per cent.[70] In the wake of this resistance to any alteration of both commission rates and agent's rebate, the Stock Exchange was forced to amend its proposals.[71]

The problem was that there were major divisions between the membership of the London Stock Exchange. These were not simply between jobbers and brokers but between large and small firms and those doing a high volume institutional business and those catering for individual investors. As the Chairman of the Stock Exchange, R. F. M. Wilkinson, remarked in 1966, with a hint of exasperation, 'with over 300 firms it impossible to get anything like unanimity of view and back-seat drivers and vested interests are not unknown'.[72] Though the one-man-bands were being eliminated there remained an enormous diversity between small and large partnerships, with the largest increasingly operating as companies. Within jobbing, for example, a two-man firm could handle approximately 100 actively traded issues while the likes of Wedd, Durlacher covered entire groups of securities. Reflecting this change was the decision in 1968 to group jobbers by firm, not market, on the floor of the Stock Exchange because the largest firms were now so diversified.[73] For stockbroking the differences were even greater, ranging from the small partnership with its list of long-established private clients to the private company employing an extensive staff to handle the affairs of clients such as insurance companies or pension funds.[74]

In contrast the largest brokers were extending their range of operations into fund management and corporate takeovers. In 1960, members were not permitted to be involved in the running of a unit trust because of both any conflict of interest and a belief that they took business away from the Stock Exchange by matching bargains internally. Nevertheless, four years later, in 1964, Phillips & Drew were allowed to establish a unit trust, the Barbican Investment Fund, as way of catering for the needs of private investors. John Prust & Co. also extended their operations into the management of unit trusts. In another direction the brokers Miln & Robinson who specialized in the machine-tool industry, set up a subsidiary that

[69] Ibid., 9 Dec. 1968.    [70] Ibid.
[71] Ibid., 16 June 1969, 30 June 1969, 5 Jan. 1970.    [72] Ibid., 9 May 1966.
[73] Ibid., 15 May 1968, 1 Dec. 1969.    [74] Ibid., 6 Feb. 1967, cf. 1 Feb. 1965.

advised on management, mergers, and financing.[75] Grieveson, Grant & Co. explained in 1968 what they had been trying to do during the 1960s.

To compete, on more level terms, with the Merchant Banks, a determined effort has been made by leading firms on the Stock Exchange to build up an all-embracing service of research and investment advice, coupled with sophisticated record-keeping (for capital gains etc.) as well as dealing ability . . .

The minimum commission rules made it difficult to compete solely on price and so they were trying to add-value by improving the service they provided. However, they felt hampered in this direction by the rules and regulations imposed upon them as members of the Stock Exchange.

For some years now we have been most concerned, and so we believe have several other large firms, about the difficulty of competing with the service offered by the Merchant Banks and some Clearing Banks. We ourselves are in favour of a more competitive environment but we feel strongly that the competition should be on fair terms. At the moment we are not allowed to advertise. We are not allowed to deal outside the market or broker to broker. And so far we have not been allowed to open branch offices where we wished. The Merchant Banks can do all of these things. But a more important argument is that we operate within minimum commission rules, which the Council is not intending to remove.[76]

Faced with these hurdles they were no match for the merchant banks in fields such as fund management, new issues, company flotations, and takeovers, try as they might. The jobbers, Wedd, Durlacher, reported to the Stock Exchange in the same year that:

In the last few years the Merchant Banks have been taking over the management of an increasing number of large institutional funds with gilt-edged portfolios, formerly managed by these institutions with stockbroker advice.[77]

Here was an area that stockbrokers had played an important role in the past but were now losing out to the merchant banks, because they had the flexibility to provide the service that was required and the opportunity to compete aggressively for it. As a result, even the largest stockbroking firms were driven more and more to rely upon the basic commission business of buying and selling securities for clients, so reinforcing the commitment of so many to the fixed commission regime. Phillips & Drew, for example, with c.15 per cent of all gilt-edged commission paid on the Stock Exchange between September and November 1968 earned only £180,867 commission from it, whereas that generated from a c.2 per cent share of equities trading produced £308,000.[78]

---

[75] LSE: Council, 31 Oct. 1960, 2 Mar. 1964, 12 Oct. 1964, 3 Oct. 1966, 5 Oct. 1966; Reader and Kynaston, *Phillips & Drew*, 79–80, 87, 98, 102, 133; B. H. D. MacDermot, *Panmure Gordon & Company, 1876–1976: A Century of Stockbroking* (London 1976), 64.
[76] LSE: Council, 11 Nov. 1968.       [77] Ibid., 25 Nov. 1968.
[78] Reader and Kynaston, *Phillips & Drew*, 92.

Though the rules and regulations of the Stock Exchange did constrain the ability of some of its members, both brokers and jobbers, to compete with non-members, like banks, discount houses, and New York brokerage houses in London, there still remained clear advantages of membership. Immediate access to the trading-floor was one and this was steadily improved during the 1960s. Links between members' offices and the trading-floor were greatly enhanced with an electronic quotation service and direct telephone lines, for example. Both jobbers and brokers were provided with their own telephones rather than having to compete for the use of those available for common use. However, by the mid-1960s the Stock Exchange was concerned that this was going too far, making current prices on the floor widely available to non-members, and thus eroding the privileges of membership. By then, though, it was too late to stop the process. Using the techniques of computer technology developed for the New York Stock Exchange both Exchange Telegraph and Reuters were planning an improved price dissemination service with or without the co-operation of the Stock Exchange. As it was going to be impossible to prevent this happening, and many of its own members wanted such a facility, the Stock Exchange decided to go ahead with the development of its own service either on its own or in alliance with Exchange Telegraph and/or Reuters. In this way it would retain control and so be able to ensure only authorized access. By the middle of 1967 the Stock Exchange was ready to introduce a digital video service that would display official market prices on monitor screens in offices within a five-mile radius of the Stock Exchange. It was claimed to be the most advanced in the world. This service would be available on subscription to members and to Reuters and Exchange Telegraph, who could relay it to their clients. Restrictions, however, were imposed by the Stock Exchange on who had access to it so as to limit its use by competitors. The Stock Exchange was trying to balance carefully the needs of its own members, and their clients, for immediate access to current prices and a desire to prevent non-members from using these prices to develop a rival trading system.[79]

The finances of the Stock Exchange were also improving in the 1960s, following on from the pattern set in the late 1950s. Inflation reduced considerably the real value of the debt created when the proprietors were bought out, and the proportion of income that needed to be used to pay interest on the annuities. This did pose some feelings of guilt, leading the Stock Exchange to consider in 1960 if there was any way they could reward the original owners, by permitting them to share in the rising income being generated. However, it was discovered that if it did this it would lose the privileges it enjoyed as a mutual organization not run for profit, which reduced considerably the taxation it paid.

[79] LSE: Council 22 Feb. 1960, 25 Apr. 1960, 31 Aug. 1965, 7 Nov. 1966, 5 June 1967, 23 Oct. 1967; LSE: *Annual Report*, 1964/5.

There was also a reluctance to make a commitment for future payments which could not be sustained if the income of the Stock Exchange failed to grow in future. Thus no action was taken.[80] What made the difference between simply covering the expenses involved in running the Stock Exchange and making a profit, were the additional sources of revenue that had been created. Prime among these was the charge for quoting securities, both initially and annually. Whereas in 1961/2 the entrance and subscription fees from members totalled £0.9m., quotation fees added a further £0.4m., which was the current gap between revenue and expenditure. During the 1960s the dependence upon listing fees for income grew with the charge increased, extended to British and Commonwealth government stocks, and made annual. By 1968–9 quotation fees were almost equal to those paid by the members, running at £1.2m. per annum compared to £1.3m., and so helped the Stock Exchange generate a surplus of £0.9m. In fact without the fees paid by companies for having their securities quoted, the Stock Exchange would have been seriously loss-making. In 1968/9 the subscription and entrance fees paid by members, plus their payment for services, came to £1.6m., or only two-thirds of total expenditure, which was £2.5m. At the same time the steady surplus that the Stock Exchange was able to generate allowed it to accumulate a capital reserve, which had grown from £1.8m. in 1962 to £3.2m. by 1966. Consequently, in the 1960s the finances of the Stock Exchange had been transformed through quotation fees and inflation without the need to provoke the anger of the members by imposing considerably higher subscription charges. When an attempt was made in 1966 to raise additional revenue, by levying a turnover charge, it was defeated by the members. The subscription fee was raised to 250 guineas per member, plus proportionate charges for clerks, but this was relatively modest considering the declining value of money.[81]

Faced with this improvement in its finances the Stock Exchange was again able to plan for the rebuilding which had been deemed necessary towards the end of the Second World War. Preparation for this was undertaken through purchasing the freehold of the site they did not own and neighbouring buildings. The North British Insurance Company building cost £1.1m. in 1960, for example. When estimates for a new building were drawn up in 1961 the maximum cost was put at £4.9m. with another £750,000 for furnishing and fittings. In return the Stock Exchange would get a modern building for their own use plus offices capable of generating an income of £284,000 per annum. Though this new building would be equipped with modern telecommunications equipment, providing external connections for all brokers and jobbers, these would not be permitted on the trading-floor, so preserving its role as the centre of all dealing activity.

[80] LSE: Council, 2 May 1960, 7 June 1960.
[81] LSE: Council, *Annual Reports*, 1961/2–1968/9; LSE: Council, 16 July 1962, 22 June 1964, 1 Mar. 1965, 8 Nov. 1965, 18 Apr. 1966.

The threat posed to the physical market by telephone and teleprinter connections was understood but the belief remained that the convenience of a central face-to-face market was both necessary and could be preserved. However, worries about the fixed costs involved in the rebuilding delayed the project. Eventually by the mid-1960s it was becoming imperative that something was done, even if it was not a full rebuilding. At the very least an extensive refurbishment was required as well as a need to create space for modern telecommunications and computing equipment. This was estimated at 25 per cent of a new building. By then the cost of a new building was put at £11.6m., or more than twice the 1961 estimate, which further strengthened the opposition of those who believed that such a project could not be self-financing, but would have to be paid for out of considerably increased subscription fees or other levies on the membership. However, it was no longer possible to do nothing. It was now essential that a new telephone system was installed if the Stock Exchange was going to continue to function as a market while some degree of modernization, costing around £2m., had become essential. Neither the telephone system nor the modernization would provide any extra revenue while a new building would be partly self-financing, because of the office rents it could generate. There was also the added incentive that if they were given planning permission to proceed, the office space they could provide would command premium rates, because of the current ban on office-building by the Labour government. Thus, the decision was made to proceed with the new rebuilding and, eventually, despite the prohibition on new office development in London, they were given the requisite planning permission. Once complications with the Post Office, on their relocation, had been overcome and a loan of £10m. raised, rebuilding began. A completely new building emerged by the end of the decade.[82]

The other facilities provided by the Stock Exchange for its membership were also both improved and extended, though this was done more slowly in London compared to Paris. Computerization of the Settling Room continued so increasing its capacity while keeping down the rise in costs. The introduction in 1964 of an IBM 360 was estimated to save £42,600 per annum in running costs, for example. Similarly, it was estimated in 1966 that the new computer meant that a processing task that had previously taken 876 man-hours could now be done in 68.5. Such was the capacity of the computer by then that it could be used for other processing tasks in the Stock Exchange. In addition, the range of services provided for the membership were progressively extended. A Central Stock Payment Scheme was created in 1963. This handled payments between members in the same way that the Settlement Department met the need to move securities around. Furthermore the Central Delivery Department handled the physical

[82] Ibid., 6 Mar. 1961, 20 Nov. 1961, 24 Dec. 1962, 10 May 1965, 14 July 1965, 20 July 1965, 6 Sept. 1965, 29 June 1966; LSE: *Annual Reports*, 1960/1–1968/9.

movement of both documents and money between members. When the set-tlement payments and delivery service all came into full operation the Stock Exchange would be able to provide its membership with a cheap and effi-cient means to complete the transactions negotiated on the trading-floor or over the telephone. The Central Delivery Department, for example, was handling 8–10,000 cheques daily in 1963, and this rose to 20–25,000 on account days. However, though a pilot scheme for the Central Stock Payment scheme, involving allotment letters, came into operation in June 1963, the introduction of the full scheme was still not in place by March 1965. Though the saving to the members was estimated at £28,000 per annum the cost to the Stock Exchange was to be £83,701 per annum. Many members simply did not believe that they would save money but did believe that they would have to pay for the service. Nevertheless, the scheme was proceeded with, becoming effective in May 1966.[83]

This opposition to the introduction of new central services had made the Stock Exchange more conscious that it had to offer its members services that continued to be cheaper and better than those they could obtain from other suppliers. Consequently, in 1968, when they introduced a computer-ized probate valuation service they ensured that brokers were charged less than the fee that they, in turn, charged their customers. Of course the Stock Exchange itself laid down the minimum fee that was charged for such a service! Even so there was a slow take-up of the service and it was not self-financing. The Stock Exchange as an institution was attempting to provide its members with more and more of the facilities and services that it per-ceived that they required. On top of a trading-floor and a regulated market it now handled the settlement of sales, the payment for purchases, the phys-ical delivery of cheques and share certificates, and the provision of current price information. All these were to be paid for either on subscription or by being charged for, and the Stock Exchange saw them as potential sources of income. However, as with both the Settlement Department in the past and the probate valuation service currently, there was no indication that the Stock Exchange was able to price its services so as to make them profit-able, responsive as it was to the criticism of members. At the same time it had less need to make them profit centres in its own right as long as the quotation fees continued to grow and so cover the rising expenses of the Stock Exchange. Certainly the members were extremely reluctant to cover the costs of running the Stock Exchange, and the expanding range of ser-vices it provided, by paying increased subscription fees or any other similar charges.

In many ways the Stock Exchange was coming into conflict with its own

---

[83] LSE: Council, 9 Jan. 1961, 6 Feb. 1961, 2 Mar. 1961, 24 Apr. 1961, 17 Dec. 1962, 4 Feb. 1963, 25 Feb. 1963, 8 Apr. 1963, 22 June 1964, 29 Mar. 1965, 9 Aug. 1965, 15 Nov. 1965, 21 Nov. 1966, 8 Apr. 1968; LSE: *Annual Reports*, 1967/8, 1968/9; FLP, *The Stock Exchange: A History of Rebuilding* (London 1972), 6, 15, 31, 59.

members. As firms got bigger they were in a position to carry out more of the back-office functions themselves, with their own staff and their own computing equipment. This was especially so as a lot of broking and jobbing activity could be seasonal and cyclical creating opportunities to utilize underemployed staff remuneratively. Under these circumstances the larger firms were reluctant to pay either directly, or indirectly via their subscriptions, for a service that they were able to undertake themselves. This even applied to the price dissemination service with two firms—Exchange Telegraph and Reuters—eager and able to provide it on a subscription basis. It was only the Stock Exchange's desire to retain complete control over who had access to the service that drove them to do it themselves, for the initial idea had come from outside. In fact, by the end of the 1960s there was a growing criticism that the Stock Exchange was not providing the service that its members required. Improved as the Settlement Department was, for example, it handled only the most actively traded securities leaving brokers and jobbers to arrange the others between themselves. The problem was that the services provided by the Stock Exchange were neither minimal, as in the past when almost everything had been left to members, nor comprehensive where everything apart from the actual buying and selling, would be handled for the membership. As the brokers J. & A. Scrimgeour complained in 1968

... the real problem facing the Stock Exchange today is not the fact that some business may be done outside, but the difficulty of handling profitably the enormous volume which can only be done inside the House.[84]

Large stockbroking firms such as Scrimgeours were looking for cheaper ways to execute the large number of small deals that passed through their hands, and did not find that the facilities provided by the Stock Exchange offered much help.

During the 1960s the Stock Exchange exerted a growing control over its membership, both in terms of the services it provided and the rules and regulations it imposed. Nevertheless this control was not total.[85] This can be seen over the question of the admission of women. The Stock Exchange had no specific rules barring women members but was reluctant to accept them, citing the complications involved if the woman had acquired British nationality through marriage or both husband and wife were members but in different firms, including a jobber and broker. Until 1966 no firm ruling had to be made but in that year Miss Muriel Bailey applied for membership. She was a clerk with the stockbrokers James Flower & Sons, where her performance and abilities would have qualified her for a partnership, if she had been a man. As only members could be partners she wanted admission to secure that position. She even offered to not enter the trading-floor

<hr />

[84] LSE: Council, 25 Nov. 1968.     [85] Ibid., 13 Feb. 1961, 8 Jan. 1962, 22 July 1963.

if that would lessen opposition to her application. In her application she gave a brief resumé of her career

I started in the City in 1925 as a shorthand typist with the firm of Chandler & Co. (the Senior Partner, Mr. Lionel M. Walter, being a friend of my father's). About 1934 I joined Jas. Flower & Sons. When the war broke out there were so few of us left that the firm managed to get me exempted from the Forces, and in consequence I became responsible for the running of the office. Towards the end of the War I started to build up a personal business and over the period of years have been very successful, and can say with no hesitation that all my clients, both male and female, have the utmost confidence in me.

Faced with such a strong application the sub-committee dealing with admissions was unwilling to either accept or reject on its own authority. They noted that

While there are no rules which specially prohibit the admission of women members, the Committee appreciate that the consideration of any application from a woman candidate could involve matters of principle to which the Council may wish to give consideration before being required to decide by ballot whether or not to admit a woman member.[86]

Forced to give a judgement the subcommittee was in favour of admitting Miss Bailey but pointed out that any agreement to enter the Stock Exchange could not be made binding under the rules. Unfortunately, canvassing among the membership revealed that if women were permitted access to the trading-floor then their admission would provoke strong opposition. Nevertheless, the Council of the Stock Exchange agreed to back the admission of women, but with no access to the trading-floor, though that was seen as the first step towards unrestricted membership. This was then put to a vote of the entire membership in April 1967 where it gained the support of 55 per cent. As a majority of 75 per cent was required, the application was rejected. Miss Bailey decided to keep her application on record, which Council agreed to, so maintaining the pressure on them to find a solution. However, another poll on the admission of women a year later, had an even worse result. Only 663 members voted in favour while 1,366 were against the admission of women. Faced with this double rejection, despite the backing of the governing council of the Stock Exchange, Miss Bailey abandoned her attempts to gain membership, and the issue then lapsed.[87]

The Council of the Stock Exchange met a similar rebuff over nationality. The Stock Exchange had tightened up its nationality requirement under the influence of nationalism during the First World War, so that only British subjects could be admitted. As with the admission of women, faced with the inquiry from the Monopolies Commission the Stock Exchange was keen

[86] LSE: Council, 28 Nov. 1966.
[87] Ibid., 5 Dec. 1966, 9 Jan. 1967, 16 Jan. 1967, 10 Apr. 1967, 8 May 1967, 1 Apr. 1968, 23 Nov. 1970.

to show that it was a relatively open and flexible institution moving with the social and international currents of the time. This the admission of women and foreigners would have done, deflecting criticism from the other question of fixed commissions which the Council wanted to preserve at all costs. Unfortunately, the question of foreigners came up not against a hostility towards Germans caused by bitter memories of two world wars, but a fear among many members of the competitive power of New York brokerage firms operating from London. Consequently, the Council's request to drop or change the rule restricting membership to British-born people was rejected by the membership in 1969. Though the Council could see the risks involved they were also aware of the opportunities that could come in the international market if foreigners could become members, and aware that stock exchanges abroad would look for some reciprocity if British firms were to gain membership there. However, the majority of members did not see it that way, being more concerned to defend their business in British securities for domestic customers against large and well-capitalized American firms.[88]

## Continuing Competition

In many ways it was a pity that the members of the London Stock Exchange were so hostile to the admission of both women and foreigners for these were two groups who, at least, wanted to become members. More generally the Stock Exchange continued to offer both uncertain and unattractive career prospects in the 1960s, as it had in the 1950s. The price of nominations, for example, which were a necessary precondition to membership, peaked in 1960/1 and then fell to almost nominal levels in the mid-1960s, before staging something of a recovery toward the end of the decade.[89] By the 1960s the Stock Exchange had come to regard nominations as a positive handicap. If nominations were not taken up shortly after the retirement of a member they lapsed, so acting to reduce, progressively, the total membership of the Stock Exchange. A total of 600 had lapsed since their introduction. Conversely, when the price was low or non-existent members were reluctant to retire because they would get little for their nomination. At the same time, when the price of nominations was low firms had a tendency to make clerks members as a way of increasing their presence on the trading-floor without doing much to bring in extra business. The abolition of nominations had been proposed in 1960 but was opposed by those who wanted to restrict numbers for the benefit of existing members. One was P. B. Winch who wrote to the Council to express the view that 'At the present time there is plenty of work for all but taking the longer view it may well be proved

[88] Ibid., 23 Sept. 1968, 9 Dec. 1968, 22 Dec. 1969.
[89] Ibid., 24 Sept. 1962, 2 Nov. 1964, 20 Feb. 1967, 21 Oct. 1968, 2 Apr. 1969.

that the House is in fact over-populated.'[90] After the lean years of the mid-1960s it was finally carried through in 1969, becoming effective on 25 March 1970. Those holding nominations were to receive a fixed fee of £1,000 as a compensation, when they retired. To finance this all new members would have to pay an additional £1,000 on entry. Overall, between 1960/1 and 1968/9 the total membership of the Stock Exchange had shrunk by 125 from 3,423 to 3,298. The low had been reached in 1966/7 when it fell to 3,208 before staging a modest recovery towards the end of the decade. Between 1963 and 1967 a total of 275 more left the Stock Exchange, through death, retirement, bankruptcy, and disillusionment, than joined it.[91]

To replace these losses the Stock Exchange had to rely upon those who could be recruited through family and friends, as with sons joining their fathers, along with those who had worked their way up from positions such as clerks and messengers. Those who did join the Stock Exchange from other parts of the City often did so because their prospects there had disappeared rather than because of the special attraction of becoming a broker or jobber. Henry Garton became a member in 1960 after a career with the small merchant bank, Hart, Son & Co., since 1937/8, ending up as a partner. When this was taken over by Samuel Montague in 1960 he was made redundant.[92] Another group were those who had gone abroad to make careers for themselves in the colonies. With independence in the 1960s they discovered that they were no longer welcome and that stockbroking was looked on unfavourably by the new regimes. One such person was John Donovan, who had joined the Nairobi stockbrokers Francis Drummond & Co. in 1955/6, after training with Bisgood, Bishop & Co. in London. Though he had formed his own firm there in 1959 he decided in 1963 to return to London reflecting that

I now feel that Democratic African Socialism in Kenya and stockbroking, may not be compatible in the future, and I wish to return to London for political and family reasons, and become a member of the London Stock Exchange.[93]

He had already been preceded in 1962 by C. W. Hickman who had gone to Kenya in 1950 after being a member of the London Stock Exchange since 1943. Hickman also had his own firm and had been chairman of the Nairobi Stock Exchange. The other group who saw a future for themselves as members of the London Stock Exchange were those small private client brokers located in and around London. Traditionally they had conducted their business through brokers belonging to the Stock Exchange. However,

[90] LSE: Council, 18 Feb. 1960, cf. 21 Nov. 1964, 21 Apr. 1969, 23 June 1969, 13 Oct. 1969, 1 Nov. 1969; LSE: Annual Report, 1969/70.
[91] LSE: Council, 2 Aug. 1965, 13 Dec. 1965, 24 Oct. 1966; LSE; Annual Reports, 1960/1–1968/9.
[92] LSE: Council, 26 Sept. 1960, cf. A. Gleeson: People and Their Money: 50 Years of Private Investment (M & G Group 1981).
[93] LSE: Council, 25 Nov. 1963, cf. 19 Nov. 1962.

they began to recognize in the 1960s that the advantages of membership now outweighed the costs. As members they could deal directly with jobbers while the fixed commission regime did not apply to transactions between members. Twenty-three of them joined the London Stock Exchange over the 1968/9 period.[94]

The admission of these provincial brokers was representative of London's changing relationship with the other British stock exchanges. On the one hand London needed these other brokers for they fed it business from investors located elsewhere in the British Isles. On the other hand they competed with London brokers as they enjoyed a lower cost structure, because of rents and wages, and were not restricted by the London Stock Exchange's rules and regulations. Throughout the 1960s the London Stock Exchange tried to find a way of balancing these conflicts in its relationship with the provincial stock exchanges, for it needed to retain their custom without extending to them privileges which would allow undercutting. It was expected, for example, that London brokers would rebate a share of the commission to provincial brokers on the business they generated but not to a degree that these brokers could compete with London on price.[95] However, the developments in the 1960s were undermining the London Stock Exchange's dominance of the domestic securities market, though the continuing improvement of the telephone system need not have done. It permitted ever closer links between London brokers and their provincial clients, for example. By 1968 Maquire, Kingsmill & Co. had built up an extensive national connection using telephones, teleprinters and telex, manned by a staff of 27, including three partners, in addition to which were office personnel. As a result they estimated that over the 1964–8 period they had handled 320,000 transactions generating a commission of £766,000. However, they were one of the few firms of London brokers doing this type of business.[96]

Instead, it was the provincial stock exchanges that took advantage of the improvements in telecommunications to enhance their ability to compete with London. Try as it might the London Stock Exchange could not prevent provincial brokers gaining access to latest prices via the teleprinter and, using these and the telephone, they were able to deal between each other, so avoiding paying a London broker a share of the commission they received. From that the next stage was the formation of regional stock exchanges, like the Scottish and the Northern, that eliminated any barriers or charges between provincial brokers.[97] These regional stock exchanges also invited any stockbroker resident in their area to join, having previously confined membership to those resident in the major cities such as Glasgow

---

[94] LSE: *Annual Report*, 1968/9.
[95] LSE: Council, 10 Oct. 1960, 17 Oct. 1960, 30 Jan. 1961, 12 Oct. 1964, 14 Feb. 1966, 19 Sept. 1966, 18 Mar. 1968, 8 Apr. 1969.
[96] Ibid., 17 Oct. 1960, 28 Dec. 1960, 27 Feb. 1961, 27 May 1968.
[97] Ibid., 6 Nov. 1961, 27 Nov. 1961.

and Manchester. These country brokers had, traditionally, traded through London where they had long-established links with individual brokers. By joining a regional stock exchange these country brokers obtained both direct access to the jobbers operating there and the discretionary commission rates available to members, both of which were denied to them by London. By the mid-1960s the members of the London Stock Exchange were acutely aware that these new regional stock exchanges posed a serious threat to the business that had, in the past, come to them.[98]

London stockbrokers were gradually abandoning the country business as a result apart from that which came via the banks, believing that they could not compete directly with the provincial brokers. Provincial brokers enjoyed lower costs, more flexibility in charging customers, and regulations that permitted them to operate as both brokers and jobbers. Many firms that had once done a country business were forced to close, such as Beckhuson, or contract, like Stratham, or merge, as in the case of Marshall & Kerr Ware, due to the competition and loss of business. One firm affected was Lumsden & Co. who complained in 1969 that

In the last few years Country Jobbing has greatly increased and from many of the smaller country brokers it is now quite exceptional to receive orders in all the leading stocks. The oddments and second-class stocks come here as before, and dealing in them is often barely remunerative.[99]

A small number of London brokers responded to this challenge by setting up branches outside London, so as to gain direct access to potential clients. In the past such branch offices had not been permitted but, in the mid-1960s, they were accepted as necessary if London was to compete with the provincial brokers. One of the firms in the forefront of this policy of establishing branches was J. & A. Scrimgeour. In 1967 it merged with a number of the small local brokers with whom it had long been associated. The result was a London-based firm with 12 branches as widespread as Salisbury, Scarborough, Stockton, and Swindon. It expected to provide '. . . a far more efficient country-wide service . . . ' and aimed to cultivate the private client business.[100] However, they remained unusual as most London brokers had not chosen to establish branch networks. Instead, those that did set up the odd branch did so to cater for specific and often established clients. In 1966, for example, the brokers Simon & Coates wanted to establish a branch office in the Channel Islands, specifically St Helier in Jersey, to service the merchant banks and North American brokerage houses now located there for tax reasons. Altogether, by the beginning of 1969 the 10 largest London

---

[98] LSE: Council, 23 Aug. 1965, 17 Jan. 1966, 10 July 1967, 23 Oct. 1967, 18 Mar. 1968, 8 Apr. 1969.

[99] Ibid., 2 Sept. 1969, cf. 3 Jan. 1967; W. A. Thomas, *The Provincial Stock Exchanges* (London 1973), 261–3, 272, 277, 287; W. A. Thomas, *The Stock Exchange of Ireland* (Liverpool 1986), 205.

[100] LSE: Council, 14 Aug. 1967, cf. 20 Sept. 1965, 14 Mar. 1966, 9 Oct. 1967.

stockbroking firms had only 16 branch offices between them and 13 of these belonged to Scrimgeours.[101]

The ability of the members of the London Stock Exchange to compete with provincial brokers by establishing branch networks was, however, severely constrained by its membership of the Federation of Stock Exchanges in Great Britain and Ireland. The idea of creating a single organization covering all brokers and jobbers in the British Isles had waxed and waned over the course of the twentieth century. It was revived again in 1962 when London set up a committee to consider the possibility of forming a national stock exchange, driven by the desire to eliminate the competition posed by country jobbing in particular. After two years of discussion it was decided to form a Federation rather than push for full unification, as that still faced insurmountable obstacles, particularly direct access to London jobbers. Out of this Federation, which came into existence in 1965, the London Stock Exchange expected to get an agreement to phase out country jobbing. In the process they accepted the restriction that no branch office could be established where any member firm operated that belonged to the London Stock Exchange, the Associated Stock Exchange, and the Provincial Brokers Stock Exchange (110 smaller towns). Effectively this prevented the London stockbrokers from expanding geographically. Even the acquisition of a provincial firm by a London broker, or mergers, could be prevented if others already operating in that location lodged an objection with the Federation. As the Federation failed to take any action against country jobbing, through outlawing dual capacity, but did stop the spread of branch offices, the London Stock Exchange had restricted the ability of its members to compete with non-members and gained nothing in return. Simon & Coates, for example, were stopped from establishing the branch office in St Helier, while Chapman & Rowe could not establish themselves in Brighton by taking over a local broker there. The same happened to W. I. Carr, Sons & Co. in Northampton and Scrimgeour in Newcastle. There were a few concessions, such as Messel's takeover of Daffern & Stephenson, a Coventry firm of brokers but even there they were prevented from then expanding into Birmingham. The rules of the Federation were used effectively by provincial brokers to stop London brokers gaining a foothold in their area, to the increasing annoyance of those London brokers who were pursuing a policy of creating national branch networks. As it was there was a growing feeling in London that either the restriction on the formation of branches should be dropped or London should leave the Federation.[102]

The London Stock Exchange had agreed to the Federation, and its rules, in the belief that it was but a stage on the way to a full merger, which would

---

[101] Ibid., 28 Nov. 1966, 13 Jan. 1969.

[102] Ibid., 19 Mar. 1962, 9 Mar. 1964, 10 May 1965, 6 Sept. 1965, 19 Sept. 1965, 14 Mar. 1965, 28 Nov. 1966, 9 Oct. 1967, 9 Dec. 1967, 12 Feb. 1968, 18 Mar. 1968, 8 Apr. 1968; *The Federation of Stock Exchanges in Great Britain and Ireland* (1964), pp. i, iv, 17, 35–6.

bring all stock exchanges, brokers, and jobbers in the British Isles under its control. This would strengthen the London Stock Exchange when negotiating with the Bank of England and the government and make it easier to impose fixed commission charges and such rules as single capacity. With that goal in sight the Council of the Stock Exchange drove through the policy of Federation despite opposition from a few members at that time. Neither the Council nor the members were aware of the full implications that membership of the Federation would have for London's ability to compete at a time when the telephone and regionalization were allowing the provincial brokers to not only bypass London but also take business away from it. The assumption was that country jobbing provided a service for matching deals in local stocks, not in competing with London in selected lines. However, until the London Stock Exchange permitted all brokers wherever located, to both deal directly with jobbers and to trade between each other at negotiable rates, those excluded from such opportunities would seek to establish alternative market arrangements for themselves. The failure to recognize this fundamental need and an inability to deliver it, because of the desire by the majority of their own membership to maintain their exclusive trading rights, meant that the Federation formed in 1965 was an inevitable failure. As this became clear in the years that followed, there was a growing hostility among the members of the London Stock Exchange to the whole principle of Federation. The feeling was that too many concessions had been made to the provincial brokers and London had gained nothing in return. One possibility was for London to offer some kind of associate membership which would give those who joined access to London brokers and jobbers on somewhat more favourable terms. In particular brokers outside London but in the Home Counties might be then persuaded to continue doing business through London rather than joining the Midlands grouping centred on Birmingham, which was formed in 1966. However, this idea also foundered because the London Stock Exchange was unwilling to grant the concessions these brokers wanted, especially direct access to jobbers and reduced rates of commission. Many of its small broking members feared the influx of new competition.[103]

Gradually there was the realization that only full unification could achieve what both the Council of the London Stock Exchange and the majority of non-member brokers wanted. Until that happened there was an extreme reluctance by the provincial stock exchanges to give up their trading-floors, and the broker/jobbers that serviced them. Conversely, many of the members of the London Stock Exchange were worried by the sudden competition that an expanded membership would pose, as unification would allow provincial firms to join without either an entrance fee or a nomination. Many small London brokers would become indistinguishable

[103] LSE: Council, 27 Nov. 1961, 10 May 1965, 16 Aug. 1965, 23 Aug. 1965, 18 Oct. 1965, 7 Mar. 1966, 25 May 1966, 24 Oct. 1966, 3 Jan. 1967.

from provincial firms, equally accessible by telephone, and with cost advantages in terms of staff and rent.[104] They were already aware in 1967 that

A substantial number of orders both large and small are now married in the country exchanges with our without the assistance of the country jobbers. Prices at which the deals are done are based on the London Jobbers quotation.[105]

With direct and unhindered access to London it was realistic to expect this competition to intensify, making it certain that many of the London Stock Exchange's membership would resist any move towards unification. Nevertheless this is exactly what was under discussion in the late 1960s. This desire for the creation of a single unified stock exchange was driven by the largest firms of both jobbers and brokers. To the jobbers such a creation seemed an inevitable and sensible solution for the current difficulties. Durlacher's pointed out that it would remove the increasingly troublesome competition from the provincial broker/jobbers with 27 firms operating that way in 1966. Wedd Jefferson sought to show the general advantages it would have for the securities market

. . . a market will operate at its maximum efficiency when it sees all the business: to the extent that business bypasses the market, so the efficiency of the market is impaired. For this reason we are of the opinion that a single Stock Exchange with one trading floor would be the ideal solution to the problem of the securities system in this country . . .

Within this integrated market the large jobbers hoped to thrive by providing the central market place for all, as they expected all business to gravitate to London once all brokers had direct access to them, bypassing London brokers and their commission charges. Conversely the large London brokers were not worried about the loss of business for they saw opportunities through nation-wide expansion. Cazenoves, therefore, backed the formation of a single exchange, while another firm of brokers, Gilbert Eliot & Co. expressed their confidence in the outcome.

. . . the perpetuation of old established geographical limitations is having the effect of preserving many ineffectual broking firms in the provinces, who are themselves often competitors of the London Stock Exchange, at the cost of the natural expansion of London firms of superior efficiency.[106]

Ranged against the large brokers and jobbers were the smaller and more numerous brokers who felt threatened by any change, especially one that brought in extra competition. These were firms like Pim, Vaughan & Co. and Hope, Dodgson & Co. who had no confidence that they would gain through unification and were keen to prevent a rapid influx of new

[104] Ibid., 7 Feb. 1966, 14 Mar. 1966, 1 Aug. 1966, 17 Oct. 1966, 23 Oct. 1967.
[105] Ibid., 3 Jan. 1967.
[106] Ibid., 10 Sept. 1966, cf. 3 Oct. 1966, 17 Oct. 1966, 7 Nov. 1966, 9 Mar. 1970.

members. In 1970, for example, in addition to London's membership of 3,359 there were another 984 members of other British stock exchanges (excluding Dublin and Cork). This would add an additional 29 per cent to the membership with almost all being stockbrokers, so intensifying the competition for the available business.

Yet again another half-way house was proposed, in an attempt to persuade the provincial brokers to accept the end of dual capacity and London brokers to permit greater integration. The suggestion was the creation of a jobbers network. All brokers would have direct access to their local jobbers and, in turn, all these jobbers could deal with each other free from the constraints of the minimum commission rules. Thus, though a provincial broker could not buy and sell directly with a London jobber, they could deal indirectly, through their own jobbers, and not have to pay commission. Inevitably this provoked opposition from those within the London Stock Exchange who would lose out in such an arrangement. The brokers L. Powell, Sons & Co., who specialized in providing a dealing service for members of the provincial stock exchanges, believed that such a proposal would destroy what still remained of their business after regionalization. Though much of the opposition did stem from firms that would be adversely affected there was a feeling that the proposal would undermine the market in London by spreading it among all the major cities in the British Isles, through London jobbers opening branches outside London.[107]

J. & A. Scrimgeour, with considerable practical experience of the national market through their branches, considered that the proposal flew against current trends in technology. What they felt was happening was that markets were becoming geographically larger, serviced from particular centres.

The function of a market is to bring buyers and sellers together in a single concentrated area for the maximum convenience of dealing and with a view to attracting the maximum turnover. Modern communications media are such that the tendency is for fewer markets to service much larger areas. The existing tendency under the jobbing system is for consolidation into much smaller numbers of large firms. These large firms provide the convenient and concentrated catalyst organisation for marrying buyers and sellers.[108]

Such was their analysis of the position in 1968. Where less actively traded securities were concerned, which the provincial exchanges catered for, Scrimgeours suggested the creation of a secondary market in addition to that provided by the London Stock Exchange. Clearly, to a firm trying to build up a national business they saw no future for geographically distinct exchanges in the British Isles but rather their replacement with nationwide stockbroking firms channelling business to London, where sales and

[107] LSE: Council, 16 Jan. 1967, 18 Mar. 1968, 29 Apr. 1968.
[108] Ibid., 20 Apr. 1968, cf. 10 June 1968, 14 June 1968, 8 July 1968, 15 July 1968.

purchase could be more easily matched, both in active and non-active securities.

This view was supported by many of the major London brokers, such as Joseph Sebag & Co., and, quite quickly by the London Stock Exchange itself, and so the plan was dropped. However, the provincial stock exchanges were not ready to accept that the only trading-floor, in a unified stock exchange, would be in London. As a result an impasse had been reached by July 1968. The provincial stock exchanges were happy with the Federation because it curbed the power of the London brokers to invade their territory through the establishment of branches. In contrast London was very unhappy because of the curbs and the failure to do anything about country jobbing. The feeling grew more intense

... London should only remain in the Federation, which was universally unpopular with London members, if there remained the prospect of progress being made towards a united Stock Exchange.[109]

However, such progress could not be made unless London granted far greater access to its trading-floor than hitherto and that it was reluctant to do, even through devices such as the jobber network. Eventually, by September 1969 those in favour of unification had triumphed in London, faced with the unwillingness of the provincial stock exchanges to contemplate anything other than a single stock exchange in which all members had the freedom to deal directly with all other members, whether brokers or jobbers. In return the provinces accepted that any member could open a branch wherever they chose and that dual capacity would cease after a two-year period of adjustment. Though these principles had now been accepted the detail of how to achieve a unified stock exchange remained to be worked out, with opposition to be expected at every stage.[110]

Unification between London and its foreign counterparts was never a possibility in the 1960s but here also the relationship was changing. Through a combination of improvements to communications and a lessening of barriers to the international movement of money and capital, stock exchanges were once again coming into competition with each other. In 1962 the International Federation of Stock Exchanges was formed, consisting of mainly European exchanges.[111] This exposed the London Stock Exchange's ambivalent attitude towards such activities as arbitrage. Arbitrage was acceptable if it brought business to London but not where it either diverted business away or was used as a device to bypass the fixed commission charges or undermine the rules on single capacity. The result was an attempt to extend and refine the rules on arbitrage which, cumulatively, made the activity almost impossible to conduct by a member of the Stock Exchange. There

[109] Ibid., 15 July 1968.
[110] Ibid., 1 July 1968, 20 Jan. 1969, 21 Sept. 1969, 31 Nov. 1969.
[111] Ibid., 8 Jan. 1962.

was the growing suspicion that jobbers were using arbitrage concessions to offer a dealing service direct to major international investors, such as foreign banks, so cutting out brokers and the commission they charged. The result was a ban on jobbers conducting arbitrage in anything other than the specific securities in which they made a market. This limited their ability to conduct balancing, if not matching transactions, between London and foreign financial centres, which was of great advantage for money-market and foreign-exchange activities. By 1967 jobbers were little involved in arbitrage as a result.[112]

These restrictions were unfortunate for the 1960s did see a revival in the international trading of securities, benefiting from the relaxation of exchange controls in Europe and growing world prosperity. At the same time growing restrictions on the use of the dollar, by the United States government, encouraged the search for an alternative venue for such transactions other than New York. As London was still an important international financial centre, and had retained many of its traditional links, it was an obvious location for such activity, presenting new opportunities for the members of the London Stock Exchange. The brokers, Vickers da Costa, were among the first to spot the possibilities of a global operation. They linked up in 1963 with Markus & Stone in New York, Julius Bar in Zürich, and J. D. Anderson in Johannesburg, to trade dollar, not sterling securities. As they put it, 'We are of the opinion that the geographical and time situation of London between European centres and New York is capable of exploitation.'[113] Another firm of brokers, L. Messel & Company, who had strong ties with the merchant bank, S. G. Warburg & Co., were of the same opinion. However, to capture this market the London Stock Exchange would have to alter its rules and regulations both on what its members could do and the charges they made to non-members. Successful arbitrage, for example, was conducted using joint-account trading, in which all expenses, profits, and losses were shared between the member and the counter-party on the foreign stock exchange. Almost by definition this conflicted with the Stock Exchange's rules on commission as nothing was charged on either a sale or purchase. Again, there were demands for this concession to be dropped as some members saw that it would allow a few to avoid the minimum commission rates and offer a discount service to favoured overseas clients. However, as the brokers Vanderfelt & Co., who did a large South African business, pointed out '. . . this form of business would be brought to a standstill', if commission had to be paid, because the margins involved were so small.[114] As much of the membership viewed

---

[112] LSE: Council, 22 Feb. 1960, 12 June 1961, 21 Aug. 1961, 16 Jan. 1967.
[113] Ibid., 21 Jan. 1963, cf. 29 Apr. 1963; cf. P. Einzig, *The Euro-Bond Market* (London 1969), 7, 11–12, 23, 65, 147, 195; E. W. Clendenning, *The Eurodollar Market* (Oxford 1970), 1, 7, 23, 27, 40, 205.
[114] LSE: Council, 4 July 1963.

with hostility those conducting a foreign business it was difficult for them to obtain the concessions they needed.

The problem was that only a small minority of the Stock Exchange's membership were actively involved in any kind of foreign business, let along the more specialist branch of arbitrage, and so they were vulnerable to attack by those who resented their privileges. In 1967 it was estimated that only, at most, 40 of the 250 stockbroking firms were continuously interested in foreign business while 12 dominated it. Altogether, it was estimated for 1966 that brokers' commission on dealings for overseas clients generated £1.4m. while arbitrage produced a further £0.9m., or £2.3m. in total. With a membership of c.3,400 for that year this would have represented a small proportion of their collective income. That same year turnover on the London Stock Exchange was £31.6bn. which, if it produced an average 0.5 per cent commission, would generate a total income of £108m., making the overseas portion a mere 2 per cent. The importance of overseas earnings for the Stock Exchange did grow, with commission and arbitrage producing £3.5m. in 1967. Altogether it was estimated that between January and March 1969 turnover in UK equities, for overseas residents, was 4.5 per cent of total turnover in ordinary shares on the London Stock Exchange. Clearly it had increased but it continued to be dwarfed by the business for British investors.

Despite the vast potential that foreign business was increasingly seen to possess, the London Stock Exchange was unable to capture it.[115] It was always difficult, for example, to fix a commission rate that was not out of line with the going market rate. Certainly by the mid-1960s those brokers handling an international business, such as Vickers da Costa, were of the opinion that the commissions they had to charge were losing them orders to non-members. The Stock Exchange was sensitive to the needs of its members to stay competitive and did try to adjust rates in response to their requests, though they were reluctant to make any radical changes which would undermine the captive business in domestic securities for British investors. A special rate for bargains in Eurodollar bonds and other foreign currency loans did prove competitive in 1968, for example.[116] The problem went deeper than fixed commissions though. Under the rules of the London Stock Exchange not only had commission to be paid by both the seller and the buyer but the transaction had to be passed through the market so as to give the jobber his turn on the deal. This ensured that each broker received commission and the jobber profited from the spread between buying and selling prices. In contrast non-members were willing to buy and sell Eurodollar loans and Eurobonds commission free, making their profit from any difference in price they could achieve. The result was the business in

[115] Ibid., 21 May 1961, 16 Jan. 1961, 16 July 1962, 29 Apr. 1963, 13 May 1963, 16 Jan. 1967, 3 Apr. 1967, 10 July 1967, 25 Mar. 1968, 28 July 1969.
[116] Ibid., 27 June 1966, 10 June 1968.

such securities, which was growing rapidly, continued to bypass the Stock Exchange.

By 1968 it was estimated that 60 per cent of the trading in Euro-Currency Bonds was in London, totalling $15m. per day, but only 1 per cent passed through the London Stock Exchange. Part of this was even handled by London Stock Exchange members, such as Vickers da Costa, Straus Turnbull, and Rowe & Pitman, who dealt directly between overseas and British clients, but never brought any of the business to the jobbers on the floor of the Stock Exchange, as they were expected to do. What was required, if the Stock Exchange was to capture this business, was permission for brokers to buy and sell without charging commission and for jobbers to deal directly with non-members, both at home and abroad, because each could then compete with non-members on equal terms. Such a move was in direct conflict with the principle of single capacity, only relaxed to a limited degree for arbitrage, and so the Stock Exchange could not accept such a radical departure from its rules.[117] This was despite the fact that those doing such a business made it clear that without such a dispensation they would lose out to non-members in Eurobond dealing.

The brokers Rowe & Pitman wrote in 1965:

We have acted as brokers to all the foreign currency loans issued in London by Hambros Bank Limited, totalling approximately $240m. during the past eighteen months. As you are aware, these issues have been made in large quantities in London recently, by other houses as well as Hambros, and the Authorities are agreed that it is of great importance to the position of London as an international capital market, and consequently to the UK balance of payments, that borrowers should continue to be attracted to London rather than to other financial centres. Clearly, the relative attraction of London in this regard depends, among other things, on the ability of London to provide the most efficient and active market in the securities after they are issued: if foreigners are able to deal more effectively than we are, and if the real market is therefore established abroad, London's position as the leading issuer is bound to be called into question.

With the above considerations particularly in mind, we have attempted for some time to fulfil our obvious duty as brokers to these issues by assisting to make a market in the bonds. The experience which we have thus gained causes us to admit that the present Stock Exchange rules actually inhibit the growth of such a market in London. The rules of the Stock Exchange are, of course, primarily designed to regulate dealings in securities (whether domestic or overseas) between residents of this country, and, to a lesser extent, between foreigners and residents in domestic securities. They were never intended to be relevant to dealings between foreigners in overseas securities. These foreign currency loans, though issued in London, are placed almost exclusively overseas, and are not normally attractive to residents of this country. Dealings subsequent to the issue therefore take place almost entirely between foreign sellers and foreign buyers, who have no reason to use London as

---

[117] LSE: Council, 23 Aug. 1965, 8 July 1968, 4 Nov. 1968, 2 Dec. 1968.

the medium for their transactions unless it can show itself to be more competitive than other centres.[118]

What Rowe & Pitman wanted was permission to charge whatever they felt was appropriate. The Council of the Stock Exchange was in no position to grant this in the 1960s because of the threat it posed to the captive domestic market. Thus, the London Stock Exchange lost this business in international securities because of its inability to give those members involved the flexibility they required.

Instead, transactions in international securities in London were dominated by non-members, especially a growing number of European banks and US brokerage houses. Merrill Lynch established a London office in 1961, for instance, and they were followed in 1963 by Weeden & Co., a New York firm of over-the-counter (OTC) brokers with an aggressive policy of undercutting existing commission rates. In turn these non-members attracted business away from the London Stock Exchange as they could offer a better market in international securities.[119]

The Stock Exchange's response was to introduce more restrictions on the freedom of its members to buy and sell with whomsoever they chose. Brokers were already expected to use the services of the jobbers wherever possible and that was reinforced by a ban on any dealings with the London branches of foreign brokerage houses. This was in the belief that,

Undoubtedly a better market in dollar securities could be established in London if the Jobbers saw more of the business. Brokers are transmitting an increasing volume of business directly overseas as recompense for statistical services and the desire to obtain reciprocal business.[120]

Despite opposition to this ban within the Stock Exchange, especially from those firms doing an international business, the restriction was not repealed. There continued to be strong support for any measure designed to drive business into the Stock Exchange through restrictive practices, rather than a desire to either attract it in through competitive policies or a willingness to allow members to seek the best deal wherever it was to be found.

However, this measure proved futile for the market in dollar securities continued to dwindle on the London Stock Exchange with brokers still directing business to American brokers in either London or New York. Stockbroking firms such as Laurence, Keen & Gardner, Chase, Henderson & Tennant, and Fielding, Newson-Smith & Co. made it clear in 1964 that any such restriction was completely impractical.

[118] Ibid., 23 Aug. 1965, cf. 12 June 1961, 3 Mar. 1969.
[119] Ibid., 26 July 1965, 2 Aug. 1965, 16 May 1966; Einzig, Euro-Bond Market, 65–6, 68, 76–8, 80: Clendenning, Eurodollar Market, 7–8, 40; Sir Paul Newall, Japan and the City of London (London 1966), 25, 35–6; H. Bonin, Société Générale in the United Kingdom (Paris 1996), 61, 98.
[120] LSE: Council, 12 June 1961, cf. 24 July 1961, 20 Nov. 1961, 4 Dec. 1961, 26 Aug. 1963, 28 Oct. 1963.

... for overseas business we are not able to have a sufficient knowledge of, and day to day contact with, the markets of the world to select investments for our clients to the best advantage ... we have to rely on the advice of overseas broking firms in making our selections. The London branches are particularly well placed to assist us in this matter, and in fact they do assist us.

In return these London branches expected the brokers to favour them with any business that resulted, which is what happened though such orders were routed via their overseas offices, creating additional expense and unnecessary delay, because of the ban on direct dealing. They were also of the opinion that it was impossible to revive the market in overseas securities on the London Stock Exchange, no matter what measures were taken

It is our experience that in all but the market leaders, jobbers base their London quotations on the overseas markets' closing prices of the previous day, adjusted for changes in the dollar premium. In fact there is no genuine market in England. In the case of American over-the-counter securities, we find jobbers unwilling to obtain a price unless they can expect an order, whereas London agencies of overseas firms obtain lists of quotations for us daily.[121]

Though there was an interest in foreign securities among British investors in the 1960s the combination of high taxation and exchange controls prevented any real expansion, so that the size of their holdings were insufficient to support a market in London. Hence the only market was abroad, principally New York, and it was to there that buying and selling orders would, inevitably, be directed. This gave New York brokerage houses an advantage over their British counterparts and they exploited it to the full by not only establishing direct contact with British investors, like the insurance companies and pension funds, but accompanied that by establishing branches in London.

By 1968 it was estimated that there were 19 New York brokerage houses with branches in London and, in that year, they made tentative enquiries about being permitted to join the London Stock Exchange. These enquiries did not meet an outright rejection, despite the obvious obstacle that it would involve the admission of non-UK citizens. Though there was the fear that allowing New York brokerage firms to become members would allow them to capture American business still in British hands, there was also the possibility that it would bring more buying and selling from the United States to London. The London Stock Exchange was well aware of the changes that were taking place in international investment in the 1960s and the opportunities it was creating both for itself and its members. Their assessment in 1968 was:

The movement towards international broking brought about by the large funds of the oil sheikhs and the international Dollar or Deutschmark issues is tending to

---

[121] LSE: Council, 15 June 1964, cf. 6 Jan. 1964.

bring into being international brokers. If this movement continues London must either join in or opt out. If we opt out we may encourage some other continental centre to replace London. If we join in we will no doubt attract a lot of New York firms.

At that stage they concluded that, '. . . there is no reason of principle why any member of another Exchange, of whatever nationality, should not be elected to membership of this Exchange.'[122] They did recognize, though, that such a radical step would involve fundamental changes in the London Stock Exchange's own rules and practices.

This matter of principle was put to the test when the American brokerage firm of Hallgarten & Co. expressed a desire to join the London Stock Exchange in September 1968. They claimed to be the first US firm to have established an office in London, opened in 1912, and conducted an international business from there for institutional clients. Initially this application was received favourably, with the Stock Exchange concluding that,

. . . it must be to the advantage of London as a financial market to attract US brokers here rather than let them go to Paris, Zurich or Amsterdam. No doubt such brokers will take some business away from the purely local brokers but protection of vested interest has seldom lasted long. The main object must be to bring as much business as possible in UK securities to London.[123]

However, when put to a vote on the Committee responsible for admissions it was decided, by a majority of 6 to 5, that members of overseas stock exchanges could not join London. The reason given was to protect those brokers who '. . . could suffer very severely from the competition of the financially more powerful American firms.'[124]

This decision was a blow to the Council of the Stock Exchange, who had supported the candidacy of Hallgarten & Co., and they remained committed to seeking ways and means of admitting members of foreign stock exchanges. Unfortunately for them the majority of members did not share their view, being, as usual, concerned with protecting their position in the domestic market from all potential competitors.

What the Council of the Stock Exchange were fully aware of was that a number of its own membership were following this course of action by opening branches abroad and joining foreign stock exchanges, and this could be jeopardized if London showed no reciprocity. As early as 1962 two London brokers, Spencer, Thornton & Co. and Stoop & Co., were granted permission to open offices in other countries in order to compete more effectively, for the growing international business, with the continental banks and American brokers who maintained offices in London. The first such office opened was that by Spencer, Thornton & Co. in Brussels, spurred by the belief that it was that city which was going to become the

---

[122] Ibid., 10 June 1968, cf. 11 Mar. 1968.   [123] Ibid., 23 Sept. 1968.
[124] Ibid., 9 Dec. 1968, cf. 8 July 1968.

financial central of Europe, because of its central position in the European Economic Community. More realistic was Vickers da Costa branch office in Luxembourg in 1963, because that country's favourable tax laws made it an attractive location for financial activities. By 1966 a total of seven stockbroking firms had foreign offices while another 21 maintained strong overseas connections. The next step came in 1967 when Cazenove & Co. opened a branch in the United States and became members of the Pacific Coast Stock Exchange. They were soon followed by Rowe & Pitman and Joseph Sebag & Co., while W. I. Carr joined the Hong Kong Stock Exchange in 1969. Throughout the London Stock Exchange raised no objection. Nevertheless, the number of member firms who established overseas offices remained tiny with hardly more than an office each. They were certainly no match for the New York firms that were using London as their base for global expansion in the 1960s. Major firms like Phillips & Drew did not participate, seeing their future purely in terms of the domestic market.[125]

This expansion through foreign branches by London brokers in the 1960s hardly compensated for the decline in the network of agents, or remisiers, that had sustained their international business in the past. The prohibition on members giving their remisiers more than 25 per cent of the commission income they generated, combined with the declining importance of the London Stock Exchange as an international market for securities, steadily reduced the incentive these agents had to channel business to London. In 1962 the broker Vivian Gray & Co. claimed that remisiers had '. . . virtually ceased to exist . . .'. By 1964 there were only 25 remisiers, now renamed 'overseas representatives', attached to London brokers compared to several hundred before 1939. A few firms, like Williams de Broë still maintained a network of such agents but it had been largely replaced by banks and international broking firms with branch offices in major financial centres. The Stock Exchange's attempt in 1967 to make it easier to attract foreign nationals as agents, by giving them access to the trading-floor for a three-months training period, was of little value when the whole way of conducting a global securities business was changing.[126]

When the London Stock Exchange was called upon to change its policy on its members' operations in foreign countries, as with advertising, branches, or membership of other exchanges, it did show itself to be relatively flexible in the 1960s. The problem was that the changes needed to not only capture but retain an international business were also of a domestic nature and went to the very heart of the rules and regulations by

[125] LSE: Council, 5 Feb. 1962, 16 Apr. 1962, 7 Jan. 1963, 8 Apr. 1963, 28 Dec. 1966, 23 Oct. 1967, 27 Nov. 1967, 11 Dec. 1967, 18 Mar. 1968, 12 May 1969; Reader and Kynaston, *Phillips & Drew*, 113.
[126] LSE: Council, 16 July 1962, cf. 30 July 1962, 11 Feb. 1963, 21 Dec. 1964, 26 June 1967, 17 June 1968, 2 Dec. 1968.

which it had operated for most of the century, being steadily developed and reinforced over time. It was thus unable to adjust its ways of operation sufficiently to meet the needs of the market in the 1960s with the result that its international business gradually ebbed away into the hands of non-members, many of whom were European banks and New York brokerage firms. By the middle of the 1960s, for example the London Stock Exchange had given up its last hope of retaining the American market even though there remained some trading in London in such stocks as General Motors, Ford, Chrysler, A. T. & T., General Electric, IBM, Standard Oil, and Texaco.[127] This loss was blamed, almost entirely, on circumstances beyond their control. This was summed up in an investigation conducted in 1964:

Investing by a UK national in the USA now involves a double risk—the risk of security fluctuation and that of exchange fluctuation. During most of the post-war years there has been a noticeable premium on investment dollars and this has almost eliminated the big pre-war market. While the total amount of investments held by UK nationals in the USA is greater than pre-war, they are now much more held by institutions than individuals. The institutions in their turn have formed their own USA connections and deal directly by means of the telephone. In pre-war days, US brokers doing business in the UK were largely confined to those with offices in London, and it was considered by them to be permissible to deal with an institution in Scotland, but in London dealing was done through London brokers. The arrival of the regular Trans-Atlantic air service and efficient telephones changed this situation, making it possible for any American Broker (whether from Chicago, Boston, San Francisco or Texas, as well as New York) to fly to this country for a few days and later keep in touch by telephone. This influx from America made it essential for existing US brokers to call on institutions in order to compete and, moreover, the aeroplane facilitated visits to the USA by UK investors. This direct contact between USA brokers and British institutions, aided by the resultant elimination of the London commission, channelled most institutions business out of London brokers' hands direct to the USA. Even that part which is given to London brokers is often directed to a USA firm (e.g. Merrill Lynch & Co.).

All the above factors have caused the market to lose the turnover on which they relied and, as a result, they can only make prices based on the US price. There is no doubt that they attempt to be competitive and to make as close a price as possible but in the end most of their bargains have to be undone in the USA, involving them in expenses that in aggregate must average a USA commission. . . . the true malaise which has hit the London market is that many orders no longer come to London brokers at all. As a result, those London brokers who do have a substantial US business, tend to concentrate on special deals, selling groups and placings, where they are on a fully competitive basis and also get paid a commission that is remunerative, something which is probably hardly true of the present American commission.[128]

---

[127] Ibid., 1 May 1961, 12 June 1961, 29 Apr. 1963, 2 Dec. 1963, 23 Dec. 1963, 6 Jan. 1964, 3 Feb. 1964, 12 Oct. 1964, 31 Jan. 1966, 25 Sept. 1967.
[128] Ibid., 16 Mar. 1964.

The best that could be expected was that American brokers would share commission with their British counterparts, which they were refusing to do. Canadian brokers did share commission and there remained something of a Canadian market in Britain, mainly because of the size of the holdings relative to those retained in Canada. Nevertheless, even there institutions tended to direct business to Toronto and Montreal, or the London offices of Canadian brokers.

With the loss of the North American market, what still existed of the London Stock Exchange's once commanding presence in international securities focused largely on South African and Australian mining securities. British investors were still major holders of mining stocks, especially gold, which was seen as a hedge against inflation. In addition much of the dealing in London was on behalf of international investors who saw London as a central market for such securities. In 1968, at the time of another boom in Australian mining stocks, 163 firms of brokers and eight firms of jobbers were involved in such dealings, with extensive operations between London and the major Australian stock exchanges.[129] In the mid-1960s there was also appearing in London a market in European securities, but this was largely ignored by the Stock Exchange as the turnover was low. Most sales and purchases were thus handled by the merchant banks, outside the Stock Exchange, in the 1960s.[130] Thus, though the City of London developed rapidly as an international financial centre in the 1960s, the Stock Exchange profited little from this. It continued to lose its American market, failed to develop one in either Eurobonds or European shares, and retained a presence only in Australian and South African mining securities. None of this was through ignorance, but an unwillingness to allow its members to respond to the needs of the international institutional investors who were interested in such securities.

## MONEY AND CAPITAL

Between 1960 and 1970 the nominal value of securities quoted on the London Stock Exchange did rise by £16bn., or by 51 per cent, but this was driven by the issues of shares by both existing and newly converted British businesses. Even more spectacular was the market value of these securities which grew by £62.4bn. or 138 per cent, reflecting their revaluation by investors in the face of inflation. By 1970 55 per cent of the market value of all securities quoted on the London Stock Exchange were those issued by industrial and commercial concerns, compared to only 40 per cent in 1960. A further 15 per cent came from financial and property companies. In contrast, the market value of the National Debt, and allied securities,

---

[129] LSE: Council, 25 Apr. 1960, 4 Sept. 1967, 12 Feb. 1968, 10 June 1968.
[130] Ibid., 9 Mar. 1964, 6 Apr. 1964.

had halved as a proportion of the total over the same period, falling from 33 per cent to 17 per cent, while overseas government or railway securities were now of little significance. Judging from market values the London Stock Exchange in the 1960s was overwhelmingly a market for the issues of British domestic businesses (*c*.51 per cent—1960, *c*.70 per cent—1970) and international resource companies (*c*.10 per cent). (Tables 10.1 and 10.2.)

Table 10.2. London Stock Exchange: Nominal and market values of securities quoted in 1960 and 1970 (%)

| Category of security | Nominal value | | | Market value | | |
|---|---|---|---|---|---|---|
| | 1960 | 1970 | Difference | 1960 | 1970 | Difference |
| British government | 58.4 | 45.7 | − 12.7 | 31.9 | 15.0 | − 16.9 |
| UK public bodies | 2.4 | 4.4 | + 2.0 | 1.4 | 1.6 | + 0.2 |
| TOTAL | 60.7 | 50.2 | − 10.5 | 33.2 | 16.6 | − 16.6 |
| Colonial governments | 2.6 | 1.6 | − 1.0 | 1.5 | 0.5 | − 1.0 |
| Foreign governments | 5.3 | 4.2 | − 1.1 | 0.5 | 1.3 | + 0.8 |
| Colonial/Foreign public bodies | 0.4 | 0.2 | − 0.2 | 0.2 | 0.1 | − 0.1 |
| TOTAL | 8.3 | 6.0 | − 2.3 | 2.1 | 1.9 | − 0.2 |
| Banks/discount houses | 1.4 | 3.1 | + 1.7 | 2.7 | 5.6 | + 2.9 |
| Financial, land, and investment | 2.8 | 4.7 | + 1.9 | 4.9 | 5.4 | + 0.5 |
| Insurance | 0.3 | 0.7 | + 0.4 | 2.4 | 2.0 | − 0.4 |
| Property | 0.7 | 2.0 | + 1.3 | 1.1 | 1.6 | + 0.5 |
| TOTAL | 5.3 | 10.5 | + 5.2 | 11.2 | 14.6 | + 3.4 |
| Railways, trams, canals, docks | 1.5 | 1.0 | − 0.5 | 1.0 | 0.6 | − 0.4 |
| Gas, electricity, and water | 0.5 | 0.6 | + 0.1 | 0.8 | 0.3 | − 0.5 |
| Telegraph and telephone | 0.1 | 0.3 | + 0.2 | 0.1 | 1.6 | + 1.5 |
| TOTAL | 2.1 | 1.9 | − 0.2 | 1.9 | 2.5 | + 0.6 |
| Commercial/Industrial | 15.3 | 23.4 | + 8.1 | 33.8 | 51.0 | + 17.2 |
| Breweries/Distilleries | 1.6 | 2.5 | + 0.6 | 2.7 | 2.3 | − 0.4 |
| Iron, coal, and steel | 1.7 | 0.8 | − 0.9 | 2.8 | 1.3 | − 1.5 |
| Shipping | 0.6 | 0.5 | − 0.1 | 0.6 | 0.5 | − 0.1 |
| TOTAL | 19.2 | 27.2 | + 8.0 | 39.9 | 55.0 | + 15.1 |
| Mining | 1.8 | 1.9 | + 0.1 | 4.8 | 7.7 | + 2.9 |
| Oil | 2.1 | 2.0 | − 0.1 | 6.4 | 1.6 | − 4.8 |
| Plantations | 0.4 | 0.3 | − 0.1 | 0.5 | 0.1 | − 0.4 |
| TOTAL | 4.3 | 4.2 | − 0.1 | 11.7 | 9.4 | − 2.3 |

*Source*: As Table 10.1.

These securities did not attract the interest of only domestic investors, though it was British institutions and individuals that did dominate to an overwhelming extent. In the 1960s US investors started to become involved, attracted by those British companies with an extensive international business, such as the Anglo-Dutch concerns of Unilever and Shell or major operators like ICI and BP.[131] Vickers da Costa estimated in 1966 that between 300,000 and 400,000 individual US investors had holdings in UK companies. Worryingly for the London Stock Exchange around 200,000 of these, or between half and two-thirds invested through the medium of American Depository Receipts (ADRs). These were British shares repackaged for the American market by New York banks and brokerage houses. This made them more acceptable to US investors and suitable for trading there, but not in London, as the Stock Exchange refused to quote them. Vickers da Costa reported that

A considerable number of UK securities are officially traded on the New York and American Stock Exchange. Many more are actively dealt in 'over the counter' between members of these Exchanges and of the National Association of Securities Dealers.[132]

At that time this was considered of little importance by the London Stock Exchange but it did represent a potential threat, considering the established position of New York brokers in London and their strong links with British financial institutions, who were the main investors in such securities. If this market did develop further it could begin to attract British investors away from members of the London Stock Exchange. This had already happened in selected securities domestically, with the competition from the regional stock exchanges. A combination of the provincial stock exchanges and New York brokerage houses was beginning to erode the London Stock Exchange's command over that market which was now at the heart of its activities, namely the trading in UK ordinary shares. Though trading in gilt-edged stock continued to dominate turnover on the London Stock Exchange, growing from £16bn. in 1965 to £19.5bn. in 1969, that in UK equities was rising even faster, reaching £8.7bn. in 1969 compared to £3.5bn. in 1965. More importantly for the membership of the Stock Exchange it was the buying and selling of domestic equities that generated most of the commission income compared to the much more competitive gilts market. In 1969 85 per cent of commission income came from equities.[133]

Reflecting this increasing reliance on domestic equities trading as the focus of its members business was the Stock Exchange's declining importance within the money market. Securities quoted on the Stock Exchange

---

[131] LSE: Council, 19 Feb. 1968, 28 July 1969.   [132] Ibid., 24 Jan. 1966.
[133] LSE: Quality of Markets, April–June 1990, Tables I and III; Reader and Kynaston, *Phillips & Drew*, 92.

did continue to offer a temporary and remunerative home for short-term funds. However, the Stock Exchange's own rules made such operations less attractive than in the past. The failure, for example, to permit forward trading, or trading for the account, in government stock, made it difficult to conduct risk-free sale and buy-back operations on the Stock Exchange, and so the business was arranged elsewhere. Here the blame lay with the Bank of England, rather than the Stock Exchange in the 1960s. The Bank of England did not want its existing arrangements with the discount houses exposed to competition and so it stopped the Stock Exchange from introducing a facility that would have permitted that. As it was the attempts to stop bond washing during the 1960s did, progressively, limit the ability of members of the Stock Exchange to provide the type of market that those in the money market required. Stamp duty and capital gains tax also made it uneconomic for institutional investors to buy and sell securities on a continuous basis, where the costs outweighed the profit to be made or led them to search for other ways of adjusting their exposure to interest, exchange, or other fluctuations. Thus most money-market activity took place outside the Stock Exchange, such as in the unregulated Eurobond market or the trading in certificates of deposit between banks.[134]

Bereft of much of the turnover that money-market operations would have generated, the London Stock Exchange was ever more dependent on activity in the capital market for its existence. Within this its role was largely that of providing a market rather than making an active contribution to the provision of finance or the conversion from private to public status. The government itself had a well-developed system for obtaining long and short-term finance, and the Stock Exchange was but one element within it. The chain of command ran from the government through the Treasury and the Bank of England to the Stock Exchange. Mullens, the government broker, was used to relay the government's instructions and wishes to the market or even undertake direct intervention as with the use of tap stock.[135] Though the market's response was never wholly controllable by the Bank of England, there was never any question that Stock Exchange would not provide a forum where central and local government securities could be traded.[136] For corporate securities the merchant banks had established a dominant position by the 1960s, relegating stockbrokers to smaller issues

---

[134] M. Collins, *Money and Banking in the UK: A History* (London 1988), 362–5, 373–5; E. R. Shaw, *The London Money Market* (London 1975), 8, 32, 77–9, 92, 98–9, 114, 122, 138, 144; W. M. Scammell, *The London Discount Market* (London 1968), 93; G. A. Fletcher, *The Discount Houses in London* (London 1976), 93, 163, 166–7, 175–6, 247; Clendenning, *Eurodollar Market*, 1–2, 7–11; Bonin, *Société Générale*, 61; Newall, *Japan and the City of London*, 25, 122; Einzig, *Euro-Bond Market*, 73, 78–80; LSE: Council, 25 Apr. 1960, 7 June 1960, 18 Aug. 1961, 11 Dec. 1961, 31 Aug. 1964, 24 Oct. 1966, 2 Dec. 1968, 2 July 1969.

[135] Wainwright, *Mullens*, 96–8.

[136] K. Burk, *Morgan Grenfell, 1838–1988: The Biography of a Merchant Bank* (Oxford 1989), 195, 224; A. J. Merrett, M. Howe, and G. D. Newbould, *Equity Issues and the London Capital Market* (London 1967), 2–3.

or retailing an issue to their clients for a share of the commission. Those brokers involved in the floating of new companies or the raising of additional capital found themselves squeezed between the merchant banks, who handled the larger issues, and the semi-official ICFC (Industrial and Commercial Finance Corporation) that invested directly in small companies for an equity stake. The likes of Rowe Swan & Co. and Cazenoves, for example, who had once played a prominent role in the new issue business, retreated from it in the 1960s.[137]

In terms of the new issue market the Stock Exchange's great strength was its ability to use its existing market for securities as a way of putting additional ones into circulation easily and cheaply. This could be done via either introductions or placings which were ideal for small to medium-sized issues. However, because of the essentially private nature of these methods the Stock Exchange increasingly restricted their use in the 1960s, worried about any public or government outcry regarding exclusion or market manipulation. As a placing was calculated to cost, in 1964, 0.5 per cent of the amount raised, plus commission to brokers and other agents, whereas an offer for sale cost 1.25 per cent on the amount even before the heavy additional expenses such as advertising were included, the result was to limit the market that the Stock Exchange provided to the larger new issues. The Stock Exchange took further steps in 1966 to discourage small and medium-sized issues by setting a higher minimum on the size of a new issue that it would grant a quotation to. No company with a market value of less than £250,000 could obtain a quotation on the Stock Exchange and no individual issue of securities was to be less than £100,000. Accompanying this was a requirement that at least 35 per cent of an issue be sold to investors, forcing owners of a company to relinquish more control to outsiders, and so discouraging them from making an issue of securities. The result was that the London Stock Exchange lost new issues in small lines of securities, with provincial stock exchanges picking up some of the business, while the merchant banks dominated the volume end.[138]

These restrictions on the size of new issues, by the Stock Exchange, led to larger companies being favoured, as their issues of securities could more easily bear the costs of a public prospectus and the charges made by merchant banks. As a result the Stock Exchange's own actions contributed to the growing scale of business units in Britain with organic growth and, especially, mergers, creating ever-larger companies. This takeover activity in turn, did generate much activity on the Stock Exchange as it became a

[137] LSE: Council, 2 Oct. 1961, 10 July 1967, cf. D. Kynaston, *Cazenove & Co.: A History* (London 1991), 204, 231; R. Coopey and D. Clarke, *3i: Fifty Years Investing in Industry* (Oxford 1995), 85–7, 96.

[138] LSE: Council, 9 Mar. 1964, 10 Jan. 1966, 19 Jan. 1970; W. A. Thomas, *The Finance of British Industry, 1918–1976* (London 1978), 163–74; Coopey and Clarke, *3i*, 95; R. Roberts, *Schroders: Merchants & Bankers* (London 1992), 418, 452; Merret et al., *Equity Issues*, 5–10.

market for control rather than money and capital. However, though the Stock Exchange's policy of both new issues and quotations was a factor in this development, much more fundamental forces were at work. The government's own taxation policies, for example, including capital gains tax, corporation tax, and dividend restrain in the 1960s, encouraged firms to merge in order to both avoid tax and to obtain access to finance. At the same time the tax treatment of income encouraged the institutionalization of investment rather than individual ownership. One estimate suggested that between 1957 and 1970 institutions increased their ownership of ordinary shares from 38 per cent of the total to 55 per cent. These institutions, like insurance companies and investment trusts, or the merchant banks managing pension funds, favoured larger issues for these were more easily bought and sold as circumstances changed. The passage of the Trustee Investment Act in 1961, which permitted pension funds to invest in equities also greatly increased the importance of institutional investment in that area.[139]

Generally, the problem for the London Stock Exchange in the 1960s was that it took its quasi-public role far more seriously than that of creating and maintaining an orderly but dynamic securities market. When the Italian automobile manufacture FIAT applied for a quotation in 1962 it was rejected on the grounds that its accounts did not meet UK accounting standards because, '. . . the grant of quotation would lead investors to believe that adequate information to assess the merits of the security was available'.[140] When the Stock Exchange did quote risky stocks such as Australian mining securities, the result was widespread criticism when such securities did not fulfil the prospects that the investing public expected of them.[141]

Nevertheless, by 1970 the Stock Exchange had become increasingly aware that its caution and restrictions had lost it important components of the national and international securities market with alternative trading growing up even in London and in corporate securities which it had previously ignored.[142] The problem was that it was easier for the Stock Exchange, and the bulk of its membership, to concentrate upon protecting their

[139] S. J. Prais, The Evolution of Giant Farms in Britain: A Study of the Growth of Concentration in Manufacturing Industry, 1909–70 (Cambridge 1976), 4, 8, 64, 87, 90–1, 116, 123–4; L. Hannah, The Rise of the Corporate Economy (London 1976), 173, 211–16; L. Hannah and J. A. Kay Concentration in Modern Industry: Theory, Measurement and the UK Experience (London 1977), 83–6. Thomas, Finance of British Industry, 153–4, 218–21, 230, 234–5; R. Speigelberg, The City: Power without Accountability (London 1973), 169, 191, 223; J. Moyle, The Pattern of Ordinary Share Ownership, 1957–1970 (Cambridge 1971), 7, 11, 13; C. Courtney and P. Thompson, City Lives: The Changing Faces of British Finance (London 1996), 80; W. A. Thomas, The Big Bang (Oxford 1986), 17.

[140] LSE: Council, 19 Nov. 1962, 28 Oct. 1963, 9 Mar. 1964, 6 Feb. 1967; Roberts, Schroders, 443, 457; Burk, Morgan Grenfell, 224. Quoted in Courtney and Thompson, City Lives, 90, cf. J. Attali, A Man of Influence: Sir Siegmund Warburg, 1902–1982 (London 1986), 225, 236–8.

[141] LSE: Council, 1 June 1964, 11 July 1966.

[142] Ibid., 3 Apr. 1967, 28 July 1969, 26 Jan 1970.

# II

# *Prelude to Change, 1970–1979*

## GROWING THREATS

In the course of the twenty-five years since the end of the Second World War the London Stock Exchange carved out for itself a successful niche within the British financial system. The security of this niche depended upon preserving a close working relationship with the Bank of England and the Treasury, regardless of which political party formed the government of the day. In return for supervising the securities market this relationship gave the Stock Exchange the power necessary to preserve an essentially anti-competitive structure. It was able to impose and maintain a system of mandatory fixed charges upon its members, exclude potential rivals from direct access to the market, and limit the effect of those forces which undermined its control. Inevitably all this involved costs to the Stock Exchange, for its rules and regulations both stifled change among its own members and alienated those who might have joined. This had the consequence of reducing the role it performed within the securities market to a position where it could only command the buying and selling of long-dated UK government debt and the shares of British industrial and commercial companies. This did give it an important position within the domestic securities market and one capable of generating a safe and attractive income for its membership. However, all that was to change in the 1970s, despite the fact that the rivalry of the provincial stock exchanges was finally neutralized in that decade. A combination of technological change, international liberalization, growing discontent among institutional investors, and an unwillingness by the government to tolerate its restrictive practices, all conspired to pose a serious threat to the London Stock Exchange. It was forced to give way on a number of issues while among its own membership the demands for change gained momentum. Nevertheless, the structure of the Stock Exchange remained largely unaltered in the 1970s, which was itself no small feat considering the developments of that decade.

The management of the London Stock Exchange were well aware that constant vigilance, accompanied by appropriate action, was necessary if the position that had been carefully built up since the war was to be maintained. In July 1971 they noted that:

... the pre-eminent position of London as a securities market is not unchallenged and the principal difficulty in maintaining such a position lies in the maintenance of competitiveness.[1]

Acting on a suggestion from Nicholas Goodison in October 1972 they took the step of setting up a special committee to undertake long-range strategic planning for the Stock Exchange, rather than responding to events and demands as they unfolded, which had been the position in the past. By July of the following year this committee was in a position to report on the specific roles they saw the Stock Exchange performing. This all related to the provision of a fair and orderly market for securities that suited the needs of both members and investors. They also produced an agreed aim which was to make the London Stock Exchange the largest and most efficient in Europe. To this end, in October, a reorganization of the Stock Exchange was proposed, reflecting the fact that it was now a large organization, with 900 staff and an expenditure of £4.5m., existing in a more competitive and cost-conscious environment. The object of the reorganization was to give the Council of the Stock Exchange, consisting of elected but unpaid members, more time to plan for the future and take strategic decisions, rather than supervise the day-to-day running of the institution. Eventually in November 1974 the Stock Exchange appointed a Chief Executive— Robert Fells—to take responsibility for its day-to-day running.

In January 1976 the architect of these reforms, Nicholas Goodison, was elected Chairman of the Stock Exchange, a position to which he was re-elected in 1979, on the recommendation of D. H. Leroy-Lewis who was '. . . convinced that Mr Goodison was the right person to lead the Council . . .'. This was despite the fact that a view existed which wanted to limit the chairmanship to one five-year term because of the way Braithwaite stifled debate and change throughout the 1950s.[2]

However, streamlining the organization and functioning of the Stock Exchange, and giving it strategic aims, did little to alter the fundamental problem it faced of implementing any new policy against the wishes of the majority of the members. In a situation where each member had a vote, no matter how large or small their business, the opportunity and ability to obstruct change was immense, if it involved them in any extra payments or threatened their immediate livelihood. An attempt was made in 1975 to reduce the power of the individual member by switching to the firm being the representative unit, with the number of votes each could cast being related to the size of their staff. This was quickly defeated with any decision being put off until 1982. The continuing power of the individual member was exhibited in 1978 when an attempt to reduce the size of the

[1] LSE: Council, 5 July 1971.
[2] Ibid., 15 Mar. 1971, 22 Mar. 1971, 9 Oct. 1972, 3 July 1973, 16 Oct. 1973, 27 Nov. 1973, 12 Nov. 1974, 17 June 1975, 11 Dec. 1975, 6 Jan. 1976, 25 June 1979.

Council to 30, so as to make it a more effective body, was rejected by a membership concerned about any loss of influence.[3]

Consequently, the room for manœuvre possessed by the Council of the Stock Exchange continued to be constrained by the ability of the membership to block new proposals if they conflicted with their wishes. This presented the Stock Exchange with a serious problem for change was being required of it by the government. It was becoming more and more difficult to satisfy the interests of both government and the members during the 1970s. The Stock Exchange was well aware that in return for carrying out the government's wishes it received valuable benefits. Though stamp duty was considered a burden, restricting the growth of business, the more favourable treatment of transactions handled by members compared to non-members did limit the development of a viable outside market in domestic securities. However, the government was becoming more sympathetic to those in the City, such as the banks and insurance companies, who were complaining about the costs they bore, through fixed commission charges, because of the monopoly position occupied by the Stock Exchange. The investigations by the Monopolies Commission into the supply of professional services was making the Conservative government (1970–4) aware of these costs, much to the Stock Exchange's consternation.[4] In February 1971 they sought advice from Christopher Tugendhat, the MP for the City of London and Westminster. His view was that, '. . . neither (Nicholas) Ridley (President, Board of Trade) nor the Civil Service are very familiar with Stock Exchange procedures, or particularly inclined in your favour,' and he added the advice that, 'I feel sure that it would be a good thing for you to take the initiative and explain why you behave as you do.'[5]

Clearly concessions from the Stock Exchange were expected. If the Stock Exchange was to preserve its structure of fixed minimum commissions, which it regarded as a priority, it would have to give way in other areas, such as being more flexible on whom they admitted and permitting more competition between members. However, none of these changes would be welcomed by the membership, and they had to be convinced by the Stock Exchange if changes were to be implemented. The Stock Exchange did offer one concession early in 1972 by abandoning its rule that refused a quotation to any company that competed with its members by undertaking a stockbroking business. The Stock Exchange agreed that it was unacceptable for it to use its power to grant or withhold a quotation as a way of protecting itself from outside competition.[6]

By itself it was an inadequate concession and the investigations of the Monopolies Commission continued throughout the early 1970s, touching

---

[3] Ibid., 24 July 1972, 20 Aug. 1974, 11 Dec. 1974, 31 Dec. 1974, 11 Feb. 1975, 19 Aug. 1975, 23 Sept. 1975, 4 Nov. 1975, 3 Feb. 1976, 17 Jan. 1978.
[4] Ibid., 4 Jan. 1971, 1 Feb. 1971.  [5] Ibid., 1 Feb. 1971.
[6] Ibid., 8 Mar. 1971, 31 Jan. 1972.

upon a number of matters where the Stock Exchange did control the freedom of its members to operate as they chose. One such area was the vexed question of advertising, which divided the membership itself. Despite pressure from some members there continued to exist a strict prohibition on advertising.[7] A number of the larger firms, such as Vickers da Costa, found this ban especially restrictive as they had to compete with non-members, like merchant banks, who could advertise. They complained in 1970 that

We really do think that we should receive more support in our efforts to keep investment business with member firms, and not allow so much to be diverted to other institutions.[8]

There was even a reluctance to allow them to be named in TV, radio, and newspaper reports. The issue came to a head in February 1971 when the Monopolies Commission concluded that there was '... often a close connection between advertising restrictions and price restrictions'.[9]

Keen to deflect attention away from fixed commissions the Council of the Stock Exchange decided to liberalize advertising, but they acted without realizing the degree of opposition that existed among the membership. Smaller firms, in particular, feared that they would lose clients to the larger firms through advertising campaigns. Even some of the larger firms opposed advertising, feeling it would lower the status of the profession, as with Cazenoves, or because it would increase costs without bringing in extra business, such as Spencer, Thornton. Nevertheless, it was the larger firms, like Vickers da Costa and Buckmaster & Moore, who fully supported the move. When a vote was taken in May 1971 it was found that only 780 members wanted the freedom to advertise while 1,392 did not, defeating the proposal by a majority of 612. Consequently the Stock Exchange was unable to offer the dropping of advertising restrictions as a response to the Monopolies Commission report. The matter then rumbled on in the Stock Exchange until February 1972, when, under pressure from Hoare Govett, it was agreed that members could advertise but only overseas. This victory by the smaller firms, whose business was entirely focused on the domestic market, proved short-lived. In August 1973 the government referred the whole question of the Stock Exchange's restriction on advertising to the Monopolies Commission prompting the Council to propose, once again, liberalization. After considerable opposition from the smaller firms, and without another poll, advertising was eventually approved in November 1973, being extended to agents acting for brokers in January 1974. In 1976 TV advertising and direct mailing was even permitted. Unfortunately for the Stock Exchange once set in motion the investigation by the

[7] LSE: Council, 11 May 1970, 26 May 1970, 26 Oct. 1970.
[8] Ibid., 12 Oct. 1970.     [9] Ibid., 15 Feb. 1971.

Monopolies Commission into advertising continued, touching on the issue of fixed commission charges in August 1974.[10]

Whether a rapid liberalization of the restrictions on advertising would have avoided the Monopolies Commission investigation is open to question. The issue of restrictive practices generally was one being tackled by successive governments from the early 1960s onwards. Nevertheless, it did bring the Stock Exchange's restrictive practices to the attention of the government, leading to a full-scale enquiry. In September 1974 the Stock Exchange received a letter from the Board of Trade indicating that it would have to register the rules and regulations that governed its operations with the Office of Fair Trading. If it was found that, after inspection, these rules and regulations restricted competition in transactions in securities or could be considered not in the public interest, they would then be referred to the Restrictive Practices Court. The long road that was to lead to the 'Big Bang' of 1986 had begun, and it was initially prompted by a refusal of the membership to make any serious concessions to meet the mood of the time, despite the advice of their own Council.[11] Similar opposition was mounted against the admission of both women and foreigners, which had also been recommended by the Monopolies Commission in 1971. Again the Council was in favour of such proposals. The admission of foreigners was quickly accepted, reflecting the growing cosmopolitan nature of the City of London from the mid-1960s onwards.

The admission of women, however, was a different matter and there was much more opposition to them becoming members of an exclusively male club. When a poll was held in May 1971 the proposal to admit women was, as in the past, decisively defeated by 1,287 votes to 955 or a majority of 322. Again, the Stock Exchange had misjudged the mood of the times for the issue was then taken up in Parliament, where there was growing pressure for the government to intervene and ensure that women were admitted. This focused on Miss Fookes who indicated that she was keen to become a member. The government resisted the pressure and did not force the Stock Exchange to admit women.[12]

However, the Stock Exchange's case was becoming untenable because it had no rules specifically preventing women from becoming members. Their standard response, as in January 1972, was that:

. . . no suitable candidate has ever been refused admission to membership provided he is prepared to pay the normal costs of membership.[13]

[10] Ibid., 15 Mar. 1971, 29 Mar. 1971, 5 Apr. 1971, 13 Apr. 1971, 19 Apr. 1971, 24 May 1971, 9 Aug. 1971, 20 Dec. 1971, 24 Jan. 1972, 31 Jan. 1972, 21 Feb. 1972, 17 July 1973, 16 Oct. 1973, 6 Nov. 1973, 22 Jan. 1974, 13 Aug. 1974, 22 June 1976.
[11] Ibid., 10 Sept. 1974.
[12] Ibid., 8 Mar. 1971, 29 Mar. 1971, 13 Apr. 1971, 24 May 1971, 12 July 1971.
[13] Ibid., 10 Jan. 1972, 16 Oct. 1973.

As a private club the Stock Exchange could determine its own policy on admissions but it was clear that it discriminated against women because suitable female candidates did exist. Muriel Bailey, for example reappeared in May 1972, applying for membership, though now as Muriel Wood, her married name. By then the London Stock Exchange's attitude towards female members had changed for the proposed merger of all British stock exchanges would, automatically, introduce women members to London because there were already 13 female members of other stock exchanges. Faced with the inevitability that women would be able to transact business on the floor of the London Stock Exchange, when the merger took place, it was decided to pre-empt the issue. By a vote of 24 to 5 the Council of the Stock Exchange agreed to accept applications from women for the year commencing 25 March 1973. On 1 March 1973 7 women had been elected to membership of the London Stock Exchange and this doubled in April. The first of these was Muriel Wood who was elected on 1 January 1973, when she was already 66 years old. More typical was Mrs Susan Shaw, of Shaw & Co., who was 38 when she became a member in March 1973. Though female members were now acceptable, women clerks were not permitted on the trading-floor, unless specific permission was given. That came to an end in June 1973 when it was decided that there were now no grounds for their exclusion. Miss Diana Craig, a clerk with J. M. Finn & Co., was the first one given access to the floor. Henceforth all applications from male and female clerks were to be treated equally, allowing women to enjoy the same career path as men.[14]

The London Stock Exchange continued to enjoy a close working relationship with the government of the day, whether directly with the Chancellor of the Exchequer and the Treasury or indirectly via the weekly meeting between the Chairman of the Stock Exchange and the governor of the Bank of England. Under the Conservatives (1970–4) the Stock Exchange was worried by its public image because they were aware that adverse publicity would provoke government pressure and even intervention. The Stock Exchange was also often exasperated at those government actions which undermined the operation of the market that they provided, such as those dealing with taxes and controls. One incident that particularly annoyed them was the late intervention by the government in the takeover bid for Wilkinson Sword by the British Match Corporation. The bid was made on 23 May 1973 but was not referred to the Monopolies Commission until 29 June, or over a month later, creating a great deal of uncertainty in the market. The brokers for British Match, Fielding, Newson-Smith & Co., observed, with a great deal of anger,

... the orderly and effective conduct of sophisticated and efficient capital markets cannot be maintained against a background of such dilatory and lethargic government performance.[15]

[14] LSE: Council, 1 May 1972, 5 Mar. 1973, 17 Apr. 1973.
[15] Ibid., 10 July 1973.

Critical as the Stock Exchange was of the Conservative government they had even more cause for concern when Labour came to power in 1974, and remained there until 1979. In the face of a government that believed that intervention by the state was more effective than the forces of the market in financing industry, the Stock Exchange, once again, began to worry about whether it would be left with a role.[16]

The actions of the Monopolies Commission and then the Office of Fair Trading, under a Conservative government, had posed threats to the way the Stock Exchange operated but not to its importance and survival. However, from the mid-1970s onwards, under a Labour government, its very existence was again in question. It was a lot easier for the government of the day to attribute poor economic performance to the way particular components of the British financial system operated, and seek to reform them, than to address more fundamental and wide-ranging problems.[17] In response all the Stock Exchange could do was to state the needs of the market and stress the risks involved with direct government intervention.

Throughout the many years during which the services provided by the Stock Exchange and by the financial community have been refined and developed, the basic principle has been that successful and professional operations must be founded on confidence and trust both between practitioners in the market and their clients. This has been fostered to the point where the public generally accepts the services provided are properly conducted and administered.

It then went on to add that this was best done by those directly involved because of their expertise and speed of response. They then concluded that

The very complex inter-relationships and internal operations of those City bodies which form the financial system, are best regulated by each individual body under the general supervision of the Bank of England.

Furthermore, self-regulation was so much better suited to the international operations that many in the City were engaged in giving as the reason,

Because self-regulation is based on the voluntary acceptance of authority by those to whom it is applied, it can extend beyond the bounds of national legislation and apply with equal force to those outside its jurisdiction.[18]

However, to a government looking for solutions to national economic problems and unsympathetic to the market, these were not arguments that convinced. Furthermore, the case for self-regulation was undermined by international comparisons with the United States, where a much greater degree of state intervention had existed since the 1930s, in the form of the Securities and Exchange Commission. The OECD had even begun an investigation into financial markets, with suggestions that reform was required before a European-wide market could come into existence.[19]

---

[16] Ibid., 23 Oct. 1973, 4 Feb. 1975, 5 July 1977.   [17] Ibid., 4 Feb. 1975.
[18] Ibid., 4 Mar. 1975.   [19] Ibid., 29 Apr. 1975.

Consequently, in the mid-1970s there was beginning to build up a momentum which challenged the right of the Stock Exchange to be the sole authority for the securities market. Out of this came the formation in 1978 of the Council for the Securities Industry (CSI) which was to take over responsibility from the Stock Exchange. The Stock Exchange was to come under the control of this Council, along with other components of the securities market, and the whole organization would be supervised by the Bank of England. Such a move was, in a way, inevitable with the gradual fragmentation of the market in the 1960s and 1970s, and with the growing volume of Eurobond trading in London, little of which took place on the Stock Exchange. Nevertheless, it did pose a serious threat to the role of the Stock Exchange for a major pillar of its post-war survival was that it acted as an interface between the securities market and the government.[20]

At the same time there continued to be the threat to the way the Stock Exchange operated from the Restrictive Practices Court (RPC). The Stock Exchange were trying to delay the formal investigation into their rules and regulations by requiring time to prepare both documentation and a defence. However, by January 1979 the Office of Fair Trading would wait no longer. It was reported to Council that

... a letter had been received from the OFT to the effect that the Director-General had concluded that he could not properly defer any longer the commencement of proceedings and that he intended to issue the notice on or about 22nd January 1979.[21]

An approach to the government to exempt the Stock Exchange from the Restrictive Practices Act also failed. The last hope was the defeat of the Labour party in the general election, with a government coming into power that was more sympathetic to the financial market.

In the City there was also diminishing support for the Stock Exchange. Many regarded its failure to adjust its costs and practices to changing needs as an impediment to their own ability to compete in an increasingly international business. A report by the Inter-bank Research Organisation in 1973, for example, on the future of London as an international financial centre, concluded that the London Stock Exchange was a 'closed shop' and implied that it was not doing enough to attract business to London.[22] The Stock Exchange's changing attitude towards the CBI is a measure of its loss of power and influence in the course of the 1970s. In 1970 the CBI invited the Stock Exchange to join but were rebuffed on the grounds that,

[20] LSE: Council, 14 Feb. 1978; A. Cairncross, 'The Bank of England', in G. Toniolo (ed.), *Central Banks, Independence in Historical Perspective* (Berlin 1988), 66.

[21] LSE: Council, 9 Jan. 1978, cf. 19 Jan. 1978, 9 Feb. 1979, 23 Oct. 1979.

[22] Inter-Bank Research Organization, *The Future of London as an International Financial Centre* (London 1973), 3–7, 13–14.

The CBI, correctly or not, tends to be identified with the Tory Party, whereas the Stock Exchange at all times is concerned to establish and maintain its freedom from any political affiliations.[23]

At that time the Stock Exchange was so confident of the position it had established for itself, in its relationship with the Bank of England and the government, that it did not need to bolster it by membership of a body such as the CBI. Conversely, in November 1979, with another Conservative government in power, the Stock Exchange took the decision to apply for membership, seeing a need to cultivate influential friends in order to defend its position against the hostile attack of both the government and other sectors of the business and financial community. The relationships that the Stock Exchange relied upon to preserve its customs and practices crumbled away in the 1970s, leaving it facing a somewhat uncertain future.

The Stock Exchange also continued to be unsuccessful in obtaining the concessions it wanted from the government. Requests for a reduction, variation, or abolition of stamp duty, for example, were regularly made to the Chancellor of the Exchequer but were ignored under the Conservatives while the Labour government doubled the rate in 1974 from 1 per cent to 2 per cent.[24] The introduction of Value Added Tax (VAT) on the services provided by its members also led the Stock Exchange to seek concessions. The Stock Exchange was worried that such a tax would destroy what remained of the private investor as they could not reclaim VAT in the way that financial institutions could. Though the Stock Exchange managed to have transactions between members declared free of VAT the commission charged by brokers was subjected to it from April 1973. Similarly, the Stock Exchange complained, to no avail, about the move of the Companies Registration Office from London as it was a major reference source for their members, dealing as they were in British corporate securities.[25] More general requests to simplify the income tax structure and to lower the top rates, in order to encourage savings and investment, also brought little response from governments during the 1970s. The incoming Labour government of 1974 even toyed with a wealth tax, setting up a Royal Commission on the Distribution of Income and Wealth. Though the Stock Exchange lobbied against such a tax there was little evidence that its view was influential with the government.[26]

In other areas of City activity there was also a tendency for the Stock Exchange to be sidelined. In terms of insider trading, for example, the City Takeover Panel was now the body responsible for co-ordinating action and introducing rules. Covering as it did all the participants in the City it was much more effective than the Stock Exchange ever could be, acting alone.

[23] LSE: Council, 7 Dec. 1970, cf. 20 Nov. 1979.
[24] Ibid., 26 Apr. 1971, 9 Oct. 1972, 2 Apr. 1974, 15 Oct. 1974.
[25] Ibid., 24 Apr. 1972, 11 Sept. 1972, 30 Oct. 1973.
[26] Ibid., 1 Sept. 1970, 24 Sept. 1974, 28 Jan. 1975, 8 Apr. 1975.

In 1971 the Panel pronounced that '. . . it is axiomatic in the City, that inside information must never be used for personal gain'. To this end it began to introduce rules to prevent the exploitation of privileged information, as in the case of companies. However, as the Stock Exchange had long been aware, such rules were ineffective unless accompanied by some real sanctions or punishments. Consequently by 1973 the Panel was coming round to the view that insider dealing should be made an offence. There was a growing feeling in the 1970s, both in the government and the City, that the Stock Exchange should no longer have exclusive power devolved to it in such areas as investor protection and insider trading for it was incapable of enforcing them. The Stock Exchange's own demand for the outlawing of insider trading indicated the need for additional support.[27]

The Stock Exchange's own rules and regulations governing members were also coming under increasing pressure in the 1970s. In 1973 it was accepted that members who had adopted the corporate form could themselves be listed on the Stock Exchange again. Again no single investor was allowed to acquire more than 10 per cent of the shares. Then, in 1975, financial institutions were permitted to own up to 10 per cent of a member. However, in the 1970s the Stock Exchange continued to use its rules on membership to restrict the growing competition from British and European financial firms. The Canadian firm of Wisener & Partners applied for membership of the London Stock Exchange in 1973 for their British operation but this was rejected, even though London allowed its own members to join stock exchanges abroad. The reason given was the fear that a failure overseas would bring down the London branch, and thus endanger other members of the Stock Exchange. Though this was a legitimate worry it disguised the main reason, which was a fear of the competition which these large, well-capitalized, international brokerage firms posed. The Council was keen to see a solution which would allow members of foreign stock exchanges to become members in London, because of the business they would bring in and the reciprocity it would encourage, but that was unacceptable to the membership as a whole. A few limited moves were made, such as allowing foreign nationals to become members and foreign firms to own 10 per cent of a member, but the London Stock Exchange continued to refuse membership to the North American brokerage houses located in London.[28]

The worry expressed over the financial stability of its members, given as a reason for restricting outside involvement, was a genuine one on the Stock Exchange in the 1970s. Under the compensation scheme the Stock

[27] LSE: Council, 13 Apr. 1971, cf. 5 Feb. 1973, 2 July 1974, 4 Mar. 1975, 7 Oct. 1975.
[28] Ibid., 27 Feb. 1970, 8 Feb. 1971, 15 Mar. 1971, 19 Apr. 1971, 17 Apr. 1973, 22 May 1973, 5 June 1973, 9 Oct. 1973, 30 Oct. 1973, 13 Nov. 1973, 21 Nov. 1973, 19 Feb. 1974, 29 May 1974; M. C. Reed, *A History of James Capel and Company* (London 1975), 104.

Exchange was regarded as guardian of its members' behaviour, not only towards each other but also in their relationship with their clients. Consequently, rather than wait for collapse or scandal to take place, the Stock Exchange increasingly scrutinized potential applicants and granted itself power to monitor their activities on a continuous basis. From 1 August 1971, all candidates for membership of the Stock Exchange had to pass the Stock Exchange examination, unless they already possessed similar qualifications. However, try as it might the Stock Exchange was never in a position to remove the risk of failure among its members, in a business that operated so much on the basis of trust and expectation. In response to such failures the Stock Exchange raised the minimum level of capital required by both brokers and jobbers. By 1973 no broking firm was to have less than £30,000 in free funds available to support its operations while the figure for jobbers was £50,000. In addition, when there were more than three partners each extra one had to have £5,000. Inevitably, this made it even more difficult for an able young man, without existing connections in stockbroking or jobbing, to start in a small way and then build up a business, as had been common in the past.[29]

However, the level of capital being set was a compromise that satisfied neither those firms doing a large speculative business, such as those conducting arbitrage or option dealing, where it was far too low, nor those doing a steady commission business for private investors who were well known to the partners. Naturally enough the private stockbrokers complained as it further raised their costs. Ransford & Co. found that a maximum of £15,000 or half the proposed rate, was all that was required, while Woolan & Co. were of the opinion that

... provided a sound investment business is carried on, allied to a well-managed office, an increase of the suggested size in the required solvency margin is unnecessary for the proper conduct of business. No practical level of solvency margins can provide protection against reckless trading.[30]

Despite opposition the minimum levels were to come into force in 1973, with smaller firms being given over 18 months to adjust. If a firm was willing to submit to high-level scrutiny and to maintain half its capital in British government 10-year loan stock, then the level of capital required could be halved.

Scrutiny and rules were to no avail in 1974 when the stock market crisis of that year swept away numerous firms and members. In the course of the year the number of stockbroking firms in London fell from 168 in 1973 to 129 in January 1975, and the number of London members dropped from 3,536 to 3,390. Though only six firms actually failed the survivors

[29] LSE: Council, 26 Mar. 1974, 1 Oct. 1974.
[30] Ibid., 26 Apr. 1971, cf. 13 Apr. 1971, 3 May 1971, 24 May 1971, 1 Nov. 1971, 26 Mar. 1973.

merged to create stronger groupings.[31] It forced the Stock Exchange to recognize that

No system of regulation whether internal or external is going to prevent occasional insolvencies in a volatile and high-risk business particularly at a time when the fall in share prices has been the sharpest ever recorded and the level of business has halved.[32]

During the collapse in the market important firms such as Chapman & Rowe, Mitton, Butler & Priest, and Tustain L'Estange had been hammered. Mitton, Butler had been the first stockbroking firm to be incorporated, having done so in 1970 to attract outside capital and to build-up reserves. By 1972 the firm had a capital of £0.2m., and was earning £50,000 per annum in commission from a large personal clientele. However, that was not sufficient to prevent it going under along with its weaker brethren. Nevertheless, the Stock Exchange's immediate reaction was to tighten up on both scrutiny and capital requirements, despite the views of particular members, such as Laurie Milbank & Co., that the result would be drive business into the hands of non-members, not burdened by such supervision and requirements. Such was the alarm on the Stock Exchange at the mounting level of compensation payments, with £0.8m. having been paid out by October and further claims expected to total £2.4m., that immediate intervention was demanded. Most members continued to believe that any cost was worth bearing if it could lead to potential failures being spotted at an early stage and thus minimize the losses that all were expected to bear. Consequently, in 1975 sole traders were finally banned, as no longer appropriate for a modern securities market, while corporate members, with partial limited liability, had to have a minimum margin of £200,000 available to finance their operations. Over and above these capital requirements the Stock Exchange set out extensive and rigorous rules on how members were permitted to conduct their own business. The booklet detailing how a firm should keep its accounts, and the disclosures it had to make, was 19 pages long while the one covering the code of conduct on dealing was 25 pages.[33] Certainly the failures of 1974 had been a great shock to the Stock Exchange. The Compensation Fund had paid out £3.5m. since 1951 and of that £1.7m., or 48.3 per cent was for 1974 alone. The growing size of individual firms had increased the risks that the Compensation fund had to bear.

Decontrol of financial activities at home and abroad was introducing a more complex and competitive environment in which it was no longer

[31] G. B. Blakey, *The Post-War History of the London Stock Market, 1945–92* (Didcot 1993), 155–66; D. Kynaston, *Cazenove & Co.: A History* (London 1991), 288; LSE: *Annual Reports*, 1974 and 1975.

[32] LSE: Council, 2 July 1974.

[33] Ibid., 9 July 1974, 15 Oct. 1974, 3 Dec. 1974, 21 Jan. 1975, 11 Feb. 1975, 4 Mar. 1975, 8 Apr. 1975, 13 May 1975, 24 June 1975.

possible for the Stock Exchange to restrict the activities of its members in such a way as to minimize their collective exposure to large losses. For the first time the Stock Exchange was forced to accept that universal compensation was no longer feasible. As a result it was decided to confine compensation to non-members with those participating in the market expected to bear the risks resulting from the business that they were engaged in. Even for outsiders a £50,000 maximum level of compensation was introduced in November 1975 for each claim. Clearly, what emerged out of the 1974 crisis was a distinction between the need to protect the individual investor from mistakes or fraud by those they employed to conduct their business, and the principle of 'caveat emptor' for the professionals involved in the market place, whether members or non-members. All the same the Stock Exchange continued to perform its post-war role of policing the market so as to remove or limit those trading practices that were inherently risky, thus continuing to restrict the ability of its members to move into those new areas that a climate of international volatility and liberalization was creating in the 1970s. Admirable as the principle of the Compensation Fund was when it was introduced, one of its by-products was to discourage innovation on the Stock Exchange because of the fear that this would lead to large losses which would have to be borne by all members, even those undertaking a safe commission-only business.[34]

## LIMITED RESPONSES

Throughout the 1970s the Stock Exchange also persevered with a system of fixed commissions despite criticisms from both the government and elsewhere in the City and the difficulty of setting rates that satisfied all members. The fixed commission regime had become such a fundamental component of the Stock Exchange's operation that its abandonment was unthinkable. The problem was that the buying and selling of securities was becoming more complex with Eurobonds, and more competitive with New York brokerage houses, that the Stock Exchange was under pressure to continuously review and amend the rates if it was to retain its position in the market. However, any change in the rates was then opposed by those members whose business was not subject to growing competition, but would suffer from a loss of income. Consequently it was very difficult to adjust rates to satisfy all. Those members who did a private client business were forever pressing for an increase in the minimum charges as they wanted to pass their rising costs onto their customers. They could easily produce evidence that much of the business they did for individual investors was uneconomic, having to be subsidized from the profits made on larger deals. Conversely those firms pressing for charges to be

[34] Ibid., 5 Jan. 1970, 2 Feb. 1970, 9 Nov. 1970, 1 Feb. 1971, 10 Jan. 1972, 24 Apr. 1972, 22 May 1972, 4 Mar. 1975, 1 July 1975, 4 Nov. 1975, 6 July 1976.

lowered could produce evidence that they were losing their customers to non-members or to direct dealing between the large institutions. As these pressures grew in the 1970s the Stock Exchange as an institution was caught in the middle.

In 1971, for example, the brokers Argentine & Christopherson, who did a private client business lobbied for an increase in commissions, arguing that

... the squeeze in profit margins is felt more acutely by small firms and that, unless some increase in commission scale is brought into effect reasonably quickly, there is likely to be an accelerated decline in the dwindling number of such firms ...[35]

However, the Stock Exchange turned down their request because it was well aware that institutional investors, especially the banks, would resist any increase by lobbying the government and the Bank of England and threatening to charge brokers more for the services they provided. In 1972 the merchant banks again put pressure on the Stock Exchange to reduce the rates of commission on large transactions, having already obtained concessions in 1970. The Stock Exchange was forced to take this seriously because of the collective power these firms possessed. Compared to the private investor the financial institutions were in a much more powerful position regarding the Stock Exchange. Their business was channelled through a small number of firms and they were represented by such trade bodies as the Accepting Houses Association, the Issuing Houses Association, and the British Insurance Association. Consequently when the insurance companies pointed out, also in 1972, that they were paying c.£10m. a year in commission charges to brokers and demanded a 25 per cent reduction in charges, the Stock Exchange had no alternative but to negotiate. They had already permitted the commission on Euro-currency bonds to be at the discretion of the broker for, otherwise, it was clear, what still remained of the business on the Stock Exchange would be lost.

Despite opposition from among the membership to any reductions, such as from H. & R. Wagner and Panmure Gordon, the Stock Exchange was forced to concede discounts on transactions over £50,000 in gilt-edged, in order to retain business for their members. London-based banks and insurance companies had to remain competitive in world terms and were no longer willing to pay higher charges to Stock Exchange members even if it did encourage the private investor by subsidizing their buying and selling. If the Stock Exchange did not reduce its rates these financial institutions would trade elsewhere. Faced with the rebellion of the institutions on the level of charges, which continued after the concessions they gained, the Stock Exchange was then forced to reconsider the question of minimum charges for small transactions. Many members were already, unilaterally,

[35] LSE: Council, 11 Jan. 1971, cf. 10 Jan. 1972, 24 Jan. 1972, 8 May 1972, 22 May 1972.

increasing charges in this area. However, this was a politically sensitive area as the Stock Exchange was keen to increase its popular appeal by encouraging small investors to buy, sell, and hold shares. Increasing the costs of transactions was hardly likely to do that and would only antagonize the government, whether Conservative or Labour.

The problem was that stockbroking firms had never devised a means of providing a low-cost service to small investors, and thus all were expected to bear their share of a level of office overheads and dealing expenses, which could only be justified for large investors. As long as costs could be covered through overcharging large investors, who were increasingly financial institutions, then there was limited need to change. It was in the 1970s that this ceased to be as possible as in the past, as these institutions now had access to alternatives at home and abroad. At the same time the inflation of the mid-1970s, combined with collapse in the market, was pushing up the costs of stockbroking firms without any compensation in terms of an increased volume of business, as had been the case for most of the 1950s and 1960s. However, it was no easy matter to increase the minimum charge. Nevertheless, the Stock Exchange was able to double the minimum commission from £2 to £4 and push up the rate from 1.25 per cent to 1.5 per cent, so providing some relief. Even so minimum commission levels were, generally, unremunerative. In 1974 it was estimated that the average bargain cost £5.24 to execute while the minimum commission was £4.00. It remained difficult to push through an increase against government attempts to control prices. There was also no desire to attract public attention to the fixed scale of charges.[36]

Action was becoming imperative though when an internal survey revealed that the last concession on volume business had reduced the commission received by an average of 7.5 per cent, and there was no compensatory increase in the level of business. This reduction was experienced mostly by the large institutional businesses, so making them reluctant to agree to any more such reductions. The one area where these large firms, like Capels, were happy to agree substantial volume discounts was in foreign securities which commanded little of a market in London. Thus the situation developed whereby the London Stock Exchange tried to maintain high fixed rates on business in domestic securities, in order to preserve the income of its members, while lowering them on transactions in foreign securities with the aim of attracting orders from markets abroad. By the mid-1970s the Stock Exchange had put in place a scale of fixed commissions which they recognized as being very competitive in transactions over £10,000. This satisfied most institutional customers and even brought in some foreign business. Conversely, they were also aware that transactions under £10,000 were expensive, making the Stock Exchange vulnerable to pressure from

[36] Ibid., 22 May 1972, 24 July 1972, 29 Aug. 1972, 16 Oct. 1972, 13 Nov. 1972, 29 Oct. 1974, 12 Nov. 1974.

medium-sized investors. This pressure could be resisted so long as these investors had little alternative to the Stock Exchange but how could they be justified to a government inquiry?[37]

By responding to the needs of the institutional investors the Stock Exchange did quieten City criticism, so helping to preserve its fixed commission structure throughout the 1970s. The other pillar of the Stock Exchange's structure was the separation of brokers and jobbers, and this it was also determined to maintain. Throughout the 1970s it was repeatedly stated how important this principle was to the successful functioning of the Stock Exchange.

Single capacity, a scale of minimum commission and a viable Compensation Fund must be maintained. Any breach of the first two could lead to reduced profitability and reluctance to support the third.

This was one such statement in May 1977.[38] During the 1970s this separation of the function of broker and jobber was increasingly seen as a key element in maintaining a standard of behaviour in London that encouraged a climate of trust, and brought in business from foreign investors. Through the commitment to single capacity any client of a broker could be certain that both the price obtained was that prevailing in the market and the advice given was impartial. In London for example, brokers were not tempted to try and unload on their clients securities which either they could or could not sell or for which they had overpaid, as was claimed to be happening on those stock exchanges where no such separation existed.

Though this separation did bring benefits in terms of investor protection, making it more difficult, but not impossible, for brokers to manipulate their clients, the principle of single capacity was becoming more difficult to maintain. Domestically, the largest financial institutions now undertook such a volume of sales and purchases that they were keen to establish direct contact with the jobbers, cutting out the brokers completely. In turn the largest jobbers like Smith Brothers, were keen to foster such contacts because they were losing business to outside dealers like the European banks and North American brokerage houses. However the Stock Exchange had made it clear early in the decade that it would not countenance jobbers trading directly with non-members, and it did not move from that position throughout the 1970s. In 1973 they had informed the major financial institutions in the City that

The Stock Exchange . . . does not and cannot exist on institutional business alone and the Council considers it important to preserve the separation of Broker and Jobber, which is the guarantee of fair treatment to the great majority of investors.[39]

[37] LSE: Council, 26 Mar. 1973, 12 June 1973, 19 June 1973, 14 Aug. 1973, 23 Oct. 1973, 26 Nov. 1974.

[38] Ibid., 3 May 1977, cf. 29 Nov. 1971, 21 Nov. 1973; 26 Nov. 1974, 9 Nov. 1976, 4 Dec. 1979.

[39] Ibid., 24 Apr. 1973, cf. 1 Mar. 1977.

Though the avoidance of conflict of interest was the reason given at the time, behind it all lay the fear that once the major financial institutions could deal directly with the jobbers the maintenance of fixed commissions would be impossible and the livelihood of numerous brokers would be ruined. Hence the implacable opposition to any erosion of single capacity on the domestic front.

Internationally, however, the situation was much more complex for many members, including some of the largest stockbroking firms, wanted a relaxation of the single capacity rule in order to compete more effectively. In 1969 the rules had already been altered to allow brokers to make markets in Euro-currency bonds, where it was necessary not only to handle sales and purchases but to deal extensively on their own account if the needs of buyers and sellers were to be met. However, this was considered to be a special case because Eurobonds were almost exclusively held by, and traded between, financial institutions who did not require the protection of broker/jobber separation. Instead, it was James Capel's activities in the United States that tested the Stock Exchange's commitment to single capacity. Having allowed brokers to join foreign stock exchanges James Capel & Co. had become members of the Mid-West Stock Exchange in Chicago. There they had begun to operate as specialists, which meant that they bought and sold both on their own account and for clients. Even worse the securities that they traded were British and South African, with BP, Plessey, and Roan Selection Trust being the most prominent. Though James Capel's operations in Chicago were run by Americans, and 65 per cent of the business were generated locally as opposed to 35 per cent from London, the London Stock Exchange ordered them to cease operating as specialists.[40]

James Capel & Co. did not accept the ruling as it would have ended the valuable business that they were building up in the United States, using their long-established expertise in those international and mining stocks that still commanded a market in London. One of their partners, David Leroy-Lewis warned the Stock Exchange that

If the position of the Stock Exchange in this country is to be maintained overseas, I believe we have got to encourage—and certainly not discourage—our member firms to take part in the growing international nature of the securities industry . . . if our member firms form overseas subsidiary organizations, they should, as far as possible be allowed to compete on equal terms with their competitors in those countries.[41]

The outcome was a fierce debate in the Stock Exchange between firms like Capels who wanted to expand internationally, and not be constrained by rules peculiar to London, and those members worried that it would destroy single capacity and fixed commissions in London. Jobbers like

[40] Ibid., 15 Nov. 1973, 10 Jan. 1972.     [41] Ibid., 29 Nov. 1971, cf. 10 Jan. 1972.

Smith Brothers and Wedd, Durlacher were especially worried as they saw their command of particular markets being lost to brokers operating on other Stock Exchanges. Wilfred Rantzen of Smith Brothers complained bitterly as his firm were the major jobbers in South African mining securities. Thus, in this case Smith Brothers argued for the enforcement of single capacity whereas later in the 1970s they were to argue the other way, indicating the fluctuating reasons behind the support for broker/jobber separation. In the end the Stock Exchange allowed Capels to act as dealers but only in securities not quoted in London. The whole question was then referred to a committee, which was to investigate single capacity and international operations.

What this investigation revealed was the growing global nature of the securities market which was being matched by the organizational expansion of European, Japanese, and American firms. By 1972 the New York brokerage house of Merrill Lynch had 48 overseas offices, and they were generating 10 per cent of the company's income. In response to this, many of the lesser stock exchanges in the United States had opened up their membership to foreign banks and brokerage houses, hoping to create an advantage over New York. Crédit Suisse (Zürich) had joined the Pacific Coast Stock Exchange while Algemene Bank (Amsterdam), Comerzbank (Frankfurt), and Crédit Lyonnais (Paris) were on the Mid-West, and Nomura (Tokyo) were members of both the Pacific and Boston Stock Exchanges. All this had implications for the future of both the London Stock Exchange as an institution and its members, for most of these banks and brokerage houses also had London branches though excluded from the London Stock Exchange. In 1972 a total of 34 US and 13 Canadian brokerage firms, for example, had offices in London, where they dealt not only in dollar stocks but in UK securities. Consequently, through the international networks of these banks and brokers it was relatively easy for London-based financial institutions to direct business world-wide, and if the members of the London Stock Exchange wanted to compete for their orders they had to be able to offer the same facilities.

All this became clear in 1972, and the Stock Exchange was forced to conclude that:

... the international markets in securities offer great opportunities to the firms which are prepared to compete for business. The problem is how to provide a framework within which member firms can compete effectively for business without encouraging irresponsibility and without upsetting traditional methods of transacting business in securities in this country.

The dilemma facing the Stock Exchange was how to preserve single capacity for brokers at home but to permit dual capacity abroad. As a compromise it was agreed to permit them to operate with dual capacity in the

United States and Canada but not in Europe. Even then it was pointed out that continental banks acted as both brokers and dealers and:

... if the Council wishes to encourage members firms to compete for the available business in Europe at an early stage rather than, as in the case of the Euro-dollar market, give competitors a head start, then there is really no practical alternative but to permit member firms overseas organizations to act in dual capacity.[42]

While the conclusions of the report regarding overseas operations were inescapable there remained many members of the Stock Exchange who were reluctant to concede the relaxation of single capacity for North American operations, let alone in Europe. One such was Somerset Gibbs, of Capel-Cure, who pointed out that if single capacity was abandoned abroad minimum commission rules would also be unenforceable, as they did not apply to jobbing operations. That would then undermine the position at home for it would be impossible to isolate British and foreign trading as markets for UK securities were appearing overseas.[43]

Despite the report and its recommendations the argument over the relaxing of single capacity abroad rumbled on through 1972, 1973, and into 1974. All the time the competition for the available business was growing as Australian and Japanese brokers opened offices in London, to add to those from the United States and Canada. The Australian stockbroking firm of Constable & Bain opened an office in London in 1971, for example. By then the whole question of what brokers could do abroad became entangled with the desire of jobbers to become members of foreign stock exchanges. Such was the global nature of the securities business in the 1970s that London jobbers wanted to expand internationally in order to take advantage of it, as well as improve their own ability to match their sales and purchases by operating on different markets. As markets grew in size in such regions as Asia and Australia they offered scope for dealers to set up profitable operations, which had not been possible in the past.[44] The major London jobbers such as Wedd, Durlacher, with their considerable experience, wanted to take advantage of this by joining these stock exchanges as dealing members. This was opposed by the smaller jobbers, like Medwin Lowy, who saw themselves being squeezed by the larger firms, able to offer keener prices and larger trades because of their global operations. More importantly it was opposed by the brokers, like Hedderwick, Borthwick & Co., and Cazenoves, who saw business moving out of London if local exchanges could offer the service currently available only in London. Cazenoves estimated that 85 per cent of their business in Australian and South African securities was done in London rather than Australia while

[42] LSE: Council, 3 July 1972, cf. 17 Jan. 1972.
[43] Ibid., 14 Aug. 1972, 25 Sept. 1972, 12 Feb. 1973, 21 Nov. 1973.
[44] S. Salisbury and K. Sweeney, *The Bull, the Bear and the Kangaroo: A History of the Sydney Stock Exchange* (Sydney 1988), 388.

Joseph Sebag & Co. claimed that 80 per cent of their Hong Kong business was completed in London. Sebag's went on to note that:

The reason the business came to London was because there was a better market here, but with a jobber locally the market would improve and the attraction of London would diminish.[45]

The majority of members of the London Stock Exchange were still committed to retaining control over their own market by preventing some of their number setting up large-scale operations abroad. The presumption remained that they had more to lose from expanding operations internationally than they had to gain, and so both brokers and jobbers obstructed each other's efforts.

In the end both brokers and jobbers began to expand internationally by ignoring those rules that made it difficult for them to do so. Jobbers were developing direct contract with non-members while brokers were evading the minimum commission rules. Faced with this situation the Stock Exchange was reluctant to either ignore it, because of the precedent that would be set, or to tighten up the rules, which would drive away business and lose them members. However, any solution could not involve a change to single capacity domestically because the Stock Exchange was convinced that:

... the principle of separation of capacity works well for UK stocks, producing a larger and free market in domestic stocks than that of any other country of comparable size ...

The problem was perceived to lie, solely, in the international sphere where brokers were now looking beyond London for the best markets in a wide variety of securities and jobbers were following suit in order to match sales and purchases at close prices. Over the years since the end of the Second World War the London Stock Exchange had lost the markets it once dominated, such as those in South African mining securities and American stocks, which were now spread among a number of separate exchanges. On these exchanges no distinction between broker and dealer was made, and it was with these dual capacity firms that the members of the London Stock Exchange had to compete. The Stock Exchange was forced to recognize that the

... maintenance of the competitive position of member firms in both London and overseas now requires that they should be allowed to act in dual capacity in International stocks: it is fundamental to the securities business that the rules are set by the dominant market—and there is no longer any significant group of non-UK stocks in which London dominates the market.

The London Stock Exchange was no longer in a position to impose its methods and rules of operations on the global financial community, as

[45] LSE: Council, 7 May 1974.

it had in the past. It now had to meet strong competition in all but British securities and could only succeed by matching the services provided by others by adopting some or all of their methods and organizations.

The solution proposed by the Stock Exchange in November 1974 was to create a category of member called international dealers, open to all existing brokers and jobbers. These international dealers could trade only in non-sterling securities but would not be bound by the rules relating to both single capacity or commissions. Essentially, members were to be given freedom to compete in the international markets in whatever they chose, freed from most of the restraints imposed upon them by the London Stock Exchange.

We only stand a good chance of London remaining the central securities market in Europe if we encourage the financial power of our member firms. We cannot do this by placing artificial restrictions on their expansion[46]

was the philosophy behind the proposals. This was a belated recognition that if the Stock Exchange prevented its members from competing with their peers not only would the international business be lost but foreign firms would, eventually, also invade the domestic market. However, in the 1970s many members continued to believe that whatever happened abroad and in international securities the British market for domestic stocks was immune from foreign competition. Consequently, there was a resistance to any changes on the international front that might set precedents domestically.

A half-way house involving giving members the freedom to operate as they chose in international markets but maintaining rigid controls in domestic ones was regarded with great suspicion by the majority of members who continued to derive most of their income from trading in UK securities for UK investors. Any relaxation was viewed not as a necessary compromise but as a dangerous precedent for domestic operations. C. M. Horner, of the brokers Scott, Goff, Hancock & Co. spoke for many when he suggested that the alternative to what was currently in place was

... a free-for-all with the consequent ending of the jobbing system as it is now and the emergence of dual capacity firms and the eventual takeover of the stock market by the banks and outside institutions.[47]

Clearly this was not what most wanted and if it could be avoided by sacrificing an international role for the London Stock Exchange, then that was a price worth paying, especially as most members would not have to meet it, as they did an essentially domestic business. Consequently, despite agreeing that the concept of the international dealer was an attractive one the proposal was eventually abandoned by May 1975. Further attempts to give greater discretion to those members competing in the markets for

[46] Ibid., 12 Nov. 1974.     [47] Ibid., 12 Nov. 1974, cf. 26 Nov. 1974, 27 May 1975.

foreign securities also foundered on the need to maintain the principle of single capacity at all times. This was in spite of the recognition, as expressed in November 1976, that '. . . the market for foreign currency securities might need to be regulated by rules and regulations different from those in the domestic market . . .'.[48] It was only with the abolition of exchange controls in 1979 that the needs of those members dealing in foreign securities once again became a priority. The effect of the exchange controls had been to cocoon the members of the London Stock Exchange from international competition, leaving them exposed and vulnerable when it was removed.[49]

The realization that the London Stock Exchange's command of British securities was under threat from abroad came at the end of a decade when many of its domestic competitors had been removed through the amalgamation with the provincial stock exchanges. By the end of the 1960s, the stage had been reached when a merger was a distinct possibility, though much detail remained to be finalized. As before, one of the main stumbling blocks to a merger was the demand from London that dual capacity be abandoned in the provinces and the demand from the provinces for direct access to the London jobbers. In the negotiations each side tried to preserve those advantages, with London threatening to withdraw from the Federation, so removing the block on branches, while the provinces hinted at further developing country jobbing, so threatening the London market. No compromise was achievable and the only way forward, if a merger was to take place, was one of '. . . complete equality of member firms to compete with each other under uniform rules, subject only to the practicalities of distance'. The provincial exchanges could retain their own trading-floors but dual capacity must be ended after a transition period of three years. This the provincial exchanges agreed to but London remained reluctant to concede direct access to its trading-floor for provincial members. It was not until December 1970 that London accepted the principle of equality for all, including direct access to jobbers. London brokers were well aware that the existence of the provincial brokers constituted a loophole in the fixed commission rules which could be exploited by major institutional investors, like the merchant banks, and that it was necessary to pay a price to close it.[50]

Even after the difficult issues regarding dual capacity and access to jobbers had been resolved, there still remained other problems that could have blocked the merger. One such was the question of the assets being contributed by each exchange to the new unified body. Those possessed by

[48] LSE: Council, 9 Nov. 1976, cf. 26 Nov. 1974, 27 May 1975, 18 May 1976, 1 Mar. 1977, 3 May 1977, 16 May 1978.

[49] Ibid., 6 Nov. 1979, 4 Dec. 1979.

[50] Ibid., 26 May 1970, cf. 9 Mar. 1970, 18 May 1970, 9 Nov. 1970, 3 Dec. 1970, 28 June 1971, 5 July 1971, 12 July 1971, 13 Dec. 1971, 10 Jan. 1972, 17 Jan. 1972.

London, consisting largely of its building in the City of London, were valued at £21m. being equivalent to £6,356 per member. In contrast, the total value of the assets owned by all the provincial stock exchanges was put at a mere £0.5m., or £500 per member, as most did not own the freehold of the buildings they occupied. The wealthiest of the provincial exchange was the Scottish with property worth £261,828 (£1,329 per member) and the poorest was either Belfast (£15,389; £453 per member) or the Northern (£72,414; £203 per member) depending upon how it was measured. However, as there was no expectation of selling the London property or capitalizing its value among the membership, it was agreed to combine the assets and share them equally.[51] The next issue that blew up was the question of the Dublin Stock Exchange, which also included the Cork Stock Exchange from March 1971. This was to become part of the unified stock exchange but was located in a separate country with its own currency. Regardless of that problem it was decided to include Dublin as it had been, and still was, such an integral part of the British securities market. At that stage currency fluctuations were not seen as a major problem.[52]

With the problems either solved or ignored the date for the amalgamation of all 'British' stock exchanges into one single organization was set for 25 March 1973, with dual capacity firms to cease operations by April 1974. Most were already in the process of converting into brokers, recognizing that they could not survive on dealing alone. Certainly it was clear from an early stage that all provincial business was already beginning to be centralized in London when it was decided to abandon work on an inter-exchange stock payment scheme because of lack of demand. As it was, the merger added a further 1,131 members to the 3,733 already belonging to London. (Northern—391; Midland and West—222; Scottish—195; Provincial—184; Ireland—109; Belfast—30). This greatly reinforced the London Stock Exchange's ability to enforce its rules and regulations throughout the British securities market as now all involved in the business had to accept them if they wanted to remain members. The last anomaly remaining were the two dual capacity firms. Rensburg & Co. of Liverpool split itself into two separate firms in February 1974 but Campbell, Neil & Co. of Glasgow managed to get a one-year extension, but were not allowed to continue beyond 5 April 1975. Consequently, by the mid-1970s the London Stock Exchange had, for the first time in its existence, administrative control over all the stockbrokers and jobbers in the British Isles. The creation of a single exchange was a long overdue move considering the increasing integration within the British securities market. The open access that all brokers now had to jobbers was a boost to the efficiency of the market as the great volume of business passing through London could justify keener prices and easier matching of bargains. In one sense it had achieved a monopoly position. Of course this monopoly

---

[51] Ibid., 12 July 1971.     [52] Ibid., 29 Mar. 1971, 13 Dec. 1971.

was, at best, a partial one and only extended to the market in British corporate securities. For UK government debt there continued to exist the market provided by the discount houses, who dominated the short-dated issues, while for foreign or international securities the North American brokerage houses and European banks were active traders. Try as they might the London Stock Exchange could not prevent even their own members trading with them. When it did restrict the activities of its members, in order to limit the growth of an outside market, the result was the loss of business, as in the case of the Eurodollar market.[53]

## TECHNOLOGY AND COMPETITION

The role of the London Stock Exchange was not simply to monitor and supervise the activities of its members, ensuring that all obeyed the rules and regulations that governed their collective activities. Integral to this was the provision of the market place itself that members used to transact business, apart from that which could be done from the office by telephone. At the beginning of the 1970s the focus of this market was still the trading-floor located within the Stock Exchange building. It was quickly recognized that this building was inadequate because of the changing structure of the membership. Amalgamation had created larger and larger firms of jobbers that wanted to be grouped together rather than spread across the trading-floor catering for specific markets as individual jobbers had in the past. The Stock Exchange responded to this need by creating a new trading-floor which was opened on 11 June 1973. At this stage there was no conception that the floor of the Stock Exchange would not continue to be the focus of its members buying and selling operations, and it was up to the Stock Exchange to provide them with the most appropriate facilities they would require. To that end the London Stock Exchange were more and more willing to permit members access to the fastest possible communications between the floor and their offices, recognizing that both locations were essential for the maintenance of an active market. Large firms like de Zoetes, Grieveson Grant, and Laurie Milbank, for example, were permitted to operate radio links between the floor and their offices in 1970 while fax machines were introduced in 1971. The Stock Exchange were also fairly relaxed about the access members had to current prices, through the Market Price Display Service (MPDS), as long as these were not sufficiently current so as to allow outside markets to develop.[54]

---

[53] LSE: Council, 23 Feb. 1970, 6 July 1970, 20 July 1970, 21 July 1970, 21 Sept. 1970, 14 Jan. 1971, 1 June 1971, 3 July 1972, 10 July 1972, 16 Oct. 1972, 19 Mar. 1973, 26 Mar. 1973, 12 Feb. 1974, 4 Mar. 1975; W. A. Thomas, *The Provincial Stock Exchanges* (London 1973), 279, 325; W. A. Thomas, *The Stock Exchanges of Ireland* (Liverpool 1986), 202, 205, 228, 236, 246.

[54] LSE: Council, 26 Oct. 1970, 17 Apr. 1973, 5 June 1973, 27 July 1970, 8 Mar. 1971, 4 Dec. 1972.

Nevertheless, the possibility of a trading system that would bypass the trading-floor by linking all brokers and jobbers offices in one system, was under discussion throughout the 1970s. The Stock Exchange were first alerted to these new development by K. H. M. Crabbe, of the jobbers R. A. Blackwell & Co., after he returned from a visit to the United States. When there he had seen a new computer system—the Block Automation System—at the New York Stock Exchange. This had the potential to match buying and selling orders electronically. There were also outside computer bureau's that were also attempting to provide electronic market places. Both excited by the potential and alarmed at the threat the London Stock Exchange immediately formed a committee to investigate the capabilities and limitations of such systems.[55] After a visit to the United States this committee reported its findings which created a dilemma for the Stock Exchange. On the one hand the Stock Exchange was keen to develop communication systems which would keep members in touch with each other, both on the trading-floor and in their offices. As the report noted '. . . a highly sophisticated communication system under the control of the London Stock Exchange could be of benefit in that it would speed up communication and possibly help to move lines of stock'. Here the only objection was on grounds of cost. On the other hand they were most unwilling to fund, or even permit, a communication system that could also be used for dealing, so bypassing completely the physical trading-floor located within the Stock Exchange building. If that took place they could only envisage it to be disadvantageous to the Stock Exchange. It would draw business away from its trading-floor, and so undermine is ability to handle large transactions at close prices because not all business was passing through it. At the same time it would make the Stock Exchange's task of policing the market more difficult as it would be impossible to monitor such transactions.

As it was, the Stock Exchange came to the conclusion that it could shelve any decision. Despite the ability of computers to match bargains that was not regarded as '. . . a serious competitor to orthodox methods of dealing where personal judgement is important'. The only area where a computer system could make a contribution was in small transactions because that '. . . usually requires little personal judgement other than dealing at the most advantageous price'. However, considering the expense of the computer system needed and the limited volume of business that would be generated by small transactions, the cost of such a dealing system could not be justified. This was despite the view of the New York Stock Exchange's expert on computer dealing systems, Andy Hays, who envisaged an eventual end to the traditional trading-floor. Though this view was supported by Jay Perry of Salomon Brothers, it was the minority view in New York

---

[55] Ibid., 6 Apr. 1970, 13 Apr. 1970.

at the time. Nevertheless, this visit to New York did make the London Stock Exchange aware of the developments taking place in the securities market that were undermining the control exercised by traditional stock exchanges. It was becoming clear that non-members had gained a significant share of the business even in those stocks quoted on the New York Stock Exchange. Weeden & Co. were one of the leading outside brokers in New York and, when dealing in selected shares quoted on the New York Stock Exchange, they accounted for around a third of all transactions. From 1964 onwards these non-members of stock exchanges had begun the development of a nation-wide dealing system based on the twin technologies of telecommunications and computing. By 1968 they were in a position to invest $15m. in such a system, which was to come on stream in 1970. This system— NASDAQ (National Association of Securities Dealers Automated Quotations) would provide instantaneous quotes on over-the-counter stocks allowing all participants to trade by telephone on the same basis, wherever located. Again, the London Stock Exchange chose to ignore these new developments though there was an obvious parallel between itself and the New York Stock Exchange.[56]

Though the London Stock Exchange may not have considered that computing technology offered either threat or opportunity, the major institutional investors of the City of London saw it as a weapon in their campaign to obtain reductions in the commission rates on volume business. In December 1971 planning for a London-based automated block-trading system was begun by the merchant banks, with the expectation that it would be in use sometime during 1973, if no concessions on commission were forthcoming. Though reductions were obtained by the merchant banks they were not considered sufficient, and so the development of the system went ahead. By September 1972 it even had a name—ARIEL (Automated Real-time Investments Exchange)—and was expected to offer a cheaper service than the Stock Exchange in those transactions worth £20,000 and over. The Stock Exchange was now taking this threat seriously, and had despatched another fact-finding mission to the United States. This discovered that three computer-based systems were now in operation, namely Instinet (backed by the New York Stock Exchange), Autex (backed by the American Stock Exchange), and NASDAQ. None had, as yet, attracted a great deal of custom, with Instinet's turnover put at 0.25 per cent of the New York Stock Exchange's own turnover. As a result the matching of buyers and sellers was proving difficult. Though the results from New York did stiffen the London Stock Exchange's unwillingness to give further concessions to the institutions, they were aware that they were running a risk that the ARIEL system would prove a success. It was backed by substantial institutional

---

[56] LSE: Council, 4 Jan. 1971; R. O'Brien, *Global Financial Integration: The End of Geography* (London 1992), 1–2; A. Hamilton, *The Financial Services Revolution: The Big Bang Worldwide* (London 1986), 16, 43.

investors who were keen to reduce their current transaction costs, which were higher than New York's, and who were unhappy with the existing price information service, which was slower than in New York. Consequently, the London Stock Exchange was persuaded to respond to the challenge by lowering its charges and improving its service. The New York Stock Exchange had already lost the markets in US government bonds, fixed interest stocks, and insurance and bank shares to non-members and was relying on legislation to recover them.[57]

Faced with this threat from ARIEL the London Stock Exchange also adopted negative tactics by prohibiting its members from using it. These negative tactics did prove effective for they removed from the system the very people—the jobbers—whom the large institutional investors wanted as market-makers. However, it did not stop the continuing development of ARIEL. At the same time the Stock Exchange started to assess the possibility of using such a system for its own use, and even considered co-operation with the Paris Bourse on the development of in-house automated dealings. There was even an attempt to buy ARIEL and bring it under the control of the Stock Exchange, where it was to be used for dealings in Eurodollar bonds, involving both members and non-members. This was turned down by ARIEL's sponsors, the Accepting Houses Committee, who continued to use it as a weapon to extract further reductions in commission changes. These were being resisted by the Stock Exchange. With the prospect of real competition from ARIEL and the possibility of NASDAQ extending its operations to Europe, encouraged by the OECD, the Stock Exchange was increasingly worried about the impact computerized dealing systems would have on its control of the market. These fears were intensified towards the end of 1973 when it was informed that the New York Stock Exchange was proposing to abandon its fixed commission charges in order to compete with the outside markets, including NASDAQ, for the business of the institutions, who accounted for almost half of its turnover.[58]

Certainly, by the mid-1970s the London Stock Exchange was fully aware of the challenge posed by computerized dealing systems, used in conjunction with the telephone. Among its own membership there had been a considerable investment in dealing rooms located within the offices of brokers and jobbers. These were only actively used in the hour before the Stock Exchange opened at 9.30 a.m. and in the hour and a half after it closed at 3.30 p.m. Having provided these dealing rooms at considerable expense, the member firms were reluctant to see them stand empty for six hours while their staff traded on the floor of the Stock Exchange. Consequently,

[57] LSE: Council, 6 Dec. 1971, 25 Sept. 1972, 22 Jan. 1973.

[58] Ibid., 19 Feb. 1973, 10 Apr. 1973, 24 Apr. 1973, 29 May 1973, 11 Sept. 1973, 18 Sept. 1973, 13 Nov. 1973, 2 Apr. 1974, 16 Apr. 1974; Hamilton, *Financial Services Revolution*, 117–18.

there was a demand for either longer trading hours on the floor of the Stock Exchange, removing the need for expensive dealing rooms, or greater investment in a computerized system that would make greater use of the dealing rooms. As it was, longer hours were generally unpopular and the investment in dealing rooms had become a necessity, whatever the Stock Exchange did. What was happening was that the process of amalgamation among the brokers and jobbers had reached such a stage that they were able to finance dealing facilities of their own that could match those available on the floor of the Stock Exchange. Advanced telecommunications already allowed those manning these dealing rooms to maintain constant contact with each other while the use of computing technology allowed them to handle both information flows and orders from numerous sources simultaneously. It was becoming possible to replicate the physical trading-floor electronically though it still did not have the capacity to cope with rapidly changing prices and a high volume of transactions involving numerous buyers and sellers—the conditions of active markets.[59]

When ARIEL did begin to operate in 1974 the Stock Exchange adopted a wait and see policy. It was prepared to withdraw discounts on commission from those who used it, such as the banks, but was reluctant to go this far and provoke even greater investment in an alternative market. What they did do was refuse permission for ARIEL to subscribe to Extel, which cut it of from direct access to both current prices and news from the Stock Exchange itself. As it was ARIEL did not prove to be a success for those that had backed it. Without the participation of the jobbers, who were in a position to act as counterparts to any deal at prices close to those currently prevailing, the financial institutions were left dealing with each other. Unfortunately for them too few were involved to make the market viable while any deal was only too visible, revealing each other's investment strategy as soon as it began. Thus the threat posed by computerized dealing systems receded in London in the 1970s, compared to New York where NASDAQ proved a success. Nevertheless, the Stock Exchange remained conscious that its floor-based trading system was under threat from the development of outside markets, aided by continuing advances in communications and computing. The growth of the market in Eurodollar bonds, which took place without any physical trading-floor, was a continuing example of what was possible. As it was, ARIEL probably achieved what its backers wanted, which was to force the Stock Exchange to give substantial discounts on the commission charged on high volume business, for this had been achieved by the late 1970s.[60]

[59] LSE: Council, 5 Feb. 1974, 19 Mar. 1974, cf. R. C. Michie, 'Friend or Foe: The London Stock Exchange and Information Technology since 1850,' *Journal of Historical Geography*, 23 (1997), 304–26.
[60] LSE: Council, 26 Feb. 1974, 19 Dec. 1973, 19 May 1975, 20 Sept. 1977.

These fears that current prices could be used to create outside markets did restrict the Stock Exchange's own attempt to develop a market information service for both its members and investors generally. Not only was the existing service to British subscribers considered unsatisfactory, because it did not offer immediate access to current prices, but there was also a growing demand for British prices from such continental European centres such as Frankfurt, Amsterdam, Zürich, and Paris. This was met by Reuters but they only supplied closing prices. There did exist a market data and information service—Datastream—which had originally been developed by the brokers Hoare, Govett & Co. for their clients. The Stock Exchange saw this as a basis for a system of its own, which would supply prices and other relevant material to the membership and selected subscribers. However, Hoare, Govett & Co. were not willing to relinquish control of the system, having built it up themselves. This left the Stock Exchange with its own Market Price Display Service, which had 231 subscribers in 1973, of whom 71 were non-members.

Co-operation with Reuters was also pursued as they were trying to develop a service that would display current prices for securities along with other financial information, such as exchange and money market rates.[61] By April 1974 Reuters had in place a system that would allow London prices to be displayed in Tokyo within four seconds. The Stock Exchange had accepted in September 1973 that:

... the world-wide provision and reception of market information through visual display screens will in future become a vital aspect of the business of the Stock Exchange and its member firms.

Not only would this be a service to its members but the provision of such a service could itself be a profitable business for the Stock Exchange. Unlike Reuters, however, the Stock Exchange were determined that no such service could also be used for dealing purposes in securities where it provided the market, as with domestic equities. In foreign securities its attitude was entirely different,

The Council of the Stock Exchange accept the existence of a trend towards the computerised visual presentation of bids and offers for securities. They are also of the opinion that there may well be a need for a 'visual floor' to facilitate international deals in Eurodollar Bonds.[62]

This was a market the Stock Exchange had lost and a 'virtual reality' trading-floor offered a possibility of recapturing it.

With the object of capturing this market in international securities the London Stock Exchange pursued a policy of active co-operation with the

---

[61] Ibid., 22 Jan. 1973, 29 Jan. 1973, 3 Apr. 1973, 17 Apr. 1973, 8 May 1973, 5 June 1973, 25 June 1973, 16 Apr. 1974.                      [62] Ibid., 11 Sept. 1973.

Paris Bourse. The idea was to distribute prices and information via computer screens. '. . . the activity and liquidity of markets can be improved if the order givers are able to follow their movements and know what transactions they could make upon them', was the principle that underlay the willingness to make current prices available, for it would both increase the number of transactions and channel them through members of the Stock Exchange. What was envisaged were two systems. One would display the prices of active stocks and be aimed at financial institutions and market intermediaries. The other would cover a greater number of stocks and would be directed towards those who required general information about the state of the market. Despite the potential of each system, especially the former, it was not to be used for dealing purposes but only to supply information.[63]

However, the discussions with Paris led nowhere and the Stock Exchange was tempted to sell its own price display system—MPDS—to Reuters, who would then broadcast London prices world-wide. It was only through the intervention of the broker Dundas Hamilton, that this did not take place. He pointed out that, by selling MPDS the Stock Exchange would be giving up control of its own price information which could then be used by Reuters as the basis of an alternative dealing system based on screens, not the trading-floor. This was the very possibility that the Stock Exchange wanted to avoid for, if they lost control over who had access to the market, their power to impose common standards of behaviour as well as fixed commissions and single capacity would disappear. As a result the Stock Exchange drew back from closer involvement with Reuters and decided to take greater direct control itself. Extel, for example, had previously collected and distributed prices but, after 1975, it was only to distribute, paying the Stock Exchange for the supply of prices. With the real threat of electronic markets, whether in the form of ARIEL or provided by Reuters, the Stock Exchange now regarded the prices generated on its floor as a major weapon in limiting the competition it faced. Without current prices it was difficult for outside markets to operate unless they also possessed such a volume of transactions that their prices reflected the state of supply and demand as accurately as those of the Stock Exchange. Such was the case with Eurobonds but was not so in domestic securities, especially after the merger with the provincial stock exchanges.[64]

When Hoare, Govett sold their Datastream service in 1976 the Stock Exchange were tempted to buy it, simply to prevent its conversion into an automated trading facility that would rival the Stock Exchange itself. However, the purchase price was considered too high and they were not in a position to block the sale. They remained in a position, though, to control access to their prices. Instead they introduced in 1977 their own

[63] LSE: Council, 8 Jan. 1974.
[64] Ibid., 21 May 1974, 28 May 1974, 29 Oct. 1974, 17 June 1975.

information and data service—EPIC—while in 1978 they began the development of a new price display system—TOPIC—so confirming their desire to control all the prices and information that emanated from the Stock Exchange. In the past the Stock Exchange had been able to maintain its control over both the market and its members by restricting physical access to the trading-floor. In the electronic age the equivalent was access to prices and data displayed on electronic screens, and the Stock Exchange was determined to extend its control to include these as well.[65] However, there were two elements to the electronic method for the same system could be used for display and dealing. At this stage the Stock Exchange's aim was to monopolize both functions but it faced competition in this from providers such as Reuters, who saw the electronic display of financial data as a natural extension of their information gathering service. There were even those in the Stock Exchange itself who saw competition with the likes of Reuters as a fruitless task and advocated co-operation instead. A report in October 1979 concluded that:

The vital part of communications was the data bank and the strength of the Stock Exchange lay in the information it held; actual dissemination however, should be left to others.[66]

The Stock Exchange could have focused on the development of an electronic market place rather than try to compete with established information providers, simply because their members generated the prices. However, at this stage the fear was that a display system could become a dealing system, and this forced the Stock Exchange to try and control both.

The other aspect of the Stock Exchange's activity that was being transformed by the advent of computers was the settlement of transactions and the accompanying payments. This had become a serious problem by 1970 because of the extra work involved in completing sales and purchases of shares compared to gilt-edged stock. In the gilt-edged market all transactions were settled by delivery to or from a jobber's account at the price and amount agreed. However, because of the volume and variety of transactions in shares, with numerous individual investors and companies involved, a clearing system operated for the most actively traded securities. This eliminated all but the original and final sale and purchase. At the same time for those numerous but less actively traded securities settlement was carried out in brokers' own offices and these were in the majority. Between two-thirds and three-quarters of all transactions were settled in the offices of members rather than centrally. With the fortnightly account period the work involved was concentrated at the end of the account, when the Settlement Department was very busy and delays often occurred. At other times the Settlement Department was inactive and over-staffed. One suggestion made in

---

[65] Ibid., 27 July 1976, 25 Aug. 1977, 1 Aug. 1978.
[66] Ibid., 2 Oct. 1979, cf. 1 Aug. 1978.

1970, in order to solve the problem was a rolling account with every deal to be completed on the 11th day after it had taken place. This was opposed by the jobbers who wanted to maintain the fortnightly account as that gave them a specified period in which to try and match sales and purchases and so reduce the need to either borrow funds to finance holdings or borrow securities to meet sales. Any move towards a rolling settlement would increase jobbers costs, as they would have to borrow both money and securities, and so the plan was dropped. A move to weekly accounts also failed for the same reason, but it was imperative that action was taken for the costs involved, especially for staff, were escalating, due to the need to meet the fortnightly peaks in demand.

During 1970 it was estimated that there were 13.3 million transactions on the Stock Exchange, as sales and purchases flowed between brokers and jobbers. Of these 77 per cent were in outstanding issues of UK shares, compared to 10.3 per cent in gilt-edged and fixed-interest securities. Furthermore, half of all transactions in shares were for £1,000 or less, though they represented only 7 per cent of the total value of the business done. The total cost of settling these transactions was put at £31.6m. of which £14.4m. (67 per cent) were staff wages and salaries, and a further £2.4m. (11 per cent) for office space. If the Stock Exchange could develop a comprehensive settlement system to meet the need for a fast, efficient, and cheap means of matching transactions, it would further enhance its value to a membership at a time when electronic developments were eroding the value of the trading-floor it provided.[67]

At an average cost to a broker of £3.18 per transaction, including gilt-edged and new issues which were handled cheaply, the settlement system in place was considered expensive. As 83 per cent of settlement expenses were borne by brokers it helped to explain their inability to offer a low-cost service and their constant pressure to raise minimum charges. The New York Stock Exchange had already put in place a computerized system for recording the movement of securities and money from buyers and sellers. In contrast, the system in London was still based on the passing of tickets from hand to hand which were then processed either in the Stock Exchange's own Settlement Department or the offices of individual brokers and jobbers, depending on the securities involved. If an electronic system could be put in place which automatically matched original and final sales and purchases, and also included billing and payment system, large potential savings could be made. Consequently, by the middle of 1973 the development of a new settlement system, involving both the clearing of bargains and payments, was well underway.[68]

[67] LSE: Council, 13 July 1970, 14 Sept. 1970, 2 Nov. 1970, 16 Nov. 1970, 3 May 1971, 12 July 1971, 9 Oct. 1972, 16 Oct. 1972, 22 Jan. 1973.

[68] Ibid., 5 Oct. 1970, 22 Jan. 1973, 29 Jan. 1973, 17 Apr. 1973, 29 May 1973, 21 Aug. 1973.

What eventually appeared at the end of 1973 was a system called SEPON—Stock Exchange Pool Nominees. Under this system all settlement activity was transferred to the Stock Exchange, away from members' offices. In return both jobbers and brokers would be provided with a simpler, speedier, and more reliable system at less cost. Though the technology to do this was in place, having been pioneered by the New York Stock Exchange, what was still lacking was a legislative and administrative framework within which this new settlement and accounting system could operate. For a fully centralized system to work the legal title to stock belonging to jobbers, as their float, and passing through the market, would have to be held by the Stock Exchange, not the members or their clients. This involved a radical change and members would have to be persuaded of the merits of the new system. Despite that obstacle the Stock Exchange firmly believed that:

With the likelihood of continuing inflation the cost of handling certificates is bound to increase and it seems inevitable that the idea of a central stock depository will become a reality and the certificate will be eliminated altogether . . . the principle of transfer by title by book entry is likely to be the cornerstone of future developments.[69]

The Stock Exchange also estimated in 1974 that the new system would save members £8.3m. per annum (brokers—£7.1m., Jobbers £1.2m.), when it became fully operational by the end of the 1970s. By the end of 1974 this paperless settlement system now named TALISMAN (Transfer accounting and lodgement for investors, stock management for jobbers) had gained acceptance not only from the membership but among City institutions generally. As a result the Stock Exchange pressed ahead with a pilot scheme, due for introduction in October 1976. This was to be followed by a phasing-in of the full nation-wide service, which was expected to be completed by July 1979.

Unfortunately, the collapse of the market in 1974, the failure of a number of major firms, and the loss of quotation and membership had seriously undermined the Stock Exchange's finances, putting the future of the TALISMAN system in doubt. Though members were to be charged for the services provided under TALISMAN, which included the checking, accounting and delivery of bargains, the Stock Exchange was now doubtful if it could recoup the cost or make it pay. By the middle of 1975 it was estimated that TALISMAN would eventually cost £15.7m., of which one-third had already been spent. However, so committed was the Stock Exchange that it contemplated selling its own building and then renting it back, in order to finance further development of TALISMAN. Instead, the Stock Exchange tower was used as security for further loans in order to bring TALISMAN to a stage where it was, at least, self-financing and even

[69] Ibid., 11 Dec. 1973, cf. 2 Jan. 1974.

revenue producing. Attempts were made to reduce the costs of the system, especially staff, but it was also decided to raise the charges for the service. Initially TALISMAN had been sold to members and the City as offering huge cost savings in the areas of settlement and accounting. Now it was being sold as a greatly improved service that would have to be paid for. If necessary, the Stock Exchange was even willing to see commission rates rise, despite likely complaints from the public and City institutions, if that was the only way its members could afford the charges necessary to make TALISMAN a financial success.[70]

The Stock Exchange had become convinced that the operation of the market was in jeopardy, because of the amount of paper generated and the costs and difficulties of handling it, that any expense was justifiable in creating a comprehensive electronic alternative. At the same time the Stock Exchange saw that control of such a system would make it an indispensable element of the securities market at the very time that alternatives, such as ARIEL, were posing a threat. Consequently, the costs of the system, and its future revenue stream, were secondary considerations to the power a central settlement and payments system would give the Stock Exchange over the securities market. In the final extremity the system could always be made to pay by making it a charge on the income of the Stock Exchange, which could be increased by charging members more and companies higher quotation fees. The Stock Exchange was not yet fully aware of the changed conditions it was operating due to a more competitive enviroment. Therefore, even under the difficult conditions of the mid-1970s the Stock Exchange pressed ahead with the TALISMAN scheme.[71]

The relationship between the London Stock Exchange as an institution and its membership was altering significantly during the 1970s. Through developments like a centralized settlement and payments system the Stock Exchange was trying to ensure that it continued to play an important part in the activities of its members at a time when the need to use the floor was in decline. The growth of electronic information systems brought to every office the news and prices that, in the past, could only have been obtained through a visit to the floor of the Stock Exchange. At the same time the growing speed and sophistication of telephone communications was providing a means of trading between offices that also reduced the need for more than a daily visit to the floor. Even the Stock Exchange's role as the intermediator between its members and the Bank of England/Treasury was in doubt in the 1970s with the adverse rulings of the Monopolies and Mergers Commission and the referral to the Restrictive Practices Court. There must have been those among the membership who were beginning to question what they got in return for their membership fees, apart from

[70] LSE: Council, 12 Nov. 1974, 15 Apr. 1975.
[71] Ibid., 15 July 1975, 19 Aug. 1975, 21 Oct. 1975, 2 Oct. 1979; LSE: *Annual Reports*, 1975–9.

rules and regulations that restricted their ability to respond to new challenges and exploit new opportunities. However, this relationship between the Stock Exchange and the membership was also shifting because of changes in the composition of the membership. Throughout the 1970s there was a continuance of the trend towards the creation of larger but fewer firms, both among brokers and jobbers.

## CHANGE AMONG THE MEMBERS

Compared to the situation in the 1950s, when the Stock Exchange consisted largely of numerous individual members and small partnerships, by the 1970s a number of large firms now dominated the business it conducted. In the mid-1970s Phillips & Drew handled c.8 per cent of the turnover in long-dated gilts, 9 per cent in short-dated, and 3 per cent in equities. Capels, Hoares, and Scrimgeours, could boast two-dozen or more partners and were supported by three dozen or more authorized clerks. Firms like these were large-scale operations employing extensive support staffs and investing extensively in offices and equipment. Their subscription to the Stock Exchange was a mere 1 per cent of their costs of operation compared to 40 per cent for the salaries of brokers and dealers, 28 per cent for office employees, and 9 per cent for rent. In addition a further 22 per cent was spent on settlement, indicating why it had such a high priority for the Stock Exchange. Large firms were able to spread their costs over a large volume and variety of business, especially from the institutions, putting pressure on the smaller firms that offered a more personal service to private clients, but found it difficult to do so profitably at minimum levels of commission. Consequently, despite the rules restricting competition between brokers, both on price and approaching potential clients, the continuing trend was all for mergers. At the very least the larger firms were able to attract the most experienced staff as they could offer them a greater guarantee of continued employment, even during a cyclical downturn in activity. At the same time the Stock Exchange's own rules on the capital required by members and the training they possessed all made it more difficult for the small firms to exist. The result was that by February 1971 the membership of the Stock Exchange was divided into only 176 firms, which was 100 less than 1964, and 154 fewer than 1953. Medium-sized firms like de Zoete & Gorton and Bevan Simpson were merging in order to create a scale of operations big enough to compete for institutional business with the likes of Hoare, Govett and James Capel. When they merged in 1970 de Zoete was the tenth and Bevan Simpson the twentieth largest stockbroking firms, whereas in 1975 they were fourth.[72]

[72] Council, 26 May 1970, 3 Aug. 1970, 9 Nov. 1970, 11 Jan. 1971, 1 Feb. 1971, 8 Mar. 1971, 29 Mar. 1971, 13 Apr. 1971, 16 Oct. 1972, 19 June 1973, 6 Nov. 1973, 29 Oct. 1974, 5 Nov. 1974, A. Lorenz, *BZW: The First Ten Years* (London 1996), 13; W. J. Reader and D. Kynaston, *Professional Stockbrokers: A History of Phillips & Drew* (London 1998), 141, 158.

Nevertheless, even then there continued to be small partnerships conducting private client business, surviving quite adequately in an environment of fixed commissions and restrained competition. One such was Burge & Co., a seven-partner firm. They noted in April 1971 that

... we find that all our more worthwhile clients come to us through private recommendation, particularly as we, being a smaller firm, can offer a more personal service than our larger brethren.[73]

However, even they had to seek institutional clients in order to survive, because of the shortage of wealthy individuals with funds to invest and willing to pay the fees that brokers charged. Stockbrokers did try to economize, faced with rising costs, especially for wages and offices. There was a continuing relocation of back offices out the City. Grieveson Grant, for example, sited its back office in Tunbridge Wells in 1971. While Phillips & Drew sent theirs to Brentwood in 1974. However, members were expected to maintain an office of some kind within 700 yards of the Stock Exchange, which meant that the costs of maintaining two offices had to be borne.[74]

These underlying forces creating mergers were given an added boost in 1974, with the collapse of business, rapid inflation of wage costs, and difficult trading conditions. In the July of that year it was reported to the Stock Exchange that '. . . many firms are seeking to merge in order to reduce costs etc.'.[75] It was estimated that in the peak year of 1972 London brokers had shared an income of £183.4m., which was comfortably above their costs of c.£100m. consisting of 70 per cent spent on employees, 10 per cent on premises, and 15 per cent on equipment and other expenses. This left the c.3,000 London brokers with an average income of c.£25,000 per annum compared to c.£2,500 for their employees. However part of this was a return on the capital invested. In contrast, the collective income of the brokers fell to £142.3m. in 1973 and then to £118.9m. in 1974, or a drop of 35 per cent. By that stage it is doubtful if this income was covering the costs of operation which had risen substantially with rapid inflation. A firm like James Capel cut its London staff by 20 per cent between 1973 and 1975, reducing it from 500 to 400 while Mullens closed its new dealing room, opened in 1972, and cut its staff from 230 to 170, or by 22 per cent. All firms were under severe pressure to cut costs. Overall, it was estimated that the total number of staff employed by London members of the Stock Exchange fell from 14,149 in December 1973 to 9,717 in December 1974, or a reduction of 31 per cent in the space of a single year. A similar contraction of employment took place among members located outside London. As this enormous collapse was spread over so many firms in

[73] LSE: Council, 26 Apr. 1971.
[74] Ibid., 17 May 1971, 12 Feb. 1973; Reader and Kynaston, *Phillips & Drew*, 147.
[75] LSE: Council, 2 July 1974, cf. 29 Oct. 1974.

different locations it largely passed unnoticed by anyone other than the Stock Exchange itself, and was certainly not lamented in the country at large. No government enquiry was launched or state assistance provided! The result for London was that the number of brokerage firms fell to 129 by January 1975 which was 39 less than 1973. Mergers continued in the late 1970s with two medium-sized brokers, Sebags and W. I. Carr, coming together in 1979. Even those firms specializing in serving private clients, like Raphaels and Zorn & Leigh Hunt saw advantages in scale, and so merged in 1976.[76]

As a consequence a small number of firms came to dominate disproportionately the Stock Exchange. By 1975 the 10 largest firms of brokers and jobbers provided almost 20 per cent of the London Stock Exchange's membership, and conducted most of the business. More importantly with stockbroking firms the size of Grieveson Grant (71 members of the Stock Exchange) or Hoare, Govett (58 members) they were more and more able to provide themselves with facilities that, in the past, they would have had access to only through the floor of the Stock Exchange. They were able to establish branches in other financial centres, invest heavily in modern communications equipment, and maintain specialist staff in their offices. As a consequence they were able to create their own network, even extending overseas, and so meet many of the needs of their institutional clients from within their own resources. Cazenoves, for example, which emerged as one of the leading institutional brokers in the 1970s had some 200 staff in London by 1979, plus offices in New York, Johannesburg, Hong Kong, and Bermuda.[77]

However, the problem in London remained the inability to either establish relationships with other financial groups like the banks, or obtain the large injections of capital necessary to compete with European banks and North American brokerage houses. There remained a rigid ceiling of 10 per cent on the level of outside ownership permitted in a stockbroking firm. This was not attractive to non-members as it offered no degree of control or possibility of integrating operations, to warrant the investment of the large sums necessary to build up either nation-wide stockbroking operations or international activities. Consequently, despite the ending of the restriction on establishing branches within the British Isles, that came with unification, it was little pursued by members of the London Stock Exchange. Instead, what took place was co-operation between brokers in different centres and a growing centralization of business in London. Similarly, though London brokers did expand their operations internationally none

[76] Ibid., 23 Dec. 1974, 7 Jan. 1975, 14 Jan. 1974, 11 Feb. 1975, 24 June 1975, 29 July 1975; Reed, *Capel and Company*, 104; S. D. Chapman, *Raphael Bicentenary, 1787–1987* (London 1987), 44–6; D. Sebag Montefiore, *The Story of Joseph Sebag & Co.* (n.p. 1970), 61–2, 66, 69; D. Wainwright, *Government Broker: The Story of an Office and of Mullens and Company* (East Molesey 1990), 91; Reader and Kynaston, *Phillips & Drew*, 150.

[77] LSE: Council, 11 Feb. 1975, 28 Oct. 1975; Kynaston, *Cazenove*, 274, 284, 286, 297–8.

came to match the activities of the New York investment banks or retail brokers, like Merrill Lynch. What the unification of the Stock Exchange in 1973 had done was create an influx of small provincial stockbroking firms. In November 1973 the London membership of 3,733 was grouped into 186 firms, or 20 members per firm, while the 1,131 members outside London were served by 205 firms, or 5.5 members each. These, like their counterparts in London, were committed to the maintenance of rules and regulations that limited the competition they had to face. That would be greatly intensified if they had to compete with a few well-capitalized firms possessing strong links with either commercial banks, and their extensive retail networks, or merchant banks, with their strong connections to institutional investors. Thus, not only were these new members committed to fixed commissions and single capacity but they also had no intention in permitting the emergence of large integrated operations. Nothing could be done about the rule changes already made, as with the ending of the ceiling on the number of partners, incorporation, and limited outside participation, but there was to be no further liberalization in the 1970s, after unification. The Council of the Stock Exchange could recognize the need to change and agree on the need to permit full competition between members and to adopt a more liberal attitude towards non-members, such as the London branches of New York brokerage firms, but such wishes did not translate into rule changes. It was only the largest firms, and especially those in London, that could spare partners to attend to general Stock Exchange affairs and serve on the various committees. Consequently, these committees were not necessarily representative of the views of the majority and were thus rejected or ignored by the membership as a whole. Whereas the London Stock Exchange had become increasingly dominated by large firms, and this had been producing change in the late 1960s/early 1970s, unification restored the influence of the small broker doing a largely private client business. Though the collapse of business in 1974, followed by the difficult conditions of the rest of the decade, with a combination of inflation and high taxation, did work to the advantage of the large institutional brokers in the long run, its more immediate impact was to encourage a conservative attitude to change. Certainly there was no willingness to see fixed commissions or single capacity abandoned, or permit any other relaxations in the rules and regulations.[78]

Whereas brokers could operate behind rules and regulations that limited competition and guaranteed fixed charges jobbers existed in a much more competitive environment. Rules did exist that tried to force brokers to bring business to the jobbers or gave jobbers a share of the income from the deals that bypassed them, but these were difficult to enforce. The growth of ever-larger stockbroking firms inevitably increased the opportunities to match

[78] Sebag-Montefiore, *Sebag & Co.*, 20; LSE: Council, 20 Nov. 1973, 12 Nov. 1974, 28 Jan. 1975, 27 May 1975, 30 Mar. 1977, 16 May 1978, 4 Dec. 1979.

sales and purchases internally, using prices from the floor, because a larger proportion of the business would be passing through these firms. Conversely, jobbers were prevented from responding to this challenge through spreading their contacts outside the restricted clientele of members of the Stock Exchange. Brokers were jealous of the exclusive access to jobbers that membership of the London Stock Exchange gave them, and keen to ensure that it stayed that way. The Stock Exchange responded to any reports from brokers concerning jobbers establishing contact with non-members by further tightening the rules. In contrast, it was much more reluctant to introduce rules that forced brokers to put their business through London jobbers, rather than outside dealers in London or abroad, or permit jobbers to establish operations on other exchanges. It was only in those markets largely lost to the London Stock Exchange, such as Eurodollars, or in specialist activities, like arbitrage, that any latitude in the rules was permitted to the jobbers. However, with much dealing taking place between offices, via the telephone, it did become more difficult to monitor the degree of external contact that jobbers had, and the purposes to which it was put. The Stock Exchange had long recognized that the buying and selling of securities internationally required jobbers to deal with non-members, and that was gradually extended in the 1970s, into the whole area of foreign securities, including those traded in London.[79]

As it was, the capacity of jobbers to provide a full market-making service continued to diminish as their numbers shrank and their capital base was eroded by inflation. By January 1975 there were only 16 London jobbers still in existence compared to 21 in December 1972, due to mergers, withdrawals, and retirements. R. A. Blackwell, for example, merged with Greenwood & Harris, Wissman Bristowe and Alfred Hick and da Costa in the 1970s, while Wedd, Durlacher amalgamated with George Hill in 1971. Finally in 1974 Wedd, Durlacher and R. A. Blackwell teamed up to form the largest firm of jobbers on the Stock Exchange. The result was that in many of the less popular groups of securities only one or two firms of jobbers made a market, leading to wider prices and a limited ability to buy and sell at will. At the same time these jobbers continued to rely, largely, on the funds provided by their partners for the capital needed to support the markets they made. Only individuals and non-financial corporate bodies could contribute and then up to a maximum of one-third of the total. Even when it was decided to allow financial companies to participate, the limit was set at 10 per cent, discouraging most of those interested. Jacob Rothschild's Rothschild Investment Trust did take a 10 per cent stake in the largest firm of jobbers, Wedd, Durlacher, but sold it back to the partnership when it was clear that it could not be further increased and there was no possibility of establishing a close working relationship. Consequently, it

---

[79] Ibid., 3 Aug. 1970, 17 May 1971, 12 Feb. 1973, 24 Apr. 1973, 19 June 1973, 31 July 1973, 4 Dec. 1973, 5 Feb. 1974, 7 May 1974, 23 July 1974, 12 Nov. 1974, 1 Mar. 1977.

was difficult for London jobbers to carry securities in the expectation of reversing the deal in the future, because they did not possess the capital reserves to fund such an operation themselves or provide sufficient margin for large loans from banks. Many of their operations were financed by bank borrowings, with interest charges amounting to £3.6m. per annum in 1973/4, but their prime object was to close any open position within the trading day or, at least, over the account period, so avoiding the need to finance holdings of securities. Thus they were not in a position to compete with the New York investment houses or European banks in the Eurodollar markets where it was necessary to finance large holdings of securities in order to supply the market when an opportunity arose. Increasingly their activities were confined to the most actively traded British corporate securities for here they were able to buy and quickly resell with little difficulty. More than ever they were simply intermediaries between brokers rather than market-makers and risk-takers, and so vulnerable to brokers matching bargains internally or between each other.[80]

## MARKET OPPORTUNITIES

Throughout the 1970s the primary aim for the London Stock Exchange was to maintain its control over the domestic market for securities. The merger with the provincial stock exchanges in 1973 was itself driven by the desire to remove a main source of competition for such a market. At the beginning of the 1970s the Stock Exchange had carried out an analysis of the business that it handled which confirmed the overwhelming importance of the domestic market for its members. A similar analysis, carried out at the same time, indicated that only 2.6 per cent of all sales and purchases were on behalf of foreign clients, plus another 1.6 per cent on arbitrage account, leaving 95.8 per cent being carried out for British investors.[81] With the unification of all British stock exchanges London was able to exert its influence over the entire market for British corporate issues. Even in companies with a strong regional following among investors, buying and selling now largely took place through London, and this became more marked as mergers and takeovers produced groups that had national or international identities rather than local or regional ones. By 1972 financial institutions already owned 35 per cent of all UK company shares and this rose to 47 per cent by 1978. Consequently, much of the buying and selling of shares was directed from London and this naturally fell into the hands of the London Stock Exchange.[82]

[80] LSE: Council, 27 Dec. 1972, 7 Jan. 1975, 11 Feb. 1975, 27 May 1975, 29 July 1975, 30 Mar. 1977; Lorenz, BZW, 16; Wedd, Durlacher, Mordaunt and Company, Members of the Stock Exchange (London 1984).

[81] LSE: Council, 26 Apr. 1970, 12 July 1971, 7 Feb. 1972, 8 May 1972, 25 Sept. 1972.

[82] Ibid., 23 Apr. 1974, 11 Feb. 1975; Thomas, Stock Exchanges of Ireland, 196–8, 228, 236, 246; Thomas, Provincial Stock Exchanges, 279, 317–18, 325; W. A. Thomas, The Big Bang (Oxford 1986), 17.

Nevertheless, despite the control that the London Stock Exchange exerted over the domestic market for corporate securities, the main business transacted, by value of turnover, continued to be in UK government debt. Turnover in British government securities grew from £27.3bn. in 1970 to £151.7bn. in 1980, or more than fivefold, while that in UK equities rose from £8.8bn. to £30.8bn. or less than fourfold over the same period.[83] Institutions also generated most of this business. In the survey done in August 1974 it was discovered that 92 per cent of all sales or purchases carried out in UK government short-dated securities were done on behalf of institutions with the average size of the deal being £0.5m. In longer-dated UK government stocks the institutions also dominated, being responsible for 88 per cent of all transactions, with an average size of £0.2m. It was only in the buying and selling of UK and Irish equities that individual investors played a prominent role, generating 21 per cent of the business in May 1974 and 29 per cent in August. Nevertheless, that still left institutions as the dominant element.

UK government debt thus continued to dominate the London Stock Exchange in the 1970s, especially with a Labour government creating ever more of it. The number of UK government stocks outstanding doubled in the 1970s, and their notional value grew ever more, from £21.1bn. to £71.9bn. (1970–80). Brokers like Phillips & Drew, with a specialist gilts department did well as a result, with profits rising from £1.4m. in 1974/5 to £3.6m. in 1978/9 as a result. Nevertheless, the focus of the members of the Stock Exchange was less and less on that market because the margins such business generated were small. The market in government debt was very competitive, with discount houses actively involved, while banks and insurance companies had the power and influence to demand volume discounts and reduced rates on the commissions charged by brokers. In another survey conducted in 1974 it was discovered that the commission income London brokers received from handling sales and purchases of UK government debt had fallen from one-third of their total income in the mid-1960s to around a fifth in the mid-1970s. In contrast the commission generated from handling the buying and selling of equities had grown from around half to about two-thirds. No wonder a major firm like Cazenoves, which had once conducted a large gilt-edged operation on behalf of institutional investors, abandoned the business in the early 1970s. Over the period 17–25 July 1972 Cazenoves estimated that only 1 per cent of its commission income came from transactions in gilt-edged compared to 93 per cent from ordinary shares and 6 per cent from debentures. Consequently, apart from a small business in foreign securities, such as mining stocks, and the interest of overseas investors in British multinationals like Shell, Unilever, BP, and ICI, the prosperity of the London Stock Exchange

[83] LSE: Council, June 1974, 5 Nov. 1974, 8, Apr. 1975; LSE: Quality of Markets, Apr.–June 1990, Tables CI and CIII.

in the 1970s rested on the market it provided in domestic corporate issues for, increasingly, British institutional investors. In the survey of 7 August 1974 it was revealed that there were only 656 transactions in short-dated gilts, though they totalled £100.3m., while there were 8,140 in UK/Irish equities for a total of £24m. Arranging the former was relatively simple and so the fee generated was correspondingly small, while the latter was more complex and time consuming, with the result that the charges were correspondingly higher. Thus, though the value of turnover might suggest that the London Stock Exchange depended on the market in UK government debt the number of transactions and the commission income of the brokers clearly revealed that the all-important market was British corporate securities.[84]

During the 1970s the nominal value of British government securities quoted by the Stock Exchange rose by £53bn. while that for industrial and commercial companies was a much more modest £11.8bn. However, in terms of market value the rise for government stock was only £44.7bn. while that for industrial and commercial companies it was £70.5bn. The result was to restrain the rise of UK government debt, as a proportion of quoted securities, to 21.7 per cent of the total market value in 1980, compared to 15.0 per cent in 1970, whereas that for industrial and commercial companies only fell from 55.0 per cent in 1970 to 47.2 per cent in 1980, of market value. More than ever the London Stock Exchange was now dominated by UK equities despite the expansion of British government debt in the 1970s. (Tables 11.1 and 11.2.) This British focus was partly forced on the London Stock Exchange because of the continuance of exchange controls until 1979, and the introduction of further government restrictions on foreign securities during the decade. Until their abolition exchange controls prevented UK residents from buying non-sterling securities unless through an authorized depository and with the permission of the Bank of England. In addition when a UK resident sold foreign currency securities 25 per cent of the money received had to be converted into sterling, with only the remaining 75 per cent being left free to use for the purchase of non-sterling issues. The result was a premium on the value of freely available dollars, which pushed up the cost of purchasing US securities. Regulations such as these greatly restricted the desire of British investors, especially individuals, from buying or selling foreign securities because of the costs and complexities it involved. These regulations also caught non-UK residents because their transactions might involve an intermediary stage, involving a sale or purchase in Britain, creating, at the very least, the problems of proving their tax-exempt status. Finally, the withholding-tax structure operated in Britain, where dividends and interest payments were taxed at source, deterred many potential foreign investors from buying UK

---

[84] LSE: Council, 7 Aug. 1972, 29 Oct. 1974, 26 Nov. 1974; Kynaston, *Cazenove*, 271, 292; Wainwright, *Mullens*, 103–4, 138; Reader and Kynaston, *Phillips & Drew*, 157–8.

Table 11.1. London Stock Exchange: Nominal and market values of securities quoted in 1970 and 1980 (£m.)

| Category of security | Nominal value | | | Market value | | |
|---|---|---|---|---|---|---|
| | 1970 | 1980 | Difference | 1970 | 1980 | Difference |
| British government | 21,638.4 | 74.652.4 | + 53,014 | 16,100.6 | 60,780.3 | + 44,679.7 |
| UK public bodies | 2,099.2 | 3,141.7 | + 1,042.5 | 1,710.4 | 2,678.1 | + 967.7 |
| TOTAL | 23,737.6 | 77,794.1 | + 54,056.5 | 17,811.0 | 63,458.4 | + 45,647.4 |
| Commonwealth governments | 735.5 | 252.1 | – 483.4 | 538.0 | 224.5 | – 313.5 |
| Foreign governments | 2,000.4 | 329.6 | – 1,670.8 | 1,403.0 | 5.4 | – 1,397.6 |
| Commonwealth/Foreign public bodies | 117.4 | 59.2 | – 58.2 | 67.7 | 241.7 | + 174.0 |
| TOTAL | 2,853.3 | 640.9 | – 2,212.4 | 2,008.7 | 471.6 | – 1,537.1 |
| Banks and discount houses | 1,470.5 | 4,370.2 | + 2,899.7 | 6,054.3 | 16,558.8 | + 10,504.5 |
| Financial, land, and investment | 2,201.4 | 3,243.5 | + 1,042.1 | 5,755.3 | 9,745.6 | + 3,990.3 |
| Insurance | 383.3 | 690.0 | + 306.7 | 2,140.1 | 5,187.5 | 3,047.4 |
| Property | 947.5 | 1,184.3 | + 236.8 | 1,758.3 | 3,591.3 | + 1,833.0 |
| TOTAL | 4,9577.7 | 9,488.0 | + 4,530.3 | 15,708.0 | 35,083.2 | + 19,375.2 |
| Utilities | 909.0 | 996.4 | + 87.4 | 2,695.7 | 4,147.0 | + 1,451.3 |
| Commercial/Industrial | 11,480.5 | 22,517.0 | + 11,036.5 | 56,105.7 | 123,114.3 | + 67,008.6 |
| Breweries/Distilleries | 1,192.6 | 1,837.1 | + 644.5 | 2,480.6 | 4,373.7 | + 1,893.1 |
| Shipping | 219.3 | 275.6 | + 56.3 | 486.1 | 623.1 | + 137.0 |
| TOTAL | 13,801.4 | 25,626.1 | + 11,8247 | 61,768.1 | 132,258.1 | + 70.490.0 |
| Mining | 891.1 | 951.1 | + 6.0 | 8,223.0 | 15,812.4 | + 7,589.4 |
| Oil | 947.5 | 3,128.4 | + 2,180.9 | 1,758.3 | 26,328.8 | + 24,570.5 |
| Plantations | 129.3 | 200.2 | + 70.9 | 136.7 | 1,320.9 | + 1,184.2 |
| TOTAL | 1,967.9 | 4,279.7 | + 2,311.8 | 10,118.0 | 43,462.1 | + 33,344.2 |
| Eurobonds: UK companies | — | 2,081.4 | + 2,081.4 | — | 1,663.2 | + 1,663.2 |
| Eurobonds: Foreign companies | — | 4,752.6 | + 4,752.6 | — | 3,931.3 | + 3,931.3 |
| TOTAL | — | 6,834.0 | + 6,834.0 | — | 5,594.5 | + 5,594.5 |
| TOTAL | 47,317.9 | 124,689.0 | + 77,371.9 | 107,413.8 | 280,327.9 | + 172,914.1 |

Sources: Stock Exchange Official Yearbook, 1970; Stock Exchange Fact Book, 1980.

securities because they could not reclaim it. Generally, the tax structure in the UK along with exchange controls made the development of an international securities business difficult, whether it involved British investors buying foreign securities, foreign investors buying British securities, or foreign investors simply using London as a convenient centre for global transactions. Try as they might the London Stock Exchange had little success in convincing the government that a relaxation of taxes, such as stamp duty, or a change in procedures would greatly assist in the expansion of this international business. In fact the government had no desire to see such business expand as it would create more opportunities for foreign exchange movements which might further destabilize the international

Table 11.2. London Stock Exchange: Nominal and market values of securities quoted in 1970 and 1980 (%)

| Category of security | Nominal value | | | Market value | | |
|---|---|---|---|---|---|---|
| | 1970 | 1980 | Difference | 1970 | 1980 | Difference |
| British government | 45.7 | 59.9 | + 245.0 | 15.0 | 21.7 | + 227.5 |
| UK public bodies | 4.4 | 2.5 | + 49.7 | 1.6 | 1.0 | + 56.6 |
| TOTAL | 50.2 | 62.4 | + 227.7 | 16.6 | 22.6 | + 256.3 |
| Commonwealth governments | 1.6 | 0.2 | − 65.7 | 0.5 | 0.1 | − 58.3 |
| Foreign governments | 4.2 | 0.3 | − 83.5 | 1.3 | — | − 99.6 |
| Commonwealth/ Foreign public bodies | 0.2 | — | − 49.6 | 0.1 | 0.1 | + 257.0 |
| TOTAL | 6.0 | 0.5 | − 77.5 | 1.9 | 0.2 | − 76.5 |
| Banks and discount houses | 3.1 | 3.5 | + 197.2 | 5.6 | 5.9 | + 173.5 |
| Financial, land, and investment | 4.7 | 2.6 | + 47.3 | 5.4 | 3.5 | + 69.3 |
| Insurance | 0.7 | 0.6 | + 80.0 | 2.0 | 1.9 | + 142.4 |
| Property | 2.0 | 0.9 | + 25.0 | 1.6 | 1.3 | + 104.2 |
| TOTAL | 10.5 | 7.6 | + 91.4 | 14.6 | 12.5 | + 123.3 |
| Utilities | 1.9 | 0.8 | + 9.6 | 2.5 | 1.5 | + 53.8 |
| Commercial/ Industrial | 24.2 | 18.1 | + 96.1 | 52.3 | 43.9 | + 119.4 |
| Breweries/ Distilleries | 2.5 | 1.5 | + 54.0 | 2.3 | 1.6 | + 76.3 |
| Shipping | 0.5 | 0.2 | + 25.7 | 0.5 | 0.2 | + 28.2 |
| TOTAL | 29.1 | 20.6 | + 85.7 | 55.0 | 47.2 | + 114.1 |
| Mining | 1.9 | 0.8 | + 6.7 | 7.7 | 5.6 | + 92.3 |
| Oil | 2.0 | 2.5 | + 230.2 | 1.6 | 9.4 | + 1,397.4 |
| Plantations | 0.3 | 0.2 | + 54.8 | 0.1 | 0.5 | 866.3 |
| TOTAL | 4.2 | 3.4 | + 117.5 | 9.4 | 15.5 | 329.6 |
| Eurobonds: UK companies | — | 1.7 | — | — | 0.6 | — |
| Eurobonds: Foreign companies | — | 3.8 | — | — | 1.4 | — |
| TOTAL | — | 5.5 | — | — | 2.0 | — |
| TOTAL | — | — | + 163.5 | — | — | + 161.0 |

Sources: As for Table 11.1.

value of the pound and threaten the precarious balance of payments position. The existence of this surrender requirement conditioned the way that British financial institutions invested abroad. Essentially, switching between foreign securities was made difficult and expensive for British investors, whether individual or institutional, because of the requirement to surrender 25 per cent of the foreign currency resulting which had been introduced as a temporary crisis measure in April 1965 by the Labour government but not removed until the end of 1977.[85]

As it was the Conservative government ignored the Stock Exchange's entreaties even extending the investment currency premium to the former sterling area in June 1972. This had detrimental consequences as dealings in those securities that could be traded elsewhere did leave London. Zürich even made a market in South African securities seeing the investment premium as an opportunity to displace London. The new Labour government, that came to power in 1974, was openly unsympathetic and made the situation even worse. Not only was stamp duty doubled but the 25 per cent surrender requirement was extended to the securities of the former sterling area. South African and Australian mining shares were one of the few international markets that the London Stock Exchange still retained by the mid-1970s. Extending that requirement to the remaining foreign securities in the 1970s dealt those markets a severe blow, as it reduced, considerably, any involvement from British investors, whether institutional or individual. Based on long-standing British interest in Australian, South African, and Hong Kong securities, active markets existed in these on the London Stock Exchange, with experienced jobbers and brokers ever ready to trade. In turn this attracted foreign investors, including those from the countries concerned, because London often possessed a better market for certain of the securities than existed domestically. It was estimated that prior to March 1974, when the 25 per cent surrender rule was extended to South African securities, only around 30 per cent of the London business done in South African gold-mining shares was done for UK residents compared to 70 per cent for foreigners. Deprived of this interest from British investors the volume of activity in gold-mining shares fell to half the January–March level by July 1974.[86]

The Stock Exchange's conclusion was that:

The market in London, although built upon the United Kingdom investors, has always been a market for the world. It now appears that we are less competitive than other markets, particularly for those customers such as the Swiss Banks, who have traditionally used the London market. There is considerable evidence that these investors now try New York and Johannesburg in South African stocks and deal

[85] LSE: Council, 1 June 1970, 24 Aug. 1970, 26 Apr. 1971, 20 Sept. 1971, 25 Oct. 1971, 19 June 1972, 9 Oct. 1972, 30 Apr. 1973.
[86] Ibid., 10 July 1972, 17 July 1972, 2 Apr. 1974, 24 July 1972, 5 July 1974, 15 Oct. 1974, 5 Nov. 1974.

directly in Australia. This has a snowballing effect on the liquidity of the London market because of the resultant loss of turnover.[87]

Not only was the international trading in securities such as these bypassing the London Stock Exchange but so was what remained of British investment, as with that of the financial institutions. That now went directly to markets abroad where it was possible to buy and sell in larger amounts and at closer prices. London brokers already possessed offices abroad through which such orders could be routed while the North American brokerage houses in London were joined by others from Australia and South Africa.[88]

The loss of part of its own market and the limited advances made generally on the international front cannot all be blamed on government policy in the 1970s though it was an important cause. The London Stock Exchange's continued unwillingness to modify its own practices, structures, and charges made, at least, an equal contribution. Changes were made in practices and charges in the 1970s but these were, always, too little and too late. Whenever the changes required posed any kind of threat to the brokers' position in the domestic securities market, as did the revision of the fixed commission structure or single capacity, then it was fiercely resisted. The result was that the measure was delayed, amended, or stopped. To most members any form of international business was either marginal, unimportant, or dangerous and so there was an extreme reluctance to extend any concessions to it in order to keep it.[89]

Among the membership it was the largest firms of brokers, like Capels, and jobbers, such as Wedd, Durlacher, that saw a promising future in the international market, especially European securities.[90] For most members of the Stock Exchange, business in foreign securities, or for foreign clients, was of minimal importance. Thus, it was impossible for the Stock Exchange to adapt sufficiently in order to expand this international business if the changes required threatened to undermine the rules and regulations that governed domestic operations.[91] When the changes required did not threaten the domestic market the Stock Exchange was able to adopt a liberal and welcoming position. However, the failure to adjust its basic rules and regulations made it almost impossible for the Stock Exchange to develop a

---

[87] LSE: Council, 5 Nov. 1974.

[88] Salisbury and Sweeney, *The Bull, the Bear and the Kangaroo*, 388; LSE: Council, 3 Apr. 1973, 20 Nov. 1973, 7 May 1974, 7 Jan. 1975, 23 Jan. 1975, 29 Apr. 1975, 1 Mar. 1977, 4 Dec. 1979.

[89] Ibid., 15 Nov. 1971, 26 Apr. 1971, 10 Jan. 1972, 24 Apr. 1972, 30 July 1972, 31 July 1972, 14 Aug. 1972, 24 July 1973, 23 Oct. 1973.

[90] Ibid., 10 July 1972, cf. 17 July 1972, 24 July 1972, 31 July 1972, 14 Aug. 1972, 18 Sept. 1972, 3 July 1973.

[91] Ibid., 30 Oct. 1973, 4 Dec. 1973, 5 Feb. 1974, 7 May 1974, 25 June 1974, 12 Nov. 1974, 26 Nov. 1974, 1 June 1971, 20 Mar. 1972, 25 Feb. 1975, 27 May 1975, 23 Sept. 1975, 1 Mar. 1977, 3 May 1977, 6 Nov. 1979, 4 Dec. 1979.

large international business. The fact that London—but not the Stock Exchange—did emerge as a major international market in securities in the 1970s indicates what was possible.[92] By the end of the 1970s, faced with the new world that the ending of exchange controls brought about, the Stock Exchange could only reflect on what might have been. As they noted in December 1979:

Overseas business came to the City but not the Stock Exchange . . .

and they went on to acknowledge that:

London brokers had lost substantially in both the primary and secondary Eurodollar markets and some of their client companies had raised loans in that market through overseas brokers.[93]

There can be no doubt that exchange controls along with close government supervision exercised by the Bank of England and the Treasury, had made it very difficult for the Stock Exchange to pursue its ambition to become the centre of the international securities market. However, it has to be said that its own failure to make the changes needed to be successful internationally, meant that the Stock Exchange itself contributed to its growing marginalization in the increasingly global market that characterized the 1970s. This can be seen clearly over the vexed question of arbitrage which needed to adopt new forms and methods in the 1970s if it was to survive as a Stock Exchange activity, but faced the opposition of most members to any relaxation of the rules for whatever reason. Minor relaxations in the rules regarding arbitrage were made during the 1970s but it was major relaxations that were required.[94]

Two new developments were taking place. First, international firms of brokers were appearing, led by the New York brokerage houses, that maintained offices in the major financial centres of the world and were members of the appropriate stock exchanges, when permitted. Naturally enough the most ambitious of the London brokers wanted to emulate these firms and so, by 1973, were operating subsidiaries in such places as Paris, Frankfurt, New York, Montreal, Hong Kong, Singapore, Sydney, and Tokyo. As a result arbitrage operations could be internalized within the same stock-broking firm, whether British, American, Australian, or South African, in the same way as it had already happened with European banks. In addition, with the improvements in communications and the declining importance of exchange and other controls, the price differentials between separate markets, for the same security, were becoming negligible or even disappearing, such was the speed of adjustment. In the Eurobond market

---

[92] Ibid., 26 Jan. 1970, cf. 8 Feb. 1971, 1 Mar. 1971, 17 May 1971, 20 Mar. 1972, 29 Jan. 1973, 17 Sept. 1974, 25 Feb. 1975.

[93] Ibid., 4 Dec. 1979, cf. 27 Dec. 1972.

[94] Ibid., 23 Oct. 1972, 18 Dec. 1972, 26 Mar. 1973, 19 Mar. 1974, 13 Aug. 1974, 31 July 1973.

there was only one electronic market place to which all major players had access, whatever their national origins. Thus, for major international securities brokers were less and less arbitraging between markets but directing their clients orders to that market place that offered the best service in terms of price, delivery amount, and cost. Arbitrage was becoming submerged beneath the global expansion of the securities business which first affected bonds and then involved equities.[95]

It was not only brokers that were being affected by these developments for jobbers were discovering that they had to operate internationally in certain securities, such as Australian mining shares, if they were to be able to match supply and demand at close prices on a constant basis. While the Stock Exchange was willing to allow brokers to set up operations abroad, though restricting their ability to do so through access to capital, it was much less willing to allow jobbers to do so. Jobbers were seen as the heart of the market in London and so could not be permitted to provide the same service for other stock exchanges. Otherwise the business that currently flowed to London brokers would be matched locally. All that the Stock Exchange would agree to was the right of jobbers to have a dealer overseas but who would only operate when the London market was closed, or to join exchanges in countries from where little business came. Stocken & Concannon, for example, were permitted to join the Boston Stock Exchange but Wedd, Durlacher were not allowed to join the Hong Kong Stock Exchange. Similarly, Wedd, Durlacher were only allowed to have a telex link to Goldman Sachs London office as a means of dealing with their New York office, but were not permitted to have direct dealings with New York brokers in London. Again, the Stock Exchange was protecting the position of the broker and his commission income, even though it put jobbers at a disadvantage in the international market by restricting the way they did business.[96] As Wedd, Durlacher observed in 1974

It has been our policy in creating the overseas Dealing Department at W. D. M. for European shares that there should be a price virtually at all times for a reasonable amount of shares on a basis competitive with what a Broker can obtain in any other parallel market. In order to achieve this, particularly in the case of securities which enjoy only a limited market in London, and where the principal market is elsewhere, it is essential to have first class communications, otherwise the jobber is at the mercy of a Broker who has more up-to-date price information than he has.[97]

As with brokers, jobbers were finding that they were dealing with an emerging global market in the 1970s and that required them to operate in and through a number of major financial centres, if they were to continue to make competitive markets in the most actively traded international issues,

---

[95] LSE: Council, 3 Apr. 1973, 14 May 1974, 28 Jan. 1975.
[96] Ibid., 31 July 1973, 4 Dec. 1973, 5 Feb. 1974, 14 May 1974, 23 July 1974, 12 Nov. 1975.
[97] Ibid., 23 July 1974, cf. 12 Nov. 1974, 28 Jan. 1975, 26 July 1977.

including those of major British multinationals. The restrictions imposed on them by the Stock Exchange made it difficult to compete in that market. The problem was that the London Stock Exchange continued to see developments in the international market as taking place through co-operation between stock exchanges rather than the global expansion of member firms. Thus, in the spirit of European co-operation there were grand designs to remove restrictions on membership, harmonize the regulations covering markets and create common systems for settling transactions and conveying inflation. However, on all these fronts there proved to be insuperable difficulties and few tangible results emerged in the 1970s.[98]

Therefore, the London Stock Exchange was not able to proceed internationally in the 1970s, as it had domestically, in creating a unified structure for the European securities market, while it was also unable to allow its members the freedom to organize and operate that would allow them to take advantage of the emerging opportunities in the global securities market. The result was that non-member finance houses, like the North American investment banks and the continental European universal banks, were able to capture the market because they already possessed the international representation and operations that were required. The 1970s witnessed the triumph of the member firm over the market organization and the actions of the London Stock Exchange helped to ensure that its membership were in no position to compete.

It was not only on the international front that the London Stock Exchange both failed to develop an institutional response to a new opportunity and stifled the ability of its own members to do so. The clearest example of such an occurrence in the 1970s was the case of options, which were of increasing popularity at a time of monetary instability following on from the collapse of the Bretton Woods system of managed currencies. Initially it was the Bank of England that was responsible for limiting the use of options in London because it regarded them as speculative and destabilizing devices. However, during 1973 the Bank had begun to appreciate how options could be used to limit rather than increase risk, as with transactions in foreign securities at a time of fluctuating exchange rates. As a result it relaxed its rules making it easier for those in the City of London, with deals sensitive to variations in the value of currencies and interest rates, to insure against adverse trends through an option contract. However, for members of the Stock Exchange the use of options was restricted to those provided by members. This worked satisfactorily for domestic securities but created severe problems for foreign securities, where option contracts were now increasingly required. As, by the mid-1970s, there was almost no active market in London in foreign securities there were also no options in such securities being offered by members. Instead, they were available from

[98] Ibid., 29 May 1973, 12 June 1973, 8 Jan. 1974, 26 Mar. 1974, 2 Apr. 1974.

non-members but the rules precluded their use. The Stock Exchange would not move from this position because it continued to view options in foreign securities as risky speculation.[99]

Nevertheless, despite the attitude of the Stock Exchange the use of options in London grew during the 1970s. The Chicago Board of Trade considered establishing an options exchange in London to cater for this demand. It was this that forced the London Stock Exchange to consider its own position, with the possibility of creating its own options exchange or collaborating with the Chicago Board of Trade.[100] After a visit to Chicago an enthusiastic report was produced which indicated that:

... this new concept is immensely attractive to large sections of the investment community, both institutional and private. They are aware of considerable demand for a European options market following upon the extraordinary success of CBOE [Chicago Board Options Exchange] during its two years of operation. The flexibility of the system enables many new types of investment strategy to be used.[101]

What was proposed was an Options Board of Europe (OBOE) which would be modelled on CBOE but owned by the Stock Exchange. There was an acceptance that the Stock Exchange had discouraged activity of this kind in the past, regarding it as speculation of little value, and that had had detrimental consequences. An options exchange was considered a way of recovering what the Stock Exchange had lost. In the light of this report the Stock Exchange immediately started to plan for the creation of a London options exchange.

This options exchange was to be entirely separate from the Stock Exchange itself, even though owned by it. It was to be located not on the floor of the Stock Exchange but on the third floor of the building and would have its own finances, management, membership, and clearing system. As such it would not compromise the rules and regulations under which the securities market operated. The Stock Exchange recognized that for the options exchange to be successful, it would have to attract the custom and even participation of the diverse financial institutions and firms of the City of London. The problem of the Stock Exchange's refusal to allow banks to join would, therefore, be avoided if the options exchange was separate. However, the proposed options exchange was not enthusiastically received by the various bodies that the Stock Exchange had to convince in order to obtain regulatory approval. The Bank of England was worried by the effects of such an exchange on the system of exchange control in place while the Labour government, through the Board of Trade, were not enthusiastic because of its perception that trading in options was little more than speculation. Nevertheless, a member of the Cabinet, Harold Lever, pressed the Stock Exchange to persevere because

---

[99] LSE: Council, 5 June 1973, 30 Oct. 1973.     [100] Ibid., 11 Mar. 1975.
[101] Ibid., 8 Apr. 1975.

. . . if the Stock Exchange felt that an options exchange provided a useful adjunct to the securities market, they would be foolish to be dissuaded from pursuing their objective by fears of political reaction.[102]

At this stage the main obstacle that the Stock Exchange faced was the financial one. The development of the TALISMAN settlement system was severely straining the Stock Exchange's finances and with the current state of the market there was little prospect of raising additional funds through charges on members or companies. Nevertheless, the Stock Exchange remained keen on the project believing that a European options exchange would make an important contribution to the operation of the securities market. However, further discussions with the Bank of England revealed a serious risk to the Stock Exchange if it went ahead and formed an options exchange. According to the Bank of England the government regarded options as highly speculative, so putting at risk the stability of the securities market and the ability of the Stock Exchange to police it. If this proved to be the case then the government would appoint a Stock Exchange Commission (SEC) to replace the system of self-regulation that had been in place since the Second World War. Whether this threat was real is unclear, considering the remarks by Harold Lever, for the Bank of England could have been using it as a means of reinforcing its long-standing opposition to options, which it had maintained since the war. Nevertheless, the Stock Exchange did take the threat very seriously, especially with a Labour government in power, and concluded that:

. . . we must balance the advantages of a European options market in London against the possibility of this hastening the establishment of the S.E.C. The continuation of self-regulation over our traditional business is more important than securing an European options market in London.

Out of this discussion came a decision to encourage and support the formation of an options exchange in another European financial centre.

. . . a joint venture in some other European centre, whether it be Paris, Amsterdam or Luxembourg, is well worth pursuing. If we cannot, for political reasons, have the whole cake in London, let us at least have half overseas.[103]

Though 'political reasons' were mentioned there must remain the suspicion that the Bank of England was keen to preserve its control over foreign exchanges by preventing the appearance of devices that would make its task more difficult.

As it was, the Dutch proved the most receptive to the initiative from London. By February 1976 the Amsterdam Stock Exchange had received permission from their Minister of Finance to investigate the possibility of creating a single European options market, with floors in both Amsterdam

---

[102] Ibid., 13 June 1975.      [103] Ibid., 29 July 1975.

and London. However, even this proposal met opposition from the Bank of England, which appeared to have set itself against any such market in London.[104] The middle of 1976 saw the Bank and the Stock Exchange on collision course over the options exchange, with the Stock Exchange deciding in June that it would 'sponsor the establishment of an options market in London under the regulatory control of the Council . . .'.[105] Nevertheless, the Stock Exchange had its own problems over an options exchange. What had not been agreed was that this options exchange should be in any way separate from the rest of the Stock Exchange, in terms of either membership or regulations, as had been originally proposed. Instead, the use of the traded options market would be restricted to members as they saw it, not as a new source of business for the Stock Exchange, but as a means of improving their ability to buy, sell, and deal in securities in competition with non-members. This decision introduced doubts about the value of the proposed options exchange if it was not to include the participation of non-members. They had been envisaged as major users but were now to be excluded. As a result the Stock Exchange abandoned its planning for a traded options market in London by December of 1976. Instead, they agreed to support the creation of the European Options Exchange in Amsterdam by having UK options listed there and permitting its members to participate in it. By January 1977 the European Options Exchange had been established in Amsterdam, and by April it was in operation. Its structure was that originally proposed in London. Though sponsored and financed by the Amsterdam Stock Exchange it was legally separate and had its own staff.[106]

Though the attitude of the government was not favourable and the Bank of England was a major obstacle, the reason why the European Options Exchange was in Amsterdam and not in London was due to the London Stock Exchange itself. So obsessed was its membership in limiting the competition they were exposed to, either inside or outside the Stock Exchange, that they were unwilling to countenance the formation of a separate market within the Stock Exchange that did not operate under the same rules and regulations, because of the precedent it would set. Thus, they gave up the opportunity for London to be in the forefront of a new market which all agreed would be of great benefit. In fact as early as July 1977 the Stock Exchange was again looking at the establishment of an options market in London. This was prompted by the worry that a market for UK securities might develop in Amsterdam if the options in those securities was traded there. The development of this London options market was given further impetus when the Board of Trade prevented members of the London Stock Exchange joining the European Options Exchange, citing legal reasons. It was not until April 1978 that permission was given. Thus, though the

---

[104] LSE: Council, 17 Feb. 1976, 18 May 1976.     [105] Ibid., 8 June 1976.
[106] Ibid., 20 July 1976, 28 Sept. 1976, 7 Dec. 1976, 18 Jan. 1977, 11 Apr. 1978.

creation of the European Options Exchange in Amsterdam had been prompted and supported by London it was soon perceived as both a threat by the London Stock Exchange and a necessity by its membership. As a substitute some member firms had formed the London Options Clearing House (LOCH) as an embryonic market in options in London. Conversely, it was not until September 1978 that the Stock Exchange itself gave permission for members—both brokers and jobbers—to join the European Options Exchange, and then only those already engaged in option trading.[107]

The Stock Exchange's own planning for a traded options market in London continued to hit difficulties that delayed its opening. As late as November 1978 the Inland Revenue informed the Stock Exchange that the taxation of option contracts was '. . . a political matter . . .' and so the government had to make a decision. Nevertheless, the market did open that month with a daily turnover during November of 626 contracts. By 28 November 10,200 contracts were open, representing an underlying stock value of £25m. However, the restrictions imposed on this traded options market in terms of membership and regulations, meant that it was not a facility generally available in the City of London, which had been originally envisaged. With London as the major financial centre in Europe, the need for such a market was, therefore, not met by the traded options market provided by the London Stock Exchange. Consequently at the end of 1979 others in the City of London proposed the formation of a financial futures exchange. This exchange would be independent of the Stock Exchange and open to all, which was the structure originally proposed for the options exchange.[108] Encapsulated in the failure of the traded options market were all the facts that stopped the Stock Exchange from making the most of the opportunities presented to it in the 1970s, with the City of London's re-emergence as a major international financial centre.

One of the Stock Exchange's problems was that it took so long to push through any new proposal that others were able to establish a prior position. This was the case with the market in the shares of smaller companies. In November 1974 the Stock Exchange observed that:

The UK market is a single market for all securities which are all dealt through the same system. This means that active and inactive securities use a system which appears to operate most effectively in active high turnover securities.[109]

With the disappearance of the provincial stock exchanges into a London-based trading system there were few opportunities for smaller companies to obtain a market for their shares. Provincial brokers and country jobbers

---

[107] Ibid., 19 July 1977, 26 July 1977, 15 Dec. 1977, 10 Jan. 1978, 18 Apr. 1978, 19 Sept. 1978.

[108] Ibid., 7 Nov. 1978, 5 Dec. 1978, 4 Dec. 1979; see D. Kynaston, *LIFFE: A Market and its Makers* (Cambridge 1997), 13–21.

[109] LSE: Council, 26 Nov. 1974.

had in the past provided a forum for such trading but the London Stock Exchange's insistence on the end to dual capacity had removed the very firms that had specialized in it. However, despite recognizing that one of the weaknesses of the new Stock Exchange structure lay in the market for the shares of smaller companies, no action was taken to remedy the situation. Other matters, such as ARIEL, OBOE, TALISMAN, and the crisis of 1974, all demanded the attention of the Stock Exchange and its membership. Nevertheless, by July 1977 it was accepted that there was a case for a two-tier market structure, which would cater for both the actively traded issues of large corporations and the less marketable shares of smaller companies. Accepting the need for special provision for smaller companies did not mean that any positive action was taken. Immediately there were raised all the risks such a market would be exposed to, namely the greater possibility of insider trading and market rigging as the shares of smaller companies were more closely held. Consequently, progress on the formation of a special market for smaller companies proceeded slowly and cautiously during the late 1970s. It was spurred by the growth of an outside or over-the-counter (OTC) market in such securities provided by non-members. In 1978 the Stock Exchange did begin planning for an Unlisted Securities Market (USM) to meet the competition but this had not reached fruition by the end of the decade. There was, as with the options exchange, the worry that creating a separate market, governed by different rules and regulations, but still controlled by and identified with the Stock Exchange, would create a precedent for change. Thus, from identification of the problem in 1974 the Stock Exchange had failed to produce a solution some six years later.[110]

Certainly it appears that during the 1970s the London Stock Exchange was less and less interested in providing a market for the shares of smaller companies, which also tended to be those that were less actively traded. Matching bargains in such securities was both time-consuming and costly compared to those of the widely held and more marketable issues of large companies. In addition, the shares of smaller companies tended to be held by individuals, and so traded in smaller amounts, compared to the large transactions by institutions in the issues of large companies. Jobbers were also unwilling to make markets in the shares of smaller companies as it was much more difficult to dispose of the securities they purchased or deliver those that they sold. Even in those securities in which they were willing to make prices the difference between buy and sell prices was a wide one to compensate for the risks that they ran. Inevitably this made such securities even less attractive to investors and so reduced even more the level of activity that they generated. The London Stock Exchange responded to this situation by making it more and more difficult for smaller companies to

[110] LSE: Council, 26 July 1977, 18 Apr. 1978.

gain a market for their shares through a quotation or listing. In 1970 the minimum public issue acceptable was £250,000, with a market value of no less than £100,000. A year later the nominal amount had been doubled to £0.5m. By insisting on a public offer for sale for most issues, in order to be seen to be treating investors fairly, the Stock Exchange was also opting for the method that most discriminated against smaller companies. The fixed costs involved in a public offer for sale were high, involving as they did advertising and printing expenditure as well as the fees of merchant bankers and stockbrokers. In contrast, introductions for shares already widely held or placings for new securities, were relatively cheap at 6–7 per cent of the amount raised on an issue of £250,000 in 1970. However, this did involve restricting the issue to a small circle of investors through circulating a stockbroker's clients or feeding the market through a jobber.[111] As the Stock Exchange noted in June 1974, with a Labour government in power,

... it would only need a single placing to be done on favourable terms for there to be an outcry from the press and politicians about shares going to favoured clients, insiders, and so on.[112]

The Stock Exchange preferred to adopt a cautious, even restrictive attitude, towards the way new issues were made because of the possible political backlash that would see an end to self-regulation and an increase of state intervention and control. Thus it favoured public offers over any other method in the full knowledge that it was too expensive for the issues that many small companies wanted to make. Charging for a listing also discouraged smaller companies. As their shares were much less traded the need for a public market place was less necessary, especially if it cost money to obtain and maintain. Though the Stock Exchange was increasingly aware that it did not serve smaller companies well in terms of the market that it provided, the situation continued unattended throughout the 1970s.[113]

Allied to the problems experienced by smaller companies was the unwillingness of the Stock Exchange to provide a market for risky new ventures rather than the conversion of established businesses into public companies and the subsequent issue of additional shares and debentures. By 1970 a five- or even 10-year record of business was required from any company wanting to issue securities, and even then the most that could be expected initially was not to raise funds for additional expansion but a sale of part of the holding of the existing owners. In the Stock Exchange's considered view

It is most uncommon for the total amount involved in such an offer to be 'new money' and it might well be very difficult for a small company to add substantially

---

[111] Ibid., 7 Sept. 1970, 29 Nov. 1971; W. A. Thomas, *The Finance of British Industry, 1918–1976* (London 1998), 166, 173.
[112] LSE: Council, 18 June 1974.
[113] Ibid., 4 June 1977, 11 Dec. 1974, 26 July 1977, 18 Apr. 1978.

to its equity base on the occasion of its first appearance in the market. It would probably be impossible for a small unquoted industrial company to raise loan money on the Stock Exchange without first having obtained quotation for its equity . . .

Clearly, the Stock Exchange no longer saw itself as a means whereby new or small companies could obtain the finance required to expand their operations. That was now the prerogative of the large and established enterprise. The Stock Exchange even acknowledged that it was now cheaper to raise money directly from a merchant bank or the Industrial and Commercial Finance Corporation than via a public quotation, especially as access to the cheapest method, a placing, was restricted. The value of a quotation came later when those running a company wanted to capitalize their investment and skills by establishing a public value for what they had created.

The Stock Exchange was not even keen for its members to play a leading role in conversions and new issues, because of the difficulties and conflict that they might become involved in. The brokers, Pember & Boyle, for example, were refused permission in 1970 to set up a subsidiary that would handle new issues. Similarly Hoare, Govett, who had handled issues for ICFC lost the role to Warburgs in 1977, as Stock Exchange rules restricted their operations in Eurobonds, which were becoming popular as a means of raising finance. Consequently, stockbrokers no longer offered a cheap alternative to the merchant banks in handling small new issues for, instead, they concentrated upon retailing those issues made by the merchant banks and providing the secondary market. The emphasis was now firmly upon co-operation rather than competition between stockbrokers and merchant banks, with one concentrating upon the secondary and the other the primary market. Stockbrokers in the 1970s were no longer dynamic elements in the primary capital market, exploiting niches ignored by the established merchant banks.[114]

When presented with the opportunity to help finance the development of North Sea oil in the 1970s, through providing a market for the shares of the companies being set up to drill for oil and gas, the Stock Exchange backed away. It stated in May 1974 that '. . . the Stock Exchange is not the proper medium for raising the initial capital required by a new company for the first stages of exploration into unproven territories.' The problem for the Stock Exchange was that the government had devolved to it responsibility over the quality of securities brought to the market. Thus, a quotation on the London Stock Exchange was regarded by the investing public as a testament to the soundness of the underlying operations. Consequently, any subsequent collapse by a listed company, with even suggestions of fraud

---

[114] LSE: Council Minutes, 7 Sept. 1970, 22 Nov. 1970; Kynaston, *Cazenove*, 272; Thomas, *Finance of British Industry*, 163, 165; R. Coopey and D. Clarke, *3i: Fifty Years Investing in Industry* (Oxford 1995), 231, 242, 410. R. Roberts, *Schroders: Merchants & Bankers* (London 1992), 448, 452–3; Reader and Kynaston, *Phillips & Drew*, 158.

or price manipulation, brought the Stock Exchange into public disrepute and the risk of direct government intervention. Thus, though the Stock Exchange was aware of the markets it was losing it was unwilling to take the risk of providing a market for new and untried ventures, especially in mineral exploration, because of the reactions that failure would bring. It did allow such companies to be traded under rule 163, where specified securities were traded on the Stock Exchange but not officially quoted. In 1973 there were 450 such securities, with many being speculative mining companies, but even that device did not guarantee immunity from public hostility and government pressure when a spectacular collapse took place. The Stock Exchange had got itself into an impossible position. It was criticized if it did not provide an open market for any company that was looking to have its securities widely held and actively traded. Conversely it was criticized if it did not ensure that only those that provided the most secure prospects based on an established and proven track record were given a quotation. If it failed to provide the market it was accused of restricting access to risk capital. If it granted the quotation and companies subsequently failed it was blamed for its lack of protection for investors. The compromise increasingly adopted by the Stock Exchange was to err on the side of caution. It only permitted those securities to be quoted and traded which offered little prospect of bringing the Stock Exchange into disrepute, regarding that as the safer option. Inevitably the result was a concentration on the securities of established British companies with proven track records. [115]

The collapse in the securities market in 1974 did force the Stock Exchange to adopt a more liberal attitude towards those applying for a quotation. By then the Stock Exchange was relying heavily on the fees it levied on companies wanting an official quotation. Income from quotation fees rose, for example, from £1.0m. in 1969/70 to £1.7m. in 1972/3 before falling away in 1974/5, encouraging the Stock Exchange to look more favourably on all who applied. At the same time a growing number of companies of all kinds found it increasingly difficult to raise the funds they needed from the traditional sources of reinvested profits, bank loans, and sales of additional securities to existing shareholders. Such were the economic, financial, and monetary conditions in Britain in the mid-1970s that the corporate sector had serious problems obtaining the finance it needed. Heavy and persistent government borrowing, was making it impossible for companies to raise loan capital, while inflation was pushing the interest rates charged by banks to high levels at a time when controls on prices and profits squeezed self-finance. Pressure was thus put on the Stock Exchange by the merchant banks to make it easier and cheaper for companies to issue securities and obtain a quotation. This was fully supported by institutional

[115] LSE: Council, 14 Sept. 1970, 6 Nov. 1973, 21 Nov. 1973, 7 May 1974.

brokers like Rowe & Pitman who worked closely with the issuing houses. The Stock Exchange in January 1975 did make placings easier and in 1977 reduced the requirement of the amount of a company's shares that had to be available to the market from 35 per cent to 25 per cent.[116]

Even these relaxations were of limited value because the ceiling of £1m. was retained, forcing companies to use the more expensive route of a public offer for sale. At the same time a major obstacle was left in place which the Stock Exchange knew would stop quoted companies from making placings. The Stock Exchange insisted that companies gave their own shareholders pre-emptive rights to any new issue if it was not made by way of a public offer for sale, and this rule remained in force. Clearly, even in the face of a major crisis in corporate funding the Stock Exchange was not willing to put its reputation at risk through a major relaxation in the rules governing new issues. The Stock Exchange continued to see itself as the regulator not only of the market and those who used it but also of the securities that were traded there. As such, like all regulators it aimed to avoid controversy by limiting the use of the market to those tried and trusted companies.[117]

As it was, the London Stock Exchange became ever more dependent in the 1970s upon the business generated by institutional investors buying and selling UK government debt and the stocks and shares of large and established British companies. Its role in the capital market was very much confined to providing a market where financial institutions traded securities in response to the public's purchase of insurance policies, saving for a pension, or deposit of money in banks and building societies. Especially after the crash of 1974 many remaining investors deserted the stock market in favour of more tangible assets such as property and works of art.[118] By the middle of the 1970s the Stock Exchange had concluded that the private investor had largely disappeared as a force in the market place.

In modern times, the great private capitalist responsible to himself exists, as far as the UK is concerned, only in the realms of fiction.[119]

Their own assessment suggested that there were no more than 77,000 serious investors who held, between them £6.9bn. in quoted UK securities and £1.0bn. in quoted overseas securities. The rest of the population were only involved in the Stock Exchange indirectly through the use made of their savings by financial institutions, such as the pension funds, merchant banks, insurance companies, commercial banks, building societies, and even their own members. Consequently, the Stock Exchange saw

---

[116] LSE: *Annual Reports*, 1970–4; LSE: Council, 11 Dec. 1974, 7 Jan. 1975.

[117] Ibid., 4 Feb. 1975, cf. 27 May 1975; Blakey, *London Stock Market*, 226; Coopey and Clarke, *3i*, 115–17, 232–3.

[118] LSE: Council, 4 June 1974, 13 Aug. 1974, 24 Sept. 1974, 29 Oct. 1974, 5 Nov. 1974.

[119] Ibid., 1 July 1975.

its future tied inextricably to the other financial institutions of the City of London.[120]

However, though the Stock Exchange compounded the problems of the British economy in the 1970s it was not responsible for the low level of investment that took place. That was a result of the international situation, with the final collapse of the post-war boom, compounded by the policies pursued by successive British governments that placed short-term social and political considerations above long-term economic prosperity. The Stock Exchange informed the government of its assessment of the economic situation on more than one occasion in the 1970s, as it tried to defend itself from the accusations of politicians and the media who had very little understanding of the dilemmas and difficulties if faced. Stung by blame for the financial and economic crisis of 1974 the Stock Exchange retorted by blaming the high interest rates on government spending and high inflation due to government economic policy.

Under present circumstances the rate of interest required by providers of loan capital, the high yield required by producers of equity capital, and the liquidity problems resulting from rapid inflation which is absorbing retained earnings, means that very few projects have a sufficient rate of return to cover the cost of capital, let alone provide a contribution to build up essential reserves.

No wonder that the brokers Laurence, Prust & Co., considered that investors were 'on strike because of the level of risk that currently prevailed'. However, the Stock Exchange did not put the blame only on the Labour government then in power for it saw the current situation building up over the 1950s and 1960s, as inflation eroded the value of fixed-interest securities while periods of dividend control undermined confidence in equities through falling yields and prices. What the Stock Exchange was recommending was a fundamental overhaul by the government of its fiscal and monetary policies, because

... it is necessary to recreate an environment where investors will be willing to put their funds at risk in equities or other securities at yields which represent an acceptable cost to companies wishing to undertake new investment.[121]

Essentially, this was a plea for greater continuity and stability in government economic policy which would give investors the confidence in the future necessary for them to purchase and hold securities.

Unfortunately for the Stock Exchange such a radical departure from post-war economic policy was not a feasible option for the Labour government then in power, troubled as it was by severe financial and monetary difficulties at home and abroad. It was easier to let the public go on blaming

---

[120] Ibid., 21 Nov. 1973, 24 Sept. 1974, 7 Jan. 1975; Kynaston, *Cazenove*, 262, 293; Roberts, *Schroders*, 445; A. Gleeson, *People and Their Money: 50 Years of Private Investment* (M & G Group 1981), 83, 118, 128–9, 135–8.

[121] LSE: Council, 28 Jan. 1975, cf. 15 Oct. 1974, 7 Jan. 1975, 4 Feb. 1975.

the Stock Exchange, or the City of London as a whole, than tackle the more fundamental economic problems apparent at the time. However, the attacks it suffered combined with the problems the Stock Exchange itself faced with the downturn in activity, forced it to re-examine what had gone wrong over the years. The Stock Exchange's conclusions were tantamount to an indictment of post-war governments, whether Labour or Conservative, for none escaped the criticisms it made. First, it tried to explain the conditions affecting the operation of the capital market under a system where companies issued transferable securities.

Under the market system, companies seeking capital are subjected to competitive constraints. As far as loan capital is concerned, the constraint is mainly the alternative outlet offered by Government in the form of their own gilt-edged securities of which, by comparison with other national markets, almost unlimited amounts are available and to which constant and increasing additions are being made . . . As far as risk-bearing share capital is concerned the considerations are quite different. Company boards will only call on their proprietors, the shareholders, to put up more funds, if they can reasonably justify to them the prospect of using these additional funds profitably.

After these brief comments indicating the major factors affecting a company's desire and ability to raise capital, the Stock Exchange then launched into a bitter catalogue of all that had happened since the Second World War to prevent the market operating efficiently and effectively. It was almost as if decades of pent-up frustration with the policies of successive governments could no longer be suppressed.

Since 1945, British companies and businesses of all kinds have been forced to operate in an environment in which the risk of the endeavour has been, or has appeared to be, disproportionate to its reward. The Governments of our Continental European and Japanese competitors used their Marshall Plan funds mainly to re-equip their industries; we used ours in large part to finance, directly and indirectly, consumption. Our fiscal policies have been mainly directed towards social equality or towards consumerism; theirs have been mainly directed towards promoting investment . . . Added to all these disadvantages have been the continuing structural change and inconsistencies of economic policy which successive British governments have inflicted upon business. No industrial nation has been subjected to the same unending sequence of nationalisation, denationalisation, renationalisation, variation of tax rates, alteration of tax structures, introduction and repeal of investment allowances, initial allowances, capital allowances investment grants, development grants, free depreciation, the Industrial Reorganisation corporation, Industry Act grants with and without string attached, the National Enterprise Board, dividend control, price controls, wages controls and similar transitory phenomena all in the space of a few years . . . overshadowing everything is the spectre of the change of government and the repeal of the enactments of its predecessor. This 'repeal system' has made long-term investment planning in the UK more difficult than in any other industrial country—a development which bears more heavily as the technological development horizon lengthens and the apparent lives of parliaments shorten.

Clearly to the Stock Exchange the origins of short-termism in financial markets were self-apparent, lying with the changing polices pursued by governments which were then reflected by the decisions taken by investment managers and company boards. The Stock Exchange continued with its indictment, concluding that

It is, then, small wonder that UK companies are unable to view the future of their enterprises with the same confidence as their competitors overseas. Confidence is the key to investment. Confidence, in this context, means the reasonable expectation that, on the assumption that the technological, industrial and commercial risks have been fairly assessed, the results of successful investment will be likely to flow back to the providers of risk capital in the form of reasonable profits and dividends. These risks are serious enough, but they are at least the risks which the businessman has been trained to assess. If to these are added risks of an arbitrary political nature, not risks to which foreign competitors are subject, it should not be a matter of great surprise that British businessmen are less inclined to commit risk funds for investment than these others. To suggest that these ills should be remedied by directing capital into industry is to attack the symptoms instead of attacking the disease.[122]

Though the Stock Exchange itself was not free from blame, being part of the mechanism that constrained and inhibited change, its contribution was tiny in comparison to the role played by successive post-war governments as politicians pursued solutions to economic problems they little understood and civil servants controlled markets and activities in ignorance of the conditions under which they operated. Unfortunately for the Stock Exchange government intervention was viewed as a solution to Britain's economic decline into the serious difficulties of the 1970s, whether by academic economists or media commentators, and so its version of events and preferred solutions were largely ignored. The investigation set up by the Labour government into the cause of Britain's economic problems, and chaired by the ex-Labour Prime Minister, Harold Wilson, continued to see the Stock Exchange and the City as the chief culprits. As in the past it was unable to discover the evidence required to prove that that was so but that did not prevent the belief having wide currency. However, by the time that Committee reported in 1979 there had been, yet again, another change of government.[123]

By the 1970s the role of the Stock Exchange was now mainly with regard to capital market for its role in the money market was a limited one. Most of the trading in short-dated government debt, whether issued centrally or by local authorities, was handled outside the Stock Exchange by the likes of the discount houses and emerging money brokers and dealers. A few Stock Exchange firms, like Phillips & Drew, Messels, and Laurie Milbank

---

[122] LSE: Council, 1 July 1975.
[123] Committee to Review the Functioning of Financial Institutions [Wilson Committee], *Report* (London 1979), cf. Thomas, *Finance of British Industry*, 230–5, 277, 280, 297.

retained a place in the market but most were giving up, as was the case of Cazenoves. Non-members had greater access to capital, negotiable charges, more flexible methods of operation, and better connections than Stock Exchange firms and so increasingly monopolized the business. Even the money brokers like Sheppards & Chase, who acted as intermediaries between the members of the Stock Exchange and the banks, found it difficult to stay in business because of outside competition. In particular they needed a much larger capital base but the Stock Exchange would not give them permission to create a structure that would allow them to do that. Again, the Stock Exchange was worried by the risks being run in large open positions and so it was not keen to promote such operations.[124] Similarly, in the trading of securities between London and other European centres, for exchange purposes, the continental European banks were playing a dominant role. With many of the securities involved being Eurobond issues, the Stock Exchange was completely bypassed. Thus, as the City of London attracted more foreign banks and financial intermediaries from Europe, Japan, and the United States than ever, they traded more and more with each other not only in money-market instruments but also securities. Members of the Stock Exchange were involved, as matching international transactions for currency purposes could include sales and purchase made through brokers. The US investment bank Kidder Peabody, for example, maintained close connections with London stockbrokers as it tried to balance clients requirements for sterling in London and dollars in New York. As in the past matching sales of the same, or even similar securities, in different centres allowed currencies to be switched while holdings remained unaltered. However, the international bond markets, along with direct transfers between banks, offered far greater scope for this in the 1970s than the equity market provided by the Stock Exchange.[125]

This did not mean that the Stock Exchange had no role to play within the money market. An estimate for 1972 suggested that around half of all turnover was conducted on credit, averaging around c.£900m. per month, which was then settled at the end of each account. The margin for loans ranged from a mere 5 per cent for short-dated government debt down to 50 per cent for minor corporate issues. Thus many securities could be held using largely borrowed funds because of their ease of resale. There was also the professional use of the Stock Exchange for money-market purposes. Financial institutions, for example, were frequently in the position of requiring cash but reluctant to dispose of securities. Thus they sold securities for cash but bought them back for the end of the account. Their investment

[124] LSE: Council, 22 Mar. 1971, 4 Oct. 1971, 4 June 1974, 1 Oct. 1974, 5 Nov. 1974, 28 Jan. 1975; Kynaston, *Cazenove*, 292.
[125] LSE: Council, 26 Apr. 1971, 14 May 1974, 4 June 1974, 5 Nov. 1974, 28 Jan. 1975; H. Bonin, *Société Générale in the United Kingdom, 1871–1996* (Paris 1996), 62, 74–5; P. Newall, *Japan and the City of London* (London 1996), 32–6, 39–40.

position remained unaltered while temporary funds obtained cost nothing more than brokers' commission and a jobbers' turn. Especially after 1974 the rates charged for such a transaction were low while the jobbers' turn was narrow on actively traded securities such as government debt or major corporate issues. Conversely, another financial institution might wish to employ temporarily available funds by purchasing securities for cash and reselling for the end of the account. Dealers in securities, whether jobbers in the Stock Exchange or outside finance houses, were forever in the position of having to borrow money to finance holdings of securities or to borrow securities for delivery to another until they were in a position to purchase them in the market. Financial institutions like insurance companies and investment trusts actively participated in this because it provided them with a means of obtaining funds while still retaining the ownership of the securities, as the dealer was obliged to replace them. All these types of transactions were possible because the London Stock Exchange continued to provide markets in a wide range of securities, that were able to supply or absorb substantial quantities without wide fluctuations in price and at relatively low charges for large orders.[126]

During the 1970s the London Stock Exchange came under attack from a number of quarters, including the government, the media, and from within the City itself. The 1970s, like every decade since the end of the Second World War, was one in which government was seen as the solution to every problem, not the cause of many. Thus the Stock Exchange as representative of a market was out of favour. Conceding lower commission rates in 1974 removed much of the criticism from within the City through there remained many who resented its restrictive practices and 'closed shop'. The criticism from, the government, however, refused to go away, especially with the Labour Party coming to power in 1974. Nevertheless, little tangible resulted from that period of hostility, whipped up by the crisis of 1974 and the poor performance of the economy in those years. More worrying for the Stock Exchange was the fact that the incoming Conservative government of 1979, though it could ignore the predictable recommendations of the Wilson Committee, was not willing to drop the referral to the Restrictive Practices court. That referral threatened the whole way the Stock Exchange had operated since the Second World War, with fixed commission and single capacity. However, it did represent a new attitude from the government for it was an attempt to reform a market not manipulate it or ignore it or bypass it, as had been the pattern in the past. The 1970s saw the continued erosion of the Stock Exchange's position in the securities market, though its merger with the provincial exchanges enabled it to monopolize British corporate issues. This was a large and active market generating substantial income for brokers and jobbers but in it the Stock

[126] LSE: Council, 7 Feb. 1972, 4 Apr. 1972, 16 Apr. 1974, 4 June 1974, 30 July 1974.

# 12

# *Big Bang*

## THE GOODISON/PARKINSON AGREEMENT

No event in the history of the London Stock Exchange has attracted more attention than Big Bang. On 27 October 1986 both fixed commissions and single capacity were abolished and these had been at the centre of Stock Exchange thinking for most of the twentieth century, and certainly since 1945. At the same time the 100 per cent external ownership of members was permitted. Whatever these changes might have meant for the rest of the City of London they certainly constituted a fundamental revolution for the London Stock Exchange. This was despite the fact that certain changes had already taken place especially in the field of international securities and international markets, where there had been limited relaxation of the rules covering both single capacity and fixed commissions. As early as 1970 members had been allowed to deal in overseas securities on equal terms with overseas competitors, and further relaxation of the rules did follow in 1983, in the wake of the abolition of exchange controls in 1979. It is clear that pressure for reform had been mounting in the 1970s, both within and outside the Stock Exchange, and this had brought results despite the opposition of many members worried about the consequences it would have for their business. Responsibility for the final transformation, when it did come, has been claimed for a variety of forces and by a variety of individuals. For some it is seen as the power of impersonal market forces whereby technological change and globalization destroyed the natural protection of a national stock exchange. Others have emphasized the political agenda and point to the role of Conservative politicians and their reforming zeal. A number see the guiding hand of central bankers with the Bank of England using its influence to enhance the competitive position of the City of London. Finally, there are those that see the process as an internal one and argue that the London Stock Exchange was already reforming itself and the interventions of others only delayed and distracted it.[1] However, historical reality is a lot more complex

I am very grateful to Sir Nicholas Goodison for reading this Chapter and making comments upon it, in terms of both substance and emphasis. However, the views expressed are my own.

[1] Among the books seeking to explain and document Big Bang are: J. J. Fishman, *The Transformation of Threadneedle Street: The Deregulation and the Reregulation of Britain's Financial Services* (Durham, NC 1993); G. Galletly and N. Richie, *The Big Bang* (Plymouth 1988);

than the simplistic views of protagonists or the observations of contemporaries. The London Stock Exchange in 1980 rested upon a series of major compromises arrived at in the past, each leading to another. Once one of these was removed so the links between them all would precipitate a process of unravelling, until a new but different stability was achieved.

Whatever the relative contribution of these, there can be no doubt that the abolition of exchange controls in October 1979 was fundamental as it created the conditions that encouraged such a profound transformation. The barriers that had once restricted the ability of British investors to buy and sell British securities on other markets vanished with the end of exchange controls. Sir Nicholas Goodison reflected in 1986 that '... the real impetus for change was the abolition of UK exchange controls in 1979. If anything should be called the "Big Bang", it was that.'[2] This view has been endorsed by, among others, Nigel Lawson, Chancellor of the Exchequer in the mid-1980s. During the 1970s London had become host to an international securities market, involving numerous foreign financial intermediaries who were not members of the London Stock Exchange. Thus, in London itself the London Stock Exchange faced formidable competition which only exchange controls had kept partially at bay as it divided the foreign from the domestic market. The ending of exchange controls destroyed the London Stock Exchange's ability to monopolize its own domestic market and impose its own rules and regulations. Even before the decade of the Big Bang had begun the Stock Exchange resembled a house of cards from which one of the central pillars had been removed. This had already been recognized by the Council of the Stock Exchange. In the *Annual Report* for 1980 Nicholas Goodison observed that 'The removal of controls will have a far-reaching effect on securities markets . . . The overall effect will be greater integration of the United Kingdom market with world markets. It will be a world in which the Stock Exchange must compete for its position.'[3]

This was a recognition that change was now inevitable and that the rules and regulations that had served the Stock Exchange well in the past, most notably in the years since 1945, were not necessarily sustainable in the

A. Hamilton, *The Financial Services Revolution: The Big Bang Worldwide* (London 1976); W. Kay, *The Big Bang: An Investor's Guide to the Changed City* (London 1986); J. J. Khoury, *The Deregulation of the World's Financial Markets: Myths, Realities, and Impact* (London 1990); S. MacLachlan (ed.), *Life After Big Bang* (London 1987); W. Moran, *The Politics of the Financial Services Revolution: The USA, UK and Japan* (London 1991); W. A. Thomas, *The Big Bang* (Oxford 1986); S. K. Vogel, *Freer Markets, More Rules! Regulatory Reform in Advanced Industrial Countries* (Ithaca, NY 1996); G. N. Webb, *The Bigger Bang: Growth of a Financial Revolution* (London 1987).

[2] *Stock Exchange Quarterly*, Mar. 1986, 8, cf. *Financial Times* (FT) 27 Jan. 1992; N. Lawson, *The View from No. 11: Memoirs of a Tory Radical* (London 1992), 626; LSE: *Annual Report*, 1980; LSE: Council, 16 Sept. 1986; J. Plender and P. Wallace, *The Square Mile: A Guide to the New City of London* (London 1985), 20.

[3] LSE: *Annual Report*, 1980.

future. The environment that successive British governments had created in that period, and which had moulded the behaviour of the Stock Exchange as an institution, had now changed. There was always a tension on the Stock Exchange between those members who found themselves constrained by the rules and regulations that governed their conduct, and so sought to change or bypass them, and those members who saw the rules as essential for the maintenance of an orderly market, and so fought to preserve them. Hence the changes introduced before 1914. The pressure from post-war governments to maintain orderly markets that were responsive to public opinion and to the interests of governments themselves, had given power to those members opposed to change. The enforcement and extension of any and all rules and regulations could always be justified in the interests of preserving this orderly market. Single capacity, for example, which had been introduced to reinforce minimum commissions, could be defended, persuasively, as being in the interest of investor protection. It ensured the separation of buying and selling transactions so that the investor received a fair price as the broker had to go through the market, and thus expose his actions to the public scrutiny of his peer group. Similarly, fixed commissions were then seen as essential if single capacity was to be preserved, for otherwise a large investor could deal directly with a jobber via a compliant broker. Together these rules allowed the Stock Exchange to police its membership and their dealings, not so much with each other but with the investing public. That was a function that governments expected the Stock Exchange to perform, and was one of the reasons it and its membership had escaped government regulation, despite the interventionist climate that followed the Second World War. However, there is nothing to suggest that the Conservative government was even remotely aware that the ending of exchange controls in 1979 had implications for the Stock Exchange, let alone ones that would undermine the whole way it had developed over the previous 30 years.

Consequently, the Stock Exchange faced a difficult period of adjustment after 1979 for it would have to review its rules and regulations in the light of a greatly altered competitive environment, which could render impossible the maintenance of both single capacity and fixed commissions. Both had already proved unsustainable internationally, as the many past debates in the Council on overseas dealings testify. However, the Stock Exchange still had to contend with the case pending with the Restrictive Practices Court (RPC). This had originated at a time when the Stock Exchange faced a much less competitive environment and so warranted investigation as it could be seen to be exploiting a quasi-monopoly position. Rather than being a spur for change, the RPC case now became a barrier to progress as it made it difficult for the Stock Exchange to plan for the future when it had to defend the past. The court case, if lost by the Stock Exchange, could endanger the maintenance of any kind of an orderly market as it might result in the whole of the rule book being outlawed. Suddenly there would be no rules or regulations. The London Stock Exchange, as an institution, had no alternative but to defend its rule book in the RPC for otherwise the whole basis of the orderly market that had evolved over the years would be lost. The Council of the Stock Exchange did try to persuade the government to drop the case or opt for another forum that did not threaten the sudden ending of the existing rules (one preferred option was a reference to the Monopolies and Mergers Commission). In both 1979 and 1980, Sir Nicholas Goodison had meetings with John Nott, the Secretary of State for Trade, for that very purpose but with no success. All that resulted was the agreement to delay the implementation of any findings by the RPC by nine months, which was regarded as of little value by the Stock Exchange as it moved to create a pre-emptive free-for-all. Preparations to fight the case thus continued at the Stock Exchange though regular contact was maintained with ministers and civil servants, both directly and through the Bank of England. There continued to be the hope that the Conservative government could be convinced that the case was not only unnecessary but harmful, as it was a diversion from the more serious task of planning for the future. This lobbying also extended to opposition political parties in case they might prove willing to drop the case if they came to power. By this stage the Council of the Stock Exchange was no longer trying to preserve the status quo for international securities as they were aware that minimum commission regimes were under attack in other counties, most notably the United States, Canada, and Australia.[4]

Though the Council of the London Stock Exchange was fully aware of the international trends against fixed commissions in the early 1980s it remained publicly committed to the principle for the domestic market as it was well aware how difficult it otherwise would be to regulate its members and their relations with their customers. Many members also relied on fixed minimum commissions as a way of preserving their income. As a result of inflation in the late 1970s/early 1980s stockbrokers had experienced rising costs, especially of staff as wages and salaries rose. Though the volume of business did rise, and with it commission income, the greatest increase was turnover in gilt-edged securities which was largely on behalf of financial institutions and was done at low rates of commission. In contrast the value of equity turnover, more of which was done for individual investors, had grown less rapidly creating severe problems for the smaller broking firms that relied on it for their income, leading to more mergers. Consequently, there was considerable pressure from many members belonging to these smaller firms to preserve minimum commissions and even to push up rates generally. These were both small firms doing a largely equity business and large firms handling gilt-edged sales. Not only did these firms want their

---

[4] LSE: Council, 4 Aug. 1981, cf. *Financial Market Trends*, 3 (May 1990), 21; LSE: *Annual Reports*, 1979, 1981, 1983, 1989.

equity business to produce a greater revenue but they were keen to see that the turnover in gilt-edged should also generate greater earnings, considering its large volume. In contrast, large firms doing a largely equity business were less wedded to fixed commissions. The pressure for increased rates annoyed the major financial institutions. They made it clear that they were unwilling to subsidize either the transactions of individual investors or the inefficiencies of smaller stockbroking firms. This pressure for increased charges also annoyed the Bank of England, concerned as it was to keep down costs in the gilt-edged market.[5] Clearly the domestic commission regime was in need of immediate reform, whatever its long-term future was, and here lay a real difficulty. There already existed on the Stock Exchange both groups dedicated to preserving the existing rule book in its entirety, including fixed commissions and single capacity, and those who saw that a degree of change and flexibility was essential for long-term survival. However, as a result of the RPC case it was difficult to review and reform the rule book in the light of the changed circumstances and so establish a new compromise acceptable to all, both within and outwith the Stock Exchange. One of the problems here was that the Office of Fair Trading, which had referred the case to the RPC, would not make it clear what practices were being objected to with the result that all rules and regulations could be declared illegal, and none of the membership wanted to see that happen. The Office of Fair Trading was unwilling to compromise its position by resolving any of these issues for the Stock Exchange, leaving it at the full mercy of the Court. In turn this enhanced the power of those members who opposed all change. It was this impasse that the Council of the Stock Exchange was desperate to escape from as they could see the need for change, but the Conservative government ignored their arguments, pleas, and lobbying. This was despite the fact that from 1980 onwards the Bank of England had become convinced that the Council of the Stock Exchange, if given the opportunity, would introduce the reforms required by the changed international cirumstances. The Bank of England even convinced the Department of Trade and Industry of this but still the government took no action regarding the RPC case, despite the efforts of David Walker at the former and Lord Cockfield at the latter.

Instead, in July 1982, the Stock Exchange was informed that the RPC case would start in October 1983. As this deadline grew nearer and nearer, it absorbed more and more of the time of the Stock Exchange's Committee members and permanent staff. The cost also mounted, driven up by the fees charged by those providing legal advice. By May 1983 it was estimated by the Stock Exchange that the identifiable costs of the RPC case had already reached £1,178,000. Of this £803,000 was in professional fees while another £375,000 was in full-time staff costs. That was before the

[5] LSE: Council, 17 Nov. 1981, 16 Feb. 1982, 16 Mar. 1982, 1 June 1982; LSE: *Annual Report*, 1982; Plender and Wallace, *The Square Mile*, 18–19, 23, 92.

case had even come to court, with January 1984 now the scheduled date for the first hearing. In addition to which was the adverse publicity the case was attracting, as the Stock Exchange was thought to be defending a privileged position and using its monopoly to force the investing public to pay high rates for the services its members provided. The fact that it was the commission charges paid by private investors that were being subsidized by those paid by institutions escaped notice.[6] Left with the responsibility of reaching some solution to this problem was Sir Nicholas Goodison, who had been knighted in the New Year's Honours List, 1981/2, '. . . for the great work he has undertaken on behalf of the Stock Exchange'.[7] With such public recognition for his services it was no wonder that he was proposed, yet again, as Chairman in June 1983. According to his proposer, J. W. Robertson, there was '. . . no person better equipped to lead the Stock Exchange into the Restrictive Practices Court action'. In reply Sir Nicholas warned that '. . . the year in prospect would be a daunting one . . .' noting that they were '. . . faced with difficult decisions irrespective of the Restrictive Practices Court case'.[8] With that single word 'irrespective' the members of the Stock Exchange could be left in no doubt that reform was firmly on the agenda no matter the outcome of the case.

Thus, increasingly in the early 1980s, the obstacle to the progress of reform on the Stock Exchange lay with the RPC case. Many on the Stock Exchange, especially on the Council, had become convinced that change was essential in the wake of the abandonment of exchange controls in 1979 but did not press for it, worried that their actions might undermine the case before the RPC. Above all they did not want the sudden free-for-all that the loss of the case might mean. Obviously, there continued to remain many members, especially those doing business in UK equities for individual investors, who remained unconvinced that change was necessary. Eventually, the strength and the arguments of the two groups would have to be tested, but that awaited any resolution of the RPC case.

The Cabinet simply refused to take the political decisions that were necessary if the Stock Exchange was to be extricated from the case and the process of change begun. They, like the Prime Minister, Mrs Thatcher, were worried that any action would be seen by the media as a Conservative government pandering to its friends in the City of London. Certainly in the period 1979–83 there was no sign of a government-driven agenda of financial reform. Rather the picture was one of government inaction, despite advice from the Bank of England and the Department of Trade and Industry, and requests from the Stock Exchange to allow it to focus on reforming itself by dropping the RPC case. Lord Cockfield, the current President of the Board of Trade, had become convinced of the need to drop the RPC

---

[6] LSE: Council, 20 July 1982, 2 Nov. 1982, 17 May 1983, 19 July 1983; LSE: *Annual Report*, 1983.
[7] LSE: Council, 5 Jan. 1982.     [8] Ibid., 27 June 1983.

case but could not persuade his cabinet colleagues at that time. It was not until the Conservative election victory of 1983 that the government eventually became receptive to Stock Exchange requests for discussion and compromise. In the new Conservative government Cecil Parkinson became responsible for the Department of Trade and Industry, to which Sir Gordon Borrie, at the Office of Fair Trade, reported. At the same time Nigel Lawson, as Chancellor of the Exchequer, took over from Geoffrey Howe at the Treasury. Both were familiar with the City of London as Cecil Parkinson had worked as an accountant there while Nigel Lawson had been a journalist with the *Financial Times*. With their understanding of financial affairs they were both sympathetic to the predicament faced by the Stock Exchange. They were thus willing to accept the advice of the Bank of England that some form of action was required in order to break the impasse that the referral to the RPC had created for the Stock Exchange.[9]

The actual sequence of events that led up to Big Bang were, however, set in train by Sir Nicholas Goodison. In the aftermath of the Conservative election victory, he wrote to Cecil Parkinson stressing the threat that the RPC case posed to the maintenance of an orderly market, and suggesting that they meet. As Sir Nicholas informed the Stock Exchange Council,

After the [General] election he had written to the Secretary of State who had invited him to the D.T.I. and had given him an outline of Government thinking. It was apparent that they would only consider exemption if we abolished minimum commissions. The government favoured single capacity. They were not sure about membership but it seemed that substantial concessions were necessary.[10]

He had then been invited '. . . to make suggestions for change which might persuade the Government to consider an exemption order.' Sir Nicholas indicated a readiness to propose changes, including the abolition of minimum commissions and amendments to the constitution of the Stock Exchange. There then followed four weeks of negotiation between the government team and that from the Stock Exchange. After all the delay, speed was now essential as the end of the parliamentary session was approaching, as was the court case itself.

By 20 July 1983 a deal had been struck. In exchange for suspending the case that was before the RPC Sir Nicholas offered to put to the Council of the Stock Exchange the proposal that they would

[9] C. Parkinson, *Right at the Centre: An Autobiography* (London 1992), 244–9; Lawson, *View from No. 11*, 398–400; Sir Nicholas Goodison, draft letter to *The Times* on Big Bang, 24 Oct. 1996; P. Thompson, 'The Pyrrhic Victory of Gentlemanly Capitalism: The Financial Elite of the City of London, 1945–90', *Journal of Contemporary History*, 32 (1997), 293; R. O'Brien, *Global Financial Integration: The End of Geography* (London 1992), 96; Hamilton, *Financial Services Revolution*, 133; Moran, *Politics of the Financial Services Revolution*, 1, 69–71; Fishman, *Transformation of Threadneedle Street*, 31–4; Vogel, *Freer Markets, More Rules!* 100–7; Khoury, *World's Financial Markets*, 128.

[10] LSE: Council, 21 and 22 July 1983.

... dismantle, by stages and with no unreasonable delay, all the rules which at present prescribe minimum scales of Commission, and to complete this dismantling by 31 December 1986.[11]

In addition, it was also agreed that the Stock Exchange would become both more accountable to non-members and more responsive to those applying for membership. To ensure accountability the Council of the Stock Exchange was now to include non-members with the number and selection being determined by the Bank of England. This gave both the Bank and other financial institutions a more visible input into decision-making within the Stock Exchange, rather than simply through the presence of the government broker on Council. Furthermore, an appeal tribunal was to be established, with a majority of non-members, to consider cases where an application for membership was rejected. This tribunal was to have the power to overrule decisions made by the Stock Exchange. Conversely, the government not only left single capacity alone but saw it as a crucial element in its policy of improving investor protection, despite Sir Nicholas's warning to them that it might very well not survive the ending of fixed commissions. Sir Nicholas had informed Cecil Parkinson '. . . that he could give no assurance, as head of the main regulatory body in the securities industry, that he could hold the central market together once MCs [Minimum Commissions] had gone.'

Under this agreement, the Stock Exchange would continue to regulate its own affairs and be given the opportunity to carry out the changes that the ending of exchange controls had necessitated, as long as fixed commissions were abandoned. As Sir Nicholas made clear to the Council of the Stock Exchange, this agreement could either be accepted or rejected for

... the proposals did not represent the beginning of negotiations. They were rather the conclusion of negotiations and represented the minimum believed to be acceptable to Government.[12]

Coming after a long period during which the Stock Exchange had tried and failed to escape a public examination of its rule book, there was a clear recognition that either this agreement was accepted or the case before the RPC had to be defended. Alternatives such as a Royal Commission and even an investigation by the Monopolies Commission had all been rejected by the government. There was even a hint from the present Conservative government that they would be less compromising and less helpful than the opposition Labour Party, if the case did come to court. It was reported that,

The Government could not influence the outcome of the Court Case. Mr Hattersley [Deputy Leader, Labour Party] had told him [Sir Nicholas] that it could; Mr. Hattersley had been wrong. The attitude of the authorities as to what they might do after a Court defeat was unknown. There was a risk in letting HMG

---

[11] LSE: Council, 21 and 22 July 1983.      [12] Ibid.

[Her Majesty's Government] become the ultimate controller of our destinies. Politicians tended to be uncertain people.[13]

Whatever the political persuasion of the government the Stock Exchange tended to distrust its motives and its honesty. Also the Director-General of the Office of Fair Trading, Sir Gordon Borrie, had already shown himself unmoved by the worries that the outlawing of the rule book could result in chaos on the Stock Exchange. Therefore, if agreement was rejected, the Stock Exchange stood to lose a lot more than minimum commissions if the RPC judgment was adverse. As it was, after years of government procrastination, the Council of the Stock Exchange had, at most, five days to discuss the agreement the implications of which they were much more aware of than the government. From hearing of the proposed deal on Thursday, 21 July 1983 the Council had to give an answer to the government by Monday, 25 July. The Cabinet was then due to discuss the entire package on Tuesday, 26 July, with a statement to the House of Commons scheduled for Wednesday, 27 July. Unless immediate action was taken to stop the case going to court, both the government and the Stock Exchange could lose control over the course of events.

A prime influence on the decision that the Council came to was a general belief that they were likely to lose the case before the RPC, no matter what preparations they made. Thus any compromise was to be welcomed, faced with the certainty of defeat which, at one blow, would end both fixed commissions and single capacity as well as any other practices deemed to be against the public interest, and so endanger the operation of the whole market. The conclusion reached was that, if the offer was accepted, the Stock Exchange

... would get certainty, we would know where we were, even if we were worried about the future. There would be an enormous release of resources in the Council and the Executive. Change would be controlled.[14]

There was an almost universal feeling among the Council members that the RPC had constituted a planning blight on the future development of the Stock Exchange, because of the management time and resources it had absorbed. One member, Peter Wills, made the point that, 'we had been dug in defending a position while outsiders had been stealing our business'. Another, Andrew Hugh Smith, claimed that '... uncertainty had been bedevilling the logical development of the market'.

Freed from the constraints of the case there was genuine optimism that the Stock Exchange was capable of repositioning itself for the future. David Steen observed that 'we have been on the defensive, arguing that the system must not change. Now a series of new dialogues must take place.' Peter Wills even went so far as to attribute this positive attitude to the RPC

[13] Ibid.    [14] Ibid.

because 'It had made us take a fundamental look at our rules and princi-ples. . . .' To that end George Nissen recommended the wider perspective of London's position in the emerging global market, noting that '. . . we had to ask ourselves whether we were trying to preserve the central market or whether seeking to maximize the effectiveness of London in international securities trading'.

After two days of discussion Council reached the unanimous conclusion on 22 July 1983 that the package agreed with the government should be accepted. The following official resolution was passed to mark their decision,

The Council authorises the Chairman to inform the Secretary of State that Council have accepted the proposal placed before them at their meetings on 21 and 22 July.[15]

The government believed it was achieving a modest victory in its policy of abolishing price fixing and liberalizing markets but was totally unaware of the far-reaching consequences of its actions. If they had been it is uncertain how far they would have pressed ahead with the demand for reform as it certainly jeopardized the system of market regulation and investor protec-tion and compensation that had developed within the securities industry since the Second World War. Though in retrospect many later commenta-tors saw in the government's actions a grand strategy to restore the City of London's position internationally, its objective at the time was much more restricted. Many also saw it as a government sell-out to the City. The *Financial Times* thought the Stock Exchange had obtained a good deal. In contrast, those managing the affairs of the Stock Exchange were much more aware of the fundamental changes that an end to fixed commissions would bring. The Council of the Stock Exchange was also aware that it had to persuade the membership to accept the changes that had been agreed with government, and that had to await a general meeting whose outcome was uncertain.[16]

On 28 July 1983 the Stock Exchange was informed that the case before the RPC had been adjourned. Legislation to bring a formal end to the RPC case had to await the outcome of the general meeting. On 16 August 1983 the Stock Exchange Council started discussions on the ways and means of dismantling minimum commissions. By October it had been decided firstly to dismantle fixed commissions on overseas securities, as the area where the competitive pressures were greatest, and where agreement already existed. At this stage single capacity was still believed to have a future by some on the Stock Exchange and others outside. The government was even willing to incorporate a statement on the preservation of single capacity in the bill

[15] LSE: Council, 21 and 22 July 1983.
[16] For example, Gallely and Ritchie, *The Big Bang*, 108; Thomas, *The Big Bang*, 1; Webb, *The Bigger Bang*, 35; Hamilton, *Financial Services Revolution*, 131–2; Moran, *Politics of the Financial Services Revolution*, 83; FT, 10 Aug. 1983, 15 Aug. 1983.

that needed to be passed exempting the Stock Exchange from the jurisdiction of the RPC. In terms of domestic securities discussions with members had produced three possible methods of dismantling the system of fixed commissions, with supporters being found for either a 'big bang' or 'class-by-class' or 'top-slicing' approach. Throughout, the Stock Exchange was being monitored by both the Bank of England and the Department of Trade and Industry in order to ensure that they were taking steps to comply with the conditions of the agreement. By 20 December 1985 five non-members had been appointed to the Council of the Stock Exchange, meeting one of the requirements.[17]

## Preparing for Big Bang

As early as January 1984 it was decided that the only feasible way of dismantling fixed commissions was the 'big bang' approach. If fixed charges were removed in one area, such as gilt-edged, that would be used by institutional investors to press for reductions in other areas, so precipitating a general and unplanned ending of minimum commissions. Similarly, a progressive reduction in rates, culminating in the complete removal of minimum charges, created problems of timing each stage in a way that would not both destabilize the structure of the market and, again, precipitate a general removal. All those complications could be avoided if a specific date was set when

Except for overseas securities, the commission on all classes of security would become negotiated at the same time, so avoiding the playing off of one area of business against another.[18]

This was all in keeping with the need to preserve an orderly market at all costs that had been at the heart of the Stock Exchange's efforts to escape the RPC case since 1980.

By then, however, the question of ending fixed commissions had become part of a general reform of the whole way the securities market operated. Faced with the inevitability of change in one central part of their operation the Council of the Stock Exchange also began to consider, seriously, the introduction of new dealing and settlement systems, involving the use of the latest technological advances. Such developments had been under discussion in the 1970s but the Stock Exchange had not pursued them aggressively at the time, confident in the ability of its existing market structure to meet all requirements. Subsequently, the RPC case had delayed consideration that might have been awakened by the ending of exchange controls. However, with the prospect of developing an electronic market place there

---

[17] LSE: Council, 2 Aug. 1983, 16 Aug. 1983, 4 Oct. 1983, 18 Oct. 1983, 15 Nov. 1983, 20 Dec. 1983; *FT*, 13 Dec. 1983.
[18] LSE: Council, 17 Jan. 1984.

was a great reluctance to begin dismantling the fixed commission structure until it was in place. As a result of this decision it became clear that the earliest fixed commissions could be ended was the autumn of 1985, for it was necessary to have a new system in place before the existing one was abandoned. Clearly the Big Bang was going to involve far more than the ending of fixed commissions. By February 1984 it was clear that single capacity could not be preserved without minimum commissions, as the government had been warned. Negotiable, or even commission-free transactions, were going to allow direct contact between non-members and the jobbers, no matter what rules and regulations were introduced on the Stock Exchange. Electronic trading systems would also make it even more difficult to police such relationships in the future. In turn this had serious implications for the government. Though single capacity had not been introduced in the interests of investor protection that was one of the functions it had come to perform. Consequently if it had to be abandoned something had to be put in its place.[19]

In addition to the dismantling of fixed commissions one area of change was already taking place on the Stock Exchange which, itself, would have profound effects on the nature of the London securities market, especially the separation between different participants. This was in the degree of outside capital permitted in stockbroking and jobbing firms. In the 1970s, this had been set at a maximum of 10 per cent for any single outside investor, which had turned out to be too low to attract serious interest. There had been a general reluctance to increase the maximum permitted level in case it led to banks and other financial institutions gaining a direct foothold in the market and so undermining the separation of function between broker and dealer. No change was proposed for brokers when the situation was reviewed in early 1982.

... Brokers had no difficulty in obtaining capital and provided that the restrictions on the amount of outside participation in Broking Firms remained at the present level there was no danger of commission cutting.[20]

In contrast, though jobbers appeared to have sufficient capital to support the markets they were making, they had insufficient to permit any form of expansion, especially into related activities such as trading in Eurobonds and financial futures. One firm had requested permission in 1980, denied at the time, to link up with a European bank so as to gain '... access to considerable extra capital to enable it to continue to operate in the Eurobonds market'. However, after a further review of the situation it became clear that access to additional capital was becoming a priority if both broking and jobbing firms were to retain even the business they currently did because of the rising costs of staff, equipment, and offices, and in order to finance transactions.

[19] LSE: Council, 7 Feb. 1984; *FT*, 12 Sept. 1983, 6 Oct. 1983.     [20] Ibid., 11 Jan. 1982.

Over the next five to ten years the provision of capital for both broking and jobbing firms was likely to be a major problem[21]

was the conclusion drawn in January 1984, by which time the Stock Exchange was willing to contemplate even more radical change. As it was, even in 1982 it was recommended that the maximum level of an outside holding was raised but only to 29.9 per cent. It was hoped that this would attract outside funds, especially from banks.

This recommendation was accepted and a few outside financial institutions were quick to take advantage of it, when it came into operation in October 1982. The US bank, Security Pacific Corporation, was one of the first, acquiring for £8.1m. a 29.9 per cent stake in the brokers, Hoare, Govett, for example. However, the real transformation of ownership came after July 1983. With the agreement to end fixed commissions, and the realization that single capacity would go, there was a sudden jockeying for position by outside finance houses, as they saw opportunities to create integrated banking and broking operations in London, which would include membership of the Stock Exchange for the first time.

Having been denied membership, and charged fixed commissions, British investment and commercial banks also saw this as an opportunity to create in London the type of integrated financial operations that existed in the United States and continental Europe. Thus, in the period before Big Bang in 1986 a number of the leading London merchant banks acquired stakes in 11 brokers and three jobbers. Warburgs teamed up with the jobbers Akroyd & Smithers and two brokers, Rowe & Pitman and Mullens. A similar course was followed by some of the major commercial banks, such as Barclays, who linked up with the jobbers Wedd, Durlacher and the brokers de Zoete & Bevan. There was also a rush of foreign banks cementing relationships with London brokers such as Phillips & Drew and Union Bank of Switzerland. The giant New York bank, Citicorp, teamed up with three brokers, Vickers da Costa, Scrimgeour Kemp Gee, and J. & E. Davy while its US rival, Chase Manhattan, contented itself with two, namely Laurie Milbank and Simon & Coates. Even the chairman's own firm, Quilter Goodison, sold a 100 per cent stake to the French bank, Paribas, in 1986.[22]

A combination of the raising of the limit to 29.9 per cent and the recognition that not only would fixed commissions end but so would single capacity, meant that entirely new possibilities were opening up in the securities market. One considered view on the Stock Exchange in Jan. 1984 was that

[21] Ibid., 19 Feb. 1980.
[22] A. Lorenz, *BZW: The First Ten Years* (London 1986), 13, 15, 16, 20; W. J. Reader and D. Kynaston, *Professional Stockbrokers: A History of Phillips & Drew* (London 1998), 173; Hamilton, *Financial Services Revolution*, 138–9; LSE: Council, 5 Oct. 1982, 21 Nov. 1982, 20 Dec. 1983, 20 Apr. 1984; FT, 29 Sept. 1983, 31 Oct. 1983, 6 Nov. 1984, 15 Jan. 1986, 8 Nov. 1988, 21 Nov. 1988, 28 Nov. 1988, 7 Dec. 1988, 16 Dec. 1988, 31 Dec. 1988, 25 Oct. 1996.

... many of the existing guidelines had been designed to protect the minimum commission structure. . . .[23]

The problem was that nobody really knew what the future prospects of these brokers and jobbers were for they had operated so long within the restricted environment created by the London Stock Exchange's rules and regulations. What did appear to be clear to all was that brokers and jobbers needed additional capital if they were to compete and the banks and finance houses were keen to provide it as they could see huge potential gains flowing from integrated operations. Until then the notion had been persevered with that all members were independent agents free from the influence or control of outside financial institutions. The relationship between brokers and commercial bankers, for example, was considered an equal one with brokers having control of the market, through privileged access to jobbers, whereas bankers dominated the users, both through their own needs and their branch networks giving access to investors. However, banks increasingly centralized their national investment activities through their head office, whether for themselves or their clients, which then dealt with a small number of large broking firms. In turn, these stockbrokers were heavily dependent upon these banks for business and so keen to operate in ways that met their requirements, but, faced with fixed commissions, brokers were limited in what they could offer institutional clients like the banks, encouraging the banks to favour integrated operations if it became possible. At the same time the ban on direct contact between jobbers and non-members, including major investors like the merchant banks, who could generate substantial business in their own right, encouraged them to consider owning jobbing firms. Hence the rush of non-members to purchase strategic holdings in brokers and jobbers, when it became possible, even when it coincided with the ending of fixed commissions and thus a more competitive environment. Barclays Bank, for example, committed itself to pay £50m. for de Zoete & Bevan and £100m. for Wedd, Durlacher, in the event of 100 per cent outside ownership being permitted on the Stock Exchange. By the end of 1986 around 65 outside financial institutions had bought stakes in 90 brokers and 15 jobbers, and these included most of the largest firms.[24]

The maintenance of single capacity had become increasingly difficult long before the agreement to end fixed commissions. More and more business could be matched within a stockbroker's own office, because of their increasing size, and then presented to the market as a 'put through' rather than being actually conducted via the jobber. Also, once exchange controls

[23] LSE: Council, 10 Jan. 1984.
[24] Ibid., 20 Jan. 1981, 16 Dec. 1981; W. A. Thomas, *The Securities Market* (Hemel Hempstead 1986), 29; H. Mcrae and F. Cairncross, *Capital City: London as a Financial Centre* (London 1984), 135–44; J. Attali, *A Man of Influence: Sir Siegmund Warburg, 1902–1982* (London 1984); Lorenz, *BZW*, 21–2, 28–31; B. Widlake, *In the City* (London 1986), 185.

had been abolished in 1979 the barriers surrounding the free flow of securities to and from Britain no longer existed. Consequently, investors in Britain were able to access, easily, foreign markets for securities rather than having to direct business through the London market. In these foreign markets there existed dual capacity firms who dealt directly with major investors, quoting buy and sell prices and transacting business commission free. In November 1982, further reductions in the minimum commissions set for overseas business had already been agreed, in order to help the competitiveness of Stock Exchange members in this area, illustrating the impact that the ending of exchange controls was already having. However, yet again a more radical overhaul was made difficult by the RPC case.[25]

In the 1980s this undermining of single capacity also came a lot closer to home with the formation of the London International Financial Futures Exchange (LIFFE). The London Stock Exchange had had the opportunity to take the lead in European financial futures in the 1970s but had failed to capitalize on it because of fears over the attitude of the Bank of England and an unwillingness to compromise over commission charges and single capacity. There was also the question of whether any financial futures market would cover all who wanted to participate or only members of the Stock Exchange. In the end the London Traded Options Market (LTOM) was formed as a defensive measure to protect the Stock Exchange's underlying market in securities. However, access to this market was restricted to members of the London Stock Exchange and bound by that institution's rules and regulations. There was no attempt to develop it as a market in its own right, meeting new needs at a time of increased fluctuations in currencies, interest rates, and security prices. Due to the relative failure of LTOM, with little business being reported until 1982, and the need for such a facility in London, others took up the challenge and proceeded to develop a financial futures market independent of the Stock Exchange. These even included members of the Stock Exchange, principally Jack Wigglesworth of Greenwells, a stockbroking firm. Though facing the same opposition to the scheme from the Bank of England, as the Stock Exchange had experienced, the backers of LIFFE persevered.[26] Throughout the Stock Exchange had been in a dilemma. A number among its members wanted to participate in the new market because of the advantages it possessed for their existing business, as well as opening up new avenues. In contrast, the Stock Exchange as an institution was worried that if large losses were incurred by those members who participated this could have serious consequences for the rest of the membership and ultimately themselves.

[25] LSE: Council, 15 Apr. 1980, 1 July 1980, 16 Feb. 1982, 30 Nov. 1982, 21 Dec. 1982.
[26] Ibid., 20 Jan. 1981, 3 Mar. 1981, 2 Feb. 1982, 1 June 1982, 7 Dec. 1982, 18 Jan. 1983, cf. D. Kynaston, *LIFFE: A Market and its Makers* (Cambridge 1997), 22–3, 27, 29, 30, 34–5, 44, 60; *FT*, 5 Mar. 1985.

There could be dangers in locating the new Financial Futures floor in the Stock Exchange in that the impression might be gained that it was regulated by the Council.[27]

Consequently, the Stock Exchange wanted to be consulted about what was happening for they were keen to protect their own position. They were worried that an Exchange dealing in financial futures contracts, involving securities such as gilt-edged stock, could evolve into an alternative market for these securities and so challenge the Stock Exchange itself.

As LIFFE took shape it did pose a problem for the Stock Exchange for, inevitably, those of its members involved in its establishment wanted to join it, with Laurie Milbank & Co., L. Messel & Company, Panmure Gordon & Co., and Wedd, Durlacher, Mordaunt & Co. being among the most prominent. The Stock Exchange was willing to permit this though membership of other exchanges in London had been denied in the past, because of fears that they would develop as alternatives to the Stock Exchange. However, two conditions were set. First, single capacity had to be observed by all Stock Exchange members operating on LIFFE, even though that exchange intended to permit dual capacity. Secondly, members could only join LIFFE through a separate limited company so that any losses they made there would not impinge on the Stock Exchange. As a result the rules of the Stock Exchange, while not banning its members from membership of LIFFE, did make it difficult and unattractive for them to join. Nevertheless, because LIFFE was going to trade a gilt-edged futures contract the major Stock Exchange firms involved in that market, both brokers and jobbers, made it clear they would join.[28] In July 1982, 27 out of LIFFE's total members of 261 were Stock Exchange firms. The Stock Exchange was even warned that 'Any artificial restrictions would lessen the influence of the Stock Exchange on LIFFE.' As it was, LIFFE opened for business at the end of September 1982 with an ex-Stock Exchange employee, Michael Jenkins, as Chief Executive. The gilts contract was introduced on 18 November 1982 and it did result in the Stock Exchange losing some business. LIFFE's system of dual capacity and negotiable commissions proved more flexible and appealing to customers than the Stock Exchange's rigid demarcation between brokers and dealers, combined with a fixed scale of charges. This was especially so for the large financial institutions who generated most of the business, and wanted to deal directly with market-makers or even participate themselves. In July 1982 32 UK banks and 56 foreign banks had already agreed to join LIFFE and more were to follow. Consequently, even closer to home the concept of single capacity was becoming unsustainable because a growing number of the Stock Exchange's own membership, especially the larger firms of brokers and jobbers, needed the flexibility to either make prices or deal directly with institutional investors, if they were to

[27] LSE: Council, 7 Apr. 1981.
[28] Ibid., 5 Jan. 1982, 19 Jan. 1982, 2 Feb. 1982, 4 May 1982; Kynaston, *LIFFE*, 47–9, 55–6.

compete successfully for business with those members, such as banks and foreign brokerage houses, who already did. Nevertheless, as late as May 1985 jobbers continued to be refused permission to act as both brokers and dealers when operating on LIFFE.[29]

What the agreement with the government over minimum commissions thus began was the unravelling of the complex web of rules and regulations that had governed the activities of members for much of the twentieth century. These rules had gradually stopped Stock Exchange members evolving in ways best suited to meet the needs of the investors they served and the markets they operated in. For some this would have involved close formal links with outside financial institutions while for others it would have meant dual capacity operations. London certainly possessed no firms like Merrill Lynch of New York. In 1983 Merrill Lynch had assets of $1.25bn. while those of one of the largest London brokers, Hoare, Govett, was a mere £30m. and that of the largest jobbers, Akroyd & Smithers, was £40m. Thus Big Bang would not only involve changes to the rules and regulations of the Stock Exchange but would have far-reaching consequences for the organization of its member firms.[30]

Also, if single capacity went the Stock Exchange's ability to ensure investor protection became much more limited, and both it and the government had to accept the new situation that would then exist. The Stock Exchange had long recognized its limitations in this direction, as in the problems over insider trading, where they had pressed for government intervention. It was only from 1980 that the government, however, began to recognize that it had a role to play in these areas, rather than leaving it up to the Stock Exchange and bodies, such as the Takeover Panel. Therefore, though the government little realized it when it pressed ahead with its policy of abolishing fixed commission on the Stock Exchange, the result was a true revolution in the securities market for so much rested on that structure. This made it very difficult for anyone, even those in the Stock Exchange, or in financial services generally, to predict what would be the outcome of the changes that were now collectively labelled 'The Big Bang'. So many other developments had taken place, and were continuing to take place, that the London Stock Exchange's new position could hardly be guessed at.

Certainly by February 1984, by which time the concept of Big Bang had been fully accepted, the Council of the Stock Exchange was fully aware of the momentous changes that were facing it. One of the members of the Council, Patrick Mitford-Slade, well articulated current feelings when he reflected that

At the time of the agreement with the government at the end of July 1983, some of the Council and many users had been sceptical about the link argument and had

---

[29] LSE: Council, 18 May 1982, 14 May 1985, cf. Kynaston, *LIFFE*, 72, 87, 112.
[30] *FT*, 12 Sept. 1983, 19 Sept. 1983.

hoped that the monitoring of change would help to preserve single capacity with negotiated commissions . . . as the debate had developed many of the sceptics had realised that with all the pressures that there would be on the system, the chances of preserving the present system were small. First, there was the growing internationalisation of the securities markets and the inevitable competition from overseas houses; second and more important, both the government and the Bank of England had adopted a 'Laissez faire' attitude . . . neither body had been of any help in attempting to preserve single capacity but seemed to be driving the City inexorably towards financial conglomeration, in order to balance the power of the foreigner, and consequently towards opening up the securities markets, which would lead inexorably to dual capacity trading.

Big Bang had become more than a decision to abandon fixed commissions on one specific date rather than phase it in over a period of time. The phrase now referred to the revolution taking place in the City of London's financial markets and institutions, reflecting both the culmination of change stemming from the introduction of Eurodollars in the 1960s, through the foreign exchange upheavals in the 1970s, to the current transformation of the Stock Exchange.

There was also a new attitude abroad which had, at last, infected the Stock Exchange after all the delays, obstructions, and missed opportunities of the past. As Patrick Mitford-Slade went on to say, 'many people no longer feared change but accepted the challenge and were anxious for change to occur as soon as possible.' What was now required was to plan for that change and ensure that it took place in as orderly a way as possible, so as to avoid serious disruption to the markets, as they had to continue functioning throughout.

The financial world was a continuous and dynamic one and so the transformation of its systems and practices had to be accomplished without shutting down at any stage. The older systems had to be kept going while the new ones were developed and tested, and then the transition from one to the other had to be accomplished without a moment's delay or mismatch. Patrick Mitford-Slade again warned how difficult this was going to be

The period of change was certain to be uncomfortable and everyone, including the authorities, must accept that a new market system would be unlikely to be as good, at least in the short term, as the old system either from the point of view of liquidity across a wide range for securities or of investor protection. However, if the Council were to be free to shape the market without too many inhibitions, it could be a better system after a time.[31]

The problem the Stock Exchange faced was the need to create a new trading system that continued to cope with both block trades from institutions and small orders from individual investors but in the context of all members being able to both make markets and deal directly with investors.

[31] LSE: Council, 7 Feb. 1984.

The simpler system of brokers buying and selling on behalf of their clients, and jobbers acting as intermediaries between brokers, was no longer possible to sustain. Thus it was not only necessary to move to negotiable commissions and dual capacity but also to a new trading system. In the meantime any interim changes or piecemeal reductions in commission rates were resisted. A small reduction in the charges made for transactions in gilt-edged was agreed in February 1984, under pressure from the financial institutions. However it was decided to hold back any further relaxation of the 29.9 per cent limit on outside participation of member firms until the date of Big Bang so as to reduce demands for the premature end to single capacity. Nevertheless, it was accepted by March 1984 that 100 per cent ownership had become inevitable, fuelling the stake-building that was taking place in brokers and jobbers by British and foreign banks and other financial institutions.[32] Thus, by early 1984 the Stock Exchange was faced with a situation where it had to plan for the ending of both fixed commissions and single capacity and devise an entirely new trading system against a background of rapid developments in information technology and the growing internationalization of the securities business. Finally, it had to incorporate the participation of major financial institutions that had been denied membership in the past.

## PRESERVING AN IDENTITY

Also, since the Second World War the Stock Exchange had become more than a market for securities for it had also attempted to provide the growing range of services that its members required, ranging from the settling of transactions once completed to the provision of relevant financial and other information. This was done both as a service to its membership and as sources of profit in its own right, supplementing income derived from membership fees, listing charges, and property rents. Since 1947, when the dual ownership structure of the Stock Exchange finally ended, its activities as a market and a business had gradually merged so that it was difficult to disentangle one from the other. The Stock Exchange now had a chief executive, as well as a chairman, whose role it was to run it successfully and profitably but, not necessarily, in the interests of the members whose priorities lay in the market rather than all the additional services. Even in 1986 this was not fully recognized for Council had concluded that:

Since settlement and Information Technology were now the financial core of the undertaking, if they were sold what was left would be hardly viable.[33]

The TALISMAN system for settling transactions in gilt-edged stocks and shares had given Stock Exchange members an edge over non-members as

[32] Ibid., 21 Feb. 1984, 20 Mar. 1984.
[33] Ibid., 3 June 1986, cf. 10 Feb. 1982, 16 Mar. 1982.

it greatly simplified the delivery of and payment for these securities, reducing the office staff firms needed to maintain for such purposes. The system was then continually extended to cover additional categories of securities, such as South African gold-mining shares, as well as improved so as to offer faster delivery times. However, the more numerous and varied the securities to be settled, and the less time available, the more complex had to be the system. The attempt to extend the system to Australian mining shares, for example, had gone badly wrong by 1985 because of technical problems. At the same time the Stock Exchange was looking for outside participation in the system, especially from banks, in order to both reduce the costs it was incurring and make the system more comprehensive.

From June 1982 the Stock Exchange was investigating an equity settlement system which would involve brokers, banks, and institutional investors. It would centralize the holding and transfer of shares and so eliminate much paperwork. The problem was that the more the Stock Exchange turned its settlement system into a general facility the less advantages it gave to its own members. There were thus those in the Stock Exchange who doubted the wisdom of proceeding further down the path of a large investment in settlement systems which, important as they were, were not central to the Stock Exchange's main function of providing the market. Even in 1982 it was suggested that this would be best left to others, but the majority view continued to be that it was a core function that the Stock Exchange should perform as a service to its membership.[34]

At a time of uncertainty the Stock Exchange tried to bolster its position both in the market and among its membership by providing additional services like settlement systems. Another service was the continuing development of the Topic Information System (TOPIC), which displayed prices and information to all members and other subscribers. In the early 1980s the Stock Exchange continued to become more and more a business in its own right, selling services to its members and others at a price that generated a healthy profit. TOPIC, for example, was referred to as an '. . . outstanding commercial success . . .' in February 1982, while at the same time those members who provided much of the information it displayed, relating to current prices of securities, were complaining of the time and cost involved in doing so, for which they received no financial benefit.[35] The problem was that there was a lack of any clear sense of purpose on the Stock Exchange as it was trying to operate both as a business and a market. Survival of the Stock Exchange as an institution was equated with its ability to generate a growing income through diversifying into such related activities as providing settlement systems and information. However, the survival of the market that it provided required more than that. It required the members to be able

---

[34] LSE: Council, 1 July 1980, 16 Mar. 1982, 30 June 1982, 1 June 1982, 21 Sept. 1982, 15 Feb. 1983, 17 Jan. 1984, 5 Feb. 1984.
[35] Ibid., 4 Nov. 1980, 17 Dec. 1980, 30 June 1981, 2 Feb. 1982, 2 Mar. 1982.

to thrive in an increasingly competitive international environment, and to that end they needed to be able to match their rivals in terms of organization, capital, costs, and methods of operation, and that was what they had not been doing, because they were held back by the rules and regulations of the institution to which they belonged. Useful and valuable as settlement and information services were they were not central to the role performed by the Stock Exchange for its membership, which was the provision of an orderly market. Even before the agreement with the government in July 1983 there were signs of growing unhappiness among the membership. It was reported to the Council of the Stock Exchange, in April 1982, that,

The membership as a whole were concerned at the increasing size of the organisation which was becoming progressively more expensive.[36]

Like many long-lived organizations when largely immune from competition, the Stock Exchange had become bureaucratic and costly over time, confusing its role as a market with an ambition to provide a comprehensive range of services for its members, whether they wanted them or not and with little regard to whether it was the most suitable and most cost-effective provider. Instead of expressing serious concern at the loss of the international market the Stock Exchange was congratulating itself in the early 1980s on the success of TOPIC which, by August 1982, was providing 6,000 pages of information to its clients. However, only 1,000 of those came from the Stock Exchange, indicating the gulf that had opened up between the Stock Exchange as an institution and the activities of its membership. As it was the Stock Exchange had entered an area in which there was growing competition from other providers, most notably the news agency firm of Reuters. There was a growing feeling on the Stock Exchange that it had gone too far into the business of becoming a provider of financial information and that it should pull back, recognizing that its prime function was the market. One conclusion reached in November 1982 was that

If a choice had to be made it might be better to sell price information rather than to develop further the means of information.[37]

Despite these reservations the Stock Exchange continued with the development of its financial information service.

In contrast, the Council of the Stock Exchange were well aware that they had to be very responsive both to users and members if they wanted to retain the gilt-edged market. As early as June 1981, long before the agreement with the government that was to produce Big Bang, reform of the gilt-edged market was being discussed. At that stage these focused on the

---

[36] Ibid., 6 Apr. 1982, cf. the view of those establishing LIFFE that the Stock Exchange was not the model to follow if they wanted to create a dynamic exchange, see Kynaston, *LIFFE*, 47.
[37] LSE: Council, 2 Nov. 1982, cf. 17 Aug. 1982, 7 June 1983; for Reuters see D. Read, *The Power of the News: The History of Reuters* (Oxford 1992), 301, 307–8, 401–3.

problems of settlement rather than trading systems. Since the First World War gilt-edged securities had been traded for cash rather than the account, as with other securities, creating problems for the delivery of and payment for stock. All transactions had to be settled, rather than only the residual balance after the cancelling out of numerous transactions through clearing. It was observed in May 1982 that:

The gilt-edged market was an extremely important part of the securities market in the Stock Exchange and was quite different from the equity market in that being a true cash market it required the provision of facilities for borrowing and lending stock. The sums involved were such that any breakdown could prejudice the workings of the money market throughout the City ... the present 'paper' system was vulnerable to surges in turnover. The temporary improvements introduced in recent years had worked well but it was doubtful if it could cope if volumes increased substantially.[38]

The Stock Exchange was keen to do all it could to accommodate the gilt-edged market, faced as it now was with competition from LIFFE's futures contracts. It proposed the creation of a transfer and settlement system that involved an integrated data network (IDN) and book entry transfer (BET) for UK government securities.

Much of the trading in government stock, notably short-dated issues, already took place outside the Stock Exchange, with the discount houses playing a prominent role. Consequently, there was no guarantee that the Stock Exchange would retain that part of the market it still held unless it improved the facilities it provided, as well as continue to remain competitive in terms of commission rates. This was recognized on the Stock Exchange for they

... could not seek to control dealings in gilt-edged securities outside the Stock Exchange, but BET and IDN would give a competitive advantage to those who were part of the system.[39]

At this stage the Stock Exchange was working closely with the Bank of England in developing improvements to the gilt-edged market that would leave the actual market mechanism intact. Co-operation continued through 1982 with the Bank of England making reassuring noises over any threat to the Stock Exchange's gilt-edged market posed by LIFFE. According to Mullens, the government broker, in January 1982,

... the Bank took the view that the spot market was of overriding importance and Liffe had a useful but peripheral function to perform.[40]

In January 1983 the Bank made it clear that it expected the transfer system for gilt-edged securities (BET), which it was developing with the Stock Exchange, to be available to non-members such as the discount

[38] LSE: Council, 18 May 1982, cf. 30 June 1981.
[39] Ibid., 18 May 1982.     [40] Ibid., 19 Jan. 1982.

houses and, later, private investors. The Stock Exchange was agreeable to this having long shared the market. By January 1984 this project, now referred to as the Central Gilts Office (CGO) had cost £7.8m. to develop, jointly funded by the Stock Exchange and the Bank of England. Annual operating costs were estimated at £2.25m. and the whole scheme was to be introduced in July 1984. However, by the beginning of 1984 the Bank of England was becoming worried about the role to be played in the gilts-market by the post Big Bang Stock Exchange. It was reported to the Stock Exchange in March 1984,

... the Bank had made it clear since the agreement with the Government in 1983, that the main planks of its policy towards the evolving Stock Exchange were that there should be a strong central liquid market and that investors should be adequately protected.

Though the Bank did have these general concerns its priority was to preserve the market for government debt, which was its direct responsibility. However, the Bank was keen to see the London Stock Exchange become a global leader in the international securities business, though the actual means used to achieve this were left to the Stock Exchange.

The Bank had made it clear that it was for the Stock Exchange to reach decisions on the future structure of the gilt-edged market, but this structure would have to be acceptable to the Bank and devised in such a way so that the Bank would be persuaded to keep the business inside the Stock Exchange.[41]

Thus, the Bank of England was pursuing a policy of supporting change in the Stock Exchange but was concerned about what might happen to the market in gilt-edged securities. What the Bank of England wanted was a single market which would be simple to regulate and this was most easily achieved if that market was within the Stock Exchange, because of the close working relationship that had grown up over the years. If the Stock Exchange would not meet the Bank's requirements then it could lose the gilt-edged market.

To reinforce its point the Governor of the Bank of England made a public speech in March 1984, of which a prior copy was sent to the Stock Exchange, illustrating the working relationship between the two financial institutions that existed. According to the Governor there was

... growing recognition that there are powerful institutions, both foreign and domestic, which are not members of the Stock Exchange, and which are quite capable of making efficient and competitive markets outside and, to an increasing extent, are already doing so. It seems to me that the market fragmentation to which this leads is unattractive and undesirable because it tends both to make market liquidity overall less than it would otherwise be and seriously to exacerbate the problem of ensuring effective market regulations . . . compelling as these arguments

[41] Ibid., 16 Mar. 1984, cf. 18 Jan. 1983, 7 June 1983, 10 Jan. 1984.

are for concentrating securities activity to the maximum extent possible through the central market provided by the Stock Exchange, no central market can expect to maintain its position, and still less to draw in additional business, unless it is at least as competitive and efficient as markets outside, and is ready to accommodate participants who would otherwise have no alternative but to undertake their business outside.[42]

From the Bank's perspective regulations and control would be much simpler if all trading was consolidated under the control of the Stock Exchange through it admitting all those involved, including discount houses, banks, and foreign brokerage houses.

However, such was the pace and degree of change unleashed by the ending of exchange controls in 1979 and the July 1983 agreement, that the Bank of England was not in control of what was taking place. What the government had seen as a modest reform to encourage competitiveness in the securities market was turning into a transformation of radical proportions because of the coincidence of timing and circumstances. In April 1984, for example, it was admitted that the proposed new Central Gilts Office could now become incompatible with the way the market was evolving and by October the whole project was in doubt. It had been designed by the Bank of England and the Stock Exchange to fit a market where jobbers and brokers had distinct roles. Instead, what emerged was a radically new structure to the gilt-edged market. What the Bank of England now proposed was a system of primary dealers who would have to establish separately capitalized subsidiaries to ensure that adequate capacity was always available to support the gilt-edged market. As the volume of gilt-edged business would, inevitably, fluctuate this meant tying up capital which might otherwise have been employed to support activity elsewhere in the securities market, such as in domestic equities or international bonds. This move indicated that the Bank of England's prime aim was to safeguard the market in UK government debt rather than mastermind the re-emergence of London as the centre of the global securities market. That was left to the Council of the London Stock Exchange.[43]

No matter what the outcome of the Big Bang was to be when it took place in 1986, the Bank of England, acting for the government, needed a system for trading the national debt. Consequently, the senior partner in Mullens, Nigel Althaus, who had been brought in from Pember & Boyle in 1982 at the Bank's insistence, and his partner Kenneth Hill, who handled the dealing in government debt, joined the Bank of England in 1986. The

[42] LSE: Council, 6 Mar. 1984 (speech reprinted).

[43] Ibid., 17 Apr. 1984, 26 June 1984, 31 July 1984, 16 Oct. 1984; *FT*, 19 Sept. 1983, 8 Nov. 1984, 5 Mar. 1985; P. Phillips, *Inside the New Gilt-Edged Market* (Cambridge 1987), 12–13; Bank of England, *British Government Securities: The Market in Gilt-Edge Securities* (London 1993), 6–14, 14–16; C. Goodhart, 'Structural Changes in the British Capital Markets', in C. Goodhart, D. Currie, and D. T. Llewellyn (eds.), *The Operation and Regulation of Financial Markets* (London 1987), 45.

Bank of England had always controlled the gilt-edged market but now, instead of acting through the government broker, Mullens, they were to do so directly. Though the Bank of England, especially David Walker, had been supportive of the Stock Exchange in its desire to free itself from the RPC case and transform itself into a more competitive market internationally, it also had its own agenda of preserving and enhancing the gilts market. At the same time it possessed neither the expertise nor the power to make the Stock Exchange into a more globally competitive market. Only the Stock Exchange itself, both in terms of the Council and the members, could do that.[44]

The reform of the Stock Exchange, especially from 1983 onwards, also produced other changes. On the back of the inquiry by Professor L. C. B. Gower into improving investor protection, the government launched a wholesale reform of the way investments and securities were supervised, with a presumption towards state regulation. Initially, the Stock Exchange had believed that a positive response from themselves would result in the continuance of self-regulation.

... the proposals in the Gower report emphasised the need for investor protection. In the light of recent development the objectives should be the creation of a fair and orderly market, from which would stem investor protection. The Stock Exchange now had the opportunity to take the initiative and should consider what the constitution, administration and funding of the Council for the Securities Industry should be and its relationship with the Government and other authorities.[45]

The Stock Exchange had a long and successful post-war record in policing the relationship between its own members and the investing public, including its compensation scheme. The Gower enquiry itself had been prompted by failures among non-member financial intermediaries and Gower himself had publicly praised the self-regulatory activities of the Stock Exchange. Though largely uncredited, the Stock Exchange had been the main instigator behind the attack on the practice of insider trading, forcing a reluctant government and an uninterested Bank of England to take action. The result was the Takeover Panel, as most cases arose from privileged knowledge regarding bids and merger proposals. It was only in June 1980 that the government went further and passed legislation to make insider dealing an offence. The Stock Exchange were happy to co-operate passing on 36 possible cases to the Department of Trade by September 1982. Of these only 2 had resulted in prosecutions. However, the Stock Exchange did not believe such a law could be enforced and were worried that it would

[44] D. Kynaston, *Cazenove & Co.: A History* (London 1991), 317; D. Wainwright, *Government Broker: The Story of an Office and of Mullens and Company* (East Molesey 1990), 107, 109, 111; R. Roberts, 'The Bank of England and the City', in R. Roberts and D. Kynaston, *The Bank of England: Money, Power, and Influence, 1694–1994* (Oxford 1995), 169; *FT*, 19 Sept. 1983, 26 Sept. 1983, 10 July 1985, 8 Nov. 1984.
[45] LSE: Council, 15 May 1984, cf. 1 May 1984.

only impede legitimate business. In fact they came to the conclusion that collective self-regulation was more effective for they had had some success in persuading the secretive Swiss banks to divulge information. In contrast, the Department of Trade let this initiative lapse. Consequently, with this track record the Stock Exchange had every reason to be optimistic that it would retain an important role in investor protection through the supervision of its members' relationships with their clients, despite the changes that were in train for Big Bang.[46]

Instead, what appeared in 1985 was a Securities and Investment Board (SIB) that was given considerable supervisory power over all aspects of investment, including the buying and selling of securities. Within this there were to be officially recognized Self-Regulatory Organizations (SROs) and investment exchanges (RIEs) that would have responsibility for particular sectors of the industry. The Securities Association was to supervise brokers and dealers, for example, taking over a function carried out by the Stock Exchange itself. The Stock Exchange itself requested, in September 1986, the right to be the recognized investment exchange not only for all equities but also gilts and options. Here however it met a challenge for part of this business was being conducted in London by non-members of the Stock Exchange. The London market in Eurobonds, for example was calculated to have a turnover equivalent to 20–30 per cent of that of London Stock Exchange and was largely handled by European banks and US brokers. There were an estimated 120 foreign securities houses in the City by this time. Though the Stock Exchange offered to act as the SRO on their behalf, without them having to join the Stock Exchange, there was a reluctance by these non-members to agree. There was the obvious fear that the Stock Exchange would use the power that self-regulation gave it to impose its own rules and regulations upon all participants in the market, whether they were members or not. The Stock Exchange thus saw the power it had exercised over the London securities market since 1945 slipping away from it, leaving it one among a number of self-regulatory bodies under the control of the Securities and Investment Board. It would no longer have privileged access to the Bank of England. The Stock Exchange thus lobbied hard to try and have non-members forced to accept its jurisdiction. Sir Kenneth Berrill, the SIB Chairman, the Governor of the Bank of England, and the Secretary of State for Trade and Industry were all approached for support. An attempt was also made to influence the views of the *Financial Times* with off-the-record briefings. No support was forthcoming and the Stock Exchange was left with no alternative but to seek some agreement with those non-members who had banded together in such organizations as the Association of

---

[46] LSE: Council, 25 June 1980, 7 Sept. 1982, 21 Sept. 1982; *FT*, 10 Aug. 1983, 10 Apr. 1986; Fishman, *Transformation of Threadneedle Street*, 40, 207; LSE: *Annual Report*, 1982; *Quality of Markets*, Oct.–Dec. 1991, 11.

International Bond Dealers (AIBD) and the International Primary Market Association (IPMA).[47]

These rival organizations threatened the Stock Exchange's status as the regulatory body for the securities industry. Having grown up on the back of trading in international securities, these new groupings could move into the domestic market and threaten the one area still dominated by the Stock Exchange. In the absence of both exchange controls and any support from either the government or the Bank of England, the Stock Exchange was acutely aware of how vulnerable it now was. Such was the size and the sophistication of the international market in securities, conducted in London by largely foreign banks and brokers, that it possessed the capacity to challenge the members of the London Stock Exchange for the business in the stocks of major British companies, especially those with an international orientation such as BP, Shell, Unilever, and RTZ. 'There is no statute obliging investors to transact their business in securities through the Stock Exchange' was Sir Nicholas's stark assessment, delivered to a meeting of the International Federation of Stock Exchanges in Stockholm in September 1984. Without some action the Stock Exchange could lose, progressively, the market in those major British stocks that were widely held internationally.[48]

In future it was only through a combination of providing the best market and a suitable regulatory environment that the Stock Exchange would be able to maintain its position. Those non-members, who had for so long picked away at the London Stock Exchange's international market but left its domestic operations relatively untouched, were now threatening to invade that territory as well. By the mid-1980s major US investment banks and brokerage firms such as Goldman Sachs and Merrill Lynch, as well as European universal banks, like Société Générale, conducted large operations in London and were eager to participate in the domestic market. With the Stock Exchange's regulatory position reduced to its own members it could not expect to bolster its position through assistance from either the government or the Bank of England. After a meeting with Sir Kenneth Berrill in January 1986, the Stock Exchange was left in no doubt that it would not be given a monopoly position within the securities market.[49]

## NEW WAYS: NEW ROLES

The Stock Exchange was now on its own. The unofficial contract that had been formed during the Second World War, and built up through the years

[47] LSE: Council, 6 Aug. 1985, 15 Oct. 1985; Widlake, *In the City*, 312, OECD, *Economic Survey 1986/7: United Kingdom Financial Markets* (Paris 1987), 38; Macrae and Cairncross, *Capital City*, 144; Plender and Wallace, *Square Mile*, 44–5; Kay, *Big Bang*, 11; Fishman, *Transformation of Threadneedle Street*, 86–9, 97.

[48] Quoted in *Stock Exchange Quarterly*, Sept. 1984, 7.

[49] LSE: Council, 19 Nov. 1985, 17 Dec. 1985, 7 Jan. 1986; F. Duffy and A. Henney, *The Changing City* (London 1989), 106; H. Bonin, *Société Générale in the United Kingdom* (Paris 1996), 97–8.

of the managed economy, had finally come to an end. One lay member of the Council (Alan Clements) suggested in October 1985 a radical solution to the new situation. The Stock Exchange should recover its old position through absorbing all those international markets that had been developed in London by non-members.

The Stock Exchange should strive to keep control over domestic securities, to exert some control over dealings in international securities, and to seek in the future to embrace the large and expanding Eurobond market.[50]

These were sentiments with which the chairman agreed but that did not mean it could be done. There already existed powerful banks and foreign brokerage houses with entrenched positions in the market and they had no desire to have their independence threatened by the Stock Exchange. The ending of exchange controls and the creation of the SIB had both merged the international and domestic securities market and created an opportunity for new but authorized markets to appear.[51]

The whole concept of designated dealers in overseas securities had been an attempt to respond to this international challenge by permitting Stock Exchange members, both jobbers and brokers, to have direct contact with the London offices of US brokers and other such firms, but to do so in such a way that denied such firms direct access to the domestic market. By October 1983 it was recognized that this attempt had failed.

. . . member firms were failing to get a reasonable proportion of the huge growth of overseas business. The importance of this now outweighed any risks which might be run in preserving intact the domestic market. The main factor which had always been regarded as supporting the domestic system—minimum commissions—was now to be removed and this put the influence which any new dealing system in international stocks had on the domestic market into a different perspective. The abandonment of minimum commissions would affect the Broker/Jobber balance and the jobbers must, if they were not to be substantially handicapped, be permitted to form organisations with the characteristics of International Dealers.[52]

At this stage all that was being suggested was the creation of firms of international dealers by either brokers or jobbers. These firms would be members of the Stock Exchange, though they could be 49 per cent owned by non-members, and they would be able to act as both brokers and jobbers so permitting them to make markets for, and trade commission-free with, non-members. They would not be permitted to trade from the floor as there was still the remote possibility, at that date, that single capacity would be preserved in the domestic market. Even so, it was recognized then that if single capacity was abandoned there would be no need for the category of

[50] LSE: Council, 29 Oct. 1985.
[51] Ibid., 21 Dec. 1982, 21 June 1983, 20 Sept. 1983.
[52] Ibid., 18 Oct. 1983, cf. 15 Apr. 1980, 17 June 1980, 1 July 1980, 16 Feb. 1982, 30 Nov. 1982, 13 Dec. 1983.

'international dealer'. Thus, when it became accepted by all that single capacity could not be sustained the need to create a special category of 'international dealer' was rendered superfluous.

Though there was a recognition on the Stock Exchange that further liberalization was essential if they were to stop the loss of business in American Depository Receipts (ADRs) to overseas markets, let alone regain it, there continued to be a reluctance to advance too quickly in allowing members complete freedom in their overseas operations. The Council of the Stock Exchange was trying to control the pace of change so that it did not destabilize the domestic market, which constituted the overwhelming bulk of its members activities. At the same time they were trying to promote orderly development in the international market, holding discussions with rival stock exchanges, such as New York while simultaneously exploring ways of creating a formal market in London for US securities as a counter to the drain of trading in the ADRs of major British companies to that centre. In Europe there was even a long-term strategy, expressed in 1984, that there would be an eventual amalgamation of all major stock exchanges. Having achieved this domestically in 1973 it was perfectly possible to envisage it taking place within the European Community, though it was recognized that there were major obstacles to be overcome.[53]

Amidst all this uncertainty and confusion experienced by the London Stock Exchange in the early 1980s, as the whole framework that had supported its market structure began to unravel, it did experience one area of success. This was the creation of an Unlisted Securities Market (USM) to cater for domestic securities that could not be granted a full quotation because of their small size, risky nature, or lack of an earnings record. In the late 1970s this was still recognized as a weakness in the British financial system, despite all the efforts of the market and the government to solve it over the years with, for example, such state-sponsored initiatives as the ICFC (which became 3I) and the National Enterprise Board. There continued to be a widespread belief that medium-sized companies were too large to rely on self-finance, assisted with bank loans, but too small to be floated publicly, with a subsequent quotation on the Stock Exchange.

The unwillingness of the Stock Exchange to grant a quotation to any company other than a substantial concern with a long track record did make it more difficult for newer and smaller companies to obtain the financial backing they required to finance further growth, other than by selling out to, or merging with larger companies. The small-scale flotations that had been so common between the wars had become a thing of the past by the 1960s and 1970s as the Stock Exchange took its role of regulator of the securities market more and more seriously. Again, the problem of the Stock Exchange being both the market and the supervisory body for the

[53] Ibid., 29 May 1984, 26 June 1984, 4 July 1984, 4 Dec. 1984, 14 May 1985, 4 June 1985.

whole industry led it down the path of caution. It was easier to police the market if the temptation of speculative issues was removed from both members and investors though at a cost of limiting opportunities available to those seeking finance for novel enterprises. Consequently, there certainly existed the possibility that, in the wake of the financial crises of the mid-1970s, there was a gap in the financial system that could be filled by a more liberal attitude towards obtaining a public market for new issues, with a less-demanding track record.[54]

The Stock Exchange's solution to the problem was to create an additional market—the USM—that would be recognized as separate from the main market, though part of it. By this device it was hoped to offer a home to securities which did not meet the strict requirements of a full quotation but still required a forum where they could be traded, if they were to attract the interest of investors. Such securities were traded under rule 163 which permitted deals to be done in stocks and shares which had not—nor could not—be accepted for an official quotation. The level of business being conducted in this way was growing but it was an unsatisfactory arrangement as it did not give investors a recognized and formal market for their holdings, and left the Stock Exchange in the difficult position of permitting trading to take place in securities over which it had exercised very little supervision. Either it had to reject these companies, further stimulating the OTC markets made by non-members or it had to create a market where these securities could be traded which would not jeopardize the reputation of the Stock Exchange. Refusing this business was not an attractive one for an analysis done in May 1981 revealed that business done under Rule 163, in the securities of companies that would be potential candidates for the USM, had grown 32 per cent by value and 48 per cent by volume, since the beginning of the year.

Spurred on by the prospects of increased business the Stock Exchange opened the USM in November 1981. Conditions for listing were simpler, cheaper, and less onerous than on the Stock Exchange proper, so attracting companies at an earlier stage of their development. This continued to worry the Stock Exchange, because of the risks it ran that one or a few disastrous issues would jeopardize the reputation it had built up of careful monitoring the financial health of those companies making new issues, and so weeding out the fraudulent and the risky. There was also the problem of a reappearance of market manipulation as it was easier for a few investors to control the stock of a smaller new issue than a large national company. Despite these doubts the Stock Exchange persevered with the USM, showing that a more positive attitude towards market developments was coming to the fore, prodded by the need to generate more turnover in equities for the membership and the threat of competition from an emerging over-the-

---

[54] R. Coopey and D. Clarke, *3i: Fifty Years Investing in Industry* (Oxford 1995), 199, 275.

counter market (OTC) provided by M. J. Nightingale & Co. The USM proved an immediate success attracting a stream of new company promotions, with many then gravitating to a full listing. By September 1986, 508 companies had floated on the USM raising £1bn. in the process. Of these 71 had moved on to the main market while those that remained had a market capitalization of £4.2bn. This compared to only 60 companies seeking a public listing in the 1976–80 period. With a listing on the USM costing from £70,000 to £120,000 compared to £230,000 to £300,000 for a full quotation it had opened up the stock market to a host of both new and established British companies, especially in more speculative areas like oil exploration and high technology. Though companies like these involved evident risks, and investors were exposed to market manipulation, because turnover was limited and the shares closely held, the USM contributed a dynamic new element to the British capital market in the first half of the 1980 stockbroking. Jobbers like Bisgood Bishop, with Brian Winterflood, and brokers such as Simon & Coates, with David Cohen, were sufficiently attracted by the potential of the USM to become experts in the securities listed there. Such was the success of the USM that the Stock Exchange was already considering in January 1985 introducing yet another market—the Third Market—to cater for even smaller issues and even riskier enterprises. This Third Market was formally set up on 26 January 1987 despite increased fears over the risks involved with such small and new companies.[55]

The Stock Exchange also designed a new index, at this time, to better reflect activity on the market. This index would also be the basis of an option contract to be traded on the Stock Exchange's own LTOM. As there was no desire to antagonize the *Financial Times*, who were responsible for the existing index, it was decided to open discussions with them on its structure and name. What was proposed was a new 100-share index that would replace the existing *FT* index. The Stock Exchange wanted the index to be called the Stock Exchange 100-share index, SEFT 100 for short, so as to gain the maximum publicity advantage. However, after discussions with the *Financial Times* it was agreed to call the index the FTSE 100 (Footsie 100) when it began on 3 January 1984. The good offices of the *Financial Times* was probably of more value at this time than the association of the Stock Exchange with an index. In any case LIFFE immediately announced plans to trade a financial futures contract based on the value of the FTSE 100.

[55] LSE: Council, 16 Sept. 1980, 5 May 1981, 16 Feb. 1982, 15 Feb. 1983, 1 Mar. 1983, 27 Mar. 1984, 22 Jan. 1985, 6 Aug. 1985, 15 Apr. 1986, 15 July 1986; D. Cobham, 'The Equity Market', in D. Cobham (ed.), *Financial Markets* (London 1992), 37; Coopey and Clarke, *3i*, 163; R. Buckland and E. W. Davis, *The Unlisted Securities Market* (Oxford 1989), 1, 7, 9, 11–14, 59, 63–5, 116, 130; LSE: *Quality of Markets*, July–Sept. 1990, 15; LSE: *Annual Report* 1981; *FT*, 12 Mar. 1984, 10 Nov. 1984, 30 Jan. 1985, 27 Jan. 1986, 10 Nov. 1986, 20 Jan. 1987, 24 Jan. 1987, 27 Jan. 1987, 28 Jan. 1988, 10 Feb. 1988, 28 Sept. 1988, 6 Feb. 1989, 30 Dec. 1996.

This was launched in May 1984 at the same time as the Stock Exchange's own option contract. Neither proved an immediate success as the Inland Revenue would not agree to a suitable tax structure. Nevertheless, it did lead to the introduction of an index that became the most widely used barometer of whether the market was rising and falling.[56]

With the USM and the FTSE index, the Stock Exchange had shown itself capable of initiating and carrying through important changes in the early 1980s. However, all this was dwarfed by the consequences of the ending of fixed commissions and the introduction of statutory financial regulation (SROs). The Stock Exchange had to deal with both problems simultaneously. As a priority it had to create a trading system which would allow the market to function when fixed commissions and single capacity disappeared. This had also to be done fairly quickly because the government and the Bank of England were unwilling to concede any delay in the timetable for dismantling the fixed-price regime, as that would be regarded by many as a Conservative government giving concessions to its friends in the City. The Stock Exchange was thus forced to take rapid decisions on both how to organize its market for the future and the trading system to be employed. It was therefore necessary to find a trading system and structure which was known to work. By the middle of 1984 the computerized trading networks used by NASDAQ along with the Toronto Stock Exchange's 'Cats' system, were being studied, and more ambitious plans were gradually being dropped.

Even at that stage a decision had been taken not to imitate the New York Stock Exchange with its system of specialists, which at least would have preserved the semblance of a broker/jobber division. On investigation it was discovered that New York's specialists were steadily losing their importance in the market, with almost 40 per cent of stock exchange turnover bypassing them completely. In addition to the specialists' growing inability to control the market within the New York Stock Exchange, they were losing more and more business to non-members as well. Consequently, the most obvious choice of introducing specialists in London was rejected. The conclusion was reached in July 1984, that:

... to introduce a specialist system with all its faults, on a largely unwilling membership would be to impose the second best at a time when the opportunity to make the right choice existed.

Having lagged in the move to introduce computerized trading systems, the London Stock Exchange now intended to overtake all its main rivals in Western Europe and North America and introduce an electronic system that would link up all its members and allow them to deal as they wished. Within that system some members would be able to become registered market-makers in specific stocks, feeding prices into the system. What was envisaged was

[56] LSE: Council, 6 Dec. 1983, 17 Jan. 1984, 3 Apr. 1984; Kynaston, *LIFFE*, 133, 152.

... a system which would take advantage of methods of communication that would enable members, wherever they were located, to see the prices made by market-makers and to be able to deal with them on the floor and by the telephone.[57]

Not only was this envisaged as being able to cope with the changes in the market, through the ending of single capacity, but there was also the hope that it would be better than that which was currently available. The majority of stocks that were traded on the London Stock Exchange generated very little activity and so no active market existed in them. Sales and purchases could only be achieved through negotiation of an agreed price, once buyers and sellers had been matched up. In contrast there were a small number of very actively traded issues in which jobbers quoted close prices and were always willing to buy and sell in large amounts. The proposed system attempted to create active markets in all quoted securities by forcing market-makers to display two-way prices for sales and purchases and guarantee to trade.

By July 1984 this new electronic market place was being referred to as SEAQ (Stock Exchange Automated Quotations) and was modelled on the New York Stock Exchange rival, NASDAQ. Though there did exist the fear that this system would lead to the trading-floor being deserted, this was not considered a strong possibility. It was not possible for the Stock Exchange to be certain about the future nature of the market, but the ending of floor trading was more predictable than they were willing to believe. The system being copied was operated without a trading-floor and was gaining business from the more traditional stock exchanges, including New York. At the same time the London Stock Exchange had had problems in the past holding some of its trading on the floor of the Stock Exchange. In January 1981 the jobbers, Smith Brothers, had declared their intention of withdrawing their dealers in gold shares from the floor of the Stock Exchange, and conducting all business in that market from their office. It was only after some pressure from the Council of the Stock Exchange that they were persuaded to rescind the move in March 1981.[58]

As it was, the Stock Exchange was able to build the SEAQ trading system into the TOPIC information network that was already in place and available to members. Though TOPIC had not been designed for that purpose, its development did form an excellent preparation for the new electronic trading system. Nevertheless, much work and investment still needed to be done.

A new central quotation database and display system for market-making prices would need to be designed together with trade-reporting software; this trading support system would represent the core of the new market.[59]

---

[57] LSE: Council, 10 July 1984, cf. 17 Apr. 1984.
[58] Ibid., 20 Jan. 1981, 3 Mar. 1981, 10 July 1984; *FT*, 13 July 1984, 20 July 1984.
[59] LSE: Council, 13 Apr. 1984.

This was the stage the Stock Exchange had reached by November 1984 and by May 1985 work on SEAQ was well advanced. When SEAQ, TOPIC, and TALISMAN were all in place, the Stock Exchange was of the opinion that they were sufficiently prepared for the era when fixed commissions and single capacity would have ended and full outside ownership of members would have begun. In June 1985 that date was set for October 1986.

Despite all the planning for and heavy investment in an electronic trading system there continued to be the expectation that the existing trading-floor would continue in use, with even worries that it would not possess sufficient capacity. At the very least there was the belief that electronic systems would always be unreliable and so a physical trading-floor was a necessity. Consequently, as late as March 1986, the Stock Exchange, in response to requests from its membership, was financing the reorganization of the trading-floor, so as to accommodate all those who intended to participate in the post Big Bang market. A few members did warn that the exercise was pointless but major jobbers, like Smith Brothers, had assured the Stock Exchange that it was necessary. Nevertheless, the emphasis was firmly on the electronic system, with expenditure on the trading-floor being cut back from November 1985 onwards. By September 1986 the Stock Exchange had in place, with SEAQ, a system that was capable of handling eight or nine transactions a second, which was only marginally less than NASDAQ. The aim was to more than double that to 20 per second so as to cope with the expected volume of business. As a first trial that Stock Exchange had introduced SEAQ international in June 1985 on which market-makers displayed the prices of 300 non-UK stocks.[60]

After further expenditure, development and testing the new electronic system for trading domestic equities was in place by 21 October 1986, and ready for the day of Big Bang, which had been set for 27 October. On that day the SEAQ worked well but TOPIC failed twice due to overloading, spoiling the celebrations for a system that had been hurriedly put together. In fact, so successful was the system that business quickly switched away from the trading-floor. Smith Brothers abandoned the trading-floor a month after Big Bang. The market had been able to exert a strong pull when most members belonged to small firms which could not afford to invest heavily in large and well-equipped computing and communications facilities and pay staff expensive salaries, plus bonuses, for their time and effort. However, long before the introduction of an electronic trading system members had been grouping themselves into ever-larger firms that could afford the necessary investment. Thus, again, it was the combination of developments that was conspiring to produce such a radical change in the structure of a securities market provided by the Stock Exchange. A

---

[60] LSE: Council, 21 May 1985, 4 June 1985, 16 July 1985, 6 Aug. 1985, 18 Mar. 1986, 15 June 1986, 16 Sept. 1986; *Stock Exchange Quarterly*, Dec. 1984, 23–4, Dec. 1985, 14–15; *FT*, 28 Dec. 1985.

physical trading-floor was sustainable if there were a sufficient number of members who found it cheaper to use the common facilities provided and which they paid for through their membership fee. However, by the mid-1980s the business transacted on the Stock Exchange was increasingly dominated by a small number of large firms, both among the brokers and jobbers. These firms found it most economical to operate from their offices, using computer screens and telephones. Thus, by January 1987 the Stock Exchange floor was being deserted by members, with soon only the traded options market being left.[61]

As it was, the real problem that emerged was that of settlement due to the volume of business, which exposed members to risk until a transaction was completed. One solution was to move to a system of rolling settlement with sales and purchases completed within a short period after the transactions took place, rather than every deal waiting until the end of the fortnightly account. Seven days was the period suggested in 1987 but this move to a rolling account was deemed impracticable under the existing settlement system. As the Stock Exchange was already working on a replacement for TALISMAN, called TAURUS, it was decided to wait until that was in place. However, these settlement problems paled into insignificance in October 1987 with the stock-market crash which began on Friday, 16 October. Such was the wave of selling that the systems were overloaded so that prices, when available, no longer reflected the current market, and some brokers and dealers resorted to not answering their telephones. By the end of that year there was a recognition that SEAQ was not delivering the quality of price information that the market required and improvements would have to take place. By then, though, there was no suggestion of returning to a physical trading-floor. Irrespective of its faults, whether predictable or unknown, the electronic market place had made itself the permanent and central element for securities trading in London. Instead there was a desire both to revive the notion of a fully computerized trading system, which would combine both display and dealing, and a much more comprehensive paperless settlement and payments system.[62]

Nevertheless, before the large firms finally took control of the Stock Exchange those members belonging to the small firms fought a strong rearguard action, as they had in the past over such changes as the use of advertising, the admission of women, or greater freedom for international transactions. In January 1985 the Council of the Stock Exchange had decided to make the move towards corporate ownership rather than individual membership, seeing this as '. . . a radical break with tradition'. This was a recognition that membership was moving towards a position where

[61] LSE: Council, 15 Oct. 1985, 5 Nov. 1985, 21 Oct. 1986, 28 Oct. 1986; *FT*, 21 Nov. 1985, 23 Apr. 1986, 3 Jan. 1987, 6 Feb. 1987, 19 Mar. 1984, 14 Oct. 1987, 19 Mar. 1984, 14 Oct. 1997.
[62] LSE: Council, 20 May 1986, 28 Oct. 1986, 3 Aug. 1987, 1 Dec. 1987; *FT*, 14 Aug. 1987.

large banks, both British and foreign, owned member firms. This was not only through existing members selling stakes in their firms to financial institutions, but through the desire of more and more banks to participate directly in the market. In August 1984 the merchant-banking firm of Schroders had set up a 29.9 per cent owned subsidiary—the maximum then permitted—and then applied for Stock Exchange membership. The rule on limited outside ownership had been designed to permit existing members to obtain additional capital but it was now being used, quite legitimately, by banks to recruit staff and set up their own stockbroking subsidiaries. The Stock Exchange could either tighten its rules on membership or it could accept what was happening, which was that companies rather than individuals or partnerships, dominated the securities market. Driving the Council of the Stock Exchange to favour corporate ownership rather than simply membership, was a need to create a structure whereby those who possessed the financial power, in terms of the business that they did, and the fees they paid could have that reflected in the decision-making mechanisms. Inevitably this meant that the individual members would have to relinquish power and this they resisted. Thus, though a new constitution had been proposed in March 1985, in which power was shifted to corporate members, it was rejected by the membership as a whole. Partners of small and medium-sized firms were still numerically superior. In the 1984 elections to Council they had showed their disapproval of Sir Nicholas's actions by pushing him into second place in the ballot. Thus the Stock Exchange was still trying to get the new constitution accepted as late as 30 September 1986. It concluded that there was a pressing need

...to identify those criteria which would persuade a 75 per cent majority of members to forgo their individual voting rights and transfer control to Firms.[63]

That pressing criteria turned out to be a payment of £10,000 per member, which was what it cost in November 1986 to put an end to the power of the individual member over policy-making in the Stock Exchange. As a result a favourable vote on the major constitutional changes was forthcoming from a meeting of members. More and more the decision taken in 1973 to merge with the provincial stock exchanges looked a mistaken one. It had been taken to consolidate the London Stock Exchange's monopoly over the domestic securities market, and to preserve fixed commissions and single capacity. However ten years later in 1983 that monopoly was already under threat with trading in ADRs abroad, while pressure from the government was to force the abandonment of fixed commissions. The larger London firms, with a number already involved in international operations or new ventures such as LIFFE, would probably have proved keener to change compared to the smaller firms more dependent on private clients

---

[63] LSE: Council, 21 Aug. 1984, 8 Jan. 1985, 12 Mar. 1985, 11 June 1985, 12 Mar. 1986; R. Roberts, *Schroders: Merchants & Bankers* (London 1992), 507; *FT*, 7 June 1985.

and domestic equities. However, the merger had considerably boosted the power of the smaller firms and so they had to be bought off. Achieving constitutional change required a 75 per cent majority and, with many members unconvinced of the need for change or convinced that it was not in their interests, it would not be easy to achieve. Consequently, persuading the membership to vote for change can be regarded as a major feat of lobbying and argument by those in favour of reform, for it could easily have been lost.

Long before the individual members were bought off the Council of the Stock Exchange was working on plans to persuade large corporate non-members to join. They were prompted in this policy by both the government and the Bank of England, as a means of stimulating competition within the markets for both gilt-edged stock and equities. However, the Stock Exchange now required little outside prompting having seen that it was impossible to protect the domestic market. There was also the continuing need to reach some agreement with the numerous securities firms operating from London but previously excluded from membership. To this end it was necessary not only to change the rules on admission but also to give the new members a major voice within the Stock Exchange, to reflect their importance within the securities market. Otherwise any attempt at subsequent change or reform could be thwarted by the individual members, in whose hands the votes lay, and whose interests were radically different from these large, highly capitalized global operators.[64] By the middle of 1985 the Stock Exchange had accepted that member firms could be 100 per cent owned, by single non-members (from 1 March 1986), which meant that they could be full subsidiaries of British or foreign banks. At the same time the Stock Exchange was actively planning how to capture the international securities market that was already active in London.[65]

By November 1985 the way to proceed was clear. The Stock Exchange had to attract as members those firms, already in London, who were conducting an international equities business. This recognized that the bond market had been irrevocably lost, as it had developed its own organization and mechanisms. However, international equity trading was still in its infancy, and so the London Stock Exchange stood a chance of capturing a significant proportion of the business taking place, but only if it could offer an attractive home for the major participants, prominent among whom were foreign firms. The introduction of SEAQ international, a variation of SEAQ, offered these global players an attractive market place where major international securities could be traded with all the rules and regulations necessary for an orderly market. This was what the London Stock Exchange had long experience in. The stumbling block was the Stock Exchange itself,

---

[64] LSE: Council, 30 Sept. 1986, cf. *FT*, 21 Feb. 1985, 9 July 1988, 10 Nov. 1988.
[65] Ibid., 8 Jan. 1985, 7 May 1985, 4 June 1985, 18 June 1985, 30 July 1985, 20 Oct. 1985, 5 Nov. 1985, 19 Nov. 1985, 17 Dec. 1985.

as it was perceived by these international firms as an expensive and bureaucratic organization that would stifle rather than promote their efforts to build up an international equities market akin to that existing in Eurobonds. The government was reluctant to see foreign firms, especially the Japanese, obtain too large a role but even it could see that it would be better if they were members, because of the international business they would bring to the Stock Exchange. Such a move would also encourage reciprocity, with British banks and brokers obtaining membership of the Tokyo Stock Exchange. Thus the matter lay entirely with the London Stock Exchange and its ability to reach an agreement with the newly formed 186 member International Securities Regulatory Organization (ISRO) regarding a merger.[66]

Considering the changes taking place in the Stock Exchange, and what was in progress for October 1986, those operating in international markets were less hostile to a merger than they would have been in the past. With no fixed commissions, permission to operate as broker/dealers and full outside ownership, most of the barriers that had once existed to Stock Exchange membership for North American brokerage houses or European banks were scheduled to disappear. There was also a general relaxing of rules that might inhibit international firms from joining, such as the need to have separately capitalized subsidiaries to trade in overseas securities. The Stock Exchange also decided to make the cost of joining relatively cheap. In February 1986 an entry fee of £20,000 was set, which compared very favourably to buying a seat on the New York or Tokyo Stock Exchanges. Even LIFFE had charged £30,000 each when it had made a new offering of seats in January 1982. These tactics quickly paid off with the New York brokerage firm of Merrill Lynch and the Japanese broker Nomura both applying for membership in March 1986. These were quickly accepted and were effective immediately without any restrictions attached. At the same time the Stock Exchange was continuing its discussions with other international firms operating in London, indicating to them that it was keen to participate in the rapidly developing international market.[67] The Stock Exchange Chairman, Sir Nicholas Goodison, made the Stock Exchange intentions clear in April 1986 when he reported that

. . . London had the opportunity of becoming the major centre for international dealings and this would be more likely if all dealers shared a unity of purpose through being members of one unified organisation.[68]

Thus, by the mid-1980s it was the Stock Exchange that was actively courting the incomers to the City of London, who had done so much to

[66] LSE: Council, 17 Dec. 1985, 21 Jan. 1986; *FT*, 9 Apr. 1984, 10 Apr. 1986.
[67] LSE: Council, 4 Feb. 1986, 18 Feb. 1986, 4 Mar. 1986, 18 Mar. 1986; Kynaston, *LIFFE*, 51; *FT*, 11 July 1986, 4 Feb. 1987.
[68] LSE: Council, 29 Apr. 1986.

build up an international business there. For so long these firms had been denied membership on one pretext or another, as the Stock Exchange feared the competition they would bring or the instability they might create. Now, all that was in the past and their membership was perceived as one of the ways that the London Stock Exchange could preserve its role in the domestic securities market and make up for lost opportunities in the expansion of the international market. What continued to worry these international firms, used to operating in London without controls, was the fact that the Stock Exchange remained an overregulated and costly organization, especially with its technological systems such as TOPIC, TALISMAN, and SEAQ. Only a change in constitution would satisfy them, giving control to corporate rather than individual members, for that would be a recognition of where the power would lie in the future. At the same time the Stock Exchange pressed ahead with the development of SEAQ international, as a way of making itself attractive to those non-members trading foreign securities. By June 1986 the system carried the prices from 35 market-makers and listed 195 stocks while, by September, it was displaying firm prices for South African and Australian securities. Eventually, this twin track approach of an electronic international market-place and negotiations to clear up differences paid off. In September 1986 there was an agreement between the Stock Exchange and the ISRO to form a single stock exchange in London catering for both internationally traded stocks of UK and foreign origin, and domestic securities.[69]

Though this gave the appearance of a takeover by the Stock Exchange of the ISRO, because the administrative and physical structure was provided by the Stock Exchange, it was much more a merger of equals. The *Financial Times* even had the view, in October 1987, that '. . . a grouping of international securities houses effectively took control of the exchange in 1986. . . '.[70] The new Stock Exchange was to be run by a Committee with equal numbers from the London Stock Exchange and the ISRO, with Stanilas Yassukovich from ISRO having an influential role in decision-making, as Deputy Chairman. All that then remained to consummate the merger was the switch to corporate control, which came about when the voting rights of individual members were bought out. Thus, at the beginning of 1987 there came into being in London a new organization named the 'International Stock Exchange', with Sir Nicholas Goodison as Chairman and Stanilas Yassukovich as Deputy Chairman. To all external appearances it looked the same as before but beneath that lay a revolution. The international firms had now secured a major and permanent stake in the future of the London Stock Exchange, seeing in it the regulatory framework and organized market place that they increasingly required to operate

---

[69] Ibid., 29 Apr. 1986, 13 May 1986, 20 May 1986, 24 June 1986, 2 Sept. 1986, 9 Sept. 1986; *Stock Exchange Quarterly*, Autumn 1986, 7.
[70] *FT*, 21 Oct. 1987.

successfully in the emerging global equities market. In April 1988 the London Stock Exchange became an officially recognized Investment Exchange, permitted to regulate both the market and the behaviour of the users.[71]

However, the ambitions of those who created the International Stock Exchange was even greater than that. When the agreement to merge the Stock Exchange and the ISRO was reached in September 1986, it was reported that:

... what had been contemplated by the Joint Working Party in the future was the organization of one major Exchange in London, covering gilts, options, UK and foreign equities, with a single co-ordinated market system and under one governance. Such a move would prevent the fragmentation of the market by perpetuating the central market itself, which would thereby be given the opportunity over the next five years of becoming the second largest in the world.[72]

Thus, on the one hand the London Stock Exchange could contemplate a situation where they occupied second position to New York in the international hierarchy. On the other they faced the prospect of relegation to a position of a minor player where they only handled retail orders in UK domestic stocks. The merger with ISRO, achieved by the end of 1986, was the first step of this ambitious plan as it brought on board the international players who could, so easily, have formed their own separate organization and market.

The next steps, however, proved impossible to achieve. The Stock Exchange, with its traded options market decided to pursue a merger with LIFFE during 1987.[73] By then LIFFE had established itself as an independent and successful exchange within the City of London. Its contract based on German government bonds had proved very successful. Consequently, LIFFE was not keen on a merger with the Stock Exchange though they were interested in taking over LTOM. In August 1987 LIFFE rejected the Stock Exchange's proposals for a merger, worried by the level of autonomy it would be allowed if it was but one element in a proposed London Futures and Options Exchange. Despite the strides the Stock Exchange had made in liberalizing its rules and regulations concerning membership and permitted activities, there remained the suspicion that its involvement would stifle the more entrepreneurial orientation of LIFFE. The Stock Exchange eventually accepted this rejection because it recognized that the further development of LTOM, with or without the involvement of LIFFE, would mean a considerable financial and managerial investment on its behalf.[74] In May 1988, for

[71] LSE: Council, 1 Sept. 1986, 16 Sept. 1986, 30 Sept. 1986, 5 Jan. 1987; *Quality of Markets Review*, Oct.–Dec. 1991, 14.

[72] LSE: Council, 9 Sept. 1986, cf. *FT*, 12 Aug. 1985, 5 Feb. 1987.

[73] LSE: Council, 24 June 1986.

[74] Ibid., 2 Mar. 1987, 1 June 1987, 3 Aug. 1987, 7 Dec. 1987, 4 Jan. 1988; Kynaston, *LIFFE*, 152, 161–4.

example, they concluded after studying the futures market that, if the Stock Exchange '. . . wanted to become the dominant force in Europe, money, time and effort would be required for further development of the LTOM'.[75] Instead, by June 1988, the Council decided that establishing the Stock Exchange as the most important market for international equities was a big enough task, and the futures market could be left to go its own way. This was especially so as it was evident that both LTOM and LIFFE faced problems, with falling turnover after the crash of October 1987, and competition from rival exchanges in continental Europe. Even under these changed circumstances LIFFE continued to want to distance itself from the Stock Exchange turning down the opportunity to rent the now almost deserted Stock Exchange floor, both because of the costs involved and the possible loss of independence. Nevertheless, co-operation continued.[76]

Thus, the Stock Exchange's ambitious plan of regaining its once dominant position in the London market, through merging with, or absorbing, rival firms and institutions failed to materialize. Nevertheless, what it was left with was a commanding position in the domestic equity market and a major role in the international equity market. There was little it could do to further its domestic position but the international market offered immense possibilities, considering the way it was expanding in the 1980s. Once having admitted the members of the ISRO the new Stock Exchange pressed ahead with its plan to capture this international market. Realizing that New York was dominant in North America and that Tokyo occupied the same position in Japan, that left London to compete for the European market. Thus the London Stock Exchange needed to be repositioned as Europe's stock exchange so as to capture business from continental Europe, away from the established markets located there, as well as filling the role of the European time zone leg in a global securities market that never stopped. To do this they continued to expand the securities traded on SEAQ international. At the same time they decided to extend membership of the Stock Exchange to those firms that did not even maintain a London office. Once it was accepted that the trading-floor could comprise an electronic network it was a logical next step to allow the participation of any acceptable member who could access the network. The Stock Exchange was now keen to ensure that membership was open to all global players and that these global players wanted to join.[77]

## A CHANGED INSTITUTION

Reflecting the completely changed nature of its membership, the Stock Exchange had also to alter the degree of control and supervision it

---

[75] LSE: Council, 9 May 1988.

[76] Ibid., 7 Dec. 1987, 4 Jan. 1988; Kynaston, *LIFFE*, 210, 223, 235–9, 255; *FT*, 18 July 1987, 10 Mar. 1988, 12 Apr. 1988, 23 May 1990, 4 Apr. 1990.

[77] LSE: Council, 16 Sept. 1986, 2 Feb. 1987, 3 Aug. 1987, 15 Oct. 1987; *FT*, 21 Nov. 1985, 6 Feb. 1987, 16 Dec. 1987.

exercised. Fundamentally, it was necessary to ensure that all those allowed to trade would obey the rules of the market and honour all sales and purchases. However, on top of that, since the Second World War, had been laid layer above layer of rules and regulations governing the behaviour of members not only towards each other but also with regard to their clients and the securities traded. Once begun, the principle of compensation, for example, was extended and refined in response to government and public pressure. The Compensation Fund was designed to compensate those clients of a stockbroking firm who had lost money through fraud or negligence, through a levy on all other members. This then gave the Stock Exchange the right to monitor the financial state of its members and the way they operated, leading to strictures on what was permissible. The post-war years had seen a continuous erosion of the independence of member firms to operate as they chose, within the market rules and regulations, as the Stock Exchange sought to limit claims on the Compensation Fund. When the stockbroking firm of Hedderwick, Stirling, Grumbar & Co. failed in 1981, for example, the Stock Exchange decided to appoint an official inspectorate with wide powers to investigate the financial affairs of members. This was despite the fact that the liquidator of that firm eventually paid 100p in the pound. The result of all this was that not only was fraud and negligence rare among the members of the Stock Exchange, despite the publicity given to cases when they did occur, but so was the ability to operate in novel ways in response to changing conditions. Even then, this monitoring and the restrictions did not stop all abuses, for it was admitted, in June 1982, that '. . . churning was a problem encountered from time to time . . .' as brokers bought and sold a client's portfolio for the commission income the transactions produced. As in other areas of its activities, the Stock Exchange faced government and media criticism whether it was over- or underregulated, for it was never possible to find a permanent compromise in a dynamic market.[78]

In the face of the changing nature of the membership of the Stock Exchange it was found that the ways of the past were no longer tenable. With members becoming subsidiaries of large banks and other financial institutions, the minimum capital requirements set by the Stock Exchange—£0.2m.—looked irrelevant as did the requirement to operate unlimited liability. Barclay's BZW subsidiary, for instance, was capitalized at £240m. in 1985. As a result the Stock Exchange was in a position where such matters as solvency and client relationships were better left to the members themselves, under the monitoring of the Securities and Investments Board (and later the bodies that supplemented and replaced it). Similarly, there was a move towards fines rather than expulsions as a penalty for breaking the rules of the Stock Exchange as most corporate members were now such

[78] LSE: Council, 6 Oct. 1981, 20 Oct. 1981, 1 June 1982, 15 June 1982, 5 Oct. 1982, 2 Nov. 1982.

important players in the market that they could not be easily excluded. BZW had a staff of 1,300 to be kept busy. Similarly, it was decided in 1986 to limit the Compensation Fund to a maximum of £250,000 per claimant as the new corporate members were unwilling to join an organization with an open-ended commitment to make payments based on the negligence or fraud of others. Eventually, in August 1988 the Stock Exchange's own Compensation Fund was wound up, being replaced by a centralized scheme for the entire securities industry. By then the Securities Association, founded in 1988, had taken over from the Stock Exchange as the supervisory body for the stockbroking profession.[79]

The ending of the Compensation Fund symbolized the changed relationship that now existed between the Stock Exchange and its corporate membership. By 1989 there were 391 corporate members of whom 248 were British while the remainder were foreign, including 52 from the USA, 17 from France, and 14 from Japan. Many were owned by larger groups engaged in a wide variety of financial activities, both in Britain and abroad. The stockbroking firm of Straus Turnbull, for example, was gradually absorbed by the French bank, Société Générale, between 1986 and 1988, after a 20-year relationship. Even in London many had interests spread over the gilt-edged market, Eurobonds, and LIFFE, in addition to membership of the Stock Exchange. Under these circumstances it was impossible to expect the Stock Exchange to police their operations generally or monitor their financial health, as it was only aware of a minor aspect of their business. Instead of the Stock Exchange policing the behaviour of its members, leaving non-members with a much less rigorous regime, all those operating in the securities market were monitored by the Securities Association, a new self-regulatory body. At least this ended the unfair competition that Stock Exchange members had experienced throughout the post-war years.[80]

Consequently the edifice of investor protection that the Stock Exchange had built up since the Second World War, when it was acting as the government's semi-official regulator of the securities industry, crumbled in the face of the changes taking place even before Big Bang in 1986. In many ways it was a task that the Stock Exchange was less and less able to fulfil as so many of the activities were outside its jurisdiction. The long-standing problem over insider trading had been an early warning that the Stock Exchange alone did not possess the authority to police all aspects of the securities business and had to seek additional support. Though there was a logic in extending the power of the Stock Exchange over the relations

---

[79] Ibid., 20 Aug. 1985, 17 Sept. 1985, 5 Nov. 1985, 8 Feb. 1986, 29 July 1986; Lorenz, *BZW*, 31; Thomas, *Securities Market*, 195; *FT*, 28 Apr. 1987, 16 May 1988, 9 July 1988, 5 Mar. 1991.

[80] Bonin, *Société Générale*, 97–8; Sir Paul Newall, *Japan and the City of London* (London 1996), 41–3; Lorenz, *BZW*, 35–7; 'Arrangements for the Regulation and Supervision of Securities Markets in OECD Countries', *Financial Market Trends*, 41 (1988), 19; LSE: *Annual Reports* 1988, 1989.

between its members into their other activities, because these could impinge on both the institution and the market, the policy had been pursued too far in the post-war years. The end result had been that the Stock Exchange had been blamed by both the government and public for any perceived abuses and wrongdoings related to securities even though almost all involved non-members, where the Stock Exchange was powerless to act. The Stock Exchange had refused membership to the financial firm Barlow Clowes and had alerted various government departments about its activities since 1984. No action was taken by these bodies until November 1987, when a series of frauds was then uncovered resulting in prosecution and imprisonment.[81]

The Stock Exchange was still left in control of vetting those securities that were eligible for trading in the United Kingdom, regardless of the market this was done in. With its long history of evaluating the quality and honesty of applications to quote securities the London Stock Exchange was the obvious competent authority for such a task. No other institution in the City of London had the staff or the experience and nor did any branch of government. However, in undertaking this role, the Stock Exchange again exposed itself to the criticism of both the government of the day and the public generally. The government, for example, was keen to see the development of a market for small companies bringing new processes, technologies, products, or services to the market. By definition these were risky ventures devoid of a track record or tangible assets and so prone to both collapse, through over-enthusiastic expansion, or fraud, because of their insubstantial nature. Consequently, when these companies failed the Stock Exchange would be criticized for adopting a lax policy on vetting new issues of securities. That criticism would come from both the government and the media, each looking for someone to blame. Conversely, the government was also concerned with fostering the growth in the number of private investors and stimulating their interest in stocks and shares. This required that these private investors should have complete confidence in the securities quoted on the Stock Exchange, because they did not have the expertise or knowledge to carry out their own investigations. Thus the Stock Exchange was expected to take a cautious and even conservative attitude towards the securities it permitted to be quoted, which made it open to criticism that it was denying young entrepreneurial companies a market for their shares and thus the finance needed for expansion. Again this criticism would come from both the government and the media. Consequently, whatever the Stock Exchange did it would face a hostile press when any new issue turned out badly, and a quoted company collapsed, or an entrepreneur complained about the inability to obtain a listing for what was expected to be a company with incalculable growth

---

[81] Webb, *The Bigger Bang*, 35; Thomas, *Securities Market*, 197; Fishman, *Transformation of Threadneedle Street*, 88–9, 165.

prospects. At the same time a compromise had to be achieved between keeping listing requirements cheap and simple, so as to attract business to London, and the need to ensure an adequate level of scrutiny and investigation, so that proper checks could be carried out. Again, whatever the outcome the Stock Exchange would face criticism that its procedures were either inadequate for the detection of fraud or slow, expensive, and cumbersome, so driving business away.[82]

For the domestic securities market the outcome of Big Bang for the London Stock Exchange was that it remained virtually unchallenged. At the same time the working relationship with the Bank of England also meant it retained the gilts market, which did grow enormously in the stock market crisis of 1987. The success of the USM also eroded the position of the emerging OTC market but, in contrast to gilts, it fared badly in the aftermath crash. What challenge there was for the London Stock Exchange in domestic equities came from overseas, with trading in the ADR's of major British companies in New York and on NASDAQ. By the end of 1987 there was active trading in the ADRs of Glaxo, Hanson Trust, Jaguar, and Reuters in the United States. However, this mainly reflected the fact that these stocks were heavily owned by institutional investors in the USA who found it convenient to trade them there, because they could escape stamp duty. The London Stock Exchange did now appear to be holding onto the sales and purchases of British investors, even in those securities popular abroad, with any loss due to the incidence of taxation not underlying uncompetitiveness.[83]

At the same time the merger with the ISRO had grafted onto the Stock Exchange the rapidly developing market in foreign equities, which was being conducted in London by largely overseas firms. The number of foreign securities houses operating in London already numbered 104 in 1980 but grew to 158 by 1989, with 78 new firms arriving compared to only 16 departing. The biggest increases were among those from other than the United States (43 rising to 55), with those from Japan (21 to 42), and Europe (13 to 24), doubling. With Big Bang the London Stock Exchange provided the main trading forum for these firms. The market value of corporate stocks quoted by the London Stock Exchange grew from £210.8bn. in 1980 to £1,834.3bn. in 1990, and most of this was due to foreign securities. By 1990 the London Stock Exchange quoted foreign corporate stocks with a market value of £1,288.3bn., and they alone constituted 61.4 per cent of the value of all the quoted securities. Added to the 26 per cent taken by UK corporate stocks, it indicated that business

[82] C. Courtney and P. Thompson, *City Lives: The Changing Voices of British Finance* (London 1996), 158, 167; OECD, *Economic Survey 1986/7: United Kingdom Financial Markets*, 37, 42; Cobham, 'Equity Market', 31.

[83] *FT*, 21 Feb. 1985, 21 Oct. 1985, 5 Nov. 1985, 20 Dec. 1985, 2 Apr. 1986, 23 Apr. 1986, 28 July 1986, 3 Aug. 1987, 24 Oct. 1987, 10 Dec. 1987, 20 Apr. 1987.

on the London Stock Exchange was now dominated by corporate equity (see Tables 12.1 and 12.2). Not only was much of the trading activity conducted by London Stock Exchange members in foreign securities it was also being conducted for foreign investors. London had already been emerging as a centre for international trading in corporate stocks, reflecting its established position in Eurobonds, and this market now became a central activity for the new London Stock Exchange, along with its continued admittance of domestic equities. By 1989 foreign equity turnover in London had reached £40bn. per annum, or one-third that of UK equities with that in French, Swedish, and Japanese securities being especially important. Of course, bond trading, whether government or corporate was now the preserve of other organizations, even though conducted by many of the banks and brokerage houses who were members of the London Stock Exchange.[84]

Without the reforms brought in at the time of Big Bang it was unlikely that the London Stock Exchange would have been able to capture this international market or even hold its position in domestic equities. Not only could foreign banks and brokers join the Stock Exchange, bringing their international business with them, but all members could now operate in a more competitive manner, meeting the needs of their customers and facing up to the challenges of rivals. In the gilt-edged market, for example, by the end of 1987 over half of all transactions now bypassed brokers, as institutional investors dealt directly with market-makers, while 90 per cent of total business did not involve any commission payment. Similarly in equities, whether domestic or foreign, the large institutions were able either to deal directly with market-makers, cutting out the brokers, or pay a much smaller commission fee. One estimate for February 1987 suggested that commissions, when paid by institutions, had fallen by around 50 per cent as a result of Big Bang.[85] The stamp duty charged by the government was now a much more serious cost than commission rates for those buying and selling securities. These lower charges, added to the London market's strength in terms of liquidity, meant that it was now very competitive, able not only to retain business in UK equities but attract that in major non-British stocks. This global business was growing rapidly in the 1980s as international equity investment grew apace. Financial institutions world-wide were searching for a hedge against inflation after the ravages of the 1970s. The average UK pension fund had 75 per cent of its funds in equities in 1989 compared to 50 per cent in 1979. In contrast fixed-interest securities, such

[84] FT, 5 Nov. 1985, 16 Dec. 1986, 14 Nov. 1987, 17 June 1989, 1 Sept. 1989, 29 Nov. 1990; LSE: Quality of Markets, Spring 1989, 27–9, Apr.–June 1990, 17–18.
[85] FT, 4 Feb. 1987, 7 Feb. 1987, 5 Aug. 1987, 24 Aug. 1987, 14 Dec. 1987, 11 Oct. 1988; LSE: Quality of Markets, Oct. 1986, 13, Spring 1989, 29, Jan.–Mar. 1990, 19, April–June 1990, 19–20, Oct.–Dec. 1990, 31.

Table 12.1. London Stock Exchange: Nominal and market values of securities quoted in 1980 and 1990 (£m.)

| Category of security | Nominal value | | | Market value | | |
|---|---|---|---|---|---|---|
| | 1980 | 1990 | Difference | 1980 | 1990 | Difference |
| British government | 74,652.0 | 128,808.3 | +54,155.9 | 60,780.3 | 124,173.2 | +63,392.9 |
| UK public bodies | 3,141.7 | 402.1 | −2,739.6 | 2,678.1 | 307.6 | −2,370.5 |
| TOTAL | 77,794.1 | 129,210.4 | +51,416.3 | 63,458.4 | 124,480.8 | +61,022.4 |
| Commonwealth governments | 252.1 | 6.3 | −245.8 | 224.5 | 3.2 | −221.3 |
| Foreign governments | 329.6 | 4,103.3 | +3,773.7 | 5.4 | 3,731.0 | +3,725.6 |
| Commonwealth/Foreign public bodies | 59.2 | 2.2 | −57.0 | 241.7 | 1.3 | −240.4 |
| TOTAL | 640.9 | 4,111.8 | +3,470.9 | 471.6 | 3,735.5 | +3,263.9 |
| UK companies | — | 70,097.8 | — | — | 546,028.9 | — |
| Foreign companies | — | 54,427.8 | — | — | 1,288,266.1 | — |
| TOTAL | 39,393.8 | 124,525.6 | +85,131.8 | 210,803.4 | 1,834,295.0 | +1,623,491.6 |
| Eurobonds: UK | 2,081.4 | 36,616.6 | +34,535.2 | 1,663.2 | 57,771.4 | +56,108.2 |
| Eurobonds: Foreign | 4,752.6 | 80,046.6 | +75,294.0 | 3,931.3 | 78,208.8 | +74,277.5 |
| TOTAL | 6,834.0 | 116,663.2 | +109,829.2 | 5,594.5 | 135,980.2 | +130,385.7 |
| TOTAL | 124,689.8 | 374,511.0 | +249,821.2 | 280,327.9 | 2,098,491.5 | +1,818,163.6 |

Sources: Stock Exchange Fact Book (1980); Stock Exchange Official Yearbook, 1990/1.

Table 12.2. London Stock Exchange: Nominal and market values of securities quoted in 1980 and 1990 (%)

| Category of security | Nominal value | | | Market value | | |
|---|---|---|---|---|---|---|
| | 1980 | 1990 | Difference | 1980 | 1990 | Difference |
| British government | 59.9 | 34.4 | + 72.5 | 21.7 | 5.9 | + 104.3 |
| UK public bodies | 2.5 | 0.1 | − 87.2 | 1.0 | — | − 88.5 |
| TOTAL | 62.4 | 34.5 | + 66.1 | 22.6 | 5.9 | + 49.0 |
| Commonwealth government | 0.2 | — | − 97.5 | 0.1 | — | − 98.6 |
| Foreign governments | 0.3 | 1.1 | + 1,144.9 | — | 0.2 | + 68,992.6 |
| Commonwealth/ Foreign public bodies | — | — | − 96.3 | 0.1 | — | − 99.5 |
| TOTAL | 0.5 | 1.1 | + 541.6 | 0.2 | 0.2 | + 692.1 |
| UK companies | — | 18.7 | — | — | 26.0 | — |
| Foreign companies | — | 14.5 | — | — | 61.4 | — |
| TOTAL | 31.6 | 33.3 | + 216.1 | 75.2 | 87.4 | + 770.1 |
| Eurobonds: UK | 1.7 | 9.8 | + 1,659.2 | 0.6 | 2.8 | + 3,373.5 |
| Eurobonds: Foreign | 3.8 | 21.4 | + 1,584.3 | 1.4 | 3.7 | + 1,889.4 |
| TOTAL | 5.5 | 31.2 | + 1,607.1 | 2.0 | 6.5 | + 2,330.6 |
| TOTAL | — | — | + 200.4 | — | — | + 648.6 |

*Sources*: As for Table 12.1.

as gilts and corporate bonds, shrunk from 29 per cent of the total in 1978 to 4 per cent in 1990. Generally by September 1989 cross-border equity holdings totalled $640bn., or 6.4 per cent of all equity holdings, compared to a negligible proportion ten years before. UK institutional investors alone held $180.5bn. in foreign equities, creating a good basis for London's international market. At the same time foreign investors, such as US pension funds, had increased their holdings of UK equities. In 1981 overseas investors owned 3.6 per cent of all UK equities but 12.8 per cent in 1991. Naturally this worked its way through into the secondary market with cross-border equity trades increasing more than tenfold between 1979 and 1986 (from $73.1bn. to $800bn.) and then doubling by 1989 (to $1,598.3bn.). Of these cross-border transactions around 60 per cent of the total passed through London with the Stock Exchange and its membership in a dominant position.[86]

As a result of the changes ushered in at time of Big Bang, the London Stock Exchange regained its competitive edge. Duffy and Henney, writing in 1989, concluded that,

The London Stock Exchange has changed from being a small, protected and comfortable club, whose members transacted business in UK securities largely on the floor of the Exchange, to become the International Stock Exchange.[87]

These changes had inevitable consequences for the members of the London Stock Exchange as a much more competitive environment was ushered in. Many of those firms that had rested complacently on the regular income generated under the fixed commission regime found the new conditions particularly difficult with a number taking the opportunity to sell out or retire from the business. Generally, those firms that had proved themselves the most competitive before Big Bang were also found to be so afterwards, whether they remained independent or because part of a larger group. Phillips & Drew, for instance, was already a very successful firm before it sold out to Union Bank of Switzerland. It had 61 partners, 550 staff, managed c.£4bn. for pension funds, and had an unrivalled reputation for the scientific analysis of investments. UBS then continued that tradition. Another successful firm, Cazenoves, despite approaches, remained independent and took the opportunity to move into jobbing in 1986, financing it through a £32m. loan. At the same time the firm expanded its institutional broking activities, attracting those who did not want to deal with a firm that was part of a larger, and competing, financial organization. In addition the firm expanded its fund management activities, with the amount controlled growing from £2.8bn. in 1986 to £5.8bn. in 1991.[88]

Opportunities on offer to Stock Exchange members were not only to be found in the international and institutional business for privatization had created a vast increase in the number of UK investors. By 1986 there were 5 million investors compared to 3 million in 1980 and this rose again to 11 million in 1991. This was despite the fact that the share of equities that they owned fell from 28.2 per cent in 1981 to 21.3 per cent in 1989, in the face of heavy buying from the pension funds. Consequently, a number of brokers, such as Phillips & Drew and Hoare, Govett, sought to cultivate these new investors by expanding their private client operations. However, they found it very expensive to serve a mass market without a retail base,

---

[86] FT, 1 Sept. 1989, 23 Dec. 1989, 26 Oct. 1991, 5 Nov. 1992, 12 Dec. 1994; LSE: Quality of Markets, Oct.–Dec. 1990, 19–20; LSE: Annual Report, 1991.

[87] F. Duffy and A. Henney, The Changing City (London 1989), 103, cf. Cobham, 'Equity Market', 53–6; M. Hart, J. Jonker, and J. L. Van Zanden, A Financial History of the Netherlands (Cambridge 1997), 169.

[88] Kynaston, Cazenove, 315–28; Roberts, Schroders, 507; FT, 10 Aug. 1983, 1 Nov. 1984, 1 June 1985, 15 Jan. 1986, 10 July 1987, 3 Nov. 1987.

and so abandoned their private clients in the wake of the 1987 crash, when investor interest waned. Instead, they specialized in the institutional business, which was more suited to their links with overseas banks. In contrast, those brokers bought by domestic banks with large branch networks, like Barclays, found it easier to develop a retail business serving individual investors. This was also true of brokers created by merging provincial firms with a long tradition of serving private clients. Allied Provincial Securities was formed in 1986, for example, from firms located in Glasgow, Manchester, Bristol, Birmingham, and Middlesborough, and so started off with 17 offices, 300 staff, and 50,000 clients.[89]

However, it was not until the aftermath of the crash of 1987, when turnover fell and competition became fierce, that many of the new combinations among the membership were really tested. Prior to October 1987 most members were making money with a booming market, whether they were dealing with institutions or individuals, global equities, or USM entrants. Though commissions on institutional business fell greatly with Big Bang the enormous increase in volume made buying and selling profitable. Also commissions charged to individual investors, with smaller transactions and more advice, changed little and even increased for many. The crash, and the inevitable downturn, exposed the fragility of many of the new creations, forcing their owners to rethink whole strategies, including closing down the entire operation.[90] Overall, it was estimated that employment in the securities business in the City of London fell from c.40,000 on the eve of the October 1987 crash, to c.35,000 two years later, or by 12.5 per cent. Such a shake-out was inevitable as there was no way that firms could predict which strategy would emerge the winner in the securities market that was going to emerge after Big Bang. Even a year after the crash it remained impossible to predict which firms had really established themselves because of the enormous changes taking place in the domestic and global securities markets. Continuing advances in communications and computing technology, allied to the liberalization of national markets, was exerting such a powerful influence that by 1988 the future had again, become very unclear for the London Stock Exchange and its members. Many of them had committed themselves to a vast investment in offices, equipment, and staff that could only be justified if it generated a large and profitable business, and that was simply not the case after 1987.[91]

[89] FT, 22 Jan. 1986, 13 Aug. 1987, 21 Oct. 1987, 29 June 1988, 15 Sept. 1988, 22 Feb. 1990, 10 Aug. 1991, 27 Oct. 1991, 21 Dec. 1994.
[90] K. Burk, Morgan Grenfell, 1838–1988: The Biography of a Merchant Bank (Oxford 1989), 257; Courtney and Thompson, City Lives, 111, 114, 125; Lorenz, BZW, 19, 48, 62, 72, 75, 79.
[91] J. Toporowski, The Economics of Financial Markets and the 1987 Crash (Aldershot 1993), 137–8, 141; FT, 5 Nov. 1987, 14 Dec. 1987, 13 Feb. 1988, 16 June 1988, 29 June 1988, 8 Nov. 1988, 14 Nov. 1988, 22 Nov. 1988, 7 Dec. 1988, 31 Dec. 1988, 19 Apr. 1989, 23 Nov. 1990.

In retrospect the problem of Big Bang for both the Stock Exchange and its membership was that it came about after such a long period when change had been limited at an institutional or business level but continued apace in the securities market. Thus, when change came it was a hurried process both technologically and organizationally, and only appeared to work because of the buoyant market conditions that existed at the time, and for a year afterwards. Once the volume of business began to die away both the Stock Exchange and its members had to re-examine the decisions taken at the time of Big Bang, and then respond positively to the new, and far more competitive, conditions of the securities market. As the *Financial Times* observed, in the immediate wake of the crash of 1987, '. . . few of the questions about the future configuration of the UK securities industry can yet be answered.'[92] This is not to say that Big Bang was a non-event, as has been claimed by some, such as Christopher Wood, writing in 1988, or Nigel Lawson, who referred to it in 1992 as having '. . . had little real impact'.[93] That betrays an ignorance of what had existed before, and what had been achieved. At the very least it represented a victory for those among the membership of the Stock Exchange who had long recognized the need for change and saw its inevitability in the wake of the abolition of exchange controls in 1979. That event alone had altered fundamentally the environment within which the London Stock Exchange had operated since the Second World War, though it took years to convince the Conservative government of that. This victory was also achieved over numerically superior numbers because many of the members, especially those conducting a private client business in the provinces, were as yet unaware of what the ending of exchange controls had done. Thus, many members saw no urgent necessity to reform or abandon either fixed commissions or single capacity, and remained keen to exclude banks from participation in the market, because of the competition they would bring, especially outside London. There was never any certainty that the membership as a whole could be persuaded to vote for measures that were essential for the long-term future of the institution to which they belonged but were not in the short-term interests of them all. It should never be underestimated how powerful were the forces of inertia on the Stock Exchange, as with any long-established institution, as events in the 1970s had shown. Members had to be persuaded to support change and those who managed that needed to be credited with their achievement.[94]

Big Bang was never part of any plan by the Thatcher government to reform Britain's financial services and increase the competitive power of the

[92] *FT*, 21 Oct. 1987. For an account of the market see S. M. Haslam and S. G. G. Peerless, *The London Securities Markets* (London 1990), and C. Pratten, *The Stockmarket* (Cambridge 1993).

[93] C. Wood, *Boom and Bust* (London 1988), 97; *FT*, 27 Jan. 1992.

[94] *FT*, 19 May 1984, 21 Feb. 1985, 1 June 1985, 21 Oct. 1985, 28 Dec. 1985, 26 Oct. 1987.

City of London. Instead it was part of a long-running attack on restrictive practices combined with exposure to the global changes taking place in securities markets that came with the ending of exchange controls in 1979. The combination of the two created the conditions that led to Big Bang, unleashing a degree of change that the government of the day never contemplated, and would probably have tried to stop if they had. What the intervention of government had done through the abolition of exchange controls was to break the stalemate between those wanting change and those opposing it in the London Stock Exchange. However, that change could have come sooner rather than later if it had been recognized that the RPC case had become an obstacle not a spur to reform.

In outward appearance the Stock Exchange looked the same after Big Bang, but internally power had now been placed in the hands of the major players in the global market place. At the level of the members the conditions that had restricted competition and controlled activities were abandoned. The result was an invasion of the securities market by major financial institutions, especially from abroad, and the creation of a very competitive environment which brought business to London. For the first time since the Second World War the London Stock Exchange was able to focus, once again, on its basic function of providing an orderly securities market and to do so in the context of an emerging global securities market.

The reason why the response to this emerging market was so long delayed did not lie with the Stock Exchange alone but in the relationship that had developed between it and the government during and after the Second World War. At no time in that period had the Stock Exchange been free to pursue its own interests for, instead, it was used by government as a mechanism for regulating the securities market, though never given the statutory position and authority possessed by the Bank of England with regard to banking. With the ending of exchange controls in 1979, in the context of an emerging global securities market, the Stock Exchange found itself fully exposed to international competition in its own domestic securities. As a result the relationship with the government no longer delivered benefits to the Stock Exchange, in terms of control over the national market, that justified the costs endured by the membership, in terms of tight regulation. As the government never appeared to recognize how it was using the Stock Exchange, it remained unaware of what the abolition of exchange controls had done. The government even believed that the ending of fixed commissions was compatible with the Stock Exchange remaining the regulatory authority for the securities market, and being given extra responsibilities for investor protection. In contrast, those running the Stock Exchange, and the members most involved in institutional business, were well aware of the competition they now faced and how important it was to respond. In turn, this response would make untenable many of the rules and regulations that the government regarded as essential for the regulation of the securities market. As long as the London Stock Exchange existed in a world partly closed to outside competition through exchange controls, it was in a position to maintain practices like fixed commissions and single capacity. Once that world was opened up, as it was by the abolition of exchange controls, practices that hampered significantly the competitive power of the membership could not be sustained for long. Thus the RPC case suddenly became an irrelevancy and now only hampered the process of change. Unfortunately, the government of the day, having responded to the increasing inability to enforce exchange controls by abandoning them, was unable to see the implications of what they had done and so follow them through. This left the Stock Exchange trapped in something of a time warp until freed by the 1983 agreement. Once the threat to the orderly market posed by the RPC case, had been removed, the pace of change on the Stock Exchange was rapid, despite the inevitable opposition from those who would be disadvantaged as a result. Reform, when carried out by an institution like the Stock Exchange was not a once-and-for-all action but a long-term process. It was that process that had led the Stock Exchange to the position it found itself in in 1979, when another radical change of direction was required. The actions of both the Labour government in the aftermath of the Second World War and the Thatcher government in the first year of office, each set the Stock Exchange on a new course with major consequences for itself and the financial system of which it was a part. In that sense Big Bang represented the first public manifestation of a revolution already underway on the London Stock Exchange, and one largely of its own making in the wake of the 1979 ending of exchange controls.

# 13

# Black Hole

## RELATIONS WITH GOVERNMENT

On 3 March 2001 the London Stock Exchange, as a formally organized securities market, will have existed for two centuries. Instead of taking comfort from such longevity, in the face of enormous change and periodic crises, many of those viewing the Stock Exchange in the 1990s doubt whether it has much of a future. An American academic, J. J. Fishman, concluded in 1993, after an exhaustive study, that, 'The Stock Exchange is an organization that has lost its direction. Its very future has been called into question.'[1] This was only echoing comments made by the *Financial Times* in 1989, and then repeated in 1994, 1996, and 1998. Such was the scale of the challenges facing securities markets world-wide by the 1990s that the role to be played by any and every stock exchange was being called into question, including that of London. One economist, R. O'Brien, even published a book in 1992 entitled, *Global Financial Integration: The End of Geography*, in which he speculated on the demise of specific physical boundaries to securities markets and their replacement with stateless electronic trading networks. He introduced his book by stating that

Stock Exchanges can no longer expect to monopolise trading in the shares of companies in their country or region, nor can trading be confined to specific cities or exchanges. Stock markets are now increasingly based on computer and telephone networks, not on trading-floors.[2]

Clearly these challenges were real ones coming both from governments and global economic forces. On the one hand national governments and central banks wanted to impose far greater control over securities markets, recognizing their importance in financial systems where the divisions between money and capital markets no longer existed. On the other hand the decline of national boundaries, with currency unions, global money and capital flows, and instantaneous international communications, created the need

---

[1] J. J. Fishman, *The Transformation of Threadneedle Street: The Deregulation and Regulation of Britain's Financial Services* (Durham, NC 1993), 269; *Financial Times* (*FT*), 4 Oct. 1989, 17 June 1994, 4 July 1996, 14 May 1998.

[2] R. O'Brien, *Global Financial Integration: The End of Geography* (London 1992), 8, 23–4, 76, 97, 103.

for supranational markets. From whatever direction the London Stock Exchange was thus under threat, not only as a regulatory organization and an organized market, but also as a professional association, for trading in securities had become dominated by the subsidiaries of the world's major banks and finance houses.

At the time of Big Bang these doubts over the Stock Exchange's future did appear to have been answered emphatically. In one brief flurry of activity the Stock Exchange had both modernized itself and secured a pivotal role within the global securities market. However, from the late 1980s onwards the London Stock Exchange both waned in importance within the British financial system and faced increasing competition from rival stock exchanges abroad. Did the dropping of the name 'International' in 1991, and its replacement with 'London', and the collapse of its attempt to create an all-embracing settlement system in 1993, symbolize the end of the hopes and ambitions that had accompanied Big Bang in 1986? Was Big Bang itself the beginning of a process in which, once begun, the Stock Exchange was stripped of its core functions within the British securities market while being unable to establish a major and permanent position on the international scene? Big Bang had certainly been accompanied by euphoria and hype, coinciding as it did with a stock market boom and an apparent renaissance of British international competitiveness under the Thatcher government. In its 50-page supplement distributed on the day of Big Bang the *Financial Times* had proclaimed that

Today's Big Bang changes the London Securities market irrevocably. The prize within the City's grasp is the leading position in the European time zone in a seamless market extending around the world.[3]

In retrospect it was unrealistic to expect such a sudden reversal in the Stock Exchange's prospects after years of decline when international markets had been ceded to others and a well-entrenched culture of restrictive practices and opposition to change had been built up. It was also unrealistic to expect that other stock exchanges would not respond to changes in London, especially if they and their national governments saw business draining away. What Big Bang had done was to give the London Stock Exchange the opportunity to reimpose its control over the domestic securities market and gain a role in a rapidly developing international equities market at the expense of a regulatory function that was becoming impossible for an organization that had no statutory backing or monopoly position. The challenge facing the Stock Exchange in this post-Big Bang, and post-crash, world was to continue responding to events and opportunities as they evolved, for there could be no certainty about the exact nature of the newly emerging securities market either domestically or globally.

One uncertainty was the level of freedom from government control that

---

[3] *FT*, 27 Oct. 1986.

the London Stock Exchange was to enjoy for Big Bang had involved not only a transformation of the securities market but also the entire regulatory environment within which it operated. Under these changes the Bank of England and the Department of Trade and Industry acquired final authority over the Stock Exchange, exercising that either directly or via the Securities and Investment Board (SIB). Though the Stock Exchange was not without influence in the corridors of power, that influence was both diluted through the existence of layers of authority and dissipated by the existence of other officially recognized securities markets in London. Eventually there emerged in 1997 the Financial Services Authority, which combined the supervision of the Stock Exchange with all other components of the financial system, reflecting the integration that had taken place since 1986. Also, once established, these statutory bodies began to extend their influence over all aspects of the Stock Exchange as they sought to control and police activities taking place there, especially those that could be considered either criminal or against the public interest. In the face of that growing power, and the loss of its own quasi-monopoly, the London Stock Exchange gradually abandoned many of the regulatory functions that it had once performed. With the formation of the Securities Association in 1988 (merged with the Association of Futures Brokers and Dealers on 1 April 1991 to become the Securities and Futures Authority (SFA)) the Stock Exchange relinquished its role in the policing of broker/client relationships. Similarly, the establishment of the Securities Institute in 1991 meant that the Stock Exchange no longer had a role to play in the professional training of brokers and dealers. One after another the London Stock Exchange ceased to perform many of the roles it had either traditionally undertaken or had acquired since the Second World War, with inevitable consequences for the power and influence it was able to wield in government circles.[4]

This also exposed the London Stock Exchange to renewed attacks on its remaining restrictive practices, which it had deemed necessary for the maintenance of an orderly market. In 1996, for example, there were still around 1,000 rules in the Stock Exchange rule book, governing the actions of its membership.[5] Though most of these could be defended, a number continued to reflect the pre-Big Bang era when the Stock Exchange had tried to use its rules and regulations to maintain a monopoly of the domestic securities market and enhance the position of its members. One of the areas that the Stock Exchange remained most sensitive to was the access to current market prices for securities given to non-members. If non-members had the same access as members then they could trade on equal terms and even set up

---

[4] Fishman, *Transformation of Threadneedle Street*, 76, 80–5, 88–9, 259; LSE: *Annual Reports*, 1988, 1993; FT, 16 May 1988, 9 July 1988, 4 Oct. 1989, 16 Sept. 1992, 25 Jan. 1996, 4 May 1998; 6 June 1998.
[5] LSE: *Annual Report*, 1996.

rival exchanges.[6] Thus the Stock Exchange attempted to prevent real or potential competitors getting access to such prices, though it was keen to make them available to others in the hope of stimulating buying and selling. Under pressure from the Office of Fair Trading (OFT) it was forced to concede access to Reuters in 1988. However, the Stock Exchange still had a rule forbidding members from quoting better prices to non-members than those available to members. Again, after complaints from a rival exchange, Tradepoint, the OFT launched an investigation in 1994 which led to the rule being abandoned in 1995.[7] Though none of these investigations produced the dramatic changes of Big Bang they were a constant chipping away of the restrictive rules and regulations that had characterized the Stock Exchange before 1986, and which it had done so much to protect with the 1983 Parkinson–Goodison agreement, much to the annoyance of the OFT at the time. By July 1996 the *Financial Times* could observe in an editorial that, 'Bit by bit, the arcane panoply of rules, privileges and obligations governing life at the London Stock Exchange is being picked apart.'[8] Possibly the OFT was, getting its revenge!

Thus, in the years after Big Bang the London Stock Exchange was subject to the constant scrutiny of outside bodies, backed by the power of the state, and was forced to modify its way of operation at their request or even seek their approval over any changes it wished to make. The rules governing the operation of the new order-driven market in 1997, for instance, had to be vetted by the SIB before their introduction.[9] This power of outside bodies over the Stock Exchange also extended to the type of securities for which it could provide a market. The Stock Exchange, for example, from the late 1980s was anxious to devise a way of making property assets more tradable, and thus more attractive to investors. However, it took until 1996 before it could convince the SIB, Department of Trade and Industry, and the Treasury that it could be done without exposing investors to undue risk or as a vehicle to escape taxation. This intervention existed despite the fact that the Stock Exchange was the approved listing authority for new corporate securities, under European Union legislation.[10]

Similarly, in its attempts to liberalize the practice of stock borrowing the Stock Exchange faced opposition. Stock borrowing was used by market-makers as a temporary means of meeting their commitments in the market. In the same way as dealers borrowed from banks, using the securities they had purchased as collateral until they could be sold, it was also necessary to

---

[6] For this general issue see Ruben Lee, *The Ownership of Price and Quote Information: Law, Regulation, Economics and Business* (Oxford Finance Group, Oxford 1995).

[7] *FT*, 22 Nov. 1988, 11 Feb. 1993, 3 Aug. 1994, 2 May 1995, 18 Aug. 1995, 28 Sept. 1995, 30 Sept. 1995, 2 Oct. 1995, 3 Aug. 1996.

[8] Ibid., 25 July 1996, cf. 18 Oct. 1993.

[9] Ibid., 20 Apr. 1988, 9 July 1988, 28 Feb. 1997, 20 May 1997, 24 July 1997.

[10] Ibid., 16 Jan. 1987, 6 Feb. 1987, 21 Mar. 1987, 22 May 1987, 22 Jan. 1988, 25 Nov. 1994, 16 Nov. 1996, 3 Jan. 1996.

borrow securities from financial institutions for delivery to customers, until they could be bought in the market. All concerned gained from the transactions but it did create chains of risk, as well as possibilities of tax evasion and it was this that the Bank of England and the Treasury objected to. To avoid that special procedures had been created in the gilt-edged market, using designated money-brokers to allow the practice to take place there. However, it was not until January 1996 that stock borrowing was opened to all, despite the fact that it was a well established practice in continental Europe and its advantages were well recognized. In fact it was accepted that any move towards rolling settlement could hardly take place without the liberalization of stock borrowing. By 1998 stock borrowing and lending had become a safe and routine business in the City of London with the £17bn. Universities Superannuation fund becoming a regular participant.[11]

One illustration of the relationship that now existed between government and the Stock Exchange can be seen from the question of insider trading. Since 1980 this had been designated a criminal offence and it was an area that the Stock Exchange was very keen to police. In order to maintain an orderly market the Stock Exchange tried to ensure that all had equal access to price-sensitive information. Any sudden and inexplicable price movements, could leave its members exposed as they had a commitment to buy or deliver at the agreed price, but might not yet have completed the other half of the deal. Thus it was the Stock Exchange that was responsible for managing company announcements, of which there were 120,000 in 1997, so that they reached all concerned at the same time. Furthermore, the Stock Exchange maintained in 1994 a 19-strong surveillance team whose task it was to scrutinize transactions for any unusual occurrence. In 1994/5 computer tracking systems alerted this team to around 1,000 suspicious transactions a day though only a total of 1,000 over the year were singled out for proper investigation. Eventually, in 1995, this produced only 45 that appeared to suggest insider trading. However, that was where the Stock Exchange's role ended for it then passed the details to the DTI for possible criminal prosecution. Over the entire 1980–94 period this only resulted in 34 trials in which more than half the defendants were found not guilty. The problem here was that, being a criminal offence, the burden of proof required was much higher than it had been under self-regulation, and so there was a reluctance to bring prosecutions and a difficulty in obtaining convictions.

The end result was that the Stock Exchange had lost the power to discipline those indulging in a practice that was disruptive to an orderly market. That was now the responsibility of the state which proved itself less effective than the Stock Exchange had been. The Financial Services Authority recognized this and announced new disciplinary powers in 1998. However, as this

---

[11] *FT*, 22 Nov. 1990, 11 June 1992, 8 Nov. 1994, 13 May 1996, 6 Nov. 1996, 10 July 1998.

was a crime that mainly affected the market itself, despite the complaints of investors and the media, it might have been best left to the Stock Exchange. Instead, what the saga of insider trading revealed was how the power of the state gradually encroached upon, and then supplanted that of the Stock Exchange, and that this had been taking place long before Big Bang.[12]

Generally, the system of statutory financial control that was introduced in 1986 to replace the Stock Exchange's mechanism of self-regulation has not been judged a success by impartial observers. Fishman, for example, writing in 1993 drew an unfavourable comparison between the enforcement of rules and regulations and the detection of infringements by the Stock Exchange and that undertaken by the SIB from 1986 onwards. This he blamed on the SIB's inability to distinguish between the need to protect the small investor and the rules required to govern trading between market professionals, wanting one set of regulations to fit all. The outcome was an expensive, inappropriate, and inflexible set of regulations which acted as a burden on the development of equities trading in London rather than contributing to the creation of an attractive and orderly market place.[13] This was a view endorsed by Vogel, another American academic, writing in 1996, who concluded that the effects of legislation had been to replace '... the informal with the formal, the flexible with the rigid, and the personal with the legalistic'.[14] By the late 1990s there was a slow realization that government intervention in the market place, while tackling some efficiencies and abuses, created others that, in the long-run could prove even worse. However, there was no sign that any government was willing to relinquish power once they had acquired it.

The Stock Exchange appeared to have very little influence over the government, whatever its political colour. The continuing levy of stamp duty on Stock Exchange transactions, which produced c.£850m. in 1993, was too valuable for any government to relinquish, even though it was acknowledged that its expense was the single most important factor undermining the London market's international competitiveness. Even the Stock Exchange's special stamp duty concessions for its membership were ended in 1996 when they were extended to all market participants. Similarly the attempt to outlaw bed-and-breakfasting transactions in the 1998 budget was calculated to lose Stock Exchange members considerable business from private investors, with little real benefit for the government or the economy.[15] Generally, it continued to be difficult for any government to be seen to favour the Stock Exchange, as with the abolition of stamp duty,

[12] Ibid., 1 Feb. 1990, 10 May 1993, 19 June 1993, 3 Oct. 1994, 21 May 1996, 9 Apr. 1998, 1 June 1998; Fishman, *Transformation of Threadneedle Street*, 193–4, 199, 207.

[13] Ibid., 114, 149–52.

[14] S. K. Vogel, *Freer Markets, More Rules! Regulatory Reform in Advanced Industrial Countries* (Ithaca, NY 1996), 93, cf. 10, 111, 116.

[15] *FT*, 11 Nov. 1991, 12 Mar. 1993, 21 Feb. 1996, 20 July 1996, 25 July 1996, 3 Aug. 1996, 20 Mar. 1997, 26 Jan. 1998, 19 Mar. 1998, 23 Mar. 1998.

while attacks were popular among both members of parliament and the populist media. Despite the enormous changes that the Stock Exchange had undergone since 1986, during which it lost most of its quasi-official status, it was still regarded as an all-powerful body that should be responsive to perceived national interest.

One example of this was the criticism it received for the decision in 1995 to drop the rule (from 1 January 1996) that all new issues over a certain size must reserve a proportion for the general public. This rule had forced companies to both make expensive public issues and to accept a lower average price than if they had sold the securities privately to a few institutions. Driven in the past by public anger, when investors were excluded from a popular issue, and government pressure, the Stock Exchange had introduced the rule, knowing that it would make the cost of finance more expensive for many companies. Under the more competitive conditions of the mid-1990s, when companies could decide to issue securities without securing a Stock Exchange quotation for them, the decision was taken to abandon the rule. However, it was perceived as an attack on the private investor, who would then be excluded from many new issues, not a contribution to the lowering of the cost of finance. The Stock Exchange continued to be seen by many as a public institution which could be used to achieve social engineering, through encouraging private investors, rather than an efficient and orderly market that had to survive against outside competition. Therefore, though the Stock Exchange itself had largely lost whatever political power it had once possessed it was expected to remain publicly accountable and receive nothing in return. In reality, the fate of the private investor had never rested with the Stock Exchange but with the government and taxation policy. This had consistently favoured collective investment and home ownership since the Second World War. In the same way it was not the role of the Stock Exchange to judge the economic or moral worth of a new issue, only whether it would lead to an orderly market free of manipulation.[16]

## Supervising the Market

With the disappearance of the London Stock Exchange's quasi-official status by the 1990s there were doubts over what role it had still to play in this area. If the rules and regulations were now set by statutory bodies, backed by the law of the land, what place was there for self-regulation? The changing nature of the membership of the London Stock Exchange was also undermining the control it could exercise. That membership was increasingly a corporate one even before individual membership was finally ended on 1 April 1992. In 1991 the then Chairman of the Stock Exchange,

[16] FT, 12 May 1993, 5 Oct. 1993, 19 Aug. 1995, 20 July 1996, 20 Mar. 1997, 13 June 1998; LSE: Annual Reports, 1989, 1991, 1997.

Andrew Hugh Smith, reflected on the transformation that had taken place, 'It is a consequence of our evolving role that the Exchange retains few elements of a club, and can in truth offer little to the individual member.'[17] By then membership of the Stock Exchange consisted of some 410 firms, of whom no less than 358 were companies. In turn many of these corporate members were the foreign-owned subsidiaries of major North American, European, and Japanese banks and brokerage houses. Most of the major London firms had been absorbed into international groupings such as the jobbers Akroyd & Smithers (United Bank of Switzerland (UBS)), and Smith Brothers (Merrill Lynch), or the brokers Rowe & Pitman and Phillips & Drew (UBS), or James Capel and W. Greenwell (Hong Kong and Shanghai Bank). One of the few among the major firms to stay independent were the brokers, Cazenoves.[18]

This changed the relationship between the Stock Exchange and its membership. Many of its members were now far more powerful than the institution to which they belonged, conducting a diverse and global financial business from offices around the world. As Andrew Large, Chairman of SIB, noted in 1995, 'It is becoming increasingly difficult to differentiate between the business of banks and securities houses.'[19]

Once the Stock Exchange had accepted not only corporate membership but also the combination of broking and jobbing with other financial activities, it became impossible to police the market in the same way as before. Instead, general rules and conditions were set by others, such as governments and central banks, who were concerned about the stability of the overall financial system or the entire financial group, rather than individual components. The capital required by firms participating in the London securities market, for example, was increasingly set, not by the Bank of England as the British central bank, but by European Union legislation. This still left the Stock Exchange with the important task of ensuring that its members obeyed the rules and regulations of the market and honoured any commitments they entered into.

A stock exchange was only more than a securities market when those participating could be certain that the counterparty to any transaction could be trusted and any transgressor punished. With a climate of trust, trading could take place on a continuous basis in full expectation that every single transaction would result in payment or delivery. Naturally this became more difficult to ensure when members were part of a large, and often foreign-based, organization conducting numerous and varied financial activities all over the world, any one of which could result in enormous losses. In turn these losses might make it impossible for members to honour their commitments causing repercussions throughout the market. In the past

[17] Ibid., 1991.
[18] Ibid., 1985, 1988, 1989, 1992; *FT*, 2 July 1988, 24 Aug. 1993, 25 Oct. 1996.
[19] Ibid., 12 July 1995.

this risk had been minimized by vetting those admitted to membership and the limitation placed on outside activities. By the 1990s it was being achieved through capital adequacy rules and the move to rolling settlement, which reduced the delay between transaction and completion. However, as that delay could never be completely eliminated there was also a growing demand for the Stock Exchange itself to provide a collective guarantee against counterparty risk, allowing all to trade freely. Though such a move would ensure that the Stock Exchange provided a direct benefit to its membership it also involved the risk that it would adopt a very cautious policy on membership. Only the largest and most stable financial institutions would be admitted, so minimizing risk. That would then create the danger that the excluded would turn elsewhere to trade, creating a rival market in the process.[20]

It was no easy matter to blend regulation and freedom in order to create an orderly market, but that was what the London Stock Exchange had to do if it was to be of real benefit to its membership after Big Bang. For most of the post-war years the Stock Exchange performed an important role for its members through its maintenance of the commission rate cartel and as an interface between the market and government. That ended with Big Bang and the Stock Exchange was thrown back on its traditional function, which was the provision of an orderly market where trading was conducted under recognized rules and regulations that greatly limited, though did not eliminate, the risks that such transactions involved. As that function had become so intermingled with the other roles undertaken by the Stock Exchange since 1945 it was no easy matter to distinguish what was necessary for the provision of an orderly market. This was especially so as the composition of the membership had been completely transformed, and bore no relationship to anything that had existed before. Consequently, the years after 1986 were inevitably ones of experimentation and trial and error as those running the Stock Exchange sought to establish a new order. There could be no doubt that such order was essential for the securities market, considering the speed and scale of turnover and the implications for all if serious defaults took place. Stock Exchange equity turnover in 1997, for example, exceeded £1,000bn. for the first time.[21]

The search for order in the parallel international bond market provided evidence enough that there still existed a role for the Stock Exchange despite the increase in state intervention from 1986 onwards and the functions performed by such independent bodies as the Securities Institute. The international bond market was the largest securities market in the world in the 1990s, and some three-quarters of the turnover took place in and between London-based participants. In 1993, when equity turnover in London was £572bn. (foreign and domestic) that in Eurobonds was

£2,866bn. or five times greater.[22] Since the establishment of this Eurobond market in the 1960s, participants had been searching for a means of minimizing the risks involved through better monitoring and regulation. This had led in 1969 to the formation of the International Association of Bond Dealers (AIBD) which in the late 1980s was recognized by British regulatory authorities as a designated investment exchange for the Eurobond market. In 1992 there was formed the International Securities Market Association (ISMA) which was both a trade association and self-regulatory body. By 1998 ISMA had about 800 members from 50 countries, being the major banks and finance houses from around the world. These members traded directly with each other by telephone and telex and ISMA's task was to try and monitor this activity with the object of reducing counterparty risk. This was not simply a failure to pay or deliver but, because of time differences, could involve a double risk. Payment could be made before delivery, leaving a bank exposed to both a loss of money and no delivery of bonds if the counterpart failed in the meantime. To avoid this ISMA, along with the London Clearing House, proposed in 1998 to set up a clearing system (Coredeal) for the international bond market that would eliminate counterparty risk. All around the world markets were rapidly growing up that required basic rules to govern transactions in order to reduce the risks involved, whether due to unexpected difficulties or deliberate fraud.[23] In 1996, for instance, it was reported that a market in European trade credit was being developed by the major banks, and that they intended '. . . to form an association to draw up standard rules for the trading of debt and the settlement of deals'.[24] The more counterparty risk was eliminated the less collateral was required to guarantee completion, with the result that capital could be used much more efficiently.

Though government, and especially their central banks were involved in the supervision of the participants in these markets, as so many were banks, the global nature of the business made national supervision inadequate. The American investment banker, Henry Kaufman, recognized the problems in 1997, writing that:

Transformation of global financial markets has proceeded at a tremendous pace. Meanwhile the infrastructure for supervising and regulatory financial institutions and markets has remained national and lagged badly behind market-place developments.[25]

[22] City Research Project, *The Competitive Position of London's Financial Services* (Corporation of London 1995), 2–7, A-5.

[23] FT, 12 Jan. 1990, 23 May 1992, 9 Aug. 1996, 9 Nov. 1996, 28 Feb. 1997, 6 May 1997, 29 May 1997, 15 July 1997, 23 Jan. 1998, 6 July 1998.

[24] Ibid., 30 Nov. 1996. For a discussion of the role of exchanges versus markets see *Financial Times, Mastering Finance* (London 1997), chs. by N. Naik, 'The Many Roles Of Financial Markets', B. Barker and R. Leftwith, 'Assessing the Costs of Security Trading', M. Blume, 'Stock Exchanges: Forces of Change', R. Krosner, 'The Market as International Regulator'.

[25] FT, 7 July 1997, cf. 6 June 1997.

He, like many others, saw the solution in terms of a supranational government agency, reflecting the regulatory experience of the United States. However, with the London Stock Exchange, and its international membership, there already existed an institution with a long history of self-regulation involving both domestic and international trading in securities, and one more in tune with the needs of market participants than any government body driven by bureaucratic controls and national interest. Consequently, in this direction alone the London Stock Exchange had a future if it possessed the drive and vision to grasp it and overcome national self-interest and state intervention. As Gavin Casey, Chief Executive of the Stock Exchange, observed in July 1998, 'There is no natural regulator of a pan-European exchange at the moment.'[26]

Though such a possibility could be seen to lie behind the changes introduced at the time of Big Bang, especially the merger with ISRO, it was not actively pursued from the late 1980s. Instead, the Stock Exchange was much more concerned with more practical matters such as competition for its information service, problems with settlement, and the need to devise a new electronic trading system. Important as all these were their dominance of the management and financial resources of the Stock Exchange reflected the continuance of a mentality that still looked back to the pre-Big Bang era rather than forward to what was now required. Clearly threats to the services that the London Stock Exchange provided would be resisted because, since 1947, it was both an organized market and a business. Settlement and information services, for example, generated much of the Stock Exchange's income at the beginning of the 1990s, while control over vital elements of the trading system, such as price display, made it central to the securities market. It was to be a slow process before the Stock Exchange could accept the loss of the income from the services it had once provided. In the provision of screen-based financial information, for example, the Stock Exchange faced increasing competition from other providers, and ones it could not stop through restricting access to current prices. These other providers, like Reuters, were also willing to invest a great deal more than the Stock Exchange in the collection of information and its electronic display, seeing in it the potential for a vast world-wide market. Eventually in 1993 the Stock Exchange was forced to recognize that it could not meet the challenge from these specialist firms and so began to sell its own systems to them. Its main information service, TOPIC, was sold in December 1994 and this was followed by the disposal of SEQUAL, its trade confirmation service, in October 1996. This left the field to a group of electronic information providers such as Reuters, ILX, ABP, Bloomberg, and Bridge, who invested heavily in a competitive battle for global supremacy. The London Stock Exchange, like other organized markets, were simply the sources of

---

[26] Quoted in *FT*, 8 July 1998.

price data which these companies sold to banks, brokers, and financial institutions.[27] There was no reason why the Stock Exchange needed to provide its members with this information service if others could do so better and cheaper. Historically this had always been the case as with the likes of Skinner's *Stock Exchange Yearbook* or Extel.

An even more traumatic loss for the Stock Exchange was the disaster over settlement services, for here the cause was not competition but an excess of ambition. At the time of Big Bang the Stock Exchange had suspended work on the replacement for its existing settlement system, TALISMAN, which was widely regarded as efficient and successful. As early as 1981 work had begun on a successor called TAURUS—Transfer and Automated Registration of Uncertificated Stock—which was then resumed in 1987. By then the Stock Exchange faced a serious settlement problem caused by a great increase in turnover and more complicated transactions with the ending of the broker/jobber split. The backlog of unsettled transactions was estimated at £3bn. to £4bn. in August 1987. However, rather than design a settlement system to reflect the new market conditions the Stock Exchange decided to modify TAURUS. With TAURUS the Stock Exchange would gain control over the whole transfer process as it would not only handle sales and purchases but also shareholder registers. This had already provoked opposition before TAURUS was suspended in 1984, and was sure to do so again, as it threatened the work already done by others, such as banks and company registrars. Unfortunately for the Stock Exchange their co-operation was essential if TAURUS was to succeed, and that was not forthcoming. Thus, though TAURUS was forecast in 1987 to be operational in 1989, in that year it was still far from completed. Luckily the crash of 1987, and the subsequent downturn in turnover, had allowed the existing settlement system to cope, but only at a cost. Settlement delays were estimated to be costing member firms £150–200m. per annum in 1989.[28]

In 1989 the Stock Exchange did begin to acknowledge the problems they faced in introducing TAURUS. Suggestions were made within the Stock Exchange to abandon the whole scheme and leave settlement to others, such as the banks who had considerable experience in clearing transactions. Unfortunately that was rejected as settlement continued to be perceived as central to the Stock Exchange's existence. Instead TAURUS was persevered with but in a modified form. All the time these delays were causing problems for member firms as they were expecting to introduce their own settlement systems compatible with that provided by the Stock Exchange. One of the problems now being faced by the Stock Exchange was that the market for which the settlement system was designed was itself changing,

[27] Ibid., 6 Feb. 1987, 4 Oct. 1989, 5 Mar. 1991, 14 Oct. 1991, 15 Mar. 1993, 23 Apr. 1993, 1 Oct. 1996, 25 Oct. 1996, 27 May 1998; LSE: *Annual Reports*, 1989, 1991, 1994.
[28] FT, 12 Aug. 1986, 14 Aug. 1987, 3 Apr. 1989, 22 Jan. 1993, 11 Mar. 1993, 12 Mar. 1993, 19 Mar. 1993.

becoming increasingly international in character and dominated by integrated banks and finance houses. At the same time every delay forced members to act unilaterally if they were not to see their competitiveness continually undermined by the high settlement costs in London and the delays in completing transactions. Faced with these mounting obstacles and delays, and the problems it was causing for its members, the Stock Exchange abandoned TAURUS on 11 March 1993. The Stock Exchange itself wrote off an investment of £75m. made 350 staff redundant, and the Chief Executive, Peter Rawlins, resigned. An estimated £320m. had also been invested by member firms in the belief that TAURUS was going to be introduced. So had ended '. . . the most challenging project ever undertaken by the Exchange . . .', as it was called in the 1992 *Annual Report*.[29]

With the failure of the TAURUS project the Stock Exchange lost the opportunity to make itself a central element in the London securities market, through the provision of the complete transfer process. Instead, the Bank of England took advantage of the Stock Exchange's difficulty and stepped in to take over the project. The Bank already controlled transfers of UK National Debt, with the Central Gilts Office, and so it was an obvious step to become involved in UK equities. The Bank of England was also concerned about maintaining the international competitiveness of the City of London, which the increasingly antiquated transfer system jeopardized, while it was also keen to reduce the risks inherent in any delay between a deal and its completion. Especially with banks and their subsidiaries so heavily involved in the securities market, after Big Bang, the Bank of England was increasingly worried about the risks they ran due to the large build up of uncompleted transfers. Hence the move towards rolling, rather than fortnightly settlement, under Bank of England pressure. Ten-day rolling settlement was introduced on 18 July 1994 and the move to five-days came on 26 June 1995. With the reduction, or elimination, of any gaps between a bargain and its completion the level of risks inherent in the securities market would be greatly reduced, though still present.

Consequently, the Bank of England's priorities in designating a transfer system were not those of the Stock Exchange. What emerged was a system—CREST—that ignored the needs of private investors, many of whom continued to hold paper share certificates, and focused on the requirements of financial institutions, whether as intermediaries or fund managers. These financial institutions were already familiar with electronic ownership and transfer records and had invested in the equipment and staff necessary to make it work. By August 1996, CREST was operational at an investment of less than £30m. and costs that allowed a much lower

---

[29] LSE: *Annual Report*, 1992, cf. *FT*, 29 June 1988, 6 Feb. 1989, 3 Apr. 1989, 4 Oct. 1989, 20 Oct. 1989, 7 Nov. 1990, 18 Sept. 1991, 10 Oct. 1991, 10 Nov. 1992, 22 Jan. 1993, 12 Mar. 1993, 3 July 1995.

charging structure than TALISMAN. In April 1997 TALISMAN was finally phased out with CREST capable of handling up to 170,000 transactions a day while it held ownership records of UK corporate securities valued at £950bn. Not only had the Stock Exchange lost a major source of income with the fiasco over TAURUS but yet another function which it had considered its own was now handled by an organization, CREST, over which it had no control.[30]

However, the collapse of TAURUS was something of a turning point for the London Stock Exchange, albeit one that was forced upon it. As long as it seemed that the Stock Exchange was going to control the transfer system for UK equities, no matter where the market lay, it had a clear and permanent future for other remunerative activities could be attached to the settlement process. With the end of TAURUS the future for the Stock Exchange looked bleak indeed, especially to those who had seen the provision of services as the key element in any survival plan. As early as January 1992 the *Financial Times* had questioned the lack of direction and drive on the Stock Exchange, seeing it extending far beyond the problems over TAURUS.

Two years ago, the London Stock Exchange . . . seemed on the point of transformation. Under new management, and with a new strategy agreed in outline, it seemed set for an upheaval to parallel the Big Bang reforms that had reshaped the City in 1986. Two years on, nothing has happened—and the securities companies which are the exchange's biggest customers are getting impatient.[31]

At least in 1992 there was the prospect that the Stock Exchange was going to emerge with control of the settlement system, but that had disappeared a year later.

Instead the Stock Exchange was forced to re-evaluate its position within the securities market, and out of that emerged a recognition that the provision of the services required by its membership was not necessarily what was required. As with so many other services the solution lay with specialist providers, often operating an international business and combining both equities and fixed-interest securities. Even if TAURUS had been brought to fruition, it would not have secured the future for the Stock Exchange unless it could have evolved into an international settlement system. The Bank of England's own Central Gilts Office was something of an anachronism by the mid-1990s. The settlement of the Eurobond trading, for example, was handled by Euroclear and Cedel, not stock exchanges or central banks.[32] As the Chairman of the Stock Exchange, Andrew Hugh Smith, could reflect,

[30] Ibid., 1 June 1993, 2 July 1993, 3 July 1995, 4 Aug. 1995, 28 Sept. 1995, 3 July 1996, 15 July 1996, 9 Nov. 1996, 16 Nov. 1996, 25 Nov. 1996, 4 Dec. 1996, 17 Jan. 1997, 22 Feb. 1997, 16 July 1997; *Quality of Markets Review*, Summer 1988, 21–2, 26–7, Summer 1989, 30, July–Sept. 1994, 13 15.
[31] *FT*, 30 Jan. 1992.     [32] Ibid., 16 July 1997, 8 Nov. 1997.

The cancellation of TAURUS does not impair London's ability to provide the world's leading international securities market. Business flows to our markets because of their depth and liquidity, and the extraordinary strength and diversity of the firms which operate them.[33]

Of course, what this left out was the exact role to be played by the London Stock Exchange. Unfortunately, in the period from the late 1980s until mid-1993 the London Stock Exchange had directed its attention towards the provision of services like settlement and information, because they brought in so much revenue, while neglecting the very reason why the Stock Exchange existed, namely the development and maintenance of an orderly market place.

Clearly central to an orderly market place was the nature of the market that the London Stock Exchange provided. As a result of Big Bang the Stock Exchange did appear to have a successful transition from a floor-based trading system to a screen-based one with the electronic display of prices in members' offices and then trading via the telephone. Market-makers remained central to the process with the added advantage that they could deal directly with major investors, like financial institutions. What had not come in was a fully electronic market place where trading could take place on-screen and a central computer match, automatically, orders to buy and sell in terms of securities, amounts, and prices.

Consideration had been given to such a facility but, as with settlement, it had been postponed because of the urgency of meeting the Big Bang deadline. Then, with the apparent success of the market-maker based trading little emphasis was given to replacing or supplementing it with fully inter-active electronic system. That only became a priority in the aftermath of the October 1987 crash, when the marketability of many of the less actively traded securities collapsed. The market-making system was ideal for those securities in which there was a high and continuous volume of buying and selling. Close two-way prices could be quoted by market-makers in expectation that they could easily and quickly reverse the deal, taking a profit from a small margin between the buy and sell price. In the active markets that accompanied Big Bang this was also the case for many less popular securities as investor euphoria extended to many smaller companies. When this euphoria ended, market-makers were unable to quote close bid/sell prices because of the difficulty they experienced in either buying or selling such securities. However, the wider prices being quoted further discouraged investors in these less popular securities, so reducing turnover again and forcing market-makers to quote even bigger spreads. Thus, by the late 1980s there was a growing recognition that the market designed at the time of Big Bang was not meeting the needs of all securities. Less than 100 (or 5 per cent) of quoted securities were highly traded while over 1,000 (or 70 per cent) were little dealt in.

[33] LSE: *Annual Report, 1993.*

These problems of inactive securities had been common to the pre-Big Bang years for it was impossible to maintain active markets in securities when there was insufficient turnover, no matter what trading system was in use. However, the collapse of turnover after 1987 had also thrown up a number of serious defects in the post-Big Bang organization of the market. Market-makers were not only obliged to quote prices in a range of securities but also buy and sell at these prices with all members. In the past jobbers could choose not to trade in an inactive security or simply agree to use their contacts in the market to find possible buyers or sellers, leaving the final decision to the broker and his client. Thus, jobbers had the discretion not only to vary prices at which they dealt, depending on the size of the transaction, and to vary the type of contract they entered in or even decline to trade. This ability to vary prices existed in the post-Big Bang trading system and was frequently used by large institutional investors to obtain a better bid or sell price from a market-maker than that quoted. However, it did leave the market-maker committed to buy or sell at the quoted prices. Furthermore the market-makers were then obliged to post their transactions for all to see, so allowing the market to move against them for others could guess that they would have to buy or sell in the near future in order to reverse the deal.

As long as business was brisk, market-makers could cope with these problems but they became serious difficulties in the late 1980s. Major market-makers, for example, discovered that smaller market-makers were dumping securities on them at the end of the day, when they could not be easily resold, causing large losses as they had to be disposed of at significantly lower prices. Similarly, it became increasingly difficult for market-makers to reverse a major deal at a profit as the market quickly reacted to any large sale or purchase as soon as it was reported. Faced with these mounting difficulties eight firms had pulled out of market-making by May 1989 while those that remained reported continuing losses, which were borne by their new owners. Clearly this was an unsustainable position and, in the absence of any positive action from the Stock Exchange itself, market-makers began to adjust the way they traded. In late 1988 two of the major market-makers, BZW and Phillips & Drew, refused to commit themselves to trade in anything other than the smallest permitted lot, in order to reduce the risks they ran. More generally market-makers began to quote very wide spreads between bid/sell prices in order to discourage dumping and give themselves greater scope for reversing sales and purchases profitably. The buy/sell spread on little traded securities, for example, widened to between 10 and 20 per cent in 1990, compared to 3 per cent in 1987. This had the inevitable result of driving brokers to find ways of completing bargains other than using market-makers, such as matching sales and purchases in-house or through direct contact with other brokers or investors. Of course, this made the situation worse for the less active securities as a smaller proportion now passed through the market-makers, encouraging them to further widen the bid/sell spread. All the Stock Exchange could offer was the right to a market-maker to refuse to deal with another market-maker and a relaxation of the disclosure rules. This curbed dumping and gave market-makers the opportunity to reverse a transaction before the market was aware of what was happening. However, these measures annoyed the brokers, who had relished full and immediate disclosure, and antagonized the press who saw it as a return to pre-Big Bang days of secrecy and collusion.[34]

It was inevitable that the new trading system would throw up problems and that adjustments would have to take place. However, by the late 1980s it was becoming obvious that a more radical reform of the rules and regulations governing the market would be required for it could not cope with both the range of securities quoted and the downturn in turnover. Even the eventual completion of SAEF—Stock Exchange Automated Execution Facility—in 1989, did little to help the situation, though it was designed to handle transactions in 1,000 shares or less, and so benefit the market for less-actively traded securities. Small transactions as opposed to transactions in small companies were fundamentally different problems. In February 1990 though deals in UK equities involving 10,000 shares or less comprised 78.4 per cent of all transactions that amounted to only 6 per cent of total value. In contrast deals involving 100,000 shares or more comprised only 6.9 per cent of the number but 78.8 per cent of the value. The quote-driven market-maker centred system coped well with the large deal but poorly with the small deal, because it was a system designed for the volume transactions generated by institutions, which dominated stock market activity in the UK. This was recognized by member firms who saw the solution in terms of aggregating the sales and purchases of individual investors. Both Kleinwort Benson in 1987 and BZW in 1988 had set up their own networks linking them to both clients and other brokers, and these systems incorporated an automated dealing service for small orders. By 1989 both these firms were processing 5,000 orders a week in this way and so were in a position to either match bargains internally or combine them into a transaction worthy of a market-maker's attention. Thus, the Stock Exchange's SAEF, completed at a cost of £4m., merely duplicated what its members were already developing and left unresolved the difficulties experienced by market-makers.[35]

Eventually in 1990 a committee was set up under Nigel Elwes, finance director of Warburg Securities, to investigate the problems now apparent in the way the market was operating and to devise a solution. This committee foundered on the fundamental differences between market-makers

---

[34] *Quality of Markets Review*, Spring 1989, 19–20, Jan.–Mar. 1990, 15–19; *FT*, 10 Oct. 1988, 22 Nov. 1988, 19 Apr. 1989, 22 May 1989.

[35] *Quality of Markets Review*, Jan.–Mar. 1990, 19; *FT*, 22 Nov. 1988, 13 Feb. 1989, 11 July 1998; LSE: *Annual Report*, 1989.

(jobbers) and broker/dealers (brokers) that had demanded an evolving compromise in the past. Market-makers wanted to be able to deal with members and non-members alike but be protected from unfair practices and outside competition. Broker/dealers wanted privileged access to market-makers and their prices, but also the right to match bargains themselves or with non-members. Reaching a compromise between these opposing wishes appeared to elude the Stock Exchange in the late 1980s and early 1990s. Attempts to match the requirements of market-makers with the liquidity of securities were not a success. Neither were the attempts to persuade brokers to route all business through market-makers. Also, inside and outside pressure made it necessary to restore full and immediate disclosure. As long as market-makers were required to make firm prices for securities which did not possess an active market, and disclose to all what they were doing, they were exposed to risks which they were reluctant to accept and sought to avoid.

In October 1992 a number of major market-makers—UBS, Phillips & Drew, Warburgs, County Natwest—took unilateral action and announced they were going to stop making markets in the shares of small quoted companies. The Stock Exchange was then forced to bring forward its preferred solution, which was nothing more than adoption of a modified form of New York Stock Exchange's specialist system, which had been rejected at the time of Big Bang. Under this system a market-maker would be given the exclusive right to make markets in particular securities, and all trading in these had to pass through them. Never had a Stock Exchange proposal, apart from its attitude towards the admission of women, so failed to match the expectations of the times. To the outside world it seemed a return to the pre-Big Bang era of restriction and monopoly, reversing the freedom and transparency of more recent years. Within the Stock Exchange it met with immediate opposition for 75 per cent of the turnover in the shares of many small companies was now matched in brokers' offices. Against such a background the Stock Exchange was forced to recognize that these proposals were simply unacceptable. However, the even more radical alternative of a move towards an order-driven market was equally unacceptable to many within the Stock Exchange, especially the largest firms of market-makers who appeared to have so much to lose. In an order-driven market buyers and sellers entered their orders which were then matched automatically by a central computer, without the need for any further intermediation. Such a system worked for other securities markets, such as those on continental Europe, and it was confidently predicted that it would deliver an improved service in London in terms of cost, speed, and pricing. There was a risk and that was that London would lose the liquid markets that had sustained its attractions in the past, for that came with the willingness of market-makers to risk their own capital in taking positions which they would then expect to unwind at a profit. This fear that removing the central role of the market-makers would destroy the London Stock Exchange's competitive advantage was a major obstacle to any radical reform of the market. It helps to explain why change was so long delayed, for the merits of an order-driven market were being advocated from 1988 onwards.[36]

This need to devise rules and regulations acceptable to all market participants was central to the very existence of the Stock Exchange. Otherwise the London Stock Exchange would be indistinguishable from the securities market, bringing forth questions concerning its future. Why should members pay fees to it, and accept its strictures, if they obtained little in return or even suffered as a result. Unfortunately, the Stock Exchange's attention was focused elsewhere. First this was on the continuing saga of TAURUS and the problems of settlement. Then, even before that had been resolved there arose a problem over the technological obsolescence of SEAQ, which lay at the heart of the Stock Exchange's trading system. This had been hurriedly put together at the time of Big Bang and incorporated an array of computing hardware and software, all of which needed replacing by the early 1990s. Thus, from 1992 onwards the Stock Exchange began the design of a new electronic trading platform, though it could have bought and modified existing systems in use elsewhere. From the outset this trading platform incorporated both information display and an order-driven capacity. Unlike TAURUS the Stock Exchange successfully managed the design and introduction of this new trading system—SEQUENCE—despite its complexity. From October 1993 onwards SEQUENCE gradually replaced SEAQ, and was finally completed in August 1996 at a cost of £81m. With the introduction of SEQUENCE the Stock Exchange had at its disposal an electronic platform that would support either a continuance of a quote-driven market, with competing market-makers, or an order-driven market, for the automatic execution of orders.[37]

## Providing the Market

By then the Stock Exchange was under mounting external pressure to reform its method of trading. The proposed introduction of specialists or sole traders in 1992 had, once again, brought the Stock Exchange to the attention of the Office of Fair Trading. The OFT had never abandoned its suspicions that the London Stock Exchange was using its rules and regulations to maintain a dominant position within the British securities market, and these were simply rekindled by the proposals to grant special privileges to members in return for making markets in specific securities. In February 1993 the OFT contended itself with voicing these suspicions but its

[36] LSE: *Annual Reports*, 1988, 1991; *Quality of Markets Review*, Jan.–Mar. 1990, 15–17, Oct.–Dec. 1990, 8, Jan.–Mar. 1991, 21, Apr.–June 1991, 5; *FT*, 19 Feb. 1990, 1 July 1991, 2 July 1991, 14 Oct. 1991, 30 Jan. 1992, 9 Apr. 1992, 5 Sept. 1992, 8 Sept. 1992, 15 Oct. 1992.
[37] LSE: *Annual Reports*, 1995, 1996, 1997; *FT*, 27 Aug. 1996.

pressure for reform did not abate. A subsequent OFT enquiry in 1995 did result in the conclusion that, '. . . numerous stock exchange practices and privileges had an anti-competitive effect'.[38]

It was not only pressure from government bodies that was forcing the Stock Exchange to re-examine the way its market was organized. Competition was now a much more potent force than it had been in the 1970s and early 1980s for it was now possible for any organization or company to apply to have its market officially recognized by the regulatory authorities. Reuters was already developing an electronic trading system, Instinet, based on its acquisition of proven American technology. A more direct rival was Tradepoint, which was a fully electronic stock exchange operating from September 1995 onwards. Subscribers to Tradepoint could have their own orders completed automatically and cheaply without the use of market-makers and their bid/sell price spreads. Even though Tradepoint was not a great success, with only 0.3 per cent of UK equity trades by February 1996 and 0.5 per cent in May 1997, it was taken as a potentially serious threat by the Stock Exchange. No longer could the London Stock Exchange ignore domestic competition. The changed regulatory environment, and the convergence of electronic computing and communication technologies, had made it possible to establish rival exchanges with much lower cost structures and far fewer restrictions than the London Stock Exchange.[39]

While the external forces for change were mounting up, internal resistance was also crumbling. Those banks and US brokerage houses that owned the major market-makers were finally beginning to assess the returns they were generating and the risks that were run. Maintaining active markets across a wide range of securities incurred high staff costs which were not justified in many cases while the commitment to buy and sell on demand, even small lots of shares, could tie up capital and risk its loss. Competition from broker/dealers matching their own bargains, because of the wide spreads quoted, had already begun to force some market-makers, like BZW, Smith Brothers, and Kleinwort Benson, to offer an automated execution service to these firms. With this experience market-makers became aware that a move to an order-driven system need not destroy them, for the services they provided remained essential to any high volume market. Thus, within the Stock Exchange the stalemate between the market-makers and broker/dealers was breaking up as the market-makers realized that the existing system, while giving them a privileged position, also placed upon them costly, and difficult demands.[40]

[38] Quoted in *FT*, 30 Sept. 1995, cf. 11 Feb. 1993, 18 Oct. 1993.
[39] *FT*, 18 Oct. 1993, 10 Dec. 1994, 4 Sept. 1995, 7 Sept. 1995, 30 Sept. 1995, 27 Nov. 1995, 27 Dec. 1995, 13 Jan. 1996, 24 Feb. 1996, 3 June 1997, 3 July 1998.
[40] Ibid., 2 June 1995, 30 Nov. 1995, 9 Jan. 1996, 21 Mar. 1996, 17 May 1996, 31 May 1996, 3 Aug. 1996, 27 Aug. 1996.

The Chief Executive of the Stock Exchange at this time, Michael Lawrence, recognized that a reform of the market was becoming essential and that the only alternative on offer now was a move towards a quote-driven system. Unfortunately, his professional career as an accountant and with Prudential Assurance, had not given him an understanding of the basic Stock Exchange tensions between brokers and market-makers, which had to be resolved not ignored if progress was to be made. He was familiar with a corporate management structure in which decisions were taken at board level and then implemented. Though parts of the Stock Exchange were like that, as with the services it provided, such a model did not operate for the market. Market-makers and broker/dealers were individual firms in their own right and were members of the Stock Exchange because it benefited them to be so. They were not employed by the Stock Exchange to buy and sell securities but, instead, paid for the privilege of doing so. Consequently, they could not be coerced but had to be persuaded that change was required, and then expected to be consulted over the nature of that change. Thus, when Lawrence tried to drive through the move to an electronic order-book system in 1995 they rebelled and he was sacked in January 1996. His eventual replacement, Gavin Casey, came from Merrill Lynch and reflected the fact that the Stock Exchange needed a chief executive who understood securities markets more than one who could run a business. In fact, the more the Stock Exchange shed services like settlement and information the more its future rested upon organizing and managing a successful market.[41]

This sacking of the chief executive did not stop the move towards an order-driven system, for that had now become inexorable. In June 1997 it was announced that the switch to order-driven trading would begin on 20 October. During the intervening months £20m. was spent on the necessary equipment and software, and rules and regulations were framed to permit the operation of an orderly market. When introduced, SETS (Stock Exchange Trading Service) could handle 3,000 transactions a minute. Gone were attempts to force brokers to use market-makers and gone were any obligations on market-makers to quote firm prices in numerous securities. Each could now choose how best to buy and sell on behalf of their clients or employ their capital and expertise to best advantage. The new system reflected the coming of age of the Stock Exchange as the attempts to impose a rigid format on the London securities market were finally abandoned. The process had begun with Big Bang but was then stalled for almost 10 years, as the Stock Exchange appeared to lose direction. Whatever else the Stock Exchange did its existence depended upon its ability to provide its members with a trading forum that combined the minimum regulation required for an orderly and disciplined market and the maximum freedom necessary for innovation and development. Even after Big Bang these aims had been obscured by the Stock

[41] *FT*, 17 June 1994, 2 May 1995, 5 Jan. 1996, 24 Jan. 1996, 24 Feb. 1996, 5 Mar. 1996, 7 Mar. 1996, 3 Aug. 1996, 14 Oct. 1996, 11 July 1997.

Exchange's aim of providing the full range of services required by its membership, extending not only from control over admission, behaviour, and listings but also to settlement and training. Only as these additional services were lost, sold, or abandoned did the Stock Exchange come to accept what its priorities really were. Hence the belated move to a market system that permitted its membership to trade in those ways that best suited themselves and their customers which, in turn, reflected the type of securities being bought and sold, the nature of the clients, and the size of the deal. What emerged, therefore, was an acceptance of variety with much business continuing to be done via market-makers rather than SETS, which was handling about a third of all transactions, by value, by May 1998.

The move to SETS was not an entirely smooth one. Members had been accustomed to a pricing mechanism in which the activities of the market-makers reduced any volatile pricing of deals. That was absent from SETS because of its automatic nature and so erratic prices were thrown up, especially at the beginning and end of the day when volume was low. This led many to criticize the order-driven system and led to demands from certain brokers and institutional investors for all transactions in particular stocks to be routed through SETS. The Stock Exchange resisted these demands but their existence suggested that the forces which had led to many of the controls and restrictions of the past, like single capacity and fixed commissions, continued to be present. Though order-driven trading had been seen by many as the solution to all the Stock Exchange's problems it was but one solution to one problem, and also created new problems. Nevertheless, what it did deliver to the London market was the continuing ability to meet the needs of the major institutional investors, who wanted direct access to market-makers, and an improved competitiveness for smaller transactions, which could now be done automatically and cheaply at better prices.[42] In a programmed trade, for example, a fund manager sold an entire portfolio to a market-maker at an agreed price, with the market-maker then quickly reselling the individual components, and making a profit on the difference between the two prices. Such transactions were running at c.£20bn. a year in 1995, and required direct negotiations and individual handling.[43] As the *Financial Times* had observed in March 1996,

For the very largest and most heavily traded shares, the method [of trading] makes little difference, there is always likely to be enough liquidity to allow large amounts of shares to be traded, whether by quote or order. The real problem is in dealing with smaller and less heavily traded shares.[44]

[42] Ibid., 5 Mar. 1996, 14 Dec. 1996, 3 June 1997, 10 June 1997, 24 July 1997, 23 Sept. 1997, 13 Nov. 1997, 8 Sept. 1997, 11 Sept. 1997, 23 Sept. 1997, 29 Sept. 1997, 14 Oct. 1997, 17 Oct. 1997, 20 Oct. 1997, 24 Oct. 1997, 6 Nov. 1997, 17 Nov. 1997, 26 Nov. 1997, 27 Nov. 1997, 29 Nov. 1997, 31 Dec. 1997, 3 Jan. 1998, 24 Mar. 1998, 30 Mar. 1998, 30 Apr. 1998, 23 May 1998, 28 May 1998, 29 May 1998, 30 May 1998.
[43] Ibid., 5 Mar. 1995.    [44] Ibid.

What SETS was designed to do was to meet the needs of less actively traded securities and those investors who dealt in smaller amounts, without jeopardizing the service that the London Stock Exchange's membership provided to the major financial institutions of the world. Of course, there was no necessity that the Stock Exchange itself should have provided SETS, only that it controlled access and determined the rules governing its use.

Gradually, in the 1990s the London Stock Exchange was concentrating upon its core functions as it shed peripheral activities that either faced growing competition or were no longer appropriate or had not proved a success. The Traded Options Market (LTOM) was eventually taken over by LIFFE on 20 March 1992, after two years of negotiation, as the London Stock Exchange finally abandoned any pretensions to add futures contracts to its trading operations. Once the Stock Exchange had missed the opportunity to become the European leader in financial futures in the 1970s the business was best left to the more specialist institutions in what was becoming an increasingly competitive global market. Faced with increasing competition in 1998, and manœuvrings by rival European futures market, it was LIFFE that toyed with a merger with the London Stock Exchange but, by then it was marginal to the London Stock Exchange's ambitions.[45] However, a similar attempt to close down the separate market for smaller companies, and merge it with the main exchange, failed. The Unlisted Securities Market (USM) had been a great success. Between 1980 and 1990 a total of 817 companies had been listed and £47bn. raised through the issue of securities.[46] In many ways it appeared to characterize the new entrepreneurial spirit of Thatcherite Britain, and may even have contributed to it, according to Sir Nicholas Goodison in 1989,

> . . . this new market did a lot to alter attitudes to risk among investors who, during the 1960s and 1970s, had become averse to risk owing to the economic and fiscal policies pursued by governments during those decades.[47]

However, the smaller companies that were listed on the USM were the very ones that suffered most when turnover fell in the wake of the 1987 crash. The more the turnover fell in small company securities the less easy they were to buy or sell and the more volatile the price fluctuations were. Market-makers therefore, widened their spreads which further discouraged buying and selling, making it impossible for holders to dispose of them without large losses, and difficult for institutions to build up significant holdings. Turnover in smaller company shares fell from £200m. per day, before the October 1987 crash, to £40m. per day in 1991, while the average spread almost quadrupled from 3 per cent to 11 per cent.

[45] *FT*, 10 Mar. 1988, 12 Apr. 1988, 23 May 1989, 4 Apr. 1990, 3 July 1990, 25 Apr. 1991, 29 Oct. 1991, 4 Mar. 1993, 11 July 1998; LSE: *Annual Report*, 1992; D. Kynaston, *LIFFE: A Market and its Masters* (London 1997), 236–56.

[46] *Quality of Markets Review*, July–Sept. 1990, 15.

[47] Sir Nicholas Goodison, 'Foreword' to R. Buckland and E. W. Davis, *The Unlisted Securities Market* (Oxford 1989).

Faced with these difficulties in the secondary market, smaller companies ceased to make new issues, as they were poorly received. By 1991 only £11.6m. of new capital was raised by USM companies compared to £308m. in 1988. The first action of the Stock Exchange was to combine the USM with the other small company forum, the Third Market, in 1990, in hope of bolstering their overall attractions. The Third Market had been badly damaged by the crash, coming so soon after its launch in 1987, and had never been a success. This move achieved little and the USM continued to decline in popularity among both investors and small companies seeking a quotation. Between 1994 and 1996 the number of companies listed on the USM fell from 207 to 30, for example, not helped by the fact that in 1991 the Stock Exchange had made it much easier to obtain a full quotation. Consequently, as early as 1993 the Stock Exchange unveiled plans to close down the USM, despite a likely adverse reaction and the possible appearance of a rival. The closure of the Third Market in 1990 had antagonized those in the City involved in a small company finance and even led to an outburst from John Redwood, the Corporate Affairs Minister, hinting that a rival market would find favour with the government. The Natwest Bank even investigated the creation of such a market in 1991, using its branch network, but the threat came to nothing. However, the planned closure of the USM did lead to the establishment of a rival market. J. P. Jenkins, a leading market-maker in small company shares, set up OFEX in 1995, to provide a forum for the trading of their securities.[48]

With the development of this rival, and government disapproval that a specialist market for the securities of smaller companies, was to disappear, the Stock Exchange succumbed to outside pressure and announced that the USM would be replaced. On 19 June 1995 AIM—Alternative Investment Market—was launched, and its success was boosted by the abolition of Rule 4.2. Under that rule it had been possible for members to trade any security on a matched basis, making the facilities of the Stock Exchange market available on an *ad hoc* basis to any company. By August 1996, 205 securities were listed on AIM and they had a market value of £4.3bn. A total of £650m. had been raised through new issues. OFEX was also flourishing for about a further 300 small companies were listed there. The critics of the Stock Exchange appeared to have been vindicated as the need for a market for the securities of smaller, and often newer and riskier companies, had been proven. Though there could be no doubt that such a market was required, it had to be questioned whether the Stock Exchange should have provided it, for the existence of OFEX and later the pan-European EASDAQ, launched in September 1996, indicated that alternatives were available.[49]

---

[48] *FT*, 14 Aug. 1990, 10 Nov. 1990, 11 Dec. 1991, 4 Mar. 1993, 18 Dec. 1993, 22 Apr. 1994, 26 Apr. 1994, 20 Apr. 1995, 17 June 1995, 20 July 1995, 4 Aug. 1996, 20 Aug. 1996, 27 Aug. 1996, 30 Dec. 1996, 20 June 1997.

[49] Ibid., 20 July 1995, 19 Dec. 1995, 5 Mar. 1996, 11 Apr. 1996, 17 Apr. 1996.

The problem for the Stock Exchange was that it was impossible to apply the same standards to the securities of small companies as to large companies. By their very nature small companies were often recently formed with no established track record and not operating to a proven formula. Thus the opportunities for investors to be swindled or simply misled were much greater. At the same time the shares of smaller companies were often closely held, creating easy opportunities for price manipulation, jeopardizing the operation of an orderly market. The *Financial Times* produced a stark assessment of the dilemma in September 1994, before AIM was even launched:

Stock exchanges everywhere face a common problem: the need to protect investors while creating an environment where small companies, in particular, can raise capital at an affordable price.[50]

If government, media and investors were willing to abide by the dictat, *caveat emptor*, as existed for any obviously risky purchase or investment, such as the National Lottery, then the London Stock Exchange could provide an orderly market for all types of securities. As that was not the case in the 1990s then the Stock Exchange was exposing itself to inevitable criticism and even intervention by making a market in smaller securities. One of its own members, Ronald Cohen, predicted as much in March 1994, after serving on the Committee that produced AIM. Consequently, within a few years the Stock Exchange was being attacked because of problems associated with some AIM companies and was forced to respond by tightening up its regulatory procedures on small companies seeking to join the market. Inevitably that would discourage many from seeking a quotation either because of the conditions to be met or the increased charges that would have to be levied to pay for investigation and supervision. That would then provoke further criticism that the London Stock Exchange was not catering for smaller companies. What was important for the Stock Exchange was that it offered a market for those companies whose size and investor interest would justify the cost of a quotation and the provision of a ready market for their securities. In 1994 94 per cent of the turnover on the London Stock Exchange was in the shares of the largest 350 quoted companies indicating how little activity the rest of the list generated, and how irrelevant AIM was to the business of the Stock Exchange and most of its members.[51]

The London Stock Exchange was only one part of the British financial system and, by the 1990s, an increasingly specialized part. At the same time such had been the changes since Big Bang that the orientation of it and its members was now firmly international. Consequently, it had neither the

[50] *FT*, 24 Sept. 1994.
[51] Ibid., 8 Mar. 1994, 26 Apr. 1994, 17 Feb. 1995, 19 Dec. 1995, 19 June 1995, 27 Aug. 1996, 17 Oct. 1996, 19 June 1997, 20 June 1997.

position nor the power to effect fundamental changes in the British capital market, regardless of the wishes of government or the criticism of uninformed sections of the media. In terms of small companies finance was a perennial and universal problem for it was never easy to raise the funds required for a novel venture, no matter how promising it appeared in retrospect. In many ways the problem for investors was not how to back winners but how to avoid backing the innumerable losers that soon faded into oblivion. Success required an insider's knowledge and a willingness to persevere in the face of adversity because of that knowledge. For that reason there have to be doubts whether the process could ever be institutionalized and whether any securities market had a role to play until a later stage, when a track record had been established. Instead, experience suggested that the finance of entrepreneurial companies was best left to individuals and informal networks, with suitable tax and other concessions, and that the role of the Stock Exchange was to provide a way of raising additional finance later when more passive investors could replace the early pioneers.[52] The Stock Exchange was criticized for failing to give a market to emerging biotechnology companies. When it did so in 1993, by relaxing its listing requirements, it was then criticized when a number proved disappointing. By 1997 30 such companies had a full quotation with a further 10 on AIM and they proved a volatile part of the market.[53]

Consequently, though the Stock Exchange had tried to end its separate small company market at the beginning of the 1990s, it had failed to do so. It had decided that the adverse reaction deemed to pulling out was greater than that of staying in, showing that the Stock Exchange remained susceptible to government pressure. It is unlikely that competition, in the shape of OFEX, could have been the deciding factor, considering how little turnover on the Stock Exchange was generated from small companies, who could easily gravitate to a full quotation when the time was opportune. Generally, whatever difficulties and setbacks the London Stock Exchange experienced in the 1990s, it continued to dominate the market for UK corporate securities. Its only real loss was that in Irish securities with the establishment of Dublin as an independent Stock Exchange in 1995 under a European Union directive. Even then 20 per cent of the turnover in Irish stocks, especially the largest and most liquid ones, took place in London. Altogether various estimates suggested that the London Stock Exchange accounted for 95 per cent of the domestic turnover in UK equities throughout the 1990s. This was despite competition from rivals such as Tradepoint,

[52] Ibid., 12 July 1991, 5 Oct. 1993, 17 Feb. 1995, 17 Oct. 1996, 28 Oct. 1996, 14 Dec. 1996, 17 Jan. 1997, 11 Feb. 1997, 11 Mar. 1997, 24 Apr. 1997, 27 Nov. 1997, cf. R. Coopey and D. Clarke, *3i: Fifty Years Investing in Industry* (Oxford 1995), 364, 382; *FT, Mastering Finance*, ch. by S. Kaplan, 'Plenty of Potential in Private Equity'.

[53] *FT*, 2 July 1993, 27 Nov. 1995, 24 Feb. 1996, 26 Nov. 1996, 24 Apr. 1997, 15 May 1997; *Quality of Markets Review*, Jan.–Mar. 1993, 17, Jan.–Mar. 1994, 13–15, Jan.–Mar. 1995, 11.

NASDAQ's London operation, and the OTC markets. One of Big Bang's objectives had been to preserve this domination of the domestic market and there was every sign that it had succeeded admirably without the need for restrictive practices or government support. This position was also achieved against a background of growing international competition for the market in UK equities. Both the New York Stock Exchange and NASDAQ traded the shares of an increasing number of major UK companies, in the form of ADR's, as part of their bid for leadership in the global securities market. By 1991 60 per cent of their ADR trading was in UK companies and they tried to expand this business aggressively during the decade. Nevertheless, in 1996 the London Stock Exchange continued to capture 90 per cent of the total turnover in UK equities, wherever it took place. The London Stock Exchange even took to listing ADRs itself in 1994, though they had been designed for the convenience of the American market.[54]

Nominally, at least, the London Stock Exchange also continued to dominate the market for UK government securities. However, ever since the reforms at the time of Big Bang control of the gilts market lay with the Bank of England. The Stock Exchange did formulate the rules governing the way its members transacted business in gilts and all those involved in the buying and selling operations had to be members. However, both these rules and those eligible to trade lay under the ultimate control of the Bank of England, which had prime responsibility for its direction and development. The balance of power in the gilts market had shifted firmly away from the Stock Exchange and towards the Bank of England, who organized it to suit the needs of the government as a borrower. It showed little concern, for example, for the mounting losses experienced by participating firms in the late 1980s as the National Debt shrank and competition was extreme. Between 1986 and 1991 the number of firms involved fell from 27 to 18. This loss of Stock Exchange control over the gilts market was but part of its lack of involvement in the bond market generally, whether issued by governments or companies. Trading in fixed-interest debt was dominated by banks world-wide and they maintained their own trading networks, organizations, and clearing systems to cope with its requirements. Thus, an area of securities trading that had once dominated the London Stock Exchange, and was fundamental to its foundation some 200 years before, was now of limited significance. Even by 1990 trading in gilts was down to 43 per cent of total Stock Exchange turnover, by value, compared to 77 per cent in 1980, with the business being handled by a few specialist firms, net of commission.[55]

[54] FT, 10 Dec. 1987, 10 June 1989, 10 June 1995, 3 July 1996, 19 June 1997, 18 Feb. 1998, 13 Mar. 1998, 29 Apr. 1998, 27 May 1998, 3 July 1998; City Research Project., Competitive Position, Annex.

[55] Bank of England, British Government Securities: The Market in Gilt-Edged Securities (London 1998), 7, 14–15; FT, 14 Nov. 1988, 9 Feb. 1989, 23 Oct. 1991, 12 Nov. 1992, 14 Nov. 1994, 21 Feb. 1995, 30 Mar. 1995, 8 May 1997; Quality of Markets Review, Apr.–June 1990, 17–18.

What had now replaced the bond market in importance for the London Stock Exchange was trading in foreign shares. Whereas in 1980 these had been virtually non-existent after years of exchange controls and restrictive practices, by 1990 it had re-emerged as a major component of total turnover on the London Stock Exchange. By 1993 the turnover in companies quoted on SEAQ international overtook that on SEAQ, and this foreign business continued to grow strongly. In particular, trading in Europe's largest companies had been attracted to London either because of the limited size of their own domestic securities market or restrictive practices on their domestic stock exchanges. Swedish companies like Electrolux, for example, that operated world-wide, needed an equivalent market for their securities and that London was able to provide. Similarly large South African mining companies were attracted to London because of the lack of depth in their own markets. In contrast the problem in major economies like Germany, France, and Italy were the stock exchange rules and regulations and government controls that restricted the development of their domestic securities markets. Thus an active market in the shares of major German companies like Deutsche Bank, Siemens, Bayer, and Daimler Benz, developed in London in the late 1980s. This was not to say that London dominated turnover in securities such as these for the bulk of transactions continued to take place in their domestic exchanges, as that was much more convenient for the vast bulk of their investors. Even in those German stocks quoted in London, 90 per cent of turnover took place in German stock exchanges, for instance, and the figure was 80 per cent for French securities.[56]

Faced with the loss of business to London, stock exchanges and governments around the world, but especially in Europe, began to remove controls and liberalize trading practices in order to compete more effectively. Paris and Madrid experienced 'Mini Bangs' in 1989 and Milan in 1991. In Germany the government repealed the turnover tax on securities in 1991, and in 1993 all the German stock exchanges amalgamated to form a single exchange under the leadership of Frankfurt. The Chairman of this Deutsche Börse, Werner Seifert, made it clear in 1997 that one of the objectives of this move was to replace the London Stock Exchange as the main equities market in Europe. These reforms did lead to the repatriation of some foreign business from London, as in the case of major Dutch stocks where the Amsterdam Stock Exchange was handling two-thirds of the transactions by 1998. Financial institutions, even British ones, like the insurance company Legal and General, looked for the best market when they wanted to buy and sell and they frequently found that it was not in London but on national stock exchanges. In 1996 this ability to access national markets had become easier because the European

[56] Ibid.; City Research Project, *Competitive Position*, Table 2.4; *FT*, 5 Feb. 1987, 17 June 1989, 11 Sept. 1989, 17 May 1990, 24 Jan. 1992, 2 June 1997.

Union had introduced a law opening up membership of all European stock exchanges to those at a distance.[57]

Attempts were made to limit the degree of competition between the various European stock exchanges by creating a pan-European market. The London Stock Exchange did participate in these from 1989, even though it had the most to lose being the only cross-country market place. As it was, agreement proved impossible to reach and the attempt was abandoned in 1991. In that year the London Stock Exchange also called off co-operation talks with NASDAQ, aimed at creating a transatlantic market. Considering how long it had taken to create a single British stock exchange such talks were probably premature, and needed to wait until the global securities market itself had developed further, national standards had been harmonized, and international barriers further reduced. Even when that had been accomplished the self-interest of individual stock exchanges needed to be overcome, and that would be no easy matter as they sought to preserve the rights and privileges of their members against those of competitors. Nevertheless, stock exchanges now existed in an increasingly competitive environment where their future was no longer secured by national boundaries and government support. Especially in Europe there could be no guarantee that the 32 existing stock exchanges would all retain their independence.[58]

This situation led, in July 1998, to an agreement between the London and Frankfurt Stock Exchanges to form a single market on which would be traded the securities of Europe's 350 largest companies, under a common set of rules and regulations. As preparation for this market each stock exchange agreed to delist the securities traded on the other which would lose the London Stock Exchange business in German stocks, which had totalled £170.3bn. in 1997, compared to Frankfurt's loss of £2bn. in UK stocks. Nevertheless, the expectation of the London Stock Exchange was that it would gain rather than lose as trading gravitated to the combined market, away from centres such as Paris, Amsterdam, Madrid, and Milan. Together, London and Frankfurt would constitute the core of a single European Stock Exchange which would possess the liquidity and expertise to attract to it all the buying and selling in European equities other than that which was local or specialist. As trading no longer took place on a physical floor, whether in London or Frankfurt, this market would exist between the offices of the members wherever they were located, and so could be extended to those who were also members of other stock exchanges in Europe. Logical as this development was, being in harmony

[57] *FT*, 7 Jan. 1991, 14 Feb. 1991, 13 May 1991, 24 Mar. 1992, 8 Oct. 1992, 16 June 1994, 23 June 1995, 26 Sept. 1995, 16 Feb. 1996, 28 Nov. 1997, 8 July 1998.
[58] Ibid., 15 Nov. 1990, 28 Nov. 1990, 23 Apr. 1991, 29 May 1991, 20 June 1991, 24 Sept. 1991, 2 Nov. 1995, 22 June 1998, 8 July 1998, 9 July 1998, 13 July 1998.

with European economic and monetary union, it had still to overcome all
the difficulties over details that had made it so difficult to reach agreement
on co-operation, let alone merger, in the past. However, by the late 1990s
the demand for stock exchanges at all levels was growing, offering opportunities at the local, regional, national, and international level, as well as
niche markets like small technology stock, if only they abandoned their
restrictive practices and co-operated.

What was taking place in the 1990s was a process of reordering in
the global securities market in which stock exchanges had to respond
both to a growing demand and new challenges. New issues by companies
and governments accompanied by the securitization of existing assets
was creating a vast expansion in the value and volume of securities in
circulation, and thus tradeable on secondary markets. By 1997 the market
value of securities quoted on the world's stock exchanges was put at
$40,000bn., split equally between equities and fixed-interest debt. This
amount had grown rapidly over the years, fuelled by the needs of business
and governments to raise finance. Privatization of state assets in Europe,
for example, had raised $186bn. between 1981 and 1996, over half of
which was British. In turn this had put into circulation securities with a
far greater market value, and was being emulated by countries all round
the world. Ex-communist or socialist states had vast assets to dispose of
and privatization was an attractive option as it both raised money for the
government and improved the efficiency of the economy. From the other
side there was a growing need to fund pension and other welfare payments
by means other than current taxation. The burden of such taxation was
becoming more and more unacceptable to populations around the world
as costs soared and numbers of those of working age shrank. The obvious
alternative were schemes in which those at work made regular savings
which were then invested so as to produce an income on retirement. Securities that promised a claim to a fixed or variable future income were, obviously important in this. Such schemes already existed, but only in a limited
number of countries. In 1996 pension fund assets ranged from around 75
per cent of GDP in the Netherlands, Switzerland, and the UK, through 60
per cent in the USA and 20 per cent in Japan, to under 10 per cent in France
and Germany. Consequently, the forces of both supply and demand were
combining to generate a global growth in the creation of securities, representing claims to future income, and this held out considerable promise for
the markets upon which they would be traded as investors, both individual and institutional, adjusted their portfolios in response to changing circumstances.

Among the securities to be held, shares were attractive. Though not offering the certainty of future income as did fixed-interest debt, especially that
issued by fiscally responsible governments, equities had the advantage of
coping with inflation. Inflation had destroyed the value of fixed-interest

investment in many countries, including Britain, over the post-war years. A sum of £100 invested in gilt-edged securities in 1945 would have grown to £1,209 by 1991, with all income invested. In contrast the same sum invested in equities would have been worth £28,513 through capital appreciation and income growth. Consequently, investors, especially pension fund managers, were acutely aware of the need to create mixed portfolios of assets which would include a substantial equity element. Bonds fell from 45 per cent of UK pension fund assets in the mid-1960s to only 8 per cent in 1991, for example.

Again, this commitment to equities varied enormously between countries, with both Britain and the United States having an advanced equity culture while much of continental Europe did not. Whereas in 1996 the ratio of stock market capitalization to GDP was 127 per cent for Switzerland, 122 per cent for the UK, 90 per cent for the USA, and 87 per cent for Japan, it was only 24 per cent for France and Germany and 18 per cent for Italy. Germany, in particular, had shown no real growth in the importance of securities in the economy for the ratio was the same in 1985, while it had grown substantially for most other countries. In 1985 the ratio was 49 per cent for Switzerland, 69 per cent UK, 48 per cent USA, 57 per cent Japan, and 13 per cent for France and Italy. Such a situation had become of serious concern to the German central bank, the Bundesbank, by 1997, worried by the need to fund future pension obligations and finance growing businesses. Thus, though there was no reason that the ratios of countries like the UK and USA were the appropriate ones there was every expectation that the level of equity issues and investment in many countries round the world would rise substantially, creating in turn a large demand for secondary trading facilities. This could even be accompanied by a reverse trend for equities in the UK if a low inflation period created a renewed enthusiasm for fixed-interest debt from companies and investors. Certainly such a trend was evident in the mid-1990s.[59]

A further element in the changing investment environment was its growing international nature, though this still remained in its infancy even in the mid-1990s. Though 15 per cent of the UK financial assets were foreign securities, the figure for the other major economies of continental Europe, such as France, Germany and Italy, was under 5 per cent. Again, with growing financial and exchange liberalization, and even currency union, there was every likelihood that the proportion would grow substantially, creating a much more international market for securities. This had been happening from the 1980s onwards. Issues of corporate securities to international

---

[59] FT, 31 Jan. 1992, 23 Oct. 1992, 23 Oct. 1996, 17 Jan. 1997, 24 Apr. 1997, 14 May 1997, 30 Apr. 1998, 18 May 1998; FT, Mastering Finance, chs. by J. J. Siegel, 'Risk and Return: Start with the Building Blocks,' K. Lewis, 'Why Financial Investors Like to Stay at Home', N. Barberis, 'Asset Allocation—Have Investors Got it Wrong', N. Rose, 'Securitization: Unbundling for Value'.

investors totalled $304.3bn. between 1983 and 1996 as businesses took the opportunity to tap cheaper and more flexible sources of capital than those available domestically. In turn this produced an enormous expansion in the volume of cross-border dealing in securities as international investors bought and sold with each other. Between 1990 and 1995, for instance, cross-border trading in securities grew sevenfold, from $5,000bn. to $35,000bn. Most of this was in fixed-interest debt being traded directly between banks and other financial institutions but a transnational equity market was developing involving a small number of multinational companies. In 1998 in Europe there existed 300 companies, operating in such fields as pharmaceuticals, oil, banking, and consumer brands, whose securities were held and traded internationally. Altogether, these companies accounted for c.65 per cent of the market value of all stock exchange quoted companies, and it was their securities that were the most heavily traded.[60]

What securities market had, therefore, witnessed over the 1980s and into the 1990s was a huge expansion in the volume and variety of business at all levels and there was every expectation that this would continue. This meant a demand for trading facilities both nationally and internationally, as investors sought out the best markets for the securities that attracted them. In most cases this would be national markets as it was there that the depth and spread of investor interest was greatest and the expertise most developed. The growing international dimension posed no threat to national stock exchanges like London, Paris, Frankfurt, Tokyo, or New York as long as these institutions showed themselves sufficiently flexible to meet the challenges posed by the disappearance of national boundaries and the convergence of computing and communications technology. In fact the ending of exchange control and the ease of communication made it easier and easier for distant investors, such as financial institutions, to trade directly on national stock exchanges. It became possible, for example, in the 1990s to trade on the Paris Bourse or Stockholm Stock Exchange from a London office. Thus it was no surprise that the London Stock Exchange's SEAQ international quotation system was increasingly bypassed in the 1990s as financial institutions chose to direct buying and selling orders to the most appropriate markets. Though the likes of Hans-Joerg Gudleff, Chairman of Barclay's Capital, could blame this loss of business on the Stock Exchange's failures in the late 1980s/early 1990s, it was more easily explained by the liberalization of national stock exchanges that made them much better markets than they had previously been.[61]

Nevertheless, this did not mean that the London Stock Exchange lost the market in foreign securities that it had acquired at the time of Big Bang. In

[60] FT, 5 Nov. 1992, 16 Feb. 1996, 30 Sept. 1996, 16 May 1997, 30 Apr. 1998, 18 May 1998.
[61] Ibid., 14 Feb. 1991, 10 Aug. 1994, 2 Jan. 1996, 16 Feb. 1996, 1 Mar. 1996, 9 Apr. 1996, 10 June 1996, 16 Mar. 1998, 14 May 1998.

the mid-1990s the London Stock Exchange continued to dominate trading in the international securities market, conducting around two-thirds of all cross-border buying and selling, including 90 per cent of that which took place in Europe. This was only to be expected for the City of London was home to the world's largest concentration of fund managers. By May 1998 it was estimated that the value of equity funds managed in London, at $1,808bn., had outstripped that of all other rival centres, including New York and Tokyo. Though this partly reflected the size and sophistication of Britain's own fund-management industry, of major importance was the fact that the City of London was used by financial institutions from all over the world as a base for their international operations, as they sought to diversify their portfolios away from a heavy reliance on domestic securities. At the end of 1996 $3,000bn. in assets were managed in the City of London, or 14 per cent of the world total, and much was managed for foreign clients. Thus the London Stock Exchange had immediately available to it the business of those who controlled the bulk of the world's securities. The constant turnover of these securities, as financial institutions adjusted their positions between sectors and countries, and in response to their own receipts, expenditure and expectations, generated a vast turnover for the stock exchanges of the world. London was ideally placed to capture not only that which was directed into British securities but also that placed in the stocks and shares of the world's largest companies, as much of that took place in and between the London offices of major financial institutions. As long as the City possessed these offices, and the London Stock Exchange offered them a cheap, flexible, and easy means of buying and selling their preferred securities, then it was in a position to continue to dominate the global securities business.[62] In the global money and foreign exchange markets critical mass was the essential factor behind the City of London success, and the same was true for securities markets, whether in equities or fixed-interest debt.

## CHANGING MEMBERSHIP

In order to capture this market the London Stock Exchange had not only to reform the way it operated by removing restrictive practices and introducing a more flexible way of trading, but it had also to include among its membership those firms handling an international business and respond to their requirements. This had been the other element of Big Bang when the participation of banks and brokerage houses from around the world was permitted for the first time. Big Bang thus witnessed, for example, the

---

[62] *FT*, 5 Jan. 1991, 10 July 1991, 8 Jan. 1992, 14 Apr. 1994, 10 Nov. 1994, 24 Jan. 1996, 16 Feb. 1996, 15 July 1996, 9 Aug. 1996, 9 Nov. 1996, 19 Nov. 1996, 29 Jan. 1997, 4 Mar. 1997, 24 Apr. 1997, 11 July 1997, 21 Jan. 1998, 6 Apr. 1998, 9 Apr. 1998, 14 May 1998, 19 May 1998, 13 June 1998; City Research Project, *Competitive Position*, Annex.

appearance in London of integrated finance houses whose activities spanned the entire range from commercial and investment banking through to both dealing and broking. A number of these were British, such as Barclays de Zoete Wedd (BZW) while others were subsidiaries of giant foreign banks such as Citibank of New York. Initially all appeared to do well, but in the aftermath of the 1987 crash many of the new combinations began to turn in huge losses, forcing their backers to reconsider their strategies. BZW, for example, lost £75m., on its dealing operations at the time leading Barclay's Bank to try and restructure its operations in 1989–90. Similarly Citibank cut back on its Scrimgeour Vickers broking operation in 1988 and then closed the entire firm in 1990. Other brokers to be closed or sold at this time included Messels (owned by Shearson of New York), Kitcat & Aitken (Royal Bank of Canada), and Hoare, Govett (Security Pacific). One of the most spectacular withdrawals was that of Morgan Grenfell, which withdrew entirely from broking and market-making in December 1988, making 450 people redundant. Generally, few of the combinations created at the time of Big Bang survived the harsher trading climate of the late 1980s/1990s. One of the last to abandon the field was Barclays, which sold BZW in 1997, having failed to integrate it into its general banking operations.

These conditions created opportunities for new entrants into the London securities market and many of these were major European banks or New York brokerage houses. Warburgs, for example, which had built up a major securities operation with the purchase of Akroyd & Smithers (jobbers) and Rowe & Pitman and Mullens (brokers) was itself purchased by the Swiss Bank Corporation in 1995. The two major German banks, Deutsche Bank and Dresdener Bank, became major participants in the London securities market with the purchase of Morgan Grenfell in 1989 and Kleinwort Benson in 1995 respectively, while the Dutch bank, ABN Amro, took control of Hoare, Govett in 1992, and its rival ING acquired Barings in 1995. When Merrill Lynch of New York, the world's largest brokerage firm, bought Smith New Court in 1995 they became the largest traders in UK securities. As a final illustration, in 1996 the Brazilian bank, Unibanco, acquired the London stockbroking firm of Stephen Rose & Partners, which specialized in Brazilian equities.[63]

Consequently, from the mid-1980s onwards foreign banks and brokerage firms built up a commanding presence on the London Stock Exchange. As this was often achieved at some considerable cost, both in money and

[63] A. Lorenz, *BZW: The First Ten Years* (London 1996), 43–4, 75, 79, 86, 165; H. Bonin, *Société Générale in the United Kingdom, 1871–1996* (Paris 1996), 98; *Financial Times* and *The Banker, International Banking in London: FBSA 50th Anniversary* (London 1997), 38; *FT*, 10 July 1987, 31 Nov. 1987, 29 June 1988, 8 Nov. 1988, 21 Nov. 1988, 28 Nov. 1988, 7 Dec. 1988, 16 Dec. 1988, 19 Dec. 1988, 31 Dec. 1988, 18 Jan. 1990, 31 May 1990, 15 Oct. 1990, 15 July 1995, 20 May 1996, 10 Oct. 1996, 25 Oct. 1996, 4 Oct. 1997, 4 Dec. 1997.

management, what it indicated were the attractions of the London securities market to these financial organizations, both through the potential to
develop large and profitable businesses there, as with Merrill Lynch, and
the need to participate in what had become the most international securities market in the world. In turn these firms acted as conduits between
London and their domestic markets. Though this could, and did, drain business away from the London Stock Exchange to exchanges abroad, it also
brought in business as securities were traded between the two markets and
foreign orders were filled in London. This had the effect of improving the
depth and spread of the London market so attracting more business, especially from major institutional fund managers who, increasingly, found a
presence in the City of London to be essential for their operations. The
strength of the London securities market did not rest on the activities of
British banks and brokerage houses but in the operations there of so many
firms from around the world for, collectively, they possessed the network
of contacts through which the global securities market functioned.

This did not mean that the British securities market was neglected or relegated to a secondary position. British banks and stockbroking firms continued to serve this market and provide it with a better service than in the
past, when an easy return was to be had from institutional clients under
the fixed commission regime. Now stockbrokers had to compete for business from both institutional and individual investors and do so both on the
quality of service they provided and the charges made. The large financial
institutions, in particular, were well aware of the power they possessed and
their ability to drive down commission rates or have business done net. By
1990 34 per cent of all transactions in UK equities were done without commission and when commission was charged the average was 0.39 per cent
compared to 0.45 per cent in 1987. As a reflection of the power of the institutional investor, when they did pay commission in 1990 it averaged only
0.19 per cent of the value, while that for the individual investor was 1.04
per cent. These institutional investors had become all important in the
British securities market, especially those managing pension funds. The
proportion of total UK equities controlled by pension funds had grown
from 26.7 per cent in 1981 to 34.2 per cent in 1993. By 1997 a mere 209
financial institutions, such as Prudential Insurance and Schroder fund
managers, controlled UK equities worth £764bn., or four times as much as
individual investors.[64]

These fund managers, especially the top 25, could thus demand a quality
of service and a level of price hardly contemplated before Big Bang, forcing
stockbroking firms to respond or lose the business. There was also little
advantage in being part of a large integrated group, as had been thought
at the time of Big Bang, for now charges were fully negotiable. Thus

[64] *Quality of Markets Review*, Jan.–Mar. 1990, 19–27; *FT*, 22 Feb. 1990, 7 Jan. 1991, 10
Aug. 1991, 2 Dec. 1994, 19 Aug. 1995, 27 May 1997, 13 Aug. 1997, 14 May 1998.

in-house brokers and market-makers had to compete for business with outside firms, and some were found wanting. Fund managers directed their orders to those firms that provided the best service, whether that was measured by transaction costs or the quality of advice. Increasingly the firms serving institutional clients had to be both well capitalized and employ highly qualified individuals. There thus emerged a group of Stock Exchange members, owned by banks, who could call upon the capital of their parent organization to employ in the handling of combined broking and dealing operations from major financial institutions. These were highly professional firms providing a specialist service for a small number of institutional clients, who were both British and non-British. One such was the subsidiary of the Hong Kong and Shanghai Bank which had formerly been the stockbroking firm of James Capel. This firm had been forced to move into market-making in 1997 in order to serve the needs of its institutional clients who wanted to dispose of holdings immediately and to deal net of commission. Another was Straus Turnbull, the broking and market-making subsidiary of the French bank, Société Générale. This firm employed 250 people in London in 1996. Even Smith New Court, one of the largest market-makers in London with an extensive business in foreign securities, saw the need for additional capital and a broking network, and so its willingness to sell out to Merrill Lynch.[65]

With institutional investors largely served by a small number of specialist firms those brokers who remained were driven to cultivate the individual investor, who had been increasingly neglected during the pre-Big Bang years. The relative importance of the individual investor had certainly declined over the years with their ownership of UK equities dropping from 54 per cent of the total in 1963, through 37.5 per cent in 1975, to 17.7 per cent in 1993. This was despite privatization and even demutualization, which only slowed down the rate of decline, as institutions increasingly focused their attentions on equities as a good long-term hedge against inflation. Nevertheless, privatization and then demutualization did lead to a great rise in the numbers of individual investors. Whereas in 1979 there were only 3m. investors in the UK by 1997 this had quadrupled to 12m. or from 7 per cent to 20 per cent of the population. As they controlled securities worth £200bn. they constituted a large potential market for stockbrokers. Traditional stockbrokers had never found a way of servicing this market because of the expense of maintaining offices and the cost of settling numerous small transactions. Firms that had tried, such as Quilter Goodison and Hoare, Govett, all gave up. However, the direct entry of the commercial banks into stockbroking created an entirely new range of opportunities. These banks already possessed huge retail networks through

[65] Ibid., 22 May 1989, 29 Nov. 1990, 26 Oct. 1991, 28 Oct. 1991, 15 Aug. 192, 1 June 1993, 10 July 1995, 13 July 1995, 15 July 1995, 23 Jan. 1997, 10 Feb. 1997, 6 Feb. 1998, 17 Mar. 1998; Bonin, *Société Générale*, 98; *Quality of Markets Review*, Apr.–June 1995, 15.

which additional financial services could be cheaply and expertly sold, at very little extra cost to themselves. The National Westminster bank, for example, recruited Chris Ring to run their retail stockbroking operation, and he had private client experience with the London stockbrokers Scrimgeour Kemp Gee and the Newcastle firm of Wise Speke. By 1996 Natwest handled 10 per cent of the UK's retail stockbroking transactions. Altogether, by the mid-1990s the four major banks—Barclays, Lloyds, Midland (HSBC), and Natwest controlled around 40 per cent of the private client business. Competition in this field was also growing with the ex-building society, Halifax Bank, developing its own share-dealing service in 1998 to cater for its millions of customers.[66]

What Big Bang had permitted was the marriage of stockbroking with the retail networks of the banks, making it possible to serve the mass market for the first time. This still left scope for independent retail stockbrokers who could concentrate upon the wealthiest segments of the population from a few regional offices. In 1995 there was an estimated 81,000 millionaires in the UK, up from 50,000 in 1991, and it was these that dominated the personal ownership of securities. What thus emerged were a number of national firms like Greig Middleton and Brewin Dolphin who could offer a personal stockbroking service backed by sophisticated back-office facilities providing research and settlement. When Greig Middleton merged with Allied Provincial in 1995 it created a firm with 48,000 clients and funds under management of £7.5bn. Similarly when Brewin Dolphin took over Wise Speke in 1998 the combined group had 64,000 clients and £12bn. under management. Firms like this were the direct descendants of the local stockbroking firms that had flourished in the past, both in London and the provinces, serving groups of moderately wealthy investors who were not active buyers and sellers of securities.

In addition to national firms like these there also existed other brokers serving particular groups of investors. One was that set up by Paul Killik, after a spell with Quilter Goodison. In 1996 he was running a stockbroking firm serving 17,000 clients in the South-East of England. There was also the likes of Cazenoves who were brokers to both major British companies and to the very wealthiest in society. In 1998 they were handling the investments of such families as the Wills, Hardings, and the Duke of Northumberland. Indicative of the wealth possessed by such individuals and families, Kleinwort Benson's stockbroking division was managing £31m. for one family at that time. At that level even brokers with a largely institutional business were keen to retain individual investors. Finally, the post-Big Bang era also saw the appearance of discount brokers, able to offer a simple buying and selling service at a low cost. One such was Sharelink, which had been set up in Birmingham by David Jones, who was

[66] *FT*, 28 Nov. 1988, 10 Aug. 1991, 23 May 1992, 29 Apr. 1994, 8 Jan. 1996, 21 Aug. 1996, 22 Feb. 1997, 2 Aug. 1997, 2 Apr. 1998, 10 June 1998, 1 July 1998.

a communications technology expert. By exploiting the ability of investors to dial a broker direct, an investor could buy and sell cheaply, once suitable safeguards regarding payment and delivery had been put in place. Eventually Sharelink was bought by the largest US discount broker, Charles Schwab, in 1995, as they extended their highly successful American operations to Britain. By 1998 internet broking was also developing in the UK, following on from its successful introduction in the United States.[67]

A lasting consequence of Big Bang was a permanent transformation of the membership of the London Stock Exchange. These now ranged from the subsidiaries of foreign banks and brokerage houses, that conducted a largely international business, to those firms conducting a personal or retail stockbroking operation for the greatly increased numbers of individual investors in Britain. The former were highly capitalized, extensively staffed, and capable of acting as temporary counterparties in their own right to meet the immediate needs of institutional clients from around the world. In contrast the latter conducted a low risk business where remuneration continued to come from the commission paid on transactions and charges for the specific services provided. Overall the prospects of both types of firm, and those who combined both functions, continued to appear promising in the 1990s. The institutional brokers/dealers benefited from the City of London's premier position as an international financial centre, which generated continuous activity as securities were bought and sold in response to changing conditions in the world's money and capital markets and the changing perceptions of fund managers. The personal/retail brokers benefited from the increased size of the investing public, stimulated through both privatizations and demutualizations and a much lower tax burden on the wealthy. Within these changes there was emerging a substantial number of investors who were keen to hold part of their wealth directly in securities rather than through institutional means, though that form was still encouraged by the complexities of the tax regime. The replacement of unit trusts by the Open Ended Investment company (OEIC) could also create a security that was tradeable on the securities market, creating even more scope for these types of brokers. Almost for the first time since the Second World War the years since Big Bang had seen the convergence of both a climate of investment in the UK conducive to the securities market and the freedom for the membership of the London Stock Exchange to respond to this in a variety of different ways.[68]

This is not to say that the London Stock Exchange and its membership were free of criticism in the 1990s. Part of this was self-inflicted as it appeared slow to respond to change and too ready to resort to restrictions and con-

---

[67] Ibid., 4 Nov. 1991, 29 Sept. 1994, 18 Jan. 1995, 7 Apr. 1995, 24 May 1995, 29 July 1995, 13 Oct. 1995, 20 Oct. 1995, 21 Oct. 1995, 27 July 1996, 19 Oct. 1996, 25 Oct. 1996, 11 Feb. 1997, 3 Mar. 1997, 21 Aug. 1997, 9 May 1998, 30 May 1998.

[68] Ibid., 26 Oct. 1991, 27 Oct. 1991, 12 Dec. 1991, 4 Jan. 1997, 7 Mar. 1997.

trols in order to bolster its position in the securities market. To a large extent that still reflected the decision made in 1947 to merge the Stock Exchange as a business, providing the forum in which trading took place with the organization which controlled the running of an orderly market. For much of the post-war years the result was to drive the Stock Exchange into a defensive position, where it sought both to protect its members from competition and to extend the services it provided. It was only with Big Bang, and the progressive unbundling of activities, that the London Stock Exchange began to re-emerge as a more highly focused organization in which the need to maintain an orderly market was given the highest priority. Still unresolved was the question of how this was to be best achieved. Certainly, there was no necessity for the Stock Exchange to control the trading mechanisms or services that its members used. It had not done so for the majority of its existence when it had proved a much more dynamic institution than in the post-war years. In fact, what emerged from Big Bang was akin to the dual control which had worked so well in the past, with responsibility now shared between the Stock Exchange, representing its members, and the regulatory authorities, reflecting the needs of the wider financial community. Though such a situation could and did produce conflict it was much to be preferred to a situation where government and its statutory bodies had control, for there was no way they could respond to changing market conditions, or the Stock Exchange was given a monopoly, for that would lead to restrictive practices and limited competition. Certainly, the more the London Stock Exchange responded to the changing needs of the domestic and international securities markets, and the less its membership used the necessary rules and regulations of an orderly market place to bolster their own positions, then the less criticism the Stock Exchange deserved.[69]

The other criticisms levelled at the London Stock Exchange were really aimed not at it as an institution but at securities markets generally. This was that the very ability to buy and sell securities quickly and easily created a short-term mentality among investors. Thus, the emphasis of companies was to produce immediate returns to satisfy their shareholders, and keep them loyal, rather than invest for the long-term. This criticism came from all quarters including both leading industrialists like Lord Weinstock, head of GEC for 33 years, or charismatic populists like Will Hutton, editor of the *Observer* newspaper.

Disengaged, uncommitted and pre-occupied with liquidity, the financial system has been uniquely bad at supporting investment and innovation,

was Hutton's observation in 1995.[70] The result has been unfavourable contrasts between the financial system of Britain, where the securities market

---

[69] *FT*, 21 Sept. 1996, 17 Dec. 1996, 21 Mar. 1997.
[70] W. Hutton, *The State We're In* (London 1995), 21, cf. *FT*, 30 Dec. 1996, 2 Jan. 1997 for Lord Weinstock.

did play an important role, and that of Germany, where banks appeared more central to the process. However, whenever detailed research has been conducted not only has it been impossible to find any evidence to support the accusation of short-termism but weaknesses in the German system of finance have also become apparent. Clearly no system was perfect but the consensus among informed observers was that securities market played a very valuable role within any financial system. Also with the 10 largest UK fund managers owning 36 per cent of the equity issued by the FTSE 100 companies it was also difficult to see how, collectively, they could be anything other than long-term holders.[71] That was certainly the conclusion from a study conducted by Paul Marsh, of the London Business School, for he concluded that

There is no evidence that shares are priced in a way which emphasises their short- rather than long-run prospects. Nor is there any evidence that the market penalises long-term investment or expenditure on R&D by awarding the shares of the company in question a lower rating—indeed quite the contrary.[72]

Instead any explanation for lack of investment in British industry is more likely to be found through an examination of the environment within which they operated, especially that created by the government through its monetary and fiscal policies. There is nothing more short-term than a political party in power adjusting its policies in order to achieve re-election in a few years time!

[71] J. Edwards and K. Fisher, *Banks, Finance and Investment in Germany* (Cambridge 1994), 1–2, 43–4, 63, 234, 240; *FT*, 8 July 1995, 1 Apr. 1997, 3 July 1997, 5 July 1997, 27 Apr. 1998; *FT*, *Mastering Finance*, chs. by P. Marsh, 'Myths Surrounding Short-termism', H. Rose, 'The Key Role of the Financial "Middleman"'.
[72] Quoted in *FT*, 7 Nov. 1990.

# Conclusion

As both a market and an institution the London Stock Exchange occupied a central position within the British financial system. As Britain was such a key component of the world economy from 1700 the result was to make the London Stock Exchange central to the operation of the international financial system, for much of the period. Thus, in dealing with the history of the London Stock Exchange one is examining an institution of immense importance and influence. Unfortunately, the role it performed went largely unrecognized by both contemporaries and later historians. The raising of capital for governments and business is largely attributed to those who actively mobilized the funds, such as the investment banks, with little comprehension of the role played by the existence of a market where the resulting securities could be traded. The provision of the credit required by industry and trade is attributed to the commercial banks, who collected and lent the savings of the nation. There is limited understanding of how the existence of transferable securities and an organized market blurred the distinctions between the short- and long-term use of such funds. The successful operation of an international monetary system before 1914, and its collapse and its reconstruction thereafter, is identified with the functioning of the gold standard and the guiding influence of central banks and not the presence of an exchange where the international ownership of assets could be traded. Throughout its history the prime function of the London Stock Exchange, as an organized market for existing securities, has been downplayed because of its association with speculation. Instead of trying to investigate the causes and consequences of this constant buying and selling, the assumption is made that, because it is rooted in the individual's desire to sell—not produce—for a profit, it does not perform a function within the wider economy. Consequently, the existence of the London Stock Exchange can only be justified by attributing to it the activities of others, such as those issuing securities and the use government and business made of the finance so obtained.

At the same time there is a tendency to see the entire period, until the more recent past, as one when markets, of whatever kind, operated autonomously. Markets were neither organized nor regulated by governments but left to the free operation of Adam Smith's hidden hand, through which equilibrium was maintained by competing forces of supply and demand. Eventually this broke down in the twentieth century and the state had to intervene. Under this scenario there is no recognition that these markets were by no means unmanaged. The very development of exchanges, whether stock or commodity, as well as a proliferation of trade and other business associations and bodies, testified to the need for organization and regulation, and the ready response from those directly involved. The era before 1939 was one not so much of *laissez-faire* but self-regulation, in which the government laid down the law of the land, leaving the organization to monitor and police the behaviour of their own members. In increasingly complex and interdependent economies the forces of supply and demand had to be modified so as to ensure the speedy completion of transactions. It was not simply price that had to be determined, but the amount, the quality, and the timing and location of delivery. All that required a great deal of trust between the participants, ranging all the way from the original producer and final consumer through the intermediaries involved. Once an economy moved away from a position of the production of a few basic goods for immediate consumption, as in a subsistence culture, systems were essential to guarantee that bargains made would be adhered to. The more complex and sophisticated the economy the more complex and sophisticated the systems in place needed to be. The motto of the London Stock Exchange—'My Word is My Bond'—could only be true in an organized and regulated market, where failure to honour a sale or purchase could and did result in a fine, suspension, or expulsion. In studying the history of the London Stock Exchange one is examining how the world's first modern economy coped with the need not only to develop sophisticated securities markets in a technical sense but also to devise the institutional mechanisms that facilitated their operation. Both factors are of vital importance in explaining what took place, assessing the results, and relating the outcome to the performance of both the British and world economies in those years. Conversely, in the years after the Second World War the state became increasingly involved in the direction and management of the securities market as the London Stock Exchange became a quasi-official arm of the government. This in turn had major consequences for its operation and the role it was able to play both domestically and internationally.

The history of the London Stock Exchange, divides into five distinct periods. The first begins in the late seventeenth century and culminates in the mid-1820s. During those years the Stock Exchange emerged as a distinct entity within the securities market, providing an organized forum for the trading of mainly UK government debt rather than corporate stocks and bonds. Covering the period from the mid-1820s until the First World War, the second period sees the London Stock Exchange emerge as one of the central institutions of both the British and the world economy. Expanding beyond its initial focus on the National Debt the London Stock Exchange increasingly provided a market for both domestic and foreign corporate stocks and bonds. Probably no single Stock Exchange ever provided a market for such a large proportion of the world's securities as London did at this time. However, this market did more than facilitate the mobilization of long-term capital for the development of the world economy. It also imparted liquidity and mobility to the monetary systems of the world, creating an integrated global economy in the process. The third period covered an era from the beginning of the First World War in 1914 to the start of another in 1939, with the virtual collapse of the international economy in between. Within the space of those 25 years, the achievements of the past two centuries were largely lost or reversed. The London Stock Exchange was returned to a position where the National Debt dominated trading, and its precise relations to the money and capital markets were uncertain. On the eve of the Second World War it was not at all clear what the future held for the London Stock Exchange. In the fourth period, covering the years from the Second World War until the 1980s the London Stock Exchange retreated almost entirely from its international role. Instead, it found a new role for itself as the semi-official regulator of the domestic securities market. This was a position it used to safeguard the interests of its members against competition. The final period began in the 1970s and is still continuing today. After appearing to consolidate its control over the domestic securities market, by merging with the provincial stock exchanges in 1973, the London Stock Exchange gradually lost the role it had gained after the Second World War. Attacks by the government on restrictive practices, criticism from the rest of the City for its charges and practices, and growing competition from non-members aided by rapid changes in communications and the ending of exchange controls, left the Stock Exchange without the support it required to resist change. When that came with Big Bang in 1986 it began a process of transformation that nobody envisaged, few wanted, and none could stop. The only certainty remaining for the London Stock Exchange, as it approached its third century, was that it only had a future if it changed, but then it had done precisely that over two centuries. In the eighteenth century the London securities market had no formal organization and concerned itself with dealing in UK government debt, or proxies for, with most of the activity driven by the short-term considerations of the money market. In the late twentieth century the London Stock Exchange was a highly organized market place for the stocks and shares of British and foreign companies, with most activity driven by the short- and long-term interests of institutional investors.

This story of change has the appeal of simplicity and an air of inevitability but the reality was much more complex than that. Though the securities market that was developing in London in the eighteenth century did grow in size and sophistication, it remained inferior to Amsterdam. Instead of a gradual overtaking of Amsterdam, to become the leading securities market in Europe, it was the upheavals of revolution and war that were instrumental in London's success. The switch of financial leadership away from Amsterdam and to London owed more to the political, military, and economic misfortunes of continental Europe between 1789 and 1815 than to the growing economic power of an industrializing Britain. The London Stock Exchange's connection with the finance of economic growth at that stage remained tenuous in the extreme, and it could thus not expect to profit greatly from the process at so early a stage. Conversely, the rise to world importance of the London Stock Exchange during the nineteenth century did owe much to the growing wealth and prosperity of Britain. The accumulation of savings and its mobilization for investment, created a need for a financial institution like the London Stock Exchange. In turn, the facilities it provided were increasingly tapped by savers and borrowers worldwide, as investors, governments, and business recognized the merits of securities as either attractive investments or cheap finance. By responding to this merging global market, through a liberal policy on the admission of members, the quotation of securities, and the degree of regulation the London Stock Exchange became one of the key institutions of the world's capitalist economy.

On the eve of the First World War there seemed nothing that could stop the onward march of securities and the stock exchanges on which they were traded, with London being the greatest of all. Even the war itself, with its vast increase in transferable debt in order to finance such an intense and prolonged conflict, should only have enhanced the position of the London Stock Exchange. However, what had been ignored was the fact that the securities market could only prosper and thrive under conditions of trust and stability. The purchase of a transferable security was, itself, an act of faith in the existence of a guaranteed future income and the ability to resell as and when required. It had taken years to build up confidence in the safety and marketability of securities, to a level where long-term debt was used for employing short-term money remuneratively and moving it around the world. Unfortunately, it was this confidence that was most affected by the First World War, and subsequent events, such as hyperinflation in Germany, the Wall Street crash, the collapse of monetary and financial systems worldwide, the imposition of exchange controls, and the repudiation of sovereign debts. Stock Exchanges were integral parts of national and global financial systems and so could not escape from the problems that affected them during and after the First World War. The London Stock Exchange withstood the shocks better than most but even it was forced to accept a much changed and reduced role for itself.

Thus, when the Second World War ended much of the trust and confidence that had underpinned the growing use of transferable securities and the free operation of markets had gone. Instead the power of government to direct, regulate, manage, and control had now become the central belief, to a greater or lesser extent, all round the world. Within this new climate all the London Stock Exchange could do was to co-operate and survive, which it did. However, in the process it gradually lost sense of the purpose for which it existed, which was the provision of an orderly and dynamic market for transferable securities. When the demand for such a market did begin to revive slowly in the 1950s the London Stock Exchange's response was a limited and tardy one, which was only partially due to the restricted environment within which it was able to operate. Though response and change took place it was insufficient for the London Stock Exchange to capture the opportunities that were available to it, especially with the City of London's re-emergence as a global financial centre from the 1960s. Even when the Stock Exchange experienced a period of rapid but belated change in the 1980s it was only sufficient for it to recover some of the position it had once occupied. To re-establish itself as one of the central institutions of a re-emerging global capitalist economy the London Stock Exchange required to recapture the openness, responsiveness, and blend of liberality and regulation that had characterized it before the First World War.

The institutional form that the London Stock Exchange took influenced its ability to respond to change. As long as control of the Stock Exchange was divided between members and proprietors, then it operated as a dynamic, open institution, and this was the case throughout the nineteenth century. Conversely, once control of the Stock Exchange fell into the hands of the membership, as was the case between the wars, it became much more resistant to change, though this took time to manifest itself. The real change came in 1947 when the members bought out the proprietors and took control of the Exchange themselves. From then on they were answerable only to themselves for their actions, and so could devise rules and regulations regarding such areas as admissions, number of members, scale of charges, and ways of operating that were to their particular benefit rather than in the interests of the securities market as a whole. This might not have been particularly serious because competition within the securities market would have limited their ability to abuse the power at their disposal. There were always alternative ways of trading securities and the London Stock Exchange and its membership had no monopoly. Unfortunately this was also a time of greatly increased government controls. Internationally the maintenance of exchange controls until 1979 insulated the London Stock Exchange from external competition. Domestically, the use of the London Stock Exchange by the government, through the Bank of England, as the means through which the securities market was controlled and policed, gave it immense power to both neutralize competition and impose its own rules and regulations. In many ways Big Bang was all about the end to that abuse of power by the Stock Exchange whose source had been government itself since 1945.

A stock exchange like London's needs to discover an evolving compromise between regulation and freedom if it is to be successful both as a market and an institution. Both elements were and are essential in the creation of an orderly *and* dynamic market place. This had been achieved by the London Stock Exchange before the First World War and it was this that was lost after the Second World War. Though the Stock Exchange itself, and its membership, have to bear some responsibility for this loss, due attention must be paid to the environment within which they operated throughout their existence. The period before 1914 was one of fairly liberal, open economies where government intervention was limited both domestically and internationally. Thus the London Stock Exchange could flourish as a market place serving a global economy. The years after 1945 were quite the reverse of that, with government control being experienced by all economies at all levels around the world. This created conditions where the existence of a market like the London Stock Exchange was threatened, encouraging its membership to adopt strategies that would safeguard their institution and their incomes. This they did successfully and it is against that they should be judged. In retrospect it is now clear that the influence of government on the post-war development of the London Stock Exchange was not a positive one. By creating a safe niche for the members of the London Stock Exchange in the domestic securities market the government discouraged them, both individually and collectively, from seizing the opportunities when they did emerge. Government control converted the London Stock Exchange from being a dynamic element in the world economy to a conservative element within the domestic economy. Possibly this explains much about the performance of the British economy in these post-war years if the pattern experienced by the London Stock Exchange is repeated in other institutions and businesses. Only when the London Stock Exchange faced these new challenges in the 1980s did it re-emerge as a more dynamic institution capable of formulating its own destiny rather than being driven by the dictates of government and the activities of non-members.

If current trends are any indicator of future requirements there is every possibility of the London Stock Exchange recapturing part of the role it had once occupied on the eve of the First World War. However, it can only do that if it shows itself to be equally open and responsive as it was at that time. The status quo is no longer an option considering the enormous changes taking place, unless the London Stock Exchange and its membership find relegation to the role of a local or regional market place particularly attractive. In contrast, the central position in the global market place has not yet been filled and an obvious candidate is the stock exchange located in the City of London, considering the concentration of money and capital market activity there. However, there is no necessity that such a market needs to be located in London, considering modern communications, nor any guarantee that the London Stock Exchange would fill that

# Select Bibliography

## PRIMARY SOURCES

This book rests upon a careful reading of the records generated by the London Stock Exchange as an institution. The main series used were:

1. Committee for General Purposes, 1798–1946
2. Committee of the Trustees and Managers, 1801–1948
3. Council of the London Stock Exchange, 1944–88

The minutes of the two Committees and that of the Council up to 1954, are lodged in the Guildhall Library, London. The Council Minutes for the period after 1954 are still retained by the London Stock Exchange. Associated with the Committees were numerous subcommittees whose records are also held by the Guildhall Library, and they were also consulted. However, I did not consult the records of the even more numerous Council subcommittees, held by the Stock Exchange, because of the vast increase in the volume of material included in the Council Minutes until the mid-1970s. All subcommittees reported to either General Purposes or Trustees and Managers Committees, and later to Council, submitting both reports and recommendations as well as supplementary papers, correspondence, and opinions.

For the post-war, and especially contemporary, history of the Stock Exchange the following were also invaluable.

4. *Annual Reports*, 1956–97
5. *Financial Times*, 1983–98
6. Stock Exchange Quarterly (became *Quality of Markets Review*), 1984–95.

(Detailed references are to be found in the footnotes.)

In addition, the *Stock Exchange Official Intelligence/Stock Exchange Yearbook* and *Stock Exchange Factbook* were invaluable sources of statistical data.


## SECONDARY SOURCES

Much of my already published work has been on stock exchange history, including that of the London Stock Exchange, or was concerned with the City of London, or finance and investment. Thus, I have not included in this bibliography references to contemporary and historical works which have been extensively used for my earlier writing. Instead, this selective bibliography lists those books and articles that have been of most use in writing this history.


## ABBREVIATIONS

The following abbreviations are used in the footnotes and Bibliography:

B. H.            *Business History*
Ec. H. R.       *Economic History Review*
E. J.           *Economic Journal*
FT              *Financial Times*
J. Ec. H        *Journal of Economic History*
LSE             London Stock Exchange

Anderson, B. L., 'Provincial Aspects of the Financial Revolution of the Eighteenth Century', *B. H.* 11 (1969).
——'Money and the Structure of Credit in the Eighteenth Century', *B. H.* 12 (1970).
Armstrong, C., *Blue Skies and Boiler Rooms: Buying and Selling Securities in Canada, 1870–1940* (Toronto 1997).
Armstrong, F. E., *The Book of the Stock Exchange* (London 1934).
Atkin, J. M., *British Overseas Investment, 1918–31* (New York 1977).
Attali, J., *A Man of Influence: Sir Siegmund Warburg, 1902–1982* (London 1986).
Balderson, T., 'German Banking 1913–1939', *University of Manchester: Working Papers in Economic and Society History*, No. 2 (1990).
Balogh, T., *Studies in Financial Organization* (London 1946).
*The Bank—The Stock Exchange—The Bankers—The Bankers' Clearing House—The Minister, and the Public: An Exposé* (London 1821).
Bank of England, *The United Kingdom Overseas Investments 1938 to 1948* (London 1950).
——*British Government Securities: The Market in Gilt Edged Securities* (London 1993).
Baster, A. S. J., 'A Note on the Colonial Stock Acts and Dominion Borrowing', *Economic History*, 2 (1930/3).
Blakey, G. B., *The Post-war History of the London Stock Market, 1945–92* (Didcot 1993).
Bonin, H., *Société Générale in the United Kingdom, 1871–1996* (Paris 1996).
Bowen, H. V., 'Investment and Empire in the Later Eighteenth Century: East India Stockholding, 1756–1791', *Ec. H. R.* 42 (1989).
Brooks, C., *Something in the City: Men and Markets in London* (London 1931).
Brown, R. L. and Easton, S. D., 'Weak Form Efficiency in the Nineteenth Century: A Study of Daily Prices in the London Market for 3 percent Consols', *Economica*, 56 (1989).
Buchinsky, M. and Polak, B., 'The Emergence of a National Capital Market in England, 1710–1880', *J. Ec. H.* 53 (1993).
Buckland, R. and Davis, E. W., *The Unlisted Securities Market* (Oxford 1989).
Burk, K., *Morgan Grenfell, 1838–1988: The Biography of a Merchant Bank* (Oxford 1989).
Burt, R., 'The London Mining Exchange, 1850–1900', *B. H.* 14 (1972).
Cairncross, A. (ed.), *The Robert Hall Diaries* (London 1989).
Cameron, R. and Bovykin, V. I. (ed.), *International Banking, 1870–1914* (New York 1991).
Capie, F. and Collins, M., *Have the Banks Failed British Industry?* (London 1992).
Carter, A. C., *The English Public Debt in the Eighteenth Century* (London 1968).
——*Getting, Spending and Investing in Early Modern Times* (Assen 1975).

Cassis, Y., 'Financial Elites in Three European Centres: London, Paris, Berlin, 1880s–1930s' *B. H.* 33 (1991).

——(ed.), *Finance and Financiers in European History, 1880–1960* (Cambridge 1992).

——*City Bankers, 1890–1914* (Cambridge 1994).

Chapman, S. D., 'The Establishment of the Rothschilds as Bankers', *Transactions of the Jewish Historical Society*, 29 (1982–6).

——*The Rise of Merchant Banking* (London 1984).

——*Raphael Bicentenary, 1787–1987* (London 1987).

City Research Project, *The Competitive Position of London's Financial Services* (London 1995).

Clapham, J. H., *The Bank of England, 1694–1914* (Cambridge 1914).

Clarke, W. M., *The City in the World Economy* (London 1963).

Clay, C., 'The Price of Freehold Land in the Later 17th and 18th Centuries', *Ec. H. R.* 27 (1974).

Clendenning, E. W., *The Eurodollar Market* (Oxford 1970).

Cobham, D. (ed.), *Markets and Dealers: The Economics of the London Financial Markets* (London 1992).

Coleman, A. C., 'London Scriveners and the Estate Market in the Later Seventeenth Century', *Ec. H. R.* 4 (1951/2).

Collins, M., *Money and Banking in the UK: A History* (London 1988).

*Commerce in Consternation* (London 1826).

Conant, C. A., *Wall Street and the Country: A Study of Recent Financial Tendencies* (New York 1904).

Coopey, R. and Clarke, D., *3i: Fifty Years of Investing in Industry* (Oxford 1995).

Cope, S. R., 'The Goldsmids and the Development of the London Money Market During the Napoleonic Wars' *Economica*, NS, 10 (1942).

——'The Stockbrokers Find a Home: How the Stock Exchange Came to be Established in Sweetings Alley in 1773', *Guildhall Studies in London History*, 2 (1977).

——'The Stock Exchange Revisited: A New Look at the Market in Securities in London in the Eighteenth Century', *Economica*, 45 (1978).

——'Bird, Savage and Bird of London, Merchants and Bankers, 1782–1803', *Guildhall Studies in London History*, 4 (1981).

——*Walter Boyd: A Merchant Banker in the Age of Napoleon* (Gloucester 1983).

Corporation of Foreign Bondholders, *The Principal Foreign Loans* (London 1877).

Cottrell, P. L., Lindgren, H., and Techoiva, G. A. (eds.), *European Industry and Banking Between the Wars: A Review of Bank–Industry Relations* (Leicester 1992).

Courtney, C. and Thompson, P., *City Lives: The Changing Faces of British Finance* (London 1996).

*Cunningham's Hand-Book of London* (London 1850).

Davies, K. G., 'Joint-Stock Investment in the Later Seventeenth Century', *Ec. H. R.* 4 (1951–2).

Davies, L. E. and Cull, R. J., *International Capital Markets and American Economic Growth, 1820–1914* (Cambridge 1994).

Dawson, F. G., *The First Latin American Debt Crisis: The City of London and the 1822–25 Loan Bubble* (New Haven 1990).

Day, J. E., *Stock-Broker's Office Organisation, Management and Accounts* (London 1911).

Dennet, L., *The Charterhouse Group, 1925–1979: A History* (London 1979).

Dickson, P. G. M., *The Financial Revolution in England: A Study in the Development of Public Credit* (London 1967).

Dintenfass, M., *The Decline of Industrial Britain, 1870–1980* (London 1992).

Dubois, A. B., *The English Business Company after the Bubble Act, 1720–1800* (New York 1938).

Duffy, F. D. and Henney, A., *The Changing City* (London 1989).

Duguid, C., *The Story of the Stock Exchange* (London 1901).

Dunning, J. H. and Morgan, E. V., *An Economic Study of the City of London* (London 1971).

Eagly, R. V. and Smith, V. K., 'Domestic and International Integration of the London Money Market, 1731–1789' *J. Ec. H.* 36 (1976).

Editors of Institutional Investment, *The Way it was: An Oral History of Finance, 1967–1987* (New York 1988).

Edwards, G. W., *The Evolution of Finance Capitalism* (New York 1939).

Edwards, J. and Fisher, K., *Banks, Finance and Investment in Germany* (Cambridge 1994).

Einzig, P., *The History of Foreign Exchange* (London 1962).

——*A Textbook on Foreign Exchange* (London 1966).

——*The Euro-Bond Market* (Oxford 1970).

Ellinger, B., *The City, The London Financial Markets* (1940).

Elon, A., *Founder Meyer Amschel Rothschild and His Time* (London 1996).

Essex-Crosby, A., 'Joint-Stock Companies in Great Britain, 1890–1930', M. Com. thesis, University of London, 1938.

Evans, D. M., *The Commercial Crisis, 1847–8* (London 1848).

Evans, G. H., *British Corporation Finance, 1775–1850: A Study of Preference Shares* (Baltimore 1936).

*Exposure of the Stock Exchange and Bubble Companies* (London 1854).

Exter, J., *Causes of the Present Depression in Our Money Market* (London 1825).

Fairman, W., *The Stocks Examined and Compared* (London 1798).

Feinstein, C. H. (ed.), *Banking, Currency and Finance in Europe Between the Wars* (Oxford 1995).

——and Pollard, S. (eds.), *Studies in Capital Formation in the UK, 1750–1920* (Oxford 1988).

Feldman, G. D., Olssen, V., Bordo, M., and Cassis, Y. (eds.), *The Evolution of Modern Financial Institutions in the Twentieth Century* (Milan 1994).

Fenn, C., *A Compendium of the English and Foreign Funds* (London 1837).

Fforde, J., *The Bank of England and Public Policy, 1941–1958* (Cambridge 1992).

*The Financial House that Jack Built* (London 1819).

*Financial News, The Stock Exchange: An Investor's Guide* (London 1933).

——*The City 1884–1934* (London 1934).

*Financial Times, Investor's Guide* (London 1913).

——*Mastering Finance* (London 1997).

——and *The Banker, International Banking in London: FBSA 50th Anniversary* (London 1997).

Fishman, J. J., *The Transformation of Threadneedle Street: The Deregulation and Reregulation of Britain's Financial Services* (Durham, NC 1993).

Floud, R. and McCloskey, D. (eds.), *The Economic History of Britain since 1700* (Cambridge 1984).

Francis, J., *Chronicles and Characters of the Stock Exchange* (London 1849).

Fraser, W. L., *All to the Good* (London 1963).

Galletley, G. and Richie, N., *The Big Bang* (Plymouth 1988).

Gayer, A. D., Rostow, W. W., and Schwartz, A. J., *The Growth and Fluctuation of the British Economy, 1790–1850* (Oxford 1953).

Geisst, C. R., *Visionary Capitalism: Financial Markets and the American Dream in the 20th Century* (New York 1990).

—— *Wall Street: A History* (Oxford 1997).

Gibson, G. R., *The Stock Exchanges of London, Paris and New York* (New York 1889).

Gleeson, A., *People and Their Money: 50 Years of Private Investment* (M & G Group 1981).

Goldsmith, R. W., *Comparative National Balance Sheets: A Study of Twenty Countries 1688–1978* (Chicago 1985).

Goodhart, C., Currie, D., and Llewellyn, D. T. (eds.), *The Operation and Regulation of Financial Markets* (1987).

Gorst, A., Johnman, L., and Lucas, G. W. S. (eds.), *Contemporary British History, 1931–1961* (London 1991).

Grant, A. T. K., *A Study of the Capital Market in Post-War Britain* (London 1937).

Green, E. and Moss, M., *A Business of National Importance: The Royal Mail Shipping Group, 1902–1937* (London 1982).

Greengrass, H. W., *The Discount Market in London: Its Organisation and Recent Development* (London 1930).

Greenwood, W. J., *Foreign Stock Exchange practice and Company Laws* (London 1911).

Hamilton, A., *The Financial Services Revolution: The Big Bang Worldwide* (London 1976).

Hamilton, R., *An Enquiry Concerning the Rise and Progress, the Redemption and Present State and Management of the National Debt* (Edinburgh 1818).

Hancock, D., 'Domestic Bubbling: Eighteenth-Century London Merchants and Individual Investment in the Fund', *Ec. H. R.* 47 (1994).

Hannah, L., *The Rise of the Corporate Economy* (London 1976).

—— and Kay, J. A., *Concentration in Modern Industry: Theory, Measurement and the UK Experience* (London 1977).

Hart, M., Jonker, J., and Van Zanden, J. L., *A Financial History of the Netherlands* (Cambridge 1997).

Hartley, R., *No Mean City: A Guide to the Economic City of London* (London 1967).

Haslam, S. M. and Peerless, S. G. G., *The London Securities Markets* (London 1990).

Hawtrey, R. G., *The Art of Central Banking* (London 1932).

—— *A Century of Bank Rate* (London 1938).

Healey, E., *Coutts and Company, 1692–1992: The Portrait of a Private Bank* (London 1992).

Hennessy, E., *A Domestic History of the Bank of England, 1930–1960* (Cambridge 1992).

Hirst, F. W., *Wall Street and Lombard Street* (New York 1931).

——*The Stock Exchange: A Short Study of Investment and Speculation* (London 1948).

H.M. *On the Analogy Between the Stock Exchange and the Turf* (London 1885).

Holden, C. H. and Holford, W. F., *The City of London: A Record of Destruction and Survival* (London 1951).

Holderness, B. A., 'The English Land Market in the 18th Century: The Case of Lincolnshire', *Ec. H. R.* 27 (1974).

Hoppit, J., *Risk and Failure in English Business* (Cambridge 1987).

Howson, S., *Domestic Monetary Management in Britain, 1919–38* (Cambridge 1975).

Hunt, B. C., *The Development of the Business Corporation in England, 1800–1867* (Cambridge, Mass. 1936).

Hutton, W., *The State We're In* (London 1995).

Institute of Bankers, *Current Financial Problems and the City of London* (London 1949).

——*The City of London as a Centre of International Trade and Finance* (London 1961).

——*The London Discount Market Today* (London 1962).

Interbank Research Organization, *The Future of London as an International Financial Centre* (London 1973).

Janes, H., *de Zoete and Gorton: A History* (London 1963).

Jeffreys, J. B., 'Trends in Business Organisation in Great Britain since 1856', (Ph.D. thesis, University of London, 1938).

Jenkins, A., *The Stock Exchange Story* (London 1963).

John, A. H., 'Insurance Investment and the London Money Market of the Eighteenth Century', *Economica*, NS, 20 (1953).

——'The London Assurance Company and the Marine Insurance Market in the 18th Century', *Economica*, NS, 25 (1958).

Johnson, J. and Murphy, G. W., 'The Growth of Life Assurance in the UK Since 1880', *Manchester School of Economic and Social Studies*, 25 (1957).

Jones, G., *British Multinational Banking, 1830–1900* (Oxford 1993).

Joslin, D. M., 'London Private Bankers, 1720–1785', *Ec. H. R.* 7 (1954/5).

Karo, M., *City Milestones and Memories: Sixty-Five Years in and Around the City of London* (London 1962).

Kay, W., *The Big Bang; An Investor's Guide to the Changed City* (London 1986).

Keyser, H., *The Law Relating to Transactions on the Stock Exchange* (London 1850).

Khoury, J. J., *The Deregulation of the World's Financial Markets: Myths, Realities and Impact* (London 1990).

Killick, J. R. and Thomas, W. A., 'The Provincial Stock Exchanges, 1830–1870', *Ec. H. R.* 23 (1970).

——'The Stock Exchanges of the North of England, 1836–1850', *Northern History*, 8 (1970).

Killik, S., *The Work of the Stock Exchange* (London 1933).

Kindersley, R. M., 'A New Study of British Investments', *E. J.* (1929–39).

Kindleberger, C. P., *Economic Response* (Cambridge, Mass. 1978).

King, W. T. C., *The Stock Exchange* (London 1954).

Kinross, J., *Fifty Years in the City: Financing Small Business* (London 1982).

Kirkaldy, A. W. (ed.), *Credit, Industry and the War* (London 1915).

——(ed.), *British Finance During and After the War, 1914–21* (London 1921).

*Knights Cyclopaedia of London* (Cambridge 1851).

Kynaston, D., 'The London Stock Exchange 1870–1914: An Institutional History', Ph.D. thesis University of London, 1983.

——*Cazenove & Co.: A History* (London 1991).

——*LIFFE: A Market and its Makers* (Cambridge 1997).

Lavington, F., *The English Capital Market* (London 1921).

Lawson, N., *The View from No. 11: Memoirs of a Tory Radical* (London 1992).

Lazonick, W. and O'Sullivan, M., 'Finance and Industrial Development', *Financial History Review*, 4 (1997).

Lee, R., *The Ownership of Price and Quote Information: Law, Regulation, Economics and Business* (Oxford 1995).

Lewis, C., *America's Stake in International Investment* (Washington 1938).

*London: A Complete Guide to the British Capital* (London 1810).

Lorenz, A., *BZW: The First Ten Years* (London 1996).

Lougheed, A., 'The London Stock Exchange Boom in Kalgoorlie Shares, 1895–1901', *Australian Economic History Review*, 35 (1995).

Lowe, J., *The Present State of England in Regard to Agriculture, Trade and Finance* (London 1823).

MacDermot, B. H. D., *Panmure Gordon & Co., 1876–1976: A Century of Stockbroking* (London 1976).

MacGregor, D. H., 'Joint Stock Companies and the Risk Factor', *E. J.* 39 (1929).

McKenzie, J. B., *The Story of a Stock Exchange Speculator* (London 1908).

MacLachlan, S. (ed.), *Life After Big Bang* (London 1987).

Macrae, H. and Cairncross, F., *Capital City: London As a Financial Centre* (London 1984).

Macrae, N., *The London Capital Market: Its Structure, Strains and Management* (London 1955).

Madden, J. J., *British Investment in the United States, 1860–1880* (New York 1985).

Marchildon, G. P., 'British Investment Banking and Industrial Decline Before the Great War: A Case-Study of Capital Outflow to Canadian Industry', *B. H.* 33 (1991).

——'Hands Across the Water: Canadian Industrial Financiers in the City of London, 1905–20', *B. H.* 34 (1992).

Martin, A., *Cazenove & Company, 1785–1955* (London 1955).

Matthews, R. C. O., *A Study in Trade-Clyde History: Economic Fluctuations in Great Britain, 1833–1842* (Cambridge 1954).

——Feinstein, C. H., and Odling Smee, J. C., *British Economic Growth, 1856–1973* (Oxford 1982).

Maughan, C., *Markets of London* (London 1931).

Meeker, J. E., *The Work of the Stock Exchange* (New York 1930).

Merrett, A. J., Howe, M., and Newbould, G. D., *Equity Issues and the London Capital Market* (London 1967).

Michie, R. C., 'The Transfer of Shares in Scotland, 1700–1820', *B. H.* 20 (1978).

Michie, R. C., 'The Social Web of Investment in the Nineteenth Century', *Revue Internationale d'Histoire de la Banque*, 18 (1979).

—— *Money, Mania and Markets: Investment, Company Formation and the Stock Exchange in Nineteenth-Century Scotland* (Edinburgh 1981).

—— 'Options, Concessions, Syndicates, and the Provision of Venture Capital, 1880–1913', *B. H.* 23 (1981).

—— 'Crisis and Opportunity: The Formation and Operation of the British Assets Trust, 1897–1914', *B. H.* 15 (1983).

—— 'Income, Expenditure and Investment of a Victorian Millionaire: Lord Overstone, 1823–1883', *Historical Research*, 58 (1985).

—— 'The London Stock Exchange and the British Securities Market, 1850–1914', *Ec. H. R.* 38 (1985).

—— 'The London and New York Stock Exchanges, 1850–1914', *J. of Ec. H.* 46 (1986).

—— *The London and New York Stock Exchanges 1850–1914* (London 1987).

—— 'Different in Name Only? The London Stock Exchange and Foreign Bourses c.1850–1914', *B. H.* 30 (1988).

—— 'Dunn Fisher & Co. in the City of London, 1906–1914', *B. H.* 30 (1988).

—— 'The Finance of Innovation in Late Victorian and Edwardian Britain: Possibilities and Constraints', *Journal of European Economic History*, 17 (1988).

—— 'The Canadian Securities Market, 1850–1914', *Business History Review*, 62 (1988), 35–73.

—— 'The London Stock Exchange and the British Economy, 1870–1930', in J. J. Van Helten and Y. Cassis (eds.), *Capitalism in a Mature Economy* (London 1989).

—— *The City of London: Continuity and Change 1850–1990* (London 1992).

—— 'The Development of the Stock Market', *Palgrave Dictionary of Money and Finance* (London 1992).

—— *Financial and Commercial Services* (Oxford 1994).

—— 'The London and Provincial Stock Exchanges, 1799–1793: Separation, Integration, Rivalry, Unity', in D. H. Aldcroft and A. Slavin (eds.), *Enterprise and Management* (Aldershot 1995).

—— 'The City of London: Functional and Spatial Unity in the Nineteenth Century', in H. A. Diedericks and D. Reader (eds.), *Cities of Finance* (North Holland, Amsterdam 1996).

—— 'London and the Process of Economic Growth Since 1750', *The London Journal*, 22 (1997).

—— 'Friend or Foe: Information Technology and the London Stock Exchange Since 1850', *Journal of Historical Geography*, 23 (1997).

—— 'The Invisible Stabiliser: Asset Arbitrage and the International Monetary System since 1700', *Financial History Review*, 15 (1998).

—— 'Anglo-American Financial Systems, c.1800–1939', in P. Cottrell and J. Reis (eds.), *Finance and the Making of the Modern Capitalist World, 1750–1931* (Madrid 1998).

—— 'Insiders, Outsiders and the Dynamics of Change in the City of London Since 1900', *Journal of Contemporary History*, 33 (1998).

—— 'Stock Exchanges and the Finance of Economic Growth, 1830–1939', in P. Cottrell, G. Feldman, and J. Reis (eds.), *Finance and the Making of Modern Capitalism* (Aldershot 1998).

Mirowski, P., 'The Rise (and Retreat) of a Market: English Joint-Stock Shares in the Eighteenth Century', *J. Ec. H.* 41 (1981).
——*The Birth of the Business Cycle* (New York 1985).
Mitchell, B. R., *British Historical Statistics* (Cambridge 1988).
Moggridge, D. E., *British Monetary Policy 1924–1931* (Cambridge 1972).
Moran, W., *The Politics of the Financial Services Revolution: The USA, UK and Japan* (London 1991).
Morgan, E. V. and Thomas, W. A., *The Stock Exchange: Its History and Functions* (London 1961).
Morton, W. A., *British Finance, 1930–1940* (Madison, Wisc. 1943).
Mortimer, T., *Everyone His Own Broker or a Guide to Exchange Alley* (London 1761).
Moyle, J., *The Pattern of Ordinary Share Ownership, 1957–1970* (Cambridge 1971).
Neal, L., 'Integration of International Capital Markets: Quantitative Evidence from the 18th to 20th centuries', *J. Ec. H.* 45 (1985).
——'The Integration and Efficiency of the London and Amsterdam Stock Markets in the 18th Century', *J. Ec. H.* 47 (1987).
——*The Rise of Financial Capitalism: International Capital Markets in the Age of Reason* (Cambridge 1994).
Nevin, E. and Davies, E. W., *The London Clearing Banks* (London 1970).
*A New Guide to the Public Funds* (London c.1825).
Newall, P., *Japan and the City of London* (London 1996).
Neymark, M. A., *La Statistique Internationale de Valeurs Mobilières* (La Haye 1911).
Nicholson, S., *A Victorian Household* (London 1988).
O'Brien, P. K., 'The Political Economy of British Taxation, 1660–1815', *Ec. H. R.* 41 (1983).
O'Brien, R., *Global Financial Integration: The End of Geography* (London 1992).
Oppers, S. E., 'The Interest Rate Affect of Dutch Money in 18th C. Britain', *J. Ec. H.* 53 (1993).
Osborn, A. S. J., *The Stock Exchange: Its Method and Practice* (London 1927).
Paish, F. W., *Business Finance* (London 1961).
Parkinson, C., *Right at the Centre: An Autobiography* (London 1992).
Patterson, M. and Reiffen, D., 'The Effect of the Bubble Act on the Market for Joint-Stock Shares', *J. Ec. H.* 40 (1990).
Paukert, F., 'The Value of Stock Exchange Transactions in Non-Government Securities, 1911–1959', *Economica*, 28 (1962/3).
Perkins, E. J., *American Public Finance and Financial Services, 1700–1816* (Columbus, Ohio 1994).
Phillips, P., *Inside the New Gilt-Edged Market* (Cambridge 1987).
*The Picture of London* (1815, 1820, 1824, 1826).
Pike, J. R., *Britain's Metal Mines* (London 1864).
Platt, D. C. M., *Foreign Finance in Continental Europe and the United States, 1815–1870* (London 1984).
——*Britain's Investment Overseas on the Eve of the First World War* (London 1986).
Playford, F., *Practical Hints for Investing Money* (London 1856).

Plender, J. and Wallace, P., *The Square Mile: A Guide to the New City of London* (London 1985).

Pocock, R. F., *The Early British Radio Industry* (Manchester 1988).

Pohlled, M., *Studies on Economic and Monetary Problems and on Banking History* (Mainz 1988).

Pollins, H., 'The Marketing of Railway Shares in the First Half of the 19th Century', *Ec. H. R.* 7 (1954/5).

Prais, S. J., *The Evolution of Giant Firms in Britain* (Cambridge 1976).

Pratten, C., *The Stock Market* (Cambridge 1993).

Pressnell, L. S., *Country Banking in the Industrial Revolution* (Oxford 1956).

Quinn, S., 'Gold, Silver and the Glorious Revolution: Arbitrage Between Bills of Exchange and Bullion', *Ec. H. R.* 49 (1966).

Randall, R. W., *Real de Monte: A British Mining Venture in Mexico* (Austin, Tex. 1972).

Reader, W. J., *A House in the City: A Study of the City and of the Stock Exchange Based on the Records of Foster & Braithwaite, 1825–1975* (London 1979).

——and Kynaston, D., *Phillips & Drew: Professionals in the City* (London 1998).

Reed, D., *The Power of the News: The History of Reuters* (Oxford 1992).

Reed, M. C. (ed.), *Railways in the Victorian Economy* (Newton Abbott 1969).

——*Investment in Railways in Britain, 1820–44: A Study in the Development of the Capital Market* (Oxford 1975).

——*A History of James Capel and Company* (London 1975).

Richards, R. D., 'The Bank of England and the South Sea Company', *Economic History*, 2 (1930–3).

——'The Lottery in the History of English Government Finance', *Economic History*, 3 (1934–7).

Riley, J. C., *International Government Finance and the Amsterdam Capital Market 1940–1815* (Cambridge 1980).

Rix, M. S., *Stock Market Economics* (London 1954).

Roberts, R., *Schroders: Merchants & Bankers* (London 1992).

——and Kynaston, D. (eds.), *The Bank of England: Money, Power and Influence 1694–1994* (Oxford 1995).

Rosenbaum, W. E., *The London Stock Market: Its Features and Usage* (New York 1910).

Roy, H., *The Stock Exchange* (London 1860).

Royal Institute of International Affairs, *The Problem of International Investment* (Oxford 1937).

Rubinstein, W. D., *Men of Property: The Very Wealthy in Britain Since the Industrial Revolution* (London 1931).

Salisbury, S. and Sweeney, K., *The Bull, the Bear and the Kangaroo: The History of Sydney Stock Exchange* (Sydney 1988).

Saw, R., *The Bank of England, 1694–1944* (London 1944).

Sayers, R. S., *The Bank of England, 1891–1944* (Cambridge 1976).

Scammell, W. M., *The London Discount Market* (London 1968).

Schubert, E. S., 'Arbitrage in the Foreign Exchange Markets of London and Amsterdam During the 18th C.', *Explorations in Economic History*, 26 (1989).

Schwartz, L. D., *London in the Age of Industrialisation, 1700–1850* (Cambridge 1992).

Scott, W. R., *The Constitution and Finance of English, Scottish and Irish Joint-Stock Companies to 1720* (Cambridge 1910–12).

Sebag-Montefiore, D., *The Story of Joseph Sebag & Co. and its Founding Families* (n.p. 1996).

Shaw, E. R., *The London Money Market* (London 1975).

Siegel, J. J., *Stocks for the Long Run: A Guide to Selecting Markets for Long-Term Growth* (Chicago 1994).

Smith, C. F., 'The Early History of the London Stock Exchange', *American Economic Review*, 19 (1929).

Spiegelberg, R., *The City: Power Without Accountability* (London 1973).

*The Stock Exchange Clerks' Provident Fund Centenary 1874–1974* (London 1974).

Sutherland, L., *Politics and Finance in the Eighteenth Century* (London 1984).

Suzuki, T., *Japanese Government Loan Issues on the London Capital Market, 1870–1913* (London 1994).

Sykes, J., *The Amalgamation Movement in English Banking, 1825–1924* (London 1926).

Thomas, D. and Donnelly, T., *The Motor Car Industry in Coventry since the 1880s* (London 1985).

Thomas, S. E., *British Banks and the Finance of Industry* (London 1931).

Thomas, W. A., *The Provincial Stock Exchanges* (London 1973).

——*The Finance of British Industry, 1918–1976* (London 1978).

——*The Stock Exchanges of Ireland, 1918–1976* (Liverpool 1986).

——*The Securities Market* (Hemel Hempstead 1986).

——*The Big Bang* (Oxford 1986).

Thompson, F. M. L. (ed.), *Landowners, Capitalists and Entrepreneurs* (Oxford 1994).

Thompson, P., 'The Pyrrhic Victory of Gentlemanly Capitalism: The Financial Elite of the City of London 1945–90', *Journal of Contemporary History*, 32 (1997).

*Thoughts on Trade and Public Spirit* (London 1716).

*The Times, The City of London* (London 1929).

Toniolo, G. (ed.), *Central Banks' Independence in Historical Perspective* (Berlin 1988).

Toporowski, J., *The Economics of Financial Markets and the 1987 Crash* (Aldershot 1993).

Truptil, R. J., *British Banks and the Money Market* (London 1936).

Vallance, A., *The Centre of the World* (London 1935).

Van Helten, J. J. and Cassis, Y. (eds.), *Capitalism in a Mature Economy* (Aldershot 1990).

Vogel, S. K., *Freer Markets, More Rules! Regulatory Reform in Advanced Industrial Countries* (Ithaca, NY 1996).

Vries, J. de and Van der Woude, A., *The First Modern Economy: Success, Failure and Perseverance of the Dutch Economy, 1500–1815* (Cambridge 1997).

Wade, R. W., *The Stockholders Association* (London 1806).

Wainwright, D., *Henderson: A History of the life of Alexander Henderson, First Lord Faringdon, and of Anderson Administration* (London 1985).

Wainwright, D., *Government Broker: The Story of an Office and of Mullens and Company* (East Molesey 1990).

Ward, J. R., *The Finance of Canal Building in Eighteenth Century England* (Oxford 1974).

Weatherall, D., *David Ricardo: A Biography* (The Hague 1976).

Webb, G. N., *The Bigger Bang: Growth of a Financial Revolution* (London 1987).

*Wedd, Durlacher, Mordant and Company, Members of the Stock Exchange, London* (n.p. 1984).

Whyte, W. H., *The Stock Exchange: Its Constitution and the Effects of the Great War* (London 1924).

Widlake, B., *In the City* (London 1986).

Wilkins, M., *The History of Foreign Investment in the United States to 1914* (Cambridge, Mass. 1989).

Williams, D., 'London and the 1931 Financial Crisis', *Ec. H. R.* 15 (1962/3).

——'The 1931 Financial Crisis', *Yorkshire Bulletin of Economic and Social Research*, 15 (1963).

Wilson, C., *Anglo-Dutch Commerce and Finance in the Eighteenth Century* (Cambridge 1941).

Wilson, J. F., 'The Finance of Municipal Capital Expenditure in England and Wales, 1870–1914', *Financial History Review*, 4 (1987).

Wincott, H., *The Stock Exchange* (London 1946).

Winton, J. R., *Lloyds Bank, 1918–1969* (Oxford 1982).

Withers, H., *War and Lombard Street* (London 1915).

Wood, C., *Boom and Bust* (London 1988).

Youeb, G., *Diamonds and Coral: Anglo-Dutch Jews and the Eighteenth Century Trade* (Leicester 1978).

Ziegler, P., *Central Bank, Peripheral Industry: The Bank of England in the Provinces, 1826–1913* (Leicester 1990).

# Index

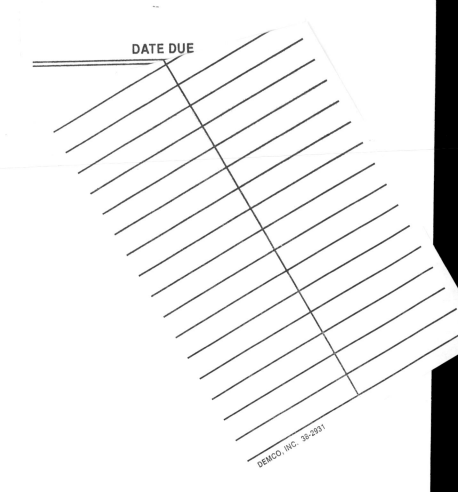

DATE DUE

DEMCO, INC. 38-2931